MASTERING
INTERNET E[XPLORER 4]

C000137743

BY GENE WEISSKOPF AND [...]

1 CD
960 pp; 7½" x 9"
ISBN: 0-7821-2133-0
$44.99

In the latest version of the popular browser suite, Internet Explorer 4 paves the way to Microsoft's "active desktop," with new features and built-in push technology. In *Mastering Microsoft Internet Explorer 4*, Weisskopf and Coleman provide complete, in-depth coverage of all the new features and show users how to get the most out of them. Perfect for every user from beginner to advanced, *Mastering Microsoft Internet Explorer 4* is an essential reference that belongs beside every Windows-based computer. The accompanying CD-ROM is loaded with valuable software, including a fully searchable, customizable electronic version of the book, Web publishing tools, and useful Net utilities.

MASTERING NETSCAPE
COMMUNICATOR 4

BY DANIEL A. TAUBER AND BRENDA KIENAN

1 CD
800 pp; 7½" x 9"
ISBN: 0-7821-2077-6
$39.99

Mastering Netscape Communicator 4 is a comprehensive, in-depth guide to using Netscape's new suite of programs to navigate the Internet and to communicate and collaborate with others. A vital reference for beginners and experienced users alike, this book demonstrates how to use Netcaster to create a constantly updated desktop, use Composer to publish your own Web page, use Collabra and Conference to work in groups, and much more. Inside, you'll find thousands of useful tips that would take hours of online time to uncover on your own.

Internet Complete

SYBEX® SAN FRANCISCO ▸ PARIS ▸ DÜSSELDORF ▸ SOEST

Associate Publisher: Amy Romanoff

Contracts and Licensing Manager: Kristine Plachy

Developmental Editor: Sherry Bonelli

Compilation Editor: Brenda Frink

Editors: Kim Askew, Bonnie Bills, Andy Carroll, Pat Coleman, James A. Compton, Ben Miller, Alison Moncrieff, Vivian Perry, Lee Ann Pickrell, Val Potter, Krista Reid-McLaughlin, Doug Robert, Peter Weverka, and Kim Wimpsett

Technical Editors: Rima Regas, Stephen Bigelow, Maryann Brown, Peggy Brundy, Asha Dornfest, Rael Dornfest, Juli Geiser, Mike Hanna, Aaron Kushner, Tom Maxwell, Bill Ross, Beth Wiley, and Dale Wright

Book Designer: Maureen Forys, Happenstance Type-O-Rama

Desktop Publisher: Tony Jonick

Production Coordinator: Susan Berge

Indexer: Matthew Spence

Cover Designer: DesignSite

Screen reproductions produced with Collage Complete.

Collage Complete is a trademark of Inner Media Inc.

SYBEX is a registered trademark of SYBEX Inc.

Mastering, No experience required., and Amazing Secrets are trademarks of SYBEX Inc.

Library of Congress Card Number: 98-86636
ISBN: 0-7821-2409-7

Printed in Canada

10 9 8 7 6 5 4 3 2 1

ACKNOWLEDGMENTS

This book incorporates the work of many people, inside and outside Sybex.

Sherry Bonelli and Amy Romanoff defined the book's overall structure and contents. Brenda Frink compiled and adapted all the material for publication in this book.

A large team of editors, developmental editors, project editors, and technical editors helped to put together the various books from which *Internet Complete* was compiled: Maureen Adams, Sherry Bonelli, Bonnie Bills, Neil Edde, Peter Kuhns, Suzanne Rotondo, and Dan Brodnitz handled developmental tasks; Kim Askew, Davina Baum, Bonnie Bills, Andy Carroll, Pat Coleman, Malcolm Faulds, Linda Good, Krista Reid-McLaughlin, Ben Miller, Alison Moncrieff, Vivian Perry, Lee Ann Pickrell, Val Potter, Doug Robert, Emily Smith, Michael Tom, Peter Weverka, Kim Wimpsett, and Shelby Zimmerman all contributed to editing or project editing; and the technical editors were Stephen Bigelow, Maryann Brown, Peggy Brundy, Asha Dornfest, Rael Dornfest, Juli Geiser, Mike Hanna, Aaron Kushner, Tom Maxwell, Rima Regas, Bill Ross, Beth Wiley, and Dale Wright. Rima Regas deserves particular thanks for helping to make sure the chapters reflect Windows 98.

The *Internet Complete* production team of designer Maureen Forys, desktop publisher Tony Jonick, and production coordinator Susan Berge worked with speed and accuracy to turn the manuscript files and illustrations into the handsome book you're now reading. Liz Paulus, Dan Schiff, Gemma O'Sullivan, Ellen Bliss, and Malka Geffen also helped in various ways to keep the project moving.

Finally, our most important thanks go to the contributors who agreed to have their work excerpted into *Internet Complete*: Laura Arendal, Pat Coleman, Gini Courter, Christian Crumlish, Peter Dyson, Brenda Kienan, E. Stephen Mack, Annette Marquis, Michael Meadhra, Mark Minasi, Janan Platt-Saylor, John Ross, Daniel A. Tauber, Gene Weisskopf, and the PC Novice/Smart Computing staff. Without their efforts, this book would not exist.

CONTENTS AT A GLANCE

TABLE OF CONTENTS

Chapter 20 □ Creating Web Pages with FrontPage Express

INTRODUCTION

Internet Complete is a one-of-a-kind computer book—valuable both for the breadth of its content and for its low price. This thousand-page compilation of information from a dozen Sybex books provides comprehensive coverage of the Internet and related Windows 98 and PC hardware topics. This book, unique in the computer book world, was created with several goals in mind:

- Offering a thorough guide covering all the important user-level features of the Internet at an affordable price

- Helping you become familiar with the essential Internet topics so you can choose your next Internet book with confidence

- Acquainting you with some of our best authors—their writing styles and teaching skills, and the level of expertise they bring to their books—so you can easily find a match for your interests as you delve deeper into the Internet

Internet Complete is designed to provide all the essential information you'll need to get the most from the Internet, while at the same time inviting you to explore the even greater depths and wider coverage of material in the original books.

If you've read other computer "how-to" books, you've seen that there are many possible approaches to the task of showing how to use software and hardware effectively. The books from which Internet Complete was compiled represent a range of the approaches to teaching that Sybex and its authors have developed—from the quick, concise No experience required style to the exhaustively thorough Mastering style. As you read through various chapters of Internet Complete, you'll see which approach works best for you. You'll also see what these books have in common: a commitment to clarity, accuracy, and practicality.

You'll find in these pages ample evidence of the high quality of Sybex's authors. Unlike publishers who produce "books by committee," Sybex authors are encouraged to write in individual voices that reflect their own experience with the software at hand and with the evolution of today's personal computers. Nearly every book represented here is the work of a single writer or a pair of close collaborators; you know you are getting the benefit of each author's direct experience.

In adapting the various source materials for inclusion in *Internet Complete*, the compiler preserved these individual voices and perspectives. Chapters were edited only to minimize duplication, to omit coverage of non-Internet tools, and to add information about cutting-edge developments. A few sections were also edited for length so that other important Internet subjects could be included.

Who Can Benefit from This Book?

Internet Complete is designed to meet the needs of a wide range of computer users. Therefore, while you *could* read this book from beginning to end, all of you may not *need* to read every chapter. The Table of Contents and the Index will guide you to the subjects you're looking for.

Beginners   Even if you have only a little familiarity with computers and their basic terminology, this book will get you up and running on the Internet.

Intermediate users   Chances are, you already know how to do routine tasks in e-mail or the Internet. You also know there is always more to learn about working more effectively, and you want to get up to speed on new Internet features. Throughout this book you'll find instructions for just about anything you want to do. Nearly every chapter has nuggets of knowledge from which you can benefit.

How This Book Is Organized

Internet Complete has twenty five chapters and three appendices.

Part I: Internet Basics   In the first four chapters of the book, we'll introduce you to basic Internet concepts, get you connected, and teach you how to use e-mail. If you've never used the Internet before, Part I will help get you oriented before you start browsing.

Part II: Browsing and More   In Part II, you'll learn how to get around the Web, news, and ftp. Chapter 5 will get you started browsing. Chapters 6 and 7 will teach you the basic features of Netscape and Internet Explorer. In Chapter 8 you'll learn how to use search techniques to locate the information you need. Chapters 9, 10, and 11 will teach you about other useful Internet tools.

Part III: AOL Amazing Secrets   Part III is a special section for AOL users. In these four chapters, you'll learn about some of the ways you can use AOL, including searching, playing games, chatting, and shopping.

Part IV: Creating Your Own Web Page   Once you've spent some time surfing the Web, you may want to post your own Web site. No worries: the chapters in Part IV give you a great introduction to all the issues you'll need to consider. You'll learn about Web site planning and design; basic HTML tags; and Microsoft's easy-to-use Web design tool, FrontPage Express.

Part V: Your PC and Hardware   If you're responsible for maintaining your own computer and for deciding what components to upgrade and when, you'll appreciate the last five chapters of this book. You'll learn how to protect your computer from physical hazards, and you'll get some guidelines for buying a new computer. If you don't want to spend thousands of dollars to get a system that's ready for the Internet and Windows 98, check out the chapters on adding RAM, multimedia, and modems. With very little money and the expertise you'll gain here, you just might give your current PC another couple of years of useful life.

Part VI: Internet User's Reference   The appendices in Part VI are designed for quick lookup—or casual browsing. There's an alphabetical reference to the essential commands and features of Windows 98, a glossary of Internet terminology you may encounter, and a comprehensive listing of HTML tags to use in your Web page design.

A Few Typographical Conventions

When an operation requires a series of choices from menus or dialog boxes, the ➢ symbol is used to guide you through the instructions, like this: "Select Programs ➢ Accessories ➢ System Tools ➢ System Information." The items the ➢ symbol separates may be menu names, toolbar icons, check boxes, or other elements of the Windows interface—anyplace you can make a selection.

This typeface is used to identify Internet URLs and HTML code, and **boldface type** is used whenever you need to type something into a text box.

You'll find these types of special notes throughout the book:

TIP

You'll see a lot of these — quicker and smarter ways to accomplish a task, which the authors have discovered based on many, many months spent testing products and using the Internet.

NOTE

You'll see these Notes, too. They usually represent alternate ways to accomplish a task or some additional information that needs to be highlighted.

WARNING

In a very few places you'll see a Warning like this one. When you see a warning, pay attention to it!

YOU'LL ALSO SEE SIDEBAR BOXES LIKE THIS

These boxed sections provide added explanation of special topics that are noted briefly in the surrounding discussion but that you may want to explore separately. Each sidebar has a heading that announces the topic so you can quickly decide whether it's something you need to know about.

For More Information...

See the Sybex Web site, www.sybex.com, to learn more about all the books that went into *Internet Complete*. On the site's Catalog page, you'll find links to any book you're interested in.

We hope you enjoy this book and find it useful. Happy surfing!

PART i
INTERNET BASICS

Chapter 1

DOORWAY TO THE WORLD: ONLINE SERVICES AND THE INTERNET

E arlier in this century, the telephone changed the way we communicated with other people and, as a result, brought the world closer together. Those same telephone lines are now providing instant access to every conceivable type of information and communication between people worldwide. At the end of this chapter, you will be able to

- ▶ Trace the history of the World Wide Web
- ▶ Identify the differences between commercial online services and the Internet
- ▶ Describe the major services of the Internet
- ▶ Identify the major roles of browsers and search engines

Adapted from *The Learning Guide to Computers*, by Gini Courter and Annette Marquis
ISBN 0-7821-1968-9   416 pages $24.99

THE BIRTH OF ONLINE COMMUNICATION

In the United States in the 1960s, concern about a nuclear attack by the Soviet Union was on everybody's mind. People were building bomb shelters in their back yards and stocking them with provisions in case the unthinkable ever happened. The U.S. military wanted to find a way to ensure that communications networks would not be destroyed, even if some of their sites fell victim to attack. So, the Advanced Research Projects Agency (ARPA) of the U.S. Defense Department funded a project to connect university computer scientists and engineers together via their computers and telephone lines. This project, called ARPANET, allowed researchers to share each other's computer facilities over long distances. Immensely more popular, however, was the use of ARPANET to exchange electronic mail (e-mail) with other users.

The next logical step from person-to-person e-mail was to find a way to broadcast the same message to multiple users. In this way, large-scale dialogues could occur with everyone reading and responding to everyone else's messages. ARPANET *mailing lists*, lists of users who all expressed interest in receiving e-mail about a particular general topic area, were developed, and a distribution system was established for the mail messages. One of the first large mailing lists was for science fiction aficionados, called SF-Lovers. With the combination of electronic mail, file transfers, and mailing lists, this network of networks, dubbed the *Internet*, was beginning to take shape.

Standardized Protocols

In 1975, Stanford University's Vinton Cerf developed a communication protocol called Transmission Control Protocol (TCP) and an addressing protocol called Internet Protocol (IP). TCP divides messages into streams of packets that are sent and then reassembled into messages at their destinations. IP addresses each packet and routes the packets across different nodes and through different networks before they arrive at their ultimate destination. By 1983, TCP/IP was established as the dominant standard for connecting computer networks. The TCP/IP standard allowed the Internet to grow from the original four host computers (the central computers in networks) in 1969 to almost 600 hosts by the end of 1983.

In 1983, the U.S. military segment of ARPANET was separated out and became known as MILNET. The Defense Department discontinued ARPANET's funding in 1989. By that time, the Internet had taken on a life of its own and no longer needed government support. Universities, laboratories, and private industries from around the world had developed essential communication links. With or without government funding, the Internet would survive.

Electronic Bulletin Boards

It was during the life of ARPANET that computer technology advanced from the era of enormous mainframes to desktop-based microcomputers. It didn't take long before personal computer owners began to show an interest in connecting with other computers from their homes and businesses. As modems and communications software were introduced into the market, the same people who championed the development of the personal computer began setting up ways to communicate with each other.

Because the Internet was developed for UNIX-based computers, it was available primarily to users in university and research settings. To address their own needs to connect with other users, personal computer owners of the late 1970s and early 1980s began to create a communication system that could run on DOS-based and Apple microcomputers. Electronic bulletin boards allowed anyone with a computer, a modem, and some relatively inexpensive software to set up a file system where other users could dial in and post messages, play games, and exchange files. People soon began to connect "on the boards." Unlike mailing lists, messages could be accessed by anyone subscribing to the bulletin board service. One person would leave a message and another would respond, then someone else would respond to the later message, and on it went. (This type of conversation, called a *thread*, often continues endlessly, long after the subject of the first message has lost its relevance.)

By the mid 1980s, electronic bulletin boards had become a popular way to "meet" other computer users, voice opinions, receive technical help, and download shareware and freeware. Today, electronic bulletin boards are still a communication option for many computer users despite or maybe because of the growth of the Internet. Many of the approximately 30,000 bulletin boards in existence in the United States are run by hobbyists who do not charge other users fees to access their computers. There are many national bulletin boards in existence today, but most boards tend to be local (so users don't have to incur long distance charges) and are often focused on a particular subject area. Boards are more intimate and more personal than the Internet and provide an easy way for people with similar interests to congregate and interact.

Commercial Online Services

As bulletin boards were growing in popularity, commercial organizations began to see the value in providing computer users with online access to information. They reasoned that if people found value in bulletin boards systems, surely there was a way to make online communication appealing enough that people would want to pay for additional services.

Two of the first commercial online information services, the Source and CompuServe, provided subscribers with a number of services for a fee based on *connect time*, the amount of time a user was actually connected to the service. The commercial information services were able to offer a wider range of services and easier access than the local bulletin boards. While many bulletin boards had only one incoming phone line to handle calls, commercial online services offered 24-hour access on hundreds of phone lines. The commercial services encouraged the involvement of the major hardware and software vendors so that computer owners could get up-to-date information about their favorite products. Soon, businesses outside the computer realm saw a value in establishing an online presence.

Although quite a few online services are in existence today, CompuServe (which eventually purchased the Source), America Online (AOL) and Prodigy are generally considered the top three commercial online information services. They each minimally offer the following types of services:

- ▶ Up-to-date news, weather, and sports information
- ▶ Electronic mail
- ▶ Computing support
- ▶ Entertainment and games
- ▶ Financial and professional information
- ▶ Travel information and reservations
- ▶ Reference and education resources
- ▶ Forums or special interest groups on specific topics
- ▶ Chat rooms for meeting people online
- ▶ Access to the Internet

CompuServe, the oldest of the remaining commercial online services, started as a data storage company in 1969 and began its online information service in 1979. From the early days, CompuServe was considered a top source for stock information, business news, professional organizations, and access to reference materials. One of CompuServe's greatest strengths is that it has access numbers in 185 countries, so business travelers can always connect to the service, receive e-mail, and have reference information at their fingertips. Figure 1.1 shows the Windows-based CompuServe Information Manager.

FIGURE 1.1: CompuServe Information Manager

A partnership between Sears, Roebuck and Company and IBM, Prodigy began operations in 1984 with a clearly identified marketing focus. In the beginning, Prodigy boasted lower connect time rates because it was supported by advertisers who would flash messages across the bottom of the Prodigy screens. If a member was interested in any of the products listed, all they had to do was click on the ad and they would be taken directly to that advertiser's information. Prodigy's competitors watched this experiment with keen interest and Prodigy's success eventually influenced the role of advertising in the other online services.

When America Online (AOL), shown in Figure 1.2, was launched in 1985, it promoted itself as the service for social users: a place where people could meet, participate in live chats, and get to know each other. AOL's People Connection and Life, Styles, and Interests sections have always been two of the most popular destinations for online socializers. In the 1990s, AOL reached out to the business sector, and today it is successfully positioned in both markets.

FIGURE 1.2: America Online's main switchboard

The World Wide Web Takes Control

The Internet continued expanding during the 1980s, as more networks were connected and more people were able to access those networks through universities and businesses. By the end of 1990, there were over 300,000 hosts connected to the Internet, a growth rate of 2000 percent in 10 years. Despite this rapid growth, the commercial online information services—with their graphical user interfaces and friendly, organized approach to accessing information—had nothing to fear from the text-based Internet. The Internet had little appeal to inexperienced users, and attracted correspondingly little commercial interest. The Internet was seen as just another source of information for those who were brave enough to enter its entangled web of UNIX, text-based commands.

What has happened in the 1990s could not have been predicted by even the most savvy business analysts. In 1992, Swiss software engineer Tim Berners-Lee introduced a graphical, hypertext navigation tool called the World Wide Web to the Internet. The World Wide Web provided the potential for the Internet to become as graphically interesting and easy to use as the commercial online services. Berners-Lee developed the Web as a convenient and efficient way to access documents stored on a number of different computer systems at CERN, the European particle-physics laboratory in Geneva where he worked. He had no intention of changing the course of human history; but within only a few short years, the World Wide Web has become an international phenomenon.

In response to the incredible expansion of the Internet, all of the commercial online services have had to undergo a dramatic shift. CompuServe is planning to abandon its proprietary software and become more closely integrated with the Internet. Prodigy has already done so. Moreover, all three major services provide direct access to the Internet through their software. Whether the commercial online information services will survive into the second millennium depends on how they redefine their corporate missions and realign their services with those exploding on the Internet.

THE INTERNET TODAY

Today's Internet is a collection of computer networks from all over the world that provide access to a number of information sources and services. While several of the services have their roots in ARPANET and early electronic bulletin boards, others have only been made possible by the development of the World Wide Web and the multimedia capacity of today's computers. All types of software and hardware companies are jockeying for the competitive advantage that can be obtained by developing new products that interface with the Web. With each passing day, a new service or innovation makes its debut on the World Wide Web. The only winners in this breakneck competition, besides consumers, are those companies that are able to take risks, develop flexible products and services, and keep the door open to new ideas.

Services of the World Wide Web

The World Wide Web is the fastest-growing marketplace, research facility, and communication tool in the world. It's possible to find information about almost any subject imaginable—from today's sport scores and stock prices to the dietary habits of an endangered Amazonian insect. You can watch movie previews, hear sound clips from the latest music CDs, listen to the news, research a subject for a paper, go on a virtual tour of the White House, explore Disney World, get the lyrics to all the Monty Python songs, go shopping, make airline reservations, and hold conversations with people from all over the globe.

All types of companies are recognizing the value of worldwide exposure to their products or services. Some of these businesses see the Web as an effective place to advertise, others see it as an opportunity to set up a new kind of business where consumers can actually shop and order products online.

What makes the Web most interesting, however, is the diversity of information that is available at no charge to anyone who logs in. You can download free software, read online newspapers and magazines, price a used car, and research any topic under the sun. It's virtually impossible to access the Web and not find something intriguing. And because the content is changing all the time, there is always something new to browse or a new site to explore.

Other Common Internet Services

Prior to the existence of the World Wide Web, Internet users had access to a number of tools to help them make use of computers on the Internet. The graphical World Wide Web has successfully incorporated many of these text-based services. As a result, it is possible to use these services without even realizing that you have left the Web. Three of the most-used Internet services that exist in both text-based and graphical forms include e-mail, mailing lists, and Usenet newsgroups.

E-Mail

Electronic mail or e-mail is probably the best know of all the Internet services. E-mail is a service that allows users to send electronic messages to other users with electronic addresses regardless of the system they are using. E-mail has provided the ability to almost instantaneously send written documents from one side of the globe to another and has changed the way people think about correspondence.

A typical Windows-based e-mail application is Netscape Mail, shown in Figure 1.3. Both incoming and outgoing mail can be filed in mail folders. The right side of the screen shows who sent the mail, the subject, and the date it was sent. The contents of the e-mail itself appear at the bottom of the screen.

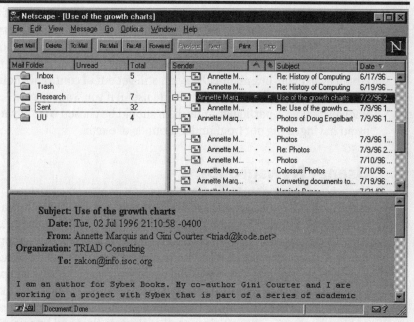

FIGURE 1.3: Netscape Mail

One of the most significant advantages of e-mail over traditional forms of correspondence is the ability to easily reply to mail received. The recipient can click the reply button, write their response, then click the send button; the response is on its way in minutes. Many people find that they correspond more efficiently and more promptly using e-mail than when using traditional forms of mail (referred to as "snail mail").

Mailing Lists

Today's mailing lists, also called *listservs*, are the direct descendants of the ARPANET mailing lists. There are literally tens of thousands of mailing lists in existence on every conceivable topic—from computer-related subjects to Voodoo. Mailing lists are a form of group e-mail. One person writes a message, which is broadcast to all the subscribers of the mailing list. Then, anyone who receives the message can reply to it, and their reply is broadcast in the same way. Because of this system, mailing lists can become overwhelming very quickly—it is not uncommon to receive 80 to 100 e-mail messages in one day. When that happens every day of the week, very few people can find the time to read them, much less respond to them. Some mailing lists archive the messages each day and send them out as packets of messages. This certainly helps in managing the e-mail avalanche, but mailing lists can still get out of control without great diligence. Although they are quite useful if you want to stay informed about a particular topic, lists should be chosen carefully to avoid having to dig out from under mounds of e-mail.

Usenet Newsgroups

Usenet newsgroups are text-based discussion groups on every topic imaginable—a more public form of mailing lists. Newsgroups are technically not a part of the Internet because they use the UNIX to UNIX Copy Protocol (UUCP) rather than the TCP/IP of the Internet. However, newsgroups have become such a popular service that most Internet providers include access to newsgroups. Anyone in the world with Usenet access can participate in a public newsgroup at any time (some groups are privately maintained and are not available to the general public). It's possible to read one or two messages (called articles) or all of them as time and interest allow.

NOTE

Because newsgroups are maintained on UNIX computers, their names reflect the UNIX naming conventions. For example, the newsgroup discussion for members of the Gumby fan club is **alt.fan.gumby**. The Alternate Trek Reality newsgroup is **alt.games.atr.rpg**.

Finding a high-quality newsgroup can sometimes be a challenge. Word of mouth is often one of the most effective methods. To find out about a newsgroup, you can read the Frequently Asked Questions (FAQ) article found in the newsgroup called **news.answers**. This article generally describes the newsgroup, its purpose, its members, and what topics are typically discussed. Figure 1.4 shows a list of some of the 25,000 Usenet newsgroups.

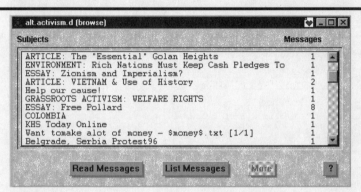

FIGURE 1.4: Usenet newsgroups using America Online

Other Internet Services

In addition to the mail-related tools, there are text-based tools used to exchange files and communicate with other computers on the Internet. Users of the Web can access these services from various Web sites. These include:

FTP   A system that lets users transfer files from one computer to another. Software programs, multimedia files, or documents can all be sent using File Transfer Protocol.

Gopher   A search tool that allows users to search through computers on the Internet through the use of a menu, it is largely being replaced by the World Wide Web. Figure 1.5 shows a typical Gopher menu.

IRC   A worldwide chat system, Internet Relay Chat allows users to type messages and receive immediate live responses from other users.

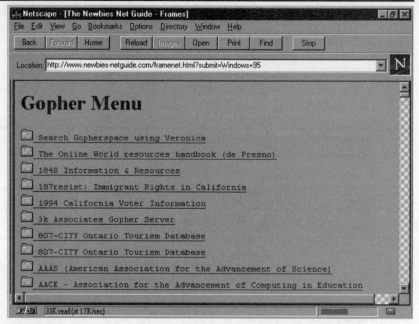

FIGURE 1.5: Typical Gopher menu accessed through the World Wide Web

Telnet   A system that allows users to access other computers, then run applications or access files that are housed there. Library card catalog databases are often set up using Telnet.

WAIS   Wide Area Information Servers provide a full text indexing system for documents searched in specific databases.

Accessing the Internet

As the demand for access intensifies, establishing an Internet and World Wide Web connection continues to become easier. There are three primary ways to gain access to the Internet:

- ▶ Students and staff of colleges and universities can gain access at no cost through their school. They may not have access to the World Wide Web, but they can usually use e-mail, FTP, and Telnet services.

- ▶ You can subscribe to a commercial online information service, like CompuServe, Prodigy, or America Online, that allow you to explore the Internet as part of the monthly fee.

▶ You can subscribe to an Internet service provider (ISP), an independent business that provides subscribers access to the Internet for a monthly fee.

A major consideration in deciding which type of access to choose used to be how many hours you expect to be online each month. Until last year subscriptions were typically based on the numbers of online hours. You can purchase plans that include from five to twenty hours per month, with an additional fee for each hour over. Many of the services also offer unlimited use plans and include a discount if you pay for a year in advance. Because of the intense competition for subscribers, pricing plans rarely remain constant in today's market. It's important to examine the pricing structure of the commercial online services and then compare them to a couple of ISPs before making a decision about which to choose.

Other questions you should consider in selecting a provider are:

▶ What services do they provide access to (e-mail, Telnet, Usenet)?

▶ What access rates can they support? A fast modem does no good if your service provider only supports slower ones.

▶ How many incoming lines do they have—how often can you expect a busy signal?

▶ Do they have access numbers in other cities so you can connect when you travel?

▶ Whom do you call if you have a problem with the service? What hours is technical support available?

NOTE

Because the Internet is no longer funded by the U.S. government, alternative methods have been developed to pay for its growth. At the current time, most ISPs and other organizations who want direct Internet access pay the telephone company a flat rate of $20,000 and a fee every month to lease a special type of telephone line called a T-1 line. Because it's a flat fee, users do not generate additional costs if they stay online. Most of the content on the Internet is placed there by volunteers or is paid for by businesses who desire a presence on the Net.

Internet Addresses

Although the World Wide Web is technically only a portion of the Internet, there are fewer services each day that cannot be accessed through the structure the Web provides. The Web combines TCP/IP, the protocol for sending documents across networks, with an entirely new method of locating and accessing documents on different networks. Berners-Lee created a simple coding mechanism involving a string of characters called a *universal resource locator* (URL) that identifies the name and address of each document available to the Web. The URL identifies:

▶ The type of server protocol used where the document is located. A server set up specifically for Web documents uses Hypertext Transfer Protocol (HTTP).

▶ The type of site: generally, World Wide Web (WWW); File Transfer Protocol (FTP), a protocol used specifically to transfer files from one computer to another; or Gopher, a client-server application that organizes the files on a server so users do not need to know or enter exact file names.

▶ The address of the host computer (*domain address*). The domain address consists of the name of the major server or *site*, the *subdomain* (usually the network, university, or company name), and the *domain* (a two or three letter designation of the type of institution).

▶ The specific location of the document on that computer's network (folders and subfolders and then the document's name).

Domain Names

Domain names are typically two- or three-character designations of the type of institution or organizations that own the domain. There are six common domain names used in the U.S.:

mil	military
gov	government
com	commercial companies
edu	educational institutions
net	companies and groups who administer the Internet
org	other organizations

Countries outside of the U.S. use a two-letter country code as their domain name.

Here's how the address `http://www.microsoft.com/msoffice/train_cert/word.htm`, where you'll find information regarding Microsoft certification, is constructed:

Protocol	http

Type of site	www
Subdomain	microsoft
Domain	com
Folder	msoffice/train_cert
Document	word.htm

By assigning an address to each document that can be accessed on the Web, documents can be accessed directly from other documents using Hypertext Markup Language (HTML) code. A link is created from one document to another. Clicking on the link sends a message to that document's host computer and the document is retrieved. Figure 1.6 shows a typical hypertext link from a search tool to a document. Underlined words designate links to other documents.

50% <u>The Nature Conservancy</u> [<u>Find Similar</u>]
URL: <u>http://csde.aces.k12.ct.us/friends/ccsi/csusa/enviro/naturcon.html</u>
Topic:
<u>/Life and Style/Environment/Groups and Organizations/By Region/United</u> ;
Review: The beauty of the Nature Conservancy is that to protect habitat, they just buy up property. You can find chapter links here and info on the Great Lakes Biodiversity Project, the East Maui Watershed Partnership and other programs.

FIGURE 1.6:   Example of hypertext links

Berners-Lee never intended for people to type in URL addresses directly. As improved methods of accessing files are developed, Berners-Lee expects that URL addresses will soon become invisible to users. In the meantime, Web users have the option of entering a URL address directly or clicking on a hypertext link that can direct them to the desired document.

TOOLS TO EXPLORE THE WEB

The World Wide Web has stimulated the development of numerous new ways to navigate the Web, to find all of the Web's buried treasures, and even to design your own exciting Web sties. You can spend all day browsing through the content on the World Wide Web (surfing), or you can target your search and have your results in just minutes. Whatever your approach, the World Wide Web provides an easy way to travel the globe without leaving your home.

Browsers

A document on the Web is called a *Web page*. The first page in a series of related documents or a site is called a *home page*. A *browser* is a software program designed to provide a friendly interface on the Web, display Web pages, and move between Web sites. A browser plays an important role in managing your interaction with the Web. Among other things, a browser lets you review Web content; save, download, copy, or print what you find; mark an address with a bookmark so you can return to the same site later; read and send mail; and record a history of where you've visited.

Competition between companies who make browsers has been fierce at times. By 1996, Netscape Navigator, shown in Figure 1.7, emerged as the clear leader in the browser wars, capturing over 85 percent of the market. While Microsoft's Internet Explorer, shown in Figure 1.8, has gone head to head with Navigator, Navigator is still the leader. Both products provide integrated e-mail and news services, bookmarks to save the locations of worthy Web sites, security features to prevent unauthorized access to information about users, and a number of other features to make browsing the Web easier.

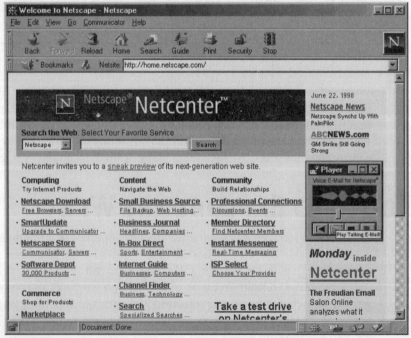

FIGURE 1.7: Netscape Navigator and Netscape's Home Page

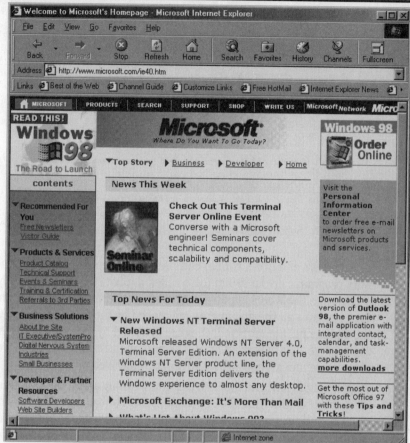

FIGURE 1.8:   Microsoft's Internet Explorer

Search Engines

A *search engine* is an application on the Web that allows you to search for particular Web sites based on key words or concepts. There are a growing number of search engines found on the World Wide Web, and each one produces somewhat different results. One of the largest search engines, Alta Vista, shown in Figure 1.9, was created by Digital's Research Laboratories in Palo Alto, California. Each day, Alta Vista indexes over 30,000,000 Web pages and 3,000,000 Usenet newsgroups and processes over 12,000,000 requests.

Doorway to the World: Online Services

FIGURE 1.9: Search using Alta Vista

Alta Vista and other similar comprehensive search engines use a software program called a spider (also called a *robot*) that automatically travels through the Web's hypertext structure, retrieves a document, and then retrieves all the documents referenced by the first document. Once the documents are retrieved, they are reviewed by index software that can analyze 1GB of text an hour. Then when users enter a search word or phrase, the index directs them to appropriate Web pages.

Learning to navigate the Web requires learning about the various search tools available and what their specialties are. For example, Yahoo is organized by subject matter, so if you're looking for collections of resources related to a single topic, it is a great place to start (see Figure 1.10). Other search engines, such as The Internet Sleuth, only reference databases that are found on the Web and the articles in them.

Each search engine has its own rules for how to conduct an effective search using that particular engine. To learn how to narrow down your search to pages directly related to your topic, it's important to read the Help files that are available on the search engine's home page. For example, if you choose to search on the word *spiders* to find out about how spiders are used on the World Wide Web, many of the search engines will return references to the eight-legged creatures as well as to the software versions. But you can narrow down the search so that only software references appear, if you know the rules of the search engine you're using. Many people figure that they can sort through the results of a broad search, but when your search returns 30,000 references, this can be a daunting task.

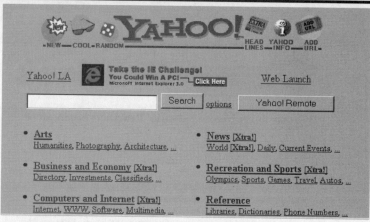

FIGURE 1.10:   Yahoo organizes searches by category.

Audio and Video

The World Wide Web is not limited to text and graphics. You can also listen to audio and view video files on the Web. In order to access most audio and video files on the Internet, users must first *download* the file (transfer the file from the host computer to their own) and then use a software application to play the file. Transferring real-time audio and video over the Internet continues to present challenges to developers. TCP/IP does not include any ability to control the speed or consistency at which information is transferred. Some packets may move quickly, while others are slowed down because of congestion at a particular network's site.

Streaming technology has provided an adequate but far from ideal solution to the audio and video problem. Audio and video streaming applications begin playing the file as it is being downloaded, rather than waiting until the entire file is received. This means that the user does not have to wait for the file to be completely downloaded. Audio streaming is being used successfully to "broadcast" the content of radio shows such as Gina Smith's *On Computers*, a weekly Saturday afternoon radio talk show, as shown in Figure 1.11. However, while it's important to note that the quality of the transmission is still affected by the traffic load on the Internet and the user's modem speed, the streaming software available today does a more than adequate job.

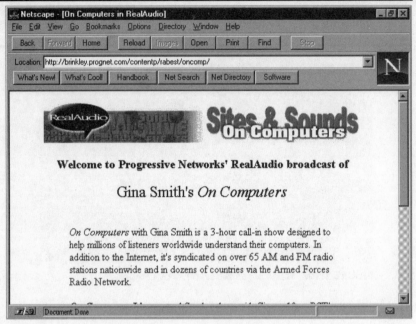

FIGURE 1.11:   Gina Smith's *On Computers* Web page

New audio and video technology is constantly being improved and transmission and quality problems are being corrected. Streaming audio and video are commonplace on the Internet.

BECOMING A CONTRIBUTOR TO THE WEB

One of the most exciting elements of the Internet is that everyone can participate. The Web is not only a tool for locating information, it is also a tool for disseminating information. Anyone who wants to can become an Internet publisher, by creating their own Web pages and using hypertext links to connect them to other pages and other Web sites. A small business can have as much of a presence on the Web as a major corporation. In fact, some of the most popular Web sites belong to innovative entrepreneurs who see the Web as an opportunity to compete with Goliath. Race, gender, age, and physical ability are no longer factors when the Internet becomes your communication medium. All you need is some knowledge about how Web sites are created, a little ingenuity to make your site interesting, and a willingness to try something new.

Creating a Web Page

Hypertext Markup Language (HTML) is used to create Web pages and specifically to link one page to another on the Web. HTML is a set of text codes, called *tags*, that format a document so it can be read by a Web browser. Many applications exist that write HTML code for you while you use special design tools to create a Web page. Major word processing applications like Microsoft Word and Corel WordPerfect have HTML designers available for their products. These products are somewhat limited in the available design features but are improving with each new release. Fonts pose a special problem to Web page designers because the person viewing the document must have the font on their system that the designer used to create their page. Until this problem is resolved, good designers designate substitute fonts as backups in case the preferred font is not available.

Once your page is created and the links are verified, you can upload it to your ISP's computer and instantly become an active participant in the World Wide Web. (ISPs may charge a fee to activate your site and maintain it after it is up.)

Making a Web Page Come Alive

Adding some excitement to Web pages, a programming language called Java entered the scene. Java is a flexible object-oriented programming language that can easily cross over from one operating system platform to another without difficulty. This feature makes it ideal for use on Web pages that will be viewed by many different types of computer systems. In simple terms, *object-oriented* means that the data and all the programming code needed to manipulate the data is bundled with the object. Rather than having to include an entire application with each Web page, only the code for the particular object appearing on the page needs to appear there. What this means for the Web is that Java applets (small applications) can be attached to Web pages to create animated objects (for example, a bird flying across the page or text flashing on and off), interactive games and puzzles, and other multimedia events that are activated while the page is being viewed. Java has become a very popular way to draw attention to a particular Web page and make it stand out from the rest.

Virtual Reality

The Web may just be in its infancy but some say that a programming language, called Virtual Reality Modeling Language (VRML), will change the graphical Web into a 3-D environment. Sites created with VRML will allow users to "walk through" a city, examine an object from all sides, or navigate through a virtual office. VRML promises to be an exciting advance in Web technology, but because it is dependent on processor and connection speeds, it will be a while yet before all users are able to benefit from this innovation.

WHAT'S NEXT?

Now that Gini Courter and Annette Marquis have given you an overview of the Internet, you're ready to get online. In the next chapter, you'll get your computer connected.

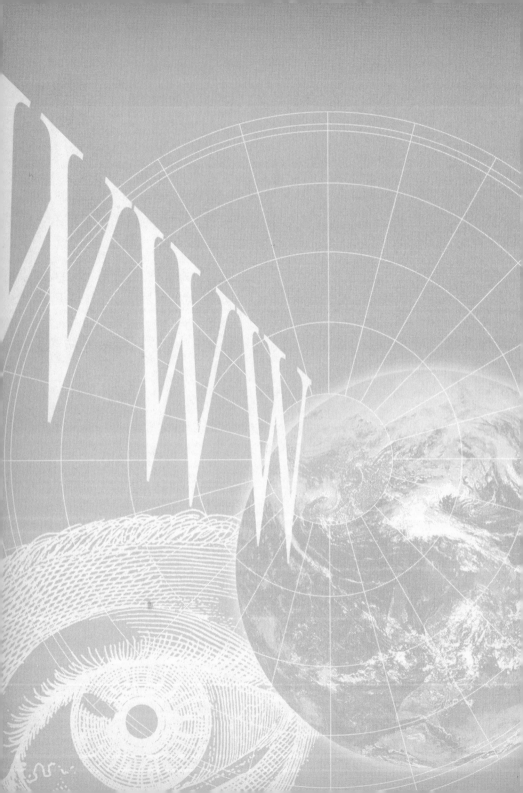

Chapter 2

CONNECTING TO THE INTERNET

Before you can use an Internet application program, you must connect your own computer to the Internet. In this chapter, you will find information about choosing an Internet service provider; making the connection through a modem, a LAN, or other link; and installing and configuring your system for a TCP/IP connection.

If you already have an Internet connection that supports other TCP/IP Internet client programs, you may be able to use it with your browser. If that's the case, you can skip this chapter.

NOTE

This chapter comes from a book about Internet Explorer, but the information here applies to setting up a connection for any Internet browser.

Adapted from *The ABCs of Microsoft Internet Explorer 4*,
by John Ross
ISBN 0-7821-2042-3   400 pages $19.99

WHAT KIND OF CONNECTION?

Choosing a way to connect your computer to the Internet is a trade-off between performance and cost; more money gets you a faster link between your own system and the backbone. While the difference between file transfers through a modem and a high-speed link can be dramatic, the cost of improved performance may not always be justified. For most home users and many small businesses, a dial-up telephone line and a 33.6 or 56Kbps modem is still the most cost-effective choice.

If it's available in your area, you might want to consider *ISDN* (Integrated Services Digital Network) as an alternative to conventional *POTS* (Plain Old Telephone Service) lines. ISDN is more expensive and complicated to install and configure, but once it's in place, it offers much faster network connections. Your Internet service provider can tell you if ISDN service is available and explain how to order the lines and obtain the necessary interface equipment.

In a larger business, where many users can share the same link to the Internet, a connection with more bandwidth is probably a better approach. Many users can share a single high-speed connection through a LAN, so the cost per user may not be significantly greater than that of a second telephone line.

If your PC is already connected to a LAN, you should ask your network administrator or help desk about setting up an Internet account; it's likely that there's already some kind of connection in place.

As with most decisions related to data communications, the simple answer to "What kind of connection to the Internet should I use?" is "The fastest that you can afford."

INSTALLING AND CONFIGURING A MODEM

For many individuals and small businesses, the most practical way to connect is through a dial-up telephone line and a modem. *Modem* is a made-up word constructed out of *mod*ulator-*dem*odulator. A modem converts digital data from a computer into sounds that can travel through telephone lines designed for voice communication (that's the *modulator* part), and it also converts sounds that it receives from a telephone line to digital data that the computer can process (that's the *demodulator* part).

Choosing a Modem

For reasons of economy, convenience, or simplicity, you've decided to go with an inexpensive connection to the Internet through a modem and a telephone line. What now? If you don't already have a modem, go find one. There are three things to consider when you choose a modem: speed, form, and compatibility.

Modem Speed

The speed of a modem is the maximum number of data bits that can pass through the modem in one second. You might find some extremely inexpensive 9600bps (bits per second) modems, but that's really too slow for programs like Internet Explorer. Don't waste your time or your money. Anything slower than 14,400bps is most useful as a paperweight or a boat anchor.

Today, almost all new modems have maximum speeds of either 28,800 or 33,600bps. Even faster modems that operate at 56,000bps (also called 56K) are now beginning to appear, but at least two different incompatible types are available. Before you buy a 56K modem, check with your service provider to make sure it will work with their modems. For most people, it's probably best to wait until a single standard emerges and the price drops before buying a 56K modem.

A fast modem is good enough for many users, especially because most households and offices already have at least one telephone line, so there's no added expense for installing a new circuit. Even if you decide you need an additional phone line for your modem, the cost will still be less than the price of a high-speed network circuit.

Modem Form

Modems come in three forms: internal, external, and on a credit-card size PCMCIA card (also known as a PC Card). Each type has specific advantages and disadvantages:

- Internal modems are expansion cards that fit inside your PC. They're the least expensive type of modem, and they don't require special data cables or power supplies. Because they bypass a bottleneck in your computer's COM ports, internal modems can actually handle data transfers faster than external modems rated at the same speed. However, internal modems are a nuisance to

install, and they don't include the status lights that show the
progress of your calls.

▶ External modems are separate, self-contained units that are easy
to install and move between computers. They cost more than
internal modems, and they need separate AC power outlets. In
order to use an external modem, your computer must have an
unused serial (COM) connector.

▶ PC Cards are small, lightweight devices that fit into the PCMCIA
slots on many laptop computers. They're the most convenient
modems for people who travel with their PCs, but they're also the
most expensive.

Modem Compatibility

The third thing to consider when you choose a modem is compatibility
with standards. In order to connect your computer to a distant system,
the modems at both ends of the link must use the same methods for
encoding and compressing data. Therefore, you should use a modem that
follows the international standards for data communication. The important standard for 28,800bps and 33,600bps modems is called V.34; the
standard for slower modems is V.32bis. Don't even consider a modem
that doesn't follow one of these standards.

Installing a Modem in Windows 98

After you physically connect the modem to your computer, you must also
notify the operating system that there's a new modem in place.

In Windows 98, communications control functions are located in a
central application programming interface (API) that moves data between
your modem and individual communications programs. One of the benefits of this design is that you can configure Windows 98 to work with your
modem just once, rather than repeating the process for each application
program that uses a modem.

Windows 98 should automatically detect your modem when you turn
on your computer. If you're using an older modem ("older" means anything made before late 1995), Windows 98 may choose an incorrect
modem configuration for you or may be unable to detect the modem at
all. In that case, you'll need to add it to the configuration manually.

WARNING

If Windows 98 is unable to detect your modem, you should make sure the modem is properly connected. All modems provide some information to the Operating System while the computer boots. It is unlikely that a modem will provide no information at that time.

If you need to manually configure Windows 98 for your modem, follow these steps:

1. Click on the Start button to open the Start menu.

2. Move the cursor to Settings and click on the Control Panel command in the Settings sub-menu.

3. When the Control Panel window opens, double-click on the Modems icon. The Modems Properties dialog box, shown in Figure 2.1, will appear.

4. If Windows 98 has already detected your modem, its name will appear in the Modems Properties dialog box. If the correct modem is already listed, you can close the dialog box now—skip to step 7. If there is no modem listed or if the name on the list does not match the modem you want to use, click on the Add button to run the Install New Modem wizard.

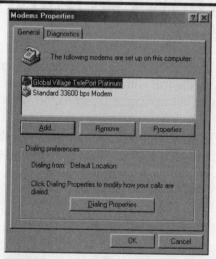

FIGURE 2.1: The Modems Properties dialog box identifies the modem currently installed in your system.

5. The Wizard will look for a modem on each of your COM ports. If it fails to find a modem, it will ask you to specify the make and model and the port to which the modem is connected. If it finds a modem, but it does not recognize the make and model, it will use one of the (Standard Modem Types) options. If your modem came with a Windows 98 installation diskette, put the diskette in your computer's drive and click on the Have Disk button to load the configuration software for your modem. If you don't have a disk, don't worry about it; the (Standard Modem Types) settings will almost certainly work just fine.

6. When the Wizard completes the installation, it will return you to the Modems Properties dialog box, which should now include the modem that you just installed in the list of modems. If the list shows more than one modem, you can select the ones you're not using and click on the Remove button, but it's not really necessary; Windows 98 will identify the active modem every time you turn on your computer.

7. Click on the Close button and close the Control Panel to complete the installation.

SETTING UP WINDOWS 98 DIAL-UP NETWORKING

If your ISP has not given you automatic configuration software, you must set up a Dial-Up Networking profile that will dial your ISP's closest telephone number whenever you start Internet Explorer or some other Winsock-compliant application program.

Creating a new profile is not difficult, but it's a little more complicated than simply clicking on an option in the Setup Wizard. To configure a Dial-Up Networking connection profile, you must complete two separate procedures: load the software and create a connection profile.

Loading the Software

If you didn't load Dial-Up Networking when you installed Windows 98, you must add it before you can connect to the Internet. Follow these steps to add the software:

1. Open the Control Panel.

2. Double-click on the Add/Remove Programs icon.

3. Click on the Windows Setup tab to display the Windows Setup page of the dialog box.

4. Select the Communications item from the Components list and click on the Details button.

5. Make sure there's a checkmark next to the Dial-Up Networking component and click on the OK button.

6. When you see a message instructing you to insert software disks, follow the instructions as they appear.

7. When the software has been loaded, restart the computer.

8. The Control Panel should still be open. Double-click on the Network icon.

9. Click on the Add button to display the Select Network Component Type dialog box, shown in Figure 2.2.

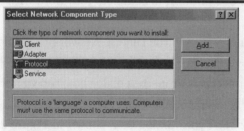

FIGURE 2.2: Use the Select Network Component Type dialog box to set up Dial-Up Networking.

10. Select Protocol in the list of component types and click on the Add button.

11. Select Microsoft from the list of manufacturers and TCP/IP in the list of network protocols. Click on the OK button.

12. You should see TCP/IP in the list of network components. Click on the OK button to close the dialog box.

Creating a Connection Profile

Once you've added support for TCP/IP networking, you're ready to set up one or more connection profiles. Follow these steps to create a profile:

1. Start Dial-Up Networking from either the My Computer window on the Desktop or the Programs ➤ Accessories menu.

2. Double-click on the Make New Connection icon.

3. The Make New Connection Wizard will start. The name of the computer you will dial is also the name that will identify the icon for this connection profile in the Dial-Up Networking folder. Therefore, you should change the name of this profile from "My Connection" to the name of your service provider. If you have separate profiles for telephone numbers in different cities, include the city name as well. For example, if you use SPRYnet as your access provider, you might want to create profiles called SPRYnet Chicago and SPRYnet Boston.

4. Click on the Next button to move to the next screen, and type the telephone number for your ISP's PPP access.

5. Click on the Finish button to complete your work with the Wizard.

6. You will see a new icon in the Dial-Up Networking window. Right-click on this icon and select the Properties command.

7. When the Connections Properties dialog box, shown in Figure 2.3, appears, click on the Server Type button.

8. When the Server Types dialog box, shown in Figure 2.4, appears, choose the PPP option in the drop-down list of dial-up server types.

FIGURE 2.3: Use the Connections Properties dialog box to configure Dial-Up Networking.

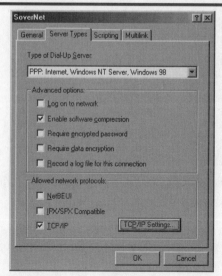

FIGURE 2.4: Use the Server Types dialog box to set up a PPP connection.

9. Make sure there are checkmarks next to these options:

    ▶ Log on to network

    ▶ Enable software compression

    ▶ TCP/IP

10. Click the TCP/IP Settings button.

11. Ask your ISP how to fill in this dialog box. You will probably use a Server Assigned IP Address and specific DNS addresses, but your ISP can give you the exact information you need.

12. Click the OK buttons to close all the open dialog boxes.

To confirm that you have set up the connection profile properly, turn on your modem and double-click the new icon. When the Connect To dialog box, shown in Figure 2.5, appears, type your user ID and password and click on the Connect button. Your computer should place a call to the ISP and connect your system to the Internet.

FIGURE 2.5: The Connect To dialog box shows the name and telephone number of your ISP.

If you have accounts with more than one ISP, or if you carry the same computer to different cities, you can create separate connection profiles for each ISP or each telephone number.

When you start Internet Explorer or any other Internet application program, the application will automatically open your default Dial-Up Networking profile and set up a connection. If you have more than one profile, you can select one that is not the default by double-clicking the icon for that profile in the Dial-Up Networking window.

CONNECTING TO THE INTERNET THROUGH MICROSOFT NETWORK

Along with all those other service providers, Microsoft has an Internet access product of their own. The Microsoft Network (MSN) was established as an online information service that would compete with AOL and CompuServe, but a few months after it was launched, Microsoft announced that MSN would be converted to a service with content areas that are extensions of the Internet.

Microsoft wants you to use their Internet access service, so they've made it extremely easy to load and configure a Windows 98 Dial-Up Networking connection to MSN. If you already have an account with MSN, or if there's an MSN telephone number that supports Internet access within local calling range of your office or home, the Microsoft service may be the easiest (but probably not the least expensive) way to set up a Windows 98 Internet connection.

When you install Internet Explorer, the Setup Wizard will ask if you want to connect through Microsoft Network or through some other service provider. If you choose MSN and state that you don't already have an MSN account, the Wizard will step you through the process of finding a local telephone number and establishing a new account. If you already have an MSN account, you can easily add Internet access:

1. Double-click on the MSN icon.

2. When the Sign In window appears, click on the Settings button.

3. Click on the Access Numbers button.

4. In the Microsoft Network dialog box, choose Internet and The Microsoft Network as your service type.

5. Click on the Change buttons to select the closest Primary and Backup telephone numbers.

6. Click on the OK buttons to close all the dialog boxes and save your selections.

When setup is complete, you will have a Dial-Up Networking connection profile for Microsoft Network, and if you specified a backup telephone number, a separate backup connection profile.

CHANGING THE DEFAULT CONNECTION

When setup is complete, you will have a Dial-Up Networking connection profile for each of your ISPs. Internet Explorer and other Winsock-compliant programs will use the current default to connect your computer to the Internet whenever you start the programs.

To change the default, follow these steps:

1. Right-click on the The Internet icon on your Desktop and select the Properties command from the menu.

2. When the Internet Properties dialog box appears, click on the Connection tab.

3. Click on the Settings button to display the dialog box shown in Figure 2.6.

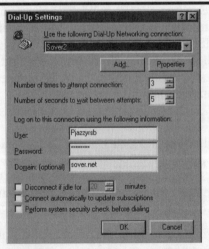

FIGURE 2.6: Use the Dial-Up Settings dialog box to change the default connection profile.

4. Choose the name of the Dial-Up Networking connection profile you want to use from the drop-down list.

5. Click on the OK button to close the dialog box.

Using Alternative Connection Methods

A telephone connection (via a modem) is the most common and least expensive way for individuals to reach the Internet; but it's not your only option. If they're not available now, high-speed data services will probably become available from your telephone company, cable TV service, and other new information utilities within the next few years. You can also use Internet Explorer with high-speed network connections through a corporate LAN or a campus-wide network.

Each of these services requires a special network interface device that allows your computer to send and receive data more quickly than the COM port can handle it. The specific hardware and software requirements are different for each type of connection; your network service provider will tell you exactly what you need.

As far as Internet Explorer is concerned, the only difference between a dial-in connection to the Internet and a faster network link is the amount of time it will take to download and display Web pages and other files.

What's Next?

So you're connected to the Internet. Now what? Turn to the next chapter, where Christian Crumlish will show you how to use this connection to send and receive electronic mail.

Chapter 3

COMMUNICATING WITH E-MAIL

T his is the real stuff. The reason why you're on the Net. E-mail! Instant (more or less) communication with people all over the globe. Once you can send and receive e-mail, you're wired.

This chapter will cover the most basic e-mail concepts—mainly, how to send and receive e-mail. If you have an internal network at your office and you're already familiar with how to send and receive mail, you can probably skip this chapter (though you might want to read the parts about how to write an Internet e-mail address to send mail beyond your network).

Adapted from *The Internet: No experience required.*, by Christian Crumlish
ISBN 0-7821-2168-3   528 pages $24.99

NOTE

When you get used to sending e-mail, you'll find that it's as useful a form of communication as the telephone and doesn't require the other person to drop whatever they're doing to answer your call. You can include a huge amount of specific information, and the person you sent mail to can reply in full in their own good time. And unlike the telephone, with e-mail you can edit your message before you send it.

E-mail is the lifeblood of the Internet. Daily, millions of written messages course through the wires, enabling people all over the planet to communicate in seconds. One reason for the widespread use of the Internet as the international computer network is that it's a flexible enough system to allow just about any type of computer or network to participate. The upside of this is that whether you have a Mac, PC, or more exotic type of computer, whether you connect by modem or from a network, and no matter what e-mail program you have, you can still send and receive e-mail over the Internet.

The downside is that there are so many different e-mail programs available that I can't hope to cover each one in detail, so I'll start off by explaining the most common activities associated with e-mail, the kinds of things you'll want to know how to do no matter what program you have. I'll use generic terminology in this part of the chapter, such as Inbox and Outbox, even if some specific programs use different terms for the same ideas. Focus on the concepts and the standard features, not what they're called in one program or another. Then, I'll cover specific commands and tips for a heaping handful of the most common e-mail programs—chances are you'll be using one of them.

In the unlikely circumstance that you have none of the specific programs that I cover, the first part of the chapter will still provide you with a list of actions to look for in the help portion of your e-mail program or to discuss with your system (or network) administrator.

If you do most of your e-mailing at work, your e-mail program may actually be *groupware*, functioning also as a calendar, an address book, a scheduler, a bulletin board, and a way to collaborate. Groupware programs can also connect you to co-workers across intranets.

YOUR E-MAIL PROGRAM MAY DEPEND ON YOUR TYPE OF SERVICE

If you have a typical dial-up account, or if you connect to the Internet through a network at your work or school, then you'll run a stand-alone mail program in your normal operating environment. If you get your Internet access through a commercial network, such as America Online or CompuServe, then you'll use their built-in mail programs, and sending mail over the Internet will require only that you use the proper sort of Internet mailing address. If you've got a Unix shell account, then you'll handle your mail either by running a Unix e-mail program (such as Pine) or by setting up an offline mail program, such as Eudora, that will run in your normal computer environment and will connect with your shell account only when you need to send and receive mail.

WORKING WITH E-MAIL

These are the things that you will do most often with e-mail:

▶ Run the mail program

▶ Send mail

▶ Read incoming mail

▶ Reply to mail

▶ Delete mail

▶ Exit the mail program

NOTE

In Chapter 4, *Refining E-Mail Messages*, Christian Crumlish will show you some additional e-mail tricks you might find useful, such as how to forward mail and create an electronic address book.

Running an E-Mail Program

You start most e-mail programs the way you do any program, usually by double-clicking an icon or by choosing a program name from a menu (the Start menu in Windows 98, the Apple menu on a Mac). If your Internet connection is not already up and running, your e-mail program may be able to start that process for you.

TIP

If you have to log into a Unix shell, then you'll start your mail program (probably Pine) by typing its name at the Unix prompt and pressing Enter.

Your e-mail program will start and either show you the contents of your Inbox (the mailbox where your new messages arrive) or will show you a list of all your mailboxes (in which case you'll want to open the Inbox).

NOTE

There are some new free Internet accounts (such as HotMail and Juno.com), that offer Web-based e-mail access. The accounts are paid for by advertising you have to keep on your screen while you're connected. To find out more about them, go to http://www.HotMail.com or http://www.Juno.com in your Internet browser, as described in Chapter 6.

In addition to an Inbox where just-arrived messages appear, you'll automatically have an Outbox in which copies of your outgoing messages can be saved (some programs will do this automatically), and usually a deleted-messages or Trash mailbox where discarded messages are held until they are completely purged. Figure 3.1 shows a Microsoft Outlook 98 Inbox and Inbox for Microsoft Outlook Express, which is part of Microsoft Internet Explorer 4.

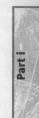

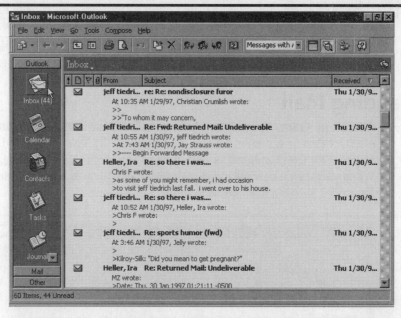

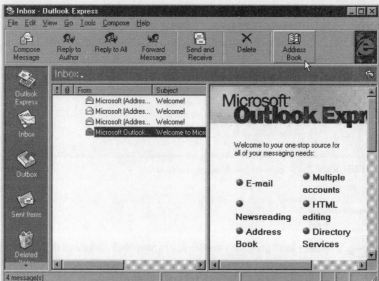

FIGURE 3.1: The first screen shows my Microsoft Outlook 98 Inbox with messages listed in the order they were sent, from the most recent to the oldest. Compare that Inbox to the one shown next for Microsoft Outlook Express, which comes with Microsoft Internet Explorer 4.

Mailboxes generally list just the sender's name and the subject line of the message (and probably its date as well). When you double-click a message in any of your mailboxes, the message will open up in a window of its own.

Sending Mail

All mail programs have a New Message or Compose E-Mail command, often located on a message menu, and they usually have a keyboard shortcut for the command as well, such as Ctrl+N for New Message. When you start a new message, your program will open a new window. Figure 3.2 shows a new message window in Eudora.

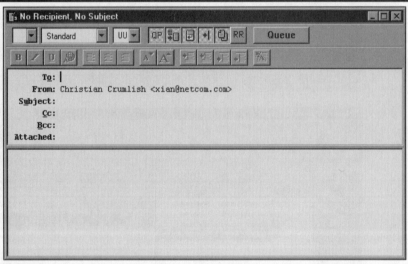

FIGURE 3.2: A blank New Message window

TIP

Most e-mail programs enable you to save addresses and then select them from an address book or list of names rather than type them in directly. See Chapter 4, *Refining E-Mail Messages*, for more information.

Type the address of the person to whom you wish to send the mail. The person's address must be of the form *username@address.domain*, where *username* is the person's identifier (the name they log in with); *address* is the identifier of the person's network or machine on the network (the address might consist of several words—the host and subdomain—separated by dots); and *domain* is the short code at the end indicating whether the address is a business (.com), a non-profit (.org), a university (.edu), a branch of the government (.gov), a part of the military (.mil), and so on. (Some e-mail programs require special text before or after the Internet e-mail address.)

By the way, all the rules mentioned in the previous category apply only to sending mail over the Internet. Generally, if you're sending mail to someone on your own network (or another member of your online service or a subscriber of your service provider), you only have to specify the username, not any of the Internet information.

TIP

The easiest way to send mail to someone is to reply to mail that they've sent you. If you're not sure exactly how to form someone's e-mail address, ask them to send you some mail and then simply reply to it. That's what I always do.

One of my addresses is xian@netcom.com (you pronounce the "@" as "at," and the "." as "dot"). I log in as "xian," my service provider is Netcom, and Netcom is a commercial business.

Sending Mail to People on Other Networks

Many people have Internet addresses even though they are not, strictly speaking, on the Internet. Most other networks have gateways that send mail to and from the Internet. If you want to send mail to someone on another network, you'll need to know their identifier on that network and how their network address appears in Internet form. Here are examples of the most common Internet addresses:

Network	Username	Internet Address
America Online	Beebles	Beebles@aol.com
AT&T Mail	Beebles	beebles@attmail.com
CompuServe	75555,5555	75555.5555@compuserve.com
Fidonet BBS	1:2/3	f3.n2.z1@fidonet.org
MCI Mail	555-7777	555-7777@mcimail.com
Microsoft Network	Beebles	beebles@msn.com
Prodigy	Beebles	beebles@prodigy.com
SoVerNet	Beebles	beebles@sover.net

As you can see, the only tricky ones are CompuServe (for which you have to change the comma in the CompuServe address to a dot in the Internet address) and Fidonet, for which you have to reverse the order of the three numbers and then put them after f, n, and z, respectively. (If you are only given two numbers, in the form a/b, then assume that they are the n and f numbers and that the z number is 1 (one).)

NOTE

Not all Internet and e-mail addresses end in .com. Some ISPs' addresses end in .net, .org, .gov, .mil, or .edu.

Here's how to create an e-mail message:

1. After entering the recipient's address in the Address box, press Tab and then type a subject in the Subject box (keep it short). This will be the first thing the recipient of your mail sees.

TIP

The subject you type in the subject line should be fairly short, but should be a good description of the contents of your message. Good subject lines can help recipients categorize their mail and respond more quickly to your messages. If they are using Inbox filters, described in Chapter 4, they may be presorting their e-mail according to the contents of the subject line, making the subject even more important for getting your mail noticed.

2. If you want to send a copy of the e-mail message to more than one recipient, you can either:

   ▶ Type that person's address on the Cc: line.

   ▶ Type multiple addresses in either the To: or Cc: line, separating each address by a comma. In some e-mail programs, the addresses may appear on separate lines.

TIP

In almost all e-mail programs, you can press Tab to jump from box to box or from area to area when filling in an address and subject. Generally, you can also just click directly in the area you want to jump to in most programs.

3. Press Tab until the insertion point jumps into the blank message area.

4. When you are done, send the message or add it to a *queue,* a list of outgoing messages to be sent all at once. Press the Send button, or select File ➢ Send.

TIP

Most e-mail programs can word-wrap your message, so you only have to press Enter when you want to start a new paragraph. I recommend leaving a blank line between paragraphs, to make them easier to read. Figure 3.3 shows a short e-mail message.

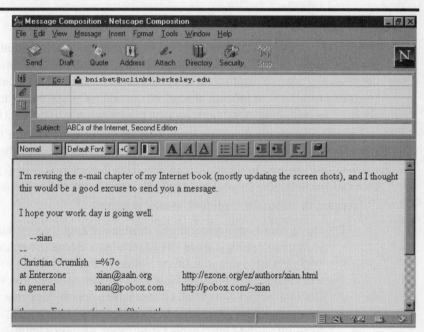

FIGURE 3.3: A short e-mail message to a friend

Some e-mail programs allow you to filter messages, which is the same thing as sorting them according to some criteria as they come into your Inbox. The post office sorts mail according to zip code; you can use your e-mail program to automatically sort messages according to who sent them, the subject, the date they were sent or received, or any other category that is useful to you from an organizational standpoint. See Chapter 4 for more on message filters.

TIP

You can sort your messages in many e-mail applications, according to categories and other criteria. Certain e-mail programs also allow you to flag messages according to the urgency of the response needed or other priorities. Check in your application's Help menu or under the File or Edit menus (in Windows programs) for commands such as Sort or Categorize. These options provide you with powerful organizational tools and transform your messages into valuable records that can be filed and retrieved for later reference. See Chapter 4 for more about sorting.

Reading Mail

Whenever I connect to the Net, the first thing I do is check my e-mail. It's like checking your mailbox when you get home, except that the contents are generally more interesting—and usually don't contain bills! Some mail programs combine the process of sending queued messages with checking for new mail. Most also check for new mail when you first start them.

Unread (usually new) mail typically appears with some indicator that it's new, such as the Subject line appearing in bold, or a bullet or checkmark appearing next to the new messages. This is supposed to help you pick out the messages you haven't read yet, so that you don't miss any.

Here are the steps for reading an e-mail message:

1. Open your e-mail program by double-clicking its shortcut icon or selecting it from the Start menu. Some programs begin by displaying your Inbox contents, and with others you will need to click on a Get New Mail button, or select File ➢ Get Mail or Get New Mail. Others have a special Mail menu selection, where you choose Mail ➢ Get New Mail, or Mail ➢ Read Incoming Mail. Display your Inbox with the command appropriate for your program.

2. To view the contents of a mail message, highlight it in the Inbox window and press Enter (or double-click it). The message will appear in its own window, much like an outgoing message. Figure 3.4 shows an incoming message in Microsoft Internet Mail.

3. If the message continues beyond the bottom of the window, use the scroll bar to see the next screenful.

4. After reading the message, you can close or reply to the
    message.

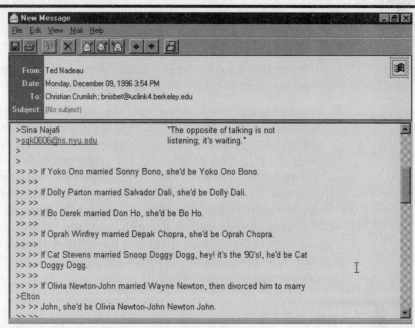

FIGURE 3.4: Here's an e-mail message I received.

TIP

I keep my mail around until I've replied to it. I could save it to a mailbox (as
described in Chapter 4) but then I might forget about it. When my Inbox gets too
cluttered, I bite the bullet and reply to mail I've been putting off, and then delete
most of it.

Replying to Mail

Somewhere near the New Message command (probably on the same
menu or button bar), you'll find the Reply command. When you reply to
an e-mail message, your new message is automatically addressed back to
the sender, and depending on your e-mail program, you may be able to
easily quote the message you received.

TIP

If you start to reply by mistake, just close the message window and don't save the reply if prompted.

To reply to an e-mail message, follow these steps:

1. Highlight the received message in the Inbox or open the message, and then select the Reply command.

2. Your program will create a new message automatically addressed to the sender of the message you're replying to. Some mail programs will also automatically include the contents of the original message (or will give you the choice of including the contents or not). Often, especially with e-mail programs that were designed primarily for use on the Internet, the included message will appear with a ">" character at the beginning of each line to indicate that it is quoted text, although different mail programs have different ways of showing quoted messages. Some, for example, just indent the quoted material (see Figure 3.5).

TIP

Any Web addresses mentioned in e-mail messages to you can function as clickable links in many of the newer programs, such as Netscape Messenger, Microsoft Outlook Express, and Microsoft Outlook 98. To use these links, click on the highlighted address, which will probably be underlined or depicted in a different color, such as blue. You will be transported to the Web site using that address. Microsoft Outlook and Outlook Express users can also add Web shortcuts as file attachments. Just click the Web icon to head for that site.

3. Sometimes, you'll want to reply to everyone who was sent a copy of the original message. Most e-mail programs offer a variation on the normal Reply command that includes all original recipients in your reply. Select Reply to All or a similar command to send your reply to everyone.

4. Tab to the subject line and type a new subject if the old one isn't very meaningful anymore. (People often fail to change the subject line of messages, even when the conversation has evolved its way onto a new topic.)

5. Add other recipients if necessary or tab your way into the message area to type your reply, and then choose the Send (or Queue) command when you are done.

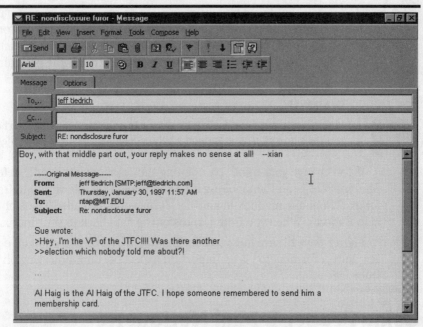

FIGURE 3.5:   A reply with the original message included

TIP

E-mail tends to take on a life of its own, with people forwarding you messages from other people asking for help, information, you name it. Sometimes people send you long chains of related messages, often called *threads*. To avoid confusion when replying to a message forwarded to you, or when replying to many recipients, direct the mail program to "retain the original text," or however the command is worded, so that people reading the message will know what you are talking about and will know the history of the issue. However, if the thread starts getting too long, try to abbreviate it as described below in the *Using Proper E-Mail Netiquette* section.

Deleting Mail

If you have read a piece of mail and you're positive that you have no need to save it, you should delete it so it doesn't clutter up your Inbox (and waste precious hard-disk storage space). To delete a message, you typically highlight it and press Delete (or click the Delete or Trash button, if there is one). In most programs, this moves the message to the Deleted-Mail or Trash mailbox until you empty the trash (or quit the program).

WARNING

In some programs, you don't get a chance to undelete a message, so be sure you know how your program works before deleting messages willy-nilly.

If you change your mind, try opening the Trash mailbox (or Deleted-Mail mailbox) and then looking for a command that allows you to transfer mail from one mailbox to another. It may even be called Transfer (as it is in Eudora). When you find it, transfer the mail back to your Inbox.

I cover ways to save messages in Chapter 4. The next section on e-mail etiquette, or *netiquette*, is an important aspect of communicating on the Internet.

Using Proper E-Mail Netiquette

Like any social system, the Internet has evolved to the point where its users observe a variety of informal rules for interacting politely. Collectively, these rules are known as *netiquette* and most of them can be inferred through the application of some common sense to various social situations.

For example, it's generally not considered good manners to misquote what someone said when talking to someone else, to take their words out of context, or to repeat something that was told to you in confidence (though the media and gossips often commit such acts!). Think of e-mail as a kind of online conversation. If people send you messages containing sensitive material, don't forward them on to others without the author's permission.

If you retain only part of the original text of messages in your replies (to keep the replies from becoming too long), be sure it is not misleadingly taken out of its full context (and likely to be misinterpreted). And please do not intersperse your own comments with the retained pieces of other people's messages so that it's not clear to the recipients who wrote what.

Keep Your Messages Brief and Tactful

When you write messages to business associates and colleagues, stick to the point and be informative. Break up large blocks of text into smaller paragraphs. Reread your messages and run a spell check before sending them—this will give you a chance to minimize mistakes, fix poorly organized sentences, and reconsider bad word choices.

PREPARING MESSAGES OFFLINE

The majority of ISPs across the nation, today, charge a monthly flat rate, as do most telephone companies for local calling. However, if your e-mail message is going to be a long one, it might be better to write it up in your word processing application and take advantage of all the formatting features (bulleted lists, columns, tables, etc.) that are not usually available in e-mail programs. Save the long message (as a text file if you are sending it to someone who does not have a word processing program compatible with yours) and send it as an attachment to a brief message that simply states, "attached you will find my comments on ..." Not only will the message look better, but (if you do *not* have a flat-rate ISP) you will save lots of connect-time charges because you are writing it *offline*, while not connected to your service provider's network. The recipient will also save connect-time charges by quickly downloading the long message and reading it offline too.

If your e-mail application, online service, or Internet access provider has an offline reader or an option for working offline, you can use that feature while reading or composing mail. For example, Microsoft Internet Explorer 4 has a File ➢ Work Offline command and Microsoft Outlook Express's Tools ➢ Send and Receive function asks you if you want to hang up when finished collecting and transmitting your mail.

If you are writing to friends (or potential friends in usenet groups or chat rooms), you can relax a little more, but still hold back on anything that could be considered offensive, even if you think it's funny and you are sure that your friends will, too. Seemingly innocuous statements said in spoken conversation can take on a whole new meaning when written down. Figures of speech, jokes, and your own private way of referring to situations or people seem a lot more serious when viewed in writing.

WARNING

The old adage about never saying or putting anything in writing that you would not want to see in a headline the next day applies to e-mail and the Internet. Now you also have to worry about your words appearing on someone's Web page or showing up when someone searches the Web, a chat service, or a newsgroup. Journalists search the Web for juicy opinions every day. There's no law preventing potential employers from checking you out on the Web and uncovering some embarrassing thing you wrote or posted years ago.

When replying to messages, try to minimize the amount of quoted text that you keep in your return message. Leave enough so it's clear what you're replying to (people don't always remember exactly what they wrote to you.) However, as mentioned at the beginning of this section, don't send abbreviated message bits attributed to other people that could be taken out of context. Just use your good common sense!

Don't Fly off the Handle

I'm trying to not give you too much advice about how to behave on the Net, for several reasons. First, I assume you are an adult and can decide for yourself how to behave. Secondly, the Net has a strongly interactive culture, and you will receive plenty of advice and cues from others if you overstep the bounds of good behavior.

Nevertheless, I will point out that e-mail is a notoriously volatile medium. Because it is so easy to write out a reply and send it in the heat of the moment, and because text lacks many of the nuances of face-to-face communication—the expression and body cues that add emphasis, the tones of voice that indicate joking instead of insult, and so on—it has become a matter of course for many people to dash off ill-considered replies to perceived insults and therefore to fan the flames of invective.

This Internet habit, called *flaming*, is widespread and you will no doubt encounter it on one end or the other. All I can suggest is that you try to restrain yourself when you feel the urge to fly off the handle. (And I have discovered that apologies work wonders when people have misunderstood a friendly gibe or have mistaken sarcasm for idiocy.)

TIP

If you are the sort to flare up in an angry response, or if you find yourself getting emotional or agitated while composing a response to a message that upsets you, save your message as a draft rather than sending it right away. Most e-mail programs provide the option to save a draft message. You can review the draft message later when you have calmed down, and you can decide then whether you want to send it, or you can send the draft to a disinterested third party and ask them if it is too harsh before you send it out.

Exiting an E-Mail Program

When you are finished sending, reading, and replying to mail, you can quit your program or leave it running to check your mail at regular intervals. You can quit most mail programs by selecting File ➤ Exit or File ➤ Quit.

USING E-MAIL VIA ONLINE SERVICES

If you connect to the Internet through an online service, then your e-mail program is usually part of the general program interface. Of the three popular online services, both AOL (America Online) and CompuServe have built-in e-mail windows. The third, MSN (Microsoft Network) connects to whichever mail program your system is using as a default.

AOL (America Online)

America Online (also known as AOL) is the most popular online service today. It has an easy-to-use e-mail interface, both for sending mail to other members of the service as well as for sending Internet mail. Figure 3.6 shows what the America Online e-mail program for Windows looks like.

TIP

America Online lets you compose messages offline; then you can log in and send them in something called Automatic AOL (formerly known as a Flash Session), so you're not paying for connect charges while racking your brain over what to write.

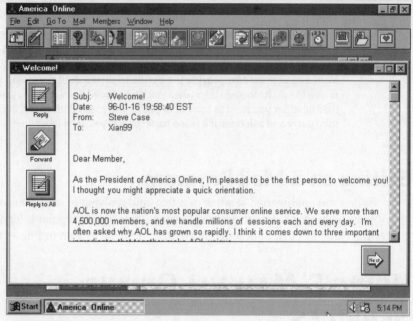

FIGURE 3.6:   America Online's e-mail program is very easy to get the hang of.

Here's how to create e-mail with America Online:

1. Open your America Online program by double-clicking on the America Online icon on your desktop, select Start ➤ Programs ➤ America Online ➤ America Online in Windows 98. (See the next sidebar for information on opening programs in Windows 3.1 or on a Macintosh.)

2. After logging on in the Welcome window, create e-mail by choosing Mail ➤ Compose Mail or by clicking on the Compose Mail button in the main America Online screen.

3. Type the recipient's address (if they're on AOL you can just use their *screen name*, which is what AOL calls a username) in the Compose Mail window.

4. Press Tab twice to jump to the Subject box and type a subject line.

5. Press Tab again to get to the message area and type your message.

6.   When you're done, click the Send or the Send Later button.

Send Send
Later

START YOUR APPLICATION BEFORE FOLLOWING THE STEPS!

Remember, in all of the steps discussed in this chapter and in the rest of the chapters in this book, you should first start the program by double-clicking on the desktop icon or by selecting Start ➤ Programs ➤ *program name* in Windows 98. If you are using an earlier version of Windows or a Macintosh computer, you can create shortcuts (known as aliases in Applespeak) and drag them out onto your desktop, where you can then double-click them to start your application).

To create a shortcut in Windows 3.1, go to the File Manager and search through the directories, (known as folders in Windows 98 and Macintosh parlance) on your hard drive or on your network until you find the program file for your application. This file will be stored in a folder named after the application, such as AOL for America Online, and may have a tiny, yet distinctive, logo icon in front of the file name. The file's extension will also be .exe, which stands for executable and means that the file so named is a program file. Click on this file, hold down the control key and drag a copy of the file out to the desktop where it will assume a box-like icon shape.

Apple users can do the same thing, except that after they find the program file (which does not have a .exe extension) on their hard drive or network, they click on it to highlight it, then select File ➤ Make Alias from the Finder menu. A shortcut to the file, the *alias*, appears right below it, and this is what should be dragged to the Apple desktop.

After you send some e-mail you will probably receive some return messages, which you can open and read.

Here's how to read e-mail with America Online:

1. To read new mail, select Mail ➤ Read New Mail in the America Online screen, and then double-click the title of the message in the New Mail dialog box.

2. Read the message and close the window when you're done. Once you've read a message, AOL moves it to the Old Mail dialog box.

3. To read an old message, select Mail ➤ Check Mail You've Read. As with new mail, double-click the title of the message you want to read.

4. AOL also keeps copies of outgoing messages. To read them, select Mail ➤ Check Mail You've Sent.

5. Close all open dialog boxes when you're done.

TIP

If you have received new mail since the last time you logged on, the Welcome dialog box will tell you, "You have new mail." Click the picture above the message to open the New Mail dialog box.

To reply to a message, click the Reply button (or click Reply to All to send your reply to all the recipients of the original message). This opens up a new mail window just like the kind you get when you send a new message.

To delete a message, select it and then click the Delete button at the bottom of the dialog box.

WARNING

You can't undelete AOL e-mail messages.

CompuServe

After America Online, CompuServe is the next most popular online service. If you're using one of the other services, the commands will likely be very similar to either AOL or CompuServe. To use the steps detailed below, first open CompuServe. In Windows 98, select Start ➤ Programs ➤ CompuServe ➤ CompuServe Information Manager, or use one of the methods described in the sidebar, *Start Your Application Before Following the Steps!*

Here's how to send e-mail using CompuServe:

1. Choose Mail ➤ Create/Send Mail (or click the Mail Center button) to send mail.

2. In the Recipient List dialog box, type the recipient's name and address or click on the recipient's name in the Address

Book and click on Copy, and then click the OK button when you're done.

3. Write your message in the Create Mail dialog box (see Figure 3.7).

4. Click the Send or Out-Basket button when you are finished writing.

FIGURE 3.7: With CompuServe, click the Send button to send the message immediately or click the Out Basket button to store the message until the next time you connect.

TIP

CompuServe lets you compose any number of messages offline and put them in your out-basket to send later. You can then use the Mail ➢ Send/Receive All Mail command to send and receive all your mail as quickly as possible so you can get back offline.

To retrieve mail on CompuServe, choose Mail ➢ Get New Mail. Double-click on a message to read it. To reply to a message, click the Reply button at the bottom of the message window. To delete a message, click the Delete button at the bottom of the window and then click on Yes.

If you want more information about CompuServe's mail feature, choose Services ➤ Go ➤ Mailcenter.

WARNING

CompuServe e-mail messages cannot be undeleted.

MSN (Microsoft Network)

Microsoft Network works more like a direct-access Internet service provider, making the connection for you and then allowing you to communicate using Web browsers and stand-alone e-mail programs.

If you're a Windows user (and most MSN customers are) your mail will work with whatever default e-mail program you're using. Microsoft Exchange (formerly Microsoft Mail) came with Windows 98. Microsoft Outlook 98 (a lot like Exchange, but with other groupware capabilities) comes with Office 97. Microsoft Outlook Express accompanies Microsoft Internet Explorer 4 and provides e-mail functions without the calendar, scheduler, and contact manager. You can download the Microsoft Internet Mail program from the Web. All these, as well as third-party programs such as Qualcomm's Eudora and Pegasus Mail can send and receive your MSN mail for you.

See the sections *Eudora* and *Microsoft Exchange or Internet Mail or Outlook*, coming up, for more on specific mail programs.

TRYING OUT POPULAR E-MAIL PROGRAMS

Well, now you know the basic e-mail moves no matter what program you have. In the rest of this chapter, I'll detail the specific commands for most of the popular e-mail programs (listed here in alphabetical order). Look ahead to see if I cover yours and just read that section unless you're interested in checking out another program.

Eudora

Eudora is one of the most popular and dependable Internet e-mail programs. It can work on a network connection, with a PPP or SLIP dial-up account, or as an offline mail reader with a Unix shell account.

TIP

A free evaluation copy of Eudora (called Eudora Lite) or a 30-day trial version of Eudora Pro, can be downloaded from http://www.eudora.com. Be sure to bookmark Qualcomm (the company that now owns Eudora) and subscribe to their mailing list for announcements. It makes frequent improvements to the program all the time, to both Windows and Mac versions as well as to the Professional and the free Lite versions. Therefore, if you've been using Eudora for a while, you may have a slightly out-of-date copy of the program, and some of your specific commands or menu names may differ from my instructions. Either upgrade to the latest version of Eudora or poke around the menus for similar commands.

Most of the useful Eudora commands are available on the Message menu (shown here).

These steps will guide you through Eudora e-mail creation. Don't forget to start Eudora first, as described earlier in the sidebar, *Start Your Application Before Following the Steps!*

Here's how to create and send e-mail using Eudora:

1. Select Message ➤ New Message (or press Ctrl+N in Windows, Command+N on the Mac).

2. Type the address of the person to whom you wish to send the mail and press Tab a few times until the insertion point

jumps to the area below the gray line. Figure 3.8 shows a short e-mail message.

3. When you are done, click the Send button in the upper-right corner of the message window. The button might read Queue instead of Send. That means that it will be added to a list (a queue) of messages to be sent all at once when the program checks for new mail.

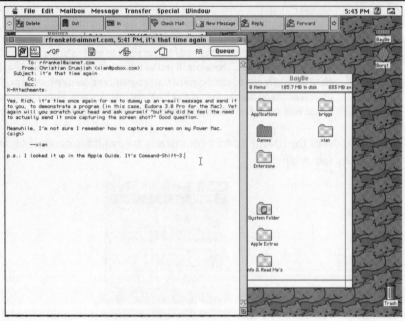

FIGURE 3.8: A new message window in Eudora for the Macintosh

Eudora makes it easy to check your Inbox for new mail, too:

1. Select File ➤ Check Mail or press Ctrl+M (or Command+M on a Mac). Eudora will connect to something called a *POP server* (POP stands for *Post Office Protocol*, but you can forget that) to pick up all your mail.

2. Unread mail will appear with a large dot (or bullet) in the left column of the Inbox (see Figure 3.9). To view the contents of a mail message, highlight it in the window and press Enter (or double-click on it).

3. After reading the message, you can close its window or select Message ➤ Reply (or Ctrl+R) to reply to the message. If you start a reply by mistake, just close the message window and don't save it when prompted.

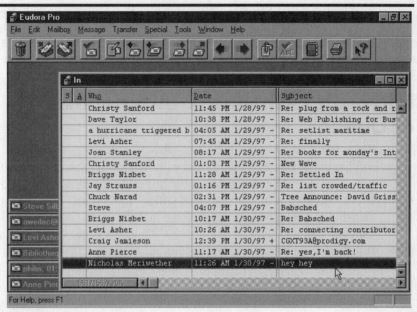

FIGURE 3.9: The Inbox of the Windows version of Eudora

TIP

If you want to reply to everyone who was also sent a copy of the message, press Ctrl+Shift+R instead of Ctrl+R (or hold down Shift while selecting Message ➤ Reply).

After you have sent and received a number of messages, you may need to clean up your Eudora Inbox by deleting old messages. Use the following options to delete messages and undelete (restore) messages that you deleted by mistake.

▶ To delete a message, place the highlight on it and click Delete (or click the Trash icon at the top of the mailbox window). This moves the message to the Trash mailbox. It won't actually be deleted until you empty the trash (Special ➤ Trash).

▶ If you change your mind, select Mailbox ➤ Trash to open the Trash box and look at the list of deleted messages. Highlight the message you want to rescue, and then select Transfer ➤ In to move the message back into the Inbox.

When you are finished sending, reading, and replying to mail, you can quit Eudora or leave it running so you can check your mail. To quit Eudora, select File ➤ Exit (or File ➤ Quit in the Macintosh version of Eudora), or select Ctrl+Q (or Command+Q for the Mac).

Microsoft Exchange or Internet Mail or Outlook

When Windows 95 came out, Microsoft Mail was superseded by the Microsoft Exchange program distributed with the new operating system. (They were similar, but Exchange had more Internet capabilities, among other improvements.) With the release of Office 97, Microsoft has once again distributed a renamed and upgraded e-mail program, Outlook 98. But Outlook is more than an e-mail reader. It's also a groupware program, suitable for collaboration, discussions, scheduling, and so on.

Internet Mail (often distributed along with its sister program Microsoft Internet News, or in a jumbo package with Internet Explorer 3 as well) was Microsoft's first true Internet-oriented mail program. With Internet Explorer 4, it's being replaced with Microsoft Outlook Express (Mail), a custom version of the Outlook groupware program that comes with Office 97. You can download Microsoft's latest e-mail software from the Microsoft Internet Explorer Web site (`http://www.microsoft .com/ie`), shown in Figure 3.10.

Fortunately, the e-mail features of Outlook 98 and Express are similar to those of Exchange (with, again, a few improvements here and there). I'll use Outlook 98 and Outlook Express for my examples here, but you can follow along even if you use Exchange (or, for that matter, Microsoft Mail).

Outlook can handle Internet mail, network mail, and mail from MSN. You can start Outlook 98 by double-clicking on the Outlook 98 icon on your desktop or by selecting Start ➤ Programs ➤ Microsoft Outlook. You can open Outlook Express by selecting Start ➤ Programs ➤ Internet Explorer ➤ Outlook Express, or by clicking on the miniature Launch Outlook Express icon in the taskbar tray near the Start button.

Part i

FIGURE 3.10: Microsoft's Internet Explorer Web site is the source of free trial versions of new Internet software, but it can take a while to download the software, plus you have to answer a bunch of questions for the marketing department.

Both versions of Outlook start you off in a window showing two panes. The pane on the left shows the various features of the program that are available, with your Inbox first and foremost (see Figure 3.1). The pane on the right shows you the contents of your Inbox (but you can click the large Inbox button at the top of the list of messages to choose another mailbox and Outlook will show its contents below).

NOTE

Outlook Express has a big Preview pane that shows you the contents of the highlighted message. You can turn this Preview on or off, and change its appearance and location with the View ➤ Layout menu selection.

Here's how to create a new Outlook e-mail message:

1. Select Compose ➤ New Mail Message (Ctrl+N). This will open up a new message window.

2. Type an address and press Tab to get down to the Subject box where you can type a subject.

3. Tab down to the message area and type your message. Click the Send button in either Outlook 98 or Express. If you are accumulating messages to send in bulk with Outlook Express, select File ➤ Send Later, then click on the Send and Receive button in the main Outlook Express window when you are ready to send them all.

To read a message in your Inbox, just double-click its subject line. The message will appear in its own window. To reply to the message, select Compose ➤ Reply in Outlook 98 or Reply to Author or Reply to All in Outlook Express (Ctrl+R). Outlook will supply the recipient's address. Proceed as if you were sending a new message.

To delete a message, just highlight it and click the Delete button or press the Delete key on your keyboard. It will be moved to the Deleted Items folder until you specifically open that folder and delete its contents (even then Exchange will warn you that you are permanently deleting the message).

TIP

To undelete a message, open the Deleted Items folder and select the message you want to restore. Then select File ➤ Move, choose the Inbox folder from the dialog box that appears, and click OK.

To exit Outlook 98 or Express, select File ➤ Exit.

If you're still using Internet Explorer 3 (or if you started with 3 and you like the mail program that came with it), then you may be using Microsoft Internet Mail for e-mail. Internet Mail starts you off in a window showing two panes (see Figure 3.11). The upper pane shows the contents of your Inbox (but you can choose a different folder in the Folders drop-down list on one of the toolbars), and the lower pane shows the contents of the currently selected message. Many useful commands also appear on the toolbar (which you can customize, if you like).

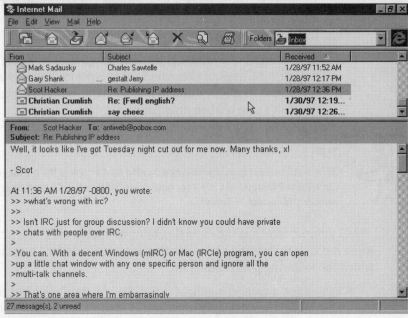

FIGURE 3.11 My Inbox as shown by Microsoft Internet Mail

Microsoft Internet Mail, or MS Internet Mail, uses e-mail creation commands that should be familiar to you after reviewing all of the other e-mail applications covered in this chapter.

Here's how to send a new e-mail message:

1. Select Mail ➤ New Message (or press Ctrl+N in Windows, Command+N on the Mac).

2. Type the address of the person to whom you wish to send the mail and press Tab twice.

3. Type a subject and press Tab again. Then type your message.

4. When you are done, click the Send button in the upper-left corner of the message window.

You will probably also recognize MS Internet Mail's sending and receiving menu selections. Here's how to read and reply to e-mail:

1. Select Mail ➤ Send and Receive or press Ctrl+M (or Command+M). Unread mail will appear with a bold subject line.

2. To view the contents of a mail message in the lower pane, select its subject in the upper pane (or double-click it to open the message in a new window).

3. After reading the message, you can select Mail ≻ Reply to Author (or Ctrl+R or Command+R) to reply to the message. If you start a reply by mistake, just close the message window and don't save it when prompted.

TIP

If you want to reply to everyone who was also sent a copy of the message, press Ctrl+Shift+R instead of Ctrl+R (or hold down Shift or the Command key while selecting Message ≻ Reply).

MS Internet Mail has the same flexibility as other e-mail programs when it comes to deleting and recovering mistakenly deleted messages, which the following points illustrate:

▶ To delete a message, highlight it and click on the Delete button. This moves the message to the Deleted Mail folder. It won't actually be deleted until you delete it from this folder.

▶ If you change your mind, select the Deleted Mail folder to view the list of deleted messages. Highlight the message, and then select Mail ≻ Move To ≻ Inbox to move the message back.

When you are finished sending, reading, and replying to mail, you can quit Internet Mail or leave it running so you can check your mail later. To quit, select File ≻ Exit (or File ≻ Quit on a Macintosh).

NETCOMplete

NETCOMplete (formerly NetCruiser) is an all-in-one Internet program from Netcom, for both Windows and the Macintosh. NETCOMplete has its own e-mail program, but it also allows you to run third-party programs, such as Eudora, Pegasus, or Internet Mail.

Here's how to activate the NETCOMplete Mail module:

1. Click the E-Mail button (or select Internet ≻ E-Mail).

2. To send mail, click the Compose button (or select E-Mail ➤ Compose). This brings up a compose window.

3. Type the recipient's address and press Tab twice. Type a subject and press Tab twice again.

4. Type your message and click the Send button when you are done (see Figure 3.12).

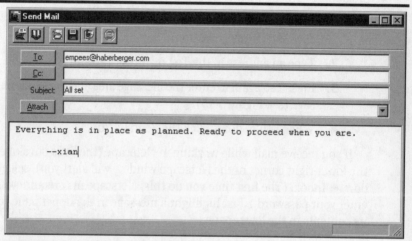

FIGURE 3.12 NETCOMplete's Compose window has all the standard e-mail trimmings.

The E-Mail window has three panes. The top two show the list of folders (with your Inbox selected) and the subjects of messages in the current folder. The bottom pane shows the contents of the currently selected message.

When you want to reply to messages, delete messages, or exit from NETCOMplete itself or just from the mail module, use these commands:

▶ To reply to a message, click the Reply button.

▶ To delete a message, click the Delete button (the Trashcan icon).

▶ To exit the mail module of NETCOMplete, just close the window.

▶ To exit NETCOMplete, select File ➤ Exit.

Netscape Messenger

Netscape Communicator 4 (the successor to Navigator 3 and Navigator Gold) sports a full-featured mail program called Netscape Messenger. It's a redesigned version of Netscape Mail. (It now looks more like Microsoft Internet Mail. Meanwhile Netcom's NETCOMplete now looks the way Netscape Mail used to look!)

Using Netscape Messenger for e-mail is a lot like using many of the other programs I've mentioned. Here's how to create and send an e-mail message:

1. First select File ➤ Compose Message (or press Ctrl+M or click the Compose button).

2. Type an address in the To box. Press Tab and type a subject.

3. Press Tab again to enter the message area and type your message (see Figure 3.13).

4. When you're done, click the Send button.

If you receive mail while working in Netscape (the little envelope in the lower-right corner of the Netscape window will alert you), select Window ➤ Inbox. (The first time you do this, Netscape may require you to enter your password.) Just highlight a message in the upper pane to see its contents in the lower pane.

TIP

Remember that any Web addresses mentioned in Netscape Messenger e-mail messages you receive will function as clickable links. That means when you finish reading, all you have to do is click on a highlighted word to go to that Web page and start surfing.

Here are some other Netscape Messenger commands you will find useful:

▶ To reply to a message, click the Reply button, press Ctrl+R (Command+R on the Mac), or select Message ➤ Reply ➤ To Sender.

▶ To delete a message, just highlight it and click the Delete button. Netscape will move the message to a Trash folder.

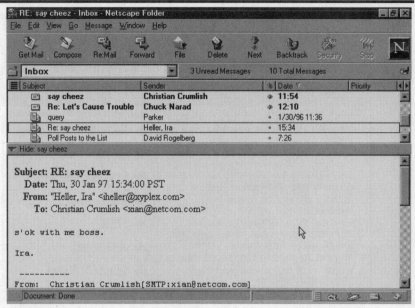

FIGURE 3.13 The Netscape Messenger window lists messages in the top pane and shows the contents of the current message in the hideable lower pane.

▶ To undelete a message, select the Trash folder in the drop-down folder list just above the top pane, select the message, and then choose Message ➤ File Message ➤ Inbox.

You can close the mail window and keep Netscape running if you want—in Windows 98, click the close button in the upper-right corner; on the Mac, click the close button in the upper-left corner—or you can quit Netscape entirely by selecting File ➤ Exit (or, on the Mac, File ➤ Quit).

Pegasus Mail

Pegasus is a popular, free e-mail program that can run on networks and over dial-up Internet connections.

TIP

You can download Pegasus from its Web site, shown in Figure 3.14 (http://www.pegasus.usa.com/).

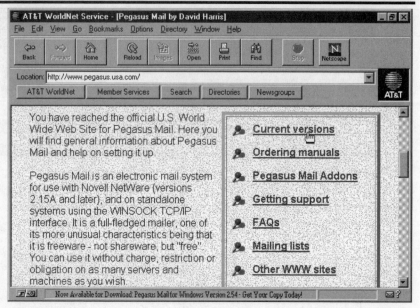

FIGURE 3.14   The all-new Pegasus Web site has lots of information on Pegasus Mail.

When you are ready to send Pegasus messages, follow these steps:

1. Select File ➢ New Message (or press Ctrl+N).

2. Type the recipient's name, press Tab, and type a subject. Then press Tab two more times to get down to the message area and type your message.

3. When you're done, click the Send button to either send your message immediately or put it in a queue, depending on how your version of Pegasus is set up.

4. To send all queued messages, select File ➢ Send All Queued Mail.

To read new mail, select File ➢ Read New Mail (or press Ctrl+W). This opens the New Mail folder. (Once you've read a message, it will automatically be moved to the Main mail folder after you close the New Mail folder or exit Pegasus.)

The following commands will help you check for new Pegasus messages, read, reply, or delete messages you've received, and finally exit Pegasus:

▶ To check for new messages, select File ➢ Check Host for New Mail.

▶ To read a message, double-click it.

▶ To reply to an open message, click the Reply button.

▶ To delete a message, click the Delete button.

▶ To exit Pegasus, select File ➢ Exit.

Pine

If you're determined to get your hands dirty and log in directly to a Unix account to read mail with a Unix mail reader, then here's a quick rundown of the most useful commands in everybody's favorite Unix mail program, Pine.

TIP

Another popular Unix e-mail program is Elm. For information about Elm, send mail to mail-server@cs.ruu.nl with no subject. As your message, type on two separate lines *send NEWS.ANSWERS/elm/FAQ* and *end*.

Here's how you create and send e-mail using Pine in the Unix environment:

1. Start Pine by typing **pine** (yes, all lowercase—it matters) at the Unix command prompt and press Enter.

2. Pine starts you off at a main menu. To enter your Inbox, type **i**.

3. To send mail, type **c**—and don't press Enter. Pine will start a new message (see Figure 3.15).

4. Type the recipient's address, press Tab, and type a subject. Press Tab again until you're in the message area. Then type your message. Pine will handle word-wrapping, so you only have to press Enter when you're starting a new paragraph.

5. When you're done, press Ctrl+X to send the message.

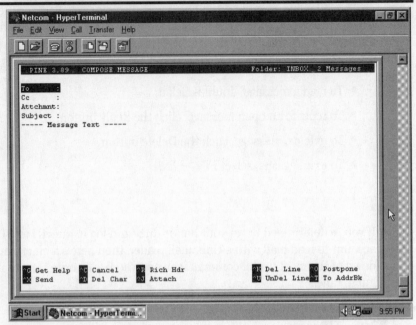

FIGURE 3.15 Pine is a *full-screen* editor, so it works something like a *normal* Windows or Mac program, even though it's text only and runs in Unix.

The following list summarizes the commands for some specific Pine functions:

Function	Type
To run Pine	Type **pine** and press Enter
To move between listed messages	Press the up and down arrow keys
To read a message	Highlight it in your Inbox and press Enter
To send mail	Type **c**
To return to your message list	Type **i**
To reply to a message	Type **r**
To delete a message	Type **d**
To undelete a message	Type **u**
To quit Pine	Type **q**

WHAT'S NEXT?

Now that Christian Crumlish has shown you how to use typical e-mail programs, you may have noticed that the steps for sending, receiving, replying to, and deleting messages are almost the same in all of these applications (excepting Pine, of course). Even if you find yourself working with an e-mail program different from the ones profiled in this chapter, you will probably be able to figure it out because you know all about basic e-mail functions now. It's time to move on to Chapter 4, *Refining E-Mail Messages*. There you'll learn about more advanced e-mail tasks.

Chapter 4

REFINING E-MAIL MESSAGES

O nce you've mastered the basics of e-mail—sending, reading, and replying to messages—there are just a few more e-mail functions you'll want to know about. Some of them are basic and available in just about every e-mail program, such as forwarding a message to a new recipient, sending mail to more than one person at a time, and saving old messages somewhere besides in your Inbox. Other more advanced or sophisticated features vary from program to program.

SENDING MAIL TO MORE THAN ONE PERSON

Sometimes you'll want to send a message to more than one recipient. You can usually do this in one of several ways. Most programs allow you to list multiple recipients in the To line, usually separated by commas (some programs require that you

Adapted from *The Internet: No experience required.*, by Christian Crumlish
ISBN 0-7821-2168-3   528 pages $24.99

use a different character, such as a semicolon, to separate addresses). Most also have a Cc line. As with traditional paper office memos, the Cc line in an e-mail message is for people who should receive a copy of the message, but who are not the primary recipient.

NOTE

When you reply to a message, if you select the Reply to Sender option, your reply will be sent only to the person in the To line. If you select Reply to All, your reply will be sent to everyone in the Cc list as well.

Most programs also offer a Bcc line, which lets you list one or more people to receive blind copies of that message. This means that the primary (and Cc) recipients will not see the names of people receiving blind copies.

WARNING

You can typically include as many names on the Cc: line as you want, but some mail servers will choke on a message if its headers are too long.

SENDING FILES VIA E-MAIL

It sounds too good to be true. Just "attach" a file to an e-mail message and it zips across the globe to your recipient, without having to be put on a disk and sent by mail or courier. Naturally, it's not that simple. Some files are just too big to send this way (anything close to a megabyte is probably too big). But even with files of a more appropriate size, you may encounter hitches. Most of the problem is in coordinating between computer types, file types, compression formats, and encoding formats. Getting all the elements to work out can be a little like trying a combination lock. But I'm getting ahead of myself. Let's start with what an attachment really is.

NOTE

Each online service or Internet service provider is a little different, so you can experiment with the size of files you can send. Some services limit the size of files you may attach to messages, while others will take anything, but the transmission may become extremely slow. You can compress files to make them smaller and you can send each file in a group of files in separate messages to keep the size low.

How Attachments Are Created

One of the most important functions of e-mail is its ability to let you send files called *attachments* along with your messages. An attachment is a data file, in any form, that your program will send along with your e-mail message—it could be a word processor file, a picture, a spreadsheet, or any other kind of file. Each e-mail program is different in the way it handles file attachments, and some of the online services still don't let you send or receive files over the Internet. Also, because different programs have different ways of *encoding* attached files (translating the files into a form that can be shipped over the Internet), you may have to compare details with your sender or recipient to make sure that both of your programs can "speak" the same code. All major mail clients now have much improved MIME capabilities.

Internet mail generally consists of only straight text files, although there are protocols for sending other forms of information. For example, most mail programs use *MIME* (*Multipurpose Internet Mail Extensions*) to send other kinds of data, including color pictures, sound files, and video clips. Depending on the e-mail program you are using, if you are sent e-mail with a MIME attachment you will see placeholders for all the MIME files—even if you are not actually able to see the pictures, hear the music, or view the movies. You may be asked if you want to view each file or save it.

Working with Different File Formats

Quite aside from e-mail issues, you might be trying to send a file that your recipient doesn't have the right application for reading, so that's another thing you may have to work out in advance. For example, if you use Word for the Macintosh and your recipient uses WordPerfect for DOS, then you may have to save your file in a format that your recipient's program can understand; this may involve both of you poking around your programs' Open and Save As commands to see what options are available.

When you receive a file attachment, your e-mail program will usually decode it and tell you where it's been placed (unless it doesn't recognize the coding format, in which case you'll get a bunch of garbage at the end of the message and no file attachment—if this happens, you'll need to negotiate with the sender as I just discussed). We will look at techniques for sending and attaching files later in this lesson when we examine individual e-mail programs.

FORWARDING MAIL TO SOMEONE ELSE

If someone sends you an e-mail message and you'd like to send a copy of it to someone else, most mail programs let you select a Forward command.

WARNING

Never send mail to a third party without the express permission of the original sender. Also, be sure to use a reply separator, such as a solid horizontal line, between all of the forwarded e-mail messages, to delineate where one person's response ends and another begins (most e-mail programs add reply separators automatically). This will avoid confusion about who wrote what and will avoid uncomfortable situations for both you and those who send you e-mail.

The Forward command is often on the same menu or toolbar as the Reply command, and it works in almost the same way. The difference is that your mail program won't insert the original sender's e-mail address into the To line. Instead, the To line will be blank so you can fill in the address of the person you are forwarding the message to. The original message will automatically be included in the new message, often with some characters (like the standard ">" Internet e-mail quoting character) or other formatting to distinguish it from what you yourself write.

Here's how to forward e-mail messages:

1. Open your e-mail program and either highlight or open the message you want to forward.

2. Click the Forward command in the toolbar of your e-mail program, or use a command such as Message ➢ Forward, or Mail ➢ Forward. A new message window will appear with the forwarded message included in the text area.

3. Type the recipient's e-mail address on the To line and then Tab your way down to the message area.

4. Edit the message if you want, or add your own note to the beginning, perhaps explaining why you are forwarding the message.

5. Then send the message as usual.

TIP

There is also a Redirect option in Eudora Pro and Eudora Light. This option automatically sends the e-mail "as is" to someone else, without adding headers to the body of the message, but adding "By way of ..." and your name to the To: field.

CHECKING YOUR SPELLING

Most e-mail programs now offer spell-checking (so the traditional excuses for sloppily edited e-mail messages are vanishing fast!), but the specific techniques vary from program to program (as you might expect). It's a good idea to check the spelling in a message before sending it, especially if the message is long, formal, or for some business purpose.

NOTE

For more on using specific e-mail programs, flip forward in this chapter.

If you write your messages ahead of time using a word processing program, then you can use your word processor's spell checker to check the message. You may find this easier than working with two different spell checkers.

ATTACHING A SIGNATURE

On the Internet, it's traditional to include a short *signature* at the end of each message. An e-mail signature is a few lines of text, usually including your name, sometimes your postal (*snail mail*) address, and perhaps your e-mail address. If you are including a signature in a business message, you might wish to include phone and fax numbers, and maybe the company Web page address. Many people also include quotations, jokes, gags, and so on. Signatures (also called *sig blocks*, *signature files*, *.signatures*, or *.sigs*) are a little like bumper stickers in this respect.

TIP

You can never be too careful when using company online resources, so consider adding a disclaimer to your signature block if you post to Usenet groups or mailing lists from a corporate e-mail address. The disclaimer can identify your views as solely your own and not those of the company.

Some e-mail programs do not support signature files, particularly those designed for local networks and those of some online services where signatures are less common, but many do and more are adding the feature all the time. Here's my current signature (I change it from time to time):

```
--
Christian Crumlish                    http://www.pobox.com/~xian
Internet Systems Experts (SYX)        http://www.syx.com
Enterzone                             http://ezone.org/ez
```

It includes my name, the address of my home page on the Web, the name of my company and its home page address, and the name of my online magazine with its address.

WARNING

Test your signature block with various e-mail systems to see if it still looks good at the receiving end, especially if it uses unusual fonts, has a logo or other graphic, uses tabs, or is formatted in columns. Some of these features do not translate well to other programs, where monospaced fonts may be substituted for fancier proportional fonts.

NOTE

Some e-mail programs let you include a graphic, such as a company logo, in your signature. For example, Microsoft Word, Outlook 97, and Outlook Express all have commands you can use to import graphics files into your signature file. Just be sure to format the signature in such a way that it looks good even for those who do not have graphics support in their e-mail setup, so that the absence of the logo or graphic will not detract from the appearance of your message. This is an easy way to cultivate a professional presence on the Internet.

FILING YOUR MESSAGES

Even after you have deleted all the messages you've replied to or no longer need to leave lying around in your Inbox, your undeleted messages can start to pile up. When your Inbox gets too full, it's time to create new mailboxes to store those other messages.

NOTE

Your e-mail storage should conform to your general scheme of organization. I arrange mine alphabetically, chronologically, and/or by project, depending on the person involved. Think about the best system for yourself before you find your Inbox filled with 200 messages to sort. If your e-mail program allows you to save your own messages that you have sent to other people, you will also need to organize them before they accumulate and become unmanageable.

Different programs offer different commands for creating mailboxes and transferring messages into them, but the principles are more or less the same as those used for real-life filing. Don't create a new mailbox when an existing mailbox will suffice, but do file away as many messages as you can (even if you have to create a new mailbox to do so), to keep the number of messages in your Inbox manageable. When you find yourself scrolling up and down through screenfuls of message lists trying to find a particular message, you know that your Inbox has officially become disorganized.

TIP

You can also save your messages as text files or word processing files to move them outside of the e-mail program. This way you can store them with other files related to the same topic. Select File ➤ Save As in your message window and select a text file type. Or, select the message contents, press Ctrl+C (or Command+C) to copy it to the Clipboard, open your word processor, and paste the message into a document with Ctrl+V (Command+V), then save the new file.

DEALING WITH E-MAIL FROM SEVERAL ACCOUNTS

You may find yourself with more than one e-mail account. It can happen more easily than you might think. All you need is to get a personal e-mail account and then get Internet access at work (or vice versa), and *Voilà!* you've got multiple accounts to manage. How do you keep things straight?

There are several approaches. One is to try to keep any e-mail accounts you may have totally separate. This approach is ideal for keeping work and personal life separate or for keeping a public address and a private backchannel for friends and emergencies.

On the other hand, some people get a personal account just to get access to an existing work account, in which case there's no reason to store the mail in separate places. Then the problem becomes how to consolidate all your mail and make sure you're not missing any of it. (A related problem is how to look at your mail when at home without deleting it from your main workspace.)

There are two ways to consolidate mail from multiple accounts, both of which will make sure you get all your e-mail. One is to set the secondary account (or all the accounts but one) to automatically forward mail to your primary address. However, this is not always possible. Even if it is, the methods vary from system to system, and you should check with your system administrator and ask about "automatic forwarding of e-mail."

Even easier, many mail programs can be set up to check multiple addresses (or check some automatically and others only when you manually request it). If you have to deal with multiple accounts and you prefer to co-mingle all your mail, I'd suggest getting your hands on a mail program (such as Eudora Pro or Microsoft) with this capability.

When you want to check your work mail from your home computer, you need an e-mail application that supports remote mail connections. Microsoft Outlook 98 has this capability, and it even allows you to quickly download just the message headers from your work account. Then you can select the specific messages you want to download, to minimize connection time.

MANAGING AN ADDRESS BOOK

Once you start using e-mail regularly, you will probably find yourself typing a few addresses over and over, or trying to remember some long and confusing ones. Fortunately, most e-mail programs enable you to create aliases (sometimes called nicknames) for these people. Aliases are shorter words that you type instead of the actual address. These lists of addresses and aliases are usually grouped together in something called an address book. Modeled on real-world address books, these windows or modules often have room for other vital information (such as street addresses, and phone and fax numbers).

Some e-mail and groupware programs share a single address box with other applications on your computer, so your contact information is available to various programs.

When you type an alias or choose a name from an address book, your e-mail program inserts the correct address into the To line of your message (some programs can also insert an address into the Cc line).

You can also set up an alias for a list of addresses, so you can send mail to a group of people all at once. I've got an alias for a group of people to whom I send silly stuff I find on the Net (no one's complained yet) and another one for contributors to my online magazine.

TIP

When you make up an address book entry or alias for an e-mail address, keep it short—the whole point is to save yourself some typing—and try to make it memorable (although you can always look it up if you forget).

Send Mail to Postmaster@

If you know someone's domain, such as the company where they work, or you know they're on one of the online services, you can try sending mail to postmaster@*address* and asking politely for the e-mail address. Internet standards require that every network assign a real person to postmaster@*address*, someone who can handle questions and complaints. So, for example, to find someone at Pipeline, you could send mail to postmaster@pipeline.com and ask for the person by name.

THE E-MAIL CAPABILITIES OF ONLINE SERVICES

Two of the traditional online services, AOL and CompuServe, still make you do your e-mail using their basic program. Because you can't switch to a better, stand-alone program when one comes along, you won't usually have the newest features. Still, AOL is slowly adding features to its software.

NOTE
Remember, before you use any of the commands in the following sections, you must open your mail program by double-clicking on its desktop icon or, in Windows 95, by selecting Start ➤ Programs ➤ *program-name*, (substituting the name of your program for the italicized word).

America Online (AOL)

The AOL mail program is still pretty rudimentary compared to the most popular stand-alone programs. It may soon be possible to use any e-mail program you want to pick up your AOL mail.

Here are a couple of important America Online e-mail features you will use often:

▶ Forward America Online mail to another address by clicking on the Forward button in the message window.

▶ To send mail to multiple addresses, just type the addresses in the To box, separating them with a comma, or press Tab and type some of the addresses in the Cc box.

Filing America Online messages is another vital function you will want to know about, before messages pile up in your Inbox and you cannot find anything. Here is how to create a new folder for filing messages:

1. Select Mail ➤ Personal Filing Cabinet.

2. In the dialog box that appears, click the Mail folder and then click the Add Folder button.

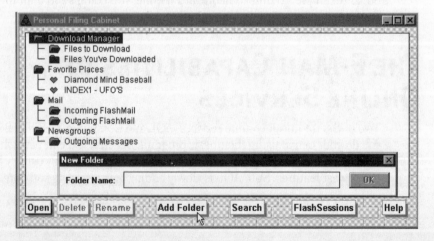

3. Type a name for the new folder and then click OK.

To file a message in any of your folders, select its subject in a mail window and drag it to whichever folder you want.

Attaching Files to AOL Messages

Until recently, you couldn't attach files to AOL messages sent over the Internet, but now you can. Remember which directory (or folder) contains the file you wish to attach to your message, so that you can quickly go there and attach the file without spending a lot of time searching for the attachments.

Here is the quickest way to attach files to America Online messages:

1. While in the Compose Mail window, click the Attach button.

2. Select a file in the Attach File dialog box that appears (this looks just like the typical Open dialog box you see in any normal program) and then click OK.

The file will be attached using the MIME format. Make sure your recipient's e-mail program can understand that format. You can also receive files sent to you from Internet e-mail addresses—as long as the sender's program can send MIME attachments.

TIP

If someone is planning to send you more than one file, ask them to send each one in a separate message. When this book went to press, AOL could only handle one attached file per message (although you can get around this limitation by creating a single compressed file, such as a zipped archive, containing many files).

Downloading Attached Files from AOL Messages

When you receive a message with an attached file, two buttons will appear at the bottom of the message window: Download File and Download Later. Use one of the two options, depending on your plans:

▶ Click Download File to download the file immediately (the message will also give you a rough estimate of how long the download should take).

▶ Click Download Later to leave the file waiting until you're ready to download it.

Using the AOL Address Book

AOL provides you with an address book for managing your e-mail addresses. To add an address to it, use these procedures:

1. Select Mail ≻ Edit Address Book.

2. In the Address Book window that appears, click the Create button, type a name in the Group Name box, press Tab, and then type the e-mail address in the Screen Names box.

3. Click OK to add the name to the address book.

Once you've entered some addresses, it's easy to use your address book to send a new message:

1. In the Compose Mail dialog box, click the Address Book button.

2. Choose a name and its associated e-mail address and then click the To button.

3. Click OK to insert the corresponding address into the To box.

AOL's mail program does not include a spell checker or a way to attach signatures to outgoing messages.

If you want more information about AOL e-mail, select Mail ≻ Post Office for up-to-date information.

CompuServe

CompuServe's e-mail has simple instructions for performing the usual e-mail functions:

▶ To forward mail to another recipient, click the Forward button in the Read Mail window, then proceed as you would with a normal message.

▶ To send mail to more than one recipient, simply repeat the normal procedure in the Recipient List dialog box to add each recipient (except don't click OK until you've selected all the recipients you want).

TIP

Don't forget to start CompuServe by double-clicking on its desktop icon or by selecting Start ➤ Programs ➤ CompuServe ➤ CompuServe Information Manager in Windows 98. You must be in the CompuServe Information Manager program before you can use the programs described here.

Filing CompuServe Messages

You can also file your CompuServe e-mail messages with basic commands. However, CompuServe's e-mail program allows you to create new folders during the filing process. The following steps show you how to file messages and optionally create new folders if needed:

1. Open your CompuServe Inbox (called an In-basket in CompuServe) by clicking the In-Basket button in the CompuServe toolbar, or by selecting Mail ➤ Get New Mail or Mail ➤ In-Basket.

2. Highlight a message in the In-Basket window and open it by double-clicking on it or by clicking the Open button.

3. In the Read Mail window, click the File-It button to file an e-mail message. This brings up the Store Message dialog box, also known as the Filing Cabinet.

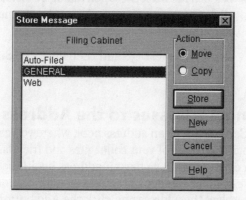

4. The list of folder names in the Filing Cabinet include preloaded folders, such as General and Auto-Filed. Use one of the following options, depending on whether these generic folders suit your filing plans:

    ▶ Highlight the name of the folder you want to file your message in and click the Store button.

▶ Click the New button to create a new folder. Type the folder name in the Add New Folder dialog box, then click OK. Highlight the new folder name in the Filing Cabinet and click the Store button to move the file there.

5. Click the Close or Cancel button to close the Filing Cabinet and click Close when you are done with your Inbox.

TIP
You can open the Filing Cabinet containing your stored CompuServe messages by selecting Mail ➤ Filing Cabinet or typing Ctrl+F.

Sending a File as a CompuServe E-Mail Attachment

Use CompuServe's File Attachment feature to include files with your messages. If you have written long memos or reports in your word processing program, you can reuse them by attaching the file to a short message.

1. Create the message as usual and then click the Attach button (or select Mail ➤ Send File).

2. Select a file from the Open dialog box that appears and then click OK twice (CompuServe always makes you confirm everything).

3. Type your message and then click the Send or Send Later button.

Adding Addresses to the Address Book

CompuServe includes an address book where you can store the names and e-mail addresses of your colleagues and friends. To add an address from an existing message to your address book, click the Address button in the Read Mail window. In the Add to Address Book dialog box that appears, select the address and click the Add button.

At any other time, you can add an address to your address book by selecting Mail ➤ Address Book. Then click the Add or Add Group button, and click OK. Fill out the Add to Address Book or the Add Group to Address Book dialog box and then click OK twice.

CompuServe does not currently have a spell checker or a way of attaching signature blocks to mail messages.

The Microsoft Network (MSN)

MSN works perfectly well with stand-alone e-mail programs, whether you use a Microsoft mail product, such as Mail, Exchange, Outlook 98, Outlook Express, or Internet Mail; or a competing product, such as Eudora, Pegasus Mail, or even Netscape Messenger. For information on Microsoft e-mail programs, see the following section, specifically the portion entitled *Microsoft Exchange or Internet Mail or Outlook*.

E-MAIL TRICKS WITH SPECIFIC PROGRAMS

The e-mail techniques and features I've outlined should bring you up to speed as a full participant in the e-mail world of the Internet. In the rest of this lesson, I'll revisit the most popular e-mail programs to tell you which of the features I've described are available and exactly how to use them. Again, unless you want to check out the other e-mail programs, look ahead to see if I cover your program and read just that section (they're in alphabetical order).

Eudora

The professional edition of Eudora, Eudora Pro, has just about every state-of-the-art Internet e-mail feature you could wish for (in both the Windows and Macintosh versions). The freeware Lite version continues to develop gradually as well and is a bargain at the price.

Before trying out the features below, be sure to start the Eudora program by double-clicking its desktop icon.

Sending, Forwarding, and Formatting Eudora Messages

Eudora's messaging features provide all of the basic e-mail functions, along with some extras that you may find useful. Here are some of the Eudora options:

- To send a message to additional recipients, type their e-mail addresses on the Cc or Bcc lines, separated by commas if there are more than one on any single line. If you wish to send the same e-mail to more than one recipient from your address book, you may also insert a recipient by first placing the cursor in the To, Cc, or Bcc lines, and then choosing the insert option under the edit menu.

▶ To forward a message you have open, select Message ➤ Forward. Then proceed as you would with a new message.

▶ To redirect a message you have received to someone else without comments, choose Redirect in the Message menu, and then add the recipient in the To line.

TIP

If you want to add some explanatory text before the forwarded message, but you don't want the forwarded message to have the ">" symbol before each line, select Message ➤ Redirect instead of Message ➤ Forward.

▶ If you wish to format your message, you can add MIME-encoded formatting with the Pro version of Eudora. Use the formatting button just above the To line in the message window or select the formatting options from the Edit ➤ Text submenu.

NOTE

Eudora does not create HTML formatting, but it does treat any URL (Web address) as a live hyperlink.

Transferring a Eudora Message to a Mailbox

You can transfer messages out of the Inbox to a different mailbox named Business Correspondence, Shopping, or any category you wish to file messages under. Please note that when you transfer a message, the message itself is moved to the new mailbox, not a copy of the message.

1. To transfer a message to a mailbox in Eudora, select the message and pull down the Transfer menu.

2. Either choose an existing mailbox from the menu or select New.

3. In the New Mailbox dialog box that appears, type a name for the mailbox and then click OK.

You may also create new mailboxes by pulling down the Mailbox menu and choosing New. You will then be prompted to name the mailbox. You may want to check the Make it a folder option if you think you will want to create new mailboxes inside of the one you are creating.

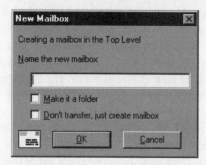

Now, why would anyone want to create a mailbox inside a mailbox? Well, sometimes the general subject category under which you file messages, has distinct subcategories, and if you like to keep things in an orderly manner, you may decide to file things separately while still keeping them together. Figure 4.1 illustrates this "nesting" technique.

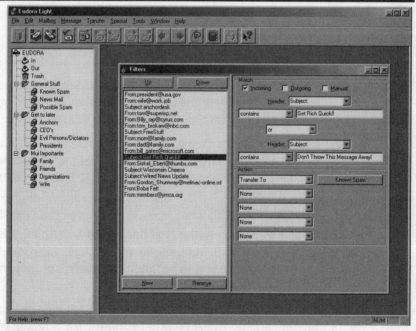

FIGURE 4.1: Creating and nesting mailboxes

Filtering Incoming E-Mail in Eudora

When you start developing carpal-tunnel syndrome from "hand-filing" all your mail as it comes into your Inbox, it's time to start looking for an e-mail program with filters. The most basic use of a filter is to recognize a type of mail, usually by one of its headers (such as who it's from, who or what mailing list it was sent to, or what it's about), and to automatically transfer it out of your Inbox and into the appropriate folder (or mailbox, depending on what your program calls it). More sophisticated filters can send automatic replies, forward mail to other recipients, perform multiple actions (such as both replying to a message and saving the message in a specific folder), and so on. Eudora's Filtering capabilities are quite powerful and handy if you will be receiving a lot of mail, or if the incoming mail is either to several e-mail accounts, or several family members. All of the mail, if properly filtered, can be made to go into different mailboxes as it is downloaded. The way you can tell whether there is new mail in a Eudora mailbox, is when the name of the mailbox is underlined as you pull down the Mailbox menu.

To set up a simple filter for keeping your messages neatly filed, follow these steps:

1. Select Tools ➤ Filters to open the Filters dialog box.

2. Click the New button.

3. Checkmark the Incoming and Manual checkboxes by clicking on them. Checkmark the Outgoing checkbox as well, if you plan to sort your own outgoing mail with this same filter.

4. Click in the Header drop-down list box and choose the header by which these e-mail messages can be recognized. Select Any Header for the broadest possible net. Headers can be any name in the To line, any name in the From line, or any topic in the Subject line.

5. Choose a criterion in the next drop-down list (usually Contains will work well, but there are many interesting choices), and then type the text to be found (or avoided or compared with) in the box to the right.

6. To further qualify the filter, add a second criterion by clicking the drop-down list box that currently reads Ignore and change it to And, Or, or Unless.

7. Select an action in the first Action drop-down list box (you will probably want Transfer To, but again there are many interesting options).

8. If you choose Transfer To, click the button to the right and select a folder into which the filtered mail should be transferred automatically (see Figure 4.2).

9. Add up to four additional actions, if you are ruthless enough.

10. Close the window and save the changes when prompted.

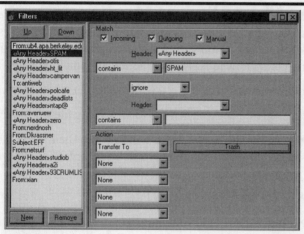

FIGURE 4.2: The simplest filter you can make with Eudora—straight to the circular file

Checking Multiple E-Mail Accounts with Eudora Personalities

You can set up Eudora (at least in the Pro version) to check multiple accounts with the Personalities feature.

1. To set up a new "personality," first find and select the Options or Settings command. (Its exact location on the menu differs in the various versions of the program, but it's over on the right somewhere!)

2. Choose the Personalities category in the dialog box. Now you can add additional addresses to your original, or "dominant," personality.

3. Click the New button to create a new personality. Enter the basic e-mail server and address information required for any account.

4. Click Check Mail if you want Eudora to look for mail on this account any time you tell it to check for mail.

5. Click Leave Mail on Server if the mail will have to be accessible to some other e-mail program as well—one at home or at work, perhaps.

Attaching Files to Eudora Messages

Eudora messages can also have files attached to them. Eudora's design lets you work intuitively with the drag and drop method, or use the keyboard or menu commands to add attachments, as explained here:

1. When you want to attach a file, first start a new message.

2. Then, use one of these actions to attach the file:

   ▸ Drag the file from a folder window into the Eudora message window (this only works in recent Windows versions of Eudora).

   ▸ Select Message ➤ Attach File.

   ▸ Press Ctrl+H or Command+H.

3. Choose a file from the Attach File dialog box (it's just like a normal Open dialog box).

4. Click OK to attach the file.

Depending on your version of Eudora, you might have the choice of several different formats for attached files, including MIME, *UUencode*, and *BinHex*—all different ways of translating files into a format that lets them travel across the Internet. Discuss the options with your intended recipient to find a format in common. The person you send the coded file to will need a program that decodes the file into a format usable in standard programs.

Adding a Name to Your Eudora Address Book

Eudora's address book feature is great for saving the e-mail addresses of people with whom you correspond. It is not easy to remember e-mail addresses, so remember instead to enter new addresses in your address book as soon as you get a message from someone new. Here are the steps for adding addresses in Eudora:

1. Highlight a message from the person whose e-mail address you want to save and then select Special ➢ Make Address Book Entry (or press Ctrl+K).

2. Type a short, memorable name in the Make Address Book Entry dialog box that appears.

3. Click the Put It on the Recipient List checkbox if you want to be able to select the address book entry from a pop-up menu (this is useful if you expect to send mail to this address regularly).

4. Click OK to add the new name to your address book.

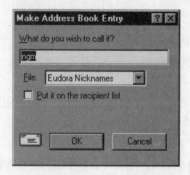

Now, whenever you want to use the address book entry, just type the short name instead of the full Internet address. You can also use address book entries in a couple of other ways, as outlined here:

▶ If you added the address book entry to the recipient list, then you can send or forward mail to the address by selecting Message ➢ New Message To ➢ *Short-Name* or Message ➢ Forward To ➢ *Short-Name*, where *Short-Name* is the name of the address you want. Eudora will do the rest.

▶ If you forget an address book entry, select Tools ➢ Address Book (in earlier versions of Eudora, it was Window ➢ Nicknames—so poke around a little if you can't find the command), select the address book entry you want, and click the To button. Eudora will copy that address into a new message window.

NOTE

Until the most recent versions of Eudora, saved addresses were called "nicknames." Now, more in line with other e-mail programs, Eudora calls them "address book entries." (They really work the same as before, if you're used to the older versions of the program.)

Using Eudora's Spell Checker

The free version of Eudora doesn't have a spell checker, but the commercial version does. To check the spelling in a message, select Edit ➢ Check Spelling. Eudora will scan the message for words it doesn't recognize. If you've ever used the spell checker in any standard word processor, then you should be familiar with this drill:

- ► To skip a suspected word, click Ignore.

- ► To accept a suggested correction, click Change.

- ► To make your own correction, type it in the Change To box and then click Change.

- ► To add the word in question to the spell checker's dictionary, click Add.

Creating an E-Mail Signature with Eudora

Eudora also has a signature feature similar to the ones discussed for other e-mail programs. Here's how to use it:

1. Select Tools ➢ Signatures ➢ New (the free version of Eudora only permits one signature).

2. Type your signature and then close the window and agree to save it when prompted. If you create multiple signatures in Eudora Pro, you can set which one you want as the default in the Signatures category of the Options dialog box (the Settings dialog box on a Macintosh).

Eudora will automatically append this signature to all your outgoing mail unless you choose None in the Signature drop-down list box at the top of the new message window.

Microsoft Exchange or Internet Mail or Outlook

Microsoft Exchange and its newer counterparts, Outlook 97 and Outlook Express, use similar commands to accomplish the same messaging goals, such as forwarding messages or sending mail to more than one person. Here are some commands you will probably use a lot:

▶ To forward a message in Microsoft Outlook 97 or Express (or Exchange), click the Forward Message (in Outlook Express), or Forward button (in Outlook 97 and Exchange). You can also choose Compose ➢ Forward or press Ctrl+F in any of these programs and then proceed as you would with a new message.

▶ To send mail to multiple recipients, type their addresses in the To box—separated by semicolons, not commas—or type additional addresses in the Cc box.

TIP

The command to forward a message in Internet Mail is Mail ➢ Forward).

Using Microsoft Word in Outlook

Outlook 97 can take advantage of all of Microsoft Word's formatting power for creating sophisticated messages with fonts, graphics, and many other features. However, the person receiving the message needs Outlook 97 or Microsoft Word to view the enhanced formats.

If you have Microsoft Word and would like to use it for composing and formatting Outlook 97 mail, follow these procedures:

1. Open Microsoft Outlook by selecting Start ➢ Programs ➢ Microsoft Outlook or by double-clicking on the Outlook desktop shortcut.

2. Select Tools ➢ Options and select the E-Mail tab.

3. Click Use Microsoft Word as E-Mail Editor.

4. Click OK.

Creating More Message Folders

As you begin to accumulate messages, replies, and copies of original messages you sent to others, you will need additional folders to store them in for easy retrieval. Fortunately, creating new message folders isn't difficult.

In Outlook 97 or Express, it's quite easy to add new message folders to your set of personal folders:

1. Select File ➢ New Folder (or press Ctrl+Shift+E) in Outlook 97. In Outlook Express, choose File ➢ Folder ➢ New Folder.

2. In the New Folder dialog box that appears, type a name for the folder and click OK.

Once a folder is created in Outlook, moving a message into the folder is even easier. In both Outlook 97 and Outlook Express, simply click the message and drag it to the folder (in the left pane).

Internet Mail uses a slightly different method to create folders.

1. In the main Internet Mail window select File ➢ Folder ➢ Create.

2. Type a name for the folder in the Create New Folder dialog box that appears and then click OK.

To move a message to a folder in Internet Mail, just click it and select Mail ➢ Move To ➢ *Folder-Name*, where *Folder-Name* is, of course, the name of your destination folder.

Sorting Outlook Express and Internet Mail Messages with Filters

Microsoft Outlook Express and Internet Mail have some of the simplest types of filtering possible: mail with specified text in one or more of four headers can be automatically filed in a specified folder.

NOTE

Outlook 97 has no filtering, however you can download the Inbox Rules Assistant from Microsoft's Outlook Web page to give it filtering capabilities "after the fact." Select Help ➢ Microsoft on the Web ➢ Free Stuff in Outlook 97 to get there, or go to http://www.microsoft.com/OfficeFreeStuff/Outlook.

These steps will get you started with the setup of an e-mail message filter in Outlook or Internet Mail.

1. Select Mail ➢ Inbox Assistant, then click Add.

2. In the Properties dialog box that appears, type text in one (or more) of the top four boxes to single out the messages you want to filter. Any message that has the text you typed in its corresponding header field(s) will be moved where you specify.

3. Select the folder you want the e-mail transferred to in the Move To drop-down list (see Figure 4.3).

4. Click OK to save the filter and then add more filters if you wish. Internet Mail lists your filters in the Inbox Assistant dialog box (in plain English, such as "Move to 'Likely Spam' if Subject contains 'Money'").

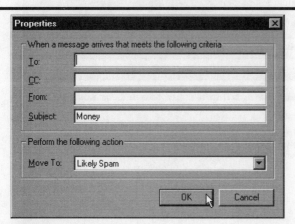

FIGURE 4.3:   With Internet Mail or Outlook Express you can sort your messages as they arrive.

You can also set up Outlook 97 to check mail from multiple different types of services (select Tools ➢ Services to see the options), but you can't set it up to check for mail on, say, two different Internet e-mail accounts. (Internet Mail can't do this, either.)

Attaching Files to E-Mail Messages in Outlook or Internet Mail

In Outlook 97, Outlook Express, or Internet Mail, use one of these options to attach files to your messages:

▶ Use Explorer, My Computer, or File Manager to open the window the file is in, click the file, and drag it into the new message window.

▶ Select Insert ➤ File and choose the file you want from the Insert File dialog box that appears and then click OK. Figure 4.4 shows an attached file in an Outlook message.

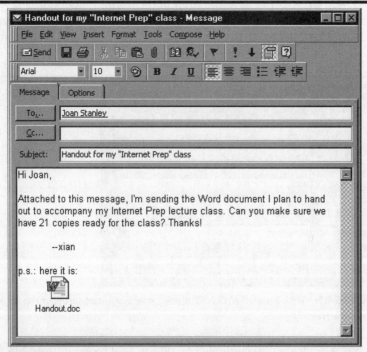

FIGURE 4.4: Outlook inserts an icon representing the attachment into your message at the insertion point. Your recipient double-clicks on the icon to open the attached file.

Using the Outlook or Internet Mail Address Book

Outlook's address book is useful for keeping track of all the e-mail addresses associated with your friends and business associates. Here's how to update the address book with new names:

1. To add a name to your address book, select Tools ≻ Address Book (or press Ctrl+Shift+B) and then select File ≻ New Entry (or press Ctrl+N).

2. In the New Entry dialog box that appears, choose Internet Mail Address and click OK.

3. Type a name for the address, press Tab, and type the e-mail address.

4. When you're done, click OK.

Using address book names in Outlook messages is even easier than adding them:

1. To send a message to someone in your address book, create a new message as usual, but instead of typing a recipient's address, click the To button to the left of the To box.

2. Select a name from the address book list and click the "To—>" button.

3. Then choose OK to copy the address to the e-mail message.

The Internet Mail address book uses much the same procedure for adding new names, but addresses are called "contacts."

1. Select File ≻ Address Book.

2. Click the New Contact button or select File ≻ New Contact.

3. Type a name for the address, press Tab, and type the e-mail address.

4. When you're done, click OK.

Correcting Spelling Errors in Microsoft E-Mail Programs

All of the Microsoft e-mail products have spell checkers. In the Outlook 97 or Express message window, select Tools ≻ Spelling (or press F7) to check the spelling of a message. In Internet Mail, it's Mail ➤ Check Spelling (or F7.)

Exchange, Internet Mail or Outlook will start scanning the message for words it doesn't recognize. If you've ever used the spell checker in Word or any other standard word processor, then you should be familiar with this drill:

- ▶ To skip the word in question, click Ignore.

- ▶ To accept a suggested correction, click Change.

- ▶ To make your own correction, type the correct word in the Change To box and click Change.

- ▶ To add the word in question to the spell checker's dictionary, click Add.

Formatting an E-Mail Message with HTML in Internet Mail or Outlook Express

Your messages will resemble Web pages if you use Outlook Express or Internet Mail HTML formatting to add colorful fonts and even graphics. Just the two steps here give you this capability:

1. Select Format ➤ HTML. A new formatting toolbar will appear at the top of your message.

2. Select the text to be formatted and use the buttons on the new toolbar to add HTML formatting, such as bold and italic, bulleted lists, alignment (center, flush left, or flush right), and text color.

NOTE

Outlook 97 permits formatting (but not HTML formatting). There are even templates (try Compose ➤ Choose Template to see some examples) with preset formatting. Internet Mail and Outlook Express both offer HTML formatting.

Using E-Mail Signatures in Outlook, Exchange, or Internet Mail

Microsoft Outlook Express, Outlook 97, and Microsoft Exchange all support signature files. These files retain your personal or professional information and add it to your messages according to your instructions.

Here are the steps for creating a standard e-mail signature in Outlook or Exchange:

1. Select Tools ➤ AutoSignature. This brings up the Auto-Signature dialog box.

2. Type your signature and click Add to put this signature at the end of new messages. (You can also prevent the signature from being added to messages you reply to or forward.)

3. Then click OK.

Internet Mail has its own way of adding e-mail signatures to messages as shown in the following steps.

1. Select Mail ➤ Options.

2. Click the Signature tab of the Options dialog box.

3. Either type your signature, or identify an existing signature file as follows:

   ▶ To type a signature, click Text, type your signature, and click Add to put this signature at the end of new messages. (You can also prevent the signature from being added to return and forwarded messages.)

   ▶ To use an existing signature file, click File and type (or browse for) the existing file name and path.

4. Then click OK.

NETCOMplete

NETCOMplete provides the same type of e-mail commands as the other e-mail programs. Read on for the little details about using NETCOMplete features.

Forwarding Mail or Sending Mail to More Than One Person with NETCOMplete

You can easily forward mail with NETCOMplete or send mail to more than one person with these commands:

▶ To forward mail in NETCOMplete, click the Forward button or select Message ➤ Forward. Then proceed as you would for a new message.

▶ To send mail to multiple recipients, just type additional e-mail addresses on the To line, separated by commas, or press Tab and add the additional addresses to the Cc line.

Creating a New NETCOMplete Mailbox Folder and Moving Messages to It

Keep your NETCOMplete Inbox organized by moving messages into specific folders. These folders can be named according to message subjects, work projects, message senders, message recipients, or dates.

1. Select Mailbox ➢ Folder Setup and then click the Add button on the Folder Setup dialog box that appears.

2. Type a name for the new folder and then click OK twice.

To transfer a message to a this new folder or a different folder just click its subject in the upper-right pane and drag it to the folder icon in the left pane.

NOTE

NETCOMplete does not offer filters for sorting your incoming mail, nor does it have any facility for checking multiple mail accounts (though you can use a program such as Eudora instead of NETCOMplete's built-in mail module).

Attaching a File to a NETCOMplete E-Mail Message

NETCOMplete's Send Mail window features a toolbar with an Attach button expressly for attaching files to your messages, as described here:

1. When you want to send an attached file with an e-mail message, click the Attach button in the Send Mail window.

2. Select a file in the Open dialog box that appears and then click OK.

Adding Names to the NETCOMplete Address Book and Using Them in Messages

When you receive e-mail from someone new and you want to keep the address available, NETCOMplete provides a quick way to get it into the address book:

1. To add an address to your address book you must first have a mail window open, and then select Settings ➤ Address Book.

2. Click the Add button.

3. Type a name for the address, press Tab, and type the e-mail address.

4. Click OK (twice).

Using the address book when sending new messages is also easy:

1. Select E-Mail ➤ Compose.

2. Click the To button in the compose window.

3. Select the name you want, click To, and click OK.

NOTE

NETCOMplete currently does not have a built-in spell checker, it doesn't permit formatting of e-mail messages (HTML or otherwise), and it does not allow you to attach signature blocks to messages.

Netscape Messenger

Netscape's newest e-mail offering, included in the Netscape Communicator 4 suite, supplies all of the functionality described in preceding sections for other programs, as well as some advanced filtering capabilities.

Setting Up Netscape Messenger

Setting up Netscape Messenger to receive your e-mail and News is easy. Before trying out the steps I describe, open Netscape Messenger by double-clicking on your Netscape Communicator desktop shortcut (or alias), or by selecting Start ➤ Programs ➤ Netscape Communicator ➤ Netscape Messenger. Select Edit ➤ Preferences ➤ Mail and Groups. The first item you can set preferences for is the appearance settings for both mail and news (font, size, color, etc.), if you wish to make changes to those, click Mail and Groups in the left pane (Figure 4.5).

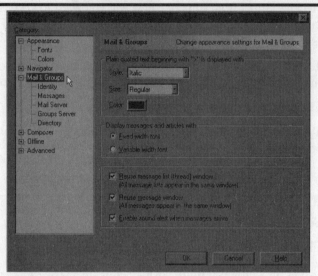

FIGURE 4.5: Setting up Mail and Groups appearance settings for Netscape Messenger

The next set of items, and the most important one, is Identity. Once you are finished making changes to the appearance settings, click Identity. The first item you will be asked to fill in is your name. The next two items are your e-mail and reply-to address. Those are usually the same, and should look something like xyz@abc.com. So, you will need to type in the same thing twice. See Figure 4.6 for an example of how to fill in the fields in Identity. If you have a business, or belong to an organization for which you will be doing e-mail correspondence, then you should fill in the organization field as well. The next item is Signatures. The way to set this is to create a Wordpad file with the information you want to appear in your signature, and then, check the box and click Choose. Once you have clicked on Choose, you will be prompted to navigate through your hard drive to select the file you created in Wordpad.

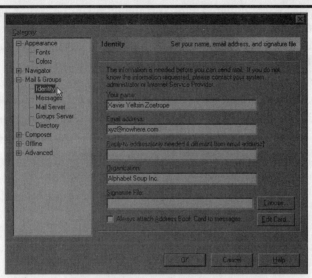

FIGURE 4.6: Setting up your Identity in Netscape Messenger

Setting your preferences for outgoing messages is simple. Click Messages in the left pane. In this window, you can set the way your messages will be formatted for others to see. If you will to send messages with HTML formatting, then you should check the first box. You have the option, when corresponding back and forth with the same person, to quote back the sender's message as part of your reply. This feature is nifty, especially when you need to reply to a long message, and need to do it point by point. The quoted text appears with greater than > signs at the beginning of each sentence. The accepted way of replying to a message on a point by point basis, is to insert your reply in between the sender's paragraphs, like so:

> > I found some pictures of you when you were six months old, and am going to make copies. Would you like me to send you some?

> Yes, it would be very nice if you could send me two copies of each. Thanks.

In the next block, you can set your preferences for the way outgoing messages are treated and filed. If, for example, you plan on sending work related e-mail messages from your home computer, and would like to have a copy of outgoing mail messages on your work computer, you should check the first box Automatically E-Mail Copies of Outgoing Messages to self. If you have a separate work account but will use your home e-mail address for work related mail, you should fill in the "other e-mail address" field, and your outgoing e-mails will be sent to that address. The next box, Groups, is for mail you will be sending in Newsgroups. You can set it up in the same way as regular outgoing e-mail.

The next group of settings have to do with where you file your outgoing messages within Messenger. Simply check the box and then using the pull down menu, choose where to file the messages. See Figure 4.7.

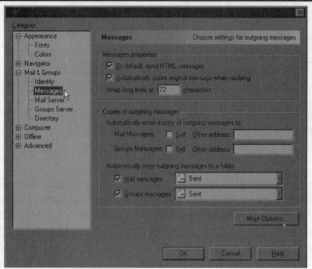

FIGURE 4.7: Setting up the Messages in Netscape Messenger

Let's go back to the left pane again to set preferences for Incoming Mail, by clicking on Mail Server. See Figure 4.8 for an image of this window. This is where you tell Messenger where to get your mail from, so you should have your account information handy. The first item to fill in is your account user name. If your e-mail address is xyz@nowhere.com, then all you should type in is xyz. For the second and third items, you should refer to the sheet or booklet your Internet service provider supplied to you when you opened your account with them. If you do not have one, call them, but the information usually looks something like smtp.nowhere.com and mail.nowhere.com for the first and second items respectively. This is not always the case though, so if it does not work for you, call your ISP's technical support line.

The next group of items has to do with the type of mail server used by your Internet service provider. Again, this is information you should be able to glean from an information booklet given to you by your Internet service provider. However, POP3 is the most prevalent type of server, and therefore the safest pick. The next item is very important. Click the More button at the bottom of the screen. This will bring up the More Mail Server Preferences Dialog box (see Figure 4.9 for a screenshot). There you will be able to tell Messenger to remember your mail password, and how often to check your mail while you are online.

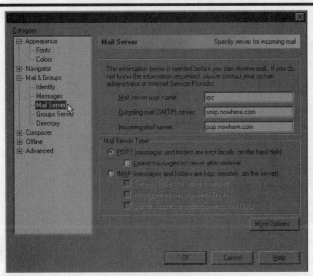

FIGURE 4.8: Setting up your Mail Server preferences in Netscape Messenger

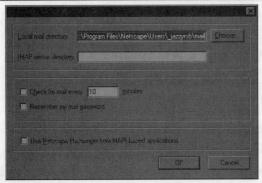

FIGURE 4.9: Setting additional Mail Server preferences in Netscape Messenger

Back to the left pane again. This time, we are going to tell Messenger where your ISP's News server is at. This, again, is information that you should have been given by your Internet service provider. See Figure 4.10 for an example of how it might look.

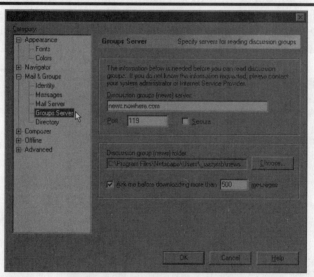

FIGURE 4.10: Setting up Groups Server for Netscape Messenger

The last item on the left pane, Directory, is quite a nifty feature. Let's say, you thought you had the address of a colleague in your address book, but it isn't there. Messenger will search your address book for it first. If it does not find it there, you can set it to look at one of the Search Engines on the Internet. I have mine set to search on the Whowhere search engine. See Figure 4.11.

Forwarding Netscape Messenger Messages and Sending Mail to More Than One Person

Netscape Messenger has a full complement of messaging features, including mail forwarding and the means to send mail to more than one person at a time. Here are the basic forwarding and sending options:

▶ When you want to forward a message, click the Forward button (or select Message ➤ Forward or press Ctrl+L or Command+L). Then proceed as you would with a new message.

▶ To send mail to multiple recipients, type the addresses in the Mail To box, separated by commas, or enter additional addresses in the Cc box.

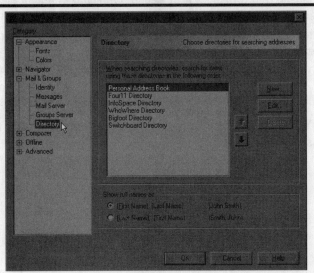

FIGURE 4.11: Setting up the Directory search features for Netscape Messenger

Creating New Folders for Filing Messenger E-Mail

Messenger also allows you to create new folders for filing messages. Here's how you do it:

1. Press Backspace to get to your Message Center (your master mail folder).

2. Select the folder in which you want the new folder to appear (or select Mail to create an upper-level folder).

3. Then select File ➤ New Folder.

4. Type a name for the new folder in the dialog box that appears and then click OK.

Filing Netscape Messenger Messages in Folders

Netscape Messenger (and the rest of the Communicator suite) has a
revamped menu structure that gives toolbar buttons mini-menus of their
own. This means that it really is even easier and faster to file messages in
Messenger than it is in other e-mail programs, because you do not have to
open a folder window or use a dialog box to find the folder where you
want to put the message.

1. Highlight the message to be moved.

2. Click the File button (or select Message ➤ File Message).

3. Choose the destination folder from the menu that pops up
   (subfolders appear on submenus).

Filtering Netscape Messenger E-Mail

Netscape Messenger's rules for filtering e-mail are quite specific and give
you more flexibility in organizing your mailbox than other mail filters.
Most of the time you can use the existing rules provided by Netscape. If
none of these rules are customized enough for you, you can construct
unique rules for your own mail management needs.

Here's how you create a new filter for incoming messages:

1. Select Edit ➤ Mail Filters.

2. Click the New button on the Mail Filters dialog box.

3. In the top half of the Filter Rules dialog box that appears,
   enter a name for your filter (see Figure 4.12).

4. Choose one of the nine different aspects of the message to
   base your filter on (such as the subject, the priority, or who's
   on the Cc list).

5. Choose one of the six different comparison criteria (Contains, Doesn't Contain, Is, Isn't, Begins With, and Ends With) and then enter the text that is to be looked for or avoided in the third box.

6. Click the More button if you want to add additional criteria.

7. Below the More button, choose from six actions (usually you'll want Move to Folder,—some of the instructions are more suited for discussion groups than for private e-mail), and then choose a folder (if applicable).

8. Finally, you can enter a description if you wish, and click OK.

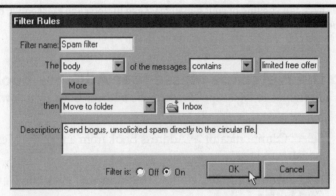

FIGURE 4.12:   You can put together sophisticated filters easily with Netscape Messenger.

NOTE

Netscape Messenger has no provision, as of yet, for checking mail from multiple accounts.

Attaching Files to Messenger E-Mail

Netscape Messenger's provisions for attaching files to e-mail are quite simple. You can also attach web page links to your messages with these commands:

1. Select Message ➢ New Message to open the Composition window. Or you can click the New Message button in the Messenger toolbar or type Ctrl+M.

2. Address your message and type your message in the message body. To attach a file to the message, click the Attach button.

3. Choose File (as you can see, you can also attach Web pages, among other things).

4. In the dialog box that appears, choose the file you want to send, and then click Open.

5. Click the Save button or the Send button to save a draft or send your message on its way.

TIP

To check the spelling of your e-mail message in Netscape Messenger, choose Tools ➤ Check Spelling in the Composition window.

Using the Netscape Messenger Address Book

You can add names to Netscape Messenger's address book by following these steps:

1. Select Communicator ➤ Address Book from any of the Messenger windows.

2. In the Address Book window that appears, click the New Card button.

3. Enter the name, e-mail address, and nickname, and then click OK.

4. Select File ➤ Close to close the Address Book window.

To use the addresses in your new messages, do one of the following, depending on how good your memory is:

▶ In the Message Composition window, type the nickname on the To line.

▶ If you don't remember the nickname you made up, click the Address button, select the name, click To, and then click OK.

NOTE

You can add any HTML formatting (or insert hyperlinks or even graphic images) to your message using the convenient toolbar in the Message Compose window. (Insert links and images with the Insert Object button furthest to the right.)

Adding a Signature File to Messenger E-Mail

Messenger's signature file feature does not include much formatting support, but you can create basic signature files and add them to your messages with a minimum amount of fuss.

Here are the steps for creating and adding a signature file:

1. First, use a text editor or word processor to create and save a text file containing the signature you want to have at the end of your e-mail messages.

2. Then, in Netscape, select Edit ➤ Preferences. Double-click the Mail & Groups item in the Category list in the Preferences dialog box.

3. Click Identity in the Mail & Groups list item and type the full path and file name of your signature file in the Signature File box (or click the Browse button to find and select the file, and click OK).

4. When you're done, click OK.

TIP

If your signature exceeds the recommended four lines (this rubric is a widely accepted netiquette standard, though many people violate it), Netscape will warn you, but all you have to do is click OK again to accept it.

Netscape Collabra

Using Netscape Collabra to post to a news group involves sending and receiving messages over the Internet. There are only two real differences from e-mail. One, messages are not directed to individuals, but to the group. Subscribers receive all messages sent to the group, thus creating the discussion format that makes news groups so popular. Two, messages are not permanently stored in an account on a server somewhere. Each time you want to read a posting you must logon and download the headers for each message. When you find the post you want to read Collabra downloads the entire message. When you are finished, unless you have saved copies of all the messages you read, Collabra purges its caches of any extraneous data, namely the messages. Let's take a look at how you can make Collabra work for you.

Part I

Getting News Groups

Sure, setting up an e-mail account is easy. All you do is tell Messenger who you are and it gets your mail. Simple. Okay, so subscribing to news groups is not quite as easy, but if you are interested in holding diverse discussions on topics that interest you, e-mail won't do it. And honestly, it's not all that hard to do.

NOTE

Okay, you caught me. You can do the same thing in e-mail, but you are limited to text-based discussion. If you are a member of a photography group that exchanges shots of landscapes you would tie up everyone's e-mail server shuttling huge graphic files back and forth. Not something people want to spend time on the Internet for, regardless of how nice the pictures might be. News groups allow you to only download the messages you want to read. That's the nice way to do it. Trust me.

First, let's make sure Collabra is open. If you are using Navigator or any other Communicator component simply do any of the following:

▶ Select the Collabra item from the Communicator menu.

▶ Go to Start ➤ Programs ➤ Netscape Communicator ➤ Netscape Collabra.

▶ Click the little voice balloons in the Component Bar, whether floating or docked.

The first thing you will notice is its striking similarity to Messenger. This is not a mistake on Netscape's part, but an easier way to get into news groups (at least in Netscapes thinking). If you have never delved into the realm of joining a news group, let's look now.

Locate the Subscribe button on the toolbar and click it. The Subscribe to Discussion Groups window will open and, if you are connected to the Internet, download the group's list from your ISP's news server.

NOTE

If you did not enter this information into the Preferences dialog box when you first started Communicator the program will prompt you to enter it now. Most ISP's news servers' URLs begin with news and look like this: news.kewl.com or nntp.chrysler.com.

Be prepared to wait a few moments as all the groups are loaded into Collabra. Because most new servers maintain at least 100 groups with at least 5 sub groups and usually more like 50 sub groups, this may take a while. Have a soda or coffee and a danish. When the groups are loaded the file list window will begin to fill up. When it is finished you can do one of three things:

▶ Locate a group by entering in known portions of the name.

▶ Search for a keyword.

▶ Check for new groups.

We will focus on the first two. If you are already subscribed to groups, you should see something similar to Figure 4.13 below.

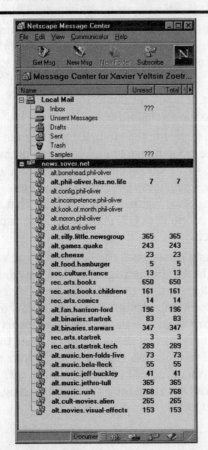

FIGURE 4.13: The main Mail and Groups window

The All Groups tab is where the main group list will appear after you download them from your news server. At the top of the pane is a text field. As you enter letters into the field Collabra tries to locate the closest match to the current criteria. For example, typing an **A** yields the a.* group root, typing **AL** yields Alabama.*, and typing **ALT** yeilds alt.*, a very popular root group. As you continue to enter letters it continues to try and match your entries. A try for Alt.Philly.* got me alt.phil oliver.has.no.life. If you know the name of a group or are mostly clear on the name, then this can work for you.

On the other hand, if you are completely unfamiliar with the available groups you can perform a search for pertinent discussion groups. Click the Search For a Group tab and again, enter a word into the text field, except this time click the Search Now button. Collabra will collect all of the matches you made and combine them in the single window, allowing you to browse the results. Enter a search for Family and you get a huge list of groups that collect people with particular family names. Unfortunately, you also get Alt.binaries.pictures.naturism.family proudly listed at the top.

Now that we have a clear idea of how Communicator handles subscribing to news groups, let's get into the mechanics of it.

There are three columns that appear in the group list as shown in Figure 4.14. The first column is the group name, or the root name of the group (for example, alt.* or comp.*), the second Subscribe, and the third, Messages. Clicking on the small dot in the Subscribe column changes the dot into a check mark (see Figure 4.15), indicating that a subscription will be set as soon as you click OK. (Clicking on the Subscribe button has the same effect.)

If you need to add another news server, click the New Server button in the lower right-hand corner of the All Groups page. The Add New Server dialog will appear where you will enter the new servers address. If navigating the entire list of groups seems maddening, click the Search For A Group tab. Enter the search information into the text field and press Enter or click Search Now. A list of matches should appear (not all things are reflected in a news group). If you search was successful, you can subscribe to the group here. When you have finished subscribing to the groups that interest you and click OK to exit the Subscription dialog, you will be returned to the Message Center.

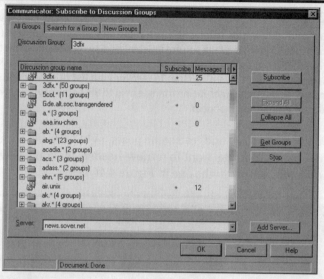

FIGURE 4.14:   The news group subscription dialog showing a complete listing of all groups downloaded from the news server

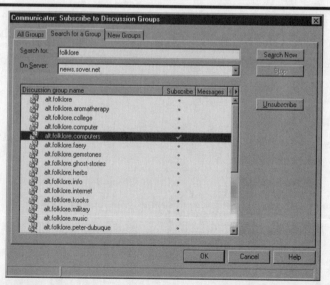

FIGURE 4.15:   A subscribed group shown in the Search page of the Subscription dialog

NOTE

You did nothing wrong. Communicator has a strange way of dealing with newly subscribed to groups. When you are finished adding groups and leave the subscription dialog, the Message Center collapses your list back into the news server item. Why? I haven't a clue. To recover your list of subscribed groups, simply click the small right-facing triangle next to the name of your news server and your groups will reappear.

Now you're ready to go and read some posts, right? Double-click the name of the news group you want to retrieve headers for and a new window will open up, similar to the one in Figure 4.16 below.

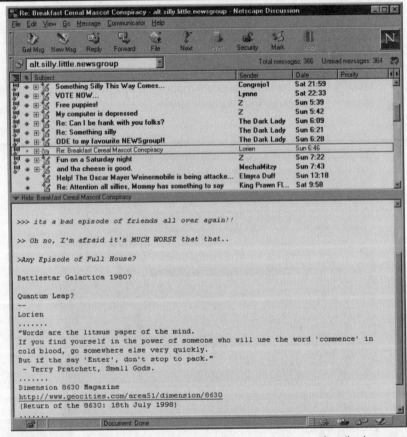

FIGURE 4.16: The Netscape Discussions window displaying a subscribed news group and its messages

> **TIP**
>
> Headers are a portion of the message that contains the title, author, e-mail address of the author, and other information about the message. The Header does not contain the actual message text itself. That has to be downloaded when you request to read it.

The upper portion of the window contains the header information for the messages that can be retrieved from the server, if you wish to read them. A decision to read a message is often made based on the content of the title of the message. To read a particular message click the message name in the upper panel. After the server sends the message to Collabra it is displayed in the lower section for your reading pleasure.

After you receive your first news group posting it's time to celebrate by sending a reply. Click the Reply button and a familiar message window will appear like the fictional message in Figure 4.17 below. Enter the text and photographs of the family trip to Bogota and click the Send button. *Voilà!* Posting sent. If you check for new messages a few minutes later you should see your first posting added to the list.

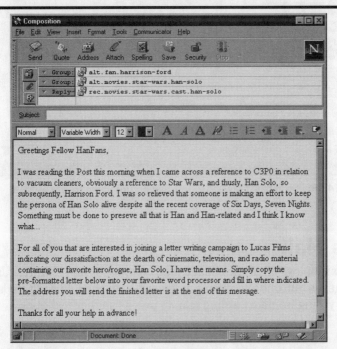

FIGURE 4.17: A message ready to be sent to eager Han Solo fans

To switch to another subscribed news group click the newsgroups list box as shown in Figure 4.18 below. The new groups messages will be loaded and you can move on to responding to people on that list.

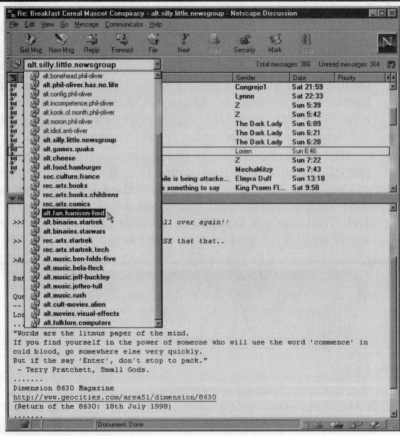

FIGURE 4.18: Switching between subscribed groups in the reader window

Pegasus Mail

Pegasus employs all of the usual e-mail commands and features. Use the Pegasus buttons and menus as described in the following steps to do everything from forwarding mail to using your address book.

Forwarding Pegasus Mail or Sending Messages to More Than One Person

Your Pegasus Mail messages can be forwarded to other people and you can send forwarded messages or other types of messages to more than one person with the following options:

▶ To forward a message, just click the Forward button at the top of the message window. Then proceed as you would with any new message.

▶ To send an e-mail to multiple recipients, type the addresses in the To box, separated by commas, or enter additional addresses in the Cc box.

Managing Pegasus Mail with Folders

Like most of the other mail programs profiled in this lesson, Pegasus Mail has a folder feature for storing messages so that you can find them later when you want to refer back to them.

Here's how to create a new folder:

1. First select File ➤ Mail Folders to open the Folders dialog box.

2. Click the New button, type a name for the new folder, and click OK.

To move a message from one folder to another, double-click the folder currently containing the message, highlight the message you want to move, and drag it to the new folder.

Attaching Files to Pegasus Messages

File attachments are an important part of Pegasus Mail messages because the program supports many different Internet file types. When you start sending messages with attachments to many different people on many different systems, you might have to experiment with these file formats to see which one works best and gets the information to your recipients in a usable format. These steps will get you started:

1. Click the Attach button on the left side of the message window.

2. Select a file in the bottom part of the window that appears, and then click the Add button (top right).

3. Choose one of the wide variety of file-encoding formats from the Encoding drop-down list, or allow the mailer to choose one for you.

4. Then click the Editor button (on the left side of the window) when you're ready to return to typing your message.

5. When you're done typing the message, you can just click Send.

TIP

If PC users—especially on a local-area network—sometimes have trouble accessing the path the folder is in, you may have to move the file around in File Manager.

Creating and Using a Pegasus Address Book

The address book feature in Pegasus Mail is a little different from other e-mail address books because you have to create the address book before you can add names to it. The advantage to this setup is that you can have more than one address book. For example, you could have Business and Personal address books to store the names and addresses of business associates and friends separately. Some people might get listed in both books, however, if you are fortunate enough to have friends at work!

1. To create an address book, select Addresses ➤ Address Books, and then click New in the Select an Address Book dialog box that appears.

2. Type a name for the address book and then click OK.

3. To open an address book, select Addresses ➤ Address Books and double-click the name of the address book you want to open.

4. To add a name to the address book, click the Add button. Pegasus suggests the name and e-mail address from the currently selected message, but you can type in any name.

5. Press Tab seven times to get to the E-Mail Address box and type a different e-mail address, if you like. Then click OK.

When you want to send e-mail to someone in one of your address books, you have two choices:

- ▶ Type their name in the To box.

- ▶ Open the address book (as just described), scroll down to select the person you want, and click the Paste button. Then click Close.

Correcting Misspelled Words in Pegasus Messages

You can access the spell-checking feature by selecting Edit ➢ Check Spelling. Pegasus will start scanning the message for words it doesn't recognize. If you've ever used the spell checker in any standard word processing program, then you should be familiar with how it works:

- ▶ To skip the word in question, click Skip.

- ▶ To accept a suggested correction, click Change.

- ▶ To make your own correction, type the correct word over the suggestion and click Change.

- ▶ To add the word in question to the spell checker's dictionary, click Add.

Pegasus will tell you when you've reached the end of the message and ask if you want to start over from the top. Click No (unless you want to). Then click Close.

Creating and Adding Signatures in Pegasus Mail

Use the Pegasus Mail Signature feature to create signature blocks that you can use repeatedly in different messages. This is especially useful for business messages, because it saves you the time of retyping your name, title, company name, address, phone and fax numbers, e-mail address, and all the other contact information usually included on a business card. Just type it once and save it in a signature file, then reuse this file in all your messages.

Follow these steps to make your signature file:

1. Select File ➢ Preferences ➢ Signatures ➢ For Internet Messages.

2. Type your signature in the dialog box that appears and click the Save button.

Pine

Pine uses simple letter commands rather than menus and buttons to implement e-mail features, but the end results are the same as for the programs that run under Windows and the Mac OS, described earlier in this lesson.

Forwarding a Message in Pine

Pine may be a simple mail program, but you can still forward messages, and Pine even adds a reply separator between the message you type and the message you are forwarding. Use these steps to forward Pine messages to other Pine users:

1. When you receive a message you want to forward to another person, press **f**.

2. Pine will put you in the Forward Message screen, which is exactly the same as the Compose Message screen except that the message area will include the original message, preceded by

    ------Forwarded Message------

3. Proceed as you would with a normal message.

Sending Pine Messages to More Than One Person

Pine also supports sending mail to many people at one time. You can add more than one address to either the To line or the Cc line in the Pine message using these options:

▶ To send mail to multiple recipients, type each e-mail address on the To line, separated by commas.

▶ Or, type additional e-mail addresses on the Cc line, also separated by commas.

TIP
You can always go back to your INBOX folder by pressing **g** (for Go to) and then Enter to accept the default.

If you want to save a piece of mail for future reference, press **s** either in the index or while reading the mail. Pine will suggest Saved-Messages as a folder name, but you can replace it with anything you like.

Looking at Message Folders with Pine

Pine provides message folders for storing messages in an orderly manner. You can file messages in folders that reflect the message subject, sender, or other topics and revisit them later with these procedures:

1. To look at the contents of a folder, press **l** to see a folder list.

2. Press the Tab key to get to the folder list you want to see, and then press Enter.

3. When you are done and want to go back, press the letter **l** to get back to the folder list and choose the INBOX folder.

Attaching Files to Pine Messages

You can also send a file with Pine. Here are the steps for adding file attachments to Pine messages.

1. In the Compose Mail screen, press Tab twice to get to the Attachment line.

2. Then press Ctrl+T. This will bring up a list of the files in your Unix directory.

3. Using the arrow keys, select a file and press Enter. Pine will send the file as a MIME attachment.

Creating and Using a Pine Address Book

To create an address book—a list of e-mail addresses you regularly send mail to—press a (from the Main Menu screen). This brings up the Address Book screen.

To add a new address to the Pine address book:

1. Press **a**. Pine will prompt you with

   ```
   New full name (last, first):
   ```

2. Type the last name, a comma, and then the first name of the person whose Internet address you want to add to your address book. Then press Enter and Pine will prompt you with

   ```
   Enter new nickname (one word and easy to remember):
   ```

3. Type a short nickname and press Enter. Then Pine will prompt you to

   ```
   Enter new e-mail address:
   ```

4. Type the person's address and press Enter. The new address will be added to the address book.

5. Press **i** to return to the INBOX folder index, or press **m** to return to the Main Menu.

Now, whenever you want to use the nickname in the address book, just type it instead of the full Internet address. Pine will do the rest.

Adding Addresses to the Pine Address Book

Pine's address book supplies all of the usual address book functions and even has a nickname feature for storing address book entries. All you have to remember is the nickname and Pine will retrieve the person's e-mail address.

You can also take an e-mail address off a recent message and send it to the Pine address book with these steps:

1. To automatically add the sender of the current message to your address book from the Folder Index screen, press **t**.

2. Type an address book entry for the sender and press Enter.

3. Press Enter twice to accept the full name and address of the sender.

NOTE
Pine does not permit you to add formatting to message text (HTML or otherwise). Pine has no message filtering capabilities, either.

Checking Message Spelling with Pine

Even though Pine may not have all the bells and whistles of its non-Unix counterparts, it does provide the essential spell-check feature for proofing your messages before they "go public." Here are the steps involved:

1. To check the spelling of a message, press Ctrl+T (while in the message area itself).

2.   Pine will highlight any suspicious word and prompt you to correct it and press Enter—but Pine won't suggest any possible spellings. Press Enter to make the correction.

Adding Signature Files to Pine Messages

Pine's signature file function operates much like that of other e-mail programs. You can add all of your professional information to the signature file and it will be added at the end of all your Pine messages. The only disadvantage to the signature file is that it will appear on all your messages, not just the ones you select to have signatures.

1.   Create a text file named `.signature`. To do so, at the Unix prompt, type **pico .signature** and press Enter.

2.   Type whatever you want for your signature (but keep it under four lines as traditional netiquette dictates).

3.   Then press Ctrl+X, type **y**, and press Enter.

TIP

The required location of the signature file might vary from one system to the next, so if your signature file does not appear at the end of your messages, ask your system administrator where it should be stored.

Your signature will appear at the end of your e-mail messages. When you reply to a message and quote the text in your reply, Pine will put your signature at the beginning of your new message, before the quoted text. The idea is for you to write your message before the signature and then delete as much of the quoted text as possible (while still letting it make sense).

WHAT'S NEXT?

You have just completed a very thorough examination of the e-mail capabilities of some of our most celebrated Internet programs. Now that you are an e-mail expert, it's time to push on and master the mysteries of the World Wide Web.

PART II
BROWSING AND MORE

Chapter 5

INTRODUCTION TO WEB BROWSING

One of the newest media available over the Internet is the World Wide Web. The Web (or sometimes WWW, w3, or W3) is a huge collection of interconnected hypertext documents. Hypertext documents can contain links to other documents, to completely different kinds of files, and to other sites on the Internet. With a Web browser, you can jump from one link to the next, following the trail of links in any direction that interests you. Not everything on the Internet is available via the Web, but more and more of it is being linked together.

The beauty of the Web is that the browser programs with which you "read" the Web are incredibly easy to use. This gives you access to all kinds of data, programs, news, pictures, and so on, without having to master the syntax of difficult protocols and arcane Unix commands.

Throughout the rest of this book, there will be references to the Web. It has become such a ubiquitous *front end* (way to connect) to the Net that much of your use of the Net will take place through a Web browser.

Adapted from *The Internet: No experience required.*, by Christian Crumlish
ISBN 0-7821-2168-3   528 pages $24.99

How Is the Web Being Used?

More and more day-to-day applications are gaining the capability to browse the Web and display documents in Web format (HTML). The competition among Web browsers is fierce, with Netscape and Microsoft duking it out for the dominant share of the market. Every sought-after browser includes e-mail and news modules as well, with Web (HTML) editors being another common feature. Upcoming releases of popular browsers will blend together your desktop view of your own computer with the Web interface. (More on that later.) Meanwhile, in-house *intranets* these days incorporate most of the features of Web sites while local, small-scale networks operate much like the Internet.

Those are the changes taking place in the world of tools. On the Web itself, commercial sites keep sprouting up like mushrooms, although there is no proven business model yet for making money on the Web.

Cramming the Web with Content

Companies have rushed to post their own Web sites, where they provide everything from customer service to upcoming product information and online ordering capabilities (if you can get through). Any information or material added to a Web site, even fiction and graphics, is referred to as *content*. The Web has more content than a university or library because the Web is a collection of data from many universities, libraries, businesses, and so on.

All kinds of companies have set up shop on the Web—not just mega-corporations such as Coca Cola and IBM. Any organization that can afford space on a Web server can display its wares (or its philosophy, or both) online. This gives Web users access to many new products, services, and business ideas that would have been difficult to find before Internet use became so widespread.

If you are in the market for energy-saving compact-fluorescent lighting or solar panels for your home, for example, check out the Real Goods Solar Living site at http://www.realgoods.com (see Figure 5.1). This site has its own set of specialized Web links that will lead you to sites sponsored by the US Environmental Protection Agency, including Solstice: Internet Information Service of the Center for Renewable Energy and Sustainable Technology (CREST) at http://www.solstice.crest.org. Explore Solstice for a little bit and you can reach the CREST Global

Energy Marketplace (GEM) at `http://gem.crest.org`, where you can click on your state to find local energy information. Chances are, if you have a special interest or purchase to make, there is a site out there that you can use, with links to other related sites that might help you out, too.

WHAT IS HYPERTEXT?

On the Web, hypertext is simply text with links. *Links* are elements of the hypertext documents that you can select—often presented as underlined words or icons. Click on a link and you'll be transported to the document it's linked to (or to a different part of the displayed document). If you use Windows, then you've got hypertext right in front of you, in the form of Windows help files. Whenever you select options from the Help menu of a Windows program, you are shown a hypertext help document with definitions and links available at the click of a mouse.

In addition to taking you to other documents, links can take you to Gopher servers, FTP sites, Telnet sites, Usenet newsgroups, and other Internet facilities. Links can also take you to other programs and connect you to pictures, sounds, movies, and other binary files.

Once we start considering other media besides text, the term hypertext is replaced by the word *hypermedia*. But the basic idea is the same: links. An advantage of hypermedia over traditional media is that it allows you to navigate through all kinds of related documents (and other kinds of files), using one simple procedure—clicking on a link.

One limitation of hypermedia is that, for now, you generally must follow links that other people have created, so the medium is not yet fully interactive. Of course, you can always make your own Web page. Also, there's a lot more text out there than hypertext. A Web browser can lead you to a plain text document as easily as to a hypertext document. You won't be able to jump anywhere else from a plain text document, so it's a sort of cul-de-sac, but you can always turn around.

Part ii

FIGURE 5.1:   Find everything from compact-fluorescent lighting to worm com-
posters at the Real Goods Solar Living site at `http://www.realgoods.com`.

NOTE
A cornucopia of job-related Web sites has sprung up, where you can design
your resume, browse job listings, or pick up interview tips.

Business needs aside, the Web's greatest strength may be its capacity
for entertainment. You can find everything from literary 'zines to science
fiction film guides. Sports enthusiasts, of course, have many Web sites to
choose from, including sites supporting the growing field of fantasy fran-
chises, where players have their own fantasy teams and create rosters from
real players. You can find out about the local activities of your favorite organization by following links from the organization's parent Web site, such as
the Habitat for Humanity site shown in Figure 5.2.

FIGURE 5.2: Find out about local branches or organizations from the Web page of their headquarters. Habitat for Humanity's Web site at http://www.habitat.org has many links to pages about its work.

NOTE

This overabundance of Web content brings problems, too, such as slower and slower browsing speeds and information overload. Run a search for the term "computer" on the Web and you could wind up with almost one million *hits*. Each hit is an individual site that matches your search term and, in this case, has something to do with computers. Fortunately, you can refine your searches, as you will learn in Chapter 8.

You don't always have to go out and look for things on the Web, though. Now there is also *push* technology (also called Webcasting or Netcasting), which allows you to direct your browser to find and obtain information from specific sites for you while you are off doing something else. This innovation is available in Microsoft Internet Explorer 4 and Netscape Net-caster, part of the Netscape Communicator 4 application suite.

Saving Time with Webcasting

A brave new method for delivering content to your screen via the Web, called *Webcasting* or *Netcasting*, allows your browser to surf the Web for you. You can set up your Webcasting software, such as Netscape Net-caster or Microsoft Internet Explorer 4's Active Channels, to deliver any kind of information you like to your desktop, including stock market reports, up-to-the-minute sports results, and even weather reports. This new push technology promises to give Web users finer control over their Web surfing activities and to improve the quality of the information pulled in.

As Web content expands and draws in more Web users, the amount of time spent waiting to get through to sites and waiting for Web pages to load has increased. This results in frustrated Web users who are sick of waiting around on the Web to see new sites or popular pages. Netcaster minimizes browser delays by downloading any Web site you specify to your hard drive, where you can browse each page in the site at your own pace, which is probably faster than pages will load while you are online.

Next week, something new will appear on the Web's horizon because the Web is in a constant state of change. When you learn how to browse the Web, you will have a valuable skill that will enable you to remain informed about new developments in all kinds of subjects, not just computers. Your ability to browse the Web and develop effective search strategies for finding things could lead to personal, as well as professional, growth and opportunities.

WEB ADDRESSES (URLs)

As you know, Web addresses can be long and somewhat cumbersome. Fortunately, most of the time you're browsing the Web, you won't have to type in Web addresses yourself after the first one, because you'll be fol-lowing links that have the URL encoded into them. You can also copy Web addresses from e-mail and other sources and paste them into your browser, rather than having to retype them. Another beautiful feature of most Web browsers is URL-saving *bookmarks*, which we will cover later in this lesson.

Enterprising search engine companies have also given us Web sites designed around their search software, such as Yahoo!, Excite, AltaVista, and Infoseek. You can go to these sites, use the interactive search form to find a list of Web addresses relating to your search criteria, and click on the links in the search list to go to the sites. You still have to type in some of the search terms, however.

NOTE

While graphical browsers such as Netscape Navigator are certainly a pleasure to use and a great way to surf the Net, reading the Web with Lynx can be just as fascinating—after all, it's the information itself that is most interesting on the Net.

WEB BROWSER BASICS

Generally, when you start a browser, you begin at a home page, a starting place you designate (or your browser designates) for your Web-crawling sessions. This will either be the default home page for your browser or a custom home page that you have specified. Some e-mail programs, such as Eudora, now allow you to double-click a URL in an e-mail message to automatically start up your most recently installed browser and bring up the selected Web page.

NOTE

Hypertext documents on the Web are commonly referred to as pages. All of the Web pages linked together and maintained in the same file on a server (network computer) are called a Web site. Companies, organizations, and individuals maintain Web sites, either on their own servers or on a server maintained by an online service or access provider.

Most online services offer access to the Web in two ways: with a built-in, licensed browser (usually Netscape Communicator or Microsoft Internet Explorer), or by enabling you to launch an external browser program alongside the main access program. Direct-access ISPs also permit you to run whichever Web browser you like over the dial-up connection (and most people opt for Netscape Communicator or Microsoft Internet Explorer).

Part ii

HTTP, HTML, AND URLS

Don't get thrown by the alphabet soup of acronyms you're confronted with when you start looking into the Web. URL, as I mentioned before, stands for Uniform Resource Locator and is simply a form of address that all Web browsers can understand. URLs always take this form: *protocol://host:port/dir/filename*. The *www* you see in Web addresses is part of the host name and refers to the World Wide Web portion of the Internet.

So, the URL gopher://gopher.spinaltap.micro.umn.edu:70/00/fun/Recipes/Balls/tofu-balls tells a browser to "use the gopher protocol to connect to the host machine called gopher.spinaltap.micro.umn.edu (somewhere at the birthplace of Gopher in the University of Minnesota), connect to port 70 there, look in folder 00/fun/Recipes/Balls, and get the file containing the tofu-balls recipe."

The protocol generally used to connect to hypertext documents is called HTTP. HTTP stands for Hypertext Transfer Protocol because browsers use it to transfer hypertext documents to you. If that protocol is called for, the URL will begin with http: (other protocols are ftp:, telnet:, and so on—there's also a protocol called file:, which is equivalent to ftp:).

The other confusing acronym you will come across is HTML. HTML stands for Hypertext Markup Language, and it is the code used to mark up text documents to turn them into hypertext documents. Hypertext documents on the Web generally end in the extension .html and contain funny-looking text tags, like this: <TITLE>.

NOTE

The Web is growing more popular all the time, and you may experience delays connecting to busy addresses. Attempts to follow links may even result in *timing-out*, meaning that some computer along the line gives up and you get an error message. If this happens, just try again—first right away and then, if necessary, during off-hours (late at night or on the weekend).

Figure 5.3 shows the Netscape home page that comes up automatically when you start Netscape Navigator (unless you change it to start at a different page).

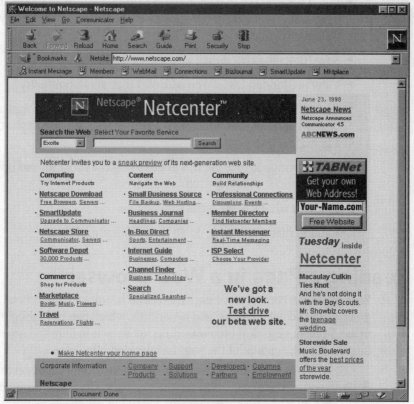

FIGURE 5.3:   Unless customized, Netscape Navigator starts you off at the Netscape home page.

Now that you're connected, you can:

▶ Follow the links that interest you. At any point, you can retrace your steps or bring up a complete history of where you've been this session and then jump immediately back to one of those pages. However, if you back up to any main page of links during the session and branch off on another series of links, that new sequence of links will replace the previously visited sequence in your history list.

▶ Go to a specific Web address (URL) when you start your browser. Generally, to stop it from loading the default home page, you click on the Stop button and enter an address directly.

▶ Insert bookmarks that enable you to jump back to an interesting page without having to retrace your steps or bring up a history of where you've been.

▶ Save (download) or e-mail interesting documents and files.

▶ View the hidden URL (Web address) that a link points to.

▶ Customize your program's home page so that you always start at a page with links that interest you, rather than having to start at a generic home page.

▶ Access online help to get tips about using the program and information about the Web itself.

▶ Find out what's new on the Net.

Read on to discover how to do all these things and more.

Reading a Page in a Web Browser

Web pages can consist of formatted text and headings; illustrations; background art and color effects; and hyperlinks, which can be highlighted text or art. In most graphical browsers, links are shown in blue and are underlined unless the creator of the page has decided otherwise.

Often a page won't fit on the screen all at once, depending on the design used by the person who created the page. Graphical browsers use scroll bars, just as other programs do, to enable you to see material that doesn't fit on the screen. If you're hunting for a specific piece of information on a long document page, try searching for keywords, which can usually be done with a menu command.

TIP

If you find browsing too slow, if pictures take too long to load, or if your browser has trouble displaying some of the art on some of the Web pages, consider turning off automatic picture loading. Most browsers have an option on one of their menus for doing so. You'll still be able to load any specific pictures you want to see, or even see all the art on a page at once, but it will make your browsing go much more quickly and smoothly.

Following a Link

In graphical browsers, following a link is as simple as positioning the mouse pointer over the link and clicking once. You will know the pointer is over an active link because it will change shape—in Netscape Navigator it changes to a little hand. Keep in mind that you only need to click once on Web links—we are all so used to double-clicking that at first it may be difficult to get out of the habit.

All browsers have a Back command, often a shortcut button, for retracing your steps back to the previous page. Once you've gone back, you can also go forward, using the Forward command, to return along your original path to the furthest point you had gotten to. Also, you can usually bring up a *history list* (on a menu in a graphical browser; on a separate page in a text-only browser) of all the pages you've been to since you started the most recent series of links.

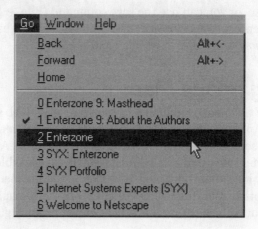

WARNING

The history list will actually show you only the pages you've visited sequentially from your starting point. Any time you back up and then follow a different link, you will lose the history path beyond the point you backed up to. For example, if I go to sites A, B, C, and D, then back up to B and then go to E, my history path will read A, B, E.

Knowing Where to Go

It's hard to get oriented in the Web because there's no real starting point. Your default home page should provide some pretty useful places to start though. I recommend surfing around for a while to see where these points lead.

In most browsers, if you have a specific Web address in mind (perhaps one you saw in an advertisement or one that was e-mailed to you), you can type in the URL and visit the Web page directly, without having to follow a trail of links to get there.

Also, at any time, you can return to your default home page. Graphical browsers have a Home button, often decorated with an icon representing a house, for this purpose.

Saving or Mailing a Document

If a Web page contains information that you want to send to someone or that you want to save on your own computer, you can either use your browser's mail command to send the document to yourself or to someone else, or you can use the save command (File ➤ Save As in graphical browsers) to save a copy of the document on your hard disk, much the same way you'd save a file in a word processor.

Clicking Image Maps

One of the most common navigation devices at Web sites is the image map. An image map is a clickable image with different regions, each of which sends the browser to a different destination. At well-designed Web sites there are often two main image maps: a clickable banner at the top of the site's home page, and a smaller navigation menu at the bottom of every other page. Some image maps are actually maps, such as those found at Web sites that function as city or regional guides.

Dealing with Frames

More and more of the Web pages you'll see are divided up into frames—sections of the screen with separate content devoted to different purposes. These frames actually partition the Web page into multiple windows, some of which may have their own sets of scroll bars. All of these windows can be a problem if you do not have a huge monitor because you can only see a small portion of the contents of each frame without extensively scrolling through the frame. Even worse, you cannot drag the frames around or resize them like you can drag and resize windows in your desktop applications. Sometimes you have to use one frame's set of scroll bars to scroll around enough in that frame to access the scroll bars of another frame, the one with the content you actually wanted to see.

Most sites have kept at least their home pages frame-free, so as not to alienate the people whose browsers don't "do" frames, not to mention those who find them cumbersome or distracting. Hopefully frame technology will become more advanced so that you can move the frames or close the ones you do not want to look at, but for now, they can be challenging.

NOTE

Some sites use frames to keep you oriented to their site regardless of where you link to. The frame from the original site stays on the screen even when you are looking at content from another site reached by following a link from the first site.

Basic frame types include a narrow navigation frame and a full content frame. Sometimes frames are also used to keep an advertisement on the screen as you scroll through the content of a site. Figure 5.4 shows a typical navigation frame for the Discovery Channel's Web site.

Keeping Track of Floating Windows

Another recent Web-interface development is the use of additional floating windows. While many browsers allow you to right-click (or, on the Mac, click and hold) a link to pop up a list of options, and then choose to open the linked page in a new window, Web developers are now also creating links that automatically open a new window for you. Some sites also pop up a small window without a menu that you can use as a control panel. It can get confusing if you're surfing the Web for a while and end up with multiple windows open on your screen.

Remember to close secondary windows when you're done with them, to minimize the confusion of having multiple windows open. As you practice browsing the Web, you will figure out which method for switching among windows works best for you. Three ways of window switching that do work well are clicking on another window, using Alt+Tab in Windows, or selecting a window from a menu. Remember to use your Back button anytime you've ended up somewhere you didn't mean to go.

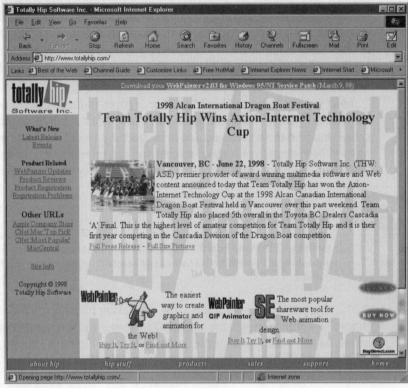

FIGURE 5.4: Discovery Online (http://www.discovery.com/), the Web site for the Discovery Channel, has a navigation frame on the left. This frame stays on the screen as you jump to different pages, displayed on the right.

NOTE

Site maps are becoming more common for complex commercial Web sites with many subordinate pages. These maps are generally reached via an icon in the frame or on the home page. The maps can be graphical depictions of a site or a simple outline of the site showing the way subpages branch off from main pages. The maps usually have live links so that you can click on any location in the map and go immediately to that page. See Figure 5.5 for an example of a site map.

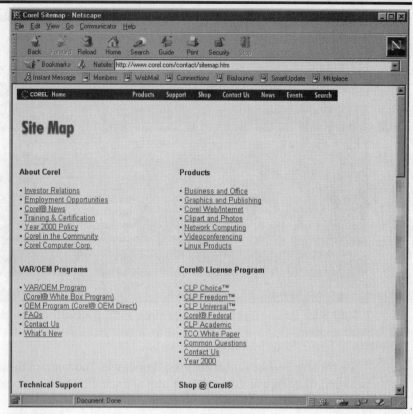

FIGURE 5.5:   Corel, a Canadian software publishing firm, has a detailed site map with links to all of its Web pages. Corel's site is at `http://www.corel.com`.

What to Do About Applets

The current trend in livening up Web pages (at least at the high-budget end) involves embedded Java "applets" (little applications or programs), often along the lines of ticker tape or animated buttons. Most browsers will let you turn off the Java interpreter if you don't want to be distracted or slowed down by these gadgets. Figure 5.6 shows a page of the HotWired "channel" called Synapse, a sort of online magazine. The frame at the bottom contains a fancy image map that's really a Java applet. Each area of the "map" changes or lights up when you move the pointer over it.

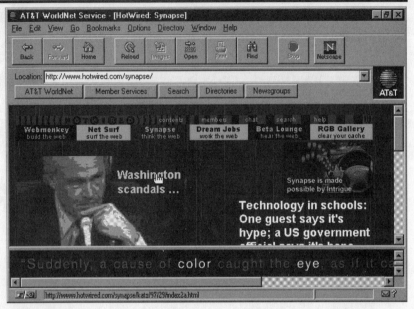

FIGURE 5.6: Synapse uses frames, image maps, and applets without exploding your computer.

Personally, I prefer a more stripped-down style. Too many of these bells and whistles will slow my computer to a grinding halt, or worse yet, crash my browser (or the whole shebang).

Browsing an Intranet

Organizations, companies, and other groups that share space and networked computers are creating smaller versions of the Internet in the form of internal *intranets*. These intranets contain documents formatted with HTML like those you find on the Web, and they are a good place to store policies, manuals, databases, and every other type of record that used to be on a piece of paper in a filing cabinet.

The whole point of an intranet is that once it's set up, you can browse it (or transfer files, or send mail, or print on shared printers, and so on) just as you would over the "real" Internet. This means you can use the same software, the same type of browser. The content and uses of an intranet naturally differ widely from the content and uses of public Web sites. However, if your intranet is set up well, you won't ever notice where you're connecting to. You'll just grab the files you want, send your messages, set up meetings, and join discussions without pausing to think about whether you're doing so on your local intranet or on the Internet "out there."

WARNING

Then again, you *should* pause to think about whether you're about to communicate with a private group, such as your colleagues or supervisors, or with a public group on the Net, no matter how familiar the software tools feel.

Wandering in Gopherspace

Gopher is a sophisticated Internet system that lets you look at data and files from different computers and networks without regard to the type of computer the client (you, more or less) is running on. If you run Gopher from a character-based Unix account, you see things as lists consisting of text entries. If you run a Gopher client on another platform, the menus and items will look appropriate to that type of computer. (For example, a Macintosh Gopher program will show the menus as folders that open up into windows.)

At one time, the Internet Gopher was one of the most useful and seamless tools on the Net. Then the Web came along and Web browsers could do everything Gopher browsers could and more. Web browsers can even connect to Gopher sites, so there's precious little reason to have a separate Gopher program now. Many dedicated Gopher programs come with extensive bookmarks that make it easier to find specific information in Gopherspace, though, so you may want your own Gopher program. Even if you plan to use your Web browser when entering Gopherspace, you'll still want to read up on Gopher at this point.

NOTE

Gopher is so-called either because it can "go fer" stuff and bring it to you or because the mascot of the University of Minnesota (where Gopher was created) is a gopher; it is not named after the Love Boat character played by (now former US Representative) Fred Grandy.

All Web browsers make perfectly adequate Gopher clients. One way to end up in Gopherspace from the Web is to click on a link that (whether you realize it or not) is linked to a Gopher address. This process is a little like tumbling down a rabbit hole. You'll leave the graphics and formatting of the Web behind and enter a limited (but still hyperlinked) world of folders and documents.

The other way to start browsing Gopherspace with a Web browser is to type a Gopher address into the address box, for example,

```
gopher://gopher.netcom.com/
```

Documents are shown with a document icon. Menus are shown with a folder icon. Figure 5.7 shows the Netcom Gopher server viewed in Netscape Navigator.

Getting Around the Gopher Menus

Browsing Gopherspace is just a matter of pointing and clicking on links, just like anywhere else you visit using a Web browser. Clicking on any icon or link takes you to a subdirectory or opens a document. If you wish to leave a subdirectory or document and go back to the main menu, just click on the Back button, as you would on the Web.

Reading Gopher Documents

Eventually, your selections will lead you to a document, which will appear unformatted and in a typewriter-like typeface. Read the document as you would any Web page, scrolling down if necessary.

Bookmarks in Gopherspace

If you find your way to or stumble upon an interesting Gopher site, you can make a bookmark to it as you would for any Web page or other resource in your browser. (More about bookmarks a little later on in this lesson.)

NOTE

Gopher has been around almost as long as the Internet. Many universities, government agencies, and organizations have a long-established Gopher "presence." That's why Gopherspace is a fascinating archive of information, some of which is not available on the Web. However, Gopher sites may not be updated as often as you would like, so the information culled from this resource may not be completely current. Of course, some Web sites contain out-of-date information, too.

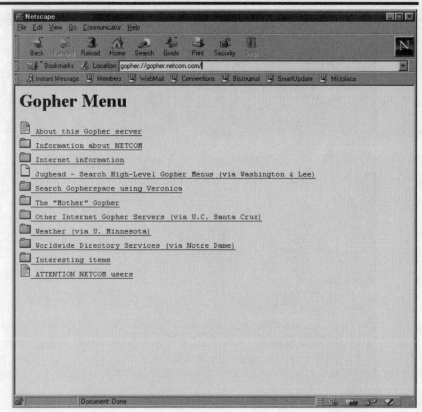

FIGURE 5.7: The main menu from the Netcom Gopher server in Netscape Navigator.

Peeking behind the Scenes

If you need to see the URL associated with a specific link, you can do so. For instance, in most browsers, when you place the pointer over a link, the associated URL appears in the status bar at the bottom of the program. Some browsers enable you to copy a URL by right-clicking or clicking-and-holding the link. You can then paste it into another document for future reference or paste it into an e-mail message to tell someone else how to get to the page in question.

If you want to see how a Web page was constructed, you can generally view the source file underlying a page. In graphical browsers, you do this by selecting View ➤ Source (or something similar). Figure 5.8 shows the source underlying the Netscape home page.

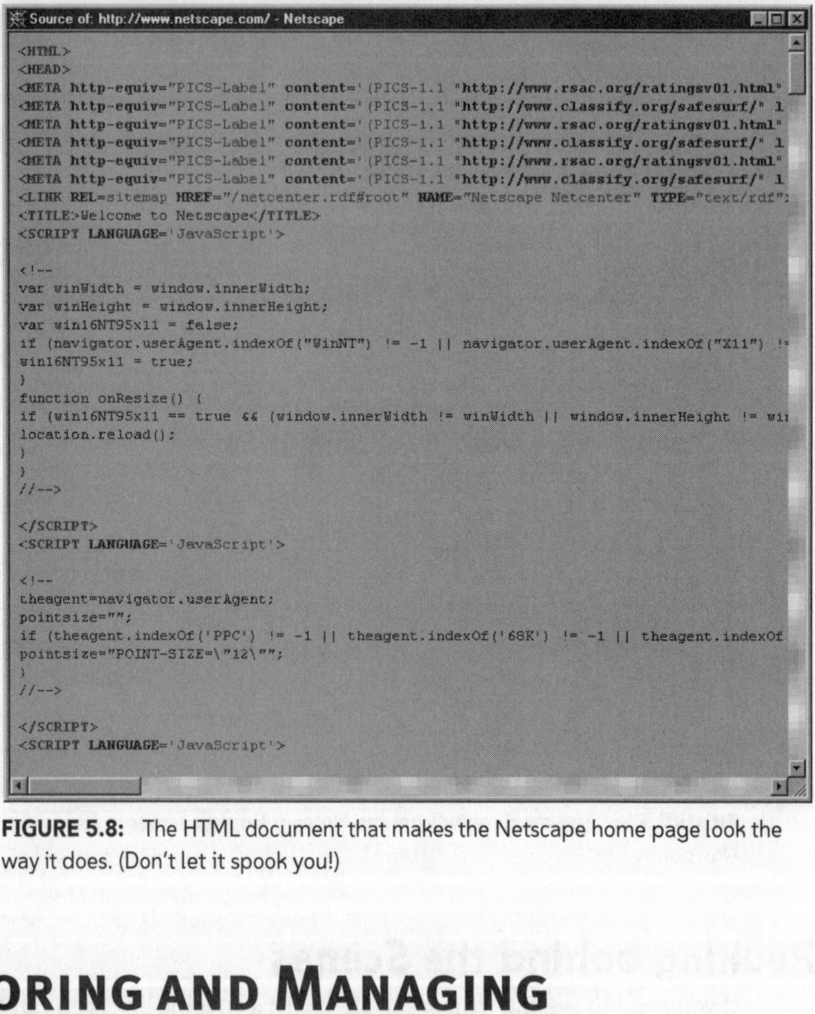

```
Source of: http://www.netscape.com/ - Netscape
<HTML>
<HEAD>
<META http-equiv="PICS-Label" content='(PICS-1.1 "http://www.rsac.org/ratingsv01.html"
<META http-equiv="PICS-Label" content='(PICS-1.1 "http://www.classify.org/safesurf/" 1
<META http-equiv="PICS-Label" content='(PICS-1.1 "http://www.rsac.org/ratingsv01.html"
<META http-equiv="PICS-Label" content='(PICS-1.1 "http://www.classify.org/safesurf/" 1
<META http-equiv="PICS-Label" content='(PICS-1.1 "http://www.rsac.org/ratingsv01.html"
<META http-equiv="PICS-Label" content='(PICS-1.1 "http://www.classify.org/safesurf/" 1
<LINK REL=sitemap HREF="/netcenter.rdf#root" NAME="Netscape Netcenter" TYPE="text/rdf";
<TITLE>Welcome to Netscape</TITLE>
<SCRIPT LANGUAGE='JavaScript'>

<!--
var winWidth = window.innerWidth;
var winHeight = window.innerHeight;
var win16NT95x11 = false;
if (navigator.userAgent.indexOf("WinNT") != -1 || navigator.userAgent.indexOf("X11") !=
win16NT95x11 = true;
}
function onResize() {
if (win16NT95x11 == true && (window.innerWidth != winWidth || window.innerHeight != wir
location.reload();
}
}
//-->

</SCRIPT>
<SCRIPT LANGUAGE='JavaScript'>

<!--
theagent=navigator.userAgent;
pointsize="";
if (theagent.indexOf('PPC') != -1 || theagent.indexOf('68K') != -1 || theagent.indexOf
pointsize="POINT-SIZE=\"12\"";
}
//-->

</SCRIPT>
<SCRIPT LANGUAGE='JavaScript'>
```

FIGURE 5.8:   The HTML document that makes the Netscape home page look the way it does. (Don't let it spook you!)

STORING AND MANAGING YOUR FAVORITE WEB SITES AS BOOKMARKS

As you travel around the Web, you can record interesting destinations by making bookmarks (also called Favorites or Favorite Places in some browsers, and Items in a Notebook or Hotlist in others). Once you've made a bookmark, you've created your own personal shortcut to a favorite destination. You won't have to find your way back to the page in question next time you want to go there.

Make bookmarks as often as you want. You can always weed out your bookmark list later, but it's very difficult to find a page you stumbled across by trying to retrace your steps later.

Organizing Bookmarks

At first, all your bookmarks will fit on a menu, but eventually you'll have too many to fit and you'll have to open a window to see them all (each browser has its own version of these features). Once the bookmark window is open, you can usually cull the list by clicking on and deleting (or dragging to the trash) any out-of-date, duplicate, or no-longer-interesting bookmarks.

As your bookmark pile grows, it becomes something like an address book—another thing to manage! The easiest way to deal with bookmark overflow is to create folders (they usually appear as submenus on the bookmark menu) for different categories your bookmarks fall into and then occasionally sort them out (Figure 5.9).

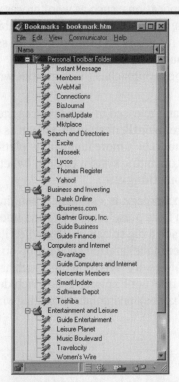

FIGURE 5.9: Some of these Netscape Navigator 4 bookmarks are sorted by category.

NETCASTS DIRECTLY TO THE DESKTOP WEB

Alongside the rapid development of Web browsers is a growing tendency to include Web features in the basic operations of your computer. There are several different ways this can take place. The latest release of Netscape Navigator, called Navigator 4 (something akin to the Gold releases of earlier versions), is now part of an application suite called Netscape Communicator 4 and features a substitute desktop oriented toward the Web, intranet browsing, and browsing your own computer as if it were a Web site. The standard Communicator components consist of Netcaster (for Webcasting), Messenger (for e-mail), Collabra (for discussion groups and sharing work), Composer (for making Web pages), and Conference (for online meetings and presentations). Microsoft has accomplished something similar with Internet Explorer 4.

Meanwhile, standard business applications, such as word processors, databases, and presentation programs, are starting to include the capability to open documents from the Internet (or across an intranet), and to save and convert documents to Web format (HTML). Apple's Cyberdog browser (discussed later in this lesson) approaches the same idea with modular application parts.

As more programs are developed and released in Java (such as the experimental Java version of the Corel WordPerfect Suite, known as Corel Office for Java), the Web may turn out to be a more important "platform" for your computer software than the operating system you run (whether that is Windows, MacOS, Unix, or something else).

Netcasting, also known as push technology, is a system for sending information to your computer screen from preselected news and information sites. The PointCast Network made a big splash in 1996 when its software (particularly the screen saver mode) started showing up on computer monitors left and right. State-of-the-art Web browsers (such as Netscape Navigator 4 and Microsoft Internet Explorer 4) and Web/desktop tools (such as Microsoft Outlook Express) incorporate Netcasting windows directly into the interface.

CHANGING YOUR START PAGE

The commands differ from browser to browser, but most Web browsers allow you to change your start page (the first page that comes up when you start the program) to a different page (or even to a list of your bookmarks) so you can start exploring the Web from any vantage point.

Generally, the way you change your home page is to go into the Options or Preferences area of your browser and either specify an exact URL or tell the browser to use the current page as the new home page. Why would you change your page? Well, you might find a useful page out there on the Net that connects to most of your favorite sites. Or you might want to use one of the directory or search pages as your new starting page.

GET EFF'S INTERNET GUIDE AS HYPERTEXT ON THE WEB

The Electronic Frontier Foundation has published a hypertext version of its Internet Guide on the World Wide Web. Point your browser at `http://www.eff.org/papers/eegtti/eegttitop.html` to go to the main page for the Guide.

WEB HELP AND INFO

There are a number of helpful resources for the Web, both hypertext and plain text documents. Try the WWW FAQ, an excellent document. Its URL is `http://www.boutell.com/faq/`. The W3 Consortium is the official source of information about the Web, and you can connect to their home page at `http://www.w3.org/`. (But be forewarned, much of their information is highly technical!) Many individual browsers also offer dedicated help files, accessible through a menu command. I'll cover some specific browsers and their help functions at the end of this chapter.

GETTING TO THE WEB VIA ONLINE SERVICES

For a while, the online services licensed versions of Mosaic, the first graphical Web browser, and tried to compete with the leaders in the browser race, Netscape Navigator and Internet Explorer. More recently, they've conceded that game and have made it possible for their users to connect to the Web with any Web browser they choose. Your installation disk for an online service may come with a specific browser (if the service has cut a deal with the browser's maker), but you'll still be able to download and use alternative browsers if you wish.

America Online (AOL)

AOL's built-in Web browser is a licensed version of Microsoft Internet Explorer. Before you start it, launch AOL by double-clicking on its icon or selecting Start ➤ Programs ➤ America Online ➤ America Online. Any of the following methods will start the AOL browser:

- ▶ Look for the Internet Connection area of the main AOL window and choose World Wide Web.

- ▶ Double-click on any AOL content on the Go To menu that includes the word Web at the end of its title.

- ▶ Go to the keyword Web by selecting Go To ➤ Keyword ➤ Web.

Figure 5.10 shows the AOL home page that comes up automatically when you connect to the Web without specifying a particular site.

Using Netscape Navigator with AOL

To run Netscape Navigator with AOL, first download the entire Communicator suite (go to keyword Netscape by selecting Go To ➤ Keyword ➤ Netscape) and install it. Then, simply connect via AOL and double-click on the Communicator icon on your desktop or select Start ➤ Programs ➤ Netscape Communicator ➤ Netscape Navigator. Navigator will use the AOL connection to show you the Web.

WARNING

Before you download files or programs from the Internet, invest in some anti-virus software for your computer and learn how to use it. Make sure the anti-virus program is turned on before you start your downloads. You can also use the anti-virus software to scan files downloaded from the Web before you got the anti-virus program or to scan files someone gave you on a floppy disk or other removable media. If the software finds a virus in your files, it can usually repair them and can even remove the virus from your hard drive in some cases.

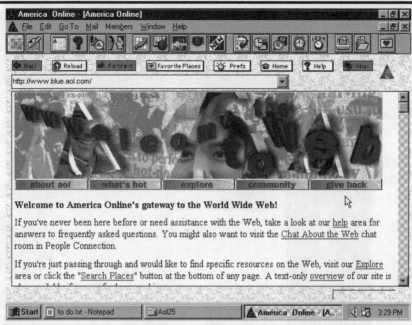

FIGURE 5.10: America Online's browser starts you off at the AOL home page.

TIP

You can also download an external version of Microsoft Internet Explorer from `http://www.microsoft.com/ie` (via the AOL Web browser) and install it to use with AOL.

CompuServe

The latest version of CompuServe comes with a built-in edition of Microsoft Internet Explorer (though it's also possible to run an external browser, such as Netscape, once you're connected). The new CompuServe interface switches to the Web browser seamlessly when you enter a Web address in the Page box.

Figure 5.11 shows the CompuServe home page that comes up automatically when you click the Internet button on the main menu.

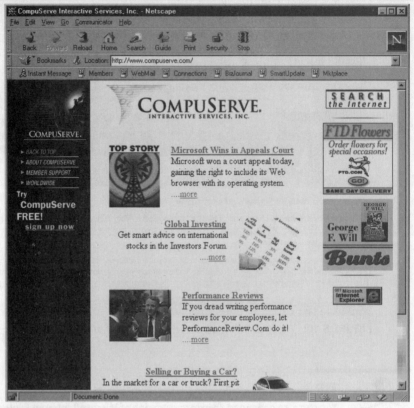

FIGURE 5.11:   The Internet Explorer browser built into CompuServe's slick new interface starts you off at this CompuServe home page.

Changing to a Different Browser in CompuServe

You can choose an external Web browser or change the browser Compu-Serve summons up by using these procedures (after the browser is installed):

1. Select Access ➤ Preferences and click the General tab on the Preferences dialog box.

2. Click the Use External Internet Browser checkbox. Compu-Serve will use the browser listed in the Internet browser box (which will be Internet Explorer, if you haven't tampered with it yet).

3. If you want to select a different browser, click the Select button, make your way to the browser you want (look for Netscape under `c:\Program Files\Netscape\Communicator\Program`; look for Internet Explorer under `ProgramFiles\Microsoft Internet` or `Program Files\Plus!`), select it, and click on OK.

4. Then click on OK again to close the Preferences dialog box.

The next time you click on the Internet button in the main menu or enter a URL in the Page box, CompuServe will launch your chosen browser.

The Microsoft Network (MSN)

About two years after its debut, MSN retooled itself as a Web-based online service. When you connect to MSN, you automatically have a PPP connection you can use to run any Internet program, including any browser you wish. More importantly, the new MSN interface is a specially adapted version of Internet Explorer, which is now being used as more than just a Web browser. Some buttons in this interface are directly linked to Web sites. To go directly to one of these predefined Web addresses, move the mouse pointer to the address box to open it up and click on the name of the page you want to jump to.

Once connected to MSN, you can also run, separately, any Web browser (such as Netscape Navigator) through the MSN connection.

The main MSN page with their On Stage display is shown in Figure 5.12 and is located at `http://www.msn.com`. The large central area, where MSNBC's global logo is depicted, features a series of glowing active links advertising MSN's new content sites. You can click on these as the logo cycles through the different "channels" available to reach the sites, but you can also reach them from the "channels" at the bottom of MSN's On Stage page. The channels light up as you pass your mouse over them, indicating that they are active and can be clicked on. Channel 1, for example, is reserved for MSNBC news.

Part ii

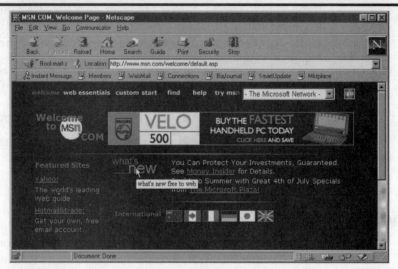

FIGURE 5.12: The Microsoft Network's new look inlcudes links to content channels that light up when you pass your mouse pointer over them.

SURFING THE WEB WITH YOUR WEB BROWSER

The program you choose to travel the Web with is largely a matter of taste, need, and budget. In fact, you may eventually end up with more than one browser on your hard drive.

Microsoft Internet Explorer 4

Internet Explorer works seamlessly with the Microsoft Network, but it also stands alone as a Web browser that can work with any Internet connection. It's available for both Windows and Macintosh, though it's much more popular on the Windows side.

NOTE

Chapter 7 contains really detailed information about browsing the Web with Internet Explorer. Check it out for more information.

Netscape Navigator 4

The latest version of Netscape Navigator is included in a jack-of-all-trades suite of products called Netscape Communicator 4. The actual Web browser part of the program is still called Netscape Navigator (as were the most recent few versions). A "professional" package, with additional tools, called Netscape Communicator Pro, is also in the works.

Netscape Navigator (commonly referred to as just Netscape) is the world's most popular Web browser, although Microsoft Internet Explorer is challenging its formidable hold on the market.

You can start Netscape by double-clicking any of the Netscape desktop shortcuts or by selecting Start ➤ Programs ➤ Netscape Communicator ➤ Netscape Navigator (or by choosing Netscape Navigator from your Apple menu). By default, it will take you to the Netscape home page.

NOTE

For information about browsing with Netscape Navigator, see Chapter 6.

WHAT'S NEXT?

Now that you have completed this chapter, you have an overview of Web browsers, but that's only the beginning. In the next chapter, you'll learn the nitty-gritty workings of Netscape Navigator.

Part ii

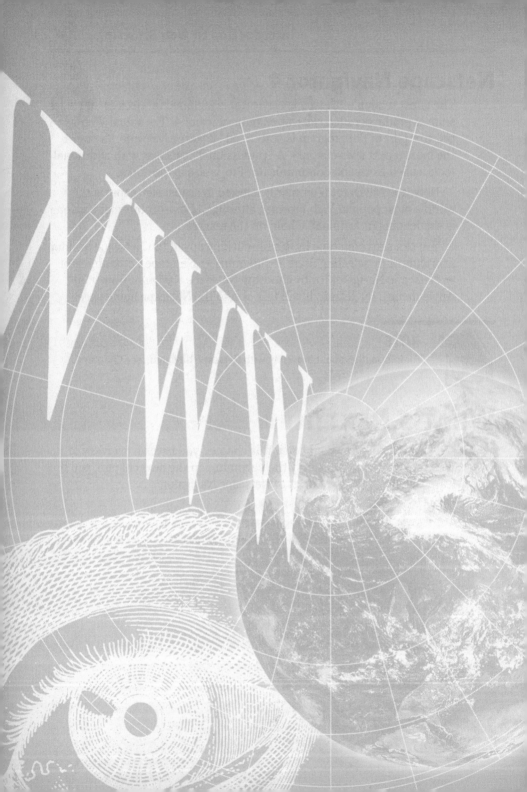

Chapter 6

AN INTRODUCTION TO NETSCAPE NAVIGATOR

L et's get working with Netscape Navigator. In this chapter, you'll learn how to start the program, how to open and save Web documents, and how to switch between documents and other hypermedia (sound and video, for example) via hot links. You'll also get a good look at navigating through *frames*, which are like window panes within a document.

STARTING NETSCAPE NAVIGATOR

Launching Netscape Navigator is easy. To start Navigator, follow these steps:

1. Start your Internet connection. (How you do this depends on the sort of Internet service you have.)

Adapted from *Mastering Netscape Communicator 4*, by Daniel A. Tauber and Brenda Kienan
0-7821-2077-6   800 pages $39.99

TIP

If your computer is on a LAN that is connected to the Internet, you may not have to do anything special before you start up Navigator. You may be able to skip over step 1, straight to step 2, to launch Navigator.

2. Now start up Navigator. You can do this in one of two ways:

    ▶ Double-click the Desktop's Netscape Communicator icon, shown here (Navigator, the Web browser, will launch by default):

Netscape
Communicator

or

    ▶ From the Windows 95 Start menu, select Programs ➢ Netscape Communicator ➢ Netscape Navigator.

Either way, Netscape Navigator, the central component of Communicator, will open.

THE COMMUNICATOR CONNECTION TWO-STEP

Before you can start using Communicator, you must start the connection software that you use to access the Internet (unless you are on a LAN that already has access to the Internet).

Here's how it works: You start your connection software—it can be Windows 95 Dial-Up Networking, Netcom's Netcomplete, or whatever you choose—which then connects your computer to the Internet. This software "introduces" Communicator to the Internet—it is a vital link in your Internet connection. (At one time, this could be accomplished only through the use of special SLIP/PPP software, but nowadays that software is included in both Windows 95 and NT.) Your connection software and your provider will then do a little dance together, passing back and forth the TCP/IP packets that make it possible for you to run Communicator (which is on your machine). Voilà—the Internet accepts your machine as a little network hooked into the bigger, more exciting network called the Internet, and you're on your way!

If all goes well (and it surely will), the Netscape Navigator window will open, and the Netscape icon in the window's upper-right corner (that nifty N in a box) will become animated. This tells you that Navigator is transferring data, which will appear in a second in the form of a Web page. Whenever Navigator is "working" (downloading a document, searching, and so on), the Netscape icon is animated. It stops when the action has been completed.

When you first start Netscape Navigator, you'll see the Welcome to Netscape home page, with its sleek, colorful graphics. You can change this start-up home page to something else if you like.

The home page is where you begin, where Navigator first lands you on your Internet voyage. Think of it as one of many ports of entry into the Web. The Web, you'll recall, doesn't just go from here to there—it's a *web*. It doesn't really matter where you start, because everything's interconnected.

You can return to the start-up home page (the one you see when you start a Netscape Navigator session) at any time simply by clicking the Home icon on the Navigator Command toolbar.

TIP

You can always return to Netscape's own home page, no matter what else you've chosen as your start-up home page, just by clicking the N icon in the upper-right corner of the Netscape Navigator window.

If you followed the steps earlier in this chapter and have Navigator running now, try clicking the Search button in the Navigator window's toolbar. This brief exercise will test your Internet connection. The Netscape icon should become animated, and in a few seconds Netscape's Search page should appear.

Now try clicking the Back button. The Netscape icon will again become animated, and Netscape's home page will reappear.

HOME, HOME ON THE HOME PAGE

The start-up home page—any home page, for that matter—may be anywhere on the Web, or it may be on your own machine. Home pages provide a lot of information and change frequently; so you may not want to zip by a Web site's start-up home page. Instead, take the time to review it when it pops up.

You are not limited to seeing the Welcome to Netscape home page at start-up—you can make it so that Navigator won't load any home page on start-up, or you can start up with one of any number of home pages that you find on the Internet. You can even create your own home page. If you change the start-up home page and want to find the Welcome to Netscape home page again, you can use its URL, which is http://home.netscape.com. Or you can just click the N-for-Netscape icon (the one that becomes animated when Web page files are arriving) in the upper-right corner of the Navigator window.

LOOKING INTO THE INTERFACE

Let's look at the parts of the Navigator window. Figure 6.1 shows you what's what in that window. We'll describe those items and tell you how to use them in this section.

TIP

Via the View menu, you can display or hide any of the toolbars, including the Navigation toolbar, the Location toolbar (which also contains the Bookmarks button), and the Personal toolbar. Or, you can click the blue arrow buttons at the left of any toolbar to collapse it (and again to expand it later). You may want to hide this stuff if and when you want the content you are viewing to be larger.

Title Bar   In the title bar you can see the name of the page you are currently viewing.

Menu Bar   The menu bar in Navigator is similar to menu bars in other Windows applications: It provides you with drop-down menus. When you move the mouse to the menu and click a selection, choices appear.

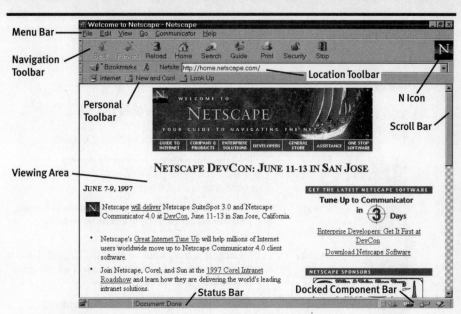

Menu Bar

Navigation Toolbar

Location Toolbar

Personal Toolbar

N Icon

Scroll Bar

Viewing Area

Status Bar

Docked Component Bar

Part ii

FIGURE 6.1: Here's the Navigator window with all its parts labeled so that you can see what's what.

Navigation Toolbar   The Navigation toolbar performs some fairly common actions. It's like other Windows toolbars in that all you have to do is click the icon for the specified action to occur. (If you point at a tool for a few seconds, a ToolTip will appear, telling you what the tool does. The ToolTip is simply a text box that shows you the name of the tool at which you are pointing.) Take a look at Table 6.1 for more information about the Netscape toolbar icons.

TABLE 6.1: The Netscape Toolbar Icons

THE TOOL	ITS NAME	WHAT YOU DO WITH IT
Back	Back	Jump back to the previous page document in your History list (that is, the page you were viewing just prior to the current page).
Forward	Forward	Jump forward to the next page or document in your History list. (If you're on the last item in the History list, this icon is dimmed—it looks grayed out.)
Reload	Reload	Refresh the contents of the viewing area.

	Home	Return to the start-up home page.
	Search	Visit Netscape's Search tools page.
	Guide	Visit one of the Netscape Guide Web pages.
	Print	Print the Web page you're currently viewing.
	Images	Turn on images (this "smart" button appears only when you have the auto-loading of images turned off).
	Security	Investigate security information—if this button is active (if it's not grayed out), you can click it to find out about the relative security of the content in view.
	Stop	Cancel the process of loading incoming content.

TURNING IMAGES ON AND OFF

Images load automatically unless you tell Netscape to do otherwise. If you have a slow Internet connection and prefer to decide whether you want to view pictures on a Web page, you can turn off the auto-loading of images. To toggle auto-loading on and off, from Navigator's menu bar, select Edit ➤ Preferences. The Preferences dialog box will appear, with a list of categories shown in it. In the list, select Advanced. The contents of the dialog box will change to reflect your choice. Locate the check box labeled Automatically Load Images and either select it (to toggle images on) or deselect it (to toggle them off). Now click OK; the Preferences dialog box will close and the Navigator window will reappear. The next time you load a page, your change will have taken effect. Note that when auto-loading is turned off, the Images button will appear on Navigator's Command toolbar. You can then click the Images button if you like, to load images on the Web page you are currently viewing.

Location Toolbar   On the left side of this toolbar is a blue folder icon followed by the word *Bookmarks* that you can click to access... yes, *bookmarks*. The next item on the toolbar is the Bookmarks QuickFile icon, which allows you to bookmark pages quickly by dragging them to the icon. The rest of this toolbar is occupied by the Location bar (shown below), where you'll see the URL (the Uniform Resource Locator, or address) of the current document.

Bookmarks & Netsite:	http://home.netscape.com/

TIP

The label that appears next to the current document's URL will change depending on the type of server you've contacted at the moment. If that Web server is running a Netscape server product, the label will read *Netsite*. If the server is running a non-Netscape server product, it will read *Location*. From your point of view as a user, it matters not a whit which type of server software (Netscape or non-Netscape) you are accessing (as long as it works). So don't worry about this odd detail.

A FEW QUICK TOOLBAR TRICKS

Here's a sneaky trick: Click the arrow on the far right end of the Location bar, and the URLs you've most recently visited will pop up in a list. Select any one of them to visit that site again.

And another: As you type URLs into the Location box, they'll be compared automatically to any URLs you've loaded recently. If a match is perceived, the previously loaded URL will appear in the Location box. For example, if you type **www.n** in the Location box and you recently visited www.news.com, that URL will pop itself into the Location box and when you press ↵ that Web page will start to load. If the URL that appears in the box is not the one you meant to visit, however, that's nothing to worry over. Just keep typing the full URL of the site you do want to visit, and when you press ↵ that page will load.

Personal Toolbar   Below the Location bar is a very handy toolbar you can use to track sites that are of particular interest to you. For example, you can drag and drop URLs into this baby and they'll appear there as buttons. Here it is, with a few URLs already in it:

Internet	New and Cool	Look Up

Viewing Area   This is the main portion of the screen—it's where you'll see what you came to the Web to see.

Status Bar   The status bar is at the bottom of the screen. As you move the cursor around the viewing area and come across links, the cursor changes into the shape of a hand with one finger pointing, and the status bar displays the URL for the link at which you're pointing. When content is being transferred to your machine, you'll see numbers in the status bar that indicate the progress of the transfer. The status bar also contains some small but mighty icons. The padlock icon on the far left tells you whether the current page is *secure*. Along the right side of the status bar is where the component bar docks (see the upcoming description).

Scroll Bars   These are just like regular Windows scroll bars: They appear on the side of the viewing area, or possibly at the bottom, when the document is too big to fit in the window. Click the scroll bars to bring into view whatever's off the screen.

Component Bar   Netscape Communicator includes a component bar, which you can use to open one component of Communicator while you are in another component. When you are using Navigator (the browser), you can use the component bar to open Messenger (the e-mail program), Collabra (the discussion group reader), or Composer (the HTML editor). As of this writing, Netcaster and Conference do not appear here. The component bar can "float," meaning that it will appear as a tiny window within the current window, or it can be "docked," meaning that it will appear at the bottom of the current window as part of the status bar. In either case, it contains buttons for various Communicator components; to launch one, just click that button.

TIP

To make a docked component bar float, click the gray bar at the left hand side of the component bar. To dock the component bar, click the component bar window's close box. Alternately, you can use the Navigator menu bar and select Communicator ➢ Show Component Bar to display the component bar as a window, or Window ➢ Dock Component Bar to anchor the component bar to the status bar.

OPENING A DOCUMENT

You actually opened your first document when you started Navigator and the home page appeared. But let's dig around a little further and see what else we can open.

Following Hot Links

Moving around the World Wide Web is a snap, thanks to hyperlinks. It's as easy as a mouse-click on the link—each link points to some other piece of the Internet, just as Windows 95 shortcuts point to something on your hard drive.

Hypertext is nonlinear. (That means you don't have to follow a straight path from point A to point Z, but rather you can skip around from one place to another to another, back to the first, round to a fourth, and so on.) Hypertext is hypertext because it has links—*hot links*, they're often called—to other sources of information. You follow these links through a document, or from document to document, document to image, or perhaps from server to server, in any way you like as you navigate the Web. (You can think of hypertext as both the text *and* the links—it's the navigational means by which you traverse the Web.) The great thing about the Web is that you don't have to know whether the information you're looking at is in Paris, France or Paris, Texas—all you need to do is follow a link.

TIP

If you do want information about a link before you click it, just check the status bar at the bottom of your screen. There you'll see a URL for anything from another site to a sound or video file, to an e-mail address. For example, if you drag your mouse over <u>Webmaster</u> on any given Web page, you might see the URL for the Webmaster's home page, an e-mail address provided by the Webmaster for feedback, or the URL for a Help page about the site you're viewing.

If you still have the Welcome to Netscape home page open now, click a few links. Don't be shy—just click anything that looks interesting. You'll soon see why they call it the Web. Try jumping back and forth a couple of times too by clicking those tools in the toolbar (but not the component bar because that will take you off into another component of Communicator). When you've had enough, simply click the Home button or the N icon to get back to your start-up home page.

A FEW QUICK WORDS ON SECURITY

Keeping the data that passes across the Internet safe and secure is an issue that bigwigs in both business and government are discussing now and one that will soon become relevant even to the casual user.

You've probably noticed a lot of talk in newspapers and magazines and on TV about commercial ventures on the Web—merchants and malls all setting up shop and taking your credit card order or banks offering home services through their sites. You can even use the Web to buy and sell stocks. If this data (your credit card number, your bank balance and access code, or your stock portfolio) is not safe, it can be read by some eavesdropper lurking in an electronic shadow. Well, you can surely see the concern!

Fortunately, designers have kept this issue in mind when they've developed browsers. Netscape Navigator was the first Web browser to allow secure transactions to take place (between your computer running Navigator and a Web server running Netscape's secure server software.

In practical terms, this commitment to security means that when you connect to a home page on a special server, the data sent back and forth can be secure from prying "eyes."

By now you've probably noticed the Security icon (it looks like a padlock) on Navigator's command toolbar. Usually, the padlock appears "open." This indicates that the document you are currently viewing is *insecure*, meaning that a third party sufficiently motivated and equipped can look in on the data being sent back and forth and do with it what he or she will.

If, however, you are connected to a *secure* page—one where such eavesdropping is not possible because the data is "encrypted" before it is transferred and "decrypted" upon arrival the padlock will appear closed. (In addition, a dialog box will appear both when you connect to and when you disconnect from that page, telling you of the secure status of the transmission.) You can also click the toolbar's Security button any time you want to investigate the overall security of a document you are viewing.

Netscape Communicator offers even more sophisticated security with the addition of *certificates* to its features. Certificates are meant to "prove" your identity to Web servers through a system of verification. Look for this technology to become an increasingly important security feature as Web producers upgrade their sites to take advantage of new versions of Netscape's server software using certificates.

You can find out more about security in general by selecting Help ➢ Security from the Navigator menu bar. To get a directory of sites using Netscape's secure Web servers and other Netscape software, visit Netscape's Customer Showcase at `http://home.netscape .com/home/netscape-galleria.html`.

Opening a Document Using Its URL

Sometimes you're going to want to go straight for the jugular—you know where the document is, and you just want to see it without starting on a home page and skipping through a lot of hot links. Maybe your pal just sent you the URL for the Exploratorium, a really wonderful interactive science museum in San Francisco.

To open a document using its URL follow these steps:

1. From Navigator's menu bar, select File ➢ Open Page or press Ctrl+O. In either case the Open Page dialog box will appear.

2. In the Open Page dialog box (see Figure 6.2), type the URL of interest (in our example, http://www.exploratorium.edu).

Part ii

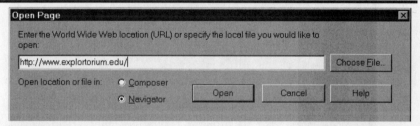

FIGURE 6.2: You can use the Open Page dialog box to open a page when you know its URL.

TIP

You can easily copy URLs from other documents and paste them directly into either the Open Page dialog box or the Location box. What's more, you needn't type the whole URL—you can just type the www. part and the domain name (dnai.com, for example), or you can even skip the rest and just type the dnai part.

3. Click Open (or just press ↵), and Navigator will find the document for this URL and display it on your screen. (See Figure 6.3.)

TIP

The Web is very *big*. And it changes all the time. From time to time you might have difficulty locating or accessing a document. The original may have been removed by its owner, the machine that holds the document may be unavailable or overworked when you try to access it, or the network path between your machine and the server might be down. If Navigator has been trying for a while to access a document without success, it will display a dialog box saying it just plain cannot locate the document. (See *Error Messages Demystified* for the dish on error messages and what to do about them.) You can go back to the document that was on screen before you tried making the jump, just by clicking OK.

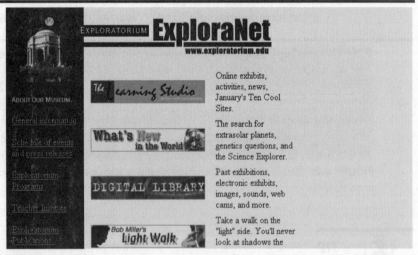

FIGURE 6.3: Here's the Exploratorium's home page. We found it using the URL a friend gave us. (Reproduced with permission from Exploratorium's Exploranet copyright ©1996 *www.exploratorium.edu.*)

TIP

If you're waiting for a page to arrive and you want to look at something else (another page, for example) while you're waiting, select File ➢ Navigator Window from Navigator's menu bar. A second window will open and in it you can look at something other than what you were trying for in the first Navigator window. You can then use Alt+Tab or the Communicator menu to switch back and forth between the two open Navigator windows. Now who said attention spans are getting shorter?

JUMPING BACK AND FORTH WHILE VIEWING A DOCUMENT

The Back and Forward icons on the toolbar provide a convenient way to jump back and forth among the hot links you've followed.

This is because Navigator tracks the documents you visit in a History list. The Back and Forward icons actually let you travel through the History list. If you have Navigator running, try clicking the Back icon to jump backward along the links you just followed, and then try clicking Forward to jump forward.

In addition to going back and forward one page at a time, try clicking the Back icon and holding down the left mouse button for a second or two. A small pop-up menu will appear, listing the last few pages you've visited. You can do the same thing with the Forward icon; the menu will list the next few pages in your History list.

There is an end to this—if you jump back to the first document you viewed in a session, or forward to the last one, you reach the end of history. The Back or Forward icon, depending on which end of history you reach, will be grayed out. (You can, as always, create more history—click another hypertext link to explore further.)

NOTE

At the bottom of many documents, you'll find a link that says something like Go Back. If you click this link, you won't necessarily go back to where you came from; instead, you'll visit the page that the Webmaster assumed you just came from (usually another page at the same site). If you want to go back to where you were before, click the Back icon on the Navigator toolbar.

GETTING AROUND IN FRAMES

Frames became a design option in version 2 of Netscape Navigator. *Frames* appear on a Web page looking like a bunch of panes within the larger viewing area window; these "panes in the window" each hold some piece of the larger whole. Like everything else in life, frames are good when used purposefully, and not so good when they're used gratuitously. In Figure 6.4, you can see News of the Day, a Web page that uses frames to enhance the organization of the page by offering a navigation frame on the left and a larger frame in which various news sources appear on the right.

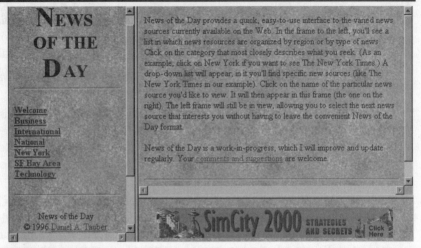

FIGURE 6.4: The News of the Day page uses frames to enhance navigation of its contents.

NOTHING'S SHOWING UP! WHAT TO DO?

Sometimes the N icon will be animated, its comets flying along, and either nothing shows up, or the text arrives *sans* images. What's going on?

When a Web server is busy, overloaded, or just plain slow, you'll get the text and basic HTML from it first and the images last. Images are a lot bigger (file-size–wise) than text, so they take longer to load. You can:

Stop Press the Stop button. Often, the images that were trying to load are mostly there, and hitting Stop will say, "Hey images! Hurry up and load!" Many times, they will.

Reload If that doesn't work, press the Reload button. In fact, if a Web page ever looks funny or incomplete in some way, try Reloading it.

Give up Sometimes Webmasters goof up, and sometimes, particularly if the Web server you're trying to access is halfway around the world, the connection is just too danged slow. Oh, well. If you really want to see that picture of Joe Namath as a baby, try your luck again some other time.

Having too many frames in a Web site is like putting too many bows on a dress—*too much*. Frames are best when used judiciously, and when no other option will do. To be fair, many sites use frames quite well—some of the most practical applications of frames are in pages that offer a table of contents in one of the frames. That index stays put (in some form or other) the whole time you're navigating the rest of the site.

NOTE
Many frames-based sites are quite apparent—there are solid lines of one sort or another, and maybe even scroll bars, that make it clear that the Netscape viewing area is being divided into little window panes. However, it has become possible to create a site that uses *borderless* frames—the usual, obvious gray lines and bars that divide the window are invisible. You may not even notice that some sites are using frames until you start navigating through them and notice that only part of the page is changing while you click around.

Whatever its purpose in a Web site, each individual frame has its own URL. It also can have its own scroll bars, various background colors, images, text, Java or JavaScript elements—anything, in short, that a non-frame Web page can have.

When you click a link in one frame, often another frame on the page will change to reflect that click. That means you can easily get lost trying to find some information that was in a frame you saw five clicks ago.

Still, using frames, you can easily get back to where you once belonged. The easiest is to use the Back button—in Navigator 4, the Back button sends you back one frame at a time until you reach the beginning of a framed-up site. You can also use the right mouse button to navigate backward—just click and, when the handy pop-up menu appears, select Back. You'll navigate backward one frame at a time.

NOTE
You can bookmark a document or a frame; this is much like putting a bookmark in a book in the sense that it helps you find where you've been without having to retrace your steps.

Part ii

QUITTING NETSCAPE NAVIGATOR

You can quit Navigator any ol' time—even when the Netscape icon (the N) is animated. When you do so, you can either close the current Navigator window, leaving any other Communicator windows open, or quit Communicator altogether. To close the Navigator window, simply do the following:

1. To quit the program, double-click the Control button in the upper-left corner of the screen, or select File ➤ Close from the menu bar. The current Navigator window will close and the Windows Desktop will reappear.

To close the Navigator window and exit Communicator altogether, do the following:

1. From Navigator's menu bar, select File ➤ Exit. The Netscape Exit Confirmation dialog box will appear.

2. Click Yes. The Navigator window, along with any other open Communicator windows, will close and the Windows Desktop will reappear.

NOTE

Remember that when you quit Navigator and/or Communicator, you are still connected to your Internet service provider, and you must break this connection, using whatever techniques are specifically appropriate. (Check with your Internet service provider to find out about that.)

WHAT'S NEXT?

Now, you know the basics of Netscape Navigator. In the next chapter, Gene Weisskopf and Pat Coleman will teach you the basics of Internet Explorer. If you're an Internet Explorer user, you'll probably want to read the whole chapter. If you're a Navigator user, you might skip the beginning part but you should go ahead and read the section called *Viewing Various File Types*—it applies to both IE and Navigator.

Chapter 7

AN INTRODUCTION TO INTERNET EXPLORER

This chapter will give you a broad overview of the way you work with Internet Explorer. We'll start at the beginning and show you the different ways you can start the program.

Later in the chapter, you'll learn about Internet Explorer's various tools, commands, and program features that help you navigate the Web and your local computer. You'll also find extensive material on the types of files that Internet Explorer can display, and we'll tell you how you can specify the way it should handle the ones that it can't display. The chapter closes with a look at how you can open the underlying HTML code for a Web page, a neat way to learn the tricks of the Web-author trade!

Adapted from *Mastering Microsoft Internet Explorer 4*, by Gene Weisskopf and Pat Coleman
ISBN 0-7821-2133-0   960 pages $44.99

STARTING INTERNET EXPLORER

Like just about all Windows programs, Internet Explorer can be started in many ways. You can also run more than one copy of Internet Explorer at a time, which allows you to view multiple documents or different sections of the same document.

To start Internet Explorer at any time, simply choose it from the Windows Start menu. In a standard installation, choose Start ➤ Programs ➤ Internet Explorer ➤ Internet Explorer. The program will start and open its *start page*, which is the page Internet Explorer displays first whenever you start it in this way.

If the start page is available on a local or networked drive on your computer or if you are already connected to the Internet, Internet Explorer opens that page immediately and displays it.

If you use a modem to connect to the Internet, however, and the start page resides there but you're not currently connected, Internet Explorer opens your Dial-Up Networking connector to make the connection to the Internet.

Dialing In to the Internet

If you normally use a network connection to access the Internet, any program can connect to the Internet as needed. That's not so when you link to the Internet through a modem and a telephone line. In that case, whenever Internet Explorer (or any other Windows application) needs access to the Internet (such as to open its start page) but does not yet have it, someone has to make that phone call to get connected.

That someone is Dial-Up Networking, which makes the call and gets connected to your Internet service provider (ISP). For example, Figure 7.1 shows the Connect To dialog box, in which you can revise or verify the user name, password, and telephone number that will be needed to make the connection.

TIP

If you want your password saved to your local disk so that you won't have to enter it the next time you connect to the Internet, select the Save Password option (the password is encrypted on your local disk).

Click the Connect button in the Connect To dialog box to make the call. You'll see status messages as the call and connection are being made. In about 20 or 30 seconds, the connection will be completed and you'll see the Dial-Up Networking icon displayed on the status bar (as shown here). Internet Explorer can now open its start page, and this connection to the Internet is also available to any Windows program that needs access to it, such as your e-mail program, an FTP client, and so on.

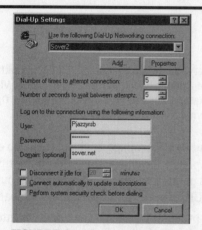

FIGURE 7.1: When a program needs a connection to the Internet, the Windows Dial-Up Networking connector makes the call over your modem.

Note that you'll see this dialog box only when you have enabled the "Prompt for information before dialing" option, which you'll find when you open the Dial-Up Networking folder and choose Connections ➤ Settings. If you have disabled this option, the call will be made as soon as the dialog box opens.

Starting from Your Start Page

The start page serves as a "home base" while you are working in Internet Explorer. You begin your leaps and bounds through the Web from the links on your start page. If you ever want to return to your start page (to return home, so to speak) during a session with Internet Explorer, click the Home button on the toolbar.

NOTE

You'll sometimes hear the start page referred to as the "home page." Even the button on the Internet Explorer toolbar that opens your start page is labeled "Home" and displays a picture of a house. Nonetheless, you should stick with "start page," the more commonly used term, to avoid any confusion with the *home page* of a Web site.

When your start page is open, you can navigate to any other page you choose. For example, you can click a hyperlink to open that link's target file, or you can choose an item from Internet Explorer's Favorites menu to go to that site.

TIP

You can specify any page to serve as the start page. You'll find this setting on the General tab in the Internet Options dialog box when you choose View ≻ Internet Options in Internet Explorer. You can also access the Internet Options dialog box by clicking the Internet icon in the Windows Control Panel.

If Internet Explorer cannot find your start page, such as when you cannot connect to the Internet, it displays a local page that offers a few tips for dealing with the problem. At this point, you can use your Favorites menu to go to a site, or you can enter a URL directly into the Address toolbar.

The start page is just like any other Web page you can open in Internet Explorer. The only thing special about it is that you see it each time you begin a session in Internet Explorer. A start page typically serves its purpose by containing one or both of the following types of content:

▸ Hyperlinks to one or more sites that you usually go to in each session with Internet Explorer

▸ Updated information that you want to see each time you start Internet Explorer, such as news, weather, stock market reports, sports scores, and so on

Starting Internet Explorer from a Hyperlink

Many programs besides Web browsers can display either text hyperlinks (which may be in a different color and underlined) or image hyperlinks; clicking the text or image opens the target file of that link. In a standard

Windows installation, when you click a link whose target is an HTML Web page, you'll find that the target will be opened in Internet Explorer.

For example, suppose someone sends you an e-mail suggesting that you check out a site on the WWW, and the text of the message includes the URL of that site. In Outlook Express Mail (and in most other e-mail programs), the text that makes up the URL is displayed in color and underlined, just as it would be in a browser. If you click the URL, Internet Explorer (or Netscape Navigator, for that matter) opens, and then it opens that site.

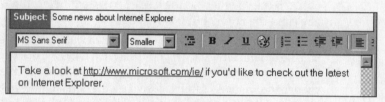

Opening an Existing Document

When you open an HTML file (one with an `htm` or `html` file name extension) in Windows Explorer, that file opens in Internet Explorer (assuming Internet Explorer is the default browser on your computer—if Navigator is your default browser, then Navigator will open).

NOTE

Quick reminder: When we refer to *Windows* Explorer, we're referring to the Explorer configuration you'll see when you're browsing your local disk drives or network drives. The *Internet* Explorer is the configuration you see when browsing Web pages.

While you're in Internet Explorer, you can choose File ➤ Open to open a specific file, either by typing the path and name of the file or by clicking the Browse button to find the file on your local or networked disk. Once you've found the file, choose OK to open it.

You can also open a file by simply dragging it from Windows Explorer or a folder window into Internet Explorer. Among the files you can open are HTML Web pages and GIF or JPEG image files (see *Viewing Various File Types* later in this chapter).

Part ii

MAKING INTERNET EXPLORER YOUR DEFAULT BROWSER

If you have installed another browser since installing Internet Explorer, Internet Explorer may not be set as your default browser, and that other browser will be called upon to open any Web pages you request. If you want to make Internet Explorer your default browser and keep it that way, here's how to do it.

In Internet Explorer, choose View ➤ Internet Options. On the Programs tab, you'll find an option called "Internet Explorer should check to see whether it is the default browser." Select this option, and close the Internet Options dialog box.

Now whenever you start Internet Explorer, it will check to see if it is still the default browser. If it finds that it isn't, it will ask if you want it to become the new default browser. If you choose Yes, it will change the Windows settings to make it the default. Now when you open an HTML file—for example, by clicking a hyperlink in a Word document that targets a Web page—Internet Explorer will be the program that opens it.

If you later install another browser that makes itself the default, the next time you start Internet Explorer, it will check to see if it is the default and prompt you accordingly.

Closing Internet Explorer

To close Internet Explorer, choose File ➤ Close, or click the Close button on the far right side of its title bar. Remember, Web browsers such as Internet Explorer are used only for viewing documents, so you never need to save anything before exiting the program.

WARNING

Even though there are normally no documents to save in Internet Explorer, you might still lose data if you exit the program prematurely. For example, when you are filling out a form in a Web page, you must click that form's Submit button to send your responses to the server. If you were to close Internet Explorer before doing so, any information you had entered into the form would be lost. Plus, if you open an OLE-compliant document, such as one from Microsoft Word, and you have its associated program installed on your system, you'll actually be editing that document in Internet Explorer. In this case, closing Internet Explorer would have the same effect as closing Microsoft Word when a document is open.

Closing Your Dial-Up Networking Connection

When you started Internet Explorer, it may have caused Dial-Up Networking to make the telephone call over your modem to connect to the Internet. In that case, when you later exit Internet Explorer, you will be asked if you want to disconnect from the Internet.

You can choose to disconnect if you're through working on the Internet for now. Doing so will close the connection so that your telephone line can receive other calls. Otherwise, you can choose to stay online and maintain the connection. You could then open your e-mail program, for example, and send or receive mail on the Internet. Or you might open Internet Explorer again, and the connection would be waiting for it.

If you do leave the connection open, don't forget to disconnect later. To do so, double-click the Dial-Up Networking icon on the right side of the Windows taskbar, then click the Disconnect button in the dialog box. Or right-click the icon in the taskbar and choose Disconnect from the shortcut menu.

A QUICK TOUR WITH INTERNET EXPLORER

Now that you've read about starting and closing Internet Explorer, let's take it on a short test ride to experience the thrill of the wind in our hair as we travel to new lands on the World Wide Web.

1. From the Windows Start menu, choose Programs ➤ Internet Explorer ➤ Internet Explorer.

2. If you connect to the Internet via a modem, Dial-Up Networking should open, dial your Internet service provider, give your user name and password, and complete the connection to the Internet.

3. Once connected, Internet Explorer opens its start page. If you installed Internet Explorer from a Microsoft source, for example, by downloading it from Microsoft's Web page, it opens the page at home.microsoft.com. The page you see in Internet Explorer will look something like the one shown in Figure 7.2.

Part ii

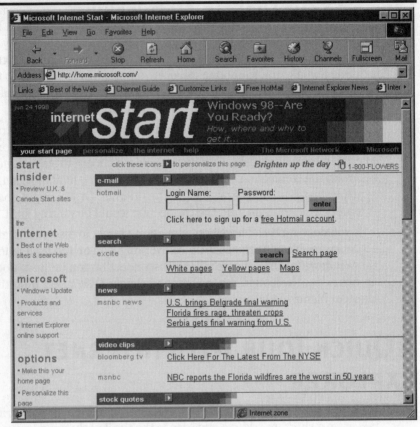

FIGURE 7.2: Internet Explorer opens your start page, where you can begin your travels on the World Wide Web.

4. At this point, you're free to click any of the hyperlinks in the current page to open a new page. Simply click a link, and off you go. Continue to click your way through several pages and see where you end up.

NOTE

When you point to a text or an image hyperlink, the mouse pointer changes to a small hand, and the address of the link's target is displayed on the status bar. Text hyperlinks are underlined and displayed in blue by default.

5. Now that you've traveled through several pages by following hyperlinks, go back through the pages you've followed by clicking the Back button on the toolbar. Each click takes you to the page you visited before the current one. Eventually you'll reach your start page.

6. Now let's go to a specific address on the Web, one of our own choosing. Either click within the Internet Explorer Address toolbar, or choose File ➤ Open. (If the Address toolbar isn't displayed, choose View ➤ Toolbar ➤ Address Bar.)

7. Enter the following URL:

    www.census.gov/datamap/www/

    and press Enter to open that page.

8. In the blink of an eye (perhaps longer if it's a busy time of the day on the Web), we've opened the Map Stats page on the Web site of the U.S. Census Bureau, as shown in Figure 7.3.

9. Just in case you'd like to return to this page at another time, you should add it to your Favorites menu. Choose Favorites ➤ Add to Favorites, and then click OK.

NOTE

When you want to return to this site, simply select it from your Favorites menu, which you'll find not only in every Explorer window, but also on your Windows 95 Start menu. You can also move this new item to another submenu on the Favorites menu.

10. Click your home state, which will open a map of that state. Let's save this picture of your state to your local disk.

11. Right-click anywhere within the map, and choose Save Picture As from the shortcut menu.

12. Specify a location and name for the new file, and click OK to save it.

Part ii

FIGURE 7.3: On the Map Stats page of the U.S. Census Bureau, you can access a wealth of information about any region in the country.

You now have a GIF image file of that map on your local disk, which you can later import into your word processor or any other program that handles GIF files. Just remember that most content you retrieve from the Web cannot be used for commercial purposes without specific permission from the owner of that content. When in doubt, drop a note asking whoever runs the Web site for permission to use the image or content.

13. Click a county within the state map, and then click the Tiger Map link, which opens an interactive map of that county.

14. Try magnifying the map by selecting the Zoom In option (as shown here) and then clicking within the map at the point you want at the center of the magnified map. In a few seconds, the new map will be displayed.

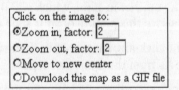

15. If you'd like to print this page, choose File ➢ Print, or click the Print button on the toolbar. In the Print dialog box, click the OK button.

SECURITY ALERT

When you click within the map to change its magnification, you may see a Security Alert dialog box warning you that you are about to send information over the Internet that could be seen by others. This is simply a not-so-gentle reminder that the Internet is not a private network. When you make a choice on a Web page and then click a Submit or Send Now button (or simply click within the map to make your choice in this case), you are sending some information over the Internet that could be viewed by others. Once you're familiar with these situations and no longer need the constant reminder, you can turn off this message in the future by selecting its "In the future, do not show this warning" option.

Now let's use Internet Explorer in a somewhat different way, to view a page from your local disk.

16. Using the Address toolbar or the File ➤ Open command, enter the drive and path to the folder where you stored the map image file you saved earlier in step 12. Press Enter when finished.

17. Internet Explorer will open that folder and display its contents; you should see the GIF file you saved earlier.

18. To go back to the previous page you were viewing, simply click the Back button on the toolbar. Or perhaps you might choose the Map Stats site from your Favorites menu to go back to that site.

We could play on this site for another dozen pages of this book, but it's time to wrap up this tour.

Don't ever worry about getting lost, because that concept just doesn't apply to your travels in Internet Explorer. Sure, you can easily forget how you reached the current page, but that's what the Back and Favorites buttons are for.

Whatever happens, you can always jump back to your start page at any time by clicking the Home button on the toolbar. Although there's nothing magical about your start page (it's just another page you can display in Internet Explorer), it's a familiar place that will have familiar content and links.

Otherwise, you can simply close Internet Explorer by choosing File ≻ Close and call it a day. If you are connected to the Internet via a Dial-Up Networking connection, you should be asked whether you want to disconnect; choose Yes to hang up.

INSIDE INTERNET EXPLORER

Now we'll look at the components that make up Internet Explorer. You'll find that Internet Explorer has many similarities to other Windows programs you have used, especially to those in Microsoft Office (Word, Excel, Access, and so on). Figure 7.4 shows Internet Explorer while displaying a Web page. As you can see, the Internet Explorer window contains many of the usual Windows components.

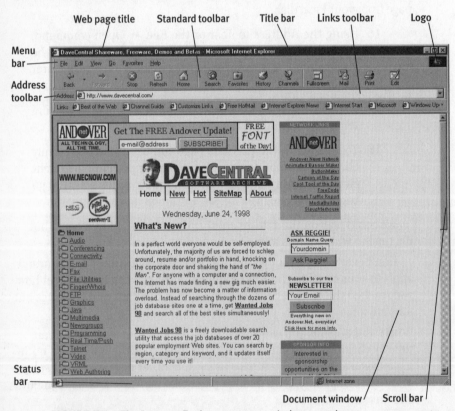

FIGURE 7.4: The Internet Explorer program window contains many components that are common to other Windows programs.

NOTE

A company or an Internet service provider (ISP) can customize Internet Explorer to make it look and act as though it were their own browser and then distribute it to employees or customers. So if your ISP or your employer gives you a copy of Internet Explorer, it may not look exactly like the one shown in Figure 7.4.

When you want to show as much of the Web page as possible, try the View ➢ Full Screen command, or click the Full Screen button on the toolbar. Internet Explorer will be maximized to occupy the entire screen, it will lose its title bar, status bar, two of its toolbars, and even its menu bar. (You can right-click a toolbar and choose Menu Bar to display it again.)

You can switch back to the normal view by choosing the Full Screen command again. The full-screen mode is the default when you open a channel from the desktop, when it's formally called the Channel Viewer.

The Components of Internet Explorer

Let's discuss the parts that make up the Internet Explorer window. Keep in mind that if a tool or an object looks similar to one you've seen in another Windows program, it most likely performs the same task in both.

Title Bar

At the top of the window is the usual title bar. It displays either the title of the Web page you are viewing (*Dave Central Shareware, Freeware, Demos and Betas Page* in Figure 7.4) or the document's file name if it is not a Web page. On the right side of the title bar are the Minimize, Maximize/Restore, and Close buttons; on the left side is the System menu. As usual, you can double-click the title bar to maximize the window (or restore it to its previous size if it was already maximized), or you can drag Internet Explorer by its title bar to move the window on the screen (assuming the window is not maximized).

Program Window

Internet Explorer's program window is shown full-screen in Figure 7.4. If it is smaller than full-screen, you can resize it by dragging any of its corners or sides. You'll find that the paragraphs in a Web page generally adjust their width to the size of the browser window. As you change the dimensions of Internet Explorer, the page reformats to fit the new size.

Part ii

Menu Bar

Beneath the title bar is the menu bar, which contains almost all the commands you'll need in Internet Explorer. If a command has a keyboard shortcut, you'll see the keystroke displayed next to the command on the menu. For example, you can use the shortcut Ctrl+O (hold down Ctrl and press O) instead of choosing the File ➤ Open command, or you can press function key F5 instead of choosing View ➤ Refresh.

Toolbars

By default, the toolbars appear beneath the menu bar in Internet Explorer and contain buttons and other tools that help you navigate the Web. The three toolbars are Standard, Links, and Address (top, middle, and bottom in Figure 7.4). We discuss these a little later in "Using the Toolbars." The Internet Explorer logo to the right of the toolbar is animated when the program is accessing data.

Document Window

Beneath the menu and toolbars is the main document window, which occupies the majority of your screen. The current document, such as a Web page or an image, is displayed here. You cannot display multiple document windows in Internet Explorer. Instead, you can view multiple documents by opening multiple instances of Internet Explorer (choose File ➤ New ➤ Window). Each instance of Internet Explorer is independent of the others.

Explorer Bar

When you click the Search, Favorites, History, or Channels button on the Internet Explorer toolbar (or choose one of those commands from the View ➤ Explorer Bar menu), the Explorer bar will appear as a separate pane on the left side of the window. It displays the contents for the button you clicked, such as the search options shown in Figure 7.5.

With the window split into two separate panes, you can make choices in the Explorer bar on the left and watch the results appear in the pane on the right. For example, in Figure 7.5, you can specify what you want to search for in the Explorer bar, and the results of the search appear in that same pane as a list of links you can click. When you click one of the result links, the target of the link appears in the right pane, while leaving the

Explorer bar unchanged. You can select another result link to try that target and continue through as many as you like.

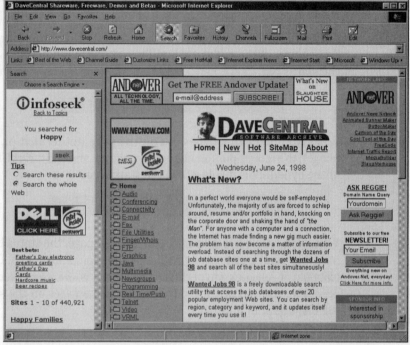

FIGURE 7.5: When you click the Search, Favorites, History, or Channels button on the toolbar, the Explorer bar opens as a separate pane on the left side of the window, where you can make choices and see the results appear in the right pane.

To close the Explorer bar, choose View ➢ Explorer Bar ➢ None, or click the appropriate button a second time, such as the Search button to close the Explorer bar in Figure 7.5.

Scroll Bars

The horizontal scroll bar is at the bottom of the document window, and the vertical scroll bar is on the right side of the document window. When a document is too large to be displayed within the window, you can use the scroll bars to scroll the window over other parts of the document.

Watch that Status Bar

At the bottom of the Internet Explorer window is the status bar. It displays helpful information about the current state of Internet Explorer, so keep an eye on it.

▶ When you are selecting a command from the menu bar, a description of the currently highlighted command appears on the status bar.

> Searches the current window for text

▶ When you point to a hyperlink on the page (either text or an image), the mouse pointer changes to a hand, and the target URL of the hyperlink is displayed on the status bar.

> http://www.sybex.com/books.html

▶ When you click a hyperlink to open another page, the status bar indicates what is happening with a progression of messages. For example, if you click a hyperlink whose target is www.sample.com/somepage.htm you might see the following messages on the status bar, one after another:

```
Finding site: www.sample.com
Web site found. Waiting for reply
Opening page: somepage.htm
(7 items remaining) Downloading picture http://. . .
```

▶ Icons that appear on the right side of the status bar give you a status report at a glance. For example, you'll see an icon of a padlock when you have made a secure connection to a Web site, and you'll see a network wire with an X across it when you're working offline.

TIP

You can use the Toolbar and Status Bar commands on the View menu to toggle on or off the display of the toolbars and status bar. You might want to hide these otherwise useful features to give yourself a little more screen real estate for displaying pages. If you want as much room as possible, try the View ➢ Full Screen command.

Getting Help

Internet Explorer offers the usual variety of program help, with a few touches of its own. When you choose Help ➤ Contents and Index, what you get is not quite the standard Windows help viewer. Internet Explorer uses a new help system that is built with HTML, just like a Web page. Nonetheless, it behaves very much like the more traditional help system. You can browse through the topics in the Contents tab, look up a specific word or phrase in the Index tab, or find all references to a word or phrase on the Search tab.

To see if there is a newer version of any of the Internet Explorer software components, choose Help ➤ Product Updates. This is the best way to keep your software current—immediately and online.

To work through a basic online tutorial about browsing the Web, choose Help ➤ Web Tutorial. Internet Explorer goes online to a Microsoft Web site and opens the tutorial page, where you can click your way through the lessons. To find answers to your questions or problems, choose Help ➤ Online Support. This will open Microsoft's online support page for Internet Explorer. It's packed with tips, troubleshooting guides, answers to common questions, and much more. It's a great place to go for up-to-the-minute solutions and fixes.

The items under Help ➤ Microsoft on the Web should prove to be quite valuable. Each takes you online to the Internet:

Free Stuff   This item finds updates to Internet Explorer, add-on programs, and freebies for users of Internet Explorer.

Get Faster Internet Access   Go to this item to learn how to get ISDN phone service from your local phone company and about how ISDN gives you Internet access at speeds more than four times faster than a 28.8 Kbps modem.

Frequently Asked Questions   Find answers to the most common questions among Internet Explorer users.

Internet Start Page   Like clicking the Home button on the toolbar, this item opens your start page.

Send Feedback   Do you have a comment about Internet Explorer for Microsoft? Would you like to report a bug or send in a request for a special feature you'd like to see in the program? Use this command to go to the feedback page, where you can tell Microsoft what you think.

Best of the Web   This item is equivalent to the Best of the Web button on the Links toolbar. You'll go to Microsoft's Exploring page, which offers a wide variety of links to interesting and useful sites.

Search the Web   This item takes you to the same site as the Go ➤ Search the Web command, where you can search the Web with several search engines, including Yahoo, Lycos, InfoSeek, AltaVista, and more.

Microsoft Home Page   Like clicking the E icon at the right of the toolbar, this item takes you to Microsoft's ever-so-humble home page. You can catch up on the latest Microsoft news, read corporate press releases, and get information for stockholders.

NOTE

The Microsoft Home Page command is *not* the same as the Go ➤ Home Page command (or the Home button on the Toolbar), which opens your own start page.

You can often learn something about an object on screen from its ToolTip. Internet Explorer displays ToolTips when you point to some of its components, such as when you point to an icon on the status bar (shown here), a hyperlink within the page, or a button on the toolbar (when the button descriptions are not displayed). Here's what a ToolTip looks like:

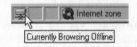

Another way to find out about an object in the current document, such as a picture or video clip, is to right-click it and choose Properties from the shortcut menu.

At the Helm in Internet Explorer

The simplest way to navigate within Internet Explorer is to click a hyperlink to open another file (the target of the link). That's probably how you'll spend most of your time while browsing, but there are plenty of commands available that can help you explore the Web, save information to your local disk, and so on.

In Internet Explorer, you can perform an action in three main ways:

- ▶ Using the menus and shortcut menus
- ▶ Using the toolbars
- ▶ Using the keyboard and shortcut keys

Using the Menus and Shortcut Menus

In Internet Explorer, you can perform just about any action by choosing commands on its menus. Many components also have shortcut menus that you access with a right-click of the mouse.

Let's take a quick look at the commands on the menu bar (you can breeze over these just to familiarize yourself with them; you won't be tested on any of this):

File   Open the current page in a new Internet Explorer window; open a file by specifying a name and URL or location; save the current page to disk; print the current page; send the current page or its URL in an e-mail message or create a shortcut to it on your desktop; choose to go to a site that you've visited earlier in this session with Internet Explorer; view the properties of the current page; choose to browse without being online (data is opened from your Internet Explorer cache on your local disk).

Edit   Select the contents of the entire page; copy selected data from Internet Explorer to another program; edit the page in FrontPage Express; find characters on the current page.

View   Hide or display the toolbars and status bar; change the size of the fonts used in Internet Explorer; cancel the downloading of the current page; refresh the contents of the page by downloading it again; view the HTML source code for the current page in Notepad; switch to full-screen mode to show as much of the page as possible; view or change the options for Internet Explorer.

Go   Go backward or forward through URLs you've already visited; open your start page; perform a search at the Microsoft search page; open another program in the Internet Explorer suite, such as Outlook Express or NetMeeting; open your Windows Address Book.

Favorites   Open a site that you have previously saved as a shortcut on the Favorites menu; add the current URL to the Favorites menu; open one of the channels you have subscribed to; open a URL from your Links toolbar; open the Favorites folder so you can rename, revise, delete, or otherwise organize its contents; create a subscription for the current page or any item already in the Favorites menu; manage your existing subscriptions.

Help   Access the help system for Internet Explorer; take the Internet Explorer Web tutorial; open a Microsoft site on the WWW to learn about Internet Explorer.

You can also invoke many of these commands from the toolbars or with shortcut keys, as well as with shortcut menus.

To access a shortcut menu for an object in Internet Explorer, point to the object and click the *right* mouse button. The choices on the shortcut menu depend on the object you click.

▶ Right-click anywhere on the page outside a hyperlink or an image, and the shortcut menu includes choices relevant to the page. You can open the next or previous page, add this page to your Favorites menu, show the properties dialog box for this page, print the page, and so on. If the page uses a background image, you can choose to save that image to a file or make it your Windows desktop wallpaper.

▶ Right-click a hyperlink, and the shortcut menu lets you open the target of that link, copy the link to the Windows Clipboard, or add the target of the link to your Favorites menu.

▶ Right-click an image, and the shortcut menu lets you save the image to a file, make that image your Windows desktop wallpaper, or copy the image to the Clipboard.

▶ Right-click selected text, and you can choose to print that text or copy it to the Clipboard.

Using the Toolbars

The toolbars in Internet Explorer (shown below) can appear in every Explorer window, whether you're viewing a Web page, folders and files on your disk, the Windows Control Panel, and so on. Two of them are also available from the Windows taskbar. They go by the names Standard, Links, and Address. You can rearrange the layout of the toolbars at any time, as discussed a little later in *Moving and Resizing the Toolbars*.

TIP

Even the menu bar now behaves as a toolbar, in that you can place other toolbars on its row or move it to one of the other rows of toolbars. When you're working in Full Screen mode (choose View ➤ Full Screen), you can even hide the menu bar.

Standard Toolbar

You'll regularly use the buttons on the first row of the toolbar, as shown above. All are shortcuts for commands on the menus. As you'll see shortly, you can choose to hide the row of descriptive text below the buttons. Table 7.1 describes each button.

TABLE 7.1: The Buttons on the Standard Toolbar

BUTTON	COMMAND	DESCRIPTION
⇐ Back	Go ➤ Back	Displays the page you were viewing before the current page.
⇒ Forward	Go ➤ Forward	Displays the page you were viewing before you went back to the current page.
✕ Stop	View ➤ Stop	Cancels the downloading of the content for the current page.

Refresh	View ➢ Refresh	Updates the content of the current page by downloading it again.
Home	Go ➢ Home Page	Opens your start page, the one you see when you first start Internet Explorer.
Search	View ➢ Explorer Bar ➢ Search	Opens the Explorer Bar on the left side of the screen and displays the search options there.
Favorites	View ➢ Explorer Bar ➢ Favorites	Opens the Explorer bar and displays your Favorites menu there.
History	View ➢ Explorer Bar ➢ History	Opens the Explorer bar and displays your browsing history there.
Channels	View ➢ Explorer Bar ➢ Channels	Opens the Explorer bar and displays your channels there.
Full Screen	View ➢ Full Screen	Switches Internet Explorer to its full-screen mode (also called Channel View).
Font	View ➢ Fonts	Changes the size or style of the default fonts used in Internet Explorer.
Mail	File ➢ Send; Go ➢ Mail	Opens your e-mail program, sends new e-mail, or opens your news reader.
Print	File ➢ Print	Prints the current page.
Edit	Edit ➢ Page	Opens the current page in your Web-page editor, such as FrontPage Express.
	Go ➢ Home Page on the Web ➢ Microsoft's Start Page	The Internet Explorer logo is animated when you are sending or receiving data. Click the logo to open Microsoft's home page.

Links Toolbar

Each of the buttons on the Links toolbar is a hyperlink to a URL (you can also access these links from the Links command on the Favorites menu). In the version we're using to write this chapter, by default, they all target Microsoft Web sites that serve as gateways to a wealth of information on the WWW (if you received a customized version of Internet Explorer, these hyperlinks may point to other locations). Microsoft updates these sites frequently, so their content will likely be fresh each time you visit.

Best of the Web   A useful collection of links to reference-related Web sites, where you might look up a company's phone number, find an e-mail address of a long-lost relative, or find sites that will help you with travel arrangements or personal finance.

Microsoft   The home page of Microsoft Corporation, where you'll find news about Microsoft and its products, a variety of support options for their products, press releases, and more.

Internet Explorer News   Valuable information about Microsoft Internet Explorer and its related applications (Mail and News, NetMeeting, and so on).

Today's Links   When you don't feel like poking around the Web on your own, you can go to the default start page for Internet Explorer, where you'll find links to what's "hot" on the Web today (at least, according to Microsoft).

Web Gallery   A good place to go when you're building your own Web pages. You'll find loads of content that you can download and incorporate in your pages. For example, you can grab images that you can use as lines, buttons, or bullets; sound files that can serve as a page's background sound; ActiveX controls and Java applets for making your pages come alive; and True-Type fonts that allow your Internet Explorer to display Web pages exactly as their authors intended when they specified those fonts.

Remember, the buttons on the Links toolbar are just hyperlinks to pages on the Web. Feel free to try them out and see what's there.

Once you've tried these buttons and have a feeling for the content on each of the sites, you may decide to revise the buttons so they point to other sites that you want to access with a click or to new buttons that point to other sites.

Part ii

To add a new button, simply drag a link from a Web page onto the Links toolbar. To delete a button, right-click it and choose Delete from the shortcut menu. To move a button, drag it to another location on the Links toolbar.

The best way to revise a button's name or target URL is to use the Favorites ➤ Organize Favorites command. Open the Links folder, and you'll find the shortcuts that make up the buttons on the Links toolbar. You can rename a shortcut, and its new name will appear on the button. Right-click a shortcut, choose Properties from the shortcut menu, and you can revise the link's target URL. You can also right-click a button on the Links toolbar to access the Properties command on the shortcut menu.

Address Toolbar

This toolbar shows the address of the file currently displayed in Internet Explorer, which might be a URL on the Internet or a location on your local disk. You enter a URL or the path to a file and press Enter to open that file.

NOTE

When you are entering a URL that you have entered once before, Internet Explorer's AutoComplete feature recognizes the URL and finishes the typing for you. You can either accept the URL or continue to type a new one. Or right-click in the Address toolbar, choose Completions from the shortcut menu, and then select one of the possibilities from the menu.

To revise the URL, click within the Address toolbar and use the normal Windows editing keys. For example, press Home or End to go to the beginning or end of the address. Drag over any of its text to select it, or hold down the Shift key and use the keyboard arrow keys to select text. When you're finished entering the new address, press Enter to have Internet Explorer open the file.

The arrow on the right side of the Address toolbar opens a drop-down list of addresses. Select one, and Internet Explorer will open that site. You visited these sites before by entering the address in the Address toolbar and pressing Enter. They're listed in the order you visited them.

Moving and Resizing the Toolbars

The toolbars in Internet Explorer are quite flexible. You can change the size or position of each one in the trio, or you can choose not to display them at all. In fact, the menu bar is also quite flexible and can be moved below one or more toolbars, or share the same row with them.

▶ To hide a toolbar, choose View ➤ Toolbar and select one from the menu; to display that toolbar, choose that command again. Or right-click any of the toolbars or menu bar and select a toolbar from the shortcut menu.

▶ To hide the descriptive text below the Standard toolbar buttons, choose View ➤ Toolbar ➤ Text Labels, or right-click a toolbar and choose Text Labels. Choose the command again to display the text.

▶ To change the number of rows that the toolbars use, point to the bottom edge of the bottom toolbar; the mouse pointer will change to a double-headed arrow. You can then drag the edge up to reduce the number of rows or drag it down to expand them.

▶ To move a toolbar, drag it by its left edge. For example, drag the Address toolbar onto the same row as the Links toolbar.

▶ When two or more toolbars or the menu bar share the same row, you can change the width of one (not the left-hand one) by dragging its left edge. In the arrangement shown below, the Address and Links toolbars are sharing the same row. You could drag the left edge of the Links toolbar to the right or left to make it narrower or wider.

▶ To expand a toolbar to display all its buttons or to make the Address toolbar as wide as possible, double-click its name on the left side of the toolbar. Double-click the name again to shrink that toolbar.

NOTE

Remember, these three toolbars are common to both Windows Explorer and Internet Explorer (the new single Explorer in Windows); the Address and Links toolbars are also available on the Windows taskbar.

Using Your Keyboard

In a world of pure browsing, you would rarely need the keyboard. In the real world, however, you might be using the keyboard quite a bit. For example, you'll frequently encounter online forms on which you will want to enter information: a feedback form for your comments; a survey form for your opinions; or a registration form that will give you access to an online newspaper.

As discussed earlier, you'll also be using the keyboard when you want to type a URL into the Address toolbar so you can open the file at that address. Many commands have keyboard shortcuts. Those that you may find useful on a regular basis are shown in Table 7.2.

TABLE 7.2:   Useful Keyboard Shortcuts

KEY	COMMAND	DESCRIPTION
Esc	View ➤ Stop	Cancels the downloading of the content for the current page. (You can also click the Stop button on the toolbar.)
F5	View ➤ Refresh	Updates the content of the current page by downloading it again. (You can also click the Refresh button on the toolbar.)
Tab		Selects the next hyperlink on the page; press Shift+Tab to select the previous hyperlink.
Enter		Activates the selected hyperlink, as though you had clicked it with your mouse.
Home/End		Moves to the beginning or end of the document.
Arrow keys		Use ↓ or ↑ to scroll toward the bottom or the top of the document. When the document is too wide for the Internet Explorer window (as evidenced by the display of a horizontal scroll bar beneath the document), use → or ← to scroll toward the right or left edge of the document.
PgDn/PgUp		Scrolls toward the bottom or top of the current document, moving approximately one screen at a time (the height of Internet Explorer's document window).
Alt+←	Go ➤ Back	Displays the page you were viewing before the current page. (The Back button on the toolbar also does this.)
Alt+→	Go ➤ Forward	Displays the page you were viewing before you went back to the current page. (The Forward button on the toolbar also does this.)

Accessing Outlook Express Mail and News

Internet Explorer and its software suite of components are an integrated package of Internet or intranet tools. While browsing in Internet Explorer, you can access Outlook Express directly from the toolbar.

NOTE

This discussion assumes that either Microsoft Outlook or Outlook Express is your primary e-mail and newsreader program. If you have not installed Outlook Express, you may not be able to perform these tasks in your own e-mail and newsreader programs.

You can send mail in several ways while working within Internet Explorer. You'll find the following commands by clicking the Mail button on Internet Explorer's toolbar:

Read Mail opens Outlook Express Mail and displays the contents of your Inbox (you can also choose Go ➢ Mail in Internet Explorer). You're free to continue working in Outlook Express as you normally would. You can return to Internet Explorer at any time in the usual ways, such as by pressing Alt+Tab.

New Message creates a new Outlook Express Mail message, as though you had clicked the Compose Message button in that program. You can also choose File ➢ New ➢ Message in Internet Explorer.

Send a Link creates a new Outlook Express Mail message that includes an attached file—a shortcut to the page that is currently displayed in Internet Explorer. The icon or the name of the attachment appears in the pane beneath the message pane. The recipient of the message can then treat the shortcut as any other shortcut, so that opening the icon will open the target page. You can also use Internet Explorer's equivalent command File ➢ Send ➢ Link by Email.

Send Page creates a new Outlook Express Mail message (see Figure 7.6) that consists only of the page that you're currently viewing in Internet Explorer. The recipient can view the page in Outlook Express Mail or click a link to open its target in Internet Explorer. You can also use the command File ➢ Send ➢ Page by Email.

Read News opens Outlook Express News in the usual way (or you can choose Go ➢ News).

NOTE
You can access your Windows Address Book from within Internet Explorer with either the File ➤ New ➤ Contact or the Go ➤ Address Book command.

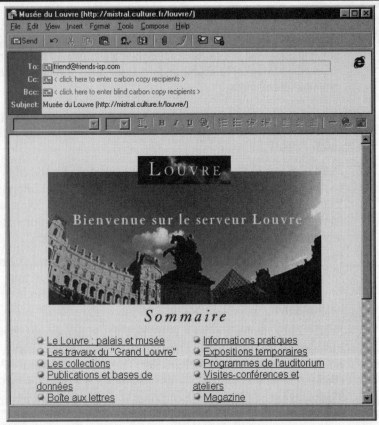

FIGURE 7.6: The Send Page command creates an Outlook Express Mail message that contains the page currently open in Internet Explorer.

VIEWING VARIOUS FILE TYPES

Internet Explorer is a browser, which means that its primary purpose is to display files, not to edit or create them. Internet Explorer can display several types of files on its own, and it can display other files with the aid of other programs. When it encounters any other type of file, you can choose to save the file to disk or let Internet Explorer attempt to open the file by passing it to the appropriate program.

NOTE

Netscape users: The information in this section applies to Navigator as well as to Internet Explorer.

Viewing Standard Web Files

When you browse, you'll encounter several types of files at virtually every Web site you visit. Internet Explorer can display all the following file types:

- ▶ .html
- ▶ .gif
- ▶ .jpeg
- ▶ .png
- ▶ .txt
- ▶ Active X files (not viewable in Netscape navigator)

Viewing Files with the Help of Other Programs

There are certainly plenty of other types of files in the world, but Internet Explorer can't display them on its own. With a little help from another program, however, Internet Explorer can handle just about any file you might encounter. This ancillary program can normally expand the file-handling abilities of Internet Explorer in two ways:

Helper or add-on   With a helper or an add-on program, Internet Explorer does not open the new file type directly; it hands the file over to the helper program. The helper may appear as a separate window of its own or as a new component within the Internet Explorer window.

Plug-in   A plug-in program allows Internet Explorer to open a new file type within the Internet Explorer window; the relationship between the two programs is almost seamless, as though the other program has been "plugged in" to Internet Explorer.

Part ii

Any individual or company can create a helper or plug-in program to extend the capabilities of Internet Explorer. Most of these applications are available free for the downloading.

NOTE

For more information about helpers, add-ons, and plug-ins, see Chapter 23.

What happens if Internet Explorer encounters a file type that neither it nor any of its associated programs can open? That's when your Windows file associations come into play, as discussed next.

Dealing with Unknown File Types

When you click a link or otherwise open a file, Internet Explorer verifies that the file type is one it recognizes. It has two ways of recognizing files:

▶ By the file's MIME type

▶ By the file's file name extension

Before a server sends the file to Internet Explorer, the server first sends the file's MIME type. This acronym stands for Multipurpose Internet Mail Extensions and is a standard method on the Internet for identifying file types. If Internet Explorer recognizes the MIME type, it will know what to do with the file, such as displaying the file itself or passing it along to another program on your system.

CRIPES! MIME TYPES YIPES!

Danger Will Robinson! I wouldn't go looking for MIME types in Internet Explorer if I were you. Why? You won't find them there. In fact, you might just drive yourself nuts trying to. Let us harken back to the days of Windows 3.1x and marvel at the thrill of Associations and we begin to see the light where MIME is concerned. If you are unfamiliar with earlier versions of Windows then you'll need an explanation of MIME and Associations. Try these:

Association; /n/, (ass•ohsh•ee•ay•shun), A sort of roadmap that tells Windows which applications to use for which filename extensions. i.e., document.doc = Word 97, picture.psd = PhotoShop, write.wri = Windows Write, and so on and so forth.

MIME; /n/, (my•mm), 1) An energetic individual that uses familiar motions to mimic reality, 2) also referred to as Multipurpose Internet Mail Extensions, MIME helps client applications, like e-mail or web browsers, determine which application to use for a file it cannot handle (i.e., RealAudio or RealVideo, QuickTime, or PDF...)

Do you feel as if you need to make some modifications to your MIME types or just curious what they look like? Here, do this:

▶ Go the the Desktop, making the My Computer (or whatever you have changed it to) icon visible.

▶ Open My Computer and go to View ➤ Folder Options.

▶ Click on the File Types tab in the resultant dialog box to make the tab active

You'll note that there is a large list of items, some familiar, some alien. Most of these items are not even related to the internet at all, but there are some important ones. The key to the kaboodle is the x-text/html MIME type that allows your browser to see Web pages in the first place. Nifty, huh?

WARNING

It's not nice to mess with Mother MIME! Unless you are very familiar with MIME or are tops at reading complex documentation, I do not suggest you modify MIME types. Doing so can cause you to lose the nifty gizmos you added in the first place.

Many MIME types and file name extensions are already associated with the appropriate programs on your computer (as discussed in the next section). For example, an HTML document has the MIME type *text/html*, a GIF image file has the type *image/gif*, and a JPEG image file has the type *image/jpeg*. You can view or revise the MIME types and program associations for files on your system, which is discussed in the next section.

When you click a link to a file, several outcomes are possible, depending on the file's MIME type and file name extension:

▶ If Internet Explorer recognizes its MIME type as one that already has an association in Windows, it will automatically open that file from the server. Internet Explorer will display the file if it can (such as with an HTML or a text file) or pass it along to the program with which that MIME type is associated in Windows.

▶ If Internet Explorer does not recognize the file's MIME type, it will look at the file's file name extension. If a program in Windows is associated with that file type, Internet Explorer will then make the following determination.

▶ If the "Confirm open after download" option in the Edit File Type dialog box for this association (discussed in the next section) is not selected, Internet Explorer will open the file immediately, using the program defined for this file in the file's association.

▶ If the "Confirm after download" option is selected, Internet Explorer will display a dialog box, asking if you want to open the file or save it to disk. When in doubt, you're better off leaving that option selected so that you'll have the opportunity to decide what to do when you encounter that file type.

▶ If the file has no association in Windows, Internet Explorer will display the dialog box shown in Figure 7.7 and let you decide how to proceed. If you decide to open the file from the Internet, you'll then have to choose the program that should be used.

▶ If the file is a viewable file for which you do not have the proper viewer software or plug-in (say, an Audio or Video file) Internet Explorer will display a dialog box and let you know what software you need and where to get it from. You will also be prompted to decide if you want to go get it right then. See Figure 7.8 for an illustration.

When you are presented with the File Download dialog box, you can choose either to open the file in its associated program (if it has one) or simply save the file to disk. For several reasons, the latter choice is often the prudent one.

First, downloading a file from the Internet puts your computer at risk of being infected with a virus—who knows where that file has been lurking? When you save the file to disk, you can later run your virus-checking program on it to see if it gets a clean bill of health.

Another reason to save a file instead of opening it is to avoid the possible chaos of having too many things happening at the same time. While you're online browsing a Web site, an incoming program file that you opened might be setting up a new game on your computer, and the resulting clash might make a messy electronic battleground.

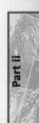

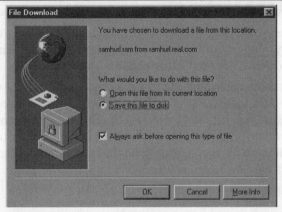

FIGURE 7.7: When Internet Explorer encounters a file that it cannot handle, you can either open the file in its associated program (if there is one) or save the file to disk.

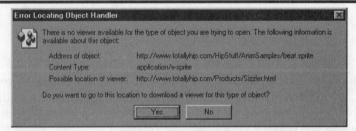

FIGURE 7.8: When Internet Explorer encounters a file for which you do not have the proper software or plugin to display.

NOTE

You may often go to a Web site specifically to download a file, such as a program update for software you own. When you click on the link to the file, Internet Explorer displays the dialog box and asks you what you want to do with the file. Unless the site tells you to do otherwise, choose to save the file to disk.

Saving a file to disk is a neat trick because you can then deal with it later. You can still install that game or patch that software, but you'll do it when the time is right. Plus, with the file safely on disk, you can make a backup copy of it, if necessary, or pass it on to a friend or coworker.

As you can see, the way in which Internet Explorer handles a file depends on whether the file has an association under Windows and whether that association is by its MIME type or by its file name extension. The next section shows how you can view, create, revise, or delete a file association.

Setting File Associations

In Windows, when you choose to open a file outside the program that created it, such as by double-clicking the file in Windows Explorer, Windows must check to see which program is associated with that file type.

Windows makes the determination based on the file's file name extension (only Internet Explorer looks at a file's MIME type when you're connected to the Web or your intranet), which is the characters after the period in the file name (after the final period if there is more than one). Here are some common file name extensions that you may recognize and the file types that Windows assigns them:

BAT	MS-DOS Batch File
BMP	Bitmap Image
EXE	Application
HLP	Help File
INI	Configuration Settings
TTF	TrueType Font file
WRI	Write Document

The extensions listed above are generic to Windows, in that those types are defined in a brand-new Windows installation. If you encounter one of these files in Internet Explorer and choose to open it, Windows takes over and performs the appropriate action.

For example, when you double-click a program file with a BAT or EXE file name extension, Windows simply runs the file. It opens an HLP file in the standard help viewer in Windows, as though you chose a command from a program's Help menu. In Windows 95, a WRI file opens in Word-Pad, and in Windows 3.1 that file opens in Write.

When you install new programs under Windows, the installation routine may add new file-type definitions to Windows. For example, when you install Microsoft Office, the following file types are defined (and there will be many more, as well):

DOC	Microsoft Word Document
WKB	Microsoft Word Backup Document
XLS	Microsoft Excel Worksheet
XLT	Microsoft Excel Template

NOTE

In this case, with the help of its ActiveX abilities, Internet Explorer can view Word (DOC) and Excel (XLS) documents. Therefore, if you have Word and Excel installed on your computer, you won't even be offered the Open/Save dialog box when you click a link to one of these files. Internet Explorer will open it.

The point to remember is this: Any file that can't be viewed within Internet Explorer is handled by the program with which its file name extension is associated in Windows (unless it has a MIME type association, which will be used first). For example, when you attempt to open a file with a WKB file name extension, Windows tells Word to open that file.

You can also create your own file associations or revise existing ones. While viewing a folder (not a Web page) in any Explorer window, choose View ➢ Folder Options and select the File Types tab. You'll see the list of file types, similar to the one shown in Figure 7.9.

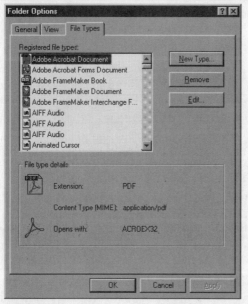

FIGURE 7.9: You can view or revise file associations or create new ones in the File Types tab.

DON'T ASK ME WHAT PROGRAM TO USE, JUST OPEN THE FILE!

How many times have you tried to open a file in Windows Explorer, only to be presented with the Open With dialog box (shown here), asking you to choose a program to use to open that file? The problem is that the file you want to open has no program associated with it under Windows, so Windows is stymied and now must wait for you to decide how to proceed. You'll also see this dialog box when you choose to open a file in Internet Explorer and that file has no association.

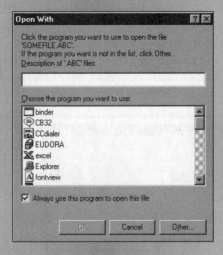

At this point, you can either choose a program from the list of associated programs already in Windows or click the Other button and select a program name from your disk drive.

For example, suppose in Internet Explorer you saved the file SOME-FILE.ABC, and in Windows Explorer you double-click the file to open it. Unless Windows on your computer has the file name extension ABC already associated with some program, you'll get the Open With dialog box.

If you know that this ABC file is, for example, a text file, you could choose Notepad from the list as the program to use to open it. If you're going to be working with more ABC files in the future, you could also select the "Always use this program to open this file" option to establish an association between any ABC files and Notepad.

If the item named Internet Document (HTML) is selected in the list of file types, then beneath the list of file types you can see that:

► The file name extension recognized for this type of file is HTM or HTML.

► The MIME type for this type of file is *text/html*.

The name of the associated program that will be used to open this type of file is Explorer. You can revise this definition by clicking the Edit button, which displays the Edit File Type dialog box (where you'll find the "Confirm open after download" option, which was discussed in the previous section). For example, you could specify that FrontPage Express be associated with the editing of this file type so that when you right-click the file name and choose Edit, the file would open in that program. To create a completely new file association, click the New Type button.

NOTE

There are no laws establishing sole rights to a file name extension! Therefore, the name and associated program for any given file type could vary on different computers. For example, the DOC extension might be used by some other program. In fact, if you were to install that program on a computer that already has Microsoft Word installed, a new association would be established for DOC files. When you later double-click a DOC file, the other program, not Word, would be the one to open it.

WHAT'S NEXT?

Gene Weisskopf and Pat Coleman took you on a whirlwind tour of Internet Explorer in this chapter and introduced you to the ways you can start the program; use its menus, toolbars, and keyboard shortcuts; and view different types of files. In the next chapter, they will teach you how to use your browser to find stuff on the Web.

Chapter 8

SEARCHING THE WEB

T he concept of browsing the Web is a great one; clicking from link to link is a wonderful way to gather information. But the aspect that makes this process truly astounding is the seemingly endless extent of the Web. From our own perspectives as users, the Web appears to be infinite in scope. No matter how many pages you could click through in one day, there would be many more new pages the next day!

NOTE

Netscape and AOL users: This chapter was taken from *Mastering Internet Explorer 4*. Searching works in a similar way in most browsers, but Netscape users should check out the notes throughout the text that let you know about the ways that Navigator works differently from IE 4. AOL users should refer to Chapter 12, which talks about searching and AOL.

The trick to using the Web is often just being able to find what you want, and that's what we're going to talk about in this

Adapted from *Mastering Internet Explorer 4*,
by Gene Weisskopf and Pat Coleman
ISBN 0-7821-2133-0   960 pages $44.99

chapter. There are many ways to find information on the Web, and you can use any number of them to corral material. The process of searching the Web can be as simple as:

1. Click the Search button on the toolbar.

2. In the Explorer bar on the left side of the window, select the search site you want to use.

NOTE

Netscape users: Netscape doesn't have an equivalent of the Explorer bar. Instead of following Step 2, you should select a search engine in the page that appears.

3. Enter some keywords to describe what you want.

4. Click the Go button (it may be labeled Submit, Seek, or Search, depending on which search site you're using), and wait a few seconds while the results appear.

5. Click any of the links that were found to open that site, and see if that site contains what you want.

You can follow many paths while making a search, as you'll see in the sections that follow.

PERFORMING A SEARCH IN YOUR BROWSER

You can initiate a search in several ways. Each of them can end up taking you to the same site, so feel free to experiment with them all to find the method that seems the most convenient.

You'll find that there are generally two ways to search the Web:

By keyword   Search for all pages that contain the keywords you specify. If you query with the keywords *bicycle* and *tours*, you'll find any pages that contain either one or both of those words, even if the mention is only a short "We do not conduct bicycle tours."

By topic   Browse through categories of topics until you find the category that interests you. You might start at the Leisure category, continue through the Travel subcategory, then on to a Bicycling subcategory, and finally into a Touring category for links to Web sites that relate to bicycle touring.

ENDLESSLY INDEXING THE WEB

The ability to search the Web for specific sites or files relies on one tiny factor: the existence of searching and indexing sites that you can access to perform the search. These sites are often known as Web spiders, crawlers, or robots, because they endlessly and automatically search the Web and index the content they find.

Search sites literally create huge databases of all the words in all the pages they index, and you can search those databases simply by entering the keywords you want to find. Despite the size of this vast store of information, they can usually return the results to you in a second or two. This is definitely a Herculean task with Sisyphean overtones (sorry about the mixed myths), because the Web is huge and continues to grow with no end in sight. Plus, a search engine must regularly return to pages it's already indexed because those pages may have changed and will need to be indexed again. Don't forget that many pages are removed from the Web each day and that a search engine must at some point remove those now invalid URLs from its database.

We'll be looking at some of the more popular search sites on the Web in this chapter. To give you an idea of just how big a job it is to search and index the Web, the AltaVista search site at www.altavista. digital.com recently reported that its Web index as of that day covered 31 million pages from 1,158,000 host names on 627,000 servers. AltaVista also had indexed 4 million articles from 14,000 newsgroups. On top of that, this search site is accessed more than 31 million times each day.

Keeping track of what's on the Web is definitely a job for that infinite number of monkeys we've always heard about.

Searching with the Explorer Bar

When you want to perform a search of the Web in Internet Explorer, you begin with the Explorer bar, which you can open by selecting View ➢ Explorer Bar ➢ Search, or clicking the Search button on the toolbar. Internet Explorer opens its Explorer bar, the separate pane on the left side of its window, while the page you had been viewing is displayed in the right pane. Figure 8.1 shows Internet Explorer with its window split into the two panes.

TIP

You can close the search bar by choosing View ➤ Explorer Bar ➤ None, clicking the Search button on the toolbar, or clicking the Close button at the top of the Explorer bar. In this way, you can toggle the search bar open or closed while still retaining the results of the last search you performed.

Once the Explorer bar is open, performing the search is as easy as entering the keywords you want to search for and selecting a search site from the list. For example, in Figure 8.1, I entered the search criteria **Form 1040** in the text-entry field (see *Searching the Web by Keywords* for tips on using quotes and logical operators when you create your query), and I selected the site named Infoseek. To perform the search, simply click the Seek button.

NOTE

Netscape users: Netscape doesn't have a search bar. To begin a search in Netscape, click the Search button. You'll be taken to the Net Search Web page, where you can select a search engine to use. Once you've selected a search engine, enter the keywords you want to search for. The results will appear in the browser window.

In a second or two (or more if the Internet or the search site you chose is having a busy day), the results of the search will appear in the Explorer bar, as shown in Figure 8.2. In this example, some 1,904 results were found, although only the first 10 are displayed in the search bar. You can click a link at the bottom of the results to view the next 10.

NOTE

If none of the results looks right, you can create an entirely new search by entering new keywords into the text-entry field and clicking the Seek button, or by selecting a different search site and starting from that one.

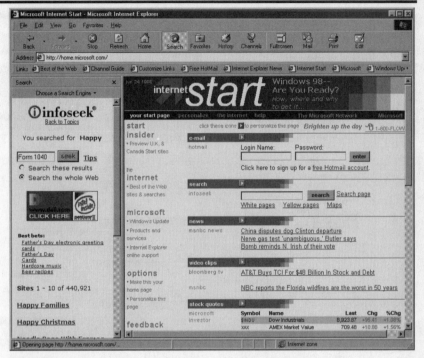
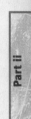

FIGURE 8.1: The Explorer bar allows you to perform a search in one pane and then sample its results while keeping those results on the screen.

Each result is a link to the page that was found to contain the keywords you entered. The Infoseek search site, like most others, arranges the resulting links in order of their likelihood of matching your query. If you point to one of the links with your mouse, a ToolTip displays information about it, as shown below:

- ▶ A short description of the target page, or the first few lines of text found on that page

- ▶ A percentage that describes the likelihood that this page meets your search criteria

- ▶ The size of the result's target file, which gives you fair warning before you decide to open it

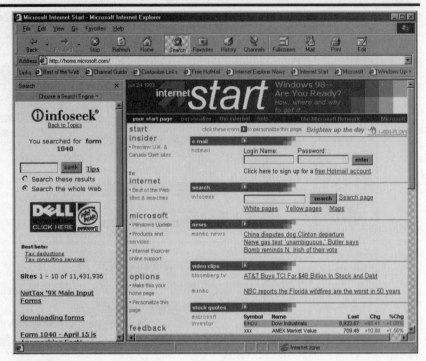

FIGURE 8.2:   After you click the Seek button in Internet Explorer, the results of the search will appear as links in the search bar.

▶ The URL of the target page, so you'll have an idea of where this file resides

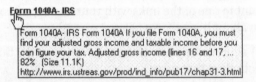

In Internet Explorer, you can click a link in the search bar to open its target in the right pane. Figure 8.3 shows Internet Explorer after one of the links in the Explorer bar was clicked. The target page appears on the right, where you're free to work in it as you would with any other page. In fact, if this looks like a page you'll want to spend some time with, click the Search button to close the Explorer bar so you'll have the entire screen for the target page.

NOTE

Netscape users: Since Navigator doesn't have a search bar, when you click a link from a search engine, you'll leave the search site in order to view the site you've found. To get back to your search results, you can simply use the Back button in your browser.

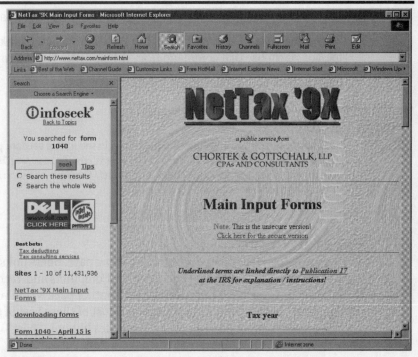

FIGURE 8.3: When you click a link in the Explorer bar, its target is opened in the right pane.

TIP

When you're viewing one of the resulting pages from a search and you like what you see, don't forget to add that page to your Favorites menu. That way you'll be able to return to that page without performing another search. See *Saving the Results of a Search* later in this chapter.

Later in this chapter, you'll read about creating more complex queries on some of the other search sites. Now let's look another way to perform searches, using Microsoft's own aggregate search page.

Searching with Microsoft's Search the Web and Best of the Web Pages

You can perform a variety of searches through two of Microsoft's pages:

Best of the Web   Click the Best of the Web button on the Links toolbar, or choose that command from the Favorites ➢ Links menu.

Search the Web   Choose Go ➢ Search the Web.

NOTE

Netscape users: If you'd like use the pages discussed in this section, you can check out Best of the Web at http://home.microsoft.com/exploring/exploring.asp, and you can check out Search the Web at http://home.microsoft.com/access/allinone.asp.

Best of the Web

This page, which is also called the Start Exploring page, offers links to a variety of topics such as Business and Finance, Computers and Technology, Living, and News. Each link takes you to another page where you'll find more links to sites within that category. (Most of these best of the Web sites are generally solid, well-established sites but only "best" according to someone at Microsoft.)

The links you'll find here are updated frequently, so when you have a spare moment, you may want to stop by and see what's new.

Search the Web

On the Best of the Web page, you'll find a group of icons labeled Search the Web. Each icon is a link that leads you to a different area of Microsoft's Search the Web page, which is shown in Figure 8.4. You can also access this page in Internet Explorer with the Go ➢ Search the Web command. Its URL is home.microsoft.com/access/allinone.asp.

The Search the Web page offers you a huge variety of search engines and options. To perform a search through one of the search sites, simply click that site's name. The page for the site you select is then displayed in the right side of the window, where you can enter the keywords you want to search for and click the Go button (named Seek on the Infoseek site).

The results page will open from the Infoseek site in this case, not the Microsoft site and will display the results as links you can click. You can continue to use the Infoseek site if you want, or return to the Search the Web page to perform a different type of search.

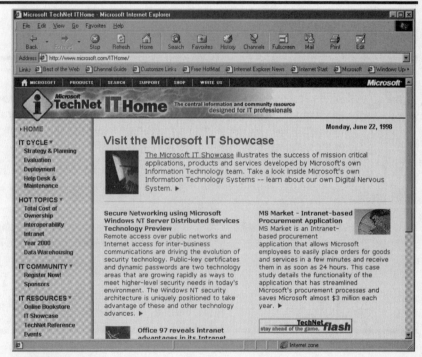

FIGURE 8.4: The Search the Web page lets you perform a search from a variety of search sites.

TIP

When you have a results page open with its list of result links, such as at Infoseek, you don't have to leave that page in order to follow one of those links. Simply right-click a link and choose Open in New Window from the shortcut menu. The target will be displayed in a new browserwindow, leaving the search page available in the other window. Press Alt+Tab or click the taskbar to switch back to the search page as needed.

Searching with the Address Toolbar

You can also perform a search right from the Address toolbar in your browser. Begin a query in the Address toolbar with the word Go or Find or with a question mark. Follow that with the topic you're interested in, for example, you might try any of the following three searches:

```
go weather Honolulu

find "border collie"

? "12-meter yacht"
```

SAVING THE RESULTS OF A SEARCH

When you perform a search that returns a list of pages, don't forget that you might want to save some of those pages so that you can return to them in the future. You can save the results of a search in several ways:

▶ Choose File ➤ Save As and save the page that displays the list of search results to your local disk, so you can open that file at any time to access those links.

▶ Right-click a link in the search results list, or open that page and add that page to your Favorites menu (your Bookmarks menu in Netscape).

▶ Open a page and save it to your local disk.

▶ Copy selected text or images from a page to another document.

SEARCHING THE WEB BY KEYWORDS

The most common way to search the Web is by entering keywords: Show me all pages that contain the words "cooking" and "French." In not much more than an instant, you'll be presented with a list of links to pages that contain those words. At many sites you can search the Web or newsgroups by keywords, and with most you go through the following steps:

1. Select the search site you want in your browser windowor open the home page for that site.

2. Enter the keywords you're searching for in a data-entry field.

3. Click the Go or Search button.

4. Wait a second or two while the search site scans through its database and displays a page of results. For most search sites, each result includes a title for the page (based on the page's HTML title), which is actually a link right to that page, and a short description of the page.

5. Click one of the result links to open that page.

TIP

When you open a page via a result link from a search page, that page will contain the words you were searching for. But there's no guarantee that those words will be used in a context that's meaningful to you. Therefore, you might want to the Edit ➤ Find (Ctrl+F) command to find your keywords on that page and see whether they are relevant.

The differences between the various keyword search sites are minor compared with the tremendous job any one of them can do for you. After all, how would you like to sift through a few dozen *million* pages trying to find those that contain a few specific words?

Some of the more popular keyword search sites include:

Search Engine	URL
AltaVista	www.altavista.digital.com
Infoseek	www.infoseek.com
WebCrawler	www.webcrawler.com
Lycos	www.lycos.com
HotBot	www.hotbot.com

Performing a search by keyword can really be quite simple, but it can also be somewhat of an art. You'll get a glimmer of this the first time a search site finds several million pages that contain your keywords.

WARNING

Searching the Web is one time that you might run into a Web site whose content you find inappropriate or just plain disgusting. No matter what your tastes or moral standards might be, there's bound to be a site somewhere that flies off the scale of your Taste-o-Meter. So use caution when browsing through the list of results from a search, and realize that although all of them contain some or all the words or phrases you were searching for, some of these topics may not be what you wanted at all.

Part ii

The search process will vary somewhat between the search sites, so you may need to use a somewhat different syntax to perform the same search at different sites. Nonetheless, some concepts apply to all of them, and you can generally follow some rules with success.

Although every keyword-search site claims to search the entire Web, performing the same query at different search sites will produce different results. This phenomenon might only have to do with how recently each site updated the pages that happened to be contained in your results. It might also have to do with how well the various sites carry on their searches and index their results. Whatever the differences, if a search is an important one that will have a limited number of results, taking that search to several sites will ensure that you're covering the possibilities.

Searching for a Simple Series of Words

The easiest way to perform a keyword search is to simply enter the words and hit the Go button. Let's try out a simple search at the AltaVista search site (www.altavista.digital.com).

If you're interested in bicycling in the Pacific Northwest, simply enter **bicycling in the Pacific Northwest** in the search field and click the Search button. In an instant or two, the results will be displayed on the page, as shown in Figure 8.5.

TIP

According to the folks who know at AltaVista, about 75 percent of all Web pages are in English, which can make it difficult when you'd like to search for pages in another language. AltaVista has thought about that, and implemented multi-langage searches. Just select a language from the drop-down menu before you click the Search button.

Notice that AltaVista tells you how many pages (documents) were found in its index; in this case it's 71,750 (see Figure 8.5). Only the first 10 are shown; you access the rest via links at the bottom of the page.

At the bottom of the page, you'll also see how many occurrences were found for *each* of the words you specified: 31,384 for *bicycling*, 273,755 for *Northwest*, and 857,780 for *Pacific*. If you think that's a lot, notice also that the words *in* and *the* were found hundreds of millions of times but, thankfully, were ignored.

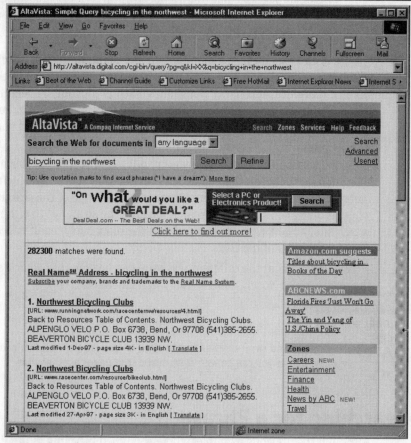

FIGURE 8.5: Performing a simple search at AltaVista produces a wide range of relevant pages.

TIP

Even though the relevance of the results may range far and wide, they are ranked so that the pages with the most likely matches are at or near the top of the list. AltaVista assigns the highest rank to pages on which the keywords appear closest to the beginning of the page, such as in its title. Below that in ranking are pages on which the keywords appear close to one another. Finally, pages are ranked by the number of your keywords that appear within them (but not the number of times they might appear in a page).

AltaVista looks for pages that contain any of the words you specify, which is an OR relationship—find pages that contain this word *or* this word *or* this word, and so on. Some sites, such as HotBot, by default do the opposite with your simple search and will only find pages that contain all the words you specify. This is an AND relationship—find pages that contain this word *and* this word *and* this word, and so on.

Keep this issue in mind when you try out a new search site, because the difference between the two styles is astronomical in scope. Including more words in an AltaVista search broadens the scope of the search, whereas doing so in a HotBot search narrows the scope. With either search site, however, you're assured that the most likely result pages will appear at the top of the list.

Now let's look at the different ways you can narrow your search so that the results more closely match what you really want.

TIP

AltaVista and several other search sites let you create a customized search page, just as you can do with customized start pages at other sites.

Searching for a Phrase

Although the previous example, where you typed **bicycling in the Pacific Northwest**, seemed like a reasonably specific query, the AltaVista search site included all pages that contained any of those words, producing the broadest possible list of results.

To really enter a specific phrase as your query, enclose the text in double quotation marks and type **"bicycling in the Pacific Northwest"**.

When you enter keywords in this way, most search sites will look only for this exact phrase and will ignore all pages that might contain only a word or two. For example, the results of searching for *sled dogs* would return thousands of pages that happen to include the word *sled* or *dogs* anywhere in the page, and not just those pages that contain both words in the context of dogs that pull sleds. This would be the time to enclose the phrase in quotes and type **"sled dogs"**. Doing so would return only pages that include that specific phrase and would shorten the list of results drastically.

Unfortunately, in the bicycling example, the phrase we used might be a little too specific. Only that exact string of text will be looked for, which could easily eliminate some good bicycling pages that might not happen to include it. What might work better is to limit the search only to those pages that contain all these words.

Requiring That a Word Must or Must Not Exist

To require that a word in your query be found in the resulting pages, precede the word with a plus sign. Using our bicycling example, in AltaVista you could search only for pages that include both the word, "bicycling" and the phrase, "Pacific Northwest" and eliminate pages that contain only one of those (about 99 percent of the pages found in the first search!). To do so, type **+bicycling +"Pacific Northwest"**.

To exclude a word or a phrase from a search, precede it with a minus sign. For example, when searching for information about a mouse for your computer, you could eliminate some obvious mouse references to shorten the list of results, by typing **+mouse +computer −Mickey −rodent −rat -pet**.

NOTE

Use only lowercase letters in a query unless you want the search to be case-sensitive. In other words, searching for "president" will find all instances of that word, whereas searching for "President" will only find those instances in which the first letter is capitalized. However, be sure to capitalize words when you only want that specific spelling. For example, when searching for a restaurant named *The Brown Cow*, spell it exactly that way to avoid all pages that simply refer to brown cows.

Using Logical Operators

All the search sites have some method for you to specify the logical operators AND and OR in your queries (at the AltaVista site, you can use these
operators when you choose their Advanced search option). You use OR to
require that two words or phrases can appear separately in a page; you
use AND to require that both appear together somewhere in that page. In
the previous section, you saw how preceding a keyword with the plus sign
makes that a required word in the query. If you precede two words with a
plus sign, such as by typing **+mouse +computer** you are creating an AND
relationship. You are looking for *mouse* and *computer* in the same document. If you did not use both plus signs, you would be creating an OR
relationship.

At the HotBot site, you can select the relationship from a drop-down
menu. Choosing "all the words" creates an AND relationship between
the words or phrases you enter in the query. If you choose "any of the
words", it's an OR relationship between them all.

At the WebCrawler site, you can literally include the words AND and
OR in your queries (the case of the words doesn't matter) by typing, for
example, **mouse and computer**.

NOTE

Because AltaVista ranks a result higher if that page contains more of your query
words, there's less reason for you to worry about creating a logical relationship
between the query terms.

You can create an OR relationship in an AltaVista query to include
words that might relate to the subject you're interested in, such as by typing **bike biking bicycle bicycling +"Pacific Northwest"**.

By including multiple variations of a word, you may be able to find
more pages that are on your topic of interest. The next section shows how
you can widen or narrow a search by using wildcards.

Broadening a Search with Wildcards

You can use the asterisk, *, in an AltaVista query to search for any and all
characters in place of the asterisk, so that typing **bicycl*** will help you find
bicycle , *bicycles*, and *bicycling*, and typing **bicycl*s** will help you find
only *bicycles*.

WARNING

The asterisk is truly a wildcard, in that it will find all the words that include the text you've entered before or after it, not only those words you might expect to find. In other words, the examples above would also find all occurrences of *bicyclette* or *bicyclettes* on a French Web site.

Another reason to try to include wildcards whenever you can is that, although computers never make mistakes, people just love to! While working with these queries on AltaVista, I mistakenly entered the query **bicyl***, which returned 700 pages in the results! In fact, the first few dozen results contained that misspelling in their page titles, which is the key ranking factor for AltaVista.

Granted, those pages undoubtedly also contained many instances of the correct spelling of bicycle, so they would have been found had we spelled the word correctly. Nonetheless, experiment with the use of wildcards or with variant spellings if the word you are searching for:

▶ Might only be included once or twice in a page, so that you would miss it if the spelling did not match yours precisely.

▶ Is often misspelled, such as *lazer* for *laser*, or *Laser Jet* for *LaserJet*.

▶ Has accepted variations in its spelling, such as *CD ROM* and *CD-ROM* or *floppy disc* and *floppy disk*.

Searching through Page Elements

At most of the search sites, you can limit your search to specific elements of the Web page. For example, at AltaVista you preface what you're looking for with the name of the page component and a colon. At other search sites, look at the Help page to see how you should format a query.

To search for the word *bicycle* only in page titles in AltaVista, type **title:bicycle**. Only the titles of the pages in this Web index will be searched, and all other portions of the page will be ignored. Some of the other page components you can search include:

text   searches only the normal text in the page that you would see were you viewing the page in Internet Explorer.

link   searches only within HTML anchor tags in a page, allowing you to find all pages that contain a link to whitehouse.gov, for example (see the next section).

image   searches only within HTML image tags, allowing you to find references to specific image files, such as `monalisa.jpg`.

domain   searches only within pages from the domain you specify, allowing you to limit a search only to URLs that are in the *gov* (U.S. government) or *uk* (United Kingdom) domains, for example.

You can combine these constraints to find, for example, pages that have *bicycle* in their title, the word *touring* in the normal text on the page, and are only in the British domain:

```
title:bicycle text:touring domain:uk
```

At AltaVista, enter these page component keywords in lowercase, don't forget the colon, and don't include a space on either side of the colon.

Finding Who Links to Whom

If you have a Web site of your own, you'd probably like to know what other sites on the Web contain links to your site's URL. Several search sites make it easy for you to perform this type of search by using the *link* keyword mentioned in the previous section.

At the AltaVista and Infoseek sites, enter the query in this way: **link:http://www.sample.com**.

At the HotBot search site, enter the URL and set the search options so you are searching on *the Web* for *Links to this URL*.

SEARCHING THE WEB BY CATEGORY

So far in this chapter we've looked at how you can search the Web for all pages that contain one or more keywords or phrases that you specify. As mentioned at the beginning, searching the Web in this way is much like looking up a word in the index of a book, where you will find the page numbers of all references to that word in the book. If you think of the Web as the book and URLs as page numbers, you've got the idea.

Now we're going to look at another way to search the Web that isn't quite so literal. With this method, you go to the search site and browse through a category of topics. This method of searching the Web is more like browsing through the table of contents of a book, where the book is broken down by categories (chapters or sections). You can turn to a chapter that seems to relate to the topic you're interested in, but there's no way to tell just what you'll find there. You might be disappointed, or you might be quite surprised to find other topics that mesh quite nicely with the one you wanted.

NOTE

Most of the concept search sites can also perform a literal, keyword search of the Web, so you can attack your query from either direction.

Some of the more popular concept search sites include:

Search Engine	URL
Yahoo	www.yahoo.com
Excite	www.excite.com
Magellan	www.mckinley.com

Yahoo is probably the most well-known site, no doubt because it was the first. The Magellan site is owned by the company that owns the Excite search site, and it uses the same database of Web sites. But Magellan is notable because it has a team of editors who actually visit thousands of sites, rating them and writing short reviews of them. Magellan also has a special category of *Green Light sites* that contain no material that would be unsuitable for children (according to the standards in effect at Magellan).

When you access the Yahoo site, you'll be presented with the page shown in Figure 8.6. As you can see, there is a familiar search field at the top of the page, but beneath that are two columns of categories. You can click one of the categories to open a page of subcategory links, and you can continue to click until you narrow the search to a page that contains links to actual Web sites in the chosen subcategory.

TIP

Some Yahoo categories have an [Xtra] link tacked onto them. Each of these opens a page of current news headlines about the topic. For example, click the [Xtra] link on the Health category to see headlines relating to issues in health.

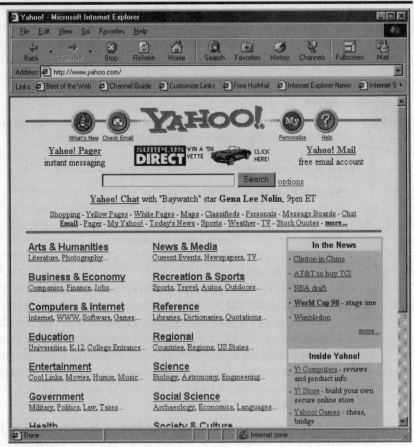

FIGURE 8.6: At the Yahoo search site, you can click your way through categories of topics to find the one that interests you. (Copyright ©1994–1997 Yahoo! Inc. All rights reserved.)

Choosing the Right Path

Before you can even begin a search through the categories of Yahoo, you need to have an idea not only of what you're looking for but also of *why* you're looking for it! For example, suppose you want to find sites that relate to bicycling. Sounds simple, but realize that categories can overlap. Many categories could include some aspect of bicycling.

Are you interested in bicycling from a rider's standpoint? If so, you might start with the Recreation and Sports category. If you're looking for a list of bike stores on the Web, you might start with the Business and Economy category. If laws relating to bicycles in your state are your primary interest, you could start with the Regional category.

Some topics are more easily categorized and will be easier to find. For example, if you want to learn about creating Web pages, you could click your way through the following links (in Yahoo syntax, categories are separated from subcategories with a colon):

```
Computers and Internet: Internet: World Wide Web: Authoring
```

Sometimes following a minor interest by browsing through Yahoo can produce impressive results. For example, while you were on your way to the Authoring page in Yahoo, you might take a sidetrack through the categories

```
Computers and Internet: Information and Documentation: Data
Formats: HTML
```

You would find a wealth of information that is only slightly off the subject you were intending to find, but surrounds it, overlaps it, and expands upon it.

Clicking through the Yahoo Categories

Let's attack the bicycling topic from a rider's point of view and say that we want to know about bicycling in the Pacific Northwest, which we searched for earlier with a keyword search.

Start by clicking the Recreation and Sports link on the Yahoo home page. This opens another page that lists the main subcategories for Recreation and Sports, including Amusement and Theme Parks, Automotive, Dance, Drugs, Motorcycles, and Travel. There are no specific links to bicycles, so we're still feeling our way along at our current location:

```
Recreation:
```

We could try the Travel link to branch out in a travel-related direction, but let's click the Sports link to head in a more bicycle-specific direction. The Sports link opens a page of sports-related links, one of which is called Cycling (no, not Bicycling; you have to keep your wits about you when you're looking for subjects of interest).

Part II

TIPS FOR NAVIGATING YAHOO

Each main category on the home page has several popular subcategories listed below it. If one of those subcategories looks relevant, click it to go directly to that topic's page.

To the right of many subcategory links in Yahoo, enclosed in parentheses, is the number of Web sites that will be found within this category. For example, if you see

`Baseball (2778)`

this means that a total of 2,778 Web sites are listed within the Baseball category. This doesn't mean that all those sites are listed on the next page. Rather, it means that the Baseball link will lead you to that many sites beneath it.

When a subcategory is followed by an at symbol, such as

`Recreation: Sports: Art@`

this category is not in a direct path from your current location. In this case, the Art category actually belongs in

`Arts: Thematic: Sports`

In other words, the Art link is one instance in which categories overlap.

Keep in mind that Yahoo places the links to Web sites (if there are any) beneath the category links on the page, so be sure to check down below, as there just might be a site that you will want to investigate.

As shown here, at the top of each Yahoo category page, you'll find the path that you've taken to reach the current category, as well as a search field. The path gives you a quick frame of reference for your current location. You can use the search field as you would a literal keyword search site, and you can choose whether to search all of Yahoo or only those sites that fall within the current category (Sports in this case).

TIP

The larger Yahoo categories will have a Sub Category Listing link near the top of the page, which you can click to see the entire list of subcategories for a topic. The topics will be arranged in an indented, outline format. These lists can be *very* long, however, so don't bother opening one unless you're going to be searching for a variety of subcategories within that topic.

Clicking the Cycling link is an obvious choice at this point. It opens a page that contains not just more subcategory links, but some actual links to Web sites that fall into this category (remember to look below the category links for the site links). Eureka! We're getting down to the details.

You can look at any of the site links that seem interesting, but if none do the trick, you should still be happy that the category links on this page

    Recreation: Sports: Cycling

are much more relevant. In fact, just about any one of them might lead to topics that relate to bicycling in the Pacific Northwest. This is actually a hurdle of sorts because it leaves too many options open. But it is also an opportunity to explore other aspects of bicycling that might end up showing you much more than you expected to find.

For our search, clicking the Tours and Events link seems like a good choice. In fact, right at the top of its target page at

    Recreation: Sports: Cycling: Tours and Events

is the category link Tour Operators@, which steps outside of our current category and points to

    Business and Economy: Companies: Sports: Cycling: Tour
    Operators

Before you follow that tempting link, however, take a look on the current page at the links to Web sites, as shown in Figure 8.7. All of them relate to companies or organizations that conduct bicycle tours, many of which operate in the Pacific Northwest.

Where to go from here? You can see that finding sites via categories is a subjective and variable undertaking. If you were to repeat a search a day or two later, you might take a completely different route through the categories.

Part II

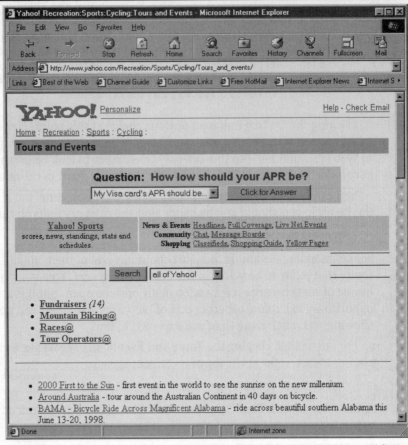

FIGURE 8.7:   As you narrow your search through the Yahoo categories, you'll find Web site links outnumbering the category links. (Copyright ©1994–1997 Yahoo! Inc. All rights reserved.)

FINDING PEOPLE ON THE INTERNET

Some search sites specialize in finding people, and you'll be amazed at how fast you can locate that high school chum you used to hang out with or a dozen people who all go by your name.

Of course, you can use any of the search sites we've discussed so far in this chapter to find people's names when they appear in Web pages. Simply search for the person's name, but be sure to enclose it in quotes to get only that name.

With the people-finding search sites, you can find an individual's e-mail address, telephone number, or mailing address. If you want to find out where that person is right now, well, you'll have to wait a few years for that.

You can access several of these sites from Microsoft's search page, Search the Web, which you can open with Go ➤ Search the Web or by going directly to:

```
home.microsoft.com/access/allinone.asp
```

All these people-finding sites are quite simple to use, and you'll know soon enough if the results are helpful or not.

Let's try the WhoWhere site as an example. You can access it either from Microsoft's Search the Web page or at the URL www.whowhere.com. Figure 8.8 shows the WhoWhere home page.

You can search for a person's e-mail address from this page or for his or her phone number and mailing address. For example, to find an e-mail address, simply enter the person's name in the Name field (quotes aren't required), and in the Domain field enter their e-mail server domain name, such as att.net or aol.com.

TIP

If the person's name is reasonably unique, you can try entering only his or her name. You might get lucky and find only the person you're looking for or perhaps just a few people with that same name. With any luck, you'll be able to decide which one is most likely the one you're looking for.

Click the Find button, and in a second or two the list of results will be displayed. Each result is a *mailto* link to that person's e-mail address, so clicking a name creates a new message to that person in your e-mail program.

To find a person's mailing address and phone number, enter as much as you know about that person in the Last Name (required), First Name, City, and State fields, and then click the Find button. The results won't be a link this time, but will be the information you might find in that person's local phone book.

If you want to ensure that someone else will be able to find you through this site, you can register your own name, e-mail and mailing addresses, and phone number with WhoWhere via the Add/Update link. If you're so inclined, you can also add more personal information about yourself, such as your hobbies, your place of employment, and where you went to school.

You'll also want to check out the other search features available at the WhoWhere site, which you can see in the left-hand column in Figure 8.8.

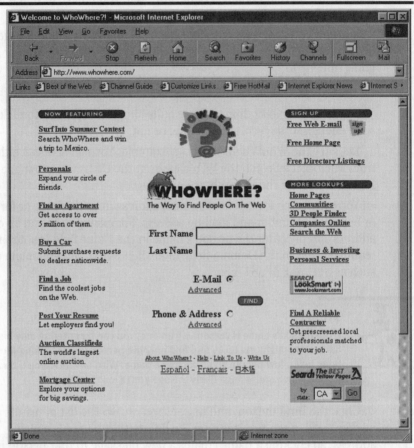

FIGURE 8.8: You can search for people through search sites such as the WhoWhere site.

TIP

One of our favorite search sites on the Internet is that of the United States Postal Service, where you can find the Zip code for any street address and also verify the correct formatting of an address. You can access this site at www.usps.gov/postofc/.

SEARCHING THROUGH NEWSGROUPS

Newsgroups are the place to go to exchange information with people of similar interests. You can use Outlook Express News to access Usenet (the User Network) and its tens of thousands of newsgroups. You can read articles (messages) that were posted by other people, respond to those that interest you or for which you have an answer, post your own questions, and generally just browse about to see what looks good.

Usenet has a mountain of information but, just like the Web, finding what's relevant is the hard part. Fortunately, most of the Web search sites also let you search newsgroups. Creating a query is much the same as when you search the Web. However, the results will often range far and wide in relevance, because a newsgroup article is simply one person sending a message that happens to contain the words or phrases you were searching for.

Searching through Newsgroups at AltaVista

To search through newsgroups at the AltaVista search site, choose Usenet instead of The Web from the drop-down menu labeled Search. Then enter your query as you would when searching the Web, and click the Search button when you're finished.

For example, to find all newsgroup articles that mention bicycling and the Pacific Northwest, you could try typing **+bicycling +"Pacific Northwest"**. Figure 8.9 shows the results from this query.

NOTE
Don't forget that a message that includes your search keywords doesn't necessarily relate at all to the act of bicycling in the Pacific Northwest. The mention of your search terms could be as irrelevant as "my friend John likes bicycling to work . . . doesn't Microsoft have a subsidiary called the Pacific Northwest?"

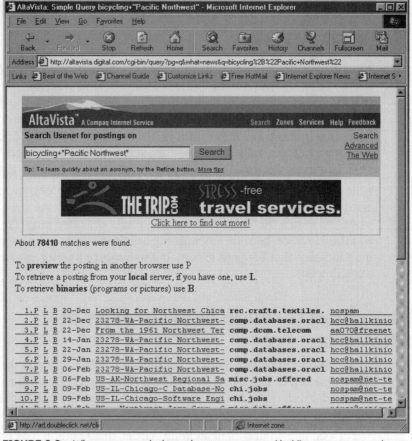

FIGURE 8.9: When you search through newsgroups at AltaVista, you can read the articles in the results list or send e-mail to an article's author.

Looking from left to right in Figure 8.9, each item in the AltaVista results list contains the following:

▶ The item number and a small icon; click either one to open this article in a new browserwindow.

▶ The L link, which you can click to open the article in your news-reader program.

▶ The B link, which you can click to download the article as a plain text file. This would allow you to convert any binary files that are attached to the article, such as an image file.

▶ The date the article was posted.

▶ The article header (title), in which the author describes the subject of the article; click the header to open the article in your browser.

▶ The newsgroup to which the article was posted.

▶ The e-mail address of the article's author (which may or may not be the author's actual address).

NOTE

To post articles to a newsgroup, you'll need to use a newsreader program such as Outlook Express News, although the Web site Deja News (discussed next) allows you to read and write to newsgroups through your Web browser.

You can narrow your newsgroup search to specific elements of a newsgroup article, just as you can with Web pages when searching the Web (see *Searching through Page Elements* earlier in this chapter). To search the text only in article headers, use *subject*, as in:

```
subject:bicycling
```

Other elements you can reference include *from* (the sender's e-mail address), *newsgroups* (the newsgroup name), and *summary* (the body of the article).

Searching through Newsgroups at Deja News

Perhaps the premier site for newsgroup-related information is Deja News at www.dejanews.com. Its search engine not only indexes all the articles that pass through thousands and thousands of newsgroups, but also archives them so that they'll always be available (Deja News claims to have upwards of 100 million articles). Most newsgroup servers regularly delete articles after a few days or weeks to make room for newer ones, so Deja News is the place to go when you're searching for in-depth information or when you want to recover articles you saw in a newsgroup months earlier.

You can also search for newsgroups by topic. Instead of getting a list of articles in the results, you get a list of newsgroups that are ranked by the number of times your query keywords are contained in their articles. This not only gives you a quick look at which newsgroups might be of interest to you, but you can also click one of the results to display a list of headers from all the articles in that newsgroup that contain your query keywords. You can then click one of the articles to open it in Internet Explorer.

With the Power Search feature in Deja News, you can perform a very detailed search of newsgroup articles, both in their current index of newsgroups (compiled from articles during the previous two or three months) or in their archived index of newsgroups. Figure 8.10 shows the Power Search form where you specify any or all of the criteria for the search.

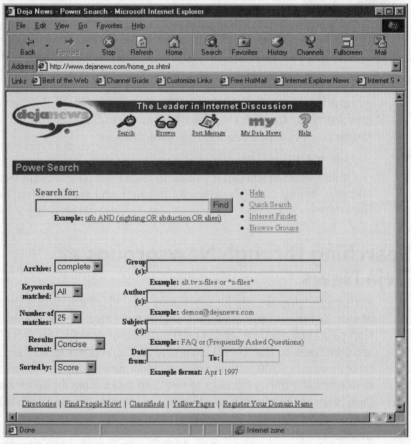

FIGURE 8.10: With the Deja News Power Search, you can easily fine-tune the scope of a Usenet search.

To increase the power of a Power Search, you can create a Search Filter. The filter lets you narrow the scope of the search by limiting it to a range of dates, newsgroups, authors, or subjects. Plus, when you've applied a Search Filter, your search automatically looks through both the current and archived set of newsgroup articles.

NOTE

When you are creating a new newsgroup message (article) in Outlook Express News (or any other newsreader), you can specify that newsgroup search spiders exclude your article from their indexes. Simply include the text *X-no-archive: yes* in the message's first line, or look in your newsreader for a command that puts this flag in the message header. Realize that your message will still appear publicly in that newsgroup, but most spiders will respect your request and not index your article.

BEING FOUND ON THE WEB

It's important to be able to find things on the Web, but it's just as important *to be found* on the Web when you have a Web site that you don't want the world overlooking. Of course, without your doing anything at all, the pages in your site will probably be found soon enough by one or more of the search sites, as they blast through the Web, indexing all that they find.

But if you really want to make your Web site known to the world as soon as possible, you'll want to go to the search sites instead of waiting for them to find you:

▶ Include a list of relevant and somewhat relevant keywords in each page, which will ensure that your site is included in the results when someone searches for a keyword that relates to your site, even though that word may not be contained in any of your pages.

▶ Register your Web site with as many search sites as possible so that you won't have to rely on chance for them to know of your existence.

Part II

TIP

If you want to cover the most ground in the least amount of time, use services that, for a fee, will register your Web site with many search sites. You can find a list of these services in the Yahoo category Computers and Internet: Internet: World Wide Web: Announcement Services.

Of course, being found on the Web is usually the whole point, but you can also work to exclude your Web site or some of its pages from the various search sites, as you'll see later in this section.

Including Keywords in Your Pages

A Web author can take advantage of the fact that just about all search sites recognize the HTML <META> tag when they are indexing a Web page. This tag allows the author to specify the description of the page, as well as a list of keywords. Both types of information are critical to the likelihood of your site being found through a query in a search site.

By supplying relevant keywords, your site is more likely to be included in the results of a relevant query, and the description ensures that a person reading those results will have a clear understanding of your site's purpose. The keywords you supply for a page are a supplement to the normal indexing of the page, not a substitution for it.

The <META> tag is an informational tag for Web servers and browsers, not for the person reading the page. You can use two of these tags to provide a description and keywords for Web robots that visit your site, using the format:

```
<META NAME="description" CONTENT="This is a description of
the page">

<META NAME="keywords" CONTENT="keyword1, keyword2, keyword3">
```

NOTE

If you don't provide the description in this way, a search site's indexing engine will most likely use the first few lines of text in the page, without making any value judgements about whether that text is a helpful description.

For example, if you run the Superman Fans Web site, you might include the following tags at the beginning of its home page (they're shown on multiple lines for clarity):

```
<TITLE>Superman Fans Home Page</TITLE>
```

```
<META NAME="description" CONTENT=
"Looking for the Man of Steel? We have a complete list of every
Superman comic, and lots more.">
<META NAME="keywords" CONTENT="comic, comic book, clark kent,
krypton, kryptonite, daily planet">
```

When someone searches for *Superman* at AltaVista, the results would look something like the following:

Superman Fans Home Page

> Looking for the Man of Steel? We have a complete list of every Superman comic, and lots more.

http://www.sample.com/ - size 15K - 12 Dec 97

AltaVista allows a maximum of 1024 characters in the description and list of keywords and ensures that the words in both those items will be included in its index. Infoseek uses a maximum of 200 characters in the description and 1000 characters in the keywords. Before you include the <META> tag in pages in your Web site, check with a few other search sites to get their current rules.

WARNING

In years past, search sites employed a less sophisticated algorithm when indexing Web pages. If a word you were searching for appeared many times in a page, that page would show up at the top of the list of results. This encouraged some Web authors to include a few hundred repetitions of a keyword in their pages, simply to get a higher ranking in a list of search results. This practice, often known as *spamming*, is not only frowned upon, but is also no longer effective with today's search sites. In fact, most search sites will either ignore repeated occurrences of a word or actually exclude that page from their index.

Registering with a Search Site

Most search sites let you send your Web site's URL to them so the pages in your site can be included in their indexes. This process of registering is an informal one, in that it costs nothing and requires little more than sending them your URL.

At the AltaVista search site, you can register a URL by clicking the Add/Remove URL link that you'll find at the bottom of the home page. On the Adding a New URL page that is opened, you simply enter the URL of your Web site (which must begin with HTTP) and click the Submit URL button. That's really all there is to it.

AltaVista asks that you send just one URL for your entire site, which might as well be the home page for that site. A new URL is usually added to their index within one day. Their searching program will snoop throughout your site and find and index all the other pages.

The Infoseek search site has a similar registration process, but that site does not tell you to submit just one page from the site. You can either register each page individually or create a list of pages and submit them all in one e-mail.

The easiest way to register your site at Yahoo is to locate the category within which you think your site belongs and then click the Add URL button, which you'll find at the top of the page. This opens the registration page, where you enter the URL of your site and a title and description for its listing in Yahoo. You can also enter secondary categories and regional information. The more you provide, the easier it will be to find your site on Yahoo. Be sure to take note of the three or four rules pertaining to registering business sites, personal Web pages, and the like.

Removing Pages from a Search Site

Most search sites also provide a way for you to unregister (remove) a page that's already in their index. This is actually quite important, because you won't attract many visitors to your site through searching if people have to fight their way through a dozen old and now invalid URLs.

The AltaVista search site and most others will automatically remove any page whose URL can no longer be found (the infamous "error 404" message). Therefore, you can remove a page from their index immediately simply by registering the page's now invalid URL. This will cause the Web robot to check this URL, which it will find to be invalid and will therefore remove it from the index.

Excluding Pages from Search Robots

You can also exclude a page or an entire Web site from the prying robots of search sites, although you will find that there is not yet just one accepted way to do so. One method that is used by several search sites, and may yet become an accepted standard, requires that you place a special text file called ROBOTS.TXT in the root folder of the Web server. The file includes instructions to search robots that visit the site about what can be searched and what should be excluded from the search.

NOTE

The ROBOTS.TXT file does not prevent a search robot from requesting one or more pages from the site; it only asks the robots to exclude them. In other words, it's a voluntary system that allows search sites to index the Web without getting a bad reputation from Web site administrators who either don't want the extra traffic caused by robots or want to keep some pages out of the search indexes.

Here's a ROBOTS file that asks that the entire Web site be excluded by all search robots:

```
User-agent: *
Disallow: /
```

The asterisk is the wildcard that represents any and all search robots, and the slash represents the root folder of the server and, therefore, all files and folders within it.

You can also specify individual search robots and selective folders. For example, if you want to exclude the entire site from AltaVista, and you want to exclude the folders /users and /logs from every other site, the following would do the job:

```
User-agent: altavista
Disallow: /

User-agent: *
Disallow: /users

User-agent: *
Disallow: /logs
```

You can read more about using a ROBOTS file to mitigate the effect of search robots at the WebCrawler site:

```
info.webcrawler.com/mak/projects/robots/faq.html
```

You can also ask Web robots to exclude an individual page from their search, as well as all the pages that are targeted by its links, by including a <META> tag in the page:

```
<META NAME="ROBOTS" CONTENT="NOINDEX, NOFOLLOW">
```

Again, this is not yet an accepted standard, but it is respected by several of the major search sites.

WHAT'S NEXT?

The size and scope of the Internet can actually be a hurdle to finding just the information you need. With the search sites and techniques that were discussed in this chapter, you'll be well equipped to track down and analyze the tidbits you need. In the next chapter, you'll learn about Internet news.

Chapter 9

INTERNET NEWS

News, the system that exchanges public messages through the Internet, has actually been around longer than the Internet itself. Usenet, as it was originally called, began when users of two computers at universities in North Carolina started to move messages through a dial-up telephone link between their two campuses. Today, most news moves across the Internet, but there are still a few isolated users who send and receive their messages through computers that are not connected to the Internet by using a technique called *UUCP* (Unix to Unix CoPy) and even by exchanging floppy disks or magnetic tapes. In spite of these exceptions, the exchange of public messages organized by topics is commonly known as *Internet news*.

News is one of the most popular and widely used Internet services. Participants use news for fast and efficient distribution of information about academic subjects, current events, business, hobbies, and other special interests. Each topic is discussed in a

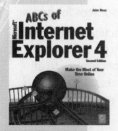

Adapted from *ABCs of Microsoft Internet Explorer*, by John Ross
ISBN 0-7821-2042-3   400 pages $19.99

separate message stream, called a *newsgroup*. There are newsgroups devoted to more than ten thousand separate topics, ranging from computer languages to popular television programs, and from cars for sale to particle physics. You might see two or three hundred new messages a day in the most popular newsgroups, but other, more obscure subjects may only get three or four messages a week.

Some newsgroups are intended for worldwide distribution; others are focused on a specific geographic region, college campus, or corporation. However, many local or regional newsgroups are distributed beyond their own borders. It's not uncommon, for example, to see a message in the Seattle.eats newsgroup from somebody who's planning to visit the area and wants to find a good seafood restaurant.

NOTE

Netscape users: Some of the information in this chapter is specific to the Internet Explorer browser. To find out about Netscape's news reader, Collabra, you'll want to read Chapter 4 in addition to this chapter.

WHAT HAPPENS IN NEWSGROUPS

If you can think of a topic, there's probably a newsgroup devoted to it. In some newsgroups, the most common messages are questions and answers or requests for help: "I just found a 1934 Crosley radio at a swap meet—can anybody tell me where to find the missing knob?" is a typical message in the newsgroup devoted to collecting and restoring antique radios and phonographs.

Because the same questions tend to come up again and again, many newsgroups contain lists of *frequently asked questions,* or FAQs. It's a good idea to look for a FAQ among the recent messages or post a message asking for a pointer to a place where you can download it, before you send your own beginner's questions to a newsgroup. For example, the FAQ for the antique radio group includes addresses for several sources for knobs.

In other groups, much of the traffic is devoted to discussions of current events related to the topic of the newsgroup. Many groups contain ongoing conversations in which one or more readers post replies to an earlier message, and then other people reply to those messages . . . . These continuing series of online replies to replies to replies are known as *threads.*

Each newsgroup has its own style. Some groups encourage newcomers; others are like the big table in the back of a local coffee shop, where the same half-dozen regulars have been gathering every day for years: strangers might be tolerated, but they're not always made welcome. After you have followed a newsgroup for a few weeks, you will begin to recognize the names and reputations of some of the regular participants and some of the shared in-jokes and local customs.

If you have experience with online services, such as CompuServe or America Online, or with non-Internet bulletin board services (BBS), the general form of Internet news will probably seem familiar to you. Internet news reaches many more users than any single online service. Discussions in other systems' conferences and forums have many features in common with Internet news, but there are many more topics and a wider variety of users than you can find in other online communities.

In most newsgroups, anybody can post a message that will automatically be distributed to every other subscriber. In order to weed out off-topic messages and prevent *ad hominem* attacks and other distractions, a few newsgroups are moderated; all messages pass through the moderator before they go back out to the newsgroup. A good moderator can keep discussions on track, send answers to common questions by e-mail, and generally keep things flowing well. Bad moderators, who insist on advancing their own opinions at the expense of those who disagree with them or who join in attacks, usually get either replaced or ignored pretty quickly.

Newsgroups are a very important part of the culture of the Internet because they encourage people to join online communities of people who share the same interests. Unlike the World Wide Web, which is still primarily a one-to-many communications medium, News is more of a many-to-many channel, where everybody can participate on a more-or-less equal footing.

Whether this is a good thing is a matter of opinion. In many newsgroups, the "noise" level of irrelevant comments and uninformed opinion is pretty high. Just because you see an article in a newsgroup, that does not mean it's automatically true or correct.

As you participate in newsgroups, it's important to remember that your postings may go to readers around the world. You can't assume that everybody who receives your messages shares your own culture and values. For example, if you're discussing the Internet itself, don't try to claim that the First Amendment protects your online freedom of speech; the American Constitution doesn't apply outside the borders of the

United States. The same thing applies to assumptions about religion. Just because you live in a small Midwestern city where everybody is either Presbyterian or Catholic, you might be exchanging messages with Hindus in Bombay or Jews in New York and Jerusalem, who might be offended by your well-meaning Christmas or Easter greetings.

If you're not prepared to defend your opinions, you may want to think twice before posting them. There's an excellent chance that somebody, someplace, will disagree and let you know about it in no uncertain terms.

The remainder of this chapter explains the way Internet news operates and describes the news client supplied in the Internet Explorer 4 suite. In addition, you'll learn about Free Agent, a freeware news client that presents the same material in a somewhat different form.

How News Is Organized

Every newsgroup has a unique name that identifies the topic of discussion within the newsgroup, and the general category, or *domain*, that includes this topic. For example, the rec.gardens newsgroup is part of the rec (short for *recreational*) domain.

Many topics have been divided into subtopics, each with a separate newsgroup, such as rec.gardens.roses, devoted to gardening information for people who grow roses. In some cases, the subtopics have been divided into still more specific groups, like rec.food.drink.coffee and rec.food.drink.tea.

The most widespread newsgroups in the seven original Usenet domains and the alternative domains that don't fit the Usenet categories. The Usenet domains are

comp	Computer-related topics
news	Topics related to Usenet news
rec	Hobbies, arts, and recreational activities
sci	Science and technology (except computers)
soc	Politics and society
talk	Debates and controversies
misc	Subjects that don't fit one of the other six categories

The alternative domains include

alt   A catch-all for alternative topics, including oddball subjects like alt.alien.visitors and alt.happy.birthday.to.me, and conferences whose originators didn't want to bother with the bureaucratic procedure involved in creating a new Usenet newsgroup

bionet   News about the biological sciences

biz   Business topics, including advertisements, which are not allowed in most other domains

clari   News from the commercial Clarinet service, supplied by United Press International, and Reuters

k12   Newsgroups for and about schools and teachers

There are several hundred other domain names, including geographic headings, institutions (such as specific universities or corporations), and network services. These secondary domains are not distributed as widely as the major ones, but your news server will probably support at least a few of them.

When you create an article for a newsgroup or a reply to somebody else's article, you send it from a client program called a *newsreader* to a news server, probably at your Internet service provider (ISP). The news server assigns a unique identity number to your article and then passes it along to all the other news servers that support the newsgroup where you posted the article.

To read news articles, you must instruct your newsreader program to complete these steps:

1. Download a list of newsgroups from the server.

2. Select the newsgroups that you want to read.

3. Download a list of available articles in a newsgroup.

4. Select and download individual articles.

With a couple of important exceptions, almost all news servers use the standard *NNTP* (Network News Transport Protocol) to exchange articles with newsreader client programs. Therefore, you can use just about any newsreader program with any server.

Part ii

USING MICROSOFT OUTLOOK EXPRESS NEWS

Outlook Express is the news and mail client supplied as part of the Internet Explorer 4 suite of Internet programs. You can open Outlook Express directly from the Windows Start menu or from the Internet Explorer browser.

To open the newsreader from the browser, use the Go ➤ News command, or click the Mail button on the toolbar and select the Read News command, as shown in Figure 9.1.

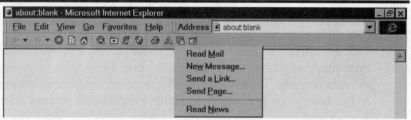

FIGURE 9.1: Use the Read News command to jump directly from the browser to the Outlook Express newsreader.

Configuring the Newsreader

Before you can start participating in newsgroups, you must tell Outlook Express where to find your news server. Outlook Express requests the information it needs to connect to your server when you install the program, but you can also change to a different server or add a new one later.

TIP

If you have accounts with more than one ISP, you may have to set up separate connection profiles for each one. Many ISPs don't allow access to their news servers unless you're connected directly to their network server.

Connecting to a New Server

To set up a new connection to a server, follow these steps:

1. Starting at the main Outlook Express screen, select Tools ➤ Accounts.

2. Click the Add button and select News. The Internet Connection Wizard will appear.

3. Type your own name, or the name you want to use to identify yourself in articles and e-mail. The E-Mail Address window will appear.

4. Type your e-mail address. If you have more than one address, use the one you want people to use when they send replies to news articles. The Internet News Server Name window will appear.

5. Type the name of your Internet service provider in the Account Name field and click the Next button. The Internet News Display Name window will appear.

6. Type the address of your news server (or NNTP server) exactly as it was supplied to you by your ISP.

7. If your ISP advises you that you must log onto the news server, place a checkmark in the option box. Click the Next button.

8. If a login is required, type your login name and password and click the Next button.

9. In the Choose Connection Type window, select the radio button that describes your connection to the Internet—either through a telephone line or a LAN. Click the Next button.

10. If you choose a telephone connection, the Dial-Up Connection window will appear. Because you have already set up a Dial-Up Networking connection profile, choose the Use an Existing Connection option and select your default connection. Click the Next button.

11. When the Complete Configuration window appears, click the Finish button.

Changing an Existing Connection Profile

To review or change any of the information in your News account, select the name of the account profile and click the Properties button. The News Account Properties dialog box, shown in Figure 9.2, shows the characteristics you entered with the Internet Connection Wizard. You can change any entry by selecting an information field and overtyping the existing information.

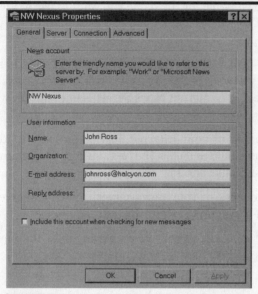

FIGURE 9.2: The News Account Properties dialog box controls the connection to your news server.

Changing the Appearance of Outlook Express

The View ➤ Layout command controls the way Outlook Express displays information on your screen. Figure 9.3 shows the Layout Properties dialog box.

Outlook Express offers these layout options:

Outlook Bar   The Outlook Bar contains icons that open your top-level Outlook Express mail and news folders.

Folder List   The Folder List is a nested list of Outlook Express mail folders and newsgroups.

Folder Bar   The Folder Bar identifies the current newsgroup or mail folder. If the Folder List is not visible, there's a drop-down menu in the Folder Bar that contains a nested list of mail folders and newsgroups.

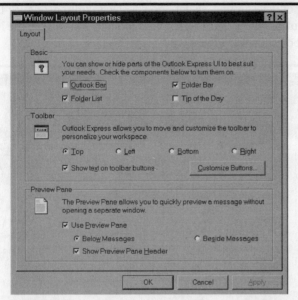

FIGURE 9.3:   Use the Layout Properties dialog box to hide or display information in Outlook Express.

Toolbar   To hide or display the toolbar, use the View ➢ Toolbar command. Options in the Layout dialog box can place the toolbar on any of the four sides of the Outlook Express Window. Click the Customize Buttons button in the Layout dialog box to add or remove a command button in the toolbar.

Preview Pane   The Preview Pane shows the contents of the currently selected article or e-mail message within the Outlook Express window. The options in the Layout dialog box control the position of the Preview Pane and whether or not it includes a header that identifies the sender and subject of the current message.

Subscribing to Newsgroups

Before you can read or contribute articles in a newsgroup, you must select that newsgroup from the thousands that your news server offers. It is possible to sample a newsgroup without a long-term commitment, but if you plan to return to the same newsgroup, you will want to subscribe to that group.

To see a list of newsgroups, select Tools ≻ Newsgroups, or click the Newsgroups button in the Outlook Express toolbar. You will see the Newsgroups dialog box shown in Figure 9.4.

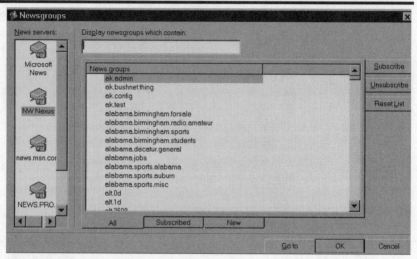

FIGURE 9.4:   Use the Newsgroups dialog box to select or subscribe to one or more newsgroups.

The first time you request a list of newsgroups from your news server, Outlook Express will obtain a complete list of all available groups from the server. It might take several minutes to download the whole list, but you'll only have to transfer it once.

If you're looking for a specific group or for newsgroups related to a specific topic, type a key word in the search field at the top of the dialog box.

To subscribe to a newsgroup, double-click the name of the group, or select the name and click the Subscribe button. Subscribed groups have a newspaper icon next to the name of the group.

To see a list of currently subscribed newsgroups, click the Subscribed tab at the bottom of the dialog box. You will see the same list in the main Outlook Express window when you select your news server.

The New tab in the Newsgroups dialog box contains a list of newsgroups that your news server has added since the last time you updated the list. It's a lot easier to choose potentially interesting newsgroups from a list of ten or twenty than from the list of all available newsgroups, which might include ten or fifteen thousand separate entries.

To discontinue a subscription, either double-click the name of the group again, select the group and click the Unsubscribe button, or use the Tools ➢ Unsubscribe from this Newsgroup command.

The Go To button at the bottom of the dialog box takes you to a newsgroup without creating a subscription. This can be useful when you want to take a look at a group before committing yourself to a long-term relationship.

Viewing a Subscribed Newsgroup

Outlook Express treats subscribed newsgroups like subfolders within larger folders assigned to each news server. There are three ways to display a list of subscribed newsgroups:

▶ Select the news server from the Outlook Bar to display a list of subscriptions in the main Outlook Express window, as shown in Figure 9.5.

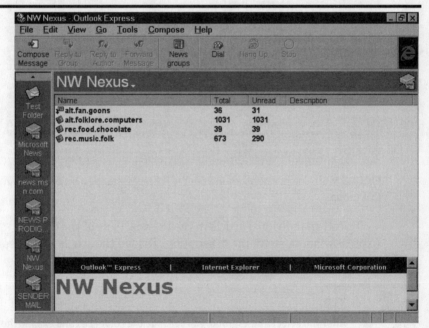

FIGURE 9.5: Choose a news server from the Outlook Bar to see the subscribed newsgroups.

▶ Use the View ➢ Layout command to display the Folder List.

▶ Click the down-arrow on the Folder Bar.

Reading News Articles

To see a list of articles in a newsgroup, select the name of the group. Outlook Express will retrieve the list of currently available articles from your news server and display them in the Subject pane, as shown in Figure 9.6. New articles appear in **boldface type**, which changes to normal type after you read them.

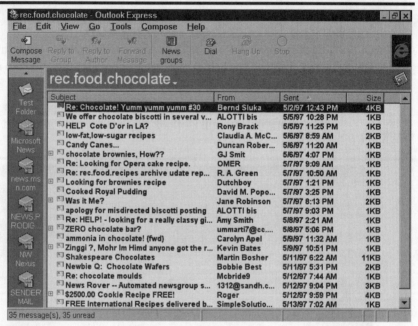

FIGURE 9.6:   Select a newsgroup from the Folder List to see a list of articles in that group.

To read an individual article in the Preview Pane of the Outlook Express window, select the description. To load the article into a separate window, double-click the description.

TIP

After you select a newsgroup, you can hide the Folder List and expand the other panes to take up the full width of the window using the View ➢ Layout command. You can add this command to your toolbar with the Customize Buttons command in the Layout dialog box.

Using News Filters

Internet newsgroups are very democratic—anybody who wants to join a discussion can write and send an article that will go to everybody else who reads the newsgroup. Unfortunately, that applies equally to people who have nothing useful to contribute to the conversation and to people who abuse the system by sending advertising, religious screeds, and other irrelevancies to hundreds or thousands of separate groups.

And of course, there's a long tradition of *flaming* in some newsgroups. A flame is an insulting (and sometimes abusive) message that attacks somebody else because the flamer doesn't like the form, style, or content of their target's participation in the newsgroup. Sometimes a single flame can grow into a full-fledged flame war, with nasty messages flying in all directions.

If you don't want to waste your time with junk articles and flames, Outlook Express allows you to apply one or more filters that automatically ignore articles from specific people or those with specific subject lines.

To set up a news filter, follow these steps:

1. Select the Tools ➢ Newsgroup Filters command. The Group Filters window will appear.

2. Click the Add button to open the Properties window shown in Figure 9.7.

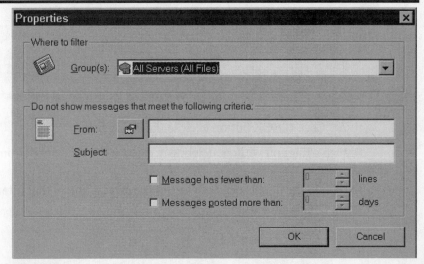

FIGURE 9.7: Use the Properties dialog box to create a new filter.

3. Use the drop-down Groups menu to select the newsgroup to which you want to apply this filter. If you want to filter all newsgroups, select the top-level All Servers (All Files) option.

4. To instruct Outlook Express to ignore articles from a particular person, type that person's name (as it appears in the From field of messages) in the From field.

5. To instruct Outlook Express to ignore articles with a specific word or character string in the subject line, type that word or string in the Subject field. If you include information in both fields, Outlook Express will only filter articles from the specified name that have the specified subject line.

6. Click the OK button. The Group Filters dialog box now contains an option that describes the new filter you just created, as shown in Figure 9.8.

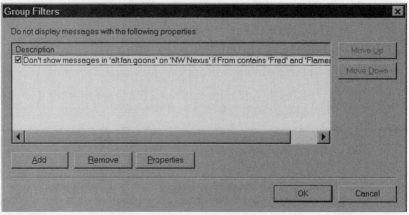

FIGURE 9.8: The Group Filters dialog box shows the terms of each newsgroup filter.

7. Click the OK button to close the dialog box.

To turn a filter off without deleting it, remove the checkmark from the description of the filter.

To change the details of a filter, select the description of that filter and click the Properties button.

Reading News Offline

It's not necessary to maintain a live connection to your news server while you read news articles. You can download individual articles or entire newsgroups and store them on your hard drive to read later. This can be particularly convenient if you use a dial-up connection to your news server or if you want to read news while traveling.

To download articles in all subscribed newsgroups, select the Tools ➤ Download All command.

To download articles in all subscribed newsgroups from the current news server, use the Tools ➤ Download This Newsgroup command

To download messages in a single newsgroup, follow these steps:

1. Select the news server from the Folder list.

2. Select the newsgroup whose messages you want to copy.

3. Select the Tools ➤ Download This Newsgroup command.

Creating and Sending News Articles

There's more to participating in a newsgroup than just reading messages from other people. Some people are permanent *lurkers* who hang around a newsgroup and never contribute, but it's generally more rewarding to participate in the discussions.

Outlook Express includes several commands (in the Compose menu and the toolbar) for submitting articles to newsgroups:

New Message   Use the New Message command to create and send a message on a new topic.

Reply to Newsgroup or **Reply to Group**   Use the Reply to Group (or Newsgroup) command to submit a message to a newsgroup that follows on an earlier message. Because the news server identifies a reply as part of a thread, many news readers (including Outlook Express) display replies directly under the original message, which makes it easier for a reader to follow the discussion.

Reply to Author   Use the Reply to Author command to send a private message via e-mail to the person who wrote a message.

Reply to Newsgroup and Author   Use the Reply to Newsgroup and Author to create a single message and send it both to
the newsgroup as an article and to the author as a private e-mail.

When you select any of these commands, the editor window shown in
Figure 9.9 appears. Type the text of your article in the main body of the
editor window.

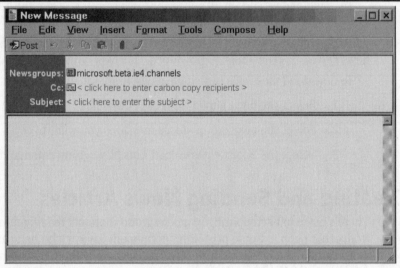

FIGURE 9.9:   Use an editor window to create an article for a newsgroup.

If you select one of the Reply commands, Outlook Express will normally load the text of the original message with a ">" at the left side of
each line. You can change the > to some other character from the Tools ≻
News Options Send tab.

It's almost always a good idea to delete irrelevant parts of the quoted
message, such as a signature block or several layers of nested quotes from
earlier messages.

If you're writing a point-by-point reply to an earlier article, it's helpful
to quote part of the original message, leave a blank line, and then enter
your reply or comment about that statement, followed by another blank
line, as shown in Figure 9.10.

When you're ready to send the article to the news server, select the
File ≻ Send Message command or click the Post Message button on the
editor's toolbar.

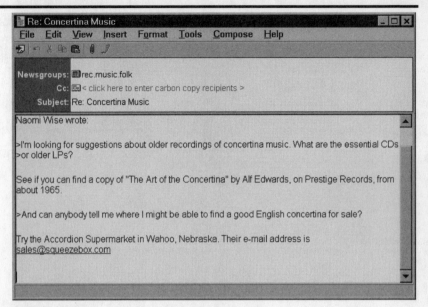

FIGURE 9.10: It's common practice to set off quotes in news articles with a > at the start of each line.

USING FREE AGENT

Microsoft's Outlook Express is an okay newsreader, but it's not your only choice. There are several third-party programs that offer different feature sets and screen layouts from the Microsoft product. One of the best is Free Agent. You can obtain a copy of Free Agent from http://www.forteinc.com/agent/. Forte also offers another newsreader called Agent with even more and better features, but you'll have to pay for that one.

One of Free Agent's nicest features is that it allows you to arrange the screen in just about any imaginable layout. Figure 9.11 shows the default layout. When you're concentrating on a particular section of the screen, you can expand that pane to fill the window by clicking the sizing icon in the upper-right corner of the pane. As Figure 9.12 shows, you can also organize the screen in many other ways: horizontal or vertical rows, or one big pane and two little ones.

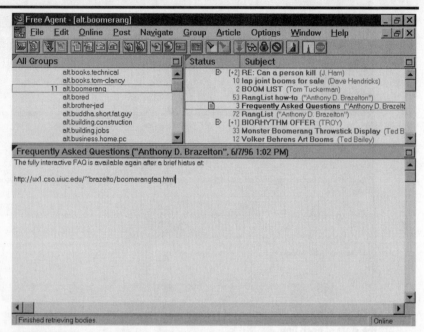

FIGURE 9.11: Free Agent can display lists of groups and articles and the text of the current article at the same time.

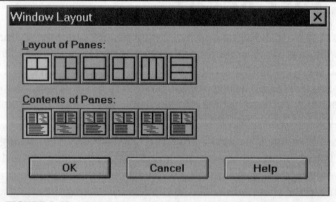

FIGURE 9.12: You can organize information in Free Agent in almost any layout.

The first time you run the program, Free Agent automatically loads the current list of newsgroups from your server. To update the list, use the Get New Groups command on the Online menu. To get another complete list, use the Refresh Groups List command.

Once you have a copy of the list of groups, you can obtain a list of articles within a particular group or subscribe to a group by double-clicking the name of the group. To switch between a list of all groups, a list of new groups, and your own list of subscribed groups, click the title bar at the top of the Groups pane. After you have loaded a list of articles, double-click a description to see the text of that article.

Free Agent isn't necessarily better than Outlook Express, but you might prefer the more flexible screen layout. Since it's free, you might want to try both programs and choose the one you prefer.

READING NEWS ON AOL

If you're an AOL subscriber, you can read Internet news by following these steps:

1. Log on to AOL and go to the keyword **Newsgroups**. The window shown in Figure 9.13 will appear.

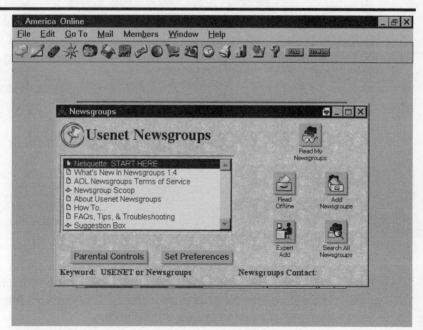

FIGURE 9.13: The Newsgroups window is AOL's gateway to Internet news.

2. To add a newsgroup to the list of My Newsgroups, click the Add Newsgroups button, select a domain, and click the List Topics button. When the list of groups within a domain appears, double-click the name of the subdomain or news-group you want. After a window appears for the newsgroup, click the Add button.

3. To open a newsgroup in the My Newsgroups list, click the Read My Newsgroup button and choose it from the list. To read an article, double-click the listing for that item. The text of the article will appear in a window like the one shown in Figure 9.14.

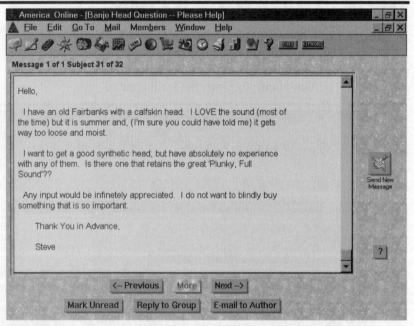

FIGURE 9.14: AOL displays Internet news articles in separate windows.

AOL's newsreader is less flexible than the programs that obtain news from NNTP servers. It's easy to use, but it lacks many features that are in Free Agent and Internet News. If you're using AOL as your only Internet service, however, you don't have any other choice.

Whichever newsreader you choose, a warning is in order: you can waste an incredible amount of time keeping up with Internet news. If you partici-pate in more than a handful of active groups, it's easy to spend several hours a day reading new articles, writing replies, and keeping up with the private e-mail that you exchange with the people you meet in those groups.

When you begin to feel that most of your closest friends are the regulars in your favorite newsgroups, you should realize that you're on the way over the edge. It's time to turn off the computer for a day or two and remind yourself that there's another world out there. Go for a walk; spend more time with your family; read a book. In spite of what your net.friends may tell you, there's more to life than an alternative reality based on typing.

WHAT'S NEXT?

Now that John Ross has taught you about Internet news, IE users will want to check out what Gene Weisskopf and Pat Coleman have to say in the next chapter. You'll learn about two nifty features: subscribing to sites and tuning in channels.

Part II

Chapter 10

SUBSCRIBING TO SITES AND TUNING IN CHANNELS

The one constant to the World Wide Web is that it seems to grow faster every day. This is a great boon for all of us, but it also introduces some rather hefty problems: How do we stay in touch with a Web site so we know when it has new information, without having to go back and visit it on a regular basis?

This chapter will offer two answers for IE 4 users: subscriptions and channels. Subscriptions are a way for you to let Internet Explorer check Web sites for new content without your involvement. Channels are Windows 98's way of implementing *Webcasting*, a technology by which content from a Web site seems to be *pushed* to you, instead of your having to go and get it. In fact, channels are really just a more sophisticated form of subscriptions, in which the parameters for a subscription are set by the Web site and are, therefore, tuned specifically for that site.

· ·

Adapted from *Mastering Microsoft Internet Explorer 4*, by Gene Weisskopf and Pat Coleman
ISBN 0-7821-2133-0   960 pages $44.99

NOTE

Netscape users: At this time, Netscape does not support subscribing to sites or channels—the Netcaster product was discontinued with Netscape Communicator version 4.04. Check Netscape's Web site (www.netscape.com) for updates on developments in Netscape push technologies.

USING SUBSCRIPTIONS TO STAY IN TOUCH

Traditionally, when you *subscribe* to something, such as a magazine or a newspaper, it regularly arrives on your doorstep or in your mailbox—daily, weekly, or monthly.

In the new world of the Internet, the concept of needing a traditional subscription no longer exists—if you want to see what's happening on the London Times Web site, just go look at it! There's no need to wait by your mailbox for the next edition.

NOTE

Because of the ease with which a Web site can be updated, many online newspapers add content to their site several times throughout the day. If this sounds totally modern and high-tech, don't forget that back in the old days, big-city newspapers printed several updated editions throughout the day. Extra! Extra!

But the ease with which you can access data on the Internet creates substantial hurdles. We tend to access not just a few sites, but dozens or hundreds. It's not just the *London Times*, but the *New York Times*, the *Los Angeles Times*, and who knows how many other *Times* throughout the world? The list goes on and on. How do you find out if a site has new content without actually going there, and how do you then find the time to download it all at the less-than-thrilling speeds of our normal Internet connections?

Signing Up for a Subscription

The answer is the *subscription*, which is the Active Desktop's way of keeping you up-to-date with your chosen Web sites. When you subscribe to one of the sites on your Favorites menu, you're telling, Windows 98, and subsequently Internet Explorer, that you want to keep in touch with that site, be notified when it has new material, and, optionally, have that material delivered to you.

NOTE

In spite of Windows 98's integrated Desktop, it's useful to remember that Internet Explorer and Windows 98 are actually separate applications.

The term *subscription* is a little misleading, because traditionally we subscribe to something by contacting the owners or publishers. But a site subscription is internal to Internet Explorer; it does not involve the publishers of a Web site. It's just a convenient term that describes an important part of the traditional subscription terminology: getting information regularly.

Subscribing to a site in Internet Explorer saves you time and effort in several ways:

▶ Internet Explorer will automatically check each subscribed site to see if it has any content that is new since the last time you visited that site. And you can have it do its checking at any time of the day or night. Imagine how much time it would otherwise take you to trudge manually from site to site, wondering if new material might be there.

▶ When a subscribed site changes or has new material, Internet Explorer notifies you and can automatically download all the new content.

▶ When Internet Explorer updates the content from a subscribed site, it stores the new content on your local drive. You can then access that new content *without* being connected to the Internet and downloading that content over your Internet connection. This means that you can do without that wire that binds you to the Net and that you can access the data from your hard disk, many times faster than you could access it from the Internet.

The bottom line is that you can come into work Monday morning and find that Internet Explorer has updated all your subscribed sites with their new content.

Subscribing to a Site

When you're adding a site to your Favorites menu, you choose whether to subscribe to that site in the Add Favorite dialog box. There are three subscription choices (the site is added to your Favorites menu no matter which one you choose):

No is the default choice, so that no subscription is set up.

Yes, but only tell me will have you notified when the site has new content.

Yes, and download will have you notified when there is new content, and that new content will also be downloaded to your local disk.

If you want to subscribe to this site, pick either of the Yes options and then click the OK button to accept the default subscription settings. You can instead click the Customize button, which starts the Subscription Wizard. It will take you through the steps of defining the subscription in the following main categories (you'll read about all of these later in the chapter):

Notification   The manner in which you will be notified when Internet Explorer finds new data on the site. By default, the item's icon in the Favorites menu displays a starlike gleam.

Download   How much of any new data will be downloaded.

Schedule   The schedule Internet Explorer will follow to check the site for new content. By default, if you have a LAN connection to the Internet, the site is checked automatically without your intervention. If you have a dial-up (modem) connection, by default you'll have to update the subscription manually, although you can choose to have the site checked automatically. You can also specify a custom schedule or choose to manually update this subscription no matter how you connect to the Internet.

You can also subscribe to a site that's already on your Favorites menu. The easiest way to do so is to find the site on your Favorites menu in the usual way, but don't open it. Instead, right-click on that item in the menu and choose Subscribe from the shortcut menu. You can also use the Favorites ➢ Organize Favorites command, find the folder that contains the item you want to subscribe to (remember that each submenu on the Favorites menu is actually a folder within the Favorites folder), right-click the item and choose Subscribe. You'll also find a Subscribe Now button in the item's Properties dialog box.

Choosing Subscribe displays the Subscribe Favorite dialog box, which is similar to the Add Favorite dialog box shown in Figure 10.1. Choose to be notified when the site has new content or to have that content downloaded, as well. Then click OK to accept the default settings, or click Customize to adjust them.

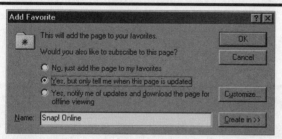

FIGURE 10.1: Subscribing to a Web site as you add it to your Favorites menu

Whether you subscribe to a new or existing site on the Favorites menu, the result is the same. In the next section, you'll see how to browse a subscribed site without actually going there.

Browsing Your Updated Subscriptions

Let's take a short tour of how subscriptions work to give you a feel for why subscriptions can be so important. You'll learn about all these steps later in the discussion of subscriptions.

When you subscribe to a Web site, Internet Explorer automatically checks that site for new content, either when you specifically ask it to (a manual update) or according to the schedule you've chosen. If the site has new content, Internet Explorer downloads as much of the new material as you specified in the subscription settings (none, by default) and then notifies you by the method you chose, such as by displaying a star on the item's icon on the Favorites menu.

NOTE

When you highlight a subscription on the Favorites menu that has new content available, you'll see a ToolTip that displays the date and time when you last accessed the site and when Internet Explorer last updated it (checked it for new content).

To view all your subscriptions, choose Favorites ➤ Manage Subscriptions. An Explorer window then displays a list of your subscriptions. You can see which ones have been updated recently, open one as you would any Internet shortcut, or right-click a subscription to view or revise its properties.

Here's where the second half of the subscription trick kicks in. If you chose to have Internet Explorer download a subscription's new content, you can browse that updated Web site while offline—you don't need to be connected to the Internet. Internet Explorer has already downloaded all the new material from that site, and it is waiting for you on your local hard disk.

BROWSING YOUR SUBSCRIPTIONS WHILE OFFLINE

When trying to browse files offline, you may sometimes see an error message indicating that the file you requested is not available offline. The amount of offline browsing you can do for any subscribed Web site depends on how much of that Web site is already on your computer in the Temporary Internet Files folder (the cache folder for Internet Explorer).

If you browse to that site regularly or have that site's new content downloaded frequently via a subscription, just about all of that site's content should now be available, because Internet Explorer has already downloaded any new material.

If, however, you click a link that targets a file you don't have on your local computer, Internet Explorer must connect to the Internet to get that file. At this point, you'll see a dialog box in which you can choose to continue browsing offline and do without that file or let Internet Explorer try to connect and go get it.

Being able to browse without being connected to the Internet means that you might let Internet Explorer update your subscriptions on your portable computer the night before you plan to travel. The next morning, you can unplug your portable from the network or telephone line and head for the airport. Once you've settled into your seat on the plane, you can browse those updated Web sites as though you were connected to them over the Internet. Not only are you free of a network connection, but Internet Explorer opens Web sites at hard-drive speeds. You will have to wait barely a second for a site to open.

Canceling a Subscription

A subscription remains in effect until you revise or cancel it completely. You'll learn how to revise one in the sections that follow; here's how to cancel one. Find the item on the Favorites menu, right-click it, and then choose Unsubscribe from the shortcut menu. You'll be prompted about the impending removal of the subscription. Choose Yes to remove the subscription, or choose No to leave it as is.

You can also cancel a subscription in the Organize Favorites dialog box in the same way. If you're going to be canceling or otherwise revising several subscriptions, it might be more convenient to do this within the Subscriptions dialog box (choose Favorites ➢ Manage Subscriptions). Right-click the site you want, and choose Properties from the shortcut menu (there is no Unsubscribe command). Choose the Subscription tab, and then click its Unsubscribe button.

When you unsubscribe to a site, you're only canceling the subscription. The site remains on the Favorites menu as before, but Internet Explorer does not check it for new content.

VIEWING YOUR CURRENT SUBSCRIPTIONS

To open a list of all your subscriptions at any time, choose Favorites ➢ Manage Subscriptions. This opens an Explorer window that lists all your subscriptions, as shown in Figure 10.2. Notice the icons to the left of each item in the list. Some are Web pages (the icon shown here on the left), others are channels (shown here in the middle), and still others are channels that have their own unique icon (shown here on the right). The channels you subscribe to are essentially special Web sites that define their own subscription download schedule, but they are nonetheless subscriptions. You'll read about channels later in this chapter.

TIP

You can also view or modify the same list of subscriptions by Exploring to the Subscriptions folder in your Windows folder.

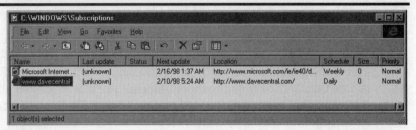

FIGURE 10.2: To view or modify your current subscriptions, choose Favorites ➤ Manage Subscriptions.

The columns of information in the list of Subscriptions are mostly from the various settings in each subscription's Properties dialog box, and they allow you to see these settings at a glance. You can easily see which subscriptions have new content, how many of them are updated daily, weekly, or manually, or which ones were updated most recently. To change the settings for a subscription, right-click it and choose Properties from its shortcut menu.

TIP

Click a column title to sort the list of Subscriptions by that column. For example, click the Last Updated column title to sort the list by the dates in that column. Click the column title again to sort in the opposite order (ascending or descending).

The Subscriptions list (or folder) is the place to go when you want to update a few, but not all, of your subscriptions. Simply select the subscriptions you want to update, and choose File ➤ Update Now, or right-click a selected subscription and choose Update Now.

When you want to go offline to browse the downloaded content of your subscriptions, you could look for each subscribed site that has the "gleam" on its icon on your Favorites menu, which indicates new content. But browsing through all the menus could be quite tedious, and the gleam doesn't tell you if a subscription includes downloading the content to your disk.

It's much easier to open your Subscriptions folder, where you'll have access to all your subscriptions with no other sites in the way.

DEFINING YOUR SUBSCRIPTIONS

As mentioned earlier, when you subscribe to a new site, you can choose to have Internet Explorer notify you when that site has new content, or download that content, as well. You'll be notified that there's new material at a site by the gleam on the item's icon in the Favorites menu. You can either choose the default schedule for that site or set your own custom schedule. In the sections that follow, you'll learn how to modify all these settings for any existing subscriptions on your Favorites menu or when you create a new subscription.

When creating a subscription for a new site on your Favorites menu, click the Customize button in the Add Favorite dialog box (look back at Figure 10.1), which starts the Subscription Wizard. Here's how to change the settings for an existing site subscription on the Favorites menu:

1. Find the site on your Favorites menu (or in the Organize Favorites dialog box or in the Subscription folder).

2. Right-click the site and choose Properties.

3. In the Properties dialog box, you'll find three subscription-related tabs with which you can view or revise the subscription settings.

    Subscription displays the current settings for the subscription.

    Receiving lets you choose how to be notified when Internet Explorer finds new content on the subscribed site and whether that new content should be downloaded. You can also limit how much content is downloaded so that you don't end up being surprised by who knows how many megabytes of new material!

    Schedule lets you choose the schedule that Internet Explorer will follow when checking the site for new content.

4. Make any changes you want to the subscription and click OK when finished.

The following sections will show you how to adjust all the subscription options so that you'll be able to tune any subscription to fit your need for updated content from that site.

Viewing Current Subscription Settings

To look at the current subscription settings for an Internet shortcut, open its Properties dialog box and select the Subscription tab, as shown in Figure 10.3. Here you'll see the name of the item as it appears on the Favorites menu, its URL, the type of subscription (notification only or notification and download), the update schedule, and the date and time when the site was last updated and when it will be updated next.

On this tab you'll also find the Unsubscribe button, which you can click to remove the subscription from this site.

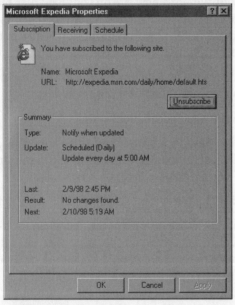

FIGURE 10.3: The Subscription tab in the Properties dialog box shows you the current settings and status of a subscription.

Choosing How You Want to Be Notified

When you are subscribing to a new Web site and choose only to be notified, clicking the Customize button in the Add Favorite dialog box (refer back to Figure 10.1) opens the first dialog box of the Subscription Wizard, which is shown in Figure 10.4. (When you have chosen to download pages, this step of the Wizard comes a little later in the process.)

Here you choose whether you want an e-mail message sent to you when Internet Explorer finds new content at this site. By default, the No option is selected.

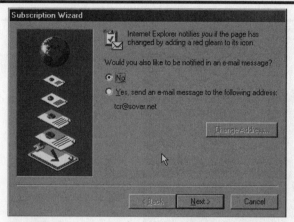

FIGURE 10.4: In this step of the Subscription Wizard, you choose whether to be notified by e-mail when new content is found at this site.

If you choose Yes, Internet Explorer notifies you by e-mail when it finds new content at this site. If you normally use an HTML-enabled mail program, such as Outlook Express, the e-mail message will actually contain the Web page. Otherwise, you will receive a plain text message that includes the URL of the subscribed site.

If you then click Change Address, you can enter a different e-mail address and mail server that Internet Explorer should use. If you're traveling, you could have Internet Explorer check your subscriptions from your desktop computer and then notify you by e-mail when a subscription has new content.

With either choice, when this site has new content, you'll be notified by a starlike gleam on this item's icon on the Favorites menu (shown here as the icon on the right; the normal icon is on the left). This simply lets you know that there's something new at this site.

When you're revising the settings for an existing subscription, look on the Receiving tab in the Properties dialog box for the Notification options; it's shown in Figure 10.5. If you want to be e-mailed when this site has new content, select that checkbox. If you need to change the e-mail address, click the Change Address button. In the next section we'll discuss how you can have Internet Explorer download any new content it finds at a subscribed site.

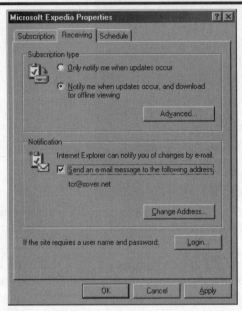

FIGURE 10.5:   The Receiving tab of the Properties dialog box

Choosing How Much Content Should Be Delivered

When you're defining a new subscription or revising the settings for an existing one, you can limit how much new content Internet Explorer will download. As mentioned earlier, if you have chosen only to be notifed; Internet Explorer simply checks the site for new content but does not download any. You can browse to the site in the usual fashion and see the new content that way. Let's look at the ways you can have Internet Explorer download that content for you—automatically and even while you're not at your computer.

When you're creating a new subscription, you have two options for downloading new content, as shown in Figure 10.6:

▶ Download this page.

▶ Download this page and pages linked to it.

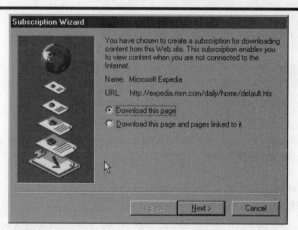

FIGURE 10.6: The Subscription Wizard lets you choose how much new content to download.

If you choose "Download this page," Internet Explorer downloads only the one page that is the target for this item on the Favorites menu. For example, if the URL for this item on the Favorites menu is:

```
www.widget.com/default.htm
```

only the page named DEFAULT.HTM is checked and, if there is new content, downloaded to your computer.

If you choose "Download this page and pages linked to it," the targets of any links on this page are also downloaded. In other words, if there are ten links on this page, you'll receive 11 downloaded pages, or whatever files are the targets for those links. Obviously, unless you know a site well, you really have no idea how many pages might be downloaded.

When you choose this second option and click the Next button, you'll see the dialog box shown in Figure 10.7, which asks you how many links "deep" you'd like to have downloaded. The default is 1 (the maximum is 3), so that only the target of each link is downloaded. If you set this option to 2, not only is the target of each link downloaded, but so are all the targets of all the links found on any of those pages.

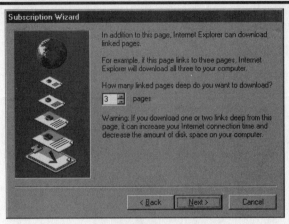

FIGURE 10.7: Internet Explorer will follow links and download their targets as many levels deep as you specify.

WARNING

When you specify a certain number of pages deep, you're creating a potential situation that is not unlike the family tree of fruit flies multiplying in a biology classroom. If the site has lots of good links, you might be committing to a life-time's supply of pages! Use caution even when specifying a depth of one page. Once you're very familiar with a site and how many links it tends to have, you can increase the depth as needed.

You have even more download options when you revise the settings for an existing subscription. As you saw in Figure 10.5, the Receiving tab in the Properties dialog box has a group of options labeled Subscription Type. If you choose the "Notify and download" option, you can then click the Advanced button to access the Advanced Download Options dialog box, shown in Figure 10.8.

This dialog box gives you a wide range of options for limiting the amount of data that Internet Explorer downloads from this site.

As you can when you're specifying a new subscription, you can choose to download the pages targeted by the links on this page. Again, use caution with this option until you are familiar with this site. Use even more caution when you choose the option to download linked pages even when they reside outside the subscribed page's Web site. This is definitely an option to leave disabled until you are familiar with a site and the links it contains. You wouldn't want Internet Explorer to attempt to download the entire World Wide Web!

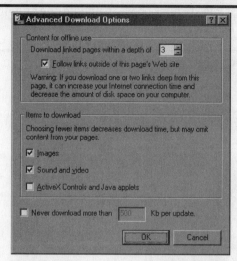

FIGURE 10.8:   In the Advanced Download Options dialog box, you can specify how much content to download from a subscribed site.

In the next group of options, Items to Download, you can choose the type of content to include or exclude from the download. To avoid lengthy downloads, deselect some or all of these options. If a page contains a deselected item, such as a video or an audio clip, you'll have to do without that content. When you select any of these data types, download times could increase drastically.

The last option lets you limit the amount of data that is downloaded when Internet Explorer updates this site. By default, there is no limit, so if you want to specify one, select this option and enter the maximum number of kilobytes that should be downloaded (remember that 1000 kilobytes (KB) is 1 megabyte (MB)).

Setting a Subscription Schedule

When you are subscribing to a new Web site and have chosen to download new content, one of the last dialog boxes in the Subscription Wizard, shown in Figure 10.9, lets you specify the schedule by which this site will be updated. You have two choices:

> **Scheduled**   You can set the precise schedule, such as at a specific time each day, every hour during the nighttime hours, once each Monday, once a month, and so on.

Manually   You must specifically choose to update one or more sites, which you can do at any time.

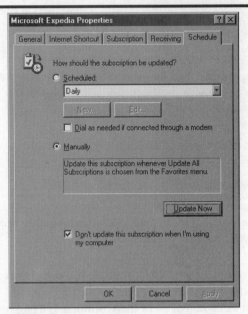

Figure 10.9: You can specify a schedule for a new subscription or choose to update it manually.

Let's look at two disparate scenarios for scheduling the updating of your subscriptions. Suppose you have a network connection to the Internet that is always live and available and that you tend to leave your computer on 24 hours a day. In this case, you can set just about any schedule you want (you'll read about custom schedules a little later in this chapter).

Whenever the scheduled time rolls around, Internet Explorer automatically connects with the Internet, goes to each subscribed site, and downloads whatever content you specified. You can schedule these updates for the evenings or weekends when they won't get in the way of your daily work routine and when the Internet and your network may be less busy, as well.

At the opposite end of the spectrum, suppose that you connect to the Internet with a modem, that you pay for your connection by the hour, and that you tend to turn your computer off at the end of the day. In this case, you'll probably want to update your subscriptions manually while you're working at the computer, as described in the next section.

Updating Your Subscriptions Manually

You can update any or all of your subscriptions at any time by doing so manually. If a subscription is set to be manually updated, this is the only way you can have this site checked for new content. But even if a site has a custom schedule, you can still choose to update it manually at any time.

You can manually update sites in several ways:

▶ To update all your subscriptions, in any Explorer window choose Favorites ➤ Update All Subscriptions.

▶ To update a single subscribed site, right-click that site's item on the Favorites menu and choose Update Now. Or if you have already opened that site's Properties dialog box, choose the Schedule tab, and click the Update Now button.

▶ To update multiple subscriptions, open your Subscriptions folder in an Explorer window by choosing Favorites ➤ Manage Subscriptions. Select one or more subscriptions and choose File ➤ Update Now; or right-click one and choose Update Now.

When the update begins, you'll see a "progress" dialog box like the one shown here. Click the Details button to see a list of all the sites being checked and the status of each one. To cancel the updating, click the Stop button. To cancel it for just one site, select that site in the details list and click the Skip button. You can also minimize this dialog box or just ignore it while it does its job.

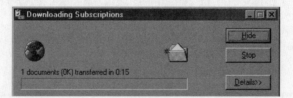

With the Manual Update schedule, there are no schedule options to set. With a custom schedule, however, there are many, which we'll look at in the next section.

CHOOSING A CUSTOM SCHEDULE

You can create a Custom schedule for a subscription that will update a site on just about any schedule you can imagine—many times each day, once each day, one day a week or a month, and so on. The Custom schedule choices are the same whether you're creating a new subscription or revising an existing one.

HOW OFTEN IS OFTEN ENOUGH?

The schedule you set for a subscription depends on several factors. First, decide how important the site is to you. Is it critical that you know as soon as possible when the site has new information, or would a day or two not really matter?

Consider how often you expect this site to get new content. Does it contain breaking news that may be updated several times a day? Have you noticed changes to the site every time you've visited it, or is it fairly static?

Don't forget that the type of connection you have to the Internet can drastically affect the process of updating subscriptions. If you have a fast, direct network connection that gives you almost instant access to the Web, checking a site for new content might happen in the blink of an eye. With a slower, dial-up connection, however, the process of connecting to the Web, checking each site for new content, and then downloading that content might take more time than you can spare for all your subscriptions.

When possible, assign each subscription to manual updating, or perhaps to the Weekly schedule, so that you can have Internet Explorer do the updating at night, when you're away from your computer and the Internet may run more briskly.

Use the Daily schedule for those sites that you really want to stay in touch with, and, when necessary, create a custom schedule for each site that requires its own schedule.

Choosing a Custom Schedule for a New Subscription

When you're creating a new subscription and choose to download content from the site, you can then choose to modify the schedule by clicking the Customize button, as shown here.

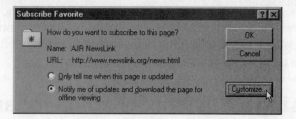

If you then select the Scheduled option (see Figure 10.9), you can select one of the existing named schedules from the drop-down menu. By default, you'll find the three schedules—Daily, Weekly, and Monthly. The actual schedule that is defined for the selected schedule is shown beneath the drop-down menu. If one of the defined schedules suits your needs, choose it from the menu and click the Next button. To change the settings for any of the named schedules, click the Edit button. To create a brand-new named schedule, click the New button. You'll read about both these choices a little later.

WARNING

Revising the definition of any named schedule, such as Daily or Weekly, changes that schedule for all subscriptions that use it. If you want to change the settings for only the current subscription, create a new schedule for it.

Allowing Unattended Dial-Up Connections

If you have a network connection to the Internet that is always active and available, you can set a schedule for any day of the week or time of day, and Internet Explorer will be able to go out and check your subscribed sites for new content.

If you have a dial-up connection to the Internet with a modem, you'll have to decide whether you want Internet Explorer updating your subscriptions automatically on a schedule. If your modem's telephone line is available 24 hours a day for its own use, there may not be a problem. But if you also use the modem phone line for voice calls, you'll have to decide when it would be appropriate for Internet Explorer to dial out automatically to update your subscriptions.

By default, no automatic updates are allowed when you connect to the Internet with a modem, and you must do a manual update, as described earlier in this chapter. You can enable automatic updates, however, by choosing the "Dial as needed if connected through a modem" option, as shown earlier in Figure 10.9. You'll have to do some planning if you share the phone line with your modem, so that the various subscription schedules don't interfere with your use of the phone.

Choosing a Custom Schedule for an Existing Subscription

To change the schedule for an existing subscription, right-click that subscription's shortcut, choose Properties, and then select the Schedule tab, which is shown in Figure 10.10. As you can see, it gives you the same two schedule options that you are offered when creating a new subscription. For the custom schedule, there's the drop-down menu with the Daily, Weekly, and Monthly choices.

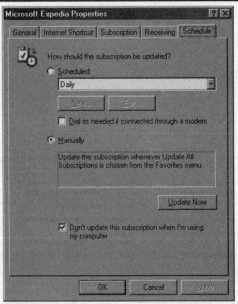

FIGURE 10.10: To revise the schedule for an existing subscription, open its Properties dialog box and choose the Schedule tab.

Creating a New Custom Schedule

When you are creating a new subscription or revising an existing one, you can click the New button to create a new custom schedule (see Figures 10.9 and 10.12). The name you specify for this new schedule will appear on the drop-down menu, along with the Daily, Weekly, and Monthly schedules.

Figure 10.11 shows the Custom Schedule dialog box that you see when you click the New button to create a new schedule. The options shown are for setting a daily schedule. When you select one of the other choices in the Days group, the options to the right change accordingly.

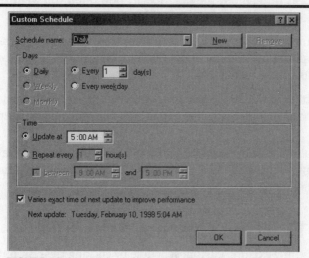

FIGURE 10.11:   You can create a new schedule in the Custom Schedule dialog box.

Creating a new schedule is a breeze. Simply select from the choices in the Custom Schedule dialog box:

1. Start by entering a name for this new schedule at the top of the dialog box, which will later appear on the drop-down menu of custom schedules. By default, a new schedule is named Custom Schedule.

2. Choose Daily, Weekly, or Monthly from the Days options, which will display the appropriate options for setting that schedule.

3. Choose the options you want for the type of schedule you're creating. For a Daily schedule, set the number of days to 1 to run the schedule every day; to 2 to run it every other day, and so on. You can choose to run it every weekday instead.

4. Select the time of day for the updating by choosing from the Time group of options. If you choose 12:00 AM, the updating starts at the stroke of midnight for all subscriptions that use this schedule.

5. Choose the Repeat Every option if you want the updating to repeat throughout the day. Specify how often you want the update to occur and between what hours.

6. Choose the Varies Exact Time option to allow Internet Explorer to shift the update time in an attempt to improve network performance.

Near the bottom of the dialog box you can see when the next scheduled update will occur. This will change as you alter the schedule, so keep your eye on it.

When you're finished, click OK, and you'll be returned to the dialog box that displays the drop-down menu of schedules, where you'll find your new schedule listed.

Editing an Existing Custom Schedule

You can revise any existing custom schedule by clicking the Edit button on its Properties ➤ Schedule tab. You'll also find the Edit button in the Web Site Subscription Wizard dialog box when you're creating a new subscription. This displays the Custom Schedule dialog box, which looks much like the one shown earlier in Figure 10.11. The only difference is that here you must select a predefined schedule name from the drop-down menu at the top of the dialog box. The schedule options will change to match those for that schedule.

Make any changes to the options that you want, and when you're finished, click the OK button. The new settings will now apply to that named schedule and will therefore affect all subscriptions that use that schedule.

NOTE

The Custom Schedule dialog box has a Remove button, which allows you to delete any of the named schedules except the defaults: Daily, Weekly, and Monthly. It also has a New button that allows you to create a new schedule name instead of revising an existing one.

VIEWING AND SUBSCRIBING TO ACTIVE CHANNELS

So far we've looked at two ways to retrieve information from the Web:

▶ By explicitly visiting a Web site, such as by entering a URL into the Address toolbar or by following a hyperlink

▶ By subscribing to a Web site

Now we'll look at a third technique, which builds on the concept of subscriptions. This major new feature of the Active Desktop is called Active Channels, and you access it from the Channels Bar that appears on the desktop when Windows 98 is started. It can deliver just the information you want and on a timely basis, where *timely* is defined by the publisher of that information.

The term *channel* suggests TV quality or TV attributes, but the technology is not quite there at this point (for which we may yet give thanks). A channel is not a site that broadcasts information (thus, the term *channel* is confusing, to say the least). It is actually a regular Web site that provides information through regular Web pages. In fact, you can view a channel just as you would view any Web site; the trick becomes evident when you choose to subscribe to a channel.

When you subscribe to a Web page, Internet Explorer visits that site from time to time and checks that site's content to see whether it has changed. You can subscribe to any site, even if it was created prior to the release of Windows 98. A channel is similar, but you can only subscribe to a channel when that site has been configured as a channel.

You subscribe to a channel simply by linking to a file that contains the site's Channel Definition Format (a CDF file). This file is provided by the publisher of the site and automatically defines the subscription to this channel in Internet Explorer. You'll see how all this works in the sections that follow.

Part ii

You can also customizes channels. Besides viewing a channel, either online or offline (if you have chosen to download its contents), you can make a channel an item on your Active Desktop, part of the Channel screen saver, or your desktop wallpaper.

Before we get into the details, let's see how channels are used. By looking at a few examples, you will be able to better understand the differences between channels and subscriptions, as well as the advantages of channels over plain browsing.

Viewing a Channel in Internet Explorer

As mentioned earlier, you can view a channel in several ways. First, you can simply go to a Web site that happens to be a channel, in any of the usual ways, such as by entering its URL in the Address toolbar. In fact, you may often encounter Web sites quite by accident that are set up to be used as channels; whether you subscribe to a channel is your decision.

When you installed Windows 98, links to a variety of channels were also installed, which you can access in a number of ways. In Internet Explorer, or from the Task Bar if you have selected the option, choose Favorites ➢ Channels. To select a channel in the Explorer bar, choose View ➢ Explorer Bar ➢ Channels, or click the Channels button on the toolbar, and your list of channels will be displayed in the Explorer bar. To close the Explorer bar, click that button again.

NOTE
The Channel Guide channel is a Microsoft site at which you will find additional channels. You'll see shortly how to visit a channel so you can subscribe to it.

You can also access the list of channels with the Favorites ➢ Channels command on the Windows 98 Start menu. Selecting a channel in this way opens the channel in an Internet Explorer window.

Viewing a Channel in the Channel Viewer

From the Quick Launch toolbar, you can click the View Channels button to open Internet Explorer in a full-screen mode known as the Channel Viewer, which is shown in Figure 10.12. The Explorer bar is displayed on the left side of the screen.

NOTE

The channels you'll see in your own Explorer bar will probably vary from those shown in Figure 10.12, in the same way that we can each have our own list of favorite Web sites. As Windows 98 is used by more and more people, you'll undoubtedly find that many Web sites will now offer you the option to subscribe to their channels from within their home page.

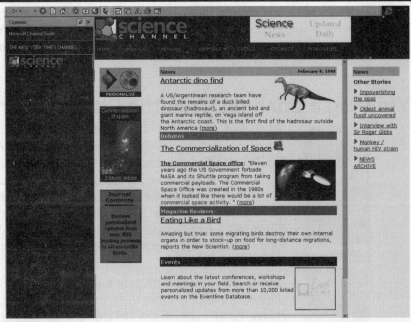

FIGURE 10.12: The Channel Viewer is Internet Explorer's special full-screen mode for the maximum viewing area.

You can also launch a channel in the Channel Viewer by selecting it from the Channel bar on the desktop, as discussed in the next section. To display the Quick Launch toolbar, right-click the taskbar and choose Toolbars ➢ Quick Launch.

You can close the Explorer bar by clicking the Channels button on the toolbar, but in the Channel Viewer, the Explorer bar will automatically slide out of the way when your mouse is not over it. Simply point to the left side of the screen to have the Explorer bar slide open again. To prevent the Explorer bar from hiding, click the pushpin button that you'll find on the right side of the Explorer bar's title bar.

When you're using Internet Explorer in Channel Viewer mode, almost all the tools in Internet Explorer are hidden, by default, leaving as much room as possible for the Web page. Only the standard toolbar is displayed, and you can even hide that by choosing the Auto Hide command from the shortcut menu when you right-click the toolbar. The other toolbars, the status bar, and even the menu bar are hidden! This really is a full-screen mode, because even the Windows Taskbar is hidden.

You can turn on these features in the usual ways. For example, right-click the toolbar and choose Menu Bar to display the menus, or use the View menu to turn on the status bar or the other toolbars. To return to the normal view in Internet Explorer, choose View ➢ Full Screen, or click that button on the toolbar.

Viewing a Channel from the Channel Bar

Yet another way to access a channel is from the Channel bar, shown at right, which can be displayed on the Active Desktop. It offers the same choices that you'll find on the Channels menu or in the list of channels in the Explorer bar, only they're conveniently placed as icons in the Channel bar, which you can access from the desktop. When you open a channel in this way, it is displayed in Internet Explorer's Channel Viewer, as discussed in the previous section.

If you don't see the Channel bar, you need to add it to the Active Desktop. From the Windows Start menu, choose Programs ➢ Active Desktop ➢ Channel Bar. You can also turn on or off the Channel bar or other items on the Active Desktop in the following way:

1. Right-click the desktop and choose Properties to open the Display Properties dialog box.

2. Select the Web tab, which is shown in Figure 10.13.

3. In the list of items, select the Internet Explorer Channel Bar by clicking its checkbox.

4. Click OK to close the Display Properties dialog box.

The Channel Bar should now appear on your desktop.

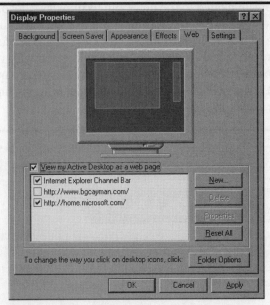

FIGURE 10.13: The Web tab in the Display Properties dialog box, where you can add items to the Active Desktop.

Subscribing to an Active Channel

In most cases, the first time you access a channel, such as by clicking its button in the Channel bar, an introductory screen at that site invites you to subscribe to the channel. Unless you're informed otherwise, no cost is involved, and most channels don't even require a registration. You simply answer a few questions for Internet Explorer's Subscribe Wizard.

Internet Explorer organizes many channels into categories. For example, when you are viewing the Channel bar on the desktop or in the Explorer bar in Internet Explorer and click the News & Technology button, you will see the names of the channels in that category:

- ► CMPNet
- ► Live Wired
- ► The CNET Channel
- ► The New York Times
- ► ZDNet

These channels are all related to the news and technology category. In the right pane of the Internet Explorer window you will see the icons that correspond to these channels. To subscribe to the CNET channel, for example, click its button to access that site. The Explorer bar with its list of channels slides to the left and is hidden (unless you leave the mouse pointer resting on it), and CNET's opening screen appears and invites you to subscribe, as shown in Figure 10.14.

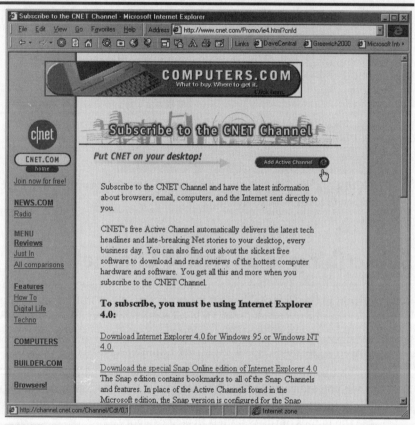

FIGURE 10.14:   CNET invites you to subscribe to its channel.

To subscribe to the CNET channel, click the Click Here to Subscribe button (most channels will have a similar way to subscribe). This button links to a Channel Definition Format file (CDF), which will trigger Internet Explorer's Subscribe Wizard.

As you can see in Figure 10.15, the Wizard for adding a channel is just about the same as the one you see when you subscribe to regular Web sites, with the following differences:

▶ The new channel is added to your Channel bar, not to your Favorites menu

▶ The default update schedule is specified by the channel's publisher via the CDF file at the Web site

You can modify the default update schedule by clicking the Customize button in the Wizard's dialog box. If you choose the option to have content downloaded, you can then choose to have only the channel's home page downloaded, or all the channel content prescribed by the CDF file. One component provided by many channels becomes part of the Channel screen saver, which you'll read about in the next section.

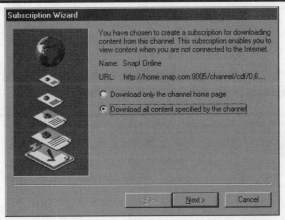

FIGURE 10.15: Subscribing to a channel is similar to subscribing to a Web site.

After completing the subscription process for the CNET channel, you will see the CNET home page, and a new icon for the channel will appear in the Channel bar on your desktop. In essence, you have subscribed to another site, except that this one is directed by its CDF file.

Using a Channel on the Desktop or in the Channel Screen Saver

As we mentioned earlier, you can also display channels as part of the Channel screen saver or as an item on the Active Desktop. Some sites will have a separate button for each display option, so you can choose to install the channel's screen saver component, its Active Desktop component, or all the content that the channel has to offer. Other sites might let you make that decision while you're subscribing to the channel, so you'll be able to choose the type of content while you're going through the Wizard.

When you configure this screen saver, you can choose which available channel to display when the screen saver is activated. Here are the steps in a nutshell:

1. Right-click the desktop and choose Properties.

2. In the Display Properties dialog box, select the Screen Saver tab.

3. On the Screen Saver drop-down menu, choose Channel Screen Saver.

4. Now click the Settings button to open the Screen Saver Properties dialog box, which is shown in Figure 10.16.

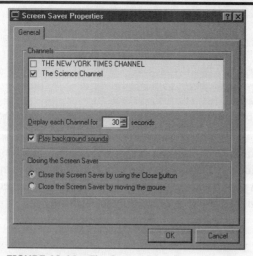

FIGURE 10.16: The Screen Saver Properties dialog box, in which you select the channels to include in the Channel screen saver.

5. Select the names of the channels you want displayed when the screen saver is activated, and then click OK. Remember, you'll only see the channels that you specifically chose to include in the Channel screen saver when you first subscribed to the channels.

6. Now click OK to close the Display Properties dialog box.

When the your computer is idle and the Channel screen saver starts up, it will connect to the Internet as needed and display the channels you have selected.

You can display pictures, Web pages, and other Web-related items on your Active Desktop, and that includes channel content, as well.When a Web site offers content designed for your desktop, it will most likely have a button to let you install just that content. When you click the button, the Subscribe Wizard takes you through the steps of downloading and installing the new item for your Active Desktop, as shown below. When you're finished and the new content is downloaded, you'll see the new item displayed on the Active Desktop.

Setting a Channel's Options

You can view or revise the settings for a channel subscription from its shortcut menu:

- ▶ Right-click the channel's icon on the Channel bar or within the Explorer bar in Internet Explorer.

- ▶ Choose Favorites ➢ Manage Subscriptions to open a list of all your subscriptions, including those that are channels (refer back to Figure 10.2 to see the Subscriptions window). Then right-click the one you want.

- ▶ Choose Favorites ➢ Channels in Internet Explorer, and right-click the channel you want.

The shortcut menu offers several choices related to channels and subscriptions. Choose Update Now, and Internet Explorer will connect to that Web site to see if there is any new content, just as you can do with any subscription. This command updates the contents of a channel on your disk, regardless of the update schedule that is specified in the channel's subscription.

When a channel has the Refresh command on its shortcut menu, you can choose that command to download the titles of the pages that make up the channel. These are displayed as hyperlinks that appear below the channel's icon.

Choose Properties to open the Properties dialog box for a channel subscription, which is shown in Figure 10.17. It should look familiar if you've read the earlier sections in this chapter on subscriptions (see Figure 10.3).

The Subscription tab gives you an overview of the current settings. You can unsubscribe to this channel or change the login parameters, if the site requires that you log in with a user name and password.

On the Receiving tab you can specify the notification method and whether Internet Explorer will merely check the site to see if anything is new or will actually download any new pages. On the Schedule tab you can specify how often the channel will be updated.

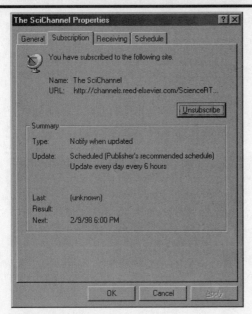

FIGURE 10.17: A channel's Properties dialog box displays the subscription settings for that channel.

WHAT'S NEXT?

The future of the Web may depend in part on our having tools such as subscriptions and channels. They allow us to maintain an ongoing relationship with the sites we value, while protecting us from the wild chaos of unlimited choices. Time will tell. But the beauty of both these tools is that they are optional—you can still browse the Web in whatever fashion you prefer.

In the next chapter, John Ross will give you a look at some of the other valuable Internet tools as your disposal.

Part ii

Chapter 11

OTHER INTERNET TOOLS: FTP, TELNET, AND DIAGNOSTICS

Web browsers are excellent general-purpose tools for moving data though the Internet to your own computer, but they're not always the best programs for certain specialized tasks. This chapter contains information about some other tools that you might want to use along with your browser. Some of these tools perform specific tasks more quickly and efficiently than a browser does; others allow you to do things that you can't do with a browser.

Some of these tools are supplied with Windows 98, and others are available from other software developers or as shareware or freeware through the Internet. All of the programs described in this chapter use the same network connection that you use for Web browsing.

The people who develop many of these programs seem to release new versions about three times a week. One of the best places to keep up with new and improved Internet tools is the Web site called The Ultimate Collection of Winsock Software

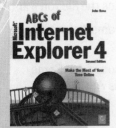

Adapted from *ABCs of Microsoft Internet Explorer 4*, by John Ross
0-7821-2042-3   400 pages $19.99

(TUCOWS), at http://www.tucows.com. TUCOWS includes ratings and descriptions of most new programs within a few days of their release, along with direct links to the developers' own home pages and sources for downloads.

USING FTP CLIENTS

FTP (File Transfer Protocol) is the Internet's standard method for moving text files, data files, and binary program files from one computer to another. You can use your browser for some FTP file transfers, but it's often faster and easier to use a dedicated FTP client instead of the Web browser.

There's an FTP client supplied with Windows 98 (in your Windows folder), but it uses a command line rather than a graphic interface. Don't waste your time with it. Much better FTP clients with point-and-click or drag-and-drop capabilities are available from online sources.

Each FTP application has a different screen layout, but the process of finding and downloading a file is essentially the same for all of them:

1. Connect your client program to an FTP server.

2. Log on to the server. Almost all public FTP servers accept the login name "anonymous," with your e-mail address as the password. If you have an account on the server, you can use your own login name and password to get access to files that may not be available to anonymous users or to upload files from your computer to the server.

WARNING

Some very popular servers will accept only a limited number of connections at one time, so the file transfer speed doesn't become impossibly slow. If you can't get through the first time you try to connect to a server, try again later, or look for another source for the file you want to download.

3. Move to the directory on the server that contains the file you want.

4. Specify the folder or directory on your own computer where you want to place the downloaded file.

5. Transfer the file from the server to your own computer. Some clients ask you to specify whether each file is ASCII text or binary data before you start the download.

6. Disconnect from the server.

WS_FTP

WS_FTP has been available for several years, but it's still one of the best FTP clients around. The developer, John Junod, now of Ipswitch, Inc., continues to offer new and improved versions. The program is free to government and academic users and to individuals for their own noncommercial use. Other users can evaluate the program free for 15 days and then order the commercial version from the developer.

You can obtain the latest versions of WS_FTP from the Ipswitch Web site at `http://www.ipswitch.com/Products/WS_FTP/index.html`.

As shown in Figures 11.1 and 11.2, WS_FTP displays the contents of a directory in your own computer (the *local system*) on the left and a directory at the distant FTP server (the *remote system*) on the right. The remote system is usually the source of your file transfers, and the local directory is usually the destination, but if you're uploading from your own computer to a server, you'll move the files from the local system to the remote system.

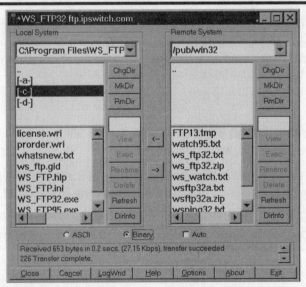

FIGURE 11.1:   The four-window version of WS_FTP shows directories and files separately.

To move to a subdirectory within the current directory, double-click its name. To move to the parent directory that contains the current directory, double-click the two dots (..) at the top of the list. To move to a completely different directory on the same computer, type the new path in the field directly above the list of files.

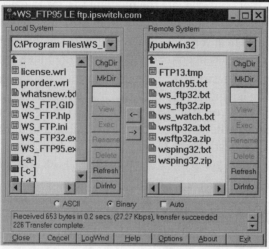

FIGURE 11.2: The two-window version lists directories and files in the same windows.

Connecting to an FTP Server with WS_FTP

To connect to an FTP server, follow these steps:

1. Click the Connect button at the bottom of the WS_FTP window. The Session Profile dialog box, shown in Figure 11.3, will open.

2. Open the drop-down Profile Name list to select a host, or type the full address of the server in the Host Name field.

3. For anonymous FTP, place a checkmark in the Anonymous Login option box. WS_FTP will use the address you specified during installation as your password. To log in to a server on your own account, type your user ID and password in the fields that request them.

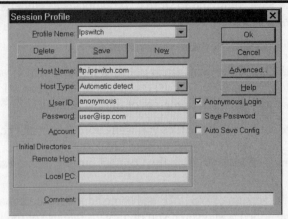

FIGURE 11.3:   Use the Session Profile dialog box to connect to an FTP host.

4. If you know the full path of the directory on the server that contains the file you want, type the path in the Remote Host field. If you leave this field blank, WS_FTP will connect you to the server's root directory, and you can move to the right place one step at a time.

5. Click the OK button. WS_FTP will display the commands and responses that it exchanges with the server at the bottom of the screen.

Transferring a File with WS_FTP

When the connection is in place, you will see the contents of the current directory on the server in the Remote System file list on the right side of the WS_FTP window. To move a file from the server to the host or from the host to the server, follow these steps:

1. Find the name of the file you want to transfer in one of the directory lists.

2. Make sure the correct file type is specified; either ASCII for text files or Binary for data files. You can assume that any file with a file name extension .TXT or .LST and files called read.me or readme are ASCII text; most others are probably binary. If you're not sure about a file, try it as binary first. Or if it's a relatively small file, click the View button to load it into a text editor; if it appears as plain text, you can use the

editor's Save command to store it. If it appears as gibberish, it's probably a binary file.

3. Select the file or files you want to transfer.

4. Click the button with an arrow pointing in the direction you want to move the file. WS_FTP will display an information window that shows the progress of the file transfer.

After you have copied all of the files you want from this host, click the Close button at the bottom of the window to break the connection. To look for files from another host, click the Connect button and repeat the whole process.

The commercial version of WS_FTP has some added features that may make it worth the added cost, even if you qualify for free use of the Limited Edition. Among other things, it supports drag-and-drop file transfer between directories, and it will resume where it left off when you reconnect after an interrupted file transfer.

CuteFTP

CuteFTP is another rather seasoned FTP client, but it has been updated and moved to the realm of shareware (sadly no longer free, but worth every dime). CuteFTP is a little less newcomer friendly, but once you have learned the ropes it has a bevy of powerful features often held over for the commercial applications. This utility is a real hummer. Registering CuteFTP will cost you $34.95 and garner you the ability to resume interrupted transfers. You can evaluate it for 30 days before commiting.

Get your copy of the latest version of CuteFTP from: `http://www` `.cuteftp.com/`

CuteFTP is similar to WS_FTP in that it displays local and remote directories on the left and right side of the main window, respectively (see Figure 11.4). Navigation around CuteFTP's main window is very similar to WS_FTP. Primarily, the main bonus to CuteFTP is that you can drag and drop file and directories back and forth between local and remote locations in the demonstration version.

CuteFTP maintains a history list of all directories visited, whether local or remote. A list box situated above each frame makes for easy retrieval of regularly visited directories. Default directories can even be set for local and remote lists.

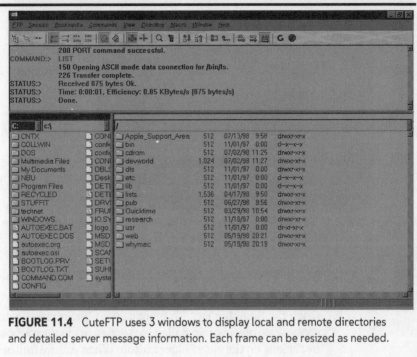

FIGURE 11.4 CuteFTP uses 3 windows to display local and remote directories and detailed server message information. Each frame can be resized as needed.

Connecting to an FTP Server with CuteFTP

To connect to an FTP server, follow these steps:

1. By default, CuteFTP opens its own Site Manager when it is first run, as shown in Figure 11.5. The Site Manager can always be reached by clicking on the left-most icon on the toolbar or selecting its name from the File menu.

2. Select a topic from the left pane and a list of FTP servers will appear in the smaller right pane. Select the desired server and click Connect. The Site Manager will disappear and be replaced by the main window.

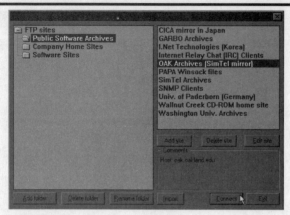

FIGURE 11.5: The Site Manager helps you connect to an FTP host and retain that information for future connections.

If the site you need is not in the initial list of bookmarked FTP sites, follow these instructions on how to add sites to your list:

1. Open the Site Manager. To manage your bookmarked sites, choose one of the preinstalled catagories or create your own by clicking on the New Folder button. When you are finished, click on the Add Site button.

2. Enter a friendly name for the FTP server that you would like to see shown in the Site Manager in the first text box. Using Figure 11.6 as a guide, enter the remaining information for the new server.

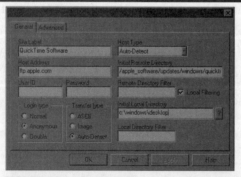

FIGURE 11.6: The Add Site dialog with the Apple QuickTime site information inserted

Keep in mind that not all of the information shown in Figure 11.6 is neccessary to logon to an FTP server. Technically you only need the Site Name and Host Address fields filled in. The remaining fields allow you to more closely pinpoint a file or specific directory and where on your drive you would like CuteFTP to look at.

Transferring a File with CuteFTP

When you have entered your site information and click on the Connect button CuteFTP will switch to the main window and begin the login process. You will see many cryptic bits of data appear in the server messages pane; they indicate the connection status and what commands CuteFTP is sending the FTP server.

When all is done, and if the connection information was correct, the contents of the remote server will appear in the right pane. If you specified a local path, that directory will appear in the left pane. You are now ready to transfer files.

1. Locate the file you want to transfer in either the local directory or remote directory list.

2. Drag the file or files to where you want them, either local or remote.

3. Click on the Yes button to ok the transfer.

4. Wait.

When you are done you can disconnect by clicking on the two small forks that are pointed at each other (the third icon from the left on the toolbar) or by choosing Disconnect from the File menu. To jump to another server, click on the lightning bolt, which displays the Quick Connect dialog, or the tiny tree structure icon on the left end of the toolbar to get back to the Site Manager.

NOTE

For more details on the commercial version of CuteFTP, go to http://www.cuteftp.com and get the latest version. The 30-day demonstration version disables download resumption after a broken connection, otherwise it is complete.

Part ii

USING TELNET CLIENTS

Telnet makes your computer a remote terminal that sends commands and receives data through the Internet to and from a distant host. When you type on your own keyboard, those keystrokes go directly to the host, just like keystrokes from a keyboard plugged directly into the host. The most common uses for telnet are remote access to a distant computer where you have an account and connection to a computer that accepts access from the public, such as a library catalog. Once the connection is in place, a telnet client program should be transparent; you should be able to concentrate on the responses you receive from the host.

Because telnet makes your computer appear to a telnet host as if it's a terminal, telnet clients are also known as *terminal emulation programs*. Different brands and models of terminals send slightly different signal formats to host computers, so many telnet programs can be configured to emulate more than one type of terminal.

The most common terminal emulation type is called VT-100, named for a very popular terminal model made by Digital Equipment Corporation (DEC). Unless the host advises you to use some other kind of emulation, VT-100 is almost always a good choice. The only common hosts that don't recognize VT-100 terminal emulation are certain IBM mainframes, which require a special IBM terminal called a Model 3270. Not all telnet clients include 3270 emulation, so you might need a separate telnet program called a TN3270 to log in to a 3270 host.

There are many Windows telnet client programs available, and most of them do at least an adequate job. In general, they fall into one of two categories:

▶ Single-purpose telnet clients

▶ Telnet clients included with general-purpose communication programs

General-purpose communications programs are usually a better choice than telnet-only applications, because they allow you to capture incoming text, send and receive files, and scroll back to read text that has disappeared off the top of your screen, among other things. The latest versions of all the popular Windows communications packages, including Pro-Comm, Crosstalk, WinComm, and QModem, can be used as Winsock-compliant telnet clients. HyperTerminal, the communications program supplied with Windows 98, does not support telnet, but you can get a free upgrade that adds this feature from Hilgraeve, the software developer who created the program for Microsoft. Hilgraeve's Web site is at `http://www.hilgraeve.com/htpe.html`.

Windows 98 Telnet

If you're using Windows 98, you probably have Microsoft's Telnet program in your \Windows directory. To start the program, follow these steps:

1. Open the Start menu and select the Run command.

2. Type **telnet** *host address* in the Open field. For example, to connect to The Well, type **telnet well.com**.

If you use the program often, you should place a shortcut to it on your Desktop, add it to your Start menu, or both.

Figure 11.7 shows the Telnet window as it appears when you start the program. To set up a connection after Telnet is already running, open the Connect menu and select the Remote System command.

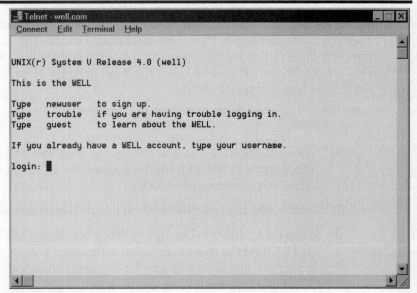

FIGURE 11.7: Microsoft Telnet is a simple terminal emulation program.

Once the connection to a telnet host goes through, you're at the mercy of that host. If you have an account on the host, you should already know how to log in and how to send commands and receive data. If you're connecting to a host that welcomes public access, it should automatically display the information you need to get started.

The Microsoft Telnet client and most other single-purpose telnet programs do not include one very important feature: you can't use them to upload or download binary program files between your PC and the telnet host. If you're using telnet to connect to a file library, you'll need a different telnet client program that supports file transfer protocols, such as XModem, ZModem, or Kermit.

HyperTerminal

Along with to Microsoft Telnet, Windows 98 also includes a terminal emulation program called HyperTerminal that can connect to other computers through a modem and telephone line. HyperTerminal was created for Microsoft by Hilgraeve, who also makes a family of commercial connectivity products for Windows, OS/2, and other platforms, called HyperACCESS.

The version of HyperTerminal that comes with Windows 98 does not include a telnet client, but Hilgraeve has released a free upgrade that adds telnet and several other useful features to the original program. Hilgraeve calls this upgrade HyperTerminal Private Edition. The free HyperTerminal Private Edition upgrade is available on Hilgraeve's Web site, at http://www.hilgraeve.com/htpe.html or on the HyperTerminal bulletin board at 313-243-9957.

To connect to a new telnet host through HyperTerminal Private Edition, follow these steps:

1. Open your Start menu, and choose the Programs menu. Select Hyper-Terminal from the Accessories submenu to open the HyperTerminal window.

2. Double-click the Hypertrm.exe icon to start HyperTerminal.

3. When the Connection Description dialog box, shown in Figure 11.8, appears, type a description of the telnet host in the Name field, and choose an icon for this connection profile. Click the OK button to close the dialog box.

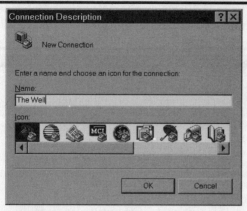

FIGURE 11.8:   Type a description of the telnet host in the Name field.

4. When the Connect To dialog box appears, open the drop-down list in the Connect Using field and select the TCP/IP (Winsock) option. The other fields in the dialog box will change to the ones shown in Figure 11.9.

FIGURE 11.9:   When you select a TCP/IP connection, HyperTerminal asks for the address of a telnet host.

5. Type the address of the telnet host in the Host Address field and click the OK button.

6. If you're not already connected to the Internet, HyperTerminal will start Dial-Up Networking and connect you to the host,

as shown in Figure 11.10. Follow the instructions that appear on your screen to log in to the remote host.

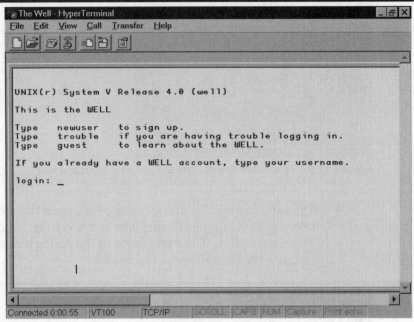

```
The Well - HyperTerminal                                    _  | | X
File   Edit   View   Call   Transfer   Help

  D | |    | |    | |

  UNIX(r) System V Release 4.0 (well)

  This is the WELL

  Type    newuser    to sign up.
  Type    trouble    if you are having trouble logging in.
  Type    guest      to learn about the WELL.

  If you already have a WELL account, type your username.

  login: _



         |


Connected 0:00:55   VT100      TCP/IP      SCROLL  CAPS  NUM  Capture  Print echo
```

FIGURE 11.10:   HyperTerminal can connect to a telnet host through your Winsock connection.

7. When you're finished using the remote host, disconnect and use HyperTerminal's Exit command to shut down the program. The program will ask if you want to save the current session. If you ever expect to return to this host, click the Yes button.

The next time you want to connect to the same host, just select the icon for that connection profile in the HyperTerminal folder. Like any other Windows 98 file, a connection profile can have a shortcut from your Desktop or your Start menu.

RUNNING DIAGNOSTIC TOOLS

When the Internet is working properly, you don't notice any of the intermediate circuits, switchers, routers, or network interconnection points. The only thing you need to know is that your computer is receiving data from a server someplace out there in cyberspace. But when you can't connect to a particular host or if data transfer seems to slow down to a crawl, it can be useful to have a better idea of what's happening between your own system and the rest of the network.

When you talk to your ISP's tech support center, they might ask you to try "pinging a host" or "running a traceroute" to a server you're trying to reach. *Ping* and *traceroute* are common Internet tools for testing the system.

Ping

Ping (Packet Internet Groper) is a tool that sends a message to a distant host and asks the host to send back a reply. When the ping client receives the reply, it displays the total duration of the exchange. Many ping clients repeat the whole process up to five or ten times and calculate an average response time. Therefore, ping can tell you two things: One, is the distant computer alive? And Two, how good is the connection?

When a ping request times out or fails completely, you can assume that there's a problem someplace between the two computers: either the distant computer is not connected to the network, or one of the intermediate processors is not working properly, or your own system or ISP has a problem. If the reply takes more than about 600 milliseconds from a host on the same continent, there's probably a problem with the network, such as a very heavy demand for resources or a network server not working properly somewhere along the path between you and the distant system.

In Windows 98, the ping utility is a DOS program. To send a ping request, follow these steps:

1. Open the Start menu and select the MS-DOS Prompt command in the Programs submenu.

2. At the C:\WINDOWS> prompt, type **ping host** and press the Enter key. In place of host, type the address of the system to which you want to send the ping request.

As Figure 11.11 shows, ping sends four echo requests and shows the success of each attempt. The section that says time=xxxms shows the number of milliseconds needed for each reply.

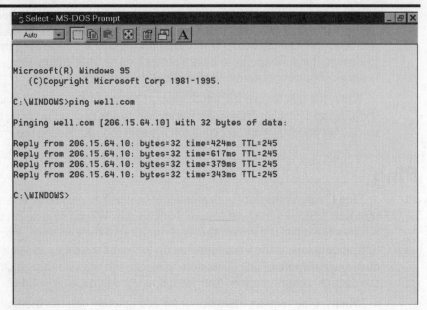

FIGURE 11.11: The Windows ping program shows the result of a ping request in a DOS window.

Traceroute

Traceroute is a standard Internet utility that identifies all of the intermediate steps between an origin and a destination. This can be fascinating information if you want to understand how data moves through the Internet, but most of us won't use it very often.

The traceroute program in Windows 98 is another DOS program. To run a traceroute test, follow these steps:

1. Open an MS-DOS window from the Start menu.

2. At the `C:\WINDOWS>` prompt, type **tracert** *host*, using the address of the distant system in place of host.

As the program steps through each link, it will display the name of each network server and the amount of time needed to obtain an echo from that server. For example, Figure 11.12 shows a traceroute test from an ISP in Seattle to The Well in San Francisco.

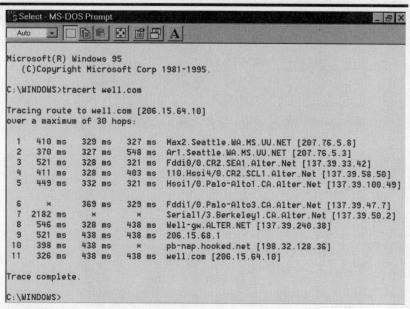

FIGURE 11.12: Traceroute identifies all of the intermediate network servers between your system and a specified host.

WS Ping

WS Ping is a graphic program that combines ping and traceroute functions into a single Windows 98 program. It was created by the same developer as WS_FTP. If you use either of these functions more often than about once a month, the program is worth having, especially since it's free for government, academic, and noncommercial home use. You can download the program from ftp.ipswitch.com/pub/win32.

Figure 11.13 shows the main WS Ping screen. To run a ping or traceroute test, type the address of the target computer in the Host field and click the button that describes the type of test you want to run.

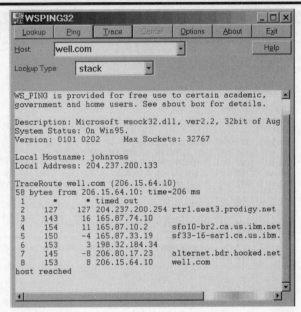

FIGURE 11.13: WS Ping combines ping and traceroute into a single program.

WHAT'S NEXT?

Congratulations. You've reached the end of Part II. If you'd like to learn about the AOL browser, turn to Part III where Laura Arendal will teach you some of the features that make it special.

PART iii
AOL AMAZING SECRETS

Chapter 12

SEARCHING WITH PURPOSE

I n the next four chapters, Laura Arendal will show you some of the Internet stuff that's particular to AOL users. In this chapter, you'll hone your searching skills—both on AOL and on the Web—and minimize extraneous and erroneous results to your searches.

TIP

This chapter covers some of the same information as Chapter 8, *Searching the Web*. (Chapter 8 originally appeared in Gene Weisskopf's *Mastering Internet Explorer 4*.) Whatever browser you are using, you should consider reading that chapter *and* this one. That way, you can see the different techniques Laura and Gene use for their Internet searches.

Adapted from *America Online Amazing Secrets*, by Laura Arendal
ISBN 0-7821-2229-9   368 pages $19.99

SEARCHING WITHIN AOL

You'll be amazed at the quality and breadth of the stuff you'll find on AOL. Not only is it safe and warm here, there's lots to sift through. To make your sifting easier and more rewarding, you'll want to use the Find button.

NOTE

Using words to search is different from using a keyword to get somewhere. *Search words* can be anything describing an area or touched on within the area; a *keyword* is an AOL word associated specifically with an area. If you tried to search for *HO*, you wouldn't find a thing. However, if you type **ho** into the Keyword/URL box and click Go, you'll immediately be connected to Heckler's Online. To successfully search for Heckler's Online, you'd need to search with a descriptive word like *humor*.

Easily accessed from the right side of the AOL toolbar, the Find button (Figure 12.1) allows you to search all of AOL or the Web, or narrow your search to AOL's channels, software area, chat rooms, member directory, access numbers, Help files, or the Internet White Pages.

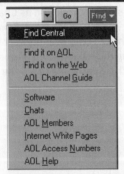

FIGURE 12.1: You have direct access to the search capabilities you're—ahem—searching for right here in the toolbar.

Even clearer than the Find menu is Find Central, the topmost menu item on the Find menu. Figure 12.2 illustrates your options for searching AOL.

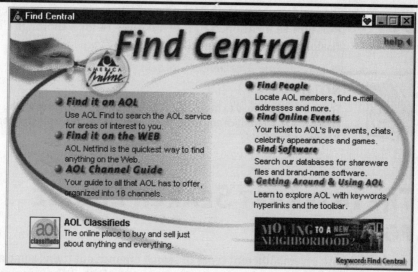

FIGURE 12.2:   AOL's search HQ

TIP

When you get the list of results to your search, you can do a cursory screen of each area by double-clicking its name to go there and then using the Find in Top Window command (Edit ➤ Find in Top Window or Ctrl+F) to see whether the item or text you want is readily accessible.

The AOL Find features in Find Central are quite easy to use, so I won't bore you with unnecessary detail. A few highlights, though, are in order:

▶ Not only can you search for people with Find People, but you can search for your soul mate through a link to AOL's personals.

▶ Under Find Online Events, you can search for special events and weekly schedules in the chat and conference rooms. There's also a What's Hot link here. Note that you can also search chat rooms via the toolbar's Find ➤ Chat.

▶ Find Software! My favorite. Besides the usual, you can check out the daily download item, which is a random shareware executable of some type or another. Useful, silly, what's the diff? Check it out!

▶ Getting Around AOL sends you right to the Member Services Online Help files, if that's what floats your boat.

▶ The insidiously inviting AOL Classifieds square deserves mention. So I've mentioned it. (See Chapter 14 for a thorough discussion of the AOL classifieds.)

NOTE

There are other ways to browse, floating soft as a cloud through the myriad areas of AOL. I introduce you to the ways and means later in the chapter, under *Browsing Left Field*.

THE INTERNET SEARCH ENGINE FOR YOU

There are several different types of search engines out there; some search the Web and Usenet newsgroups, some just the Web, some search even more narrowly, well-filtered Web sites—the G-rated stuff. There are also sites specifically geared toward searching for e-mail addresses of people and businesses.

NOTE

Though the Web is the most heavily used part of the Internet, it is by no means the whole thing. I discuss searching other parts later in this chapter under *Run with the Wolves, Burrow with the Gophers*.

In addition to search engines, there are metasearch sites, which house many search engines on one site. Some even allow you to access more than one engine to perform your search.

WARNING

I need to mention the obligatory caveat: while all the files available for downloading on AOL—including those uploaded by AOL members—are checked for viruses and functionality, everything else is fair game for yucky stuff. Be very careful when downloading a file from a Web site or Usenet newsgroup.

Web and Usenet Searches

These search engines automatically search both the World Wide Web and Usenet newsgroups for links to your topic.

AOL NetFind

Internet ➤ AOL NetFind

```
http://www.aol.com/netfind/
```

Default is Boolean OR

 With AOL's NetFind you can search the Web, search for a person, search for a business, and search newsgroups. Built on Excite's search engine capabilities, AOL NetFind searches not only for the search words you type in but also for words closely related to your search words. So if you type in **custodian,** AOL NetFind will also look for items about janitors and sanitation engineers.

Wildcards and Other Operators

+	Requires following search word to appear in each search result
-	Requires following search word to be absent in each search result
""	Place around any number of words you want searched for as a phrase

Boolean Operators

AND	Search will reveal only profiles containing both words
OR	Search will reveal profiles with either word
NOT	That word will not appear in the search results
( )	Group words together so you can search for a couple of different options at a time

AltaVista

http://www.altavista.digital.com

Default is Boolean OR

AltaVista recognizes a broad range of wildcards and Boolean operators. If you're going to search with this engine, be sure to use them; AltaVista is very powerful and can be overwhelming when not harnessed properly.

A NOTE ABOUT BOOLEAN OPERATORS

Whatever kind of Internet search you do, Boolean and other operators are your friends. Operators (words, wildcards, and other symbols) act like mathematical symbols; they tell the search engine what search words to link how. Using operators is kind of like mini-programming, if you can stand the cool-nerd aura of it.

Some search engines don't recognize all of the operators, so I carefully specify which operators work with each search engine. When using Boolean operators, uppercase them and be sure to include a space before and after each one.

I also indicate in each description what the Boolean default of each search engine is: AND or OR. A search engine that defaults to Boolean OR will, when looking for a phrase, return sites with *any* of the words, not necessarily the whole phrase. Dragsters, right?! A default to Boolean AND will return only sites containing *all* the specified search words—which is more like it.

In addition, you should know that searches are case-sensitive. As an added bonus, the Advanced Query page allows you to weight keywords.

Wildcards and Other Operators

*	Substitutes for any string of characters
?	Substitutes for one letter
-	Requires following search word to be absent in each search result
" "	Place around any number of words you want searched for as a phrase

Boolean Operators

AND	Search will reveal only profiles containing both words
OR	Search will reveal profiles with either word
AND NOT	That word will not appear in the search results
NEAR	Results will have the linked words within 10 Words of each other
( )	Group words together so you can search for a couple of different options at a time

Excite

http://www.excite.com

Default is Boolean OR

Much like AltaVista, Excite supports high-tech search strings (however, its Power Search is graphical only). Stuff you oughta know: two capitalized words next to each other are treated like a proper name, so if you wish to search for a proper name plus another word ("Bill Clinton" AND veto), put the name in quotes.

Wildcards and Other Operators

*	Substitutes for any string of characters
+	Requires following search word to appear in each search result
-	Requires following search word to be absent in each search result
" "	Place around any number of words you want searched for as a phrase

Boolean Operators

AND	Search will reveal only profiles containing both words
OR	Search will reveal profiles with either word

AND NOT   That word will not appear in the search results

( )   Group words together so you can search for a couple of different options at a time

HotBot

http://www.hotbot.com

No Boolean default

If you resist the cool geekiness that glows around every Boolean-expression user, HotBot is the site for you. It uses a graphical interface that gives you the same options as Boolean operators would—without the telltale glow.

Another advantage to HotBot is that you can search for files by their file type (Adobe Acrobat, Java, and so on). If you choose to do so, you'll want to search one file type at a time. In addition, you can save your Expert section settings for future use. The downside to HotBot is that it doesn't recognize wildcards, nor does it automatically look for plurals; thus you will want to link the singular and plural of your important search words with OR to make sure you get all the pertinent results.

Infoseek

http://www.infoseek.com

Default is Boolean AND

In addition to the below functionality, be aware that two capitalized words next to each other are treated like a proper name. Also, if you want to search for several proper names, separate them with commas. When you find a site that gives you what you need, use the Similar Pages link for more excellent results.

Wildcards and Other Operators

*   Substitutes for any string of characters

+   Requires following search word to appear in each search result

-	Requires following search word to be absent in each search result
|	Narrow by placing between a broad-category search word and a narrow-category search word (cat | Manx)
""	Place around any number of words you want searched for as a case-sensitive phrase
-	Place between words you want adjacent to each other (non-case-sensitive)
url:	Search for links to a URL
site:	Search for pages at a particular Web site
{ }	Search words in brackets will appear within 100 words of one another

Web-Only Searches

Though some of the following search engines sport links to search engines that service other areas of the Internet, they are Web-only search engines at heart.

Lycos

http://www.lycos.com

Default is Boolean OR

Lycos is another search engine where the graphical interface—including a Power Panel allowing you to customize your search—can substitute for Boolean operators. It does, however, recognize the following wildcards and operators.

Wildcards and Other Operators

+	Requires following search word to appear in each search result
-	Requires following search word to be absent in each search result
""	Place around any number of words you want searched for as a phrase

Boolean Operators

AND   Search will reveal only profiles containing both words

OR   Search will reveal profiles with either word

NOT   That word will not appear in the search results

ADJ   The words will appear next to each other

NEAR   The linked words will appear within 25 words of one
           another

FAR   The linked words appear more than 25 words apart at
           least once in result

BEFORE   Words appear in specified order but not necessarily near
           each other

O   Directly before another operator (OADJ) will force
           results to be in order you specify

/#   Use directly after ADJ, NEAR, and FAR to specify the #
           of words allowed between search words

Open Text Index

http://index.opentext.net

Default is Boolean AND

Not only does Open Text Index operate from a graphical interface, it's also case insensitive (it's nice to give those pinkies a rest from time to time). Open Text Index doesn't automatically search for plurals of your search words, so be sure to link the singular and plural of each search word with OR.

However, you can use your hard-won understanding of Boolean operators by doing a PowerSearch; here you can choose the following operators from a drop-down list.

Boolean Operators

AND   Search will reveal only profiles containing both
words

OR   Search will reveal profiles with either word

BUT NOT   that word will not appear in the search results

| NEAR | Results will have the linked words within 80 words of each other |
| FOLLOWED BY | Results will have the linked words within 80 words of each other in the order you type in |

Webcrawler

http://www.webcrawler.com

Default is Boolean OR

Wildcards and Other Operators

" "   Put quotes around any number of words you want searched for as a phrase

Boolean Operators

AND	Search will reveal only profiles containing both words
OR	Search will reveal profiles with either word
NOT	That word will not appear in the search results
NEAR/#	Results will have the linked words within the specified number (#) of words of each other
ADJ	Results will have linked search words adjacent to and in order of words you type in
( )	Group words together so you can search for a couple of different options at a time

Part iii

Searching Filtered Web Content

You can feel safe using these search engines; the search engine elves have scrutinized the content of these sites to make sure they're as pure as the driven snow.

Magellan

http://www.mckinley.com/

Default is Boolean OR

Searching with this engine's Reviewed Sites Only and Green Light Sites Only options turns up only the best in Web sites.

Wildcards and Other Operators

+   Requires following search word to appear in each search result

-        Requires following search word to be absent in each search result

""   Place around any number of words you want searched for as a phrase

Boolean Operators

AND   Search will reveal only profiles containing both words

OR   Search will reveal profiles with either word

AND NOT That word will not appear in the search results

( )   Group words together so you can search for a couple of different options at a time

Yahoo

http://www.yahoo.com

Default is Boolean AND

Another search engine in the graphical-interface category, Yahoo allows you to narrow your search through its advanced graphical search format. To get to the advanced search, click the Options button. One thing to keep in mind is that Yahoo's default is to place a wildcard after every search word. Yahoo does recognize the following operators:

Wildcards and Other Operators

*   Substitutes for any string of characters

+	Requires following search word to appear in each search result
-	Requires following search word to be absent in each search result
""	Place around any number of words you want searched for as a phrase
t:	Search word will appear in title
u:	Search word will appear in URL

Usenet Searches

If you want solid newsgroup searching and don't care one whit about the Web, you have a few good options.

AOL NetFind Newsgroup Finder

Internet ➤ Search Newsgroups

```
http://www.aol.com/netfind/newsgroups.html
```

Default is Boolean OR

Discussed in more detail under *Web and Usenet Searches*, the newsgroups you'll find through AOL NetFind are rated according to how trafficked and informative they are, their technical level, and the rationality level of the newsgroup contributors.

Reference.com

```
http://www.reference.com
```

No Boolean default

This engine will search not only Usenet newsgroups but also mailing lists and Web forums. (Web forums are message boards located at different Web sites all over the Internet.)

Part iii

Boolean Operators

AND	Search will reveal only profiles containing both words
OR	Search will reveal profiles with either word
NOT	That word will not appear in the search results
NEAR	Results will have the linked words within several words of each other

DejaNews

http://www.dejanews.com/

Default is Boolean AND

 The source for Internet Discussion Groups, DejaNews has some spiffy search capabilities. Quite well-stocked in the operator arena, DejaNews also allows you to specify whether a search word is an author, subject, newsgroup, or creation date. Thus, the search string **Dilbert ~a Adams** will find you Scott Adams' famous comic strip.

Wildcards and Other Operators

^	Substitutes for any string of characters
?	Substitutes for one letter
" "	Place around any number of words you want searched for as a phrase
{ }	Searches words alphabetically ranged between the two words enclosed by braces

Boolean Operators

AND	Search will reveal only profiles containing both words
OR	Search will reveal profiles with either word
AND NOT	That word will not appear in the search results
NEAR#	Results will have the linked words within # words of each other
( )	Group words together so you can search for a couple of different options at a time

Context Operators

~a   Author

~s   Subject

~g   Newsgroup

~dc   Creation date

Metasearch Sites

The features available at metasearch sites vary widely: some are merely Web pages that link you to one site at a time; some actually perform concurrent searches on many different search engines' indexes. Below I list the search engines featured at each site and the things that'll help you decide whether or not a site is for you.

All4One

http://www.all4one.com

AltaVista   Lycos

WebCrawler   Excite

At All4One, you type in your search string once and see your search results in the four search engines' text boxes. Boolean expressions are recognized by the search engines that normally recognize 'em.

Highway 61

http://www.highway61.com

Excite   AltaVista

WebCrawler   Infoseek

Lycos   Yahoo

This site is hip. You can tell Highway 61 how patient you're feeling (this'll get stored as a cookie so the next time you search, the Highway will remember your tolerance level) and predict the highway-crossing skills of the armadillo. Oh yeah, and get results.

Inso

http://wizard.inso.com

AltaVista	Excite
HotBot	Infoseek
Lycos	Magellan
Open Text	WebCrawler
DejaNews (Usenet only)	

Inso is a Web site that houses several search engines but doesn't integrate them. Thus you can search with one search engine at a time. However, it does help you out with advanced queries, so if your Boolean isn't so hot, you might try it.

MetaCrawler

http://www.metacrawler.com

Excite	Lycos
Infoseek	Yahoo!
Open Text	WebCrawler
and others . . .	

MetaCrawler recognizes Booleans AND, OR, and NEAR (yay!) and searches with all search engines at once, showing you the results on one page (and attributing each result to the search engine from whence it came). In addition, MetaCrawler features both MiniCrawler, an advertisement-free version of itself, and Power Search, which allows you to fine-tune your search-result screen.

ProFusion

http://www.designlab.ukans.edu/profusion/

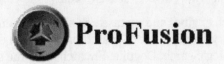 **ProFusion**

AltaVista	Excite
HotBot	Infoseek
OpenText	Lycos
WebCrawler	Magellan
Yahoo	

I like this metasearcher because you can specify that it search with the three fastest engines, the three best, all, or only the ones you pick. Moreover, it tells you which engines support Boolean operators.

SavvySearch

http://guaraldi.cs.colostate.edu:2000/form

Yahoo	Excite
WebCrawler	Infoseek
DejaNews	Galaxy
Lycos	Magellan
Shareware.com	PointSearch
LinkStar	And more . . .

A simple interface allows you to search a bunch of search engine indexes at once. Only the search engines that've produced good results to searches like yours are invoked to get you your results, but you can specifically include all or any of the search engines in your search.

Part iii

Yahoo's All-in-One Search Pages

```
http://www.yahoo.com/Computers_and_Internet/Internet/World_Wi
de_Web/Searching_the_Web/All_in_One_Search_Pages/
```

If none of the other search engines and metasearch sites I've mentioned are doin' it for ya, try Yahoo's list of search pages. From the goofily named—Coolnerds MegaSearch, Dogpile, Flycatcher—to the serious—like the Ultimate Search Page—Yahoo's page links you there.

Finding People and Businesses

If you're looking for an old buddy or a potential employer, you'll want to start off with a search engine geared specifically toward finding people and places. The search sites below have indexed a goodly amount of addresses, both e- and snail mail. Most of them require that you enter the last name of the person you're looking for, but some allow wildcards in case you're not certain of the spelling.

On AOL

Keyword **yellow pages** will take you to AOL's Switchboard, where you can perform a search for a person or business. Though the people-search options are few, the advanced option allows you to narrow the search by affiliation; from Cornell University alumni to affiliates of Ducks Unlimited, this site has 'em all.

Bigfoot

```
http://www.bigfoot.com
```

The advanced search option allows you to search Bigfoot's directory or the White Pages by name and state or e-mail address.

Four11

http://www.four11.com

This site has an excellent power search feature that allows you to type in old organizations or locations you have in common with your searchee, plus a Smart Name feature that searches for *Sue*, *Susan*, and *Susie*, even if only *Sue* is specified.

Internet Address Finder

http://www.iaf.net

Wildcards are allowed, but the scope of the search interface is rather limited.

WhoWhere

http://www.whowhere.com

WhoWhere has a couple of advanced search options to help you find that special someone's e-mail address or home phone and address.

Classmates

http://www.classmates.com

This site is specifically geared toward helping high school alumni find each other well into their golden years.

MASHA BOITCHOUK'S HOW TO FIND PEOPLE'S E-MAIL ADDRESSES PAGE

http://sunsite.oit.unc.edu/~masha/

This site has some suggestions for narrowing your search plus a slew of links to specialized search services. It's good lost-friend browsing for a rainy Saturday.

Run with the Wolves, Burrow with the Gophers

Gopher is not colorful, it isn't exciting, but it *is* extremely well organized and easy to find information on. Basically, Gopher is a hierarchical set of text links that allow you to tunnel deeper and deeper toward the object of your search by passing through logical and progressively narrower menu options.

Keyword **gopher** will take you to AOL's burrowing point, illustrated in Figure 12.3; from here you can browse neat-o Gopher sites, search Gopherspace with Veronica (like Jughead, one of Gopher's search engines), or browse through the world's Gopher sites. If you need to do some serious research, don't overlook Gopher.

FIGURE 12.3: Dig, little gopher, dig!

Browsing Left Field

Sometimes you just want to find something—you don't care what, it just has to be interesting. Start off by going to keyword **random**; this keyword will send you to whatever AOL area it picks out of a hat. The first time I browsed with Random, I went *way* left field to Dégriftour: Le Voyage à Prix Dégriffé.

If you want something in the infield, try keyword **keyword**. Here you can browse the currently definitive and up-to-date list of AOL keywords. Just like on the Internet, AOL areas come and go, so you'll want to check back here for new developments once in a while.

Another browsy thing to do if you're the festive type is to try typing in a current holiday or event as your keyword. A Halloween area often springs up in October, an Olympics area during the Olympics season, and so on.

For that just-sit-back-and-relax feeling, try exploring AOL and the Internet on a road trip. Keyword **road trip** will get you to your starting point (Figure 12.4), where you can review the scheduled road trips, sign up for as many as you like, or even volunteer to lead one. These trips go where the trip leader wants to take you, so buckle up and enjoy the ride!

The International Channel also runs its own road trips, which are a must if you're curious about other cultures. You can visit Norway or learn about how others around the world celebrate the end-of-year holidays . . . whatever the international guides are up for, you can join in on. The International Road Trip Schedule is accessible from the bottom of the AOL Road Trip schedule.

FIGURE 12.4: The '60s meet the Jetsons here at hitchhiker central.

And last but not least, take a half day to make yourself some cocoa and meander through Find ➢ AOL Channel Guide for a detailed index to AOL's Channel contents.

ROCK THE FAVORITE PLACE LIST

I won't bore you with URLs to my favorite online comics, bike magazines, and whatnot; instead, I've compiled useful sites that you can
search to find stuff you want to find. I do bore you with my favorite
hotlinks on my Website. Get there by visiting the Sybex Web site at
http://www.sybex.com and looking up *America Online AmazingSecrets*
in the catalog.

Humor

http://www.humorsearch.com/

Search the Web for humor sites. Yippee!

Maps

http://www.mapquest.com

I love this site. Here you can enter any US street address and get a
detailed map of the area—a boon if you don't like asking for directions
from gas station attendants.

MedAccess On-Line

http://www.medaccess.com

Do you hate going to the doctor? Or just hate being uninformed about
your ailments? Then this site is for you. Look anything up, from a doctor
you're thinking of going to, to your diagnosis.

City.net

http://city.net

City.net is great if you're planning a trip. Here you can get info on any
city anywhere anytime.

US Dept of Energy Computer Incident Advisory Capability

http://ciac.llnl.gov/ciac/CIACHome.html

Find the latest on computer viruses and Internet hoaxes on this very
serious site.

Amazon Books

http://www.amazon.com

Amazon has a lot of books; new books, old books, rare out-of-print books. Order through their secure server or call with your credit card number; once you set your password, you can come back and order books on that same credit card time and time again.

Get a Job

http://www.getajob.com

Search for jobs by category, company, or region, check out the library of hints for getting and keeping a job, decide whether you're an eagle or a chicken . . . it's all along the way to Getting a Life!

The Monster Board

http://www.monster.com/

A monstrous number of job listings as well as resume building tips and employer profiles await you at this site.

Auto-by-Tel

http://www.autobytel.com

Look for a new, previously owned, or leasable car through Auto-by-Tel. You'll be referred to the nearest dealership that houses their trained sales personnel, who will quote you a price that's close to cost without you having to haggle for it.

Consumer Reports

Keyword: **consumer reports**

Do a little research on the merchandise you plan to buy; make sure you know what to look for, get some hints on where to get it, and keep up with the latest recalls.

THE WELCOME WINDOW SECRET

So you know that AOL logo in the Welcome window?

Have you ever passed your cursor over it? Notice how it turns into a pointing hand when you do that? Try clicking; you've found one of AOL's Easter eggs, a little hidden treasure of an area. This area changes every day.

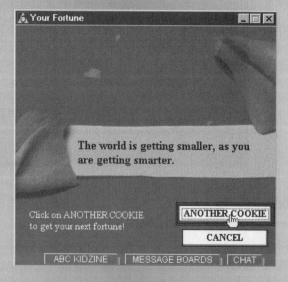

AOL's Today's News Channel

Keyword **news** ➤ Search & Explore

Browse the AOL News departments, get the best of the news, or customize a personalized to-your-mailbox news service.

WHAT'S NEXT?

Okay, AOL users. You've learned to search the Web. Time to take a break and relax! Read on to Chapter 13, where Laura Arendal will give you the straight story about playing AOL games. Learn what games to play, how to play them, and how to find people to play them with.

Chapter 13
PLAYING PREMIUM GAMES

I n our civilized society there's very little opportunity to experience the real-world challenges and adrenaline rushes of days past. No mountain lions threaten your commute to school or the office, you don't have to hunt down a bison during your lunch break to make sure you eat a decent meal at dinner, and you're not constantly on guard against attack by a neighboring tribe. Thank goodness we AOL users can play games that keep these challenges alive!

AOL offers some excellent games to hone your hunting skills and while away the hours; this chapter will tell you how to get the most out of the online multiplayer games.

Oh yeah, and for those of you who *prefer* a tigerless existence, there are logic and puzzle games to exercise your cerebral cortex.

Adapted from *America Online Amazing Secrets*,
by Laura Arendal
ISBN 0-7821-2229-9   368 pages $19.99

WHAT YOU SHOULD KNOW BEFORE YOU PLAY

Basically what you should know is that the online multiplayer games cost. Because extra money is involved, I'm going to spend some time up front talking about the lay of the pay-to-play land: how much you're being charged, how you know when you're racking up charges, what you're *not* charged for, and how to best prepare yourself to dive right into the games.

After you've been thoroughly briefed, I'll give you the lowdown on the games plus some basics to help you decide which one you want to attack first.

The Premium on Premium Games

So where do you find the coolest games on AOL? There are plenty cool games at keyword **games** (also reachable through Channels ➤ Games), but the interactive multiplayer games, which are, yes, the *premium* games, are at keyword **worldplay** (Figure 13.1).

Premium games cost money, to wit (as of this writing) $1.99 per hour on top of your usual connect-time cost. You are only charged for the amount of time you play games, so fractions of hours will run ya 3.3 cents a minute. If you're on the unlimited access plan and something of a dilettante, this is no biggie. But if you're on the limited-access plan or you're hooked on multiplayer online games, playing premium games is no small change.

NOTE

Multiplayer games—including AOL's premium games and more—can be played online for a reasonable price (a flat fee of about $10 per month) at GameStorm's Web site: http://www.gamestorm.com.

FIGURE 13.1: Your bouncing-off point to the stars, the pool table, another age . . .

When the Clock Starts Ticking . . .

You'll always be greeted by a blue dialog box before you enter a premium area, and a pleasant little dialog box will bid you farewell.

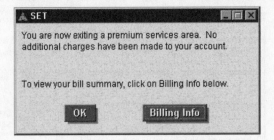

To keep tabs on your tab, either click the Billing Info button in the above dialog box, or go to keyword **billing** and click the Display Your Current Bill Summary button. These charges may take a little time to process on AOL's end, therefore may not show up on your statement immediately.

? Display Your Current Bill Summary

NOTE

If your session gets interrupted and you lose paid playing time trying to extricate yourself from a premium game, go to keyword **credit** to report the problem and get the time/money credited to your account.

Getting to the Games

There are two things you'll need to do to get into a game; you'll need to make sure your screen name has access to premium games, and you'll need to download the game to your hard drive. Instructions follow forthwith.

Ensuring Subaccount Access

First off, you should know that subaccounts are automatically blocked (through AOL default) from accessing premium games, so if you wish to play under a playful screen name (or if you want to give your kid access to these games for a special treat), you'll need to unblock premium games for that screen name. To do so:

1. Sign on as the master account screen name and, in AOL's toolbar, go to My AOL ➤ Parental Controls.

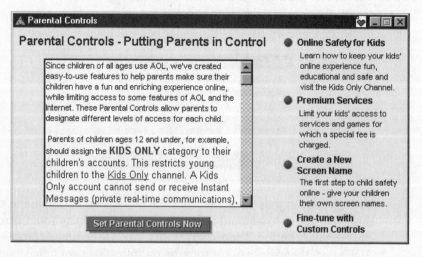

2. Click the Premium Services button on the right.

3. Notice that the master screen name has access to all premium services and the subaccount is blocked (poor Catra).

Just click the checkbox to clear it and give that screen name access to premium games.

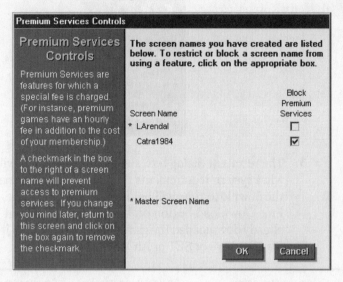

4. Click OK.

Downloading Each Game

Before you can play a game, you'll need to download it from AOL to your hard drive.

NOTE

The time it takes to download a game is, of course, not charged (unless you're on a limited-access plan). Depending on what game you're downloading and how fast your modem is, downloads can take anywhere from 30 minutes to 2 hours.

To download a game:

1. From the WorldPlay Games main screen's game list, double-click the name of the game. (You can also access it from the Game Categories list, of course.)

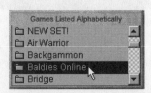

Part iii

2. Click the wiggly PLAY button on the left.

3. The resultant dialog box, shown in Figure 13.2, will tell you what system requirements the game has and, usually, what the download time will be. To download the game, click the Free Download button on the right. (Notice that if you've already downloaded the game, you can go right to it with the Play Baldies—or SET or Air Warrior . . .—button.)

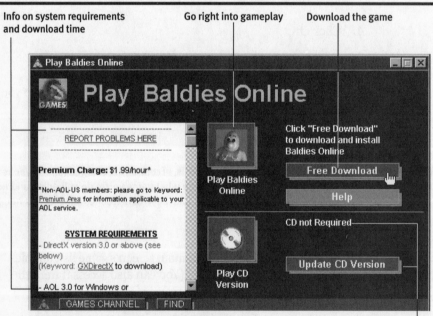

FIGURE 13.2: Your gateway to big fun

4. Click I Agree to acknowledge that you are entering a Premium Area (though, as you're performing a download, the dialog box notes that you won't be charged for your time).

5. The AOL Installer will come up with a directory path for the game to be downloaded to. If you want to put it elsewhere (for instance, if you have a directory reserved for games), just click the Change button and navigate to the folder you wish to use (Figure 13.3). Note that once you get to the folder, you'll need to click the Create Dir button and type in a sub-folder name (e.g., **Baldies**) for a complete path to be created. When you are satisfied with the download path, click OK once in the Game/New Path dialog box and again in the AOL Installer dialog box.

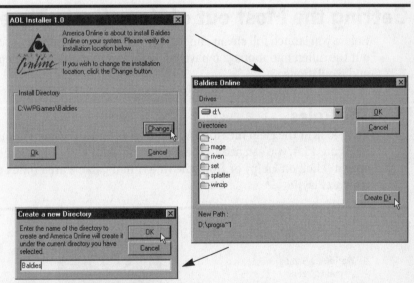

FIGURE 13.3: You may change the download directory during installation.

6. The download will begin. You can go elsewhere in AOL (except another premium area) while you're waiting for the game to be downloaded and installed, or you can do something else on your computer—or you can catch up on your homework . . .

7. When the download is done, the game will usually launch itself. Don't worry if it can't find your AOL connection this time; just exit the game, then relaunch it from the WorldPlay Games area.

TIP

Most games you can try in single-player mode before you open yourself up to heated competition/being shot at. To do the single-player thing, you can either take advantage of that first non-connected launch to play around, or you can exit AOL and start the game from your hard drive. Much of the functionality will be disabled in the single-player version, but you'll get a feel for the controls and the look of the game.

Getting the Most out of Your Game Time

Before you launch full steam and full price into your chosen game, check out the different options you have for getting comfortable with the rules and regulations.

The Rules

First, look at the Help files for FAQs and rules for each game. As shown in Figure 13.4, you can access these from the main WorldPlay Games screen (click on Help) or from the individual game's area (click on How to Play).

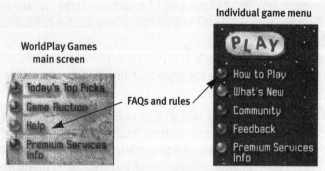

FIGURE 13.4:   Check out the Help files for each game.

TIP

Especially note how to quit a game during play. You may be able to click the Windows 95 Close button or, just as easy, press the Esc key—or you may need to wait until combat is over, then type **quit** . . .. The point is, how to quit varies with the game, and you'll want to make sure you know how to end your game session so you don't waste time and money figuring it out.

Quick Start Instructions

Some games are the play-and-learn type (you'll find this more in the puzzle and card game categories); these offer a Quickstart file. Here you can get a general feel for the game and then hone your skills by playing. The Quickstart approach is useful if you're the impatient type who'd rather figure out strategy on your own.

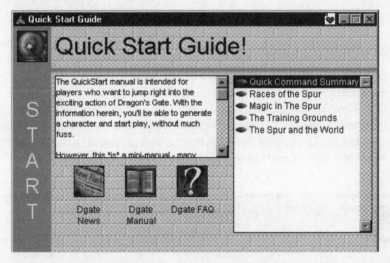

Coaching Corner

Especially if you're a beginner, you may want to take a breather in the Coaching Corner, also accessible from the WorldPlay Games main screen. Coaching will be more meaningful if you've played a game already, but it won't hurt to get some coaching before sallying forth if you're particularly nervous about a game or your bank account. Coaching Corner offers a lot of beginner classes, with the promise of more advanced classes to come.

Game Chat Rooms and Message Boards

And don't forget the ever-present AOL community; if you have specific questions about a game (or specific tips you want to share with other gamesters), drop into the game chat rooms or leave a message on the appropriate World-Play Games message board; helpful staff members patrol these boards and will answer your query in good time. Reach the chat room and message boards by clicking the Community button, found in the list on the left of each game's main area.

GOOD CLEAN FUN

As in all areas of AOL, rules of courtesy are important to abide by. Please use inoffensive language and images in chat areas, game play, and profile information; treat others with respect (in other words, no harassment, no scrolling, no impersonating other members); and resist the temptation to send chain letters or solicit other players.

In addition, when posting to message boards please post in English, English being AOL Land's official language.

Both the paid and unpaid Games areas are patrolled by staff members intent on keeping the peace, so breaking the above rules is not without consequence.

TIP

Speaking of community, an excellent way to find your way around the strange worlds here at WorldPlay is to find a mentor—a gamester with a lot of experience and patience—to guide you through the rough spots and find ways for you to gain experience points yourself. (This usually seems to involve finding an easy target for you to take on. Bloodthirsty bunch, these gamers . . .) As you move up in rank, don't forget to give back to the community what you got and look after those newbies.

Watch the Experts

For certain of the card and board games you can supplement the above learning methodologies by using the Watch option. Once you choose your card or board game, you'll notice a game table in the upper-right corner; if you wish to watch others rather than play, click the Watch button just above the game table. If Watch is inactive, either it isn't available for the game you've chosen, or the players of that particular round have opted to play in peace. (I'll show you how to set your options later in this chapter.)

Part iii

WARNING

Just because you're watching doesn't mean you're not racking up those pennies.

Test Drive a Beta Game

Lastly, a great way to play these excellent games for free is to test drive the new premium games. Find out what games are still in beta at keyword **gc test drive**. Keep in mind that *beta* means *buggy*, so you may crash in the process of play, but you won't get charged a penny for your playing time. Use the bug report forms for any problems that come up during play of a beta game.

Help!

If you need technical help with the games area, go to keyword **games help** for games tech support and try the support options shown at left.

TIP

If you have trouble launching the game you want, try exiting all the way out of the Premium Games area and then going back in. If you get a dialog box proclaiming "Server not found," it means the game is down, probably for servicing or upgrading. Try again later.

PLACES TO GO, PEOPLE TO MEET, GAMES TO PLAY

The Premium Games area offers a small but expanding selection of online multiplayer games, from adventurous fast-twitch fun to pensive logic-centered puzzles. Current offerings include:

Adventure games	Darkness Falls, Dragon's Gate, Legends of Kesmai, and Rolemaster: Magestorm
Strategy and action	Air Warrior II, Baldies Online, Harpoon Online, Heavy Damage, MultiPlayer Battle-Tech, Splatterball, and Warcraft II
Classic card	Bridge, Gin, Hearts, Online Casino, Spades, and Whist
Puzzle and board	Backgammon, CatchWord, Cribbage, SET, Spunky's Shuffle, The Incredible Machine 3, and Virtual Pool

What You Can Generally Expect

Here's what to expect when you enter the games. There are some common elements to the action adventure games and to the card and board games, so under each category I outline the basic steps you'll take to get yourself in on a game.

Adventure Games, Strategy and Action Games

Taking Magestorm as an example, here's how you get into your basic action adventure:

1. Go to keyword **worldplay**.

2. Choose your game from the scrollable list in the middle of the main WorldPlay Games screen.

3. Click Play.

4. Click the Play Game button. (Play Magestorm, in this example.)

5. Click the I Agree button, acknowledging that you understand that you will be charged for using this area.

6. The game will launch and connect to AOL. At this point you'll be alone in the private foyer, which will take many shapes depending on the game (in Magestorm, it's a library; in Splatterball it's a small store). Figure 13.5 shows Magestorm's library; most of the options available here (viewable with ToolTips-like labels) are available in all the action adventure games.

Exit Magestorm   Create a new character

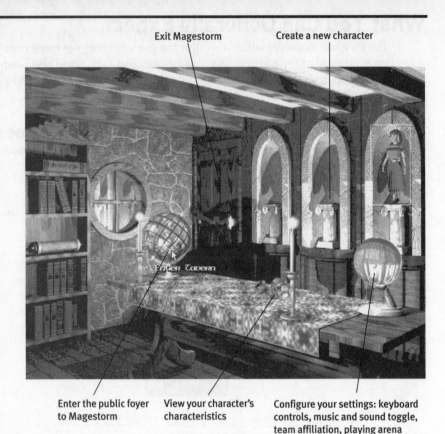

Enter the public foyer   View your character's   Configure your settings: keyboard
to Magestorm   characteristics   controls, music and sound toggle,
                                                         team affiliation, playing arena

FIGURE 13.5: You can hide out here, toying with your preferences, before screwing up your courage to enter the tavern.

7. Once you've created your character and configured your moves and location to your liking, enter the public foyer, shown in Figure 13.6. This may be called a tavern, as in Magestorm, or a clubhouse, like in Splatterball, or whatever game-appropriate title the creators have given it.

Closed to me because
my character is a Level 1   Current open matches   Private match   List of current players with level,
occupation, and whereabouts

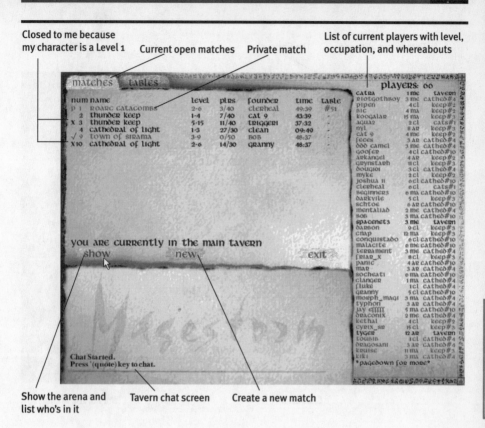

Show the arena and   Tavern chat screen   Create a new match
list who's in it

FIGURE 13.6:   There's a lot going on in this magical world.

8. From here you can peruse the list of current players and choose an existing venue for your excursion (by double-clicking on the place name in the Matches list) or create a new arena (by clicking the New button, selecting an arena and the levels allowed, and clicking Launch).

9. Once in, the other players will be alerted to your arrival. The screen will look something like Figure 13.7 (the particular graphics will change according to the game, but the layout's the same). Play on!

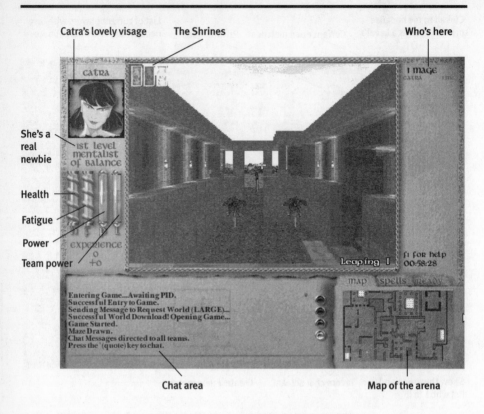

Catra's lovely visage   The Shrines   Who's here

She's a real newbie

Health
Fatigue
Power
Team power

Chat area   Map of the arena

FIGURE 13.7: Leaping about in the Temple of Ramhotep

10. When you're ready to quit, use the magic keystroke(s) you learned from the Help files (Magestorms' is the Esc key) and confirm your desire to exit. At this point you'll be able to view your billing information if you wish.

Classic Card and Puzzle & Board Games

Follow these easy instructions to start a card or board game (for instance, SET) or certain action games (like Baldies Online):

1. Go to keyword **worldplay**.

2. Choose your game from the scrollable list in the middle of the main WorldPlay Games screen.

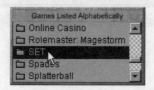

3. Click Play.

4. Click the Play *Game* button (for instance, Play SET).

5. Click the I Agree button, acknowledging that you understand that you will be charged for using this area.

6. The game will launch and connect to AOL. You can read through the Getting Started dialog boxes, or just click the Close button.

7. Create a profile and character image for yourself by clicking the My Profile button; you can customize a female or male figure (Figure 13.8), or you can choose from the large variety of images in the Image Library. Add interests and background, and you may find like souls at your playing table (Figure 13.9).

8. Select a room to enter by double-clicking on a room in the room list. You'll have a choice of beginner to advanced, special events, coaching, and game-specific challenges.

Part iii

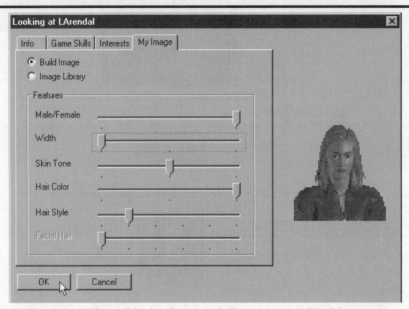

FIGURE 13.8: You could take the vaguely human route, not that anyone will believe you really look like this.

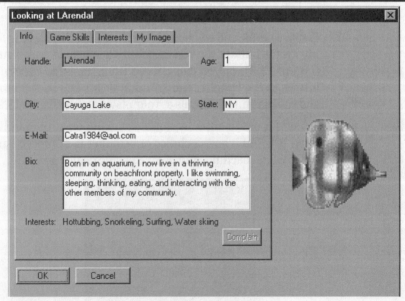

FIGURE 13.9: Or you could go for total absurdity.

9. If you're the only occupant, click New Game to start. If there are others playing, click Select a Current Game to join that group. If there's an opening at the table, you'll see an empty chair around the playing table in the upper-right corner. Click it to join; the game will start when all the chairs are filled.

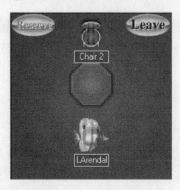

NOTE

If you're invited to join a game, click the inviting player's name or image, and the game's table and chairs will appear.

10. To start a new game, click New Game. The Create Game Table dialog box will appear. From here, choose the number of players and click the Options button.

11. The Options dialog box gives you several tabs within which you can configure your game. The Summary tab is unexciting,

so I'm going to skip directly to the General tab, shown in Figure 13.10.

View game summary,
add notes, or complain

Reserve specific
chairs

Set game
variations

How patient
you want to be

Reservation options
in case of quitters

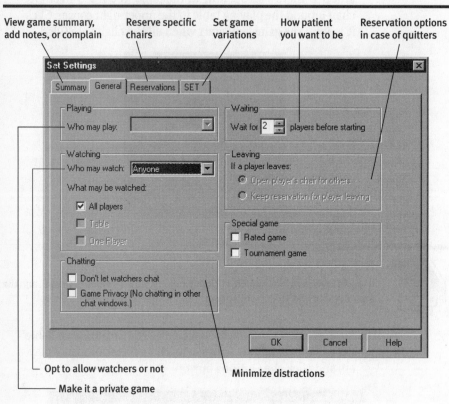

Opt to allow watchers or not

Make it a private game

Minimize distractions

FIGURE 13.10: Generally speaking, the options

12. The Reservations tab allows you to reserve a spot for a friend; at the tab, select the chair you wish to reserve, click the Reserve button, click the By Name radio button, and type in your friend's screen name. Check the spelling, click Reserve, and move on to the SET tab. The empty chair at your playing table will be tipped, with a note that it is reserved for your friend.

13. At the SET tab, choose the type of game you wish to play,
    then click OK. (Once a game has started, you can change the
    game options from the Control Panel, which is located on the
    Chat screen.)

14. When all players required are present, the game will start. All
    games have a way to chat with other players, as you see in
    Figure 13.11.

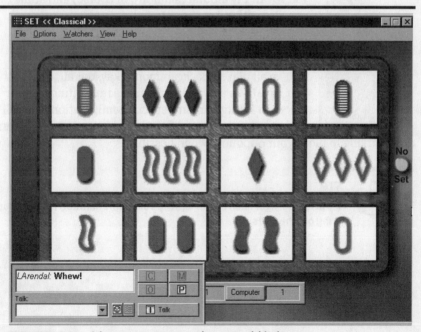

FIGURE 13.11: It's a computer-eat-player world in here.

15. When you're played out, click Exit, then Quit to leave the premium area.

16. Click OK (or view your Billing Info) to acknowledge the end of the paid playing session.

That's all I can tell you in terms of general hints; message boards and chat rooms can be really excellent ways to get the individual attention you need to feel comfortable with a game.

The Games

In this section I'm going to attempt to briefly synopsize all the online multiplayer games available on AOL so far. I'm not going to rate them; if you like it, it rocks. If you don't, it rocks for someone else. So I'll leave taste up to the individual. Here goes (alphabetically) . . .

Air Warrior II

 Get yourself an aircraft, gas up and check yer ammo, and you're on! Fly around (skillfully, of course) and strafe everyone else without getting strafed.

Backgammon

 You've all played Backgammon (okay, not all, but most of you have); it's a two-player game. After setting up your 15 pieces in Backgammon's special configuration, you roll dice and move your pieces off the board into your home trough, trying to block your opponent when possible.

TIP

If you're a Backgammon beginner, keep Voices (the narrator) on to aid you in figuring out the rules.

Baldies Online

You've got these little bald guys in red suits, and you want to set them to building, researching, and inventing. Don't forget to set some to soldiering so the non-red baldies can't get you. Basically, you want to get *them*. The most offensive group of baldies wins the day.

Some helpful, if bald, hints:

▶ Right-click on anything you want to know more about; the Baldy Help Advisor will describe it and maybe give you a few tips on it.

▶ Check your opponents' progress with the mini-map.

▶ Taunt non-red baldies. Finally, that practice at Heckler's Online comes in handy!

Bridge

Bridge is the 4-person game our parents and grandparents played, teaming off against each other across a flimsy foldout card table late into the night. Thirteen cards each are dealt out, then the madness ensues. Basically a game of bluff and call-the-bluff, with super-complicated rules, Bridge is a game you'll want to watch for a while to get the hang of.

WorldPlay offers several Bridge variations for your bidding and tricking pleasure: Chicago (Standard, Cavendish, or Duplicate), Rubber, No Score, and Whist.

NOTE

If WorldPlay doesn't satisfy your Bridge urges, try keyword **bridge**.

CatchWord

Kind of a time-pressured Scrabble, you play CatchWord by watching letters appear on the playing board and using them to form a word (found in the dictionary, not a proper noun, etc.) of at least four letters in length. You can also steal words from other players by using the word plus new letters to form another word, and, of course, you can challenge others' words.

Cribbage

Two to four players play this blackjack-like card & board game; after the cards are dealt, players lay down cards just short of or equal to 31 points. Pegs are moved around the Cribbage board in relation to a complex system of rules based on what cards and combinations of cards were played in the hand. The first player to move 121 spaces wins.

There is no inviter option in WorldPlay's Cribbage, so whoever graces your online table is who you'll play.

Darkness Falls

You may have thought that you've been doing all sorts of dark, evil things in other games, but not compared to what you'll do in Darkness Falls. It's a role-playing game where your only character choices are evil, to be played to the darkest ends in a decaying virtual town. If you've ever secretly longed to be a skeleton, zombie, demon, werewolf, vampire, or shady human, Darkness Falls is your place to explore that side of you while fighting and training to advance your skill level.

Dragon's Gate

Dragon's Gate is a role-playing adventure game involving magic, combat, middle-ages sort of stuff. You know. Advance your skills to advance your rank, casting spells and fighting foes to keep alive.

Useful things to know:

▶ Type **help** to see a list of commands. Type a command and press Enter to get a description of what the command will accomplish and how to use it.

▶ Use **set info** (type **set info help** for list of commands) to control how much information you get about the action around you.

Gin

A two-person card game involving melding (much like Hearts or Canasta) and going out (declaring *gin*) before your opponent. A succession of games is played until one player has 100 points. WorldPlay offers the following variations: Oklahoma and Hollywood Gin.

WorldPlay's Gin also offers a training mode, where the dealer decides who gets what card to help along the novice.

Harpoon Online

Join or create a team to do aquatic battle with your enemies and, with your modern and (virtual) naval weapons, prevent them from controlling the world's oceans before you do.

NOTE

Though Harpoon Online is quite difficult to learn, it's totally worth it if this type of game is your bag.

Hearts

Three to five players play, each of you trying to score fewer points than your opponents do. After your cards are dealt, discard frantically (but according to the rules)—especially your hearts—to win.

NOTE

GameStorm's card games can be found at keyword **classic cards**.

Heavy Damage

Flying your futuristic hovercraft through a virtual maze, you must search out and destroy as many other heavy-damage-wannabes as possible, all the while defending yourself from attack by same. Complete with

hipster vocab (frag or be fragged, baby!) and an arsenal to drool over, Heavy Damage packs enough action into its rules alone to get your adrenaline going.

Legends of Kesmai

Another role-playing game where you fight other characters to win points and influence, umm, the level-escalating forces that be. Medieval.

NOTE

Note that in addition to the usual Legends of Kesmai game download, you also need to download ODBC (database tools) and DirectDraw. These are available from the Legends of Kesmai How to Play area.

MultiPlayer BattleTech

Based on MechWarrior, in BattleTech you travel to where the action is and unload your weapons into your choice of other online players or droids.

NOTE

You can get a walk-through tutorial of the BattleTech way of life from the Solaris Starport Arrivals area.

Online Casino

You've got your choice of Five Card Stud, Five Card Draw, Seven Card Stud, Texas Holdem, or Omaha Holdem here at the online casino. The vocabulary will be familiar to you stone-faced Reno-goers; for you greenhorns, look under the Help menu for the rules.

Rolemaster: Magestorm

A magical role-playing game of capture the shrine (rather, blow up all shrines belonging to orders other than your own to capture an arena) and kill or be killed, get resurrected or die, bias pools of earthblood (don't ask) toward your own order . . .

SET

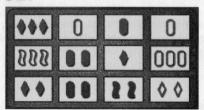

Singly, against the computer, or against up to seven other players, you can take on this pack of cards and show it who's boss. You have to match the card patterns in sets of three before your opponent(s) find the match. Said match can be of similar features or dissimilar features.

I recommend watching before playing; it takes a while to get used to the cards.

Spades

Spades is a three- or four-person card game involving bids and tricks, the objective of which is to earn the highest number of points. Read the rules.

Splatterball

It's virtual paintball, much less dangerous than the human-interface real-life kind in that big room where the ceiling's sometimes blue and sometimes black . . . Create a character, join a team, and splat as many opponents with your paint gun as you can. Capture the flag and bring it to your team's home base to gain points.

On one of the rare occasions you aren't online, power up Splatterball and practise running and splatting in single-user mode.

Spunky's Shuffle

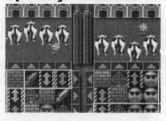

This new game pits you against either the computer or against another online player as you struggle to align your tiles toward your goal as well as to block your opponent.

It's colorful and it's silly! What more could you ask after a hard day of Heavy Damage or Dragon's Gate?

The Incredible Machine 3

Brain teasers galore; choose a puzzle (which often involves getting something, like a bouncing ball, from one place to another) and place various gadgets in the puzzle field to build a moving or appropriately angled machine to solve said puzzle.

Some helpful hints:

▶ Use the spyglass to find out what a gadget is and does.

▶ If you've placed a gadget and nothing happens, you may need to connect another gadget to it to activate it.

▶ Opponents might be friendly (chat with them for ideas) or malicious (bomb them before they bomb you), and it behooves you to find out which.

Virtual Pool

Pool is pool. A series of commands brings you a virtually realistic game of eight-ball, nine-ball, or rotation. Beer and brawling not provided.

Warcraft II

Be you Human or Orc, your object is to crush the other. However, Warcraft II is not just a search-and-destroy game. You must feed your forces and harvest resources in order to strengthen your side. And *then* you can search out the Orcs (or Humans) and destroy them!

NOTE

Find online tournament schedules for your favorite games by following this path from WorldPlay Games' main screen: Today's Top Picks ➢ Events. Tournaments are held either in the WorldPlay Games Events Room or at Love@AOL, so be sure to check the location. Note that the listed times are Eastern Standard time; plan appropriately.

WHERE TO FIND FINE NONPREMIUM GAMES

The Games channel has game demos and reviews, which you can connect to from Games Central (from Playstation's Final Fantasy VII, Nintendo's Diddy Kong Racing, to obscure PC games like Manx TT Super Bike).

If you're stuck in a game, any game (such as Riven) or you want cheat codes (for SimCity, for instance), post your request to the Games Insider community message boards. To get to the Games Insider community, go to keyword **games**, click Games Insider (on the left), and you're there. The message boards can be accessed from the list on the right: Games Central Messaging is the place.

The Game Insider area also brings you the Weekly Game news, updating you about new game happenings on AOL; the news archives give you past game reviews and news.

Other nonpremium game venues include Game Shows Online (at keyword **game shows**), which has a wide selection, or Antagonist, Inc. (keyword **ant**).

You can access the Online Gaming Forums at keyword **ogf**—forums include a freeform gaming forum, where you create a character and interact with other characters in a chat room to create a story, sim forum, strategy forum, collectible card games forum, chess forum, game designer's forum, wargaming forum—you name it, it could be there.

Be sure to check out NTN Games Studio (keyword **ntn**), which features a timed competitive trivia contest of 15 trivia questions per game. Check the daily schedule for different games.

WHAT'S NEXT?

That Laura Arendal is fun, fun, fun. Now that she's talked to you about playing games, she'll teach you how to find bargains and free stuff. In the next chapter, you'll learn the ins and outs of getting stuff *cheap* on AOL.

Part iii

Chapter 14

HUNTING FOR BARGAINS AND FREE STUFF

We all want to feel like we're getting the best deal on the products and services we buy—and if the provider offers it for free, all the better, right? Bargains, contests, and free stuff abound if you know where to look, both online and off. Offline you're on your own, but if you're after online bargains, you've come to the right place. In this chapter, I'll point you toward some good AOL and Web sites for getting your money's—or your talent's—worth.

THE GOODS

There are several places on AOL to shop for new goods and with the confidence that you're getting a bargain—plus some good places to find previously owned, new-to-you, recycled, perfectly broken-in items.

• •

Adapted from *American Online Amazing Secrets*,
by Laura Arendal
ISBN 0-7821-2229-9   368 pages $19.99

NOTE

Before you buy, ease your mind by checking out the AOL Guarantee, which you can find at keyword **guarantee**. AOL guarantees 100% purchasing satisfaction: AOL's merchants are certified by AOL (in addition to being stable businesses, AOL's merchants must agree to perform one-day order processing and e-mail turnaround as well as post complete customer service information and guarantees). In the event of credit card fraud (which is unlikely to happen), any damage is covered by AOL.

Shopper's Advantage
Keyword **sa**

For an annual fee (at publication date, just $59.95), you too can be a Shopper's Advantage member, reaping such rewards as lowest-price guarantees on merchandise, an automatic 2-year warranty with everything you purchase through clubs, access to weekly specials, and SA's top deals on quality brand-name merchandise. At SA you can search for a specific item or browse the selections. My browsing turned up the impressive offer of 12 rolls of 24 exposure Kodak film at $28.60 to members, $50.10 to nonmembers.

Magazine Outlet
Keyword **magazine outlet**

If clicking through online magazines doesn't cut it for you and you long for the days of curling up in your easy chair with Bubbles the cat warming your lap and a good zine to leaf through, Magazine Outlet guarantees the lowest prices on hundreds of magazine subscriptions.

For instance, you can save 80% off *Time*'s cover price (currently 52 issues for $30, compared to the regular subscription rate of $59.94). You can subscribe to 12 issues of *Wired* for $20 (compared to $39.95). And *American Woodworker* clocks in at 14 issues for $48. AOL's always adding magazines, so browse through once in a while to see what your current options are.

NOTE

Take these figures for what they are; impressive comparisons rather than hard fact. Prices change faster than books can be printed.

AOL Classifieds
Keyword **classifieds**

Dance with the wheelers and dealers at AOL Classifieds. Here you can post free or paid ads and browse the same for whatever post-pristine merchandise your heart desires (except for children to adopt, tobacco, firearms, alcohol, and explosives).

The difference between the free and the paid ads is that the free ads are posted on a bulletin board that's hidden a bit (and features bulletin board search capabilities only), and the paid ads are immediately accessible and searchable by region, category, or keyword.

TIP

There are a *lot* more listings in the bulletin boards, so it behooves the smart shopper to check both places. Given this fact, the paid ads, though reasonably priced, are probably not a necessary use of your money.

To get to the bulletin boards:

1. Go to keyword **classifieds** (Figure 14.1).

FIGURE 14.1: Every community has its garage sales, flea markets, and thrift stores: AOL is no exception.

Part iii

2. Click the Using AOL Classifieds icon.

3. Click Buy & Sell Bulletin Boards.

📭 Buy & Sell Bulletin Boards

4. Choose your category. Once you get into the boards, the vehicles (for instance) are broken down by models and types. Though these aren't searchable geographically, you can use the Find in Top Window command to narrow your search by model or year (as long as the advertiser put that information in the posting's subject line).

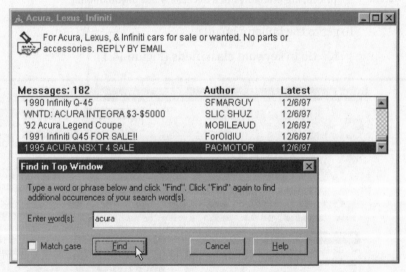

AOL Classifieds also offers you wiley traders a bulletin board, chat room, customer service, and trading guidelines.

WARNING

As with any sort of transaction, be very careful of cheats. AOL has written up some good guidelines that the smart seller and buyer will read and consider following. Find these guidelines in the Buyer/Seller folder of the Using AOL Classifieds area.

AOL Store

Keyword **aol store**

The AOL Store is like the campus store at your alma mater sans the candy counter and soda machine. Here you can buy toys, books, digital equipment, software, clothes....

The prices are comparable to your campus store and other stores out there (like CompUSA), but it's definitely worth comparison shopping at the AOL Store. You might get lucky and hit a sale—and besides, where else can you buy an AOL varsity hooded sweatshirt?

THE SERVICES

Finding the right merchandise provider is just as important as finding the goods you need, but because the human element is inescapable, it's that much more challenging. Not only do you need to find *what* you want (for instance, a ticket from Boston to LA with a stopover in Quebec), but you need to find a provider that will procure it for you at the best price, preferably in a friendly and efficient way. You will find services of all kinds on AOL—after all, cyberspace is about providing information (I'm not going to touch the reliability issue here)—so what follows are just some highlights.

TIP

Even if you don't take advantage of the extended toolbar, you can keep abreast of your AOL Perks at keyword **perks**. Special offers for AOL members include the AOL Visa, with which you can earn free AOL time, the sign-up-a-friend bonus ($20), AOL's long distance savings plan, and more.

Part iii

Traveler's Advantage
Keyword **ta**

For a yearly fee of (currently) $59.95, you get Traveler's Advantage's lowest-price guarantee (if you find a lower price on your fare, hotel, or car rental within 30 days of departure, TA will refund the difference); 5% cash back (this money usually becomes the travel agent's commission); special offers on hotels, cars, and plane fares; access to online booking arrangements; a tripfinder to help you decide on and organize your vacation itinerary; and 24-hour service.

If you travel frequently, you'll want to experiment with Traveler's Advantage (you can try it for 3 months for a buck).

Preview Travel
Keyword **preview travel**

Preview Travel (Figure 14.2) claims to be the most highly used travel service on AOL, and it's easy to see why. It keeps AOL members up to date on the latest airline, hotel, car rental, and other travel-related deals (such as the $88-$298 round-trip airfare American Airlines offered in late 1997), includes a News and Features section with weather advisories and travelers' journal entries, offers ready-made vacation packages for those of you who've planned one too many itineraries in your lifetime, plus gives you safety tips, emergency instructions, packing hints, and oh so much more.

Better yet for you infrequent travelers, there's no membership fee, though to get substantial information, you'll need to complete a brief travel profile.

AOL AutoVantage
Keyword **av**

If you're in the market for a new or used car, you can find out specs, experts' ratings, dealer and sticker prices, and past performance stats on the car of your dreams (or of your means).

FIGURE 14.2: A travel service that almost makes it unaffordable to stay home!

If you want to take it further, you can fill out the Dealer Referral Form to get a quote on the car you're beginning to think of as yours. The quoted price is nonnegotiable, but it's quite fair as it's arrived at by adding a small profit (2–5%, a dealership profit approved by Consumer Reports) to the dealer's price.

If you want to take it still further, you would then visit the local dealership that provided the quote, test drive the car, and buy it (you can also finance the car through AutoVantage if you so choose). It sure beats playing the car salesman game.

AutoVantage also offers a club membership, which is somewhat like AAA and then some. For an annual fee of $79.95 (at the time of this writing) you get 24-hour roadside service, free service at select auto service centers, car buying assistance, car and hotel deals, maps, and trip planning.

Courses Online

Keyword **courses**

The Research & Learn channel brings you a way to attend adult-education classes at universities far and wide. In addition to the personal growth and enrichment offered at AOL's Online Campus, you can earn a certification or a graduate degree with University of California Extension classes and Phoenix University's programs.

Part iii

AOL's Online Campus

 This virtual college offers such diverse courses as Basic Conversational Navajo, Essential Spanish for Health Care Professionals, Math GED Preparation, Calculus I, Breadbaking, Starting a Successful Home Based Business, and Music Theory.

Courses are $25–50, depending on how long the course runs (most courses meet online once a week for 4 to 8 weeks). As with any school, getting to class (online fees) and materials are extra.

All AOL's Online Campus new courses are free the first time they're offered. There are not many in this category, but new courses are constantly being added. For my next career, I'm eyeing that Home Farmfishing for Profit class. At the very least I'll have a new hobby!

UC Extension Online

Select classes from the UC adult-education catalog (Figure 14.3) are offered online. You can find classes on quite a variety of subjects: C Language Programming, Intro to Human Physiology, Freshman Composition & Literature. To take a class, you enroll whenever the mood strikes you and then can take up to one year to complete the course.

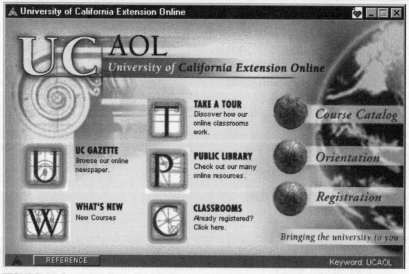

FIGURE 14.3: Relax from a hard day at the office by spending some quiet time with your Calculus primer.

Course prices are comparable to UC Extension's real-world prices; Freshman Lit, for example, is $375 (textbooks extra).

UC Extension Online offers certificate programs in Hazardous Materials Management and Computer Information Systems Analysis and Design.

Phoenix U.

Phoenix University's online campus is geared toward allowing working adults to earn an undergrad or grad degree in their (your) spare time. Don't get too excited, though, unless you were planning on getting that degree in a business-related field.

Undergraduate degrees offered are BSs in Business Administration, Business Information Systems, and Business Management. Graduate degrees you can earn are an MA in Organizational Management and MSs in Business Administration, Business Administration in Technology Management, Business Administration in Global Management, and Computer Information Systems.

Again, because the school is accredited, the cost is real-world; undergrad courses are $365 per credit, graduate courses $460 per credit.

The Motley Fool School
Keyword **motley fool**

Investing. It's what your parents are always urging you to do. If you feel at a loss when it comes to putting your money in someone else's hands, get the online investment skinny from the Motley Fool. Featuring advice on investing, and even on such satellite issues as buying a car and hunting for a job, the Motley Fool will gently guide you through the fine follies of money management in the most amusing way possible.

Nolo Press
Keyword **nolo**

The folks at Nolo really believe that, for most procedures, you can get by just fine without a lawyer. Their books and software steer you down the correct legal path without making you shell out more than the cost of said books, software, and whatever processing fees are necessary to get your case through the courts.

Nolo Press also has helpful books on other topics, such as buying a house or being a responsible landlady. Not only does Nolo's site have a helpful encyclopedia of legal topics, a tip of the day, and Shark Talk—a somewhat silly, rather bloody, but quite educational legal word game—it has an astounding collection of lawyer jokes.

Downtown AOL
Keyword **downtown aol**

AOL's Online Business Directory expands your list of goods and services to choose from by listing a large variety of businesses that have offices on the Web. You can browse the list or search it by business name or keyword.

EARNING COOL STUFF

Winning stuff in contests adds an extra edge to the excellence of getting stuff free—not only was it free, you were smart enough to score it.

There are tons of contests in different areas all over AOL; your favorite areas and holiday areas might sponsor contests from time to time, so be sure to check those places in addition to the contests listed here.

Prizes range from the absurd to the sublime.

WARNING

Keep in mind that entering a contest means that you have consented, should you be a winner, to having your contest submission, name, and/or screen name used in promotions for the contest sponsor, AOL, and its affiliates. But who knows? It may be your 15 seconds of fame!

Trivia Contests

These contests test your knowledge of the little (but terribly important) details of life (or flowers, or celebrities, or...). The way the contests usually work is that if you answer all (or a certain percent, depending on the contest) of the trivia questions correctly, yours are added to the pile of answers that are then subjected to a random drawing.

1-800-Flowers

Keyword **flowers**

1-800-Flowers sponsors a birthday trivia contest each month (winners net a $10 gift certificate for flowers).

Cruise Critic

Keyword **cruise critic**

Answer trivia questions about (surprise!) cruises for a chance to win a cruise vacation. (Hint: you can find the answers by browsing the Cruise Critic area.)

Electronic Gourmet Guide

Keyword **gourmet guess**

This one's a food trivia contest; those foodies who score at least 7 of a possible 11 points go on to the random drawing stage. Prizes range from food posters to cutlery sets.

Moms Online

Keyword **moms online**

Go to the games area for your mom-ish game options, including a mother-y trivia game for which you could win MOPS (the Moms Online Point System), which are redeemable in the Mom's Online Store, the Cybershop, or at A Common Reader.

Part iii

Talent Contests

If your thing is not little pockets of knowledge but a flourishing, as-yet-unrecognized talent, AOL's talent contests are for you. Ranging from creative writing to creative graffiti, AOL's contests are sure to include something that tugs at your special muse.

The Amazing Instant Novelist
Keyword **novel**

The Amazing Instant Novelist sponsors various writing contests that cover many topics, so if writing is your thing, look it up. You could win a resort vacation, a camera, and more cool shlag.

Antagonist Inc.
Keyword **ant**.

Here are the PC, Nintendo, and Playstation game contests—and there are many. The talent contest involves downloading the targeted game demo from the contest area and then rating it as creatively and accurately as you can. Tokens net you prizes like a weekend in Washington, DC; Mechwarrior 2 game software; or a Jolt Cola Jockstrap!

Heckler's Online
Keyword **ho**

Do you have a sassy, insolent side to your creative patter? Heckler's Online has the contests for you! Pick from:

> ▶ Digital Graffiti: take the posted picture and apply your electronic spray paint.

▶ Daily Heckler's Gameroom chat room contests such as Altered States, where the gameroom hosts throw out the name of a state and you come up with as much interesting "information" about the state until the hosts call a halt to the frenzy. And then you do it again.

▶ Interactive Top Ten: HO provides the topic, you give one of the top 10 supporting statements. For example, one of the top 10 Disturbing Things to Read in Your Horoscope: *Signing an organ donor card today will save a life tomorrow* (courtesy of Mrs. Penny).

▶ Limerickization: write a limerick about the posted topic

There are many more games at HO than I've listed, so let your mouse do the scurrying to find the perfect prize-winning competition for you. Winning in any of these nets you HO tokens, redeemable at the Prize Cellar. The prizes available in the Cellar span the gamut from Hog's Breath Hot Sauce to a Sony 27" TV.

InToon
Keyword **intoon**

Click on Intoon with the News' Hot Air contest and fill in the cartoon balloon to fit (or not) the cartoon situation depicted. You could win a cartoon print—plus, of course, fame and recognition.

Moms Online
Keyword **moms online**

There are many venues for your motherly creativity at Moms Online. Click the Games icon for games, the Daily Sphinx for a daily vocabulary contest complete with silly story. The games section includes various chat and message board games such as serial story authoring, riddle solving, and anagram solving.

MOPS (Moms Online Point System) are redeemable in the Mom's Online Store, the Cybershop, or at A Common Reader.

Preview Travel
Keyword **vacations**

In the Preview Travel area, click on the Specials icon. Enter your best sob story (How badly *do* you need a vacation? Don't hold back, and you might win one!), travel photos (to win luggage), or travel tips (also to win luggage).

Urban Legends
Keyword **urban legends**

One month Urban Legends sponsored a UFO Stories contest, inviting you to share your wildest—and, of course, completely true—alien abduction story for Lost in Space paraphernalia. Check back for other contests.

Scavenger Hunts

Find it first and you win the prize! If you want to pit your keen instinct for scavenging and your mouse finger against other players, these are the contests you've been looking for.

Antagonist Inc
Keyword **ant**

Antagonist's scavenger contest involves scrutinizing the weekly demos for a riddle (tucked cleverly into any one of them) and then submitting your answer for the chance to win big. (These prizes include the Washington, DC/Jolt Cola Jockstrap range.)

Hub Music
Keyword **hub musi**

Hub Music's monthly contest involves collecting weekly clues and answering the monthly quiz questions correctly (based on the clues that have gone before) for a chance to win a $1,000 shopping spree at Tower Records.

Random Drawings

At this point you may be thinking, "To heck with the antics! I'm no circus elephant, standing on my head for the masses!" If you have no patience for showing off, but you just wanna win, try one of these random drawings.

1-800-Flowers
Keyword **flowers**

You'll find a Birthday Bonanza at 1-800-Flowers, where you can enter a random drawing for a chance to win a birthday flower cake.

Antagonist Inc
Keyword **ant**

In the PC, Nintendo, and Playstation contests area you'll find some contests where all you gotta do is enter to (maybe) win cool Nintendo, Playstation, or PC games and stuff.

HouseNet
Keyword **housenet**

Click the Rec Room icon to find the different random drawings this home-improvement site has to offer. Win a laser level that memorizes angles! Score architectural software with which to electronically daydream about your dream home!

Hub Music
Keyword **hub music**

The daily contest at Hub Music is a blind drawing for a CD or Tower Record t-shirts and other assorted goodies.

Magazine Outlet
Keyword **magazine outlet**

This contest is a good example of what you can find if you keep tabs on your favorite areas; in December, Magazine Outlet had a sweepstakes where the grand prize was 1 million dollars.

Traveler's Advantage

Keyword **ta**

Traveler's Advantage has an annual Christmas sweepstakes, where visions of winning $25,000 in cash will dance with the sugar plums in your Christmas Eve head.

GETTING IT FREE

And who can dispute the merits of finding free stuff? Cleaner (and less embarrassing) than dumpster diving, surfing AOL and the Web for free junk can be just as rewarding.

Many of the areas in AOL offer a free topic-specific newsletter, which is an excellent way to keep up with new things going on—chat schedules, hot games, whatever your interest is. And on the Internet, free stuff abounds. Below is a little list to whet your appetite; bone up on your searching skills (Chapter 12) and find your own little gems of price-less fun.

Games

Despite all the weird vibes you might get from the anthill talk at this site, you can still find some excellent demo software absolutely free at Antagonist inc. at keyword **ant**—Quake, Duke Nukem 3D, Tomb Raider 2, Andretti Racing, and more.

Virtual Flowers

Absolutely free, send your online sweetie a lovely picture of a flower arrangement at http://www.virtualflowers.com/.

Lotsa Free Stuff!

I'll leave you with a major find: WWW Virtual Sites at http://www.dreamscape.com/frankvad/free.html has links to gazillions of free things on the Web; cards, contests, screen savers, product samples, clip art, and tons more. Check it out, you'll be amazed.

WHAT'S NEXT?

Now that you've surrounded yourself with all the stuff money and talent can buy, you'll want to tell the world about it. Turn to Chapter 15, where Laura Arendal will give you the scoop on the AOL chatroom.

Part III

Chapter 15
WOWING THE CHAT ROOM

AOL is the perfect place to meet people online. For one thing, there are a lot of people there to meet, and most of them want to meet you. For another, you can flit about from room to room all night without entering the same room twice. And you can assume whatever persona you want for the evening's entertainment. If you're shy, you can lurk and listen. If you're outgoing, you can entertain the room.

Of course, there are drawbacks. There's the lowest-common-denominator factor, where the most asinine person sets the conversational tone. And, unfortunately, there seem to be a fair number of lowest common denominators in chat rooms. There's also the isolation thing; as much as you can successfully connect with people over the net, you're still just sitting in front of a computer screen in the end. And who knows if those you connect to are really who they say they are? Meeting people online adds a whole new level of anxiety to interpersonal relationships.

Adapted from *America Online Amazing Secrets*,
by Laura Arendal
ISBN 0-7821-2229-9   368 pages $19.99

However, it's still possible to find kindred spirits hanging out, willing to engage in intelligent discourse. Let's go find them!

WHICH WAY TO THE CHAT ROOM?

People Connection, the easiest and biggest floodgate to chatting, is accessible right from the Welcome window as well as from the toolbar (People ➤ People Connection). If you've used People ➤ Locate AOL Member Online to find a friend online and she's in a chat room, you can join her with the click of a button.

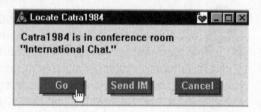

NOTE

Chat rooms and conference rooms are pretty much the same thing. Chat rooms are mostly accessed from People Connection, conference rooms from the different areas around AOL. Chat rooms are usually more unruly, and they hold 23 people max (more if there are AOL guides present). Conference rooms can hold 48 people, and the discussions are for the most part on topic. Auditoriums, where special live events take place, have virtually unlimited seating (but everyone's placed in rows, so the chatting doesn't get too overwhelming).

It's not hard to find people chatting away, but how do you find people chatting about what *you* want to chat about?

From People Connection

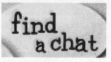

Once you get to the People Connection area on AOL (shown in Figure 15.1), you have some choices in front of you. Click Find a Chat to get the listing of featured chats shown in Figure 15.2.

FIGURE 15.1: Take off your coat and hat and dive in to find the real action.

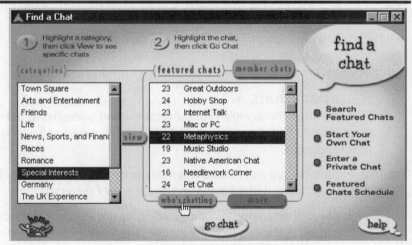

FIGURE 15.2: I'm about to check out who's getting metaphysical at this late hour . . .

Featured Chats

In the featured chats—which are AOL-created and monitored—you can check out the chat rooms by double-clicking a category in the left box, then double-clicking a room in the right box, as I've done in Figure 15.2.

Some tips:

▶ Town Square is pretty generic; you'd best be prepared to be the life of the party or be bored.

▶ Special Interest rooms bear very specific names that allow you to pick your room wisely. Many people in these rooms actually chat intelligently, with complete sentences and without expletives, about the subject at hand.

▶ Click the Who's Chatting button to check the list before you enter (and thus avoid or find certain people).

▶ If the More button is active, click it to expand the list.

▶ If you've forgotten when the Tamagotchi virtual pet chat is scheduled, click the Featured Chats Schedule button to browse through AOL's scheduled chat selection or search the feature chats (with the Search Featured Chats button) using AND, OR, and NOT to link key concepts. (See Chapter 12 for a thorough discussion of boolean expressions.)

Member Chats

In the member chats, you'll find the same sorts of categories as in the featured chats (as you see in Figure 15.3), but the chat rooms themselves are member-created.

▶ Town Square and Special Interests are usually full of all sorts of nasty rooms (in both good and bad senses of the word).

▶ You *can* find some interesting stuff going on in some of the more specific categories, like people guessing a song from the lyrics (yeah, some of these are nasty, too), people discussing abortion (in between the usual banter), and people hotly debating the merits of certain sports teams. However, most of the rooms here will promise much and deliver little—unless you just wanna goof around for a couple of hours.

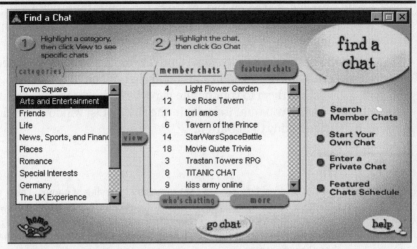

FIGURE 15.3: Member chat. Yawn.

▶ You can also create your own room in any Member Chat category by clicking Start Your Own Chat ➤ Member Chat. Give it a catchy title that'll draw people in (but not too catchy or you'll draw the wrong people, if you know what I mean and I think you do).

▶ Click the Search Member Chats button to find that special room. Unfortunately, you'll only be able to search for the exact title of the room, so you'll be doing a lot of mindreading to find a room on a specific topic (would it be Jersey Artists or New Jersey Artists or NJ Artists or . . .).

Private Chat

The private chat rooms are, well, private. They're also extremely useful for conversations with more than two other people. Say, for instance, two of your ex-coworkers—now living in Texas and Massachusetts, while you've stayed in California—are online and you all want to talk. By clicking on the Enter a Private Chat button, you can create a private chat room and IM them the name, thus inviting them in. Despite the multiple threads of conversation that inevitably get tangled during online chat, it's a great way to hang out with old friends.

Buddy Chat The easiest way to create a private room and invite your friends in is to have them in your buddy list. When they're online, gather them to your online party by highlighting the screen names you want to invite in the Buddy List window and clicking the Buddy Chat button.

TIP

You can also get into private chat rooms by guessing at names. There are certain private rooms that always exist that you can slip into without drawing too much attention to yourself, because they're often full. Given the nature of many of the member chat rooms, you'll most likely be able to guess at the names of these private rooms.

Other Chat Channels

From Channel Chat (keyword **channel chat**) you can connect to conference rooms all over AOL, get into game rooms, look for that special someone . . . . The chat opportunities from Channel Chat can be superb.

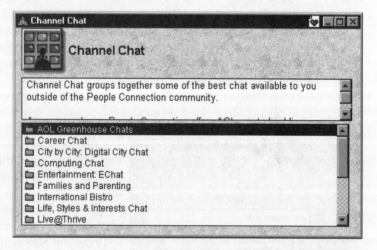

Also try your chat-room-surfing luck at AOL Live! (keyword **aol live**). Get into the Today's Live Events listing and scroll through the list of chat rooms on the bottom left; here you'll find the chat rooms associated with AOL's Channels area.

MEETING AND GREETING

It's Thursday evening, you're bored, you're wishing you had someone across the world to visit so you could take a vacation from the dreariness at home, when you realize you *could* meet someone across the world—and then go visit them. And it's almost easier done than said! Here are the best meeting spots on AOL:

Digital city: keyword **Talk of the Town**. Here you can connect with AOL members in your city or another, look for jobs, and find out what's shakin'.

Romance Channel: keyword **Romance**. What it sounds like!

Love@AOL: It's its own keyword, and it's a fave among AOLies seeking that luv-induced endorphin high.

Member Directory: People > Search AOL Member Directory. Search through the Member Directory for people claiming similar interests to yours. Use the Advanced Search tab to get way specific (more about this in *Search the Member Directory*).

Chat rooms: Search for chats on subjects that interest you; if the room members are really discussing the stated topic, you may meet some interesting folk. From chat rooms you can strike up an IM conversation or send e-mail.

Conference rooms: The same idea as chat rooms, but found outside of People Connection and thus containing conversations usually relevant to their intended topics. Start from Channel Chat (keyword **channel chat**) and AOL Live! (keyword **aol live**), but also explore your favorite AOL areas to see if they have chat rooms.

Newsgroups: keyword **newsgroups**. Check out others' opinions on a topic that interests you (e.g., world peace, fencing, doll collections) in a message-board-like forum. Strike up e-mail conversations with newsgroup members you're intrigued by.

Pen pals: keyword **Special Delivery**. Sign up to receive and/or send e-mail to other people looking for new correspondents.

Mailing lists: keyword **mailing list**. Sign up for a slew of e-mail on a topic you're similarly obsessed with. Send friendly e-mail to those who pique your curiosity.

Message boards (yes, even message boards): Opportunities to connect exist everywhere. Check out the message boards you'll find in areas all over AOL; you'll learn interesting tidbits—and you'll find people whose signatures include invitations to e-mail or IM them.

Stuff You Oughta Know

Okay, now that you've been introduced to the AOL network of chat-sters, you'll want to refine your style. Here are some tips.

Chatiquette

Don't swear. It's not very interesting conversation (and frankly, it makes you look really @#$%ing dumb).

Don't SCREAM. It's offensive.

Don't be a jerk. You'll get a rep, and you could get kicked off.

Type the first three or four letters of the screen name you're responding to when you type a response. This tactic is especially helpful if there's a bunch of people in the room and many conversations going at once.

Catra1984:   MEstu: I agree. But it's been too long, I think, to change it.

If people greet you

Hi Catra!

or wave at you

::waving at Catra::

respond in kind.

Protect Your Right to Quality Chat

You can dismiss idiots from your otherwise-pleasant experience: Double-click on the name of the rude chatter and, in the Information About dialog box that comes up, check the Ignore Member button. Once a chatter is Ignored, his comments won't show up on your scrolling chat screen anymore.

Click here to erase Catra's nonsense from view ——

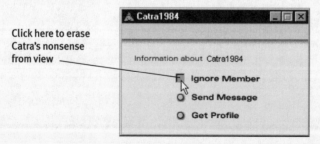

If you're experiencing continuing harassment—you've Ignored him, turned off your IMs, but he's sent you a flood of e-mail—report his butt to the Terms of Service (TOS) people. If you have evidence of TOS violations in chat or IM, type keyword **TOS** into the Go box and click Report a Violation in the Terms of Service window. If you have offensive e-mail, forward it to **TOSemail1**.

Chat Preferences

Chat

Now that you have some chat experience, you'll want to customize some of the more perfunctory chat options. From the toolbar, choose My AOL ➢ Preferences and click the Chat button.

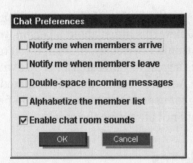

Here you can decide how you want to experience the chat room. You can keep tabs on who's coming and going, you can alphabetize for a neater, more precise experience, you can double-space the lines you see to make who said what clearer (it makes the screen scroll twice as fast, though), and you can decide whether to hear or tune out sounds.

Member Directory

Another way you can go about chatting is to search the Member Directory for people who share your enthusiasm for chess, went to your alma mater, live in the town you grew up in, whatever. To get to the Member Directory, choose People ➢ Search AOL Member Directory.

As you can see in Figure 15.4, you have some options for narrowing down your search. You can type location-specific and name-specific search words into the appropriate fields, or type keywords into the search-everything field.

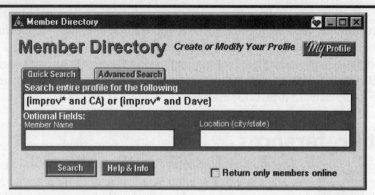

FIGURE 15.4:   If you ever meet a guy at a party and wonder whether he's on AOL, this would be a way to find out—short of actually asking him.

The Advance Search tab offers you the option of filling in everything about the person you seek. If you knew this much about a person, you'd know her screen name, don't you think?? Seriously, though, if you're looking for other Mac users, this is a great way to search for people with whom you can share resources. The Advance Search tab can be incredibly useful if the person you're looking for uses AOL's Member Profile fields in the manner intended—which will not always be the case.

Get Specific with Booleans

Boolean expressions, sprinkled liberally throughout Figure 15.4, link search criteria in a sort of shorthand. Wildcards substitute for blanks that could be anything. To use them, follow these easy rules:

*	substitutes for any string of characters	**hand** * will result in handsome, handy, handful, etc.
?	substitutes for one letter	**wom?n** will result in woman, women, womyn, womon, and so on
and	search will reveal only profiles containing both words	**cat and dog** will result in people who mention both animals in their profile
or	search will reveal profiles with either word	**Sinhalese or Sri Lanka** will result in people who mention either in their profile

( )	group words together so you can search for a couple of different options at a time	**(improv and CA) or (improv and Dave)** will result in CA residents and Daves who profess an interest in improv; the Daves will not necessarily be CA residents, the CA residents not necessarily named Dave.

Augmenting Chat

There are several ways to extend and enhance your chat experience on the fly:

Instant Message If you find someone you click with, you can always take your conversation "off-chat" by sending him an IM; from there you can chat in peace, without having to sift through the other 21 threads scrolling down your screen. Double-click on his screen name in the chat room's People Here box and click the Send Message button in the Information About dialog box.

Member Profile You can check out anyone's profile by double-clicking their screen name and, in the super-useful Information About dialog box, clicking the Get Profile button. This action pops up the Member Profile belonging to the object of your scrutiny; if you're interested in inquiring further into her hobbies, by all means ask.

Ignore Member As I discuss in several other places in this chapter, the Ignore Member button is a boon to us rational folk who don't like to be subjected to multi-line spews nor be subjected to screaming (and nonscreaming) morons. Again, double-click the screen name in the People Here box and enable the Ignore Member box. Blessed relief follows.

> ☐ **Ignore Member**

WARNING

An ignored spewer often feels slighted by the lack of response and will do anything to get your attention back. Unfortunately, it's rather easy; all she has to do is leave the room and re-enter, and the Ignore you put on her will reset.

Part III

Notify AOL If you're so offended by someone's behavior in a chat room that you feel Ignoring is too good for him, the handy Notify AOL button will allow you to record the lines in question for the Community Action Team to handle. Hate chat always falls into this category if you ask me.

NOTE

Lest you think me contemptuous of the chat experience, let me say: I'm only contemptuous of the AOL members who ruin other people's legitimate conversations, whether by rude behavior, vulgarity, or plain mean-spiritedness (like harassment).

PowerTools

PowerTools software is a real help in AOL. Found at keyword **bps**, Power-Tools has some chat-specific capabilities you'll want to explore. These include the Get In! feature, which gets you into the chat room you want to be in; chat fonts and colors, which allows you to change the font size of your chat without having to reset your whole screen appearance; inactive chat list, which allows you to ignore that special someone even if she leaps out of the room and back in; and macro capabilities, so you can create multi-line characters of your own. To use sparingly, of course.

YOUR LOOK: CHATTING IN STYLE

With the new and improved chat room options, you can have even more fun with your words and pictures (I discuss ways to find picture ideas under *Conversational Spice*). The chat toolbar allows you to change fonts, color your letters, and to bold, italicize, and underline them. That's a lot of stuff to do to one little line of text!

The best use of color occurs with the doodads you can send. One of my favorites is a rose:

@>--->---

If you color the @ red, the >> brown, and the —— green, you've got a sweet picture to send someone.

Just a note about the font change; the text in chat rooms is so small that, unless people have set their displays to show large fonts, many of the fancy fonts will look like tiny pieces of tangled yarn.

Hey, that's just not mine!

To remedy the unreadable-yarn effect, you can make the font larger, of course, but keep in mind that yarn at any size isn't easy to read, and other room members might get annoyed with you.

NOTE

If you find that chat room fonts are too small to read, you can change your system fonts by right-clicking on your desktop and choosing Properties ➤ Settings and, in the Font Size box, choosing Large Fonts. If this option is unavailable to you, choose the Appearance tab and, in the Scheme box, select any of the large options.

Other ways to have fun with your words are to use shorthands and doodads.

Conversational Spice

Typing is a lot of effort. Some of us do it well, some struggle through with two fingers and a lot of grief—not to mention spelling mistakes. There are shortcuts you can take to communicate emotions and ideas without having to explain yourself in eloquent phrases.

Shorthands

Acronyms like LOL (laughing out loud), BTW (by the way), or AFK (away from keyboard) are commonly used in chat rooms. You can find a list of other common shorthands at keyword **shorthand**. You can also make up your own. If you see an acronym you just don't get, don't be shy about asking its utterer what it means.

Not really shorthand, but very useful, are colons and brackets. Colons are often used around actions, as if the stage directions from a play are being read:

:::walks to the door laughing:::

Brackets to signal hugs:

{ { { {Catra} } } }

Doodads

Even more fun than shorthands are the little pictures people draw with Qwerty the keyboard. Doodads are emoticons' next generation; they express ideas through pictures, rather than mimicking facial expressions. For instance, rather than sending a sweetie a stick-figure kissy face, type a picture of a valentine heart. Like your writing teachers always said (and still say): show, don't tell. Doodads do just that. (Though, like emoticons, you never quite know what direction your head's supposed to be tilting; just think of it as good stretching exercise for the neck.)

<3	heart
>^..^<	cat
<^.,.^>	another cat
o/	raised hand

French Smileys

You all know about emoticons, so I won't rehash the oldies but goodies. However, there are a lot of emotiartists out there; to find some inventive smileys, go to keyword **smiley** to find French smileys.

Some of my favorites:

%\v	Picasso
:D	big laugh
> ><}}}^>	fish
@>—>——	rose
~=	a candle (message is a flame)

CDN Smileys

Go to keyword **CDN Smileys** to get the Canadian take on smileys. For instance:

(8-)	a hooting owl
@@@@@:-)	Marge Simpson (especially if the @'s are blue!)

TIP

The smiley resources available to you, my virtual emoter, are, like everything on the Internet and (to a lesser extent) AOL, in flux. To find more smileys, I recommend doing a search for *smileys* or *emoticons* through Find ➤ Find It on AOL.

Sound Files

If your soundcard exists and is working, you'll be able to hear chat room sounds—and send them!

Sending WAV Files

Send a sound to the entire room by typing **{S** *filename*. (The capital **S** is very important; **{s** won't work.) Keep in mind that you're not actually *sending* a sound file, you're reaching into another person's computer (specifically, into their C:\America Online 4.0 directory) and activating its sound file. In other words, others in the room will only be able to hear the sound files that they have installed on their computers. If you send a sound that a chatter doesn't have installed, she won't hear a thing. So if you type

> {S welcome

the chat room members whose speakers are on and sound cards are working will hear Mr. AOL say "Welcome!" as is his wont (AOL comes with Welcome.wav, so everyone has it). However, if you type

> {S leaving

only those with Leaving.wav will hear a vampire cackle merrily about leaving Windows.

If you want to combine a sentence with a sound, bracket the command and filename like so:

> {S welcome}

You might say, for instance:

> Catra! {S welcome} hello! Long time no chat!

TIP

If you accidentally land in a noisy room that you want to stay in, but you find your hangover is making you rather testy in the face of all those WAV files bouncing around, you can turn off your speakers. Or you can go to Chat Preferences, as discussed earlier in this chapter, and turn off chat room sounds until the ibuprofen kicks in.

Finding WAV Files

List More Files

To download cool WAV files, from the AOL toolbar, click Find ➤ Software ➤ Shareware ➤ Music & Sound and type event sounds into the Keywords box. You'll find some WAV utilities (which may be useful if you want to create your own WAV files), and a lot of event sounds. You'll have to hit the List More Files button a number of times to see them all.

Download Now   Download Later

To download a file, highlight the one you want and just click the Download Now or Download Later button.

Download

If you choose to delay your WAV file gratification and download the file later, you'll need to retrieve it from your Download Manager (when you're ready, of course). To do so, choose My Files ➤ Download Manager, highlight the file (or files) you wish to put on your hard drive, and click Download.

Once the WAV file is downloaded, move it into the main America Online 4.0 (or aol30) folder (C:\America Online 4.0 or C:\aol30, unless you changed this pathway when you installed AOL). Only then is it accessible to your chatting efforts.

NOTE

La Pub, your Buddy List, and People Connection have their own sound libraries. Download 'em all for an ear-splittingly good time!

WavMan

Find WavMan in AOL's software library by clicking Find ➤ Software ➤ Shareware ➤ Application (enter **WAVMan** into the Keyword box) ➤ WAVMAN32: V7.2 Chat Room Manager. You can test drive it for 30 days, after which you'll need to register it and pay a small fee for its continued use.

Not only will WavMan give you hours of fiddling fun with your WAV files, it'll also let you create an automatic answer for IMs, create aliases for your commonly used screen names (so you can type in Bente—or just B— rather than BIngesdtr), create some cool-looking waves (strings of undulating characters), and, most exciting of all, enable the anti-logoff feature.

$$(\`\cdot\,_\cdot\S(\`\cdot\,_\cdot\, ^{*\infty}*^{\infty\circ}\{(\%)\}^{\infty\circ}*^{\circ\circ}*_\cdot\,^{\cdot\cdot})\S_\cdot\,^{\cdot\cdot})$$

Your Profile

Once you enter a chat room, you are subject to scrutiny. Twenty-two other people immediately double-click your name and check out your Member Profile from the Information About dialog box.

Depending on what kind of attention you want to attract, you'll want to have a Member Profile. You could be sincere, silly, sarcastic, sensual . . . again, depending on what kind of attention you want coming your way.

To create a profile, choose My AOL ➤ My Member Profile and fill out whatever of the preset fields you want to fill out in the Edit Your Online Profile window shown in Figure 15.5. The first option, Your Name, will appear whether or not you fill it out, so you may as well fill it out so it doesn't look like you weren't paying attention. Otherwise you can ignore and embellish all you like.

The Secret to an Ultra-Cool Profile

I can't believe anyone online really cares what kind of computer you're using (and if they do, they'll ask), and how many of us have a personal quote that sums up everything about us? I mean, really.

Part III

Edit Your Online Profile

To edit your profile, modify the category you would like to change and select "Update." To continue without making any changes to your profile, select "Cancel."

Your Name:	
City, State, Country:	
Birthday:	
Sex:	○ Male ○ Female ⊙ No Response
Marital Status:	
Hobbies:	
Computers Used:	
Occupation:	
Personal Quote:	

[Update] [Delete] [Cancel] [My AOL] [Help & Info]

FIGURE 15.5: Recreate yourself in your own image.

To ditch AOL's idea of interesting personal information and create fields that actually have something to do with you (or have nothing to do with anything), follow these steps:

1. Type in what you want others to think is your name. (It's okay if you want others to think your real name is your real name. Not everyone is as cynical as I am.)

WARNING

It's safest to only use your first name online at all times, including in your Member Profile.

2. Leaving the insertion point at the end of your "name" (nudge, nudge), press Ctrl+Backspace. A square will appear in the line; this square will translate into a new line in your Member Profile.

3. Type your unique new category—such as **Favorite Bands**—followed by a colon.

4. Press the Spacebar until you've covered about 30-38 spaces total, from beginning of your new line to end, and type in your descriptive text.

5. Repeat from step 2 until you run out of space (at which point your computer will beep in consternation, and you won't be able to type anything more on that line). Your profile will look something like the one in Figure 15.6.

TIP

If you want to cram a lot of information in, don't try to line up the descriptions. The spaces you use to line things up will detract from the amount of text you can enter.

Edit Your Online Profile

To edit your profile, modify the category you would like to change and select "Update." To continue without making any changes to your profile, select "Cancel."

Your Name:	Catra☐☐Head: yes. small and perky☐☐Eyes: slitted ⦙
City, State, Country:	kibble city☐☐Paws: many. silent and clawed, instinctive toward insects, tentative toward r
Birthday:	
Sex:	○ Male ○ Female ⦿ No Response
Marital Status:	
Hobbies:	dinner☐☐Dinner: always☐☐Snacks: ain't tellin'☐☐Sleep habits: on or next to the large w
Computers Used:	
Occupation:	
Personal Quote:	

Update   Delete   Cancel   My AOL   Help & Info

FIGURE 15.6: Ever wonder what your cat is up to while you're at work?

When you're satisfied with your sincerity, sarcasm, creative nonsense, or whatever you've put together, click Update. To see yourself as others see you (whew, that's a concept!), choose People ➤ Get AOL Member Profile (Ctrl+G). In the ensuing box, type in your screen name and click OK.

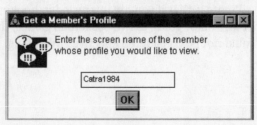

Part iii

You'll be treated to a complete view of your statement of self, probably nothing like that of my alter-ego, Catra, as seen in Figure 15.7. Notice that I lined up the first few categories, which allowed only two extra fields before another canned field, Location, popped up. When I decided neat lines weren't for me, I got as many as five "information"-filled lines in between AOL-dictated categories (Location and Hobbies). I completely ignored Marital Status (n/a for a cat, you know) and many of the others; hence, they didn't show up.

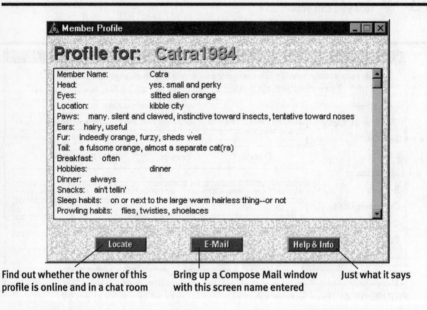

Find out whether the owner of this   Bring up a Compose Mail window   Just what it says
profile is online and in a chat room   with this screen name entered

FIGURE 15.7: Cats—on AOL?

The advantages to the creative-writing approach are: It'll be a fun read for some, you may get some appreciative IMs, and you won't be as easy a target as if you'd written Female, Single (for instance). The disadvantage to such silliness is that if you are interested in hooking up with others in your area who enjoy going to live basketball games, this sort of Member Profile could not be considered effective advertising.

NOTE

Of course, it's *your* Member Profile, and you can change it as often as you wish. Once you've found all the basketball-game-going pals you need, you can turn yourself into the cat you always wanted to be by revamping your Member Profile.

COOL AND UNUSUAL CHAT

As you'll sense as you glance through the gems I've pulled out for you below, the best chat (read: interesting, fun, intellectually stimulating) with people you don't know can be found through Channel Chat, AOL Live!, and through your favorite online forums. Here you get away from the hordes of goofs who're just looking to recreate Beavis and Butthead in their own image(s).

Of course, everything depends on who's where. Even though these sites are well away from the madding crowd, once in a while one of them gets loose and mucks up a polite conversation about Paris' Picasso museum. This is where the Ignore Member button comes in handy, as discussed earlier under *Chatiquette*.

You'll also notice that these channel chat rooms (conference rooms, really) allow a whole lot more than 23 people in at a time: 48 is the max here. Clear communication—for instance, typing in the screen name of the chatter you're responding to as well as your response—becomes important in crowds such as these.

Hecklers Online

Hecklers Online is outrageous and intelligent. Not only do they allow— heck, *encourage*—a certain amount of abuse in their chat rooms, if you pick the right night, your HO (Hecklers Online) hosts may tolerate a certain amount of profanity. (In the name of fun and good heckling, of course.)

The best part about Hecklers Online is that they're creative. It's no fun just trashing other AOLies, so you can pick from word games (rewrite a Bible verse, heckler style), graffiti art (take Al Gore into your favorite paint program for a makeover—then post it on HO!), interactive jokes, and more. Take Absurd IMs, for example. You may want to report the lamebrains who IM you for your password; Hecklers Online encourages you to play with them like a cat with a furry catnip toy. Check out keyword **HO** ➤ Funny Bone ➤ Absurd IMs to enjoy others' shenanigans and submit your own.

Heckler's Online introduction
Snert

The cat baiting the mouse

The mouse scurries away . . .

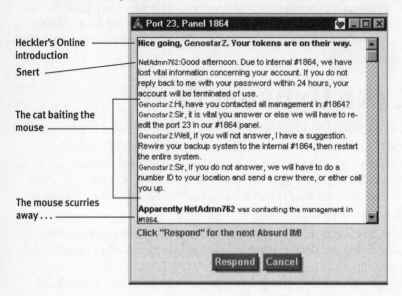

International Bistro

Keyword **bistro** will give you a chance to practice that high school French, or learn Tagalog, or just mingle with other citizens of the world.

The Front Porch

Even if you're not at all religious or spiritual, the Front Porch is pretty cool; it's an interfaith meeting ground for open-minded people to discuss ethics and their beliefs, and there is a weekly schedule of events that involves many faiths and philosophies. Like the other rooms I deem cool, the idiot factor is quite low here. Access the Front Porch through Channel Chat (keyword **channel chat**) ➤ Religion & Beliefs Chat ➤ Religion & Ethics Front Porch.

Cecil Adams' Chat

At keyword **Straight Dope** you can find Cecil Adams' straight answers to the goofiest questions. In addition, you can chat about said goofy questions.

Digital City Chat

At keyword **Talk of the Town** you'll get a plethora of chat choices. Sign up for chat with those in (or interested in) the city nearest you—or for chatting with residents of a city you want to go to. Once you select your city, you can select from a list of chat topics and times, or you can select your age group—from blastin' teens to golden gaters—from the list of free-for-all chat.

Chat Schedules

You can find some excellent chat, a la AOL Live!, at chat events with special guests. Just find areas that appeal to your tastes and check their guest schedule (usually posted prominently in the area) regularly (you'll find most of the rooms that feature special guests at AOL Live). In some areas you can sign up to get the chat schedules e-mailed to you.

Expanding Your Opportunities for Meaningful Chat

There are a lot of people yakkin' it up on AOL; about 9 million at last count. But that's only a subset of online chatters as a whole. Countless chat rooms exist all over the Internet, some of them quite creative. If you want to find regular scrollable-text chat out there on the Internet, get online and search for it . If you're ready for something more exotic, check out the venues listed below.

Part iii

Avatar Chat

Avatar chat is cool and clunky. In avatar chat, you choose an avatar—which is a 2-D or 3-D rendering of something (usually a humanoid)—to represent you, and you float through chat rooms talking to other avatars. Depending on where you decide to chat avatar-style, you may be able to pick from fictional likenesses, fantastical space-age humanoids, comic-style drawings, animals, you name it. In many chat areas, you can use an image you've created with special avatar-creation software. Some avatar chat incorporates voice, so if you have a microphone, you can represent yourself vocally.

The downside to avatar chat is that each world requires you to own its third-party software to use it. Sometimes this software is free, often it is not. Therefore you are under a bit of pressure to make sure you choose your avatar world wisely, lest you waste $30 or so. Each avatar area will have links to sites where you can buy the software, so at least they make it easy for you to fork over for the goods. Also, each avatar world is negotiated in a different way; sometimes avatars are easy to manipulate, and sometimes you'll bang your head against the wall for a long time—literally. Coordination definitely helps.

Where to Find It

To find a list of avatar chats on the Internet, type **http://www .ccon.org/** into the Keyword/URL box and press Go. You'll find that The Contact Consortium has links to all kinds of avatar-type chats.

NOTE
ClNet reviewed several avatar chats on different platforms (Compuserve, MSN, etc.), and gave Worlds Chat the highest score. Check out the review at http://www.cnet.com/ Content/Reviews/Compare/Chat/ss05d.html. Of course you have to buy Worlds' software to join in, but you can demo it free first at http://www.worlds.net.

Try Comic Chat at http://www.digital-space.com/avatars/cchat .html for a list of comic chats. Figure 15.8 shows an example of Microsoft's Comic Chat at play.

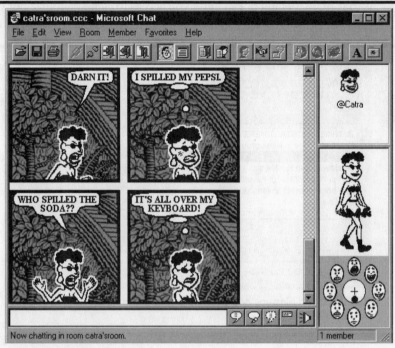

FIGURE 15.8: Catra's having a tough day.

For some more hot links to Virtual Worlds and the People Who Love Them, go to http://www.ccon.org/hotlinks/hotlinks.html. Here you'll be able to enter the realm of the avatars, find software to make avatars and avatar worlds, study the avatar phenomenon, and read others' musings about the scene.

If these links don't do it for you, just go to Internet ➢ AOL Netfind and search for **avatar chat**. You'll find enough to keep you busy for quite a while . . .

Newsgroups' Little Secret

Newsgroups are like AOL's message boards, but they're out on the Internet. A person will leave a message, and anyone can come by, read it, and respond to it.

To get to newsgroups, go to keyword **newsgroups**. The Newsgroups window, shown in Figure 15.9, is mostly self-explanatory. The big tip here is that AOL's default doesn't give you access to *all* newsgroups, but you can change that (and no, changing it doesn't violate your TOS agreement).

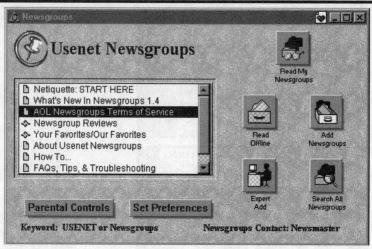

FIGURE 15.9:   Message boards for all can be found here.

To give yourself access to all Internet newsgroups, follow these easy steps:

1. Make sure you're logged on as the master account screen name.

2. In the Newsgroups window, click Parental Controls.

3. Choose which screen name to edit Parental Controls for.

4. Uncheck Block Binary Downloads.

5. Check Use Full Newsgroups List.

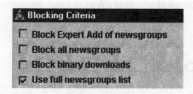

Now you'll have access to the entire newsgroup list (both AOL and Internet) and be able to download files posted on the newsgroups.

NOTE

Read the AOL Newsgroups Terms of Service, which you can find in the list on the left of the main Newsgroups window. In it you will see that, though you're about to fly freely through the Internet, you're still an AOL member and thus bound by AOL's rules.

Mailing Lists

Mailing lists are a lot like newsgroups except that the messages come to your mailbox. At keyword **mailing list** you'll find AOL's directory of mailing lists out there. These aren't all the mailing lists that exist, just the ones AOL members have discovered. AOL doesn't police the lists, so there aren't any blocks to unblock here.

When you sign up for a mailing list, you'll get e-mail from everyone who discusses the list topic via the list. When you respond to the list, your e-mail goes out to every list member. The same rules of courtesy apply here as everywhere else.

TIP

Consider signing up for a *digest* of the mailing list you're interested in. Digests are compilations of each day's mailings into one e-mail (you'll be able to distinguish these because the mailing list name will include the word *digest* or *archive*). Otherwise, you'll be buried.

PROTECTING YOURSELF

Spam is that pinkish lumpish meat byproduct that shows up in your mailboxes, either as obnoxious or rude e-mail, or just as a lot of it (such as an advertisement flung indiscriminantly out to many different message boards and mailboxes).

You don't want it; what can you do?

Nix the member profile   Basically, now that I've told you all about how to advertise who you are and find all the public places on AOL and the Internet, I'm going to tell you that the Number One way to avoid unwanted e-mails and IMs is: don't create a member profile.

Part iii

Create a public persona   Tip number two is to create a screen name specifically to be your public persona (as you've seen in this chapter, mine is Catra1984). Do everything public as that persona: lurk and chat under this screen name, sign up for mailing lists and newsgroups under this screen name, leave message board queries under this screen name. Having a public persona will help you more easily screen stuff; mail sent to your private screen name will be from friends who know that screen name, and anything you get under your public screen name can usually be tossed.

Be nice   One last tip, which as the sophisticated netizen you are you already know: Be polite in chat rooms. It's the best way to avoid a barrage of IMs and e-mails telling you to take it where the sun don't shine.

If you've been spammed, forward the e-mail, whether it's with an attachment or without, to **TOSemail1**.

Your Snert Recourse Resource

You can make it really easy to report snerts (chat cretins) if you make a log of your chat session. When you create a log, you save everything that goes on in a given session so you can look back on the stuff that happened throughout your time online. Chat screens themselves only show a certain amount of the text, so you very quickly lose sight of the precious tidbits and belly-aching humor of the first lines.

To create a chat log:

1. Go to My Files ➢ Log Manager.

2. If you want to log everything you do other than chatting, choose Open Log under Session Log (see Figure 15.10).

3. If you just want to log your chat room antics, go to a chat room.

4. Now that you're in a chat room, the options under Chat Log will be active; choose Open Log there.

5. Choose a name for your log file in the Windows dialog box that comes up and press Save. As long as you keep the chat window open (minimized is okay), AOL will log the goings-on. You can participate or go elsewhere.

6. When you're done with your session, stop the logging by pressing Close Log.

7. Whether or not you're logged on, you can read the session by choosing File ➢ Open from AOL.

8. If you want to append an earlier log file, click Append Log and double-click the file you wish to append in the Append Log dialog box.

FIGURE 15.10: Log files: just like taping your favorite TV show while you're at dinner with your parents, except you can skip the dinner with your parents part.

WARNING

Remember to delete chat logs you don't want, lest your hard drive drown in drivel.

TIP

If a log file ends up being too big for AOL to open—about 32K plus—launch Notepad or Wordpad and open it from there.

To report a chat room snert:

1. Type **TOS** into the Keyword/URL box and press Go.

2. At the Terms of Service window, choose Report a Violation.

3. Click Chat.

4. Copy and paste the snerty words into the appropriate box, type in the snert's screen name, and what chat room you were in when the snerting occurred.

UNWANTED AOL MAIL

Those announcements; the modem, the visa, the add-on software . . . the list goes on. And on. You've seen them, clicked No Thanks a million times, and really, really would just like to log on. Please. If it wouldn't be too much to ask.

To rid yourself of those commercial pop-ups, go to My AOL ➤ Preferences ➤ Marketing and double-click Tell Us What Your Pop-Up Preferences Are. (In AOL 3.0, go to keyword **marketing preferences**.)

Marketing

Checkmarking the box at the lower right will turn off most pop-ups. As the disclaimer says, you'll still see a few pop-ups related to stuff AOL has got to tell you, but believe me, it cuts down on 99% of the advertising you slog through now.

Macros and Punts

Odds are, even if you've never chatted on AOL before, your first experience in a chat room will introduce you to macros and punting. Punts—kicking others off AOL—are often preceded by macros, multiline streams of chat lines generated from punt software. Punting is illegal on AOL but rampant. Macros are not illegal but are annoying when used to excess.

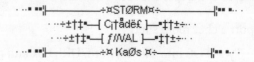

Macros can be benign, like 5-line-deep ASCII faces, or they can be mildly demonic-looking lines of text with accents littered about, looking like some strange otherworldly language.

Punters, on the other hand, can target you and freeze your screen so you have to reboot. That's when irritating becomes downright enraging.

If you get punted, copy down the screen name, reboot, and report it to the TOS Violations Community Action Team. To do so:

1. Type **TOS** into the Keyword/URL box and press Go.

2. At the Terms of Service window, choose Report a Violation.

3. Click Other, then choose IM Violations.

4. In the Cut and Paste a Copy of the IM box, type the offender's name and **IM punt**.

WHAT'S NEXT?

Now that you've learned some basics about the Web, do you want to create your own Web site? If so, you're in luck. In the next several chapters you'll get an introduction to HTML and design, and you'll learn how to use FrontPage's simple interface to make Web authoring easy.

Part iii

WHAT'S NEXT?

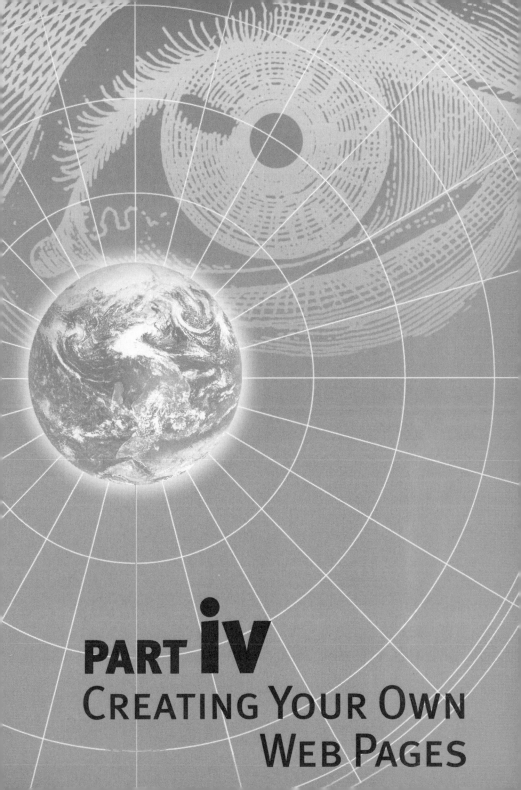

PART iV
CREATING YOUR OWN
WEB PAGES

Chapter 16

INTRODUCING WEB PAGES AND HTML

This chapter introduces you to the way in which Web documents are built with the HyperText Markup Language (HTML). You'll learn about the features of the language you'll encounter within the pages you browse in Internet Explorer.

There is no need to consider this chapter required reading if you just want to browse the Web. You can certainly use the Web without any knowledge of the HTML code that lies beneath all Web pages. But your browsing experience on the Web will be greatly enhanced if you do take the time to become familiar with the basic concepts of HTML.

Recognizing the common elements in virtually all Web pages will help you feel more at home on the Web. And if you're ready to build your own Web pages, this chapter will give you a solid background in the process.

Adapted from *Mastering Microsoft Internet Explorer 4*, by Gene Weisskopf and Pat Coleman
ISBN 0-7821-2133-0   960 pages $44.99

An Overview of HTML

You create Web pages with the HyperText Markup Language, or HTML. In keeping with the original and ongoing theme of the Internet— openness and portability—the pages you create with HTML are just plain text. You can create, edit, or view the HTML code for a Web page in any text editor on any computer platform, such as Windows Notepad.

Although creating simple Web pages in a text editor is easy, it can quickly turn into a grueling and mind-numbing task. That's why there are Web-authoring tools such as FrontPage Express, which lets you create HTML Web pages in the same way you create documents in your word processor.

Viewing HTML Pages

When you open a Web page in Internet Explorer (or any other Web browser), you don't see the HTML code that creates the page. Instead, Internet Explorer interprets the HTML code and displays the page appro- priately on the screen. If you're creating a Web page in a text editor and want to view the file you're working on, save your work and open the file in your browser. You can then continue to edit, save your work, and view the results, switching back and forth between the text editor and the browser to see the effects of your edits.

The original intent of the HTML specification was to allow Web authors to describe the structure of a page without spending too much time worrying about the look of a page—that part of the job was left to the browsers. Traditionally, each browser had its own way of interpreting the look of the page, and Web authors had to live with the fact that pages they created might appear somewhat differently in different browsers. Authors merely shrugged their shoulders and were happy that their pages could be viewed so easily from anywhere on the planet.

NOTE
After you read this chapter, you might want to turn to Chapter 19 to learn more about how HTML works.

Here's an example of the inherent flexibility that was designed into the HTML specification: Later in this chapter, you'll read about the six HTML codes you can use for creating six levels of headings in a Web page. You as an author can specify that a paragraph of text be defined as one of the six heading levels, but the HTML heading code does *not* describe what that heading should look like. It merely says something to the effect that "I'm a level two heading." It's up to the Web browser to differentiate each type of heading from the others. One browser might display the first-level heading in a large font that is centered on the page, while another browser might display it in italics and left-aligned on the page. That's why authors try to test their pages in several of the more popular browsers.

Speaking of popular browsers, the good news is that the browser market has been consolidating and standardizing. You'll find few differences in the way Internet Explorer and other browsers display the widely accepted HTML features in a page. Of course, new HTML features are being promoted all the time, mostly by Microsoft for its Internet Explorer browser and Netscape for its browser. Web authors must decide whether to include a new feature in a page, when that feature may not be well interpreted by some browsers.

HTML Elements and Tags

A Web page is made up of *elements*, each of which is defined by an HTML code, or *tag*. A tag is always enclosed in angle brackets, and most tags come in pairs, with an opening and a closing tag. The closing tag is the same as the opening tag, but starts with a forward slash.

For example, to define text as a first-level heading in HTML, you use the <H1> tag, as in:

```
<H1>This Is a Main Heading</H1>
```

A browser interprets these tags and displays the text within the tags appropriately (as shown below). But the tags themselves are not displayed within a browser, unless there is a problem with a tag, such as if one of the angle brackets was mistakenly left out (although most browsers will ignore any codes within angle brackets that they do not recognize).

This Is a Main Heading

And this is Internet Explorer's normal text.

Some tags have optional or required attributes. An *attribute* is usually a keyword that takes one of several possible values (you define each value by enclosing it in quotes). For example, the heading tag can take an optional alignment attribute:

```
<H1 ALIGN="CENTER">This is a main heading that is centered</H1>
```

NOTE

You can create a tag in either upper- or lowercase; it doesn't matter to a browser. For example, the two tags <H1> and <h1> are equivalent to a browser. In this chapter, we're using all uppercase for consistency and clarity.

The Essentials of a Web Page

Every Web page must include a few tags that define the page as a whole so that when a browser receives the page it will recognize it as such. For example, the following HTML code will produce the page that is shown in Internet Explorer in Figure 16.1 (it could also be viewed in any other browser):

```
<HTML>
<HEAD>
<TITLE>Greetings from the Web</TITLE>
</HEAD>
<BODY>
<P>Hello, world!</P>
</BODY>
</HTML>
```

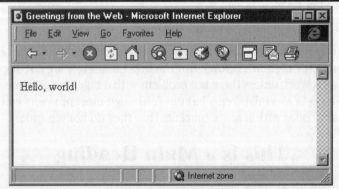

FIGURE 16.1: A sample page displayed in Internet Explorer

Remember, this code is just a text file, plain and simple. Table 16.1 lists the tags that should be included in every page so that any browser can view it:

TABLE 16.1: Essential HTML Tags for a Page

TAG	PURPOSE
\<HTML\>	Declares that the text that follows defines an HTML Web page that can be viewed in a Web browser. The closing \</HTML\> tag ends the page.
\<HEAD\>	Defines the header area of a page, which is not displayed within the page itself in the browser. The closing \</HEAD\> tag ends the header area.
\<TITLE\>	The text between this tag and the closing \</TITLE\> tag is the title of the Web page and is displayed in the title bar in Internet Explorer, as shown in Figure 16.1. The title should be descriptive, as it is frequently used by Web indexing and searching programs to name your Web page. In Internet Explorer, a page's title serves as the default name when you save the page as a favorite location.
\<BODY\>	Delineates the actual content of the Web page that will be displayed in Internet Explorer. In the example above, only the words *Hello, world!* will appear within the browser. Most of the other HTML features that we will discuss in this chapter always appear within the \<BODY\> and \</BODY\> tags in a Web page. There are several optional attributes for this tag. One of them is BACKGROUND, with which you can specify a background graphical image for the page.
\<P\>	Use the paragraph tag to mark the beginning of a new paragraph; the ending tag, \</P\>, is optional but should be included for clarity (whenever you or someone else needs to inspect or revise this code). You can include the ALIGN attribute to specify whether the paragraph should be centered or right-aligned in the page (left-aligned is the default).

There are dozens and dozens of other HTML tags you can incorporate into a Web page. The ones you use and how you use them depends only on your design, capabilities, and imagination.

NOTE

There is one important tag whose effects you won't notice in Internet Explorer, but you will appreciate when you're editing or viewing the HTML code for a page. You use the \<COMMENT\> tag to create descriptive comments within the code, which will be ignored by a browser. You can also use this combination of symbols to create a comment: \<!- This text is a comment. -\>

ADDING SPACES AND BLANK LINES FOR READABILITY

You can include extra spaces and blank lines in HTML code to make the code easier for you or others to read and interpret. When Internet Explorer (or any other browser) opens a Web page, it ignores multiple spaces within the code and displays them as a single space. It also ignores all hard returns within the code, such as when you press Enter at the end of a line of text you're editing in Notepad. Therefore, any blank lines you create in the code by pressing Enter a few times will not be displayed in Internet Explorer.

There is one HTML tag in which spaces and hard returns in the HTML code *do* count, and that is the preformatted tag, <PRE>. It instructs a browser to display the text in a monospaced font that allows you to align text precisely, such as you would when showing a program listing.

Learning HTML

As more and more of the world's documents end up as Web pages, we will all be viewing, creating, and modifying them as part of our daily routine. Learning about HTML will give you an understanding of how it works and how it looks in use, which will prove invaluable to your Web-browsing experience. But please rest assured that in this book we have absolutely no intention of molding you into a code cruncher!

With the proliferation of elegant HTML editors such as FrontPage Express, it is unlikely that a text editor will be your first tool of choice for creating Web pages. Unless you really take off in the science and art of Web-page authoring, you will probably never have to become an HTML jockey, and you will forego the pleasure of wrangling your way through screenfuls of angle brackets, slashes, and esoteric codes.

NOTE

Creating a successful Web page requires a good deal from both sides of your brain—the logical side that helps you write computer programs, and the artistic side that helps you compose a tasteful, inviting document. That's why it's important to have several people test and critique your Web efforts, since few of us can lay full claim to both sides of our brains!

You can learn about HTML in many ways without specifically studying it. Perhaps the most important method is already staring you in the face when you're browsing the Web in Internet Explorer—the pages themselves. All Web pages are built from the same text-based HTML language, so when you're viewing a page in Internet Explorer that strikes your interest, stop and take a look at that page's underlying code. You can do so in two ways:

▶ Choose View ➢ Source to display the current page's HTML code within Notepad. You can then view the code to your heart's content or save it to disk for later use.

▶ If you know you'll want to spend some time with the HTML code later on, you can save the current page to your local disk from within Internet Explorer by choosing File ➢ Save As. The resulting HTML file is the HTML code from which the page was built (but it will not include any of the graphic images from the page).

By viewing the HTML code for a page, you can get a feeling for how the page was created.

If you want to learn more about encoding Web pages, you can find countless books and even more Web sites devoted to that subject. A great place to start is Microsoft's Site Builder Network:

```
www.microsoft.com/sitebuilder/
```

It is designed primarily for "Web professionals," but the complexity and depth of the material on the site ranges far and wide. It has thousands and thousands of pages, hundreds of megabytes of downloadable software, and great links to other Web-related resources. You'll also find countless examples of what you can build in your Web site, especially when you are using Microsoft's Web technology.

Anyone interested in building or browsing Web sites will find something of value here. If you want to access the entire site, you'll need to register as a member of the Site Builder Network, which is free for a basic membership.

Another site related to the Site Builder Network is the Site Builder Workshop:

```
www.microsoft.com/workshop/
```

You could easily spend days browsing through this huge collection of information (all of which is current) about designing, building, and running Internet and intranet Web sites.

Part iv

Another site that we found via the Microsoft site is the Web Design Workgroup. This informal association of Web-page designers was founded to help other designers create truly portable Web pages that could be viewed by any browser on any computer platform:

www.htmlhelp.com

To find Web-related sites elsewhere on the Web, take a look at the following Yahoo category:

Computers and Internet: Internet: World Wide Web: Information and Documentation

A STANDARD MAY NOT ALWAYS BE ONE

The language of HTML is constantly evolving. Enthusiastic Web authors may happily include brand new and improved tags within their Web pages to produce dazzling new effects. But unfortunately, those effects may be lost on most visitors to that Web site because their browser software does not recognize those HTML features.

Officially, it's up to the World Wide Web Consortium (W3C) at the Massachusetts Institute of Technology (MIT) to define and establish new versions of HTML. Unofficially, leaders in the rush to the WWW, such as Microsoft and Netscape, regularly come up with their own extensions to official HTML in the hopes of improving the language. Eventually, many of these new codes are, indeed, included in the official HTML specification.

Skip the Programming: Use FrontPage Express

Microsoft FrontPage Express is one of the components in the Internet Explorer suite. It is essentially an easy-to-use word processor for creating HTML documents. Unlike a text editor such as Notepad, FrontPage Express is a WYSIWYG environment, in which "what you see is what you get." In other words, what you see in your document in FrontPage Express is pretty much what you'll see when you view the resulting HTML file on the Web in Internet Explorer. FrontPage Express has two important virtues:

▶ It is designed specifically to create HTML pages, so you won't find any unrelated commands or features on its menus. You don't have to think about how those options work; you simply choose them from the menu.

▶ When you create a page in FrontPage Express, you are assured that the HTML tags in that page (even though you might never see them) will be correct, with no missing angle brackets, misspelled tags, and so on.

If you're not sure what the big deal is about creating Web pages in FrontPage Express versus encoding them with HTML in a text editor, here's a simple but telling example. Shown below is some HTML code that you could create in Notepad and save to disk as an HTML file:

```
<HTML><HEAD><TITLE>Sample HTML Page</TITLE>
<H1>This Is the Main Heading</H1>
<P>Here's a bulleted list:</P>
<HR>
<UL>
<LI>Item 1</LI>
<LI>Item 2<UL>
    <LI>Item 2A</LI>
    <LI>Item 2B</LI>
  </UL></LI>
<LI>Item 3</LI>
<LI>Item 4</LI>
</UL>
<HR>
<P>...and the page continues...</P>
```

Now look at Figure 16.2 to see how you could create that page in the WYSIWYG environment of FrontPage Express. The HTML code stays hidden beneath the page you create, which appears much the way it will when viewed in Internet Explorer.

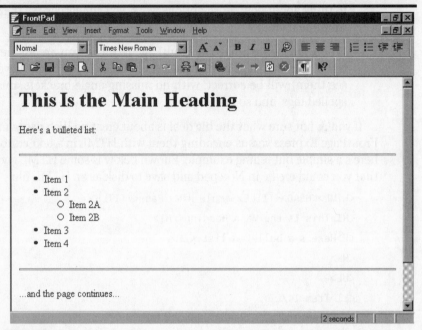

FIGURE 16.2: When you create Web pages in a WYSIWYG HTML editor such as FrontPage Express, "what you see is what you get" when that page is later viewed in a browser.

ADDING SOME STRUCTURE TO A PAGE

Just about any Web page you create will benefit if you impose some sort of structure on it. For example, think about how you would put your company's procedures manual up on the Web:

► If the manual is divided into chapters, you could make each one a separate Web page.

► You could easily re-create the manual's table of contents by making each section reference a hyperlink to that part of the manual. The reader could simply click on a section in the table of contents to open that file.

- ▶ Each chapter in the manual might have several levels of headings, which you could emulate perfectly with the heading tags in HTML.

- ▶ The body of the document would, of course, be divided into individual paragraphs.

You'll find that HTML offers several elements that let you create this type of structure in a Web page.

Using Paragraphs or Line Breaks

You create a paragraph by enclosing text within the paragraph codes <P> and </P>. Remember that Internet Explorer and other browsers will ignore any "paragraphs" you create by pressing Enter while working on the HTML code in a text editor (such as Notepad). You must specifically define a paragraph in the code by using the paragraph tag. Consider the text in the six lines of HTML code that follow:

```
<P>This is the first paragraph; its code
continues over several lines, but will be
displayed as a single paragraph in a
browser.</P><P>And this is a second paragraph
that will also be displayed as such in
a browser.</P>
```

This code would appear as two separate paragraphs in Internet Explorer, as shown in the upper portion of Figure 16.3. Note that the length of each line is determined by the width of Internet Explorer's window.

Internet Explorer and most other browsers insert some extra space between paragraphs, so in some instances, you will not want to use the <P> tag. For example, when you display your name and address in a page, you would not want extra space between each line of the address.

In those cases, use the line break tag, <BR>. It tells the browser to wrap the text that follows onto a new line, without inserting any extra space between the lines. Here is an address within HTML code:

```
John and Joan Doe<BR>The Hanford Corp.<BR>123 S Proton
Dr<BR>Hanford, WA 98765
```

You can see how this is displayed in Internet Explorer in the lower portion of Figure 16.3.

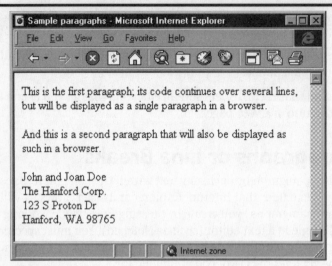

FIGURE 16.3:   You use the <P> tag to define a paragraph and the <BR> tag to create a line break.

Dividing Sections with a Horizontal Line

A simple and effective way to separate sections within a Web page is to insert a horizontal line, <HR>, also called a horizontal rule. By default, the line stretches from one side of the page to the other.

For example, if your page has a banner across the top with your company name, you could insert a horizontal line beneath it. This would separate it from a table of contents showing links to other pages, beneath which you could insert another line, followed by the main body of the page. At the bottom of the page, you could have another line, and beneath that line would be the important page identifiers, such as its URL, the date the page was last modified, a link back to a home page, and so on. An example is shown in Figure 16.4.

The <HR> tag takes several optional attributes. For example, you can specify the line's thickness (the default is one or two pixels in most browsers) and how much of the browser's window it should span (as a percentage or in pixels), such as:

```
<HR SIZE="6" WIDTH="60%">
```

which displays a line six pixels thick that spans 60 percent of the browser's window (the default is to center it in the window).

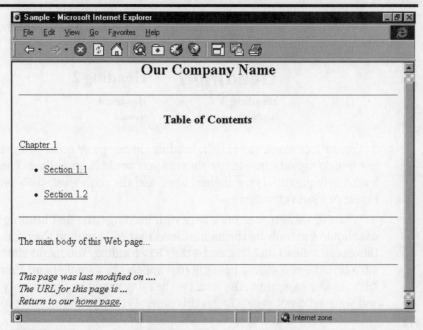

FIGURE 16.4:   You can use the horizontal rule, <HR>, to divide a page into sections.

Creating a Hierarchy with Headings

A common way to add structure to a Web page is through the use of
headings. This book, for example, uses headings to divide each chapter
into logical chunks. Its table of contents reveals the various levels of
headings, where each chapter is divided into several main headings, each
of which may contain several subheadings, and those subheadings may
contain their own subheadings.

A Web page can have a maximum of six levels of headings, the HTML
codes for which are conveniently named <H1>, <H2>, <H3>, and so on:

```
<H1>This is a two-line<BR>first-level heading</H1>
```

As mentioned earlier, no style is inherent in the headings—different
Web browsers might interpret the look of a heading in slightly different
ways. Structurally, however, all browsers will display headings so that a
third-level heading looks subordinate to a second-level heading, a second-
level heading looks subordinate to a first-level heading, and so on.

Part iv

In Internet Explorer, a first-level heading is displayed in a larger, bolder font than a lower-level heading. Shown here is a sample of the six headings within Internet Explorer.

Heading 1   ## Heading 2

Heading 3   #### Heading 4

Heading 5   ###### Heading 6

You are free to use the HTML headings in any goofy order you prefer, but it makes good sense to use them as you would in an outline. The first-level heading, <H1>, is the highest level, and the sixth level, <H6>, is the lowest or most subordinate.

When you are structuring a page with headings, the first heading you use should generally be the highest level that will occur on the page. But this doesn't mean that it must be the <H1> heading. You might start with <H2> because you want a heading that appears in a smaller font than <H1>. In this case, then, the level two heading would be the primary level, and you would not use <H1> on this page.

FORMATTING TEXT AND PAGES

Because the World Wide Web was originally conceived to be open to all, the designers of HTML avoided using literal descriptions of Web pages as much as possible. For example, the following tag would not have been appropriate:

```
<FONT FACE="TIMES ROMAN" SIZE="5" COLOR="#ff0000">
```

This tag requires a browser to have a specific, named font available that can be displayed in various sizes and requires that the browser's computer be connected to a color monitor.

But the days of trying to write to the least common denominator are waning quickly, and, in fact, the tag shown above is now a part of the official HTML specification. The <FONT> tag also illustrates two types of HTML tag attributes:

Absolute (literal)   The font type Times Roman is specified by name, and the color is specified by a hexadecimal RGB color value. There can be no doubt about how the author wanted this to look.

Relative (logical)   The font size 5, however, does not refer to an actual point size. It is a size that is relative to the browser's default font size (which is size 2 in Internet Explorer) and gives the browser a little more flexibility in how it displays the font. The author wanted the font to be larger than the browser's default, but was willing to let the browser assign the actual size.

Formatting Text

Table 16.2 shows a few of the many HTML character-formatting tags. All of them require both an opening and closing tag.

TABLE 16.2:   Basic HTML Character-Formatting Tags:

TAG	PURPOSE
<ADDRESS>	To display a Web page's author information, such as the page URL, author name, date of last revision, and so on, in italics in Internet Explorer.
<I>	To italicize text.
<EM>	To emphasize text, which Internet Explorer displays in italics; this is a relative tag compared to the more specific <I> tag.
<PRE>	To display text in a monospaced (fixed-width) font, where multiple spaces, tabs, and hard returns within the HTML code are also displayed. Use this tag when the position of characters within each line is important, such as program listings and columnar lists.
<B>	To boldface text.
<STRONG>	To give text strong emphasis, which Internet Explorer displays in bold. This is a relative tag compared with the more specific <B> tag.
<S>	To display strike-through text.
<U>	To underline text. You should generally avoid underlining text since that is how browsers indicate hypertext links in Web pages.

You can insert these tags where they are needed in a paragraph, and you can combine some tags. The browser in Figure 16.5 shows an example of HTML text formatting. That page was built from the following HTML code:

```
<HTML><HEAD><TITLE>HTML Formatting
Tags</TITLE></HEAD><BODY><P>With HTML formatting tags, you can
make text <STRONG>bold</STRONG>, <EM>emphasized</EM>, or
<EM><STRONG>bold and emphasized</STRONG></EM>. You can also
```

```
<STRIKE>strike-out text</STRIKE> or make it
<U>underlined</U>.</P>

<P>If you don't use the Preformatted tag, Internet Explorer
displays text in a proportional font, where different charac-
ters take up different amounts of space.</P>

<P>Here are two lines of 10 letters, i and M, where each line
of the HTML code also had five spaces entered between the fifth
and sixth letters:</P>

<P>iiiii     iiiii<BR>

MMMMM     MMMMM</P>

<P>Here are those letters and spaces within the Preformatted
tags:</P>

<PRE>iiiii     iiiii<BR>

MMMMM     MMMMM</PRE>

</BODY></HTML>
```

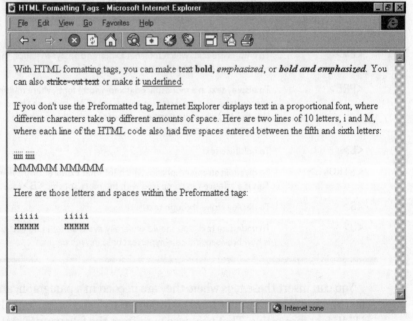

FIGURE 16.5: HTML formatting tags change the look of text in a Web page.

Formatting Pages

You can use a variety of tags to change the look of an entire Web page. You've already read about the <TITLE> tag, with which you create a title for a page. Internet Explorer displays that title in its title bar.

You can change the color of the page's background with the optional attribute BGCOLOR for the <BODY> tag. For example, the tag

```
<BODY BGCOLOR="#0000FF">
```

creates a blue background for the page.

NOTE

As with many tags, if you don't specify a color for a page, a browser that is displaying that page will use its own default color. Internet Explorer uses your Windows colors, by default, which are normally a white background with black text.

You can specify a picture instead of a color for a page's background. You don't need a large, page-sized picture, however, because Internet Explorer (and other browsers) tile the picture to fill the entire background. This allows you to use a small image file that will download quickly. You include the BACKGROUND attribute in the <BODY> tag to specify a background picture:

```
<BODY BACKGROUND="smallpic.gif">
```

If you choose a fairly dark background color or picture, you may need to use the TEXT attribute to change the default color of any text on the page. For example, the following tag creates a blue background with white text:

```
<BODY BGCOLOR="#0000FF" TEXT="#FFFFFF">
```

Part iv

Using Styles and Style Sheets

There is one tool for formatting documents in word processors that we have all grown quite accustomed to, but it has been conspicuously missing from HTML. That is the *style*, which allows you to create a named definition of a group of formats and then apply that style to any text in the document. The result is a consistent look that is easy to apply throughout the document. A second advantage to styles becomes evident when you want to adjust the look of all the text to which you've applied a style. You simply redefine the style, and that change is immediately reflected throughout the document.

In the past, HTML contained no mechanism for performing this simple, automated formatting task. But that's about to change with the acceptance of styles and style sheets in the HTML specification.

NOTE

The style sheets that Microsoft assumes will be implemented within the HTML specification are recognized by Internet Explorer 4 (and even back in Internet Explorer 3). However, because styles were not yet written into the HTML specification, few sites have taken advantage of them. Once styles are accepted, you will undoubtedly find them in use throughout the Web. In fact, FrontPage Express, the HTML word processor that comes with Internet Explorer, does not yet support styles. That's why you should use a plain-text editor, such as Notepad, to create the short examples later in this section.

Just as you would use styles in a word processor, a Web author can incorporate styles into a Web page. This can be done in several ways; the following is the simplest.

Within the <HEAD> tags for a page, you can specify style elements for various tags that will affect those tags throughout the page. For example, you could use styles to:

▶ Create a light gray background for the page.

▶ Center all <H2> headings and display their text in white.

▶ Indent the first line of all paragraphs.

Here is the HTML code that creates these effects. Figure 16.6 shows the page as it appears in Internet Explorer (with added text):

```
<HTML><HEAD><TITLE>Sample Style</TITLE>
<STYLE>
  BODY {BACKGROUND: silver}
  H2   {TEXT-ALIGN:"center"; COLOR:"white"}
  P    {TEXT-INDENT:"+10%"}
</STYLE>
</HEAD><BODY>
<H2>This Heading Is Centered</H2>
<P>This is a normal paragraph...</P>
</BODY></HTML>
```

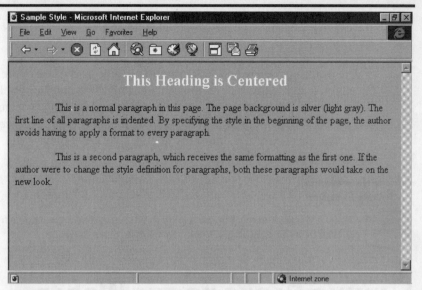

FIGURE 16.6: You can create a more consistent look in a page with much less effort when you use styles to set the formatting of HTML elements.

You could use this method to create many Web pages that all use the same styles, but there's a much more efficient way to use styles. The term *style sheet* refers to a single file that contains multiple style definitions. You can reference that file in any HTML Web page to apply those styles to that page.

Here are the contents of a style sheet (they're plain text files with a CSS file name extension) that emulates the styles shown in the previous example:

```
BODY {BACKGROUND: silver}
H2   {TEXT-ALIGN:"center"; COLOR:"white"}
P    {TEXT-INDENT:"+10%"}
```

If you save that style sheet file in a Web site (under the name NORMAL-PG.CSS in this example), you can reference it in any Web page with the following code. This code is the same as that used in the previous example; however, here the <LINK> tag replaces all the code within the opening and closing <STYLE> tags:

```
<HTML><HEAD><TITLE>Sample Style</TITLE>
<LINK REL=StyleSheet HREF="normalpg.css" TYPE="text/css"
```

```
</HEAD><BODY>

<H2>This Heading Is Centered</H2>

<P>This is a normal paragraph...</P>
```

The resulting page would look exactly the same as the one in the earlier example in Figure 16.6. As you can see from these quick examples, styles and style sheets have a great potential for easing the job of creating and, especially, maintaining a Web site. When many pages reference the same style sheet, you can simply modify the style sheet to have the changes appear in all the pages.

NOTE

If you'd like to learn more about style sheets, you'll find a great guide from the Web Design Group at www.htmlhelp.com/reference/css/.

LINKING PAGES TO THE WORLD

The little feature that creates the Web for countless computers and networks is the hyperlink. When you're reading a Web page in Internet Explorer, you can click a link to jump to a new resource (open it). That resource can be another HTML page, a graphic image, a sound or video file, or something else, and it might be located on the browser's local hard disk, on an intranet site, or on a site anywhere on the World Wide Web.

Creating a Text or Image Hyperlink

The HTML anchor tag, <A>, defines a hyperlink within a Web page and at the minimum contains two components:

▶ The text or image that you click to activate the link.

▶ The URL of the link's target that will open when you click the link.

Here is the HTML code for a text hyperlink (it's shown here on two lines, but remember that a browser ignores any line breaks in the HTML code):

```
<P>There's <A HREF="http://www.sample.com/helpindex.htm">

online help</A> when you need it.</P>
```

The text *online help* is the clickable link, and in Internet Explorer that text is underlined and displayed in blue, as shown in the top of Figure 16.7. The target of this link is the file HELPINDEX.HTM.

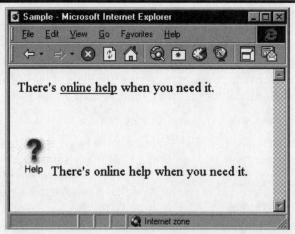

FIGURE 16.7: You can create a hyperlink from an image or from text, which is displayed in blue and underlined in Internet Explorer.

An image can also serve as a hyperlink; clicking the image activates the link. The bottom of Figure 16.7 shows an image hyperlink. In this case, the text that is next to the image serves to describe the link, but cannot be clicked to activate the link. Here's the HTML code (shown on three lines) for this link and the text to its right:

```
<P><A HREF="http://www.sample.com/helpindex.htm">
<IMG SRC="help.gif" border="0" width="46" height="51"></A>
There's online help when you need it.</P>
```

This example has the same target file as the previous example, HELP-INDEX.HTM, but the clickable portion of the hyperlink is the image file HELP.GIF. The reference to that image file falls within the anchor tags <A> and </A>, and the sentence describing the link, *There's online help when you need it,* is outside those tags.

Part iv

THE REFERENCE TO THE TARGET OF A LINK CAN BE RELATIVE OR ABSOLUTE.

When an author creates a reference in a Web page to another file, such as the target of a hyperlink, the reference can be defined as either relative or absolute.

In the two examples above, an *absolute* reference was made to the target file HELPINDEX.HTM. The reference contained the target's complete URL that defined the exact location of the file. It starts with the protocol and includes the usual host, domain, and file name

```
http://www.sample.com/helpindex.htm
```

With an absolute reference, the location of the target is "written in stone" and always points to the same file in the same location. However, this is not an advantage or even a requirement when the target of the link is stored in a location that is *relative* to the page that contains the link.

For example, if the reference to the target contained only the target file's name, such as

```
helpindex.htm
```

it would be assumed that this file resides in the same folder as the page that contains the link. Its location is, therefore, relative to the link-containing file.

Another relative reference to a target might look like this:

```
help/helpindex.htm
```

In this case, the target file resides in a folder named HELP, which resides in the same folder as the page that contains the link. The complete (absolute) URL to that file would look like this:

```
http://www.sample.com/help/helpindex.htm
```

Because the administrator of a Web site may need to change the location and directory (folder) structure of the site, a Web author will always try to use a relative reference whenever possible. In that way, if a Web site is moved to another folder on the same server or to a completely new server, all the relative references to files within that site continue to work.

Specifying Other Link Targets

You'll often find that the target of a link is another Web page, but there are other types of targets. Here are some you may encounter:

Named target   When the target of a link is a Web page, you can specify a named location within that page. That location, not the top of the page, is displayed when the page is opened in a browser. You use the anchor tag to create the name for the location, and you reference that name in the anchor tag for the link.

Frame   Later in this chapter, you'll read about the frameset, which is a Web page that you divide into multiple frames, each of which can open and display a separate Web page. When a link resides in one frame of a frameset, you can have the target for that link displayed in any of the frames in that frameset. You do so by including the TARGET attribute in the link's anchor tag, along with the name of the frame that should receive the target of the link.

Other file types   The target of a link can be any type of file. Internet Explorer can open several types of files on its own, including Web pages, text files, and GIF or JPEG image files. For other file types, it must rely on Windows 95 and request that the appropriate program handle that file. For example, sound files (WAV or AU) and movie files (MOV, MPG, or MPEG) would be played by the appropriate sound and movie player.

E-mail address   The target for a link can use an Internet protocol other than HTTP, such as the *mailto* protocol that defines an e-mail address. When the reader of the page clicks the link, the reader's e-mail program should open with a new message displayed and already addressed to the address specified in the link. The reader can create the body of the message and send it to the target address in the usual way.

Part iv

Creating a Clickable Image Map

A variation of the image hyperlink discussed in the previous section is the *image map*, which is a single image that contains multiple hyperlinks. Each hyperlink is associated with a defined area of the image called a *hotspot*, which, when clicked, activates that link. In Internet Explorer, you see only the image; there is no indication that it has clickable hotspots.

You've undoubtedly encountered image maps in many, many pages on the Web. They can be informative, attractive, and intuitive and can also transcend language, which is an important consideration on the World Wide Web.

TIP

Even though images can convey information without language, an image is nonetheless open to a variety of interpretations. Images may not even be seen when visitors to a site have turned off the display of images in their browsers to speed things up. Therefore, good Web design often means including corresponding text hyperlinks next to an image map so that a visitor to that page can either click within the image map or click one of the text links.

A typical use of an image map is literally in the form of a map: You can click on a city, state, or region to display information about that region. An image map built from a map of the United States works well when the hotspots are defined around the large, regularly shaped western states. But the plan doesn't work so well for the smaller, irregularly shaped eastern states.

In such a case, the image map would work better with a regional map of the United States. Clicking in the east would display an enlarged map of just that region of the country, and clicking in the west would display the western states, as shown in Figure 16.8.

A Web-page author can create an image map from an image in two ways:

A server-side image map is the traditional type. When you click within an image map, Internet Explorer sends the coordinates of the click (relative to the image) to the server of that Web site. The server looks up those coordinates in a table of hotspots for that image map and processes the appropriate hyperlink target. Different servers may use different systems for storing the coordinates and targets for an image map.

A client-side image map obviates any server interaction, because the hotspot coordinates are included in the HTML definition for the image map that is sent to Internet Explorer. When you click within the client-side image map, Internet Explorer looks to see which target is associated with those coordinates and then opens that target.

Here is a sample of the HTML code for a client-side image map:

```
<AREA SHAPE="RECT" COORDS="308,32 380,72" HREF="choice1.htm"
```

```
<AREA SHAPE="RECT" COORDS="223,174 365,246" HREF="choice2.htm"
<AREA SHAPE="RECT" COORDS="7,177 179,246" HREF="choice3.htm"
```

When you click within the image, Internet Explorer determines the coordinates of the point on which you clicked and finds the corresponding target for that portion of the image map, as though you had clicked a normal text or image hyperlink.

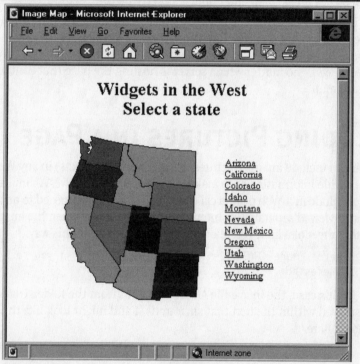

FIGURE 16.8: A geographic map can be a practical way to implement an image map.

NOTE

Working in a text editor to create the HTML code for an image map just might be the nastiest Web-programming job there is. But you can create them with ease when you use HTML editors such as the one in Microsoft FrontPage. You simply draw an outline of the hotspot within the image and then specify the target for that link.

Although it usually shouldn't matter to you which type of image map appears on a page in Internet Explorer, you'll find one advantage with a client-side map. When you point to a hotspot in the map, you'll see the URL of the link associated with that hotspot, just as you do with a normal link. When you press tab to select each hyperlink in the page, you also select each hotspot in an image map. Pointing at a hotspot not only conveniently tells you where you'll go, it also tells you that this image is, indeed, an image map and not just a pretty picture.

Finally, because all the links are processed within the browser, a client-side image map reduces the processing burden on the server. It also is more flexible than a server-side image map, because it is guaranteed to work no matter which server is hosting the page that contains the image map.

INCLUDING PICTURES IN A PAGE

You can include images (pictures or other nontext objects) in any Web page to provide information or to make the page more attractive. An image that you include in a Web page is called an *inline image*, as opposed to an image that is viewed separately in Internet Explorer, such as when the image file is the target of a link. You reference the inline image in this way:

```
There's more <IMG SRC="Images/arrow-rt.gif"> if you're
interested.
```

In this case, the image file ARROW-RT.GIF (from the folder Images) is displayed within the text that surrounds it and might look like the one shown here.

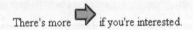

There's more if you're interested.

NOTE
The two most common graphic file formats you'll find on the Web are GIF and JPEG. The data is compressed in both types of files, so images can be transmitted much faster over a network.

Let's take a look at some of the attributes for the <IMG> tag for an inline image; all are optional:

Alternate text   When a browser cannot display graphic images, perhaps because the image file cannot be found or because the browser's image-loading capabilities have been turned off to save download time, you can include the ALT attribute in an image tag to have text displayed in place of the image.

Sizing the image   By default, Internet Explorer loads an image from the top down and displays the image in as large a box as needed. You can choose to specify an exact size for the image by including the WIDTH and HEIGHT attributes within the HTML tag (see the inline image example earlier in this chapter in *Creating a Text or Image Hyperlink*).

Aligning the image   You can use the ALIGN attribute with the LEFT, CENTER, or RIGHT options to position the image either flush-left, centered, or flush-right in the browser window. You can also use the TOP, BOTTOM, or MIDDLE attributes to align text with the top, bottom, or middle of the image.

CREATING LISTS

Using HTML, you can arrange items in lists in several ways. The two most useful ones are:

Bulleted   Or *unordered* lists, in which each item (paragraph) in the list is prefaced with a bullet; the <UL> tag begins the list.

Numbered   Or *ordered* lists, in which each item in the list is prefaced with a number; the <OL> tag begins the list. Internet Explorer applies the appropriate number to each line when it opens the page, so you can add to or delete items from the list while you create the page and not have to worry about updating the numbering.

You define each item within either type of list with the <LI> tag. The following unordered list:

```
<P>Chapter I</P>
<UL>
<LI>Section 1</LI>
```

Part iv

```
<LI>Section 2</LI>

<LI>Section 3</LI></UL>
```

Chapter I
• Section 1
• Section 2
• Section 3

looks like the example at left in a browser. The bulleted or numbered list is a fast, easy way to apply some structure to a Web page, and you'll no doubt use it frequently. As always, the way a browser formats the list, such as the amount of indention and the style of the bullets, could vary from browser to browser.

You can nest one list within another simply by beginning the new list with the appropriate list tag. This allows you to create outlines, for example, or tables of contents that have subheadings indented in their own lists. Here's the list from the example above with a second list within it:

```
<P>Chapter I</P>

<UL>

<LI>Section 1</LI>

<LI>Section 2<UL>

<LI>Part A</LI>

<LI>Part B</LI>

<LI>Part C</LI>

</UL></LI>

<LI>Section 3</LI></UL>
```

In Internet Explorer, the secondary list is indented from the primary list and displays a different type of bullet. Again, in other browsers these lists may look somewhat different. Here is the indented list from above shown in Internet Explorer (on the left) and another browser.

Chapter I	Chapter I
• Section 1	● Section 1
• Section 2	● Section 2
○ Part A	☐ Part A
○ Part B	☐ Part B
○ Part C	☐ Part C
• Section 3	● Section 3

ARRANGING ITEMS WITHIN TABLES

Another and even more powerful way to structure data within a Web page is the table. Like the tables you can create in your word processor or spreadsheet, an HTML table consists of rows, columns, and cells.

You can place just about anything you want within a cell in a table; there are few restrictions. Because of the flexibility of HTML tables, you'll find them used in countless ways in Web pages.

Sometimes a table will look like a table, with border lines dividing its rows, columns, and cells. In other cases, though, the structure of the table will be used, but its borders won't be displayed. The table serves as a convenient way to organize elements on the page without making them appear within the confines of an actual table.

Like image maps, tables are HTML elements that are best created in a dedicated HTML editor, such as FrontPage Express. You can still build a small table "manually" in a text editor, such as the table shown in the next example, but for anything more complex, you'll want to move to a more powerful editing tool.

Table 16.3 shows the basic tags with which you define a table:

TABLE 16.3:   Basic HTML Table-Building Tags

TAG	PURPOSE
<TABLE>	Begins the table definition.
<TR>	Defines a new row in the table.
<TD>	Defines a single cell within the table.

Shown below is the code for a simple, six-cell table:

```
<TABLE>
  <TR>
    <TD>Cell A1</TD>   <TD>Cell B1</TD>
  </TR>
  <TR>
    <TD>Cell A2</TD>   <TD>Cell B2</TD>
  </TR>
  <TR>
```

```
    <TD>Cell A3</TD>   <TD>Cell B3</TD>
  </TR>
</TABLE>
```

The result is a table that has three rows and two columns; the text within the <TD> and </TD> tags appears in each cell. By default, as in this example, the table has no borders. You must specifically include them by specifying the width of their lines (in pixels) with the BORDER attribute for the <TABLE> tag, so that this tag:

```
<TABLE BORDER="1">
```

would enclose all the cells in the table with a border that is one pixel wide. Shown below is the first table, on the left, and the same table with a border, on the right.

Cell A1 Cell B1	Cell A1	Cell B1
Cell A2 Cell B2	Cell A2	Cell B2
Cell A3 Cell B3	Cell A3	Cell B3

You can include the <CAPTION> tag once in a table. Any text between this tag and its closing tag is displayed as the table's caption, which by default is centered just above the table.

You use the table header tag, <TH>, instead of the <TD> tag to create a header cell for the table. Internet Explorer displays the text between the opening and closing header tags boldfaced and centered within the cell. You will often use these table headers as titles in the first row or column of a table.

By default, a table will only be as wide as the longest entries in its cells. You can specify an exact width in the <TABLE> tag with the WIDTH attribute, either in pixels or as a percentage of the browser's window. For example, this tag:

```
<TABLE WIDTH="320">
```

creates a table exactly 320 pixels wide. If you want a table to be exactly half the width of the browser's window, no matter what width that might be, use the following tag:

```
<TABLE WIDTH="50%">
```

If a table is less than the full width of a browser's window, it is aligned with the left edge of the window. You can include the ALIGN attribute in the <TABLE> tag and specify Left, Center, or Right alignment within the browser's window.

If you specify an exact width for the table, you might also want to set the width of each column with the WIDTH attribute within the <TD> tag for a cell. You can specify the width either in pixels or as a percentage of the table (not of the browser's window).

As you'll see when you create a table in FrontPage Express, you can include many other tags and attributes, such as a background color or image for the table or any of its cells, the color of its borders, and which of its borders should be displayed.

GETTING FEEDBACK WITH FORMS

So far in this chapter, all the HTML elements we've discussed have been display-oriented, in that they affect the way a page appears within a browser. Now we'll look at the HTML form, an element that not only affects the display but also allows the reader to send information back to the server.

Those two issues, display and send, are the primary pieces of a Web-based form:

▶ The form controls that you create on a Web page are displayed in a browser and can be used by the visitor to enter data, select checkboxes or radio buttons, select items from a list, and so on.

▶ Once the visitor enters data into the form, he or she must have a mechanism for sending the data back to your server. Once the server receives the data, it must have another mechanism for storing or manipulating that data.

Designing a Form

Designing a form for a Web page isn't especially difficult if, as with tables, you do the job in an HTML editor such as FrontPage Express. The forms you create for the Web look and behave much like any other computer-generated forms you may have come across. For example, an HTML form can have a one-line data-entry field (sometimes called an edit field), in which the reader can type, for example, an e-mail address.

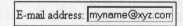

Part IV

You use the <FORM> tag to begin the form definition. As part of that definition, you specify where the data should be returned (a URL) using the ACTION attribute. The destination might be the server for the form's Web page, or it could be some other server that will accept the data. You also specify how the data should be returned, using the METHOD attribute. The POST method is a common way to handle the job.

Within the opening and closing <FORM> tags, you lay out the controls of the form. You can include any other HTML elements, as well, which will appear in the page along with the form controls. Some of the more common form control tags are shown in Table 16.4 and Figure 16.9.

TABLE 16.4:   Common HTML Form Control Tags

Tag	Form Control	Description
<INPUT TYPE="TEXT">	Data-entry field	A one-line data-entry field
<INPUT TYPE="PASSWORD">	Password field	A one-line data-entry field in which the characters you type are displayed as asterisks to hide them
<TEXTAREA>	Multiple-line data-entry field	Enter a paragraph or more of text
<INPUT TYPE="CHECKBOX">	checkbox	Select an item by clicking its checkbox
<INPUT TYPE="RADIO">	Radio button	Select one of a group of radio buttons
<SELECT>	List	Select one or more items from a list
<INPUT TYPE="SUBMIT">	Button	When clicked, sends the form's data to the server
<INPUT TYPE="RESET">	Button	When clicked, resets all form controls to their defaults

The definition for each control (other than the Submit and Reset buttons) must include a name for the control, which is sent to and used by the server to identify the data that was returned from that control. Each control can have several other attributes that define how it behaves. For example, the single-line data-entry field has the following attributes:

Size   The displayed width of the field in the form

Maxlength   The maximum number of characters that can be entered into the field

Value   The characters that appear within the field when its page is first opened or when the Reset button is clicked. You might use *(none)* as this default value, so that when the data is returned to the server, this entry indicates that the visitor has entered no data in this field.

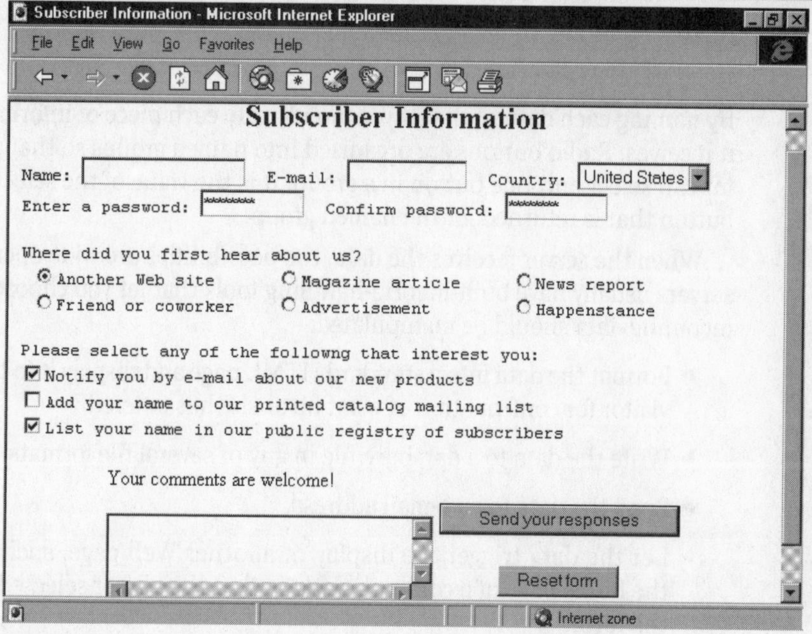

FIGURE 16.9: A visitor can enter information or select items in an HTML form.

Here is an example of the code for a data-entry field:

```
<INPUT TYPE="TEXT" NAME="COMPANY" SIZE="25" MAXLENGTH="100"
VALUE="(none)">
```

As the visitor enters information into a form, that data is still on the visitor's local computer—it has not reached the server yet.

Getting the Data Back to You

In a form such as the one shown in Figure 16.9, the visitor clicks on the Submit button (labeled *Send your responses* in the figure) to send the data back to the server. The browser collects at least two pieces of information about each control in the form:

- ▶ The name of the control
- ▶ Its current value

For example, if a visitor has entered *Pat Coleman* in the Name field, Internet Explorer sends back the following information:

```
NAME="Pat Coleman"
```

By naming each datum, the server can identify each piece of information it receives. Radio buttons are organized into named groups so that a visitor can select only one button in a group. It is the value of the selected button that is returned for the named group.

When the server receives the data, the possibilities are wide open. Web servers usually have built-in form-handling tools that let you choose how incoming data should be manipulated:

- ▶ Format the data into a standard HTML page and display it to the visitor for confirmation of what he or she has entered.
- ▶ Write the data to a database file in any of several file formats.
- ▶ Send the data to an e-mail address.
- ▶ Let the data trigger the display of another Web page, such as the home page of a company catalog that the visitor selected in the form.

Beyond using a server's built-in tools to handle the incoming data, programming work will be needed to create the necessary script or program to manipulate the data.

SPLITTING A PAGE INTO FRAMES

With the HTML feature called *frames*, you can create and display multiple Web pages within a single page. In the traditional way of browsing a Web, if you click a link in one page, a new page opens and replaces the first page in the browser.

For example, when you click a link in a page that serves as a table of contents of other pages, the target page opens, but the table of contents page is removed from the browser. By splitting a page into two frames, such as in the page shown in Figure 16.10, the table of contents page can be displayed in a frame on the left, for example, while the target of the selected link is displayed in the other frame on the right side of the browser's window. In this way, the table of contents is always available so that the reader can make another selection.

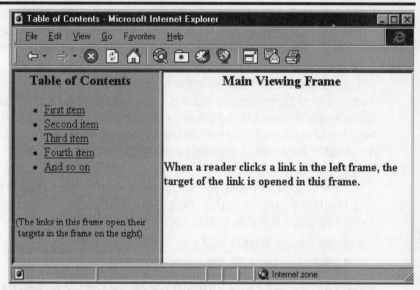

FIGURE 16.10: By splitting a page into frames, you can have a table of contents displayed in one frame, while the target of each link is displayed in the other frame.

The concept of frames is neat and simple:

▶ Create a single Web page as a *frameset*, which contains no content other than the frameset definition.

▶ Specify how the frameset should be divided into frames.

▶ Assign a Web page to each frame.

You use the <FRAMESET> tag instead of the usual <BODY> tag to begin the frameset definition in the page. For example, this tag

```
<FRAMESET COLS="33%,67%">
```

creates a frameset page that consists of two frames arranged as columns. The first frame will be in a column on the left side of the browser's window; that frame's width will be one-third of the browser's window. The second frame will be a column to the right of the first one and will take up two-thirds of the browser's window.

Part IV

You specify the source Web page to be opened in each frame with the <FRAME> tag, as in

```
<FRAME SRC="CONTENTS.HTM">
<FRAME SRC="INSTRUCT.HTM">
```

In this case, when the frameset is opened in a browser, the frame on the left displays the page CONTENTS.HTM, and the frame on the right displays INSTRUCT.HTM. You now have two Web pages sharing the same browser window.

Let's revisit the example from the beginning of this section. If the frame on the left contains an index of links, you can have each of those links display its target in the frame on the right. You do so by including the TARGET attribute in the anchor tag for the link and specifying the name of the frame (as mentioned earlier in this chapter in "Specifying Other Link Targets").

To specify a target frame, you must first name the frame. You do so with the NAME attribute in the <FRAME> tag. In the previous example, you could name the tags in this way:

```
<FRAME SRC="CONTENTS.HTM">
<FRAME SRC="INSTRUCT.HTM" NAME="RIGHT">
```

which gives the name RIGHT to the frame on the right. With that frame named, you can define each link in the index page so that its target resource appears in the named frame, such as:

```
<A HREF="SOMEFILE.HTM" TARGET="RIGHT">
```

In this way, your index remains in the frame on the left, while the target of each link is displayed in the frame on the right.

Finally, since frames are relatively new features of HTML, not all browsers yet support them. You can include the <NOFRAMES> tag within the frameset to provide a message to a browser that cannot display frames. Here's an example:

```
<NOFRAMES><BODY>
<P>Sorry, but this page uses frames, which your browser does
not support.</P>
</BODY></NOFRAMES>
```

As you can see, the <NOFRAMES> tag includes the <BODY> tag, which is not used in defining a frameset but would be recognized by a frames-unaware browser. Anything within the <BODY> tags would then be displayed in the browser.

WHAT'S NEXT?

In the next chapter, you'll learn about the design considerations involved in planning a Web site. If you want to read more about HTML, skip ahead to Chapter 19, *HTML Basics*.

Chapter 17
PLANNING A WEB SITE

As you've been surfing the Web for a while, getting to know this new communication medium, you've been observing, watching, learning, and visiting a variety of Web sites, good and bad. You've seen the power of hypertext links, become engrossed in compelling content, and experienced the excitement of animation and multimedia. You've also been disappointed by some of the utterly useless sites that litter the Web.

Now you have some ideas of your own. You have a mission, a message to share with others—you want to publish your own Web site. Perhaps you want to promote your business, espouse a noble cause, or just publish a family newsletter. Maybe you have information you want to share with the world, or you just need to share data with members of your workgroup on a local intranet.

Whatever your reasons are for wanting to create a Web site, you're probably anxious to start learning to use Netscape

The ABCs of
Netscape Composer
Michael Meadhra
Design, Create, and Publish on the Web
READY, SET, GO...

Adapted from *The ABCs of Netscape Composer*,
by Michael Meadhra
ISBN 0-7821-2065-2   368 pages $19.99

Composer. However, before you begin the nitty-gritty work of creating Web pages, you need to consider some overall issues. This chapter will get you started and will touch on some of the preliminary planning steps that are essential to successful Web site development. It's sort of like taking a trip. Before you set off, you must have a clear picture of where you are going and a plan for the route you intend to take to get there. Otherwise, you're likely to spend a lot of time wandering aimlessly, and you'll never reach your destination.

Setting Your Goal

Like any other project, a Web site begins as a concept. The Web site has (or should have) a purpose, a mission, and a reason for existence. This goal should be your guiding principal as you design your site, and everything about the site should support it. It often helps to sit down and write out a sentence or two articulating the purpose of your Web site. Perhaps your goal is to generate sales leads for a new product, or provide technical support for your customers, or furnish employees of your company with information on employee benefits and company policies. If your main goal is very broad, such as creating an online presence to build name recognition and prestige for your company, be sure to work out the approach you plan to take in achieving that goal.

The purpose of having a written goal for your Web site is to help keep your work focused. As you go through the process of developing your Web site, return to your goal from time to time for a reality check. If some aspect of your site doesn't match up to the stated goal, then something needs to change—either revise the aberrant content or restate your goal.

After you decide what you want to accomplish with your Web site, you can begin selecting and developing content. You can write the text, find or draw graphics, and locate other sites you plan to link to. You can also begin developing ideas for what you want your site to look like.

Defining Your Target Audience

When you define the goal of your Web site, a picture of your target audience should begin to emerge. Defining the target audience is an essential step in any design project, and Web publishing is no exception. You need to determine (or at least guess) who will be viewing your Web site. You need to consider the viewers' background and previous experience, their interests, their tastes, and why they might be visiting your site. One important aspect of the target audience that is unique to Web publishing is the audience's access to your Web site—the speed of their Internet connection, the capabilities of their Web browser software, and the technical expertise of the viewers themselves can all impact how you present the content on your Web page.

If your Web site exists solely as a personal statement or creative exercise, you may think you can ignore the target audience and design your site based on your own tastes and preferences. Actually, in that case, what you are really doing is defining your target audience as yourself and a small circle of friends and other kindred spirits. That's a valid approach—as far as it goes—but it's rather limited.

In practice, most people who publish on the Web do so to get their message out to a larger audience. Your goal should be to reach that audience as effectively as possible. All your Web site design decisions should be based on the needs and wants of the viewers that you envision as your target audience.

For instance, things that make a Web site fun for an audience looking for entertainment might be annoying distractions for a serious-minded researcher looking for information. A lot of graphics and multimedia effects might be just the ticket for creating an exciting Web publication on a corporate intranet where you can reasonably expect everyone to access the site via a speedy local area network. The same content may prove too slow to download practically over a dial-up connection to the Internet.

The keys to successfully communicating with your audience is to first identify the audience, and then to anticipate that audience's reaction to the various elements of your Web site design, so you can select the most effective options. You can tailor almost every aspect of your Web site to the intended audience, from the way you organize information to the kind and number of images to the colors and fonts you use.

ORGANIZING INFORMATION

Once you've laid out a goal for your Web site and defined its target audience, you can begin to think about its content and how you want to present it. The best way to start developing content for your Web site is to organize your assets. Obviously, you'll want to gather up any existing documents and images you want to work with, but your assets can also include corporate-style guidelines and samples of publications in other media, information on Web sites you admire (and may want to emulate), samples of Web sites you hate (so you can analyze what makes you hate them and avoid the same pitfalls), clip art collections and information on sources of Web art, media, and special effects. Think about the message you want to convey and which types of images, text, and other content might be appropriate. (Is it fun and lighthearted or seriously corporate?) Take inventory of what you've got and determine what is usable, what will need to be modified, and what will need to be created from scratch.

NOTE

Make sure you have the legal right to use any materials you plan to include in your Web site. For more information, a U.S. copyright law page published by Cornell University is at: http://www.law.cornell.edu/topics/copyright.html.

NOTE

Don't expect to publish on the Net via your PC with a dial-up connection to the Internet. To actually publish a document for public viewing on the Web, you'll need access to an HTTP or FTP server. If you're connected to a corporate LAN, your network administrator is probably the one you need to see about getting access to the Web server. If you use a dial-up connection to access the Web, check with your internet service provider. Most internet service providers can provide access to an HTTP or FTP server at little or no additional cost.

Creating a Storyboard

With all the materials and information you want to work with in hand, sit down with paper and pencil (or some nifty drawing software) and plot the site out (see Figure 17.1). Storyboard (sketch) your home page and each page it will link to; include all the elements you're considering (text, images, buttons, hyperlinks), and don't be afraid to make adjustments. If your original concept doesn't flow nicely, can it and start again. You can't do too much advance planning.

As you plan your Web site, you need to work on two different levels. First, you need to plan the flow of the information and the appearance of the page itself. Second, if your Web site will be anything more than a single home page, you need to design a map of the site as a whole so you can visualize how all the pages relate to each other and how they work together to create an organic whole.

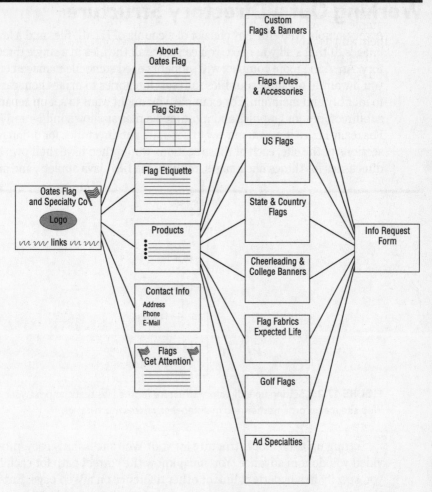

FIGURE 17.1: Sketching out a plan for your Web site helps you visualize how all the parts interrelate.

Remember that the Web thrives on hypertext links and Web users don't expect to read an entire Web site like a novel, moving from page to page in a linear fashion. They want to jump quickly to an item that interests them and then move on to something else. Viewers may enter your Web site at any point via a link from another site. So, you need to design each page of your Web site so that it stands alone and yet is part of a larger whole.

Working Out a Directory Structure

A very simple Web site may consist of a couple of HTML files and a few images. If that's all you need, you can store all the files in a single directory. Anything more complex will probably need some file management—you'll want to organize your files into subdirectories to make them easier to identify and maintain. For example, you might want to set up separate subdirectories for graphics and multimedia files as shown in Figure 17.2. For really large sites, you may want separate subdirectories for different sections of the site, each of these sections would then have their own subdirectories for things like images, multimedia files, java applets, and such.

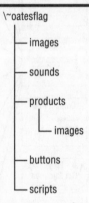

FIGURE 17.2: Setting up a directory structure for the files that comprise your Web site makes organization and maintenance chores much easier.

Setting up a directory structure for your Web site is fairly easy, provided you do it in advance. You must know the correct path for each file you specify in a hypertext link or other reference on a Web page. Entering the correct path information when you define a hypertext link is no problem. However, going back and editing a multitude of links to change all the paths is a nasty chore indeed. It's a nuisance on a small Web site; it's nearly impossible on a larger, more complex site.

To avoid this situation, you can determine what your directory structure will be, and then set up the same subdirectory structure on your local hard disk and on the Web server where you post your Web site. When you define links on your Web pages, you can choose file paths as relative to the home directory for the Web site. If you use relative addresses and have the same subdirectory structure in both locations, you can create and test your Web pages on your local hard drive and be confident that they will work the same when you post your Web site on the server. In order to do this, copy files from your hard disk to their counterpart locations on the Web server.

NOTE

You can set up directories and subdirectories on your local hard drive with your usual file maintenance tools such as Windows Explorer or a My Computer window. However, you'll need to check with the administrator of your Web server for information on creating directories and subdirectories. Usually, you'll be able to create subdirectories yourself within your own Web site, but you may need to use a utility program such as WS_FTP or FTP Explorer to do so. You might even need to perform file maintenance chores such as creating subdirectories from a Unix shell account. In some cases, the Web administrator will have to set up the directory structure for you.

Making Site Navigation Easy for Viewers

Users need to be able to move around a Web site quickly and easily to locate and access information with a minimum of fuss and bother. If you make your Web site hard to navigate, users will just leave and won't come back.

The most important factor in making your Web site easy to navigate is organization. Designing a well-organized site allows you to present information in such a way that it is easy for viewers to see and understand where things are located and how to find what they need. That's one of the reasons why storyboarding your site is so important.

But good organization alone isn't enough. For the sake of speed and ease of use, consider incorporating into your Web pages navigation aids that provide easy one-click access to key locations and sections of your Web site. You can use text links, buttons, graphic icons, or image maps (clickable images) to identify and link to important destinations, such as the home page, next page, or starting points for key topics. It is essential to make the navigational elements obvious, simple to use, consistent throughout and to place them where they are readily available to help viewers find their way around your site. For example, the buttons on the page shown in Figure 17.3 are present on every page in the site. They provide the visitor with easy and obvious links to other key pages in the site.

FIGURE 17.3: Buttons and other navigation aids help viewers find their way around your Web site.

MAKING YOUR SITE BROWSER-FRIENDLY

As discussed earlier, one of the things you must consider in defining your target audience is how that audience will access your Web site. The speed of the viewer's Internet connections is a big part of the access issue. The other major part of the access question is the capability of the viewer's Web browser software. Different brands and versions of Web browsers have significantly different capabilities. Consequently, as you design your Web site, you must consider the impact of your design decisions on those viewers with less than state-of-the-art browsers.

The HTML standard has evolved rapidly over the last few years. It's undergone some very significant changes in a relatively short time with new HTML standards, new browsers, new features, and new extensions to the language popping up every few months. Each new development has meant exciting new possibilities for Web designers. Each new development has also required changes in browser software to recognize and properly display the new features. As a result, older browsers (and even older versions of the currently popular browsers) may not display all the effects that are possible to produce with the latest browser software and the newest HTML codes and extensions. The leading browser developers seem to be in a race to develop and launch more and more new effects and entice Web designers to use them in the hopes of having their own extensions accepted as the de facto standard of the Web.

The rapid pace of change makes it hard for end users to keep up with the latest thing. By the time a new browser version can be adopted and disseminated to a large group of users (such as a large corporation or the subscribers to an online service), it may have been superseded by yet another version that is newer still. Also, some of the less popular platforms may lag a version or so behind the developments of a more popular platform such as Windows 98. As a result, large numbers of Web users are working with browsers that are one or more versions behind the state of the art and are not capable of displaying the latest, cutting-edge effects.

As you now realize, an important part of identifying the target audience is figuring out what browser versions it might be using. Some of the latest effects simply will not display properly (if at all) in an older browser. Therefore, if you want to use the latest, greatest, and most exciting effects, you will be limiting your audience to those viewers using the latest version of the most popular Web browser. If, on the other hand, you want to make your Web site available to the widest possible audience, you must avoid any effects that require the newest browser version or special add-in software and stick with accepted standards that are widely supported by old and new browsers on all platforms. The choice is yours.

Conserving Bandwidth

Another factor you will need to consider as you design your site is the size of the files that make up your Web pages. HTML files are generally quite small, even when they contain considerable quantities of text. Images and multimedia files, on the other hand, can be very large.

The time and resources required to move those large files around on the Internet can become a significant design consideration. Frequently, you will be required to pay for the amount of storage space your Web site occupies on the Web server. In addition, you might be charged for the volume of data visitors download from your site. However, the biggest problem is the time it takes for your page to appear in the visitor's Web browser window. The bigger the files, the longer it takes to download them.

Some studies suggest that a Web surfer will wait only about 12 seconds for a page to download. My own observations indicate many people are more patient than that and will wait about twice as long. Still, you can expect to have lost many of your potential viewers if your page isn't on their screens in less than thirty seconds. At the very least, slow downloads interrupt the continuity of the reading experience and make viewing your Web site a cumbersome and frustrating experience for the Web surfers who stick around.

With a direct connection to the Internet, you can download a lot of information in thirty seconds, but moving data through a modem connection is another story. The typical Web visitor accesses the Internet via a dial-up modem connection. 33.6 and 28.8K modems are now the standard, but many people still use 14.4K modems. The slower the Net connection, the less data that can be transferred in a given amount of time. Thus, the amount of data that a viewer can download in a limited time using a slow modem connection becomes a limiting factor to what you can put on your Web site. You just need to keep in mind that images, animations, sounds, and other cool effects often carry a steep price in terms of file size and, therefore, download time.

Intranet Publishing: Special Considerations

Generally, any of the techniques and principals that work for Web publishing on the Internet also apply to corporate intranets. One of the only differences between the two is that Web sites on the Internet are available to the world and Web sites and documents on an intranet have a much more restricted distribution—they are available only to other users on the same local network.

Limited distribution can be a good thing. It enables you to publish materials that would be inappropriate for just anyone. For example, a company might post its employee manual, personnel policies, project schedules, and even some confidential cost and pricing information on its intranet. The information would be readily available to employees using the intranet but inaccessible to anyone outside the company.

Because of the differences between the Internet's World Wide Web and Web sites on intranets, you need to think about the kind of documents you're likely to create for distribution in each venue. On the Internet, it's important that each Web site be able to stand on its own. Visitors to your site will probably be strangers, and you can't assume that they will have any prior knowledge of you or your topic. Intranets, on the other hand, are often used as a way for coworkers to share documents and information; you're much more likely to create individual documents and distribute them by posting them on the Web server. There is no need to build elaborate multipage sites to create a context for each document because you can reasonably expect your colleagues to share a common background and knowledge base. A simple page title may be enough to provide all the context that's needed for a page posted on an intranet.

Centralized versus Decentralized Administration

How an intranet is administrated varies greatly. Some intranets are tightly controlled by a single system administrator or a central administrative group that regulates all access to the network and all materials available on it. Other intranets are much more loosely organized with the central administration providing a basic skeleton system and allowing decentralized administration of the details by various departments and perhaps even individual users.

Posting a Web page on an intranet with a centralized administration might involve submitting a request to a person or a group who has the responsibility for maintaining Web services on the intranet. You might not be allowed to create and post Web pages yourself. More likely, you will be able to create your own Web pages, but you must submit them for approval and testing before they will be posted on the Web server.

In contrast, an intranet with decentralized Web administration might have a very informal approval process for Web pages. A designated person in each department might be able to post Web pages on the server. Or the Web server address might be announced, and anyone on the network would be able to post Web pages by simply copying HTML files to the server.

Part iv

Security and the Corporate Intranet

The Internet is pretty much open to the entire world. Anything you publish on the World Wide Web is available to anyone with an Internet connection and a Web browser. With intranets, on the other hand, you can be much more selective in who gets access to what. Typically, a corporate intranet is separated from the Internet by a firewall, a proxy server, or both. The firewall and proxy server act as gatekeepers to protect the intranet from unauthorized intrusions. These intranet security features intercept data that passes back and forth between the intranet and the Internet. They pass along information requested by an intranet user but block outsiders from gaining access to the resources of the intranet.

In addition to insulating the intranet from the larger Internet, network administrators can restrict access to Web servers, directories, and documents so that only certain users can access the documents. Restricting access to documents allows corporations to use the power of the Web to provide easy access for authorized users and, at the same time, protect sensitive or proprietary information in those documents from unauthorized users.

Typically, firewalls, proxy servers, and the various levels of access restrictions are transparent to the intranet user. They are set up and maintained by the network administrator. You'll rarely know they are there (unless you get an access denied message when you try to access a restricted resource). But that doesn't mean you can ignore the difference between the intranet and the Internet or the access restrictions. As a responsible intranet user you must be aware of the differences between e-mail addresses and URLs that are part of your corporate intranet and those that are located on the Internet. It's your responsibility to make sure that any confidential information and sensitive messages stay within the confines of the proper directories on the intranet and don't get addressed to an outside party or other unauthorized person. If your intranet is connected to the larger Internet, your systems administrator has probably set up separate Web servers for the internal system and the publicly accessible Internet. You need to be aware of the difference between the two Web servers and pay particular attention to the one where you post the pages you create. Posting a Web page containing sensitive information intended for internal use to the wrong server could have serious repercussions.

Maintaining Consistent Corporate Style

Posting Web pages on a corporate site usually means following some corporate rules concerning the content and appearance of the documents. The rules may be quite strict or very loose, but there are usually at least some basic rules about what is considered appropriate. Corporate style guidelines can make the documents on the corporate Web site easily distinguishable from outside Web pages. The guidelines may dictate colors, backgrounds, fonts, graphics, and standard navigation buttons.

MAINTAINING YOUR WEB SITE

A good Web site is rarely just a collection of static documents. Instead, a Web site is a dynamic entity that needs to be updated on a regular basis. As a result, you can't consider your job finished when you complete the process of planning, producing, and posting a Web site—you must plan to devote time to the continued care and feeding of your Web site as well. From time to time, you'll need to add new information to your Web site. But just as important, you must also cull outdated material (particularly broken hyperlinks).

In short, setting up a Web site isn't likely to be a one time project that you can just finish and forget; it's more of an ongoing commitment. However, like adopting a pet, developing and maintaining a Web site can be a rewarding experience if you're willing to invest the time it takes to reap the rewards.

WHAT'S NEXT?

In this chapter, Michael Meadhra talked to you about the important considerations involved in planning a Web site. You learned how to define your target audience, organize your information, make your site browser friendly, evaluate the special needs of intranet publishing, and maintain your Web site. It's time to turn to Chapter 18, where he will discuss the more creative considerations involved in site planning. In Chapter 18, he'll talk about the important design decisions you'll need to make. He'll discuss:

▶ Color schemes—what looks good and what's easy to read

▶ Backgrounds, including textures, watermarks, and color bars

Part iv

▶ Spicing up your layout with columns, tables, and frames

▶ Laying out text, hyperlinks, and pictures

▶ Reaching out to the reader through forms and multimedia

Once you get your site all planned out, you can turn to Chapter 19 to learn more about HTML. Or, you can read Chapter 20 to find out about FrontPage Express, which allows you to create your Web site easily using a simple word-processor–like interface.

Chapter 18

UNDERSTANDING THE ELEMENTS OF PAGE DESIGN

As you create the pages that make up a Web site, you draw upon a palette of design elements such as text, hypertext links, images, tables, and multimedia objects. You control and manipulate each of the elements to determine attributes such as color, alignment, size, and placement on the page. You also work with basic text paragraphs or multicolumn layouts, with simple images or fancy animation effects.

However, the factors that make your Web site good or bad, exciting or dull, interesting or boring, have less to do with the complexity of your design or the technical sophistication of your effects, and more to do with providing compelling content with a presentation that is appropriate for the viewing audience. All the formatting options, tricks, and techniques are just tools for presenting information. The important thing isn't the tools themselves, but how you use them to present your information.

Adapted from *The ABCs of Netscape Composer*,
by Michael Meadhra
ISBN 0-7821-2065-2   368 pages $19.99

NOTE

All the Web page design elements described in this chapter can be viewed with Netscape Navigator but not all of them can be created using Netscape Composer. While Composer makes it exceptionally easy to create basic (and some not-so-basic) Web pages and other HTML documents, the program does not support some of the more complex effects that are possible on a Web page.

SETTING THE STAGE

An artist starts a painting with a blank canvas. A Web designer starts with a blank Web page that will be the background for all the other elements of the page. That page needn't remain completely featureless—at least, not for long. You can give the background character by defining its color, its texture, or adding a picture or design. And while you're at it, you can define some other colors (such as the default colors for text and hyperlinks) as well. Then the Web page designer must consider the page layout—the arrangement of the various elements on the Web page.

Considering Colors

The default colors for a Web page are black text on a white (or light gray) background. A simple black and white color scheme is functional, providing good legibility for text on most systems, but it's drab. Adding color to your Web page can make a big difference in how that page is perceived by the viewers.

In traditional print publishing, adding color to a project means adding cost for extra production expenses and passes through the printing press. In the world of computers, on the other hand, color is essentially free. Almost all modern computer systems have at least some color capability, and most can reproduce 256 colors or more. So, using color on your Web pages costs only the time its takes you to select and specify your color choices.

The mere presence of color on your Web page can make the page more interesting. But remember, color must be used very carefully. The right combination of colors can make the page appealing and easy-to-read. In contrast, the wrong combination of colors can produce a page that is an unattractive, illegible mess. In addition, colors can have a strong emotional and psychological effect that must be considered.

The psychology of color and how color can be used to affect moods and perceptions can be an interesting study. While it is beyond the scope of this book, here are a few basic generalizations that can be helpful in selecting colors.

▶ Warm colors (red, orange, yellow) seem to advance toward the viewer; they tend to convey excitement and energy.

▶ Cool colors (blues and greens) seem to recede away from the viewer; they tend to evoke feelings of tranquillity.

The number and kind of colors you choose for your Web pages can influence a visitor's perception of your site—even before they read a single word. You can set a quiet, conservative tone (by sticking with basic black and white, and adding a few accents of navy blue or hunter green), or create a feeling of festive excitement (with liberal use of bright, high-intensity colors, especially reds and yellows).

TIP

One of the best ways to learn how to use color is to observe how other designers have used color. Study magazines, brochures, annual reports, TV, and other Web pages. Look at the colors used and how they affect your perception of the publication, and the product being discussed.

Color does more than affect moods. Your choice of colors also determines the legibility of the text on your Web page. I can't overemphasize the importance of selecting color combinations that produce legible, easy-to-read text. This point is absolutely critical!

Contrast

The main factor influencing text legibility is contrast—the relative difference between the foreground (text) and the background. Obviously, black and white provide the maximum dark/light contrast. That's why black and white is the standard for most printed material (such as this book) and the default color combination for many Web pages as well. However, you don't have to go to such extremes to maintain adequate contrast for your text to be legible. For example, you can use black or dark-colored text on a light-colored background such as light gray, light blue, beige, or yellow (see Figure 18.1). Similarly, you could use white or light-colored (light gray, cyan, yellow) text on a dark-colored (dark blue, maroon, dark gray) background. Any of these combinations should provide plenty of contrast between the text and background to make the text easy to read. On the other hand, white text on a yellow background or dark blue text on a black background (such as the sample in Figure 18.2) will be difficult to read (if not almost invisible).

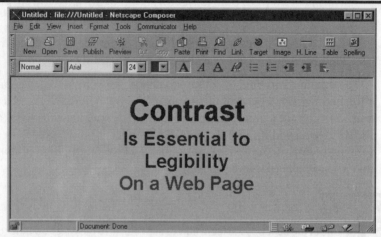

FIGURE 18.1: You don't have to stick with black and white as long as your background and text colors have enough contrast for good legibility.

Color Compatibility

In addition to the dark/light contrast, you should consider color contrast as well. Graphic artists use a tool called a color wheel to help visualize color relationships. As Figure 18.3 shows, the color wheel is a pie chart composed of six equally-sized segments. The colors are arranged in sequence starting with red and going through yellow, green, cyan, blue, and magenta to complete the circle back at red.

Pairs of colors that are opposite of each other on the color wheel are called complementary colors. Complementary colors exhibit the maximum color contrast and using them together can create visual tension. A color scheme that uses complementary colors can work if one or both colors is subdued. But using full-intensity complementary colors next to each other can create an optical illusion that is very hard to look at—the edge where the colors meet seems to vibrate. Avoid the vibrating color effect for small type at all costs—it's just too hard on the eyes!

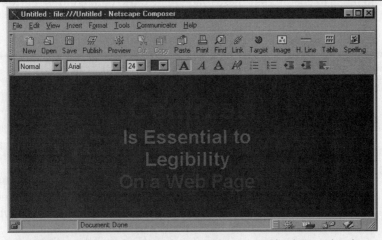

FIGURE 18.2: A lack of contrast between the text and background makes your page hard to read.

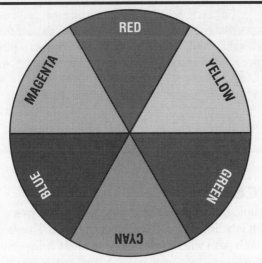

FIGURE 18.3: An artist's color wheel is a valuable reference when choosing colors.

Pairs of colors that lie next to each other on the color wheel are called adjacent colors. Adjacent colors have much less color contrast than complementary colors and are, therefore, generally considered compatible or comfortable color combinations—in other words, the colors go well together. The challenge in setting up a color scheme based on adjacent colors is to ensure that there is adequate dark/light contrast between the text and background.

SHOULD THE BACKGROUND BE LIGHT OR DARK?

Contrast is the key to legibility. Black text on a white background delivers excellent legibility due to the contrast between black and white. But what about white text on a black background? The contrast is just as good, but dark backgrounds aren't used as much as white or light-colored backgrounds. Why not?

The prevalence of light-colored backgrounds as a design element can be attributed to habit or tradition—it's what we are used to seeing in other media. Consequently, most people are more comfortable reading black or dark-colored text on a white or light-colored background. So, when you want to emphasize the content of your Web page, it's probably best to stick with the traditional light-colored backgrounds.

On the other hand, using a dark-color background and light text is a good attention-getting technique because it's a bit unusual. If you elect to use a dark-colored background, the color choice becomes very important. Darker colors tend to be more intense than lighter colors and the background color has more impact than the text color because there is so much more of it visible on the page. Therefore, the color of a dark-colored background makes a stronger impression on the viewer than the color of a light-colored background or the color of the text.

Labeling with Color

In addition to its psychological and aesthetic aspects, color serves a very practical purpose when labeling some elements of the page. This is especially important on a Web page where color helps to identify hyperlinks.

Not only do hyperlinks appear in a different color from the normal text on the page, they are also color coded to show the status of the link. In fact, when you select page colors for a Web page, you specify five different colors:

▶ Background color

▶ Normal Text—the default color for all text that isn't a hyperlink

- ▶ Link Text—the color of a hyperlink the viewer hasn't visited yet

- ▶ Active Link Text—the color of a link that has been selected and is currently loading. (You won't see much of this color. It normally appears for only a second or two.)

- ▶ Followed Link Text—the color of links that the visitor has already visited

NOTE

Although these color selections are labeled text colors they apply to the borders around images as well.

You can use color to label other elements of your Web page in addition to hyperlinks. For instance, some designers like to use a different color for headings or for picture captions to help them stand out from the surrounding text. You're free to use any color combinations you like, but beware, using too many colors can be confusing. It's usually best to select a limited palette of colors and to use them very consistently.

Beginning with Backgrounds

In the beginning, there was gray.

Initially, Web page backgrounds were almost always light gray. Actually, viewers could select their own color scheme in most Web browsers, but almost nobody bothered to change the default settings.

When the HTML standard was expanded to include tags that enabled Web authors to specify color schemes for their Web pages, colored backgrounds were created. Any of the standard system colors can now be used as solid colored backgrounds. The advent of colored backgrounds gave Web pages a whole new look; but the changes haven't stopped there.

Textures

After a solid-color background, the next step in developing an aesthetically pleasing Web page is the background texture. You can create textures because you can define an image that will serve as the background of a Web page. All the text, foreground images, and other elements of the page appear on top of the background image.

Part iv

A background image could be a single, large image big enough to fill the entire Web page. But the problem is that the Web designer has no way of knowing the size of the viewer's browser window, so there's no way to be sure how big (or small) to make the background image. Besides, a full-page sized background image would require a large image file that would be slow to download and display.

Therefore, Web page background images are usually small. The Web browser automatically duplicates the background image and displays as many tiled copies as needed to fill the browser window. The effect is similar to the tiled wallpaper on a Windows 95 desktop.

The repeating background images can be used to produce a variety of patterns. But the technique lends itself to simulating textured backgrounds such as the one shown in Figure 18.4. A very small (and therefore fast to download) image is all that's required to establish a texture such as sand, gravel, paper, or cloth. An image that is little larger is needed to create a more detailed background texture such as wood, leather, or polished stone. A good texture adds visual interest to the page without distracting the viewer from the text.

Watermarks

Of course, background images can do more than just simulate simple textures. The same basic technique can be used to create other effects. One very effective use of a background image is to repeat a logo or other symbol across the page background as shown in Figure 18.5. The result is reminiscent of watermarks on fine stationery, especially if the logo is rendered with a subtle embossed effect. Often, the embossed look isn't required as long as the colors in the logo are sufficiently subdued, so that they stay in their role of as a background, and don't conflict with the text and foreground images.

FIGURE 18.4: A textured background can add visual interest to a Web page.

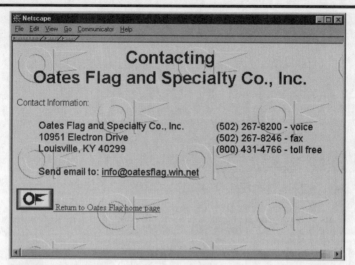

FIGURE 18.5: Repeating a logo as a background image is a good way to give your Web page a strong corporate identity.

Color Bars

Another very popular background image effect is a color bar running down the left side of the Web page as shown in Figure 18.6. This effect is often combined with a multicolumn page layout. Web designers frequently place buttons or hyperlinks in the left column over the color bar and position the body text in the remainder of the page.

The color bar effect is achieved by using a background image that is only a few pixels tall but very wide—wider than the widest browser window. Essentially, the background image is a horizontal line that consists of a section of color on the left end (to form the color bar) and the rest of the line is the desired background color. Because the background image is wider than the browser window, the browser's attempt to tile the image results in stacking copies of the background image on top of each other, line over line, to fill the height of the page. (The background image in the top graphic is thicker than necessary and includes a black border to enable you to see how the images are stacked to create the color bar effect.)

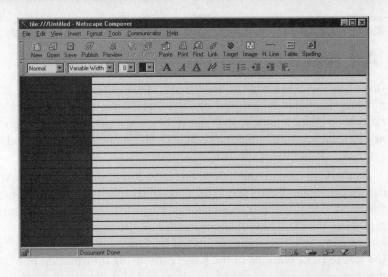

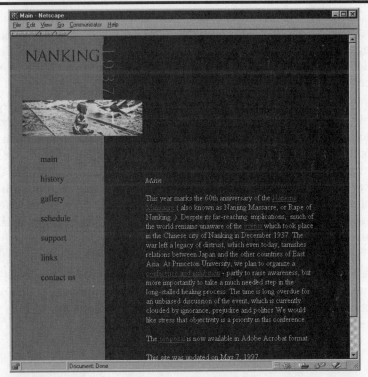

FIGURE 18.6:   A bar of color on the left side of the page is another popular background image effect.

ONE COLUMN OR TWO? DECIDING ON A LAYOUT

Given the Web's roots in the academic and scientific communities, it's not surprising that HTML and the Web started out as a utilitarian tool. Early Web pages tended to look like a thesis or a submission to a scholarly journal—pages of single-column text with a few illustrations and some formatting to set the headings apart.

As the Web has matured, designers have found ways to apply graphic design principles, developed in other media, to Web page design. Some of the most significant advances have come in the area of page layout—arranging the positions of the elements on the page. Web pages are no longer confined to a single column of text running the full width, from the left to right margins of the page, presenting information in a linear manner.

Now, single-column Web pages, such as the one shown in Figure 18.7, are only one of the options available to a Web author. The single-column page layout is simple, effective, and provides the maximum versatility for adapting to widely varying viewing conditions. It reveals information to the viewer in a linear fashion, as the viewer reads down the page.

Web pages can also benefit from the same kind of multicolumn page layouts you commonly see in newspapers, magazines, and brochures. Using multiple columns in the page layout gives the Web page author much more control over how various elements are positioned on the page. As a result, a creative Web page designer can simultaneously add to the page's aesthetic appeal and control the flow of the reader's eye across the page. Multiple columns break the page into smaller sections and they give the Web designer more opportunities to present different information on the same page.

Multicolumn page layouts can range from simple, two-column layouts such as the one shown in Figure 18.8, to three- or four-column page layouts such as the one shown in Figure 18.9. Sometimes, a column doesn't actually contain text; it may exist simply as a spacer to affect where on the page the another column of text will appear.

FIGURE 18.7: The standard Web page layout arranges all text in a single, full-width column.

Multiple columns are produced from an unusual type of HTML tags. The secret to creating multiple-column Web pages lies in the innovative use of the HTML table features. Basically, you just use a large table as a page layout grid and adjust the table settings to make the structure of the table disappear. All that is visible to the viewer then, is text and images arranged in neat columns. The technique works because there is no restriction on what you can place in each cell of a table. A single table cell can contain a whole column of text, complete with images.

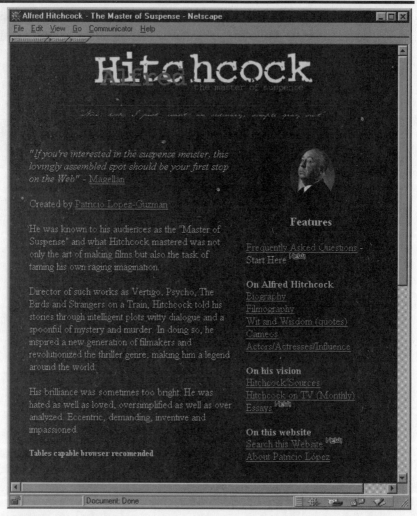

FIGURE 18.8: Breaking the text into two columns has a dramatic impact on the Web page layout.

FIGURE 18.9: You don't have to stop with only two columns.

Layout with Layers

Tables have been the tool that allows Web authors to have more control over how elements are positioned on a Web page. Now, a new development promises to raise the graphic design bar to a higher level.

A new HTML feature, called layers, will allow Web page designers to specify the exact position of each element on a Web page. Individual page elements can overlap and be turned on or off. Not only that, layers make it possible to control the order in which things appear on the page.

Layers hold the promise of some exciting, new Web page effects. This new development could make tables, as a page layout tool, obsolete. The demo page, shown in Figure 18.10, shows how the viewer can click icons to display or hide different components of the architectural rendering. It brings a new level of user interaction to the Web.

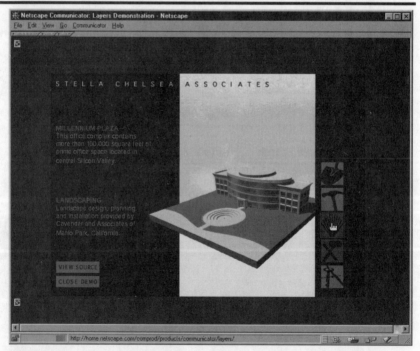

FIGURE 18.10: Viewers can assemble the building by clicking icons in this demo of the new layers feature. (Copyright 1997 Netscape Communications Corp. All Rights Reserved.)

Layers are a new technology—an extension to the HTML standard—that is not yet uniformly supported. Only the latest versions of the most advanced Web browsers can interpret and display Web pages using the layers tags. As a result, it's not yet practical to use layers on a Web page that you intend to publish for the general Web public.

PRESENTING TEXT

Let's face it, most Web pages are mostly composed of text. Consequently, the appearance of the text will have a tremendous impact on the appearance of your Web page.

Before the World Wide Web became popular, most documents viewed on the Internet typically had plain, unformatted text, and they usually appeared in a monospaced font such as courier. It was pretty ugly stuff.

The World Wide Web brought a revolutionary change in the appearance of online documents such as the one shown in Figure 18.11. The combination of HTML and a Web browser makes it practical to display text in proportional fonts and use bold, italics, different text sizes, and other types of formatting similar to what we use when we work with a word processor.

It's interesting to note how text is handled on the Web. Usually, the Web page author specifies text formatting options such as bold, italics, underline, colors, and text sizes in the HTML source code. However, it's the viewer's settings in their Web browser that mostly determines what font will be used to display the text. In fact, HTML originally provided no way for the Web author to select fonts beyond choosing between a variable width or monospaced font. This generic font selection arrangement allows viewers to select from the fonts available on their own systems and choose the ones that display attractively.

Enhancements to HTML give the Web author more control over the fonts that appear on Web pages. Any font can be applied to text in your Web page. If that font is available on the viewer's system, the Web browser will use it to display your page. For example, the page shown in Figure 18.12 uses a casual, handwriting-style font for the list of links in the left column.

FIGURE 18.11: The default font in most Web browsers is Times Roman.

The problem with specifying these types of fonts is that the list of universally available fonts is very small. Most systems will have access to some variation of Ariel (or Helvetica), Times Roman, and Courier; but that's about all. There is an assortment of fonts (such as the Comic Sans font used in Figure 18.12) available on the Internet, for use on any Web page. But not everyone has downloaded and installed these fonts. Even if they had, the list of fonts contains less than a dozen basic typefaces plus bold and italic variations.

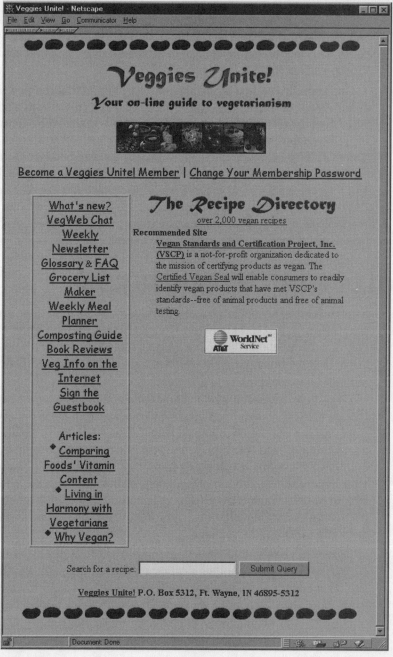

FIGURE 18.12:   This page uses a non-standard font for the links in the left column.

To address the problem of limited font availability, a new development—dynamic fonts—has emerged. Dynamic fonts stay on a Web server and are downloaded by a Web browser only when needed to display Web pages. This technology holds a lot of promise, but it hasn't yet achieved widespread acceptance.

One sure-fire method of adding a variety of fonts that the viewer will definitely see, is to create a graphic image of text that contains a special font. Then, instead of attempting to format text on the Web page to use the selected font, you simply insert the image in place of the text. Because almost all Web browsers can display images, you can be assured that the viewer will see the text as you intended. This technique, shown in Figure 18.13, works great for logos, headlines, and many other applications. Until dynamic fonts and other font initiatives become mainstream on the World Wide Web, graphic images of text are probably the best way to introduce a variety of fonts to your Web pages.

FOLLOWING HYPERLINKS

Hyperlinks are the lifeblood of the World Wide Web. More than anything else, it is hypertext links between Web pages that give the World Wide Web it's character and define the Web surfing experience. (It's no coincidence that the language of the Web is called HTML for *HyperText Markup Language*.)

Hyperlinks make the World Wide Web a unique medium. They change the way a viewer can interact with the information on a Web page. Instead of reading a Web page in a sequential, linear fashion, like a traditional printed document, the viewer can interrupt their reading to follow a hyperlink. By jumping from page to page, clicking hyperlink after hyperlink, the process of reading a Web page is transformed into a stream-of-consciousness experience. Because the viewer is an active participant, choosing what they view next, the Web becomes a more engaging medium.

Hyperlinks can lead to almost anything. The target of a hyperlink can be another Web page, another location on the current page, an image, or any other computer file available for download from the Web server.

FIGURE 18.13: To display an interesting variety of fonts, this page uses images of text that needs to appear in non-standard fonts.

As you design your Web pages, you need to give careful consideration to the hyperlinks you include. Think about what the viewer might be looking for and what they might find interesting. Use hyperlinks to provide a variety of ways to experience your Web page. Sometimes it helps to think of each Web page as an index, or table of contents, to all the targets of all the hyperlinks on the page. It's easy to see how the page shown in Figure 18.14 serves as an index to the link pages. Most Web pages must perform the same function to a lesser degree.

TIP

Make your hyperlinks clear, concise, and descriptive to give the viewer a good idea of what they will find, if they follow the link.

CREATING AN IMAGE WITH PICTURES

Images, as you well know, are another important aspect of the World Wide Web. It's the many Web page images that transform the World Wide Web from a drab world of text documents to the graphically rich experience we all know and love. Perhaps, the original developers of the World Wide Web included the ability to display images so that charts, graphs, and illustrations could be added to the dissertations and research documents they envisioned as typical Web documents. Modern Web authors have put images to use for a wider variety of purposes. Today, images are more likely to be used to add color and visual interest or to create a user interface with buttons and images maps; although, some images can convey essential information as well.

Announcing Banner Graphics

A very popular Web page design technique is to start the page with a banner graphic—a colorful image that identifies your site with some distinctive logo or illustration. The idea is, that the strong visual will make a good first impression and be more memorable than a text headline.

For example, as you can see in Figure 18.15, the logo at the top of the page unmistakably identifies the Web site. In addition, each headline on this opening page of the Web site is accompanied by a separate minibanner to give each topic a graphic identity.

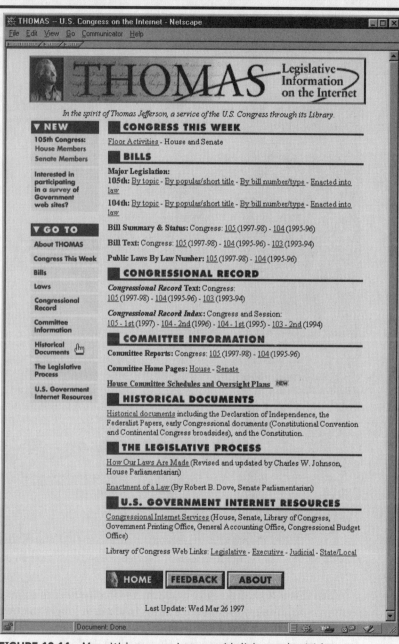

FIGURE 18.14: Many Web pages exist to provide links to other Web pages where the viewer will find the information they seek.

FIGURE 18.15: Banner graphics identify the Web site and each topic on this page.

While this is a good design approach, its effectiveness is sometimes compromised by slow execution. Images take much longer to download and display than text—especially when a user views your Web site via a dial-up Internet connection over a slow modem. Unfortunately, the viewer may have to wait a significant amount of time for the image to appear.

The only way to eliminate the problem of slow image downloads is to avoid using images of any kind, and stick to plain text. But, you would then have to sacrifice the considerable power of graphic images. The best approach is to balance the need for speed with the appeal of graphics. Choose images to convey information and not just for their random decorative value. Then, make sure every image is properly sized and compressed to create the smallest possible file, so as to keep download times to a minimum.

These guidelines apply to every image in your Web site, but especially to banner graphics, because the banner is often the first thing a viewer will see. You can't expect viewers to wait too long for that initial graphic to appear.

Say It with Pictures

Perhaps the most apparent use for images is to add pictures, charts, graphs, and illustrations to a Web page. Scanned photos such as the picture of the young girl on the page shown in Figure 18.16 can, indeed, be worth the proverbial thousand words when it comes to setting a mood. Illustrations can often communicate important information in a way that words alone can't.

In addition to the obvious uses of images as part of the main content of the Web page, they play many supporting roles as well. I've already mentioned a few of them: background images, graphics text, and banner graphics. Images are also used to place logos and symbols on Web pages. There are still more uses for images, just read on.

Navigating with Buttons

By anchoring a hyperlink to an image, you can create an image that, when the viewer clicks it, will take them to another Web page, download a file, or play a multimedia effect. As a result, the image acts like a button—you click it to make something happen.

This simple concept has a very powerful effect. It allows a Web author to make a Web page function like a graphical user interface. Of course, hyperlinks can be anchored to simple words or phrases of text, but using images can make the interface more intuitive. The buttons in the left column of the page, shown in Figure 18.17, are a good example of images that make effective hyperlinks. Images that look like the buttons we all use to control household appliances and other machines don't need instructions to click here. Their use is immediately apparent. The images of buttons can be labeled with icons, simple text (as in the figure), or a combination of both (as in the banner at the top of the page in the figure).

FIGURE 18.16: Pictures can convey data, but they also set a mood, which is sometimes equally as important.

FIGURE 18.17: The images of buttons make excellent anchors for hyperlinks. They seem to scream "Click Me!"

Using hyperlinks anchored to clickable images is a great way to provide viewers with simple, easy to understand navigation aids that help them find their way around your Web site. But all the images that anchor hyperlinks don't have to look like buttons. Signs provide another useful passageway. Images of icons and symbols, such as the ones shown in Figure 18.18, can be just as effective as rectangular button images in leading viewers to follow hyperlinks.

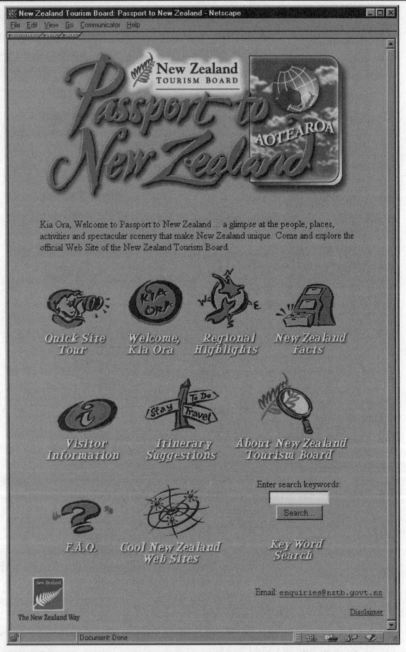

FIGURE 18.18: Images of icons and symbols also make good buttons when anchored to hyperlinks.

Finding Your Way with Maps

If an image that anchors a hyperlink is called a button, what do you call an image that anchors several different hyperlinks? The answer is an image map.

An image map is just an image that has been divided into smaller sections each of which can serve as the anchor for a separate hyperlink. As a result, clicking different portions of the image can take the viewer to different hyperlink targets.

The opening page of the Sybex Web site (shown in Figure 18.19) is a good example of an image map. The virtual desktop is a single image that contains hyperlinks to the major areas of the Web site. Click different parts of the image to take you where you want to go. For instance, to go to the online catalog page, click the shelf of books on the left side of the image; to go to a page where you can learn more about the company, click the Sybex logo on the computer screen in the middle of the image.

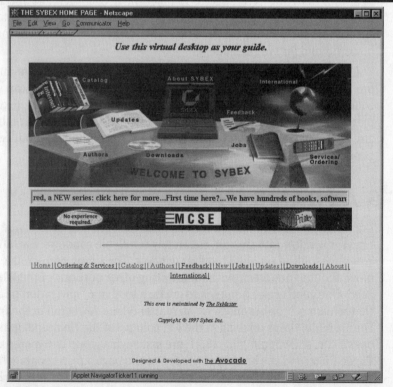

FIGURE 18.19:   An image map is one image with multiple hyperlinks attached.

Working with image maps is somewhat more complex than working with single images and hyperlinks. Defining the different areas within an image to anchor hyperlinks and setting up those links requires some specialized programming. It used to be that creating image maps required running custom programs on the Web server. Now, it's possible to create image maps that are self-contained within the Web page and function with support from the Web browser—no special server programs are required.

Adding Up Tables

A table is a way of organizing text or numbers by arranging them in columns and rows. You see tables everywhere. Invoices, bus schedules, calendars, and spreadsheets are examples of tables.

Tables might be common, but they weren't easy to produce using early versions of HTML. The way the Web browser wraps lines of text to fit within the browser window made it impossible to align text into columns by simply inserting extra spaces. To meet the need for reliable, nicely formatted tables on Web pages, newer versions of HTML have instituted special tags for defining tables. The HTML table features have become a powerful tool for Web designers.

Using table tags, you can create a table such as the one shown and Figure 18.20. Your tables needn't be as plain as this example. You can change the background and the grid lines of a table, change the text formatting, and add images and other elements (including another table) to any table cell. Tables can even serve as a page layout tool to produce multicolumn layouts.

It's a Frame Up

Frames are an HTML feature that enables the Web author to divide the browser window into smaller, separately scrollable windows. Each frame acts almost like a separate browser window. The viewer can scroll and move about in one frame without affecting other portions of the Web page. One good use of frames is to create a toolbar of navigation buttons that remain accessible onscreen no matter where you scroll in the frame. For example, the text labels in the left column of the Netscape developer's site, shown in Figure 18.21, are just such a group of hyperlinks. Those links, and the banner at the top of the page, are in separate frames and remain fixed in place as the viewer scrolls through the text in the other frame.

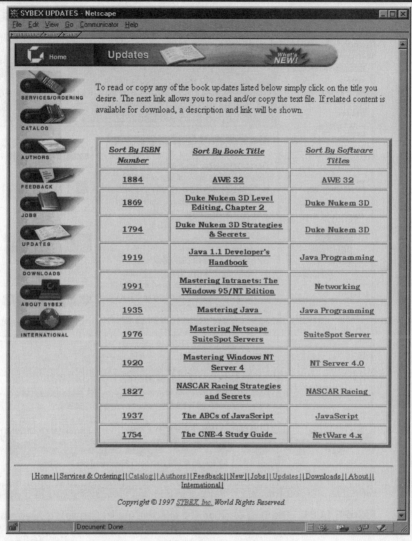

FIGURE 18.20: You can use tables to organize a Web page.

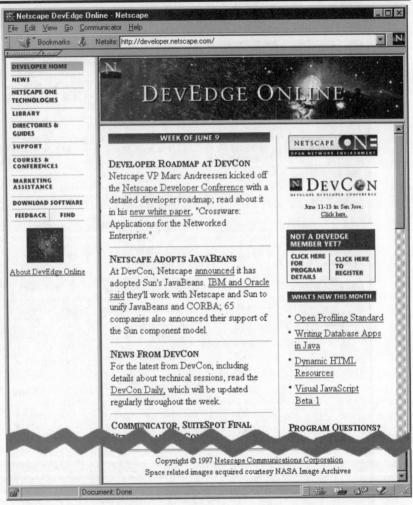

FIGURE 18.21:   The most common and effective use for frames is to keep navigation links accessible, no matter how the main window is scrolled. (Copyright 1997 Netscape Communications Corp. All Rights Reserved.)

NOTE

Visit GroundZero's site at http://groundzero.com for a several examples of frames in use. When you're ready to tackle frames yourself, visit Netscape's guide at http://home.netscape.com/assist/net_ sites/frames.html.

Frames are definitely an advanced Web page design technique. Using frames effectively requires careful planning and an understanding of the programming principles involved in making frames work.

GETTING FEEDBACK WITH FORMS

Web pages can include forms that allow viewers to submit information to the Web server for processing. For example, the Web page shown in Figure 18.22 includes Web form components that enable the viewer to specify the search parameters of the site's database of books.

Web forms work pretty much like their paper counterparts. You fill in the information and submit it (but in this case, it is submitted with the click of a button). Anyone who has used dialog boxes will recognize the text boxes, selection lists, checkboxes, and radio buttons that appear in Web forms. Using the form to solicit information, instead of an e-mail message, insures that the data will be submitted in the proper format for efficient processing.

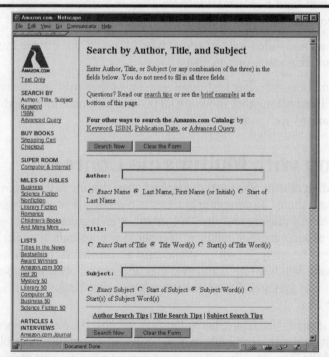

FIGURE 18.22: Fill in the form on this Web page to search for a book listed in the database. (Amazon.com site as of June 11, 1997; reprinted by permission of Amazon.com)

Web forms work with the information processing programs running on the Web server to accept submissions from viewers and send the information to the program or person that needs it. The information gathered from a Web form can be used to generate a response from a program such as a search engine, or it can be stored in a database or forwarded to a human for action.

ADDING SOUND AND ACTION WITH MULTIMEDIA

Web pages can include not only text and graphics, but sounds and moving pictures as well. Incorporating such multimedia elements can add an exciting new dimension to a Web page. It's no longer something you read—it's something you experience.

Multimedia elements can include the following:

▶ Sounds—audio information such as sound effects, music, and voices that Web surfers can hear when they visit your page

▶ Movies and Video—pictures don't have to be still; you can see live-action video clips on the Web

▶ Animation—scrolling text marquees, logos that spin and dance, and illustrations that move are all possibilities on a multimedia enhanced Web page

Interacting with Multimedia Content

Manipulating multimedia is more involved than dealing with simple text and images. Almost all computer systems can display text and images, but successfully playing multimedia content often requires some special hardware or software. For instance, in order to play sounds, a viewer's system must be equipped with a sound card and speakers. In addition to the standard Web browser, the viewer may also need a plug-in, helper application, or system software enhancement to play back the multimedia content.

Unlike images, which have been standardized on a couple of file formats, multimedia content is available in many different (often incompatible) forms and file formats. A few of the most common multimedia formats are supported by either the popular Web browsers or the Windows (or

Macintosh) system software. Otherwise, you will need to download and install special playback software for each type of multimedia content you wish to view. Not surprisingly, you'll also need special software to create each type of multimedia content. Some kinds of multimedia content even require that special software be installed on the Web server.

It takes a lot of data to reproduce sounds and motion. So, it's not surprising that multimedia files tend to be very large. Therefore, one of the problems associated with multimedia is the time it takes to download content before it can be played or displayed. Attempts to address this problem range from data compression, to defining animation in scripts that are interpreted by the browser, to a technique known as streaming—a process that enables multimedia content to begin playing as soon as a portion of the file has been downloaded.

Multimedia content is a varied lot. And the techniques for working with the different forms of multimedia are equally varied. In some cases, you can create a multimedia file using an appropriate program; then, you can add a hyperlink from that file to your Web page, just like adding any other hyperlink. When a viewer clicks the hyperlink, their Web browser downloads the file and playback begins automatically, providing they have the required playback software installed. Other forms of multimedia can be added to your Web page like images. Still other multimedia formats require scripts or special codes to be embedded in the HTML source code.

Page Design Tips

One of the best ways to learn about Web page design is to explore the Web, looking at lots of examples of Web pages. You've probably been doing that already, but you may not have really studied the Web pages you encountered. When you see a Web page you like, stop to think about what you like about it. Is it the colors or images that are appealing? Was the layout attractive and effective? Are the buttons easy to understand? How are the various pages of the site organized? Take note of the best ideas and incorporate them into the Web pages you create. Similarly, when you see a Web page you don't like, try to analyze what it is that turns you off. Was the appearance of the Web page unappealing, or was the content disappointing or poorly organized? By figuring out what went wrong with another Web page, you can avoid making the same mistakes.

Part iv

TIP

When you see a Web page containing a feature you want to emulate, you can get a closer look at how the Web author achieved the effect. When viewing the page in Navigator, choose View ➢ Page Source to open a window displaying the HTML source code for the page. If you want to study the page further, choose File ➢ Save As and save the page as a file on your hard disk for future reference.

WARNING

Don't just save a Web page on your hard disk and then use it as a template for your own pages. While it's all right to study other Web pages and learn from what other Web authors have done, it's generally considered unethical (and perhaps illegal) to actually copy the code for someone else's Web page without permission.

The following list of tips and general comments about Web page design may help to get you thinking about what makes an effective Web page:

- ▶ Web surfers are impatient. Make sure that you present something to grab their attention within the first few seconds after they arrive at your Web site.

- ▶ The title for your page is important; make it short, catchy, and descriptive. Also, make sure the title is accurate and that your page lives up to the promise of its title.

- ▶ Place important, attention getting items at the top of the page where they will appear on the first screen the viewer sees. Don't expect Web surfers to scroll down the page until after you've captured their attention.

- ▶ Keep your Web pages short. If you need to scroll down more than about three screens to reach the bottom of the page, consider breaking it up into more than one page.

- ▶ Keep your pages focused. Don't attempt to get everything on one page—use separate pages for separate aspects of a topic and tie the pages together with hyperlinks.

- ▶ Don't waste viewers' time by forcing them to wait for images to download that don't add much to the page.

- ▶ Make sure buttons and other navigational links behave as the viewer expects them to.

▶ Use compressed images and other techniques to make your page load as quickly as possible.

▶ Make your Web site browser-friendly by avoiding HTML tags and features that aren't supported by all the common Web browsers.

▶ If you include multimedia content that requires special playback software, provide a link to where viewers can obtain the software and instructions for its use.

▶ Get permission to use text or images created by someone else.

▶ Sign your work. Give viewers a way to send comments to the Web author by adding a link to your e-mail address to key pages on your Web site.

▶ Test your page and make sure every link and other feature works before you publish the page on the Web. Test it again by accessing the page from the server using different Web browsers.

▶ Retest your Web pages on a regular basis to find and fix any broken links.

▶ Keep your Web pages fresh. Remove any outdated information and add new information from time to time.

There is no formula for guaranteed success at Web page design. What works on one site, under one set of circumstances, may not work equally well under other circumstances. Besides, the Web is a new and exciting medium with lots of experimentation and innovative new developments going on all the time. That's part of the fun of the Web experience!

WHAT'S NEXT?

Now that you've got some ideas about how you might want your Web page to look, turn to the next chapter for the HTML coding that makes it all happen.

Part iv

Chapter 19

HTML BASICS

I n this chapter, you will create your first HTML document, using the traditional "Hello, World" example often used in teaching programming languages. You'll look at HTML's basic structure tags (<HTML>, <HEAD>, <TITLE>, and <BODY>) in order to learn how HTML pages should be organized. Also in this chapter, we'll introduce you to a broad range of the most commonly used HTML tags.

HELLO, WORLD: OUR FIRST HTML EXAMPLE

Let's hit the ground running and actually make a Web page. In teaching computer programming languages like C and Pascal, it's traditional to show how to create a "Hello, World" pro-gram—a program that simply puts the words "Hello, World" on the screen. Even though HTML isn't a programming language

Adapter from *HTML 4.0: No experience required.*,
by E. Stephen Mack and Janan Platt-Saylor
0-7821-2143-8   704 pages $29.99

in the same league as C and Pascal, we'll still follow that tradition by creating a "Hello, World" HTML document.

Creating the HTML Code

To create this HTML example, just start your text editor and type in the following HTML code, which we'll refer to as hello.html.

hello.html

```
<HTML>
<HEAD>
<TITLE>A Hello World Example in HTML</TITLE>
</HEAD>
<BODY>
Hello, World!
</BODY>
</HTML>
```

Netscape Navigator will display this code as a simple page, as shown in Figure 19.1.

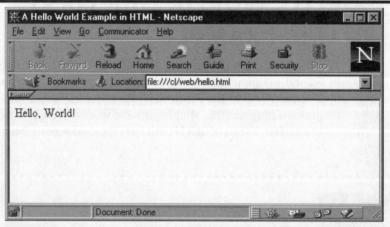

FIGURE 19.1: Navigator shows our "Hello, World" example (typed into Notepad and saved as hello.html). Notice how the title in the title bar corresponds to the text in between the <TITLE> and </TITLE> tags.

Microsoft Internet Explorer would show the page in exactly the same way.

WHICH TEXT EDITOR SHOULD YOU USE?

A text editor is a simple word processor: It only works with plain text—text editors don't do any character formatting. Your computer's operating system usually includes a rudimentary text editor, so the text editor you use depends on what kind of computer you're using. You may want to use a different text editor than the one your operating system offers.

Here are some basic text editor instructions for some commonly used operating systems:

DOS

If you're using Microsoft DOS or another version of DOS, you'll probably have access to a text editor called Edit. (If you're using a really old version of DOS, your editor is Edlin, and you'll definitely want to get a different text editor, since Edlin is frustrating to use.)

To create a file named hello.htm, type **edit hello.htm** (you won't be able to call your file hello.html since DOS limits file extensions to three letters).

To get help with Edit, select Alt+H or press F1.

Windows

In any version of Windows, use the Notepad editor (which is in the Accessories group). You can get help with Notepad through the F1 command or the Help menu.

For Windows 3 users, you'll open the Accessories group and then double-click on the Notepad icon. When you save your document, you'll need to call it hello.htm instead of hello.html, since file extensions are limited to three letters in old versions of Windows.

For Windows 95 or later, click on the Start menu, choose Programs ➢ Accessories ➢ Notepad.

Macintosh

On a Mac, use SimpleText or TeachText (they're just the same, except that SimpleText is used on newer Macintosh systems). Get help by switching on Balloon Help.

UNIX

In the UNIX world, you could try the joe, pico, vi, or emacs editors (in order from simplest to most powerful). You may need to get help from the man command (for example, man vi).

Part iv

Our "Hello, World" document uses eight basic structure tags: <HTML>, <HEAD>, <TITLE>, </TITLE>, </HEAD>, <BODY>, </BODY>, and </HTML>. Basic structure tags are the building blocks for everything else, so it's important you understand them. When creating an HTML document, people typically use the basic structure tags in the following order:

1. Start your document with the <HTML> tag, which declares you are writing an HTML document.

NOTE

HTML documents contain two sections: the head section, which describes the document, and the body section, which contains the document itself. Both of these are discussed in later sections of this chapter.

2. To start the head section, use the <HEAD> tag.

3. Inside the head section is the title of the document (notice how Navigator displays the document's title in the title bar at the top of the window). Start the title with the <TITLE> tag. Immediately after that (with no extra spaces), type the title you want for your document.

4. To close the title you need to use an end tag. End tags start with a slash. End tags are critical—if you leave off a required end tag, your document might not display at all. To end the title, use the </TITLE> tag. Again, don't put any spaces between the title itself and the end title tag.

5. To finish the head section, use another end tag, the </HEAD> tag.

6. Next, start the body section with the <BODY> tag.

7. Type the text of your document, and then close the body section with the </BODY> tag.

8. Finally, end your document with the </HTML> tag.

These tags are contained (or *nested*) within each other. The <HTML> and </HTML> tags contain the <HEAD> and </HEAD> tags, which in turn contain the <TITLE> and </TITLE> tags. Similarly, the body of your document is contained in the body section's <BODY> and </BODY> tags, which in turn are nested within the <HTML> and </HTML> tags. Figure 19.2 shows a diagram of an HTML document's basic structure and its nesting.

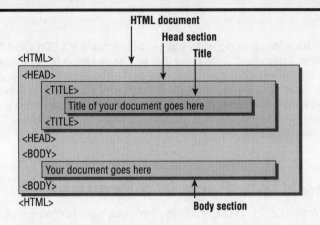

HTML document

Head section

Title

```
<HTML>
    <HEAD>
        <TITLE>
            Title of your document goes here
        <TITLE>
    <HEAD>
    <BODY>
        Your document goes here
    <BODY>
<HTML>
```

Body section

FIGURE 19.2: The basic structure of an HTML document, with elements nested inside each other in the proper order

We'll return to the topic of nesting toward the end of this chapter in *HTML's Rules of Nesting*. Also, we'll be examining each of the eight basic structure tags in detail a little bit later.

When typing in the code, you don't really have to worry about the case of the HTML tags, although it's a good idea to be consistent—if you stick to a uniform case, it will make your HTML code much easier to understand. We used all caps for the tags in hello.html because tags stand out more clearly that way; many Web designers use all caps, but plenty use lowercase as well—it's a matter of personal preference.

Furthermore, it doesn't really matter for this example what text you put in between the <TITLE> and </TITLE> tags (you could put your name or any phrase that describes this document). You could also substitute any text you desire for "Hello, World!" For example, you could type "Welcome to Cyberdyne Systems!" and then whatever text you typed will be displayed instead of "Hello, World!"

Once you've typed in the HTML code, save the text file as hello.html. (If you're using an older DOS or Windows 3 system that doesn't support four-letter extensions, save it as hello.htm instead.)

Part iv

TIP

If you're using Windows 95, make sure you're not hiding MS-DOS Extensions. Otherwise, Notepad will always save files with an extension of `.txt`—so that `hello.html` will be incorrectly saved as `hello.html.txt`. To check whether extensions are displayed, double-click on My Computer, use the View ➤ Options menu command, click on the View tab, and make sure there is *not* a check mark next to Hide MS-DOS File Extensions for File Types That Are Registered. Then choose OK.

Viewing the HTML Page in a Browser

To view the results of this HTML code in a browser, run Navigator, or whatever browser you have access to, and use the File ➤ Open Page command, or whatever seems closest. (With Navigator Gold 3, the command is File ➤ Open File in Browser; with IE, the command is simply File ➤ Open.)

TIP

For many browsers, the shortcut for the File ➤ Open command is Ctrl+O. (That's the letter "O" as in "Open," not the number o.)

As a shortcut, try to open the folder or directory where you saved `hello.html` and then double-click on the filename. (If you're on a UNIX system, typing **lynx hello.html** instead should work.) When you double-click on an HTML file, usually your default Web browser will display the file. You should see something resembling Figure 19.1. This shortcut doesn't work on every system, so if you don't see your page, you'll have to run your browser and open files manually.

WARNING

If you don't save an HTML file with an extension of `.html` or `.htm` (`.html` is preferred), then your browser won't display it correctly.

Reinforcing the Steps

To illustrate the process, here are some step-by-step instructions for creating `hello.html` on a Windows 95 system:

1. Click on the Start menu.

2. Select Programs ➤ Accessories ➤ Notepad.

3. Type in the HTML code. The end result should resemble Figure 19.3.

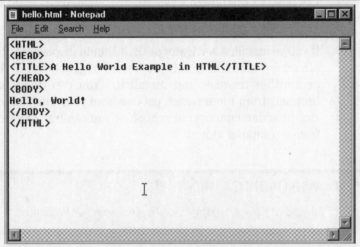

```
hello.html - Notepad                              _ □ ×
File   Edit   Search   Help
<HTML>
<HEAD>
<TITLE>A Hello World Example in HTML</TITLE>
</HEAD>
<BODY>
Hello, World!
</BODY>
</HTML>
```

FIGURE 19.3: Our "Hello, World" example, typed into Notepad and saved as hello.html

4. Use the File ➤ Save command. Double-click on My Computer and then the name of the hard drive where you save your files. Create a new folder (using the Create New Folder button), call it web, and then double-click on the new web folder to open it.

Create New Folder

NOTE

It's a good idea to have a new folder for your Web files so you can keep all of your HTML files together. You can use an existing folder if you prefer, but creating a new folder will keep things easier to manage as you work on more HTML documents.

5. In the File Name box, replace the word "Untitled" with **hello.html**, then click on Save.

6. Click on Start ➤ Programs ➤ Windows Explorer.

7. Double-click on the web folder, where you saved hello.html.

8. Double-click on hello.html.

9. If you've installed Navigator or IE, it should display your file after a few seconds. If not, you'll need to get Navigator, IE, or another browser and install it. (You can download browsers from the Internet, get one from your Internet service provider, employer or school, or you can buy browsers from a computer store.)

DOWNLOADING A BROWSER

To download Navigator or IE, visit these respective Web sites:

http://www.netscape.com/

http://www.microsoft.com/ie/

(If you need an older version of Navigator or IE that isn't available from the official sites, you can give http://www.download.com/ a try.)

It's like the old dilemma about the chicken and the egg: The easiest way to get a Web browser is...with a Web browser. This is fine if you already have one Web browser and you're just rounding out your collection with a different one, or updating to the newest version. Most versions of Windows 95 start you off with IE (older versions of Windows 95 include IE 1, while newer versions of Windows 95 include IE 3). But if you don't have Windows 95 or later, you may not have a Web browser already—so you might have to just buy a copy of Navigator from a software store.

Mission accomplished! Sure, we're glossing over some things about hello.html that will be covered in more detail later, but this example gives us a good idea of the basic structure of all HTML documents. There are only eight tags in hello.html: <HTML>, <HEAD>, <TITLE>, and <BODY>—along with their corresponding end tags. *Learning the Basic Structure Elements of HTML* later in this chapter defines each of these tags in detail. They are the fundamental tags of HTML.

INTRODUCING HTML ELEMENTS

Although many Web authors talk about tags all the time, the preferred term is *element*. An HTML element defines the structures and behaviors of the different parts of a document. We'll learn about many different elements in this chapter, such as the paragraph element (which marks a paragraph), the horizontal rule element (which creates a horizontal line), and the bold element (which makes text appear in bold). You can think of elements as the *commands* of HTML.

Most elements consist of three parts: a start tag, the content, and an end tag.

Consider, for example, the bold element: <B>shout</B>. Together, three things make up this bold element: The start tag, <B>, plus the content (in this case, the word "shout"), plus the end tag, </B>.

NOTE
If we refer to "the <B> tag," you know that we're talking about a start tag since there's no slash. End tags always have a slash, such as </B>.

Every HTML element has a start tag. We'll refer to elements like "the italics element" and let you know what the start tag is (for the italics element, it's <I>).

Some HTML elements are not required to have end tags. For example, the paragraph element uses the <P> start tag to mark the beginning of a paragraph. The paragraph's text is considered to be the content of the paragraph element. But you're not required to mark the end of a paragraph with a </P> tag (although you can if you want).

Some HTML elements have no content. For example, the horizontal rule element (which uses the <HR> start tag) has no content; its only role is to create a line. Elements with no content are called *empty elements*, and they never have end tags.

Some HTML elements are not required to have either start or end tags. The presence of such an element is assumed, even if its start tag and end tag don't explicitly appear in a document. We'll see some examples of these elements in the next section, when we learn about HTML's basic structure.

When we introduce an element, we'll tell you what its start tag is, whether it has an end tag, and whether it's empty.

The tags themselves are not case-sensitive. We show tags in uppercase solely because they stand out better in a printed book.

WARNING

Be careful not to mix up elements and tags. To quote the HTML 4.0 specification, "Elements are not tags. Some people refer incorrectly to elements as tags (for example, "the P tag"). Remember that the element is one thing, and the tag (be it start or end tag) is another." When you talk about tags, always include the angle brackets.

LEARNING THE BASIC STRUCTURE ELEMENTS OF HTML

The basic structure of an HTML document consists of the html, head, title, and body elements. In the "Hello, World" example of hello.html, we created a fully functional HTML document using this basic structure.

NOTE

The four basic structure elements (the html element, the head element, the title element, and the body element) are always present in every HTML document. However, the actual <HTML>, </HTML>, <HEAD>, </HEAD>, <BODY>, and </BODY> tags themselves are not required. Browsers can figure out where these tags are supposed to go. Only the <TITLE> and </TITLE> tags are required to appear in your HTML document.

We'll start our discussion with the html element and work our way through the other three.

Defining HTML Documents with the HTML Element

Every HTML document is simply an html element. Your document should be contained within the <HTML> and </HTML> tags. Notice how the first line of hello.html was the <HTML> tag, and the last line of hello.html closed the html element with the </HTML> tag.

The purpose of the html element is to simply declare that your document is, in fact, an HTML document.

NOTE

The <!DOCTYPE> declaration precedes the <HTML> tag and defines exactly what version of HTML you're using.

When someone looks at a file, they can recognize it as an HTML document by seeing the <HTML> tag at the top.

Each HTML element must contain two parts: the head section, which describes the HTML document but is not displayed by the browser directly, and the body section, which contains the document itself (including the document's text and its HTML markup tags). We'll discuss the head section and the <HEAD> tag first, and then move onto the body section and <BODY> tag.

Describing Documents with the Head Element

The head element is used to mark the position of the head section. The head section contains elements that define certain information about an HTML document, such as what its title is, who the author is, and reference information about the document. To create a head element, start with a <HEAD> tag, then include all of the elements you want in your head section, then end the head element with a </HEAD> tag.

In hello.html, the head section contains only the title of the document. (The title of the document is contained within the <TITLE> and </TITLE> tags, as we'll see in the next section.)

Besides the title, we could have added all sorts of things to the head section, including copyright statements and author information, but it's typical for many HTML documents to contain only a title in the head section.

The head section has many important uses other than just acting as a placeholder for the title, but these other uses are more technical, like defining relationships to other documents and incorporating advanced features like style sheets and scripts. Overall, however, the most important thing to remember about the head element is that it contains the title element.

Naming Documents with the Title Element

The title element is a strict requirement of HTML. Every HTML document *must* have a title contained within a <TITLE> start tag and a </TITLE> end tag. In turn, the title *must* be contained in the head section.

For example, we put the title element in the head section of hello .html like this:

```
<HEAD>
<TITLE>A Hello World Example in HTML</TITLE>
</HEAD>
```

Titles are displayed by browsers on top of the page, usually in the title bar. Figure 19.1 showed the title bar—but it's easy to miss it since it's so small. Here is the title bar by itself (using the title of our "Hello, World" example).

Titles are important because they are used to index and refer to the document. The more descriptive a title, the more useful it will be. A generic title such as "HTML document" or "My Home Page" won't help people remember what your page is about.

Wrapping Your Content with the Body Element

Following the head element is the body element. The body element contains the body section: Start with a <BODY> tag and end it with a </BODY> tag. Anything in between these two tags is the body section.

The body section is where the meat of the document is. Anything in the body section is displayed by the browser when you view the document. Notice how hello.html uses the <BODY> and </BODY> tags to contain all of the text to be displayed. In this case there's not much, only "Hello, World!" In most full-fledged HTML files, there is considerably more in the body section.

Now that we've seen the basic structure of HTML, it's time to see which HTML tags are most commonly used in the body of a document.

LEARNING THE TWO CATEGORIES OF BODY ELEMENTS

We've seen our first example and described the basic structure of HTML. Now we'll define the types and categories of tags that can be used in the body section. Our goal will be to create an example page more sophisticated than hello.html.

There are two basic categories of HTML elements used in the body section:

► Block-level elements

► Text-level elements

Block-level elements are used to define groups of text for a specific role, such as a heading, an author's address, a form, or a table. Text-level elements are for marking up bits of text, including creating links, inserting things like images or sounds, and changing the appearance of text (such as making text emphasized, small, or italic).

NOTE

The main functional difference between these two types of elements is that text-level elements don't cause line-breaks, while block-level elements do cause line-breaks.

Block-Level Elements

Block-level elements include tags that position text on the page, begin new paragraphs, set heading levels, and create lists.

Here are some commonly used block-level elements and their tags:

► Paragraph: <P> and </P>

► Heading, level one: <H1> and </H1>

► Heading, level two: <H2> and </H2>

► Horizontal rule: <HR>

► Centering: <CENTER>

We'll see each of these five block-level elements in action (see *Creating Your First Real HTML Page* below) after we discuss text-level elements.

Text-Level Elements

Text-level elements are used to mark up bits of text, including changing text appearance or creating hyperlinks. Some commonly used text-level elements are:

- Bold: <B> and </B>
- Italic: <I> and </I>
- Line-break:
- Link anchor: <A HREF="*URL*"> and </A>
- Image: <IMG SRC="*URL*">

The last two elements feature attributes. (An *attribute* is an optional argument inside a start tag that defines the way an element works.) In these attributes, note the URL part. Don't actually type URL—instead, that's where you'd substitute an actual URL such as http://www.yahoo.com/ or http://www.emf.net/~estephen/images/jk.gif and so on.

It's important to keep text-level and body-level elements distinct in your mind. These two types of elements behave differently from each other; we'll see exactly how as we learn more about paragraphs later in this chapter. But for now, let's see these text-level and body-level elements at work.

CREATING YOUR FIRST REAL HTML PAGE

We've now seen two types of commonly used elements. These elements might well make up about 70 percent of all the HTML tags you'll use. (However, the other elements are also important!) Using just these common tags, we can create a real HTML page. For this example, let's pretend we're creating a page for a business that sells T-shirts.

You should still have your text editor running from the "Hello, World" example at the beginning of this chapter. Switch to the text editor, create a new file (for example, using the File ➤ New command), type in the following HTML code, and save it as rupert.html in your web folder.

NOTE

If you don't want to type in this example, you can always browse to this book's Web page and download the HTML code. This example, rupert.html, is available at Sybex's Web site at http://www.sybex.com/. Click on the No Experience Required icon and navigate to the Web page for *HTML 4.0: No experience required*.

rupert.html

```
<HTML>
<HEAD>
<TITLE>Rupert's Fabulous T-shirt Company</TITLE>
</HEAD>
<BODY>
<H1>Welcome to Rupert's Fabulous T-shirts!</H1>
<H2>Fabulous T-shirts Since 1752</H2>


Our company, <B>Rupert's Fabulous T-shirt Company</B>,
is your <B><I>second-best choice</I></B> for T-shirts.
(The best choice is <A HREF="http://www.inkyfingers.com/">Inky
Fingers</A>.)


Write us at:<BR>
555 Garment Way<BR>
Alameda, CA  94412


<P>
Call us at (510) 555-9912. <I><B>We're here to help!</B></I>
<IMG
SRC="http://www.emf.net/~estephen/images/turtleshirt.jpg">


<HR>


<CENTER>Why not visit <A
HREF="http://www.yahoo.com/">Yahoo</A>?</CENTER>
```

```
    </BODY>
    </HTML>
```

Before we explain the tags that we used in `rupert.html`, let's see what this page looks like when you view it with a browser. Use your browser's Open command (from the File menu) to view the `rupert.html` file. Figure 19.4 shows the page as it is displayed by Navigator.

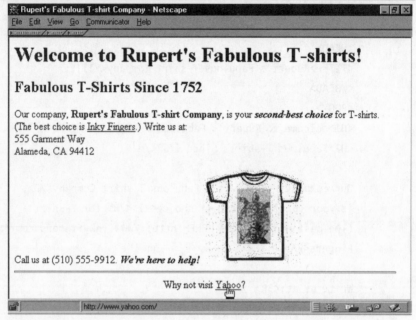

FIGURE 19.4: Rupert's Fabulous T-shirt Company page displayed by Navigator. (The toolbars have been switched off here to make the entire page fit on one screen.) Notice the different sizes for the two headings at the top of the page.

As you can see, this page has much more formatting than the "Hello, World" example. In the next few sections, we'll spend some time understanding the tags used in `rupert.html`: the headings (`<H1>` and `</H1>`, `<H2>` and `</H2>`), bold (`<B>` and `</B>`), italic (`<I>` and `</I>`), the rules of nesting, line-breaks (`<BR>`), horizontal rules (`<HR>`), images (`<IMG>`), paragraph breaks (`<P>`), centering (`<CENTER>`), and links (using the anchor element, `<A>` and `</A>`).

Understanding the Example's Headings

Examine the rupert.html example and pay attention to the sixth and seventh lines:

```
<H1>Welcome to Rupert's Fabulous T-shirts!</H1>
<H2>Fabulous T-shirts Since 1752</H2>
```

These lines contain heading elements. The first heading element is a level-one heading, enclosed with the <H1> and </H1> tags. The second heading element is a level-two heading, enclosed with the <H2> and </H2> tags.

There are six levels of headings. They range from level one, the most important (which uses the <H1> and </H1> tags), to level six, the least important (which uses the <H6> tag). Headings are always containers (meaning you need both a start and end tag). The more important headings are usually displayed in a larger font than less important ones.

The rupert.html example uses two headings. Notice in the Navigator display (Figure 19.4) how much difference there is in the font sizes on the first two lines.

Nesting Bold and Italics in the Example

In the example, Navigator displays both of the headings in bold; there's nothing you can do about that—that's just how Navigator displays normal headings. But there are three other places where bold is displayed: "Rupert's Fabulous T-shirt Company," "second-best choice," and "We're here to help!" All of these three phrases appear in bold because of the presence of the bold element in the HTML code. In addition, the last two phrases also appear in italic, due to the italics element.

Interestingly, two tags are used on the same phrases: the <B> tag *and* the <I> tag both come before "second-best choice" and "We're here to help." The order in which these two text-level elements are applied doesn't matter. Consider the two different lines of HTML code that we used in the previous example, repeated here:

```
<B><I>second-best choice</I></B>
<I><B>We're here to help!</B></I>
```

In the first line, first bold is applied, then italic. In the second line, it's the reverse. The end result is the same. In both cases, one set of tags is *nested* (contained) within the other. We'll discuss nesting in more detail at the end of this chapter, in *HTML's Rules of Nesting*.

Breaking Lines with *
* in the Example

Notice in Figure 19.4 the line-breaks after "Write us at:" and "555 Garment Way." The line-breaks occurred in these two places because of the <BR> tag (which is short for "break").

A line-break is like a typewriter's carriage return—it just takes you back to the left margin. Line-breaks are good for ending lines after short pieces of information, such as the address in this example.

While line-breaks split text onto two different lines, they do not make that text split into two separate paragraphs. The lines of the address in this example are all part of the same paragraph that starts with "Our company." Recall our earlier definition of block-level and text-level elements: Block-level elements, by definition, separate paragraphs, but text-level elements do not. Since the line-break element is a text-level element, it doesn't cause a new paragraph—just a carriage return.

Seeing the Example's Horizontal Rule

Near the end of the rupert.html file is a tag for a horizontal rule, <HR>. This horizontal rule is simply a line you can use to divide different sections. It is mostly for decorative purposes.

The <HR> tag is used by the horizontal rule element, which is a block-level element. It splits "We're here to help" and "Why not visit Yahoo?" into two separate paragraphs. Since the horizontal rule is a block-level element, you can use it to create a new paragraph automatically (splitting the text before and after the rule).

Different browsers display rules differently. For example, Navigator creates a line with a three-dimensional appearance, while IE's line is not as three-dimensional as Navigator's. Lynx, a text-only browser, displays a line with simply a row of dashes.

Comprehending the Example's Image

Perhaps the first thing your eye catches when you view the rupert.html page in Navigator or IE is the image of the T-shirt.

```
<IMG
SRC="http://www.emf.net/~estephen/images/turtleshirt.jpg">
```

The <IMG> tag requires an attribute, SRC. This stands for the "source" of the image—that is, where the image is located. Whenever you need to know *where* something is located on the Web, you use a URL. The URL of the T-shirt graphic is contained in quotes and used as an attribute value.

If you were to enter the URL into your browser's location box, you'd see just the image by itself, as shown in Figure 19.5. (The image was created by Rick Salsman of Inky Fingers to incorporate a painting by musician Syd Barrett. It can be seen at http://www.emf.net/~estephen/images/turtleshirt.jpg.)

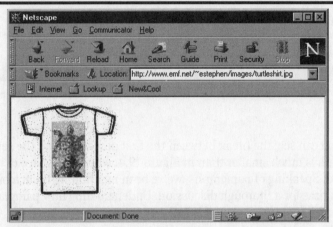

FIGURE 19.5:   Navigator displaying the T-shirt image by itself

Another term for an image on a Web page is *inline image.* That's because the image is considered to be part of the line in which it appears ("in" the "line" of text). In our sample page, the paragraph that begins with "Write us at..." is pushed down because the image is taller than the line. If the image were not included (that is, if we deleted the entire <IMG> tag), then the sample page would appear as shown in Figure 19.6.

Part IV

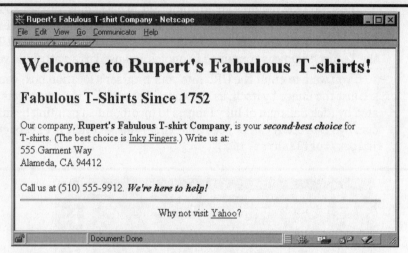

FIGURE 19.6:   Navigator's display of the rupert.html example, without the inline image

As you can see, the break between the first paragraph and the second paragraph is much smaller than in Figure 19.4, where the image is included. Speaking of paragraphs, we've been mentioning them a bit, so now it's time for a thorough discussion. Understanding how paragraphs work is an important aspect of HTML.

Understanding Paragraph Breaks in the Example

The largest difference between the format of HTML and the format of plain text is the organization of paragraphs. In plain ASCII text, determining where paragraphs start can be a problem because of some technical details about how end-of-line characters work. (We don't really want to get mired in those ASCII technical details here, right? Thought not.) To avoid any ambiguities about paragraphs, HTML uses a specific tag to mark the beginning of every paragraph: <P>.

NOTE

Optionally, you can end a paragraph with </P>. If you want to write "strict" HTML that dots every i and crosses every t, then you should use a </P>; otherwise, you can safely omit the </P> tag.

If you don't mark the beginning of your paragraphs with the <P> tag, HTML treats everything in your document as one giant paragraph. With no paragraph breaks, documents are nearly impossible to read.

TIP

Newspaper articles often use a lot of paragraph breaks, since studies have shown that shorter paragraphs are much easier to read than longer ones. Consider doing the same for your Web pages, and break up long paragraphs into several shorter nuggets of wisdom.

When interpreting your HTML document's code, browsers will always ignore carriage returns. This is actually demonstrated in the rupert.html example: Notice that we put two carriage returns in between "The best choice is Inky Fingers" and "Write us at..." in the HTML code. But these two carriage returns don't have any effect on the display of this document in Navigator, or any other browser for that matter.

Browsers ignore those carriage returns and put the two phrases next to each other, in one paragraph. In fact, if we had hit Enter 100 times to create 100 carriage returns, Navigator would ignore all 100 of them. Any extra white space in your document is ignored.

NOTE

White space is any character that takes up space but is itself invisible. Three characters are used to create white space: the space (created when you use the spacebar), the carriage return (created by pressing Return or Enter), and the tab (created by the Tab key).

Unlike a word processor where you simply press Enter to start a new paragraph or hit the spacebar a bunch of times to create some empty space, no amount of white space will start a new paragraph in HTML. The only way to start a new paragraph in HTML is to use an element's start tag, such as <P> or <H1>. (You can cause line-breaks with the <BR> tag, but as we said earlier, that's not the same thing as starting a new paragraph.)

The sole purpose of the <P> tag is to start a new paragraph. To see the <P> tag in action, study the rupert.html example again. Notice the <P> tag before the "Call us at" line. This tag tells the browser that a new paragraph should be started. We can see from the Navigator display that a new paragraph was in fact started at exactly the point where the <P> tag occurred.

Leaving off the <P> tag would make the document appear quite differently. Figure 19.7 shows the same document in Navigator if the <P> tag were removed.

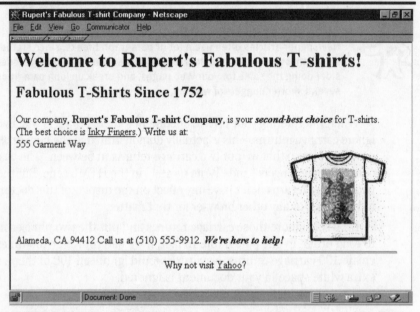

FIGURE 19.7: Navigator viewing the rupert.html example without the <P> tag. From "Our company" to "We're here to help!" is one paragraph.

All browsers, not just Navigator, would treat the text from "Our company" to "We're here to help!" as one long paragraph.

The reason for the white space in between the "555 Garment Way" line and the "Alameda, CA" line is that the image of the T-shirt is pushing down the last line. The inline image is like a giant letter that makes the entire line very tall. Imagine if the image were replaced by a giant letter T. Figure 19.8 shows what that would look like. Alternatively, we could take the image and the giant letter T out altogether. Figure 19.9 shows that result.

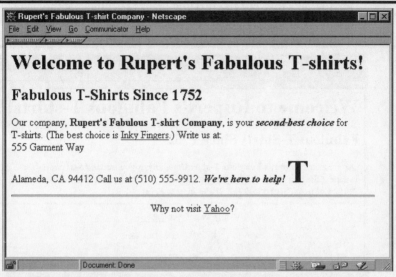

FIGURE 19.8: Navigator's display of the rupert.html example, except with the image replaced with a large capital T. Notice how the spacing for the entire line is determined by the tallest letter.

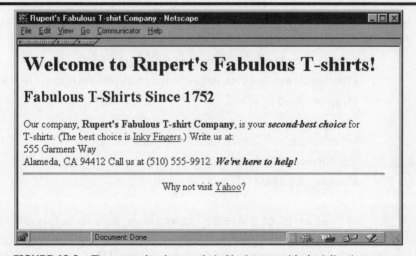

FIGURE 19.9: The rupert.html example in Navigator, with the inline image completely removed. The paragraph now has almost normal spacing.

Part iv

Finally, let's take out the two line-breaks by removing the two <BR> tags. This will make the paragraph completely normal, as seen in Figure 19.10.

FIGURE 19.10: The rupert.html example in Navigator, with all paragraph marks, images, and line-breaks removed

Let's see how the HTML code for the paragraph in Figure 19.10 would look with all the changes that we've made in this section:

```
Our company, <B>Rupert's Fabulous T-shirt Company</B>,
is your <B><I>second-best choice</I></B> for T-shirts.
(The best choice is <A HREF="http://www.inkyfingers.com/">Inky
Fingers</A>.)


Write us at:
555 Garment Way
Alameda, CA 94412


Call us at (510) 555-9912. <I><B>We're here to help!</B></I>
```

The important thing to remember is that even though there are all sorts of carriage returns and white space in this HTML code, none of it counts for making a separate paragraph. Without a paragraph element's <P> tag or other block-level element, browsers will run this code together into just one paragraph. All of the tags that are present here (<B>, <I>, and <A>) are four text-level elements, which don't cause paragraph breaks.

If you look back at Figure 19.10, you'll see that Navigator is now displaying a total of four paragraphs. The two headings each count as a paragraph, and the final line, "Why not visit Yahoo?" is a separate paragraph as well. It's a separate paragraph for two reasons: First, it is separated by the <HR> tag, which is a block-level element. Second, it is contained within the <CENTER> and </CENTER> tags, and centering is also a block-level element.

Centering Text in the Example with the Center Element

The <CENTER> tag is used to begin centering, and the </CENTER> tag is used to end centering. Anything between these two tags will be centered—including images as well as text. The two tags, plus the text between them, make up the center element.

NOTE

Technically, <CENTER> is a synonym for a block-level element called division with center alignment. The <DIV> tag for centering looks like: <DIV ALIGN="CENTER">.

Navigator and IE will redraw your page if the browser's window is resized, and the browser will use the new width of the page to determine where the center is, redrawing any centered paragraphs.

In the rupert.html example, only the line "Why not visit Yahoo?" is contained in the <CENTER> element so that's the only part that's centered.

If you recall our earlier discussion of nesting, you'll see that an anchor is nested inside the element along with the text "Why not visit" and the question mark. This anchor element makes the word "Yahoo" into a link. We'll discuss anchors next.

Linking to Example Web Sites with an Anchor

There are two links in the rupert.html example. The first link is to the Inky Fingers home page, and the second link is to Yahoo! (a popular Web page catalog). The relevant HTML code looks like this:

```
<A HREF="http://www.inkyfingers.com/">Inky Fingers</A>
<A HREF="http://www.yahoo.com/">Yahoo</A>
```

Both examples use the same type of tags—only the specific details differ. In both cases, the element being used is called an anchor element. "Anchor" is abbreviated to <A>.

The <A> tag requires the HREF attribute (short for "Hypertext Reference"), and HREF requires that a URL be specified after an equals sign (=). It's strongly recommended (though not a requirement) that you put the URL inside quotes. You can use double quotes or single quotes, but traditionally double quotes are used.

WARNING

Make sure you don't leave off one of the quotes around the URLs in your anchors. A typo like the following one will cause real problems for your page: `<A HREF ="http://www.webwitch.com/>WebWitch</A>`. The missing close quote here will cause an error that could mess up how the rest of your page is displayed. It might even make the rest of your page not be displayed at all!

Following the anchor element start tag comes some text (here, it's "Inky Fingers" and "Yahoo"). The browser will display this text as a link. (By default, link text is blue and underlined in Navigator and IE.) Your anchor text should describe what is at the other end of the link. Finally, the anchor element is closed with an end tag, </A>.

All told, the `rupert.html` example used 10 new types of elements, in addition to the basic structure. You now know how to use these new elements and tags, and we showed you what role they had in making the example work the way it did.

However, it's important to remember that different browsers display HTML documents in different ways. We've seen how Navigator displays `rupert.html`, and in a moment, we'll see this page in IE and in a text-only browser.

VIEWING PAGES IN DIFFERENT BROWSERS

It's vital to remember that different browsers will interpret your HTML code in vastly different ways. Some Web surfers may *hear* your page instead of see it, using a text-to-speech Web browser. So it's important to understand how different browsers will treat your tags.

IE and Navigator behave similarly, but not identically. Figure 19.11 shows the rupert.html example displayed in IE.

But not every browser is as similar to Navigator as IE. There are still a significant number of Internet users who access the Web through a command-line, non-graphical program named Lynx. Figure 19.12 shows the rupert.html page displayed in Lynx.

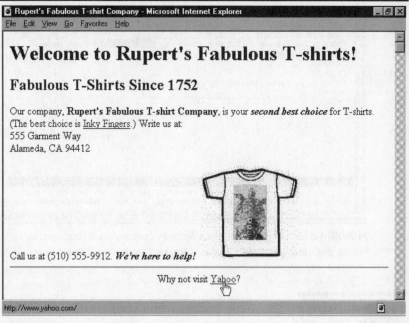

FIGURE 19.11: Rupert's Fabulous T-shirt Company page displayed by IE 4. Other than the slightly thinner horizontal rule (and the differences in the scroll bar and menu names), you'd be hard-pressed to find a difference between this version and the Navigator version we saw in Figure 19.4.

Lynx runs on many different computers, including Windows 95 and Macintosh platforms; primarily, however, Lynx is used on UNIX systems. Because Lynx is non-graphical, it displays the word "[INLINE]" (short for "inline image") where the picture of the T-shirt should be.

If you have an older type of Internet account called a *shell account*, you use a modem and a terminal emulator program to dial into the remote computer where you have your account. (Alternatively, some ISPs offer both normal Internet access as well as a shell account that you can use the Telnet protocol to access.) From a shell account's command prompt, you use the Lynx browser (instead of Navigator or IE) to access the Web.

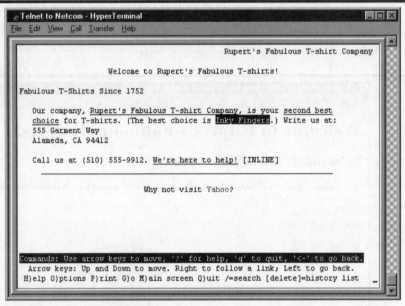

FIGURE 19.12: Rupert's Fabulous T-shirt Company page displayed by Lynx 2.7. Notice the word "[INLINE]" used as a placeholder for the T-shirt image.

NOTE

Telnet is a protocol used to log in to a remote computer. Using Telnet, you can log in to a shell account and use UNIX commands to read and send mail, work with files, and browse the Web. On Windows 95, you can use a Telnet program called simply "telnet," or you can use other Telnet clients, such as Hyper-Terminal, NCSA Telnet, and CRT. Neither Navigator nor IE have the ability to Telnet by themselves.

It's worth considering how a page looks in Lynx. Lynx is in common use in foreign countries and on older computers. Lynx is also used, along with a text-to-speech reader, to allow blind or visually impaired users to access the Web. It's not at all hard to make a page that looks great in Netscape, IE, *and* Lynx: just stick to the rules of HTML as we teach them to you.

In general, our rupert.html sample page comes across just as well in Lynx as it did in Navigator. However, there are differences in how Lynx and Navigator display HTML tags. Notice the difference in the "Welcome to Rupert's Fabulous T-Shirts!" line (Figure 19.12), which was a level-one heading: Lynx centers the heading, while Navigator just uses a larger font and bold. Many different browsers use slightly different methods for displaying headings; that's part of the power of HTML, since it allows many different types of computers and platforms to view your document. But a consequence of this flexibility of HTML is that you cannot expect to have absolute control over the appearance of your document.

Lynx, in contrast to Navigator, can't change the font size (since it can display only plain text). Instead, some versions of Lynx display the level-one heading centered and in all caps (not every version of Lynx uses all caps); Lynx shows the level-two heading as plain text, but not indented like the rest of the document.

VIEWING THE HTML SOURCE

When a browser displays an HTML document, it starts by retrieving the HTML file and then it interprets the HTML tags contained in that file. As we've seen, the browser doesn't display the HTML tags—just the *results* of those tags. When you're browsing the Web, you'll often see a page that does something interesting or attractive, and you'll want to know how it was done. There's an easy way to learn how pages do what they do: Look at the HTML code. This technique is called *viewing source* (since you're seeing the "source" of the document, and because computer programming code is often called *source code*).

NOTE

No one can "hide" their source and make it so that you can't see the HTML they used to create their page. Similarly, you can't hide your HTML code from anyone else. Anyone can view your source and see how your Web page was constructed.

We can view the source of our rupert.html example. (Even though we have access to the source on our own, through the text editor that we used to create the HTML code, it's still useful to learn the procedure of viewing source.) In Navigator 4, the command to view source is View ➤ Page Source.

NOTE

For earlier versions of Navigator, the command was View ➤ Document Source instead of View ➤ Page Source. Both commands do the same thing; only the name of the command has changed.

With IE, you can use the View ➤ Source command to see the HTML tags used to display the document. IE will display the source using Notepad (or WordPad if the source is very long). In Lynx, you can view the source by pressing the backslash key (\).

NOTE

If you are using IE to view a page that has *frames* (that is, a page with one or more different subdivisions), you'll have to choose the View Source command from the context menu for the frame. If you are using Navigator to view a page with frames, use the View ➤ Frame Source command.

In your travels on the Web, it's a good idea to frequently view the source of pages that you find interesting and try to understand the HTML code that you see. But it's also a good idea to occasionally view your own documents' source in Navigator from time to time, since Navigator will highlight any errors it sees by making the incorrect tag blink.

Speaking of errors, we'll end this chapter with a discussion of one of the principal causes of HTML errors: incorrect nesting.

HTML's Rules of Nesting

Nesting is common in HTML. Consider that the entire body section of any HTML document is nested within the body element. In turn, the body element itself is nested within the html element.

Block-level elements often contain other block-level and text-level elements. For example, a paragraph block-level element might contain some bolded text (the body element text-level element):

```
<P>

Rich ate six slices of <B>Crazy Joey's Crustacean Pizza</B> and
survived! Barely!

</P>
```

There are four main rules to remember about nesting:

▶ Elements must be completely nested and not closed in the wrong order.

▶ Text-level elements may be nested within block-level elements or other text-level elements.

▶ Block-level elements may be nested within other block-level elements.

▶ Block-level elements may *not* be nested in text-level elements.

To illustrate the first rule, consider our example of bold and italic text from `rupert.html`:

```
<B><I>second-best choice</I></B>
<I><B>We're here to help!</B></I>
```

The previous two examples show: first, italic text nested within bold text; and second, bold text nested within italic text. Both of them are correct, since the inner element is entirely contained within the outer element. Be sure not to mix up the order of the end tags. Here are the two incorrect orders:

```
<B><I>second-best choice</B></I>
<I><B>We're here to help!</I></B>
```

Both lines are in error since there is no nesting. Although Navigator and IE would do their best to understand the above two incorrect lines of HTML code (and in this case, would probably succeed in doing the right thing), there's no guarantee that your document would be displayed correctly—it's possible that the bold or italic elements would not switch off correctly and spill over into the rest of your document. To prevent things like this from happening, always nest elements completely inside other elements.

WHAT'S NEXT?

Now that you've had a quick introduction to HTML, John Ross will show you have you can use FrontPage to create Web pages *without* learning HTML.

Part IV

Chapter 20

CREATING WEB PAGES WITH FRONTPAGE EXPRESS

O ne of the most exciting features of the World Wide Web is that anybody can create Web pages and make them available to millions of other people around the world. Unlike older mass media that require complex and expensive production and distribution equipment (such as printing presses or television studios), the Web is accessible to almost anybody with a computer and some rudimentary design skills. A fifth grade class can prepare its own home page that is just as easy to find and read as one from a multibillion dollar corporation.

The Microsoft Internet Explorer suite includes a Web page editor program called FrontPage Express that provides the basic tools needed to create simple Web pages. FrontPage Express is a simplified version of Microsoft's separate FrontPage 97 HTML editor.

FrontPage Express is probably not the best choice for serious Web site designers and producers who want to include all the latest HTML features and functions in their projects, but it should be quite adequate for creating the occasional page.

Adapted from *ABCs of Microsoft Internet Explorer 4*, by John Ross
0-7821-2042-3   400 pages $19.99

Internet Explorer also includes a Web Publishing Wizard that will transfer Web pages from your PC to your ISP's Web server. If you have a permanent high-speed connection to the Internet (rather than a connection through a modem and a telephone line), you can also get free Personal Web Server software from Microsoft that allows other people to view your Web site by connecting directly to your own computer; but if you're using a separate server, you'll want to use the Web Publishing Wizard to transfer your work from your Desktop.

EDITING A WEB PAGE WITH FRONTPAGE EXPRESS

It's entirely possible to create extremely complex Web pages by typing all the code into a text document, but it's much easier to use a graphic HTML editor such as FrontPage Express that automatically adds all the document structure tags and formatting tags in exactly the right places.

FrontPage Express's basic design is similar to the layout of other Microsoft application programs that involve text editing and formatting; if you have experience with Microsoft Word or with the WordPad text editor supplied with Windows 98, you will have no trouble understanding how to use FrontPage Express.

As Figure 20.1 shows, the FrontPage Express window displays the formatted content of a Web page, with toolbars across the top of the main window. All the commands in the toolbars are duplicates of commands in the FrontPage Express menus.

Entering Text

The process of creating most Web pages begins with text. If you have a favorite word processor or text editor program, you can use that program to compose the text rather than typing it directly into FrontPage Express. To import an existing document or text file into FrontPage Express, follow these steps:

1. Save the text in the word processor or text editor.

2. In FrontPage Express, select the Open command from either the toolbar or the File menu. The Open File dialog box shown in Figure 20.2 will appear.

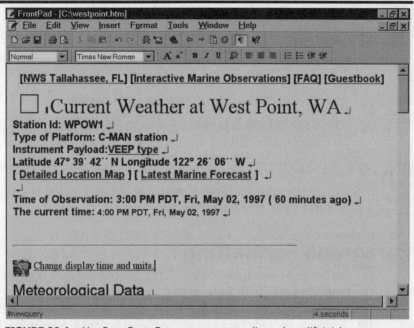

FIGURE 20.1: Use FrontPage Express to create, edit, and modify Web pages.

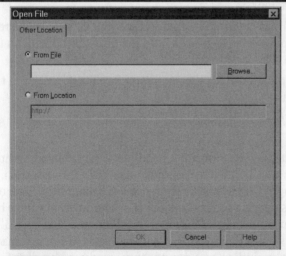

FIGURE 20.2: Use the Open File dialog box to import a text file into FrontPage Express.

3. Select the From File option.

4. Click the Browse button to locate the file you want to import.

5. In the file browser, use the Files of Type drop-down menu to select the original format of the file you want.

6. Use the file browser to find and select the file.

7. Click the Open button to enter the name and path of the selected file in the From File field of the Open File dialog box.

8. Click the OK button to load the file into FrontPage Express.

If the text on your Web page is relatively simple, it might be easier to type it directly into FrontPage Express.

Paragraph Formatting

It's important to remember that an HTML document does not include the same kind of specific formats that a word processor or desktop publisher assigns to a paragraph. In HTML, every paragraph comes with a tag that instructs the browser reading the file on how to display it. It's the browser rather than the document that determines how a paragraph format looks. That's why the same document can look quite different when you view it in different browsers.

To attach a format tag to a paragraph, place your cursor anywhere in that paragraph and select the format from the drop-down menu on the Format Toolbar.

FrontPage Express includes the paragraph formats described in the following sections.

Headings

Headings are generally used for titles, headlines, and subheads within a Web page. There are six different Heading tags, <H1> through <H6>. The largest is Heading 1, which is most often used as a main title. Each of the other headings is normally a little smaller than the one that comes before it, so you might use Heading 2 for section headings and Headings 3 through 6 for less important headlines and subheads. If you organize your Web page as an outline, you can use each numbered heading for a different level.

Normal Text

FrontPage Express calls body text *Normal* because that's what Word and other Microsoft programs use. In HTML, these paragraphs are the default style, with a <P> tag at the beginning of each one.

Lists

Lists are usually groups of short items, such as the names of people or places. Each item in a list is a separate paragraph.

HTML can handle four different list types:

▶ *Bulleted lists* are lists in which the order of the items is not important. The HTML specification calls them *unordered lists.* Most browsers display bulleted lists with a black dot at the beginning of each item. This list is a bulleted list, for example.

▶ *Numbered lists* are lists in which the order of the items is important, such as a step-by-step procedure or a list of finishes in a race. These are known as *ordered lists* in HTML. Browsers almost always attach a number to each item in a numbered list, so you should not include the numbers in your text.

▶ *Directory lists* are lists of very short items that a browser may display as either a single column or three parallel columns.

▶ *Menu lists* are lists that a browser might display as a set of indented paragraphs or possibly a bulleted list formatted differently.

Definitions and Defined Terms

As the names suggest, Definitions and Defined terms are used for glossaries and other text that provides a term and an explanation or discussion of that term. Some browsers show terms and definitions on the same line, but others place the definition in an indented paragraph under the preceding term.

Addresses

An Address is a special paragraph format used for a name and address at the bottom of a Web page. It's common practice for the owner or designer of a Web page to "sign" each page at the bottom with an e-mail address so readers can contact them. If you place a copyright notice or other legal matter on a Web page, you should also use the Address format for this information.

Part iv

Alignment

A paragraph or graphic element can be aligned to the right or left margin of the Web page, or centered. To change the alignment, select a paragraph and click one of the alignment buttons on the Format Toolbar.

Indented Paragraphs

Any paragraph format can also be indented to set it apart from the text and artwork that surrounds it. To indent a paragraph, select the text, or place your cursor anywhere within the paragraph, and click the Increase Indent button on the Format Toolbar. To move the paragraph farther to the right, click the Increase Indent button again.

To move a paragraph back to the left, select the paragraph and click the Decrease Indent button.

Line Breaks

A Web browser will normally fit a long block of text into the space available in the browser window—so line breaks will be in different places, depending on the size of the type, the width of the window, and the effect of other objects on the page. However, as a designer, you may want to force line breaks after specific words, especially in headlines. For example, if the top-level headline of your page says

Babe Ruth

Home Page

you won't want it to appear in a browser window as

Babe

Ruth Home

Page

To force a line break within a paragraph or headline (or any other text element of a Web page), move your cursor to the place where you want the break to occur, and select Insert ➤ Break. When the Break Properties dialog box appears, select the type of break you want.

Specifying a Typeface

Normally the browser displaying a Web page specifies the typeface used for all text. But because many designers want more control over the appearance of their pages, FrontPage Express offers the option of specifying a typeface for each paragraph.

To specify a typeface, follow these steps:

1. Select the text you want to change.

2. Open the drop-down menu of fonts on the Format Toolbar, and select the typeface you want to use for the currently selected text.

Character Formatting

Character formats can override the size, color, or style of text in a Web page. To apply character formatting in FrontPage Express, follow these steps:

1. Select the text you want to format.

2. Click the button on the Format toolbar that controls the type of formatting you want.

Adding Images to Your Page

In order to make the design of your Web page more interesting, you will probably want to add pictures, logotypes, or other graphic images to your text. Follow these steps to insert a graphic:

1. Move your cursor to the location where you want the image to appear. If you want the image to appear on the Web page separately from the text that surrounds it, place the cursor in a separate paragraph.

2. Click the Insert Image button on the toolbar, or select the Insert ➢ Image command.

3. When the Image dialog box appears, choose either the From File option to specify a graphic file on your own computer or LAN, or the From Location option to specify the URL of an image located someplace else on the Web.

4. Click the OK button to save your choice.

An image that occupies a separate paragraph may be located at the left or right side of a page, indented, or centered. To change the location, use the alignment and indent buttons on the Format Toolbar.

Animated images and video files work the same way. Use the Insert ➢ Video command to include a local video (.AVI) file or a file located anywhere on the Internet.

Adding Background Sounds

Used in moderation, music, sound effects (such as birds chirping), or even a friendly voice welcoming visitors to the site can add another interesting element to a Web page. On the other hand, the same recording, repeated several times, will quickly become an irritation.

To add a sound file to the current page, use the Insert ➢ Background Sound command.

Adding Links to Your Page

A hypertext link may take a user to another Web page or other file anywhere on the Internet or to another location on the same page. To add a link to your page, follow these steps:

1. Select the word, phrase, or image that you want to use as the link.

2. Click the Create Hyperlink button on the toolbar or the Insert ➢ Hyperlink command on the menu bar. The Create Hyperlink dialog box shown in Figure 20.3 will appear.

3. Choose from these three options in the Create Hyperlink dialog box:

   World Wide Web   Click the World Wide Web tab to create a link to another Web site or other Internet file. Choose the type of file from the drop-down menu, and type the full address of the target file or page in the URL field.

   Open Pages   Click the Open Pages tab to create a link to another location on the same page or to another of your own pages. Select the target page from the list of open pages and the exact location within the target page from the Bookmark field. Use the Edit ➢ Bookmark command to place a bookmark at the current cursor location.

New Page   Click the New Page tab to create a new page and create a link from the current page to that page. Type the title and URL of the target in the appropriate fields.

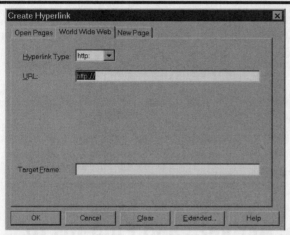

FIGURE 20.3: Use the Create Hyperlink dialog box to add a link to your Web page.

Adding a Marquee

A marquee is a line of text that crawls across the page, like the moving lights in an electric sign. To include a marquee in your Web page, follow these steps:

1. Place your cursor at the location where you want the marquee to appear. In most cases, a marquee should be a separate paragraph.

2. Select the Insert ➢ Marquee command from the menu bar. The Marquee Properties dialog box, shown in Figure 20.4, will appear.

3. Type the exact text of the marquee message in the Text field.

4. Choose the other characteristics you want to assign to the marquee, including direction of crawl, color, and number of repetitions, and select those options.

5. Click the OK button to save your choices and add the marquee to your Web page.

Part iv

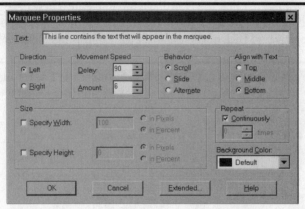

FIGURE 20.4:   The Marquee Properties dialog box controls the content and appearance of a marquee.

Adding Java, ActiveX, and Plug-Ins to Your Page

Java, ActiveX, and plug-ins are all methods for adding advanced features and functions to a Web page, including multimedia sounds and images, and direct access to other programs. To add a Java extension, ActiveX control, or a plug-in application to your page, select the corresponding command from FrontPage Express's Insert menu and complete the dialog box that specifies the specific type of program, the location of the source, and the appearance of the program or service on your Web page.

Adding one of these services to a Web page is relatively simple; however, setting up the underlying extension, control, or plug-in may be a lot more complicated. Because each service has its own requirements, you should spend some time with the specific instructions for the one you want to use or find an experienced Web designer to lead you by the hand before you try to include one of these in your own Web page.

Changing the Background

The background of a Web page may be a solid color, a single image, or the same image repeated to cover the entire page. If you don't specify any background, the browser will use the default background color specified by the user.

To change the background of a Web page, follow these steps:

1. Select the Format ➤ Background command. The Page Properties dialog box will appear.

2. To use a single background picture, select the Background Image option and click the Browse button to select a graphic file.

3. To use a tiled image as your background, select the Watermark option and click the Browse button to select a file.

4. For a solid color background, select a color from the drop-down Background menu. Remember that dark colors on a light background or light colors on a dark background are easier to read than text and background in similar colors.

5. Click the OK button to save your choice.

After you change the background of a page, take a critical look at the contrast between text, graphics, and background. If it's difficult for you to read, it's a safe bet that it will be even more difficult for other people. As a general rule, stick to light-colored backgrounds and dark text. And don't even think about trying to use a complicated photograph or drawing that will interfere with the text. Remember that your readers have hundreds of thousands of other Web sites that they can visit instead of yours; if you make the text hard to read, most people just won't bother.

Saving Your Page

When you have added all the text, graphics, links, and other elements to your page, it's time to save it. The first time you use the Save command, the Save As dialog box, shown in Figure 20.5, will appear.

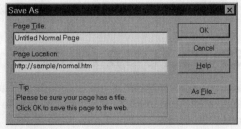

FIGURE 20.5: Use the Save As dialog box to store your page.

Follow these steps to save your page:

1. Type the title of the page in the Page Title field. The title will appear in the browser's title bar when it opens this page.

2. Type the URL of the file in the Page Location field. This URL should include the address of the server where your Web site will be located, and the full path of the file that contains this Web page. If you don't operate your own server, you will have to ask your service provider for this information.

3. If you're temporarily saving this page on your own computer, click the As File button and select a file name and location from the file browser.

If your Web page includes graphics or links to other files or if you're creating a Web site with more than one page, you should create a new folder for all the files used in your page or site. This will make it a lot easier when you're ready to set up your own Web server or transfer these pages to another server.

EDITING AN EXISTING PAGE

If you're using an existing Web page or file as the starting point for a new page, use the File ➤ Open command or the Open button on the toolbar to load a copy of that page into FrontPage Express.

After a page has loaded, you can apply any of FrontPage Express's editorial tools to change the text, figures, background, and other elements of the original page.

Remember that Web pages are protected by copyright. It's probably illegal and certainly bad form to lift the contents of somebody else's content or design into your own Web page without specific permission.

ADDING TABLES TO YOUR PAGE

Tables in HTML are a more complicated than other text because the relative positions of the table elements are important. To add a table to a Web page, follow these steps:

1. Place your cursor in the location where you want the table to appear in the Web page.

2. Select Table ➤ Insert Table.

3. Specify the number of rows and columns you want to include in the table, the alignment, border width and other layout elements, and the width of the table. Click the OK button to save your choices.

4. Type the text you want in the first cell of the table.

5. Press your Tab key to move to the next cell, and type the text you want in that cell.

6. Repeat the process for each additional cell in the table.

7. Select each cell, row, or column, and use the FrontPage Express formatting commands to specify the style and type-face you want to use for the text in the selected cell, row, or column.

To add more rows or columns to a table, or to make other changes to the layout and arrangement of a table, use the other commands in the Table menu.

ADDING FORMS TO YOUR PAGE

As you know, Web page can include interactive elements such as text boxes, drop-down menus, and radio buttons, along with the text and graphic images. When visitors to your site use a form, they send an instruction to a server to perform some kind of action, so you must specify the type of action when you set up the form fields.

Because you must coordinate the activities of more than one program and different Web servers require different kinds of configuration, setting up form fields is not something that a beginning Web designer should attempt without help.

To include form fields in your own Web page, follow these steps:

1. Place your cursor in the location where you want the form field to appear. A form field may be a separate paragraph, or it may be within an existing block of text.

2. Select Insert ➤ Form Field to open a submenu of form types, or use the Form Fields Toolbar.

3. Select the type of form you want to use.

4. When the interactive element appears on your page, type the text that should accompany the button, menu, or other object.

5. Right-click the form field and select Form Properties from the right-click menu.

6. Choose the type of form handler you want to use to handle the information from this form field.

7. Click the Settings button to open another dialog box (which is different for each type of form handler) where you can specify the details of this transaction.

8. Repeat for each additional form field.

SENDING YOUR PAGE TO A SERVER

If you connect to the Internet through a telephone line and a modem, it's not practical to use your own computer as a Web server because it won't be possible for other people to view your Web pages when you're not connected. Therefore, you will have to transfer your pages from your computer to a Web server with a permanent network connection.

The Web Publishing Wizard makes this transfer fast and easy. As you work through the Wizard, it will ask for the following information:

File or folder name   If you specify a single folder, the Wizard will transfer that file to the server; if you specify a folder, the Wizard will transfer all of the files in that folder.

Name of your Web server   The administrator of your Web server can provide a name for your site.

Your Internet service provider   Use the drop-down menu to select the name of your ISP. If it's not listed, select <Other Internet Provider>.

URL or Internet address   The administrator of your Web server will tell you what URL to use for your Web pages. If the service provider publishes an FAQ (a list of Frequently Asked Questions) or other guidelines, that document probably contains the information you need. If not, ask the administrator or help desk.

Connection type   Choose either a connection through your LAN or a dial-up connection.

Web server authentication   Type the login name and password for your account at the Web server. In most cases, they will be the same as the ones you use to log in to any other Internet connection, but your service provider will give you the specific information you need.

Subfolder containing your Web pages   Most Web servers assign a folder to each user. You may want to create separate subfolders for each Web page or set of pages. The Wizard will display your top-level folder as a default; to create a subfolder, type a slash and a name for the subfolder.

URL for your home root   The Wizard will obtain this information from your Web server.

SETTING UP A PERSONAL WEB SERVER

In most cases, it's more practical to place your Web pages on a Web server maintained by an ISP; but if you have a permanent connection to the Internet or you want to set up an internal Web site for other users on the same LAN, you can use Microsoft's free Personal Web Server software to use your PC as a server. As the previous section explained, you won't want to use the Personal Web Server if you connect to the Internet through a telephone line and modem because other people won't be able to find your Web site when you're not connected. The Personal Web Server program is available for free download from http://www.microsoft.com/ie/iesk/pws.htm.

The Personal Web Server software includes servers for both HTTP and FTP clients. Therefore, you can use the server to distribute both Web pages and general files.

To configure Personal Web Server after you have downloaded and installed the software, follow these steps:

1. Open the Windows Control Panel.

2. Double-click the Personal Web Server icon. The Personal Web Server Properties dialog box will appear.

3. If it's not already open, click the General tab. As Figure 20.6 shows, the General tab shows the address of your Personal Web Server and the location of your default home page.

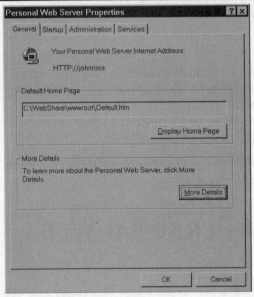

FIGURE 20.6: The Personal Web Server Properties dialog box controls the program's configuration.

4. Talk to your network administrator or ISP to confirm the Internet address for your Web Server. If the address shown for your Personal Web Server is not correct, follow the procedure later in this section to change it.

5. The default Home Page is normally the top-level page of your Web site. To see the default page, click the Display Home Page button. To specify a different default page, change the path.

6. Click the Startup tab. If the Web server State box shows that the Web server is stopped, click the Start button.

7. If you want the Web server to start whenever you start your computer, select the Run Automatically option.

8. Click the Services tab to display the dialog box in Figure 20.7.

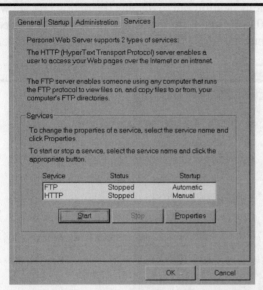

FIGURE 20.7: Use the Services tab to activate the HTTP server, the FTP server, or both.

9. Use the Start and Stop buttons to turn the FTP server or HTTP server on or off. The Web Server State option on the Startup tab must be running before you can turn on either or both servers.

10. To change the startup options, home root directory (folder), or default home page for either the FTP server or Web server, select the type of server you want to change and click the Properties button.

11. When the configuration is complete, click the OK button to save your choices.

Your Personal Web Server address is the Internet DNS address that other people will use to connect to your computer. You must obtain this address from your network administrator or Internet service provider.

The Personal Web Server uses your Computer Name as the Web server address. In almost every case, you will have to change the Computer Name you assigned when you installed Windows 98.

To change your Internet address, follow these steps:

1. From the Control Panel, double-click the Network icon.

Part iv

2. Click the Identification tab to display the dialog box shown in Figure 20.8. If there's no Identification tab visible, select Add ≻ Client ≻ Add ≻ Microsoft ≻ Client for Microsoft Networks.

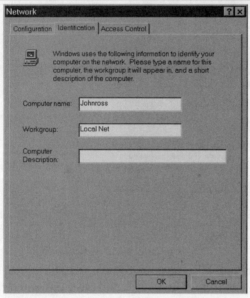

FIGURE 20.8:   Use the Network Identification tab to change your Computer Name.

3. Type the Web server address you obtained from your network administrator or ISP in the Computer Name field.

4. Click the OK button to save your changes.

Whether you transfer your Web pages to another server or use your own PC as a Personal Server, you should test your new Web site by trying to view it from other locations. It's important to get an idea what your pages look like to other users. You might be surprised by what you see because different browsers can interpret the same HTML code quite differently. Try as many different browsers as you can find, including both Windows and Macintosh computers. If you can connect through more than one Internet service provider (try several ISPs and online services), check the site through each of them.

Finally, ask at least one other person to test your site for you and to check for misspelled words and other typographical errors. It's always better to learn about errors from a friend on the first day your site is on the Web, instead of hearing from a complete stranger after it's been out there for several weeks or months.

WHAT'S NEXT?

You can't use the Internet without a computer. The next chapters are a reference–how to shop for a computer, how to keep your computer up to date, how to configure your modem, and more.

PART V

Your PC and Hardware

Chapter 21

A BUYER'S GUIDE TO PCs

I f you're the kind of person who fixes your own or someone else's PC, then you're likely to be the kind of person who's often looking to the *next* PC, the latest-and-greatest machine. Perhaps your palms itch when you see that someone else owns a dual processor Pentium II system, when all you can afford is a Pentium 133. You eye 9GB hard drives the way teenage boys eye Corvettes.

Or maybe you're not that way. Maybe computers are just a tool for you, a platform upon which to get some work done. But you've found that your current platform just isn't strong enough to support today's software: Windows 98 requires at least 16MB of RAM and a Pentium 120 in order to be useful; for most purposes you'll want at least 32MB and a faster processor. And you need to know how to either upgrade your existing machines, or buy new ones that won't offer as much trouble when it's time to upgrade again in a year or two.

Adapted from *The Complete PC Upgrade & Maintenance Guide*, by Mark Minasi
ISBN 0-7821-2151-9   1520 pages $59.99

It's a good time to upgrade; with prices these days, everybody can own some of the fastest PCs on the planet. Buyers with tons of money don't have much advantage over the rest of us now. (Unless, of course, you've *got* to have a 200 MHz Pentium-based notebook with the active matrix screen and 2-gig 1.75-inch drive.) And cheap Pentiums come *just* in time for those of us who are Windows users: Windows 98 is the best excuse that I know of for buying a new Pentium II.

But *which* one to buy? Well, I'm not going to tell you *that*: there are zillions of honest vendors out there that deserve your money. I'd just like to give you some advice on how to make sure that your vendor is one of the good ones.

I tell my clients that when they're going to buy a PC, they should consider four things: compatibility, serviceability, upgradability (I know, it's not a word), and price/performance.

Because I'm concerned about those things, I recommend that people avoid many of the big names in the PC business and buy a *generic* computer, rather than a *proprietary* computer.

PARTS OF A GENERIC PC

Before I go any further, let me clarify what I mean when I say "generic" and "proprietary." *Generic* refers to the majority of machines available today. Generic machines are PCs consisting of a few separate industry standard parts. Those parts include:

A standard case   If you buy a computer with an unusually shaped case, as you'd see in the "slimline" PCs or some of the more interesting offerings from large vendors, then you'll find that all of the boards inside the computer may be unusually-shaped as well. That means that you won't be able to easily locate replacement parts, should you need them. It also means that you can't put an industry-standard ("generic") power supply in your system. That's undesirable because there are some very nice power supply alternatives these days, such as super-quiet fans or power supplies with built-in battery backup.

A motherboard   The circuit board inside the case that contains the PC's CPU chip, its memory, and its expansion slots. On that motherboard there should be *eight* expansion slots, rather than the three that you find on some computers these days, so that you can add expansion boards to your PC now and in the future. Be aware that the vendor may have filled a number of them already. You have a sound card, a video accelerator, a drive controller, and/or something like a wave table for your Sound Blaster 16 or a 3D Accelerator card for your 2D video card).

An I/O board A board that acts as an interface—an "ambassador," essentially—between the motherboard and your hard disk, your floppy disks, two serial ports, and a parallel port. The disks are, of course, the essential storage devices that you keep your data on. A PC also contains the hard disk and floppy disk drive or drives. You'll use serial ports for your mouse and modem—the device that lets your PC communicate with other computers over the phone—and the parallel port will let you attach your PC to a printer.

A video adapter board This allows your PC to display images on a video monitor. It will probably be an SVGA board. SVGA is Super Video Graphics Array, a common video standard. I'll recommend SVGA accelerators a bit later.

That's just a generic overview. I'll zoom in on particular features you should be looking for in a few pages.

PROBLEMS WITH PROPRIETARY PCS

How is one of these generic PCs different from a proprietary PC? Well, you find most of the same functions in a proprietary PC, but you find all of them on a single circuit board, a kind of "workaholic" motherboard. The big problem with proprietary computers is that you can't upgrade them easily, nor can you fix them for a reasonable price. Proprietary computer motherboards are typically shaped differently from each other, and from generic motherboards, making it impossible for you to replace an old or damaged proprietary motherboard with anything but another motherboard of the exact same make and model. As motherboards of that particular make and model are only available from that particular vendor (by definition, since the motherboard is proprietary), it may be expensive or impossible to get a replacement. Likewise, it's almost certainly impossible to get an upgrade.

For more specific problems with proprietary designs, let's return to my four criteria.

Part v

Compatibility is at stake because if the vendor did anything wrong—for example, if the company chose a mildly incompatible video chip, as AT&T did for some of their systems—there's nothing you can do but either throw away the computer or hope that the designer was far-sighted enough to allow you to disable the built-in video function so you can go out and spend more money on a separate video board.

Upgradability is a concern because the one-board design is "all or nothing." It's not shaped like other one-board designs—for example, Compaq's one-board design looks nothing like IBM's one-board design—so you can't replace the board with a better third-party offering.

Serviceability is a problem for reasons touched on above. A generic design like a Gateway 2000 is a safe buy in many ways, not the least of which is that even if Gateway goes bankrupt tomorrow (very unlikely), the entire machine is composed of generic parts that can be bought at *thousands* of clone houses around the country. And this isn't brain surgery; you've seen in this book that you can break down and rebuild a PC in about 30 minutes, and, in some cases, leaving it better than when you started.

And what about *price/performance*? First of all, notice that I put this last. That's because compared to what computers used to cost, *any* PC is a bargain, even if you pay list price for one made by IBM. As regards the proprietary computers: in theory, a single-board design can be faster and cheaper for many reasons. You don't see that in actual fact because single-board designs tend to be used primarily for notebook computers, an environment which, by available space alone, disallows expansions cards.

You don't need to buy a big name to get big performance, reliability, or flexibility. Look in your local paper's business section for the names of companies near you that can sell generic PCs. It couldn't hurt if your company offers service through a national service company like GTE, Wang, or TRW. Then choose that fire-breathing 333 MHz Pentium II you've always wanted and put it to work for you—and smile, knowing that you've bought the security of easy upgrades and independence from any single vendor.

CHOOSING A MARKET NICHE

Where will you buy your PC? People in some companies are only allowed to buy from IBM or Compaq; others put machines together from parts. Computer dealers basically fall into three categories.

First tier   IBM and Compaq. The *definitions* of compatibility. Price/performance tends to be fairly low, innovation minimal or gimmicky. Despite past reputations, these two, and others that fall into this category, have been forced into the future by the smaller "screwdriver" shops. Their unlikely competition, which sold better, cheaper, upgradeable, and more compatible systems, chewed away the profit margins. This means that IBM, Compaq, Gateway 2000, Hewlett Packard, and Packard Bell all use a mostly industry-standard modular approach to system design. This is great for compatibility and upgradability, but you still pay an inflated premium for the name. You will most likely be offered a 3 year service contract over the often included 1 year on-site service contract, and, if you have to ship it out for service, you can expect it back in a reasonable time period.

Second tier   Micron, Acer, Sony, Digital, Quantex, and others. These companies tended toward the "modular generic" architectures for years, generating the competition from the first tier companies. Pros: better price/performance than first tier. Upgrade hardware (e.g. more RAM, better video, faster modem) will be more available, although this won't be true with the "small footprint" machines, which tend to be much less expandable. Cons: There is no storefront to take a broken machine to. Sure, there is that 1-year on-site service contract, but you spend at least an hour on the phone convincing technical support that your problem should be seen to be believed. You'll also typically have a 3–7 day wait for a service person to contact you and make arrangements to come to your home or office. Dead-On-Arrival hardware is somewhat common.

Third tier   Also known as "Screwdriver," "box shovers," or "Three Guys and a Goat PCs." This group gets a scary reputation that's really not deserved. Yes, some of them are sleazy, deceptive, and unreliable, but then those are adjectives that have been aptly applied to some of the *big* names in the business, too. On the positive side, these companies are always aware of the fact that every sale is a significant portion of their total business, and they'll do just about anything to get a multiple-machine contract with a large company or government client. You usually needn't worry about shoddy parts, as they're putting together pieces made by fairly big U.S., Taiwanese,

AND THE WINNER IS...

Surprise! The biggest winner in this highly competitive climate is you, the consumer. There has not always been competition in the personal computer market. Back in the golden days of the first personal computers, IBM and Apple Computer were the big players, and they held all the cards. Apple had immense success with the Apple II+ and IIe, while IBM monopolized the business market with its rather uninteresting, but usable IBM PC XT. When IBM finally licensed their platform to other manufacturers, there was a small explosion in the personal computer market.

These computers, however, had some proprietary technology that varied from clone-maker to clone-maker. Most machines of the time were not 100% compatible with each other. IBM readjusted their license a few years later and coined the term "PC compatible," making possible the systems we are most familiar with today. The smart companies that heeded IBM's ominous, and powerful, license agreement still exist today. The others dropped like flies on a cold winter day. As the PC compatible platform slowly came to dominate the market, it also became a battleground.

Each clone-maker developed and introduced new "standards" for each basic technology. One of the most topsy-turvy skirmishes was over video. MDA, Hercules, CGA, EGA, VGA, XGA, XGA-2, SVGA, VESA SVGA, and UVGA are all so-called video standards, each very different from the other and all coined by different companies. Technically, SVGA isn't even a standard. It's a term that describes a *range* of resolutions and color depths that a video card and monitor *may* support. Fun, eh?

Many other battles like the last one are waged every day, to the benefit of every consumer, but the big rough and tumble in today's market is who can get to line cheaper and faster. They fight for supremacy in the sub-$1000 PC market, and you can buy a fully loaded Gateway 2000 300MHz Pentium II computer with a 17" monitor for around $2000, among many others. It's hard to feel bad about that.

Korean, and Japanese vendors. If you look at the sum total of all third-tier vendors, you'll see that between them they use only about three or four suppliers for any given part (drives, motherboards, controllers, etc.). That means that if you really look at the companies that are *supplying* those parts—Micronics,

DTK, AMI, Chips & Technologies, Adaptec, G2, and others—you'll see that they're pretty large and reliable companies. The absolute best part about these machines is that they're the simplest to upgrade and maintain. They also have the best price/performance in the group, and compatibility is usually as good as the second-tier machines.

CHOOSING PC PARTS

In the process of choosing a PC, I look at what it's made of in order to decide if it's the kind of machine that I'm looking for. Let's look at the important parts of a PC and summarize what you should consider when buying one.

The CPU

If you're buying today, buy 200 MHz Pentium MMX or faster computers. The Pentium is a well-built fast chip that offers 100 percent compatibility with earlier chips as well as terrific speed. Are you missing much buying one of these rather than a Pentium II? Not really. The Pentium II is a faster CPU by all means, but the Pentium MMX is no slowpoke.

The fact of the matter today is that the CPUs are leveling out in speed, despite what the benchmarks say. What's *not* getting faster, however, are the peripherals. CPUs are hundreds of times faster than XT-level CPUs; modern peripherals, however, are only dozens of times faster than XT-era peripherals. Take the money you're saving by not buying the latest and greatest CPU and spend that on a faster bus and faster peripherals. (There are exceptions; some processes are very CPU-intensive and will benefit from a faster processor.)

The Bus

The *bus* is what brings the CPU and all the peripherals together and communicating efficiently. There are ISA, MCA, EISA, VESA, and finally, SCSI and PCI, the common adapter bus formats today. Then there's AGP, or Advanced Graphics Port. All systems today come with a mix of PCI and E/ISA slots on the motherboard, and most new Pentium II motherboards come with an AGP slot for the special video accelerator card. Watch out for older VESA Local Bus implementations, which are no longer supported and do not support Plug-and-Play.

Which brings me to my next bus requirement: Plug-and-Play. Make absolutely sure that your new machine will support Plug-and-Play as implemented by Windows 9x; that's an important qualification, because a good number of vendors have a loose interpretation of what Plug-and-Play means. The simplest hard-and-fast test is "does it work with Windows 98?" This problem, however, is dwindling swiftly as vendors realize the benefits of fully supporting the PnP API from Microsoft.

Not every board needs to be a PCI board, although that is preferable. You should be pretty sure, however, that the following adapters are PCI:

- ▶ The video adapter
- ▶ The SCSI host adapter or EIDE/ATAPI host adapter
- ▶ Any LAN cards
- ▶ Any video capture or sound capture hardware

RAM

Windows 98 runs best in a 32MB environment, but 16MB will do if your budget doesn't allow. Make sure you get a motherboard with *processor cache,* more commonly known as L2 Cache, of at least 512K, with the ability to increase that to 1MB. The option used to be very expensive, but it's now quite reasonable.

ROM BIOS

The BIOS is an important part of compatibility. Buy from one of the big three—Phoenix, Award, or AMI. That way, it's easy to get upgrades. Nice BIOS features:

- ▶ User-definable drive types
- ▶ Bus speeds that can be set in the setup
- ▶ Fast A20 gate that speeds up Windows
- ▶ Processor cache enable/disable

Motherboard/System Board

This is the board that contains the above items. If you're buying from a first- or second-tier company, you'll end up with their board. From a third-tier place, look for motherboards from Micronics, DTK, Mylex, Chips & Technologies, and AMI.

Hard Disks

You're probably going to end up buying ATAPI or Enhanced IDE-type drives, mainly because they're so amazingly cheap, fast, and reliable. Just back the silly things up *regularly*, because there's only a limited array of repair options open to you. Best buys these days are probably the 2.1GB drives (Seagate, Maxtor, and Conner make them) for about $230.

Floppy Disks

I've seen too many problems with Mitsubishi drives to recommend them; TEACs seem the most trouble-free. Don't bother with the 2.88MB floppies; nobody else uses them, but you might want to look into getting a Zip drive for easily expandable storage of 100MB per disk.

Video Board

Get a bit-blitting video accelerator board to support modern graphical operating systems. (Also called *bit-block transfer*, bit-blitting is a graphics function that copies a rectangular array of bits from memory to the screen.) Any accelerator based on the S3 chip set will be easy to support, as S3 drivers are common for any operating system. Alternatively, look at one of the two market leaders: either an accelerator card from Diamond or one from ATI. If you're into computer games, look at any card that takes 8MB of RAM and supports the 3Dfx accelerator API.

Video Monitor

Buy a monitor based on the resolution at which you'll use it. If you're doing regular old VGA (with a resolution of 640 dots across the screen by 480 dots down the screen), buy a 14-inch VGA monitor; it'll cost around $120. For the SVGA 800 × 600 resolution, get a 15-inch multisyncing monitor that can handle that resolution. For 1024 × 768, buy a monitor that's at least 17 inches diagonally. And *do not* buy interlaced 1024 × 768: sure it's cheaper, but the lawsuits from your employees going blind will be expensive. Buy noninterlaced. And only worry about it at 1024 × 768: nobody I know of tries to interlace 640 × 480 or 800 × 600. My favorite for a 17-inch monitor is the Viewsonic 17G.

Mouse

Although I hate to put more money in Microsoft's pocket, the Microsoft mouse seems the best of all the ones I've worked with. But $30 for a mouse? Arggh.

Printers

Well, they cost a little more, but it's hard to go wrong with HP laser printers. The series 6 produces beautiful output. If you need only an ink-jet printer, Epson makes the most incredible ones—you know, the ones that can print color art like a photograph. All that for starting around $199. Simply amazing!

Serial Ports

Look for serial ports based on the 16550 UART chip. It's built for multitasking, and you won't get any better than 33.600 out of your 56K modem without one.

Parallel Ports

Make sure that your parallel ports are Enhanced Parallel Port (EPP) interfaces. They're faster, and they're bidirectional. Bidirectional parallel ports are essential for modern printers, which send status information back to the PC over those ports.

FROM WHOM SHOULD YOU BUY?

When I ask this question, I don't mean whether you should buy from Dell, IBM, or Jeff and Akbar's House of Clones; instead, I mean, "Should you buy direct from the manufacturer, via mail order, or at a store?"

Well, if you're a really large company, then it probably makes sense to go straight to Compaq or whomever and negotiate a specific deal. But if you're a hobbyist or a SOHO (small office/home office) shop, then you'll have to examine your strategies.

You can probably buy cheapest from mail order. *But* if you do that, then returning defective merchandise involves shipping things around, getting RMA (Return Merchandise Authorization) numbers, and the like. That can be a hassle.

Going to a big computer retailer is just a fast way to waste money, so I'm not intending to shove you into the arms of Computerland or the like. But there are many small businesses whose main line of work is to sell computer parts, software, supplies, and systems at a reasonable price. These local vendors often offer prices that aren't that much more expensive than mail order. (Besides, the nice thing about local stores is that I like my vendors within choking distance....) And patronizing your local PC store means that when you need that disk drive on Saturday, you need only run down the street to get it, rather than waiting a week for it to ship.

That's not to say that mail order doesn't make sense. Mail order firms are more likely to have the latest and greatest software and hardware. Their prices will, again, be lower than the local store's. They may even know more about the product than a local vendor might. But take it from a veteran—there are a few things to be sure of.

▶ First, use a credit card. It's your line of defense when mail order companies get nasty. If you didn't get what you wanted, then just box it up, ship it back, and cancel the charge. Years ago, Dell used to charge a 15 percent "restocking fee." (They may still, but I refuse to do business with them, so I wouldn't know.) They sent me a hard disk that had clearly been dropped. When it worked, it registered seek times in the hundreds of milliseconds, despite what their ad promised. They tried to convince me that the drive was just what I wanted, but I knew better, and sent it back. They tried to charge me a restocking fee, so I just complained to Citibank, and Dell backed off.

▶ Second, find out who you're talking to. If the person responds, "operator 22," (I suppose his friends call him "2") ask to speak with a supervisor. You're about to give this guy your name, address, phone, and credit card number, and he won't even tell you who he is? Write the name down. Also get a confirmation number or order number.

▶ Third, only buy the product if it's in stock. Back-ordered things can take months to arrive, and by the time they do, you'll be charged the older (and higher) price. Get the salesperson to check that it can ship today. If not, don't make the order.

▶ Ship it overnight or second-day. By default, mail order companies use UPS ground, which can take anywhere from one week to a millennium to arrive. Second day is usually only a few dollars more, and then you can get a guaranteed delivery date out of the salesperson.

▶ Once you have the product, keep the carton that it came in for 30 days. That way, if a problem arises, then it's easy to ship it back. And if you do have to ship something back, then by all means insure it.

Just follow those rules, and you'll have some great luck getting things through the mail.

WHAT'S NEXT?

If you're having trouble getting your computer connected to the Internet, turn to Chapter 22. There, the folks at PC Novice/Smart Computing will walk you through the steps involved in installing your modem.

Chapter 22

Installing External and Internal Modems

While internal modems traditionally have ranked among the most difficult pieces of hardware to install, the toils are worth the frustration. A modem-equipped computer opens a whole new world of possibilities; for home users, a modem provides the connection to the Internet. Most newer computers for the home market already contain internal modems; and if that's your case, you can skip this chapter. But if you don't have one, and you're ready to get connected, read on. Here we'll provide step-by-step instructions for installing external and internal modems and provide advice for dealing with installation headaches.

NOTE

Although most external and internal modems connect to the PC in the same manner, the location and setting of COM ports and IRQs usually differ. We'll explain a common installation scenario, but you may encounter some different situations.

Adapted from *PC Upgrading & Maintenance: No experience required.*, by PC Novice/Smart Computing
0-7821-2137-3   544 pages $24.99

MODEM BASICS

A modem, or modulator/demodulator, lets your computer exchange information across telephone lines with another modem. It does this by converting a computer's digital signal to an analog signal that can travel over phone lines, and then converting the signal back to a digital form a computer can understand. Some modems can exchange data only; others, called fax/modems, can send and receive fax messages. Other modems add voice capabilities, letting you record messages on your computer.

Modems are available in internal and external versions. An external modem, the easiest to install, connects to a port on the back of your computer and sits on your desk. If you'd rather save the port (and desk space), you can install an internal modem, which is contained on an expansion card.

NOTE

An expansion card provides additional features for your computer and plugs into a narrow socket inside the computer, called an expansion slot.

IRQ Nightmares

Making your computer communicate with a modem, especially if it's an internal model, can be a nightmare because of conflicts with IRQ settings and COM ports. An *interrupt request line* (IRQ), is the hardware line over which devices send interrupts, or requests, for service to the microprocessor. IRQs are assigned different levels of priority, allowing the microprocessor to determine the importance of each request. Unless each hardware device has a different IRQ setting, conflicts may occur. A *COM port* is a serial communications port. Different hardware devices connect to the serial ports, and the operating system uses different COM port designations (such as COM1, COM2, COM3, and COM4) to identify the connections. Two hardware devices cannot use the same COM port.

External modems, used in tandem with software, take care of the settings for you, making them simple to install. Although internal modems have become easier to install, you still may encounter some IRQ or COM port conflicts. Many times the modem's factory settings will prevent these conflicts, but, if they don't, you'll have to correct the settings manually. The ease-of-use that comes with external modems isn't free; such modems cost $20 to $50 more than their internal counterparts.

CHANGING MODEM SETTINGS

COM1 sometimes isn't available for a modem because it may host the mouse connection. And if your modem won't work on COM2, you'll have to change the modem's settings.

Most newer modems, and those from major manufacturers, use DIP (dual inline package) switches to configure the COM port and IRQ settings. Rocker DIP switches simply need to be flipped on or off (like an electric light switch), while Slide DIP switches are slid into the on or off position. The configuration of the DIP switches—which you'll find in groups of two, four, or six, depending upon your type of modem—determines the COM port and IRQ settings.

The DIP switches can be located in various places on the expansion board. Many times, the factory settings will suffice for installation of your modem. If not, you'll need to adjust the DIP switches. The modem's documentation should show the correct settings for your modem. If your modem contains no such documentation, you have two choices: Use a trial-and-error approach or call technical support.

Some modems contain pins with a plastic jumper switch. You must move the jumper switch to cover various pins to change the COM port settings. Mainstream modems usually don't use these pins. If you *must* change the COM port setting of your mouse or network connection, though, you probably will find this configuration on the expansion board.

THE EXTERNAL MODEM

To install an external modem, you only need a flat-head screwdriver and a modem cable. Many external modems don't include these cables in their packaging, so check the box or directions inside; if a cable isn't included, you can find one easily at a computer store. You will not need to open your computer's case to perform this upgrade.

Part V

Connecting the Modem

First, turn off the computer. Take all the components out of the box and follow these steps:

1. Plug one end of the modem cable into a vacant port on the back of your computer and the other into the back of the external modem. On our computer, the end with a nine-pin plug went into the computer while the 25-pin plug went into the modem. To firmly attach the plugs, you may need to turn the screws on either side of the plug into the port. The screws to the port on the back of the computer were easily fastened with our fingers, but those on the sides of the modem plug required a flat-head screwdriver.

NOTE

The port on the back of the computer that you plug your modem into will correspond to the COM port you'll be using. If you plug your modem into a serial port labeled *A*, this corresponds to COM1.

2. Locate the cord plugging into your phone line. Plug this cord into the back of the modem, at the port labeled *Line*. If you still want to use a phone on this line, take the gray phone cord that came with your new modem and plug one end into the port labeled *Phone* on the back of the modem and plug the other into the port on your phone.

3. Now, plug the small, round end of the power cord into the small, round port in back of the modem; on ours, it was labeled *AC*. Then plug the power supply into a wall outlet or into your surge protector.

You're ready to test your external modem.

Checking Your Work and Finishing Up

Next, we turned on our computer and the modem to check the connection. (On the Hayes Accura 28.8 V.34 + Fax we used, we turned the modem on by flipping a switch to the "1" position.) If the lights are working, you're ready to install the communications software.

If the lights on the modem are *not* working, there are four possible causes:

- ▸ You may not have securely connected the ports and plugs.
- ▸ You may have something plugged into the wrong port.
- ▸ There may be a problem with your modem.
- ▸ You may have the wrong kind of modem cable.

If all goes well to this point, you can turn on your computer and install the communications software. Follow the on-screen prompts. Eventually it will ask which COM port to use. We chose COM1 because we plugged the device into Port A. Since you are installing the modem in Windows 98, an Installation Wizard will walk you through the process, especially if your modem is a Plug-And-Play device, which most of them are.

THE INTERNAL MODEM

We installed a Hayes Accura fax/modem which, by virtue of being an internal device, was a little more difficult to install than the external model described earlier. A Phillips screwdriver is a necessity when installing an internal modem.

Choosing the Right Slot

Internal modems can use either an 8-bit or a 16-bit expansion slot. (The expansion slots are at the back of the computer.) Most modem expansion cards have just one connector about 4 inches long. If your modem requires a 16-bit slot, the expansion card will have a second connector (about 2 inches long) behind the first. Your computer probably has a mixture of 8- and 16-bit expansion slots; the 8-bit slots are shorter and have room for only one connector. If possible, you'll want to install the modem in a slot that has empty slots on either side, which will help reduce electrical noise and interference that sometimes, although rarely, inhibits modem communications.

After you've selected an expansion slot, you'll need to remove the corresponding metal plate blocking the expansion slot's hole in the computer case. Remove the screw on top of the plate and lift the plate out from the top. Save the screw, which you'll need to fasten your modem card to the computer case. The metal plate you removed protects the inside of the computer from dust when no expansion card is installed in its corresponding slot. When you install your modem, the metal plate on the end of the card (containing the telephone line jacks) will replace the plate you just removed.

Installing the Modem

Remove the expansion card from its packaging, handling it by the edges as much as possible. Avoid touching the components on the card or the pins on the connector. Line up the connector on the expansion card with the empty expansion slot (see Figure 22.1). The connector should slide almost entirely into the expansion slot, leaving only the extreme top of the gold pins visible. It's a tight fit, so you might find it easier to roll the card into the slot by placing a corner in the expansion slot first and then fitting the remainder of the connector into the slot.

WARNING

Don't jam the expansion card into its slot; you could damage the components.

If you've properly installed the modem expansion card, the metal plate on the edge of the card will align with the empty slot in the back of the computer. You should be able to connect the metal plate of the expansion card easily to the computer's case with the screw you removed from the original plate. Don't use the screw to force the modem expansion card to line up properly; it should fit properly in the expansion slot with or without the screw in place.

TIP

One way to check the alignment of the modem expansion card is by connecting the telephone line to the modem. The telephone jacks are visible from the back of the computer. If your jacks are hidden, your board is incorrectly installed. You'll need to slide it out and start over again.

FIGURE 22.1: The connector is designed to fit into the expansion slot.

Putting It All Together: Lines and Cables

Now take the phone line (connected to the wall jack) and plug it into the jack on the back of the modem card labeled *Line*. Take the additional cable that came with your modem and plug one end into the modem jack labeled *Phone* and the other into the back of your phone (see Figure 22.2).

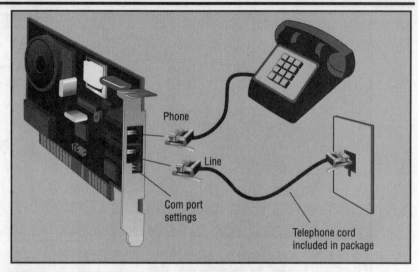

Phone

Line

Com port
settings

Telephone cord
included in package

FIGURE 22.2:   The phone line is plugged into a jack on the modem card.

At this point, you can replace the computer case cover or wait until after testing the modem to ensure it is working properly.

Reconnect the cables and turn on your computer. You should notice no changes as it boots. The easiest and quickest way to check the status of your modem is the HyperTerminal application in Windows 98.

Go to Start ➢ Programs ➢ Accessories ➢ Communications and select HyperTerminal. (If HyperTerminal was not installed when you upgraded to Windows 98, you'll need to install it using Add/Remove Programs in Control Panel.) After the splash screen clears, you will be presented with a dialog box asking you to name the connection and select an icon. When you have done this, enter the connection information into the Connect To dialog box, which shows up next.

Windows 98 uses the information you entered into the Internet Control Panel to find the modem you have installed. The name of your modem will appear in the Connect To dialog box. You should not change this unless you have been directed to by your service provider. When you've entered the appropriate information and clicked OK, another dialog box, called Connect, will open. Click Dial to log on to your provider's system.

CONSIDERATIONS FOR HIGH-SPEED MODEMS

If you're installing a 33.6 kilobits per second (Kbps) or 56Kbps modem, make sure you have a 16550 UART. In the case of a 56K modem, it is crucial that you have purchased the format that is supported by your service provider. Ask your provider if they support either K56Flex or X2 modem technology. To take advantage of the higher throughput rates offered by these modems, you need a fast UART. The speed at which the computer can communicate with the modem may be as high as 115,200 bits per second (bps); on much older machines with a slower UART, such as an 8250 or a 16450, you will experience data loss at these higher speeds, though it is highly unlikely you have a computer with such outdated hardware. If you do have an older computer the presence of these chips is especially noticeable during file downloads, when you might experience an excessive number of retries that effectively slows or lowers the overall throughput.

NOTE

A chip with the strange name of UART (Universal Asynchronous Receiver/Transmitter) manages the data sent from your communications software to the modem and resides on your computer's motherboard.

If you buy an internal modem, an outdated UART won't be an issue because the new modem card will have an updated UART chip on it, which will override the one in your system. External modems are a different story; you will have to buy an input/output (I/O) port card, which will have new COM1 and COM2 ports and an updated UART. These cards cost about $30 and will disable the COM ports that came with your system.

Modem Configuration

Beyond hardware connections, there are other steps you can take to ensure good modem performance. One thing to remember: Once you install your modem, you generally shouldn't have to mess with it again.

Part V

I'VE GOT THE MODEM, NOW WHAT?

Many questions technical support staffs frequently hear are in one or more general, yet fairly obvious, categories. If you experience problems with your modem, run through this list. You could save yourself toll-call charges and/or technical support fees by being aware of the following:

▶ Are the power connections on your modem and the computer's power supply firmly placed? A not-so-tightly placed power cord can provide sporadic power supplies and confusing error messages.

▶ If you're using an internal modem, is the modem card seated properly in its expansion slot? If it's an external modem, is it securely connected in the proper port at the back of the computer?

▶ Is your connection to the telephone line secure?

▶ Have you properly configured the modem initialization strings in your communications software? (A common initialization string is AT&F&C1&D2S7=60, but if that fails try AT&F1, an old standby that works just fine.) Other things to check: dial-up procedures, special scripts, prefixes for outgoing calls (such as 9), and autologon settings for online services that let you bypass the usual sign-on process. (Initialization strings tell the software what to expect from the modem so they'll speak the same language during a transmission.) You can eliminate the need to enter AT strings if, during installation, you pick your modem model (or a generic one) from the software's install list.

▶ Most manuals have a section on frequently asked questions; check it before calling technical support.

▶ Have you disabled call waiting? If not, add *70, as a prefix to the phone number your modem will dial. Otherwise, you could be bumped offline by an incoming call.

Sam Knox, an online services engineer for Hayes Microcomputer Products, recommends picking your modem's exact name from a communications package's configuration list. If you don't see it, pick something similar. For example, if you have the external version of a company's modem, but your software only lists the internal version, try picking that;

it's very likely they'll use the same initialization strings. Or pick the generic Hayes error-correcting setting, which won't slow down your modem transmissions or prevent you from getting online. What it will do, Knox says, is send out commands that most modems use and which should be enough to get you online. From there, he says, you can contact the manufacturer's World Wide Web site or bulletin board system to see if there's something else you can use.

Since you have Windows 98, expect relatively trouble-free installation, especially if you're using Plug-and-Play components. Some manufacturers don't intend for their products to support anything but Windows 98. Check the product's box; if you're still unsure, ask a salesperson or call the company.

Error Checking

Unlike video cards, whose device drivers seem to be updated every 30 days, modems rarely have drivers.

If a modem requires a driver, it's called a "host-controlled" modem, which means error checking is done by the software, not the hardware. Because these modems use proprietary drivers, they can run into problems with operating systems; if you're not a techno-wizard, you may want to avoid these modems.

"If a product box says 'requires Windows,' it's a big tip off that error checking is done by the software," Knox says. When software does the error checking, it requires microprocessor time, which can slow down other operations; when the checking is done by the modem, it doesn't use the microprocessor. A majority of modems, though, conduct error checking within the hardware. Knowing industry buzzwords can save you grief later, so keep your eyes open and ask salespeople or the manufacturer to clarify catch phrases you don't understand.

Installing a modem can be one of the easiest hardware installations you'll perform. It also can be one of the toughest. Unless you know your computer's configuration inside and out, it's doubtful you'll know how difficult the installation will be until you're nearly finished. After you're done, though, your modem's obnoxious grinding, squealing, and whining noises will never have sounded so good. Not to worry though; Windows 98 will take care of the dirty work.

Part v

WHAT'S NEXT?

In the next chapter, you'll learn how to use add-ons and plug-ins to extend your browser's capabilities. You'll be able to access sophisticated multimedia sites and get the most out of them.

Chapter 23

ADDING ON TO YOUR WEB BROWSER

U sing a browser on the World Wide Web used to be a fairly straightforward proposition. You could open Web pages, follow links, and even download files, but that was about it.

Then came the first plug-ins. These programs could be attached to your browser, giving it additional capabilities. Sometimes simple, sometimes extremely clever, these add-ons opened a new set of windows from which to view the Web. Now it seems that every time you turn around, there's another way of looking at stock reports from your browser or using your browser to meander about a three-dimensional world.

Most of these add-on programs are free (or at least feature a free trial period) and easy to install, but there are so many of them that it's hard to know what they do and whether you'll even find them useful. We've waded through this sea of add-ons and broken them down into the major areas of user interest.

Adapted from *PC Upgrading & Maintenance: No experience required.*, by PC Novice/Smart Computing
0-7821-2137-3   544 pages $24.99

NOTE

The terms "add-on," "add-in," and "plug-in" are interchangeable; they all refer to programs that you can add to your browser in order to enhance its performance in some way.

UNDERSTANDING THE ADD-ON STORY

There are two major areas of increased functionality provided by add-ons: multimedia and utility. Multimedia expansions can give your browser the ability to run animations, view video, or listen to audio files. The capabilities of utilities can range from being able to tell the time in Hong Kong to running Windows applications that are embedded into a Web page.

Add-ons are usually written by third-party developers who want browsers to be able to use technologies that they've developed or to be able to access information on certain types of Web sites.

Add-ons first came out for Netscape's Navigator 2.0, but now they're available for later versions of Navigator and Microsoft's Internet Explorer 3. There are a few that will function on *Mosaic* (the first graphical Web browser) and other older or more obscure browsers, but the majority of add-ons are made with the newest versions of the two most popular browsers in mind.

Some add-ons are available only for Navigator; others will work only with Explorer, but most developers have created versions for both browsers. Microsoft's add-on page (the ActiveX Component Gallery) is located at http://www.microsoft.com/activex/controls/ and at the time of this writing it boasted 103 add-ons. Navigator's page for add-ons (Inline Plug-Ins) is located at http://home.netscape.com/comprod/products/navigator/version_2.0/plugins/index.html and features 108 add-ons. Other Web pages that have add-ons can be found by searching at your favorite shareware site.

INSTALLING ADD-ONS

While some add-ons are also available as standalone applications, most need to be installed into whichever browser you're using. With Navigator, this usually entails downloading an executable file, quitting the browser, running the file, and then restarting the browser. If the add-on is not packaged in a self-executing program, users may have to place it in Navigator's Plug-In folder themselves. Because these add-ons range in size from a few hundred kilobytes to several megabytes, this can be a time-consuming process.

Microsoft has an easier, yet possibly more dangerous, option for Explorer users. At most of the pages featuring ActiveX controls, the browser will automatically install the add-on in a few minutes. The user doesn't even have to restart the browser. However, there are some who think this automation is less secure. An ActiveX add-on can have access to a user's operating system, providing the potential for disastrous results if the control was written by a malicious programmer.

One well-known ActiveX control called Exploder was written to demonstrate how dangerous add-ons could be. Exploder simply shut down PCs, but it showed how easy it would be to inflict more serious damage. Microsoft has repaired the security breach Exploder demonstrated, though other breaches are under investigation.

Navigator also may be susceptible to these types of spiteful add-ons. Microsoft claims that its security for accepting or rejecting these add-ons and other security breaches is much better than Netscape's. In fact, when we were trying a demonstration of one of the add-ons described later (Stockwatcher), Explorer wouldn't let us open the page with the stock quotes. It gave us a warning that it could be unsafe.

We have some advice for users wanting to add on to their browsers. Installing add-ons is just like any other aspect of the Internet or real life; there are some malevolent people out there, so take a little care and make sure you know what you're doing before adding any extras to your browser. The add-ons on Netscape's and Microsoft's pages have been checked out by the companies, so they are the safest bets. Before you install add-ons that you find through other sources, you may want to run them by other users or your browser manufacturer.

Part V

Getting the Most from Multimedia

Every Web browser since Mosaic has been able to view graphics; that's what helped make the Web such an attraction in the first place. But thanks to certain add-ons, being able to do no more than view standard images has begun to go the mundane way of text-based Web browsers.

Animation

Java has been an Internet buzzword recently, and it promises to revolutionize the computing industry in the future. But for now, Java programs (called *applets*) are usually little more than entertaining animations in Java-enabled browsers. There are many add-ons that emulate this ability, the most famous being Shockwave from Macromedia (http://www.macromedia.com/shockwave/).

Browsers with the Shockwave add-on can view complex animations ranging from dancing bears complete with sound effects to online games, like the one designed for Conquest of the New World from Interplay Productions (http://conquest.interplay.com). Interplay centered its site on the add-on, featuring humorous animations, a Shockwave movie, and an engrossing online battle game.

NOTE
If you go to a Shockwave-enabled Web site without the Shockwave add-on, your browser will ask if you'd like to link to a site where you can download Shockwave.

Unfortunately, Shockwave animations are quite time-consuming, even with a 28.8Kbps modem, because the animation won't play until it is completely downloaded. We tried another type of animation add-on, called Sizzler, that tries to compensate for this problem.

Totally Hip Software's Sizzler (http://www.totallyhip.com) is available for Windows (3.1, 95, and NT) and functions equally well with either browser. The installation for Explorer was painlessly completed for us through the ActiveX site, but the Navigator installation was also pretty easy. We downloaded the small (185KB) executable file, ran it, rebooted Navigator, and were ready to go. Sizzler animations get moving on-screen much more quickly than Shockwave or Java because they start their dance, bongo-beating, etc., before they are completely downloaded. You get a fuzzy image until it's loaded, but it's moving.

All these exciting new forms of animation show promise for what multimedia may soon deliver, but for now, they amount to little more than icing on a Web page cake.

Audio/Video

Sound and moving pictures have been two of the biggest detriments to rapid travel on the Internet. Audio and video files are too large to allow a transfer fast enough to support high-quality video-conferencing, movie watching, or music listening without a *dedicated connection* to the Internet. (Dedicated connections are high-speed Net connections that are constantly connected to the Net such as the T1 lines that transfer about one megabit per second and the Integrated Services Digital Network (ISDN) lines that transfer about 100Kbps.) But new technologies, especially the process of *streaming,* are moving the Internet one step closer to replacing television and radio. Streaming is the ability of an add-on to begin playing a video or audio clip as soon as it starts to download to your system. This results in nearly real-time viewing or listening with only a slight deterioration in quality.

One of the first add-ons to really take advantage of streaming was RealAudio (`http://www.realaudio.com`). RealAudio is available as an add-on or a standalone application for almost any platform, for use with any browser at any connection speed of 14.4Kbps or greater. A RealAudio-enabled browser lets users listen to news broadcasts, radio stations, and live concerts from around the world at near-stereo quality with a 28.8Kbps modem—and close to CD quality with an ISDN line.

We tested streaming video, which utilizes the same concept, except that it streams motion pictures as well as the audio. We installed the VivoActive player add-on (available at `http://www.vivo.com`) in both Explorer and Navigator. Again, Explorer automatically installed the add-on in a few seconds. For Navigator, we had to download the executable file, run it, and then restart the browser.

VivoActive, available for Windows (3.1, 95 and NT) and PowerMacs, worked equally well for both browsers. Appropriately, we watched a short video debate between Jim Barksdale of Netscape and Bill Gates of Microsoft about their future plans for the Internet. There was some delay every 20 to 30 seconds, as the player allowed the streaming to catch up, but the picture was clear and the audio was great. It was the best video we'd seen over the Internet on a 28.8Kbps connection.

NOTE

Until the Internet as a whole widens its *bandwidth* (the ability to transfer information), streaming audio and video lets those of us with slower connections enjoy some of its kilobit-hogging perks.

3-D/VRML

Virtual reality (VR) has always been high on the wish list of those yearning for technological advancement. Its goals of creating environments that engulf users in worlds of 3-D sound, images, and tactile feedback have been achieved, but only in a limited manner. Available mainly for giant corporations and the ultra-rich, VR remains largely out of reach for the common dreamer. The Internet could make it a reality for average folks, but again, only with a successful quest for greater bandwidth. VR on the Web, which is still in its infancy, presents itself in the form of 3-D images and backgrounds through the use of Virtual Reality Modeling Language (VRML) and other means.

VRML is similar to Hypertext Markup Language (HTML), the language that most Web pages are written in, but it is used to create a more realistic environment. Most browsers are just beginning to be able to recognize these 3-D pages, so add-ons are often needed.

We tested the HotSauce add-on created by Apple Computing (`http://hotsauce.apple.com`) and available for Macintosh and Windows (95 and NT), but weren't impressed. HotSauce lets Web page creators display their links as buttons in a 3-D array, supposedly making them easier to circumnavigate. We found that it just put the links in a jumbled pile. We could move link buttons out of the way to get to others, but we had a problem when we tried following the links—they often failed. HotSauce was easy to install in both browsers but was also equally mundane in both.

We decided to give another 3-D add-on a go. We tried out WIRL from VREAM Inc. (`http://www.vream.com`), which is available for Windows (95 and NT), and were more pleased with its results (see Figure 23.1). Although the files for both browsers were huge (more than 5MB), we were able to have a smaller 500KB add-on installed through the

Microsoft ActiveX page. It took about five minutes, and it was able to run all the WIRL demos.

The basic demo had three images that were activated with a mouse-click. A helicopter that took off, a cannon that fired, and a whirling WIRL logo showed the capabilities, but in a rather limited fashion. We traveled to the VREAM site for a more complete sampling. The best example we found was the "Isle of Morphos," where users could navigate either a bird or a kayak about the isle. While enjoying the view, users could control their vantage points in all three dimensions. WIRL's quality was good, the interaction was sensitive, and the extras were clever.

These add-ons indicate that virtual reality is on its way—and not just for a select few.

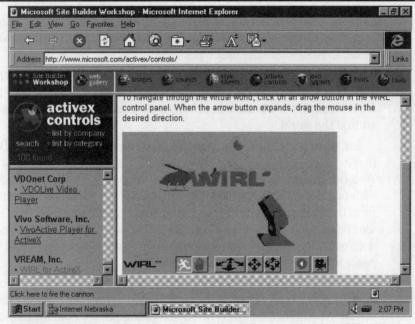

FIGURE 23.1: Microsoft's ActiveX Component Gallery installed this WIRL add-on so we could test its three-dimensional capabilities.

USING ADD-ONS

Browser add-ons are more than just glimmer and glitz. The majority are designed with a specific use in mind—something users might need or want that their browsers are currently incapable of doing. The possibilities are nearly limitless, and new, useful add-ons are being introduced every day.

Web Utilities

Of course, a major interest of browser users is how to increase the functionality of their browsers. Many utilities are just simple add-ons that slightly modify the browser, and make it more useful. For example, Cyberspell from Inso Corporation (http://www.inso.com/consumer/cyberspell/cybrspll.htm), which is available for Windows (3.1, 95, and NT) running Netscape Navigator, checks the spelling of any words, e-mail addresses, and e-mail messages that the user types.

Another useful example is EarthTime from Starfish Software (http://www.starfishsoftware.com), which is available for Windows (95 and NT). This add-on lets users check the local time in up to eight cities around the world.

Still others are much more complicated, such as DataViz's Web Buddy (http://www.dataviz.com), which is available for Mac and Windows 95. Web Buddy functions like other "offline" browsers; it will grab entire Web pages and let you peruse them at your leisure while disconnected from the Internet. But Buddy is more powerful than most. You can schedules pages for it to download, convert HTML pages into word-processing documents or images for use in graphics programs, and organize all the pages with its own bookmarking feature.

We tried Buddy for both Explorer and Navigator. It was a large download for either (more than 2MB), and we had to quit the browser and install the add-on after the download was completed, even for Explorer. But we found good uses for Buddy. If you don't have unlimited connection time and have certain pages that you regularly visit on the Web, Buddy can save you time and money.

Many of these browser-enhancing add-ons will no doubt be added to future versions of Explorer and Navigator, but until then, plugging them in may make your Web surfing easier.

Add-ons and Windows

Microsoft is dedicated to merging browser and desktop. The new upgrades to Windows 95 will implement some of this integration, and Microsoft's ActiveX and the latest version of Internet Explorer could make it happen soon. Until this bond is formed completely, however, there are many add-ons that attempt to bridge this gap.

The Word Viewer Plug-in, another add-on from Inso Corp. (http://www.inso.com), which is available for Windows (3.1, 95, and NT) and Navigator, lets users view any Microsoft Word 6.0 or 7.0 document from within Navigator.

In a similar vein, Acrobat 3.0 from Adobe Systems Inc. (http://www.adobe.com), which is available for Mac, Windows (3.1, 95, and NT), Unix, and OS/2 lets users read and navigate Adobe's Acrobat files in their browser. (Acrobat is a method of storing files that lets them be viewed on any PC with an Acrobat reader.)

Citrix's WinFrame is much more ambitious. It lets browsers run Windows applications that are embedded on a Web page (see Figure 23.2). Regardless of the user's operating system, if they have Explorer or Navigator, they can run a Windows application. We ventured to http://www.citrix.com/hotspot.htm with both browsers. Explorer automatically installed the add-on, and we only had to download a small (130KB) file for Navigator.

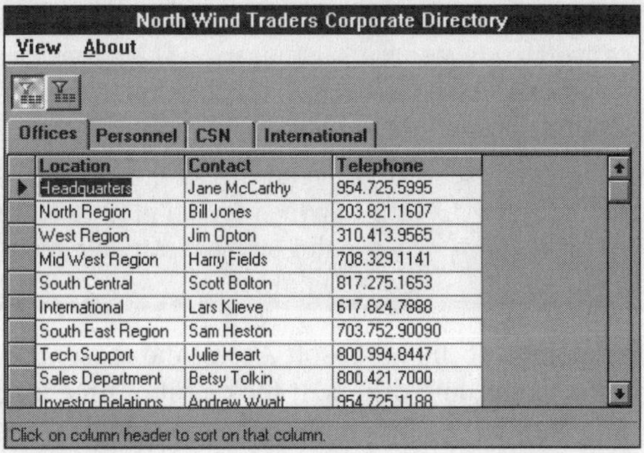

North Wind Traders Corporate Directory

View   About

Location	Contact	Telephone
Headquarters	Jane McCarthy	954.725.5995
North Region	Bill Jones	203.821.1607
West Region	Jim Opton	310.413.9565
Mid West Region	Harry Fields	708.329.1141
South Central	Scott Bolton	817.275.1653
International	Lars Klieve	617.824.7888
South East Region	Sam Heston	703.752.90090
Tech Support	Julie Heart	800.994.8447
Sales Department	Betsy Tolkin	800.421.7000
Investor Relations	Andrew Wyatt	954.725.1188

Offices | Personnel | CSN | International

Click on column header to sort on that column.

FIGURE 23.2: The WinFrame add-on from Citrix lets you run Windows applications such as this sample Rolodex embedded in a Web page.

Part V

ADD-ONS YOU DON'T ADD ON

Both Microsoft Internet Explorer 3.0 and Netscape Navigator 3.0 come with some pre-installed add-ons. Some of these are integrated so smoothly that you won't even notice them. Others open up their own windows and make themselves blatantly obvious.

Navigator has added e-mail and news capabilities since 2.0, and Explorer finally caught up with version 3.0. If you have a connection to both mail and news servers, this can save you from having to start up other programs to check and send e-mail or read the newsgroups. Having all three programs in one also lets them work together— jumping from Web page to newsgroup or newsgroup to e-mail.

Telephony, the combination of PCs and telephones, has recently created a lot of interest, most of it aimed at the use of the Internet as a way to make free or very cheap long-distance calls. If two users have the same software, they can communicate using PC microphones and speakers and only have to pay their dial-up connection charge. In short, that means you can call anyone in the world and talk as long as you want for the flat rate your Internet service provider charges, usually something like $19.95 per month. So it's no surprise that both browsers come with their own telephony software built in.

Navigator's CoolTalk provides an audio connection to anyone who also has the browser and the software. It includes a whiteboard (that lets users share graphical information as well) and a chat feature.

Explorer's NetMeeting works similarly, letting users share their voices, applications, and graphics. It also includes support for international conferencing standards and its own built-in chat capabilities.

As more add-ons demonstrate their usefulness for the average user, they will be incorporated directly into the browser platforms. Until then, we must pick and choose our add-ons to match our needs.

The site featured demos of the Microsoft Access database, the group project package Lotus Notes, and others. It took a bit of time for each program to load, and they were a bit cumbersome to navigate (there was a tracer effect that led to overlapping when we moved up or down in the browser window), but this add-on demonstrated the inevitable merger between the desktop and the Internet that will soon change the way we compute.

Doing Business with Add-ons

Of all the different types of utility add-ons, those that cover the business side of things are the most focused. These add-ons address a specific need and address it completely.

About People from Now Software (`http://www.nowsoft.com/plug ins/about_people.html`), which is available for Mac and Windows 95 using Navigator provides a browser address book. Any addresses posted to the Web with the Now Up-to-Date Web Publisher can be viewed in Navigator in a list or business card form.

Even more specific is Chemscape Chime from MDL Information Systems Inc. (`http://www.mdli.com/chemscape/chime/chime.html`), which is available for Mac, Windows (3.1, 95, and NT). Chime lets scientists view chemical information in many different structures using Navigator.

We tried out an add-on with a little more general interest. Wayfarer's Stockwatcher (`http://www.wayfarer.com`), which is available for Windows (95 and NT), gives you updates of the stocks that you have selected as they fluctuate throughout the day. It was quite a large download (more than 3MB), but it included the add-ons for both Explorer and Navigator. Unfortunately, Explorer's security kicked in, and it wouldn't let us run Stockwatcher without adjusting the safety settings.

We ran it in Navigator instead. But when we tried to run Stockwatcher from the Wayfarer site, it said we were missing some extensions and loaded them in, which took about 10 minutes. After we finally got Stockwatcher going, we were suitably impressed. There were a limited number of stocks to choose from, but you could e-mail Wayfarer and ask them to add stocks that you're interested in. By double-clicking a particular stock, we could view a 3-D chart that showed the peaks and valleys in that stock's price. As is standard in most online ticker tapes, the stock prices were delayed about 20 minutes, but we found this add-on useful—much more than a novelty.

People on the Web are as varied as people in life—different interests, goals, and dreams. There is no one set of options and abilities that could be included in a browser to match these needs. Add-ons are, and will be for some time, an excellent way to adapt your browser so that it caters to your unique desires during your travels on the Web.

WHAT'S NEXT?

Now that you've learned how to install add ons, you can read on to learn how to install RAM. The next chapter, also from *PC Upgrading & Maintenance: No experience required.*, will show you how.

Chapter 24

INSTALLING RANDOM ACCESS MEMORY

In the old days of computing with DOS, PC users didn't need to know much about memory. If a problem with memory developed, they could adjust the settings in the AUTOEXEC.BAT and CONFIG.SYS files and reboot the computer. If they wanted more memory, they installed a memory card and ran a memory management program. That's not the case now. Almost nobody runs just DOS anymore.

In fact, most people are using at least Windows 95, and many of you are using Windows 98. Needless to say, Windows 98 is a far cry from Windows 3.*x* in the memory management arena, but there are still things to keep in mind. Of course, there's the universal truth in computing, "Lack of RAM means lack of productivity," especially in an older system. If you don't have enough memory, your computer will run sluggishly, even with a fast Pentium processor.

Adapted from *PC Upgrading & Maintenance: No experience required.*, by PC Novice/Smart Computing
0-7821-2137-3   544 pages $24.99

THE FASTEST, EASIEST UPGRADE OF ALL

So, if you want to improve your computer's operation, feed it a healthy diet of more memory. No other upgrade will better enhance your computer's performance, whether it is an older system or a blazing new 333 megahertz (MHz) Pentium II. With Windows 3.1x, you needed 4MB of random access memory (RAM). Although that was a big jump in memory needs compared to the 640KB required by the early DOS-based computers, Windows limped along on 4MB. Pop another 4MB and Windows 3.1 ran much better. With Windows 95, you needed at least 8MB of RAM to handle all the advanced graphical tasks and to run one or two programs at a time.

Windows 98 Needs at Least 16MB

To get satisfactory performance from Windows 98, your computer needs at least 16MB of RAM, and probably 32 (of course, if you're a graphics, multimedia, or video professional you'll most likely opt for 128 MB of RAM, or more!). Windows manages available memory by sharing what it needs to run multiple programs, print files, operate the diskette drives and monitor, and so on. When it runs low on memory, Windows converts the overflowing data into a temporary file, called a *Windows swap file*, in space it reserves on the hard drive. As you can imagine, offloading data to and then retrieving it from the hard drive takes a toll on the computer's efficiency because getting data from the hard drive is a considerably slower process than retrieving something from RAM. When there is a large supply of RAM, however, Windows can bypass the swap file on the hard drive and maintain its speed.

Many computing novices confuse the capacity of the hard drive and the amount of RAM a computer has. Aside from electricity, memory is what drives your computer. The size of the hard drive only limits how many programs and how much data you can save to it. Having an overly large hard drive for storage won't help much if your computer is starving for memory.

It is relatively easy to install more memory. Even if you've never ventured inside a computer, you can slip more RAM chips into the waiting slots on the motherboard.

TIP

The Section *Steps to Installing RAM* walks you through the process of installing RAM.

Choosing Memory Modules

Memory is a vital component in all computers, but all memory isn't the same. Before you can upgrade memory, you must find out which type of memory chips your computer uses. You also must decide which kind of memory you want to upgrade.

Memory chips are measured by their RAM speed, which is the rate at which the modules work. RAM speed is expressed in nanoseconds (ns); rather than bog yourself down in technical definitions, remember simply that the smaller the number of nanoseconds, the faster the chip. You can install slower RAM than the other chips in your computer if you are adding to what's already there. But you cannot install a faster chip than your computer is rated to use. Check your computer's documentation to see which type and memory speed the system needs. You'll have to buy chips in multiples equal to the total memory you want. For instance, if you have 4MB now and need to upgrade to 16MB, see how many vacant memory slots there are. If the existing 4MB module is in one slot and there is only one slot remaining, you have to remove the existing module and buy two 8MB modules, one for each socket.

Here are the RAM types you'll encounter:

- **DRAM** Dynamic random access memory. This is the most common and cheapest type of memory chip. This is also the slowest type of memory because it is made up of capacitors. The computer must constantly refresh its memory by recharging the capacitors. Usually DRAM chips are hard-wired to the motherboard and can't be removed without an expert's help. You can only add more chips in the available accessory slot.

- **SRAM** Static random access memory. This memory chip is made of transistors, which do not need refreshing. Because it doesn't need constant refreshing, SRAM is about four times faster than DRAM. SRAM chips are larger than other types of memory so they are used to meet only some of the memory needs in a computer.

Part V

► **EDO RAM** Extended data out random access memory. This is the fastest, but is not necessarily the most expensive memory chip anymore. It handles memory access about 30 times faster than SRAM because it can move data in and out from different addresses at the same time.

► **VRAM** Video random access memory. VRAM is used on video boards. It is much like DRAM but has a second port to speed up the access time. Adding more video memory speeds up the time it takes the motherboard to place colors, images, and text on-screen. If the video board is slow (meaning it only has 1MB of memory), the computer's motherboard has to spend too much time creating the image on-screen. The result is a slower response to programs and other functions.

When you upgrade RAM, you must add more of the same type of memory modules. For example, if your computer has DRAM, you cannot replace it with faster SRAM or EDO RAM chips because the electronic circuits can't handle this kind of design change. However, if your video card will accept more VRAM chips, adding them will measurably speed up the computer's performance even if you don't increase the overall RAM on the motherboard.

Installing Additional RAM

Computers use three types of RAM chips, depending upon their design. Older computers used dual inline chips (DIPs) that had to be pushed directly in their sockets. DIP chips were the most difficult to install, and fortunately you will almost never encounter them in today's computers. These chips had two rows of eight "legs" called contacts. You installed them by pushing them into available receptacles. This had to be done with extreme care; if even one contact was bent during installation, your computer would not start.

The next type of computer memory to come along was the single inline memory module (SIMM), which has a single row of chips soldered to a narrow circuit card with contacts on the bottom edge. SIMMs come in several varieties: 30-pin, 72-pin, and 168-pin. To install them, hold the SIMM at an angle to match the plane of the holder in the socket. Then align the plastic pin in the socket with the hole at one end of the SIMM; SIMMs only fit in the socket one way. Push the metal contacts at the bottom of the SIMM into the socket. Finally, press the SIMM firmly into the socket, and press the SIMM back until the tabs on either side slide into position.

The more common type of memory now is the dual inline memory module (DIMM), but if you have an older PC that doesn't meet the latest design standards, you won't have this type. DIMMs are installed the same way as SIMMs, but are thicker than SIMMs because the chips are stacked one atop another. The advantage is that DIMMs can provide more memory per module at only a slightly higher cost than SIMMs.

WARNING

Before you touch the inside of the computer or handle the memory chips, make sure you discharge static electricity. If you don't, even a tiny static charge (unnoticeable to you) can permanently zap the electronic components. If you walk across a carpet while working on your computer, always reground yourself. Better yet, buy a grounding cord, inexpensively available at most Radio Shacks and other electronics stores. The cord attaches one end to the interior of your computer and the other end to your wrist; this provides an equal ground and protects your new equipment.

Planning Ahead

Upgrading computer memory is one of the best ways to give your system a longer, more useful life. Spending a few hundred dollars for memory is much better than buying a new computer. Memory slots are limited, though, so buy a module with enough memory to handle your future needs. Otherwise, you'll waste what you spend now if you decide to upgrade again later. Also, buy memory from a reliable dealer. Bargain basement deals can cost you big bucks if the memory chip goes bad or if it isn't the right type of memory for your computer.

As a guide, Table 24.1 summarizes the memory demands of common applications and activities. Although each category is demarcated with minimum and maximum amounts, any of the tasks discussed here can be run on less RAM than is specified. However, running these applications at or near the recommended maximum amounts helps ensure optimum performance.

TABLE 24.1: How Much RAM Is Enough?

AMOUNT OF RAM	APPLICATIONS
16MB to 24MB	Light word processing, e-mail, and database use with one or two open applications
24MB to 32MB	Medium administrative uses such as word processing, e-mail, fax and communications, spreadsheets, and business graphics, with one or two open applications
32MB to 48MB	Light number crunching involving spreadsheets, e-mail, and accounting software, one or two open applications
48MB to 64MB	Heavy number crunching involving spreadsheet and statistical applications, large research databases, and more than three applications open at once
64MB to 96MB	Light graphics involving word processing, page layout, and illustration or graphics software with one to two applications open at once
96MB to 128MB	Medium graphics involving basic photo editing, presentation software, font packages, multimedia, word processing, page layout, illustration/ graphics software, and more than three applications open at once

How to Install RAM

Here are two reasons to perform a memory upgrade. First, memory takes less than 10 minutes to install. And second, it can help even a weak computer immensely. That's because random access memory (RAM) is like a large library where the CPU comes to gather the data it needs to make the applications run. As mentioned above, the more RAM your PC has, the less time the CPU has to spend searching for data in the swap file, which switches some of the data from RAM to the hard drive. The less swapping you do, the faster the CPU works.

A few years ago, the average PC was equipped with 4MB of RAM. That standard was upped to 8MB, and then to 16MB. A good number of new machines today come with 32MB of RAM or more. Users who play computer games or work with desktop publishing programs might need as much as 128MB of RAM, though. Along with the progression of RAM size, chip technology has changed to the point where it's become fairly difficult to know what type of RAM is needed. "EDO," "parity," "non-parity," "single inline memory modules," and "dual inline memory modules" are some of the phrases you'll need to understand. The irony is that it's actually more difficult and time-consuming to become familiar with these terms than it is to install RAM on your PC.

NOTE

Parity RAM is a type of memory that included an extra bit (a small piece of data) to every byte to "verify" the data as it was moved around. Since RAM has been greatly improved and is much more reliable, Parity RAM is very difficult to find and not really necessary. If someone tells you that you need Parity RAM, tell them you know what's what.

Finding the Current Amount of RAM

There are three ways to discover how much memory is now in your computer.

- ▶ Type **mem** at the DOS prompt. Look under the Total column for the amount of memory you have. The amount will be listed in kilobytes (KB); eliminate the numbers after the comma to convert it to megabytes. For example, if the amount is 16,192KB, remove the 192 and add MB to the 16. You have 16MB of RAM.

- ▶ Right-click the My Computer icon on the Windows 95 Desktop. From the menu that appears, click Properties. The amount of memory your PC has will appear on-screen.

TIP

In the old days you could watch the screen as the PC booted up. The BIOS, which is built into a computer's circuitry, controls the start-up routines for peripheral devices, such as the keyboard, display, and disk drives, and runs a diagnostic test on the PC's peripheral hardware. In the process, it told you how much RAM you had. This is still true today, but if you have anything over a 100 MHz Pentium computer you probably can't read it. Why? It flashes by too fast to read!

NOTE

Adding memory will help a computer only so much. For example, we upgraded from 32MB to 64MB of RAM. After the upgrade, we saw improved performance but only by about an additional 5% (compared to the 30% increase when we jumped from 16MB to 32MB). Despite the infusion of RAM, performance was limited by the 133 megahertz (MHz) CPU installed in our PC. Therefore, you may be better off saving the money to invest in a newer computer.

Part V

Regardless of the limitations inherent in increasing your PC's RAM, there are obvious benefits to this type of upgrade RAM. For example, tests show that a 133MHz Intel Pentium processor with 32MB of RAM will easily outperform a 166MHz Pentium with 8MB of RAM. (Of course, a 166Mhz Pentium system with 8MB of RAM is practically worthless anyway.)

First Step: Open Up

There's an easy way and a hard way to know what kind of RAM you need to buy for your upgrade. The easy way is to go to the computer manual and research what kind of memory is already inside the PC. The more complicated way is to open your computer's case and determine what type of memory you need by investigating the chips that are already there.

Since the easy way needs little explanation, let's focus on the difficult path. The first step in locating your RAM is to close all open applications and turn off the power to your PC. Also, as an extra precaution, you should unplug the computer and all its peripherals. (You can leave the plugs connected to the back of your computer and devices, but remove all the plugs from their electrical sockets. This will eliminate the possibility of your getting zapped by an electrical surge.) Then remove the case to prepare for installation.

Try to determine which screws (if any) you need to unscrew in order to remove the case. Most systems will have screws running along the very edge of their cases. These are the screws you need to remove. On the system we upgraded, we didn't have to remove any screws; the case slid off after pinching two tabs in front. Your computer might be configured similarly. Make sure you don't remove any screws near your computer's fan, electrical connection, or ports—all of which can be found at the rear of the system. After the screws are removed, slide the cover toward the front or back to remove it. Ground yourself by touching the computer's metal case or power supply box or by using a grounding strap (available at your local Radio Shack).

Finding the RAM

Now we can begin to explain what you might be looking for. The first items to locate are single or double inline memory modules (SIMMs or DIMMs), which are slender circuit boards dedicated to storing RAM. They're usually green with a row of rectangular, gray chips attached to them. SIMMs fit into sockets that have metal clips on either end. The sockets are usually located near the CPU on the motherboard (see Figure 24.1). We had to remove the power supply on our computer to access the SIMMs. Other computers may allow straight access to the SIMMs.

NOTE

If your computer is less than a year old you will most likely find DIMMs, but the majority of computers out there still use SIMMs. For this reason, we will use SIMMs in all the descriptions here. Just keep in mind that RAM installation works on the same principles, regardless of type, so if you have a 80386 DX33 with 30-pin SIMMs you would install new RAM in the same way as with a day-old Pentium II 333MHz machine.

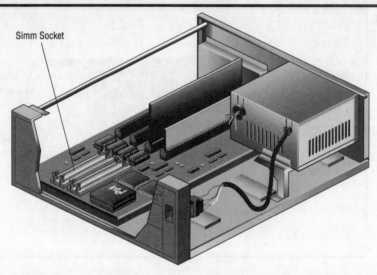

Simm Socket

FIGURE 24.1: The SIMM Sockets are usually long, white parallel channels.

If you have a newer computer (that is one powered by a Pentium or an IBM PowerPC microprocessor), it will have dual inline memory modules (DIMMs) instead of SIMMs.

You'll be able to tell the difference between the SIMMs and DIMMs by the number of pins on each type of module. The two types of SIMMs are 30- and 72-pin modules (see Figure 24.2). DIMMs for desktop PCs come in a 168-pin variety, and currently are slightly more expensive than regular 72-pin SIMMs.

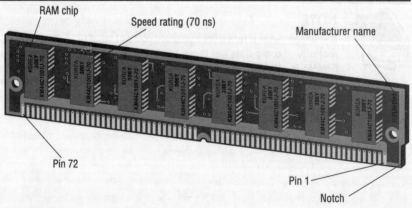

RAM chip

Speed rating (70 ns)

Manufacturer name

Pin 72

Pin 1

Notch

FIGURE 24.2: A typical 4MB 72-pin SIMM

A pin is a metal attachment on the module that allows data to pass from the PC to the rows of memory chips. Pins look like little fingers running along the bottom of the module. The number of pins is crucial because 30-, 72-, and 168-pin modules will be different lengths, and consequently are incompatible with one another. In short, you must have the correct number of pins on your module or the RAM won't fit into your computer's sockets.

No Room for More Modules

When you find the RAM sockets in your system, you may discover that the PC has no memory modules. In this case, your computer is hard-wired with a small amount of RAM on the motherboard, and you'll have to look in the user's manual to determine the type of RAM your system requires. On the other hand, you may find that your system doesn't have any empty sockets. This doesn't necessarily mean that you can't add more RAM. You'll just have to take out some of the modules already in place.

Before you do this, we need to issue one caveat. Some computers require sockets to work in tandem, meaning that two sockets must have memory modules in place in order to function. This requirement is called a *bank*. A bank of RAM could be one socket, two sockets, or four sockets. If a computer requires a two-socket bank, but only has one socket filled with SIMMs, it will fail to boot up.

Solving a RAM Space Crunch

How can you tell which type of banks your computer requires? Here's a shortcut: If you have an older computer—one with an early-model 486 CPU—it probably has a four-socket bank of 30-pin modules. Late-model 486s require one socket of 72-pin modules. Computers equipped with Pentium chips require two sockets of 72-pin modules.

NOTE

DIMMs can be installed individually, but to take full advantage of interleaving (a technology that reduces the amount of time the microprocessor must wait to access RAM), they must be installed in tandem.

Another shortcut is to deduce what kind of module you have by what is already in the PC. Assuming that you've never upgraded your RAM before, if your computer has two sockets of memory modules, it's likely that your computer has a two-socket bank. If all four of the sockets are

Part v

filled, the PC probably has a four-socket bank. If only one is filled, the PC has a single-socket bank. To be absolutely safe, call the manufacturer, ask a salesperson, or consult the user's manual.

OKAY, NOW FOR A MATH QUIZ

Let's say you have a Pentium-equipped computer, and you want to add 16MB of RAM to it. You could buy one module of 16MB, but you would be making a mistake. Why? Because one module will fill only one socket, and from our discussion here, we know that Pentium-equipped computers must have two sockets filled. Thus, we must buy two modules of 8MB, which equals the 16MB we desire.

Proper Identification

Here are four other things that you'll need to know when buying memory for your computer.

Access Speed

The speed rating of the memory chip is measured in nanoseconds. For the CPU and RAM to communicate, they have to have a speed that matches one another. Memory chips are rated at 60, 70, and 80 nanoseconds (ns).

To find the access speed of your system, find the tiny numbers and letters printed on the side of your memory chips. There's usually a series of characters followed by a dash and then a number. The number will be the chip's access speed. If there's only a one-digit number, such as a six, seven, or eight, that's okay; these numbers represent 60, 70, or 80.

NOTE

It's okay to add faster chips but not slower ones. And in this case, the lower number is faster (that is, 60ns is faster than 70ns)

EDO or Non-EDO

This is something that mainly applies to owners of Pentium-equipped computers. EDO stands for extended data out, which is a shortcut designed in some RAM chips to decrease the amount of time the CPU and memory interact. Putting EDO chips in a non-EDO computer won't do any harm. Putting non-EDO chips in an EDO computer won't hurt anything either; however, the computer won't boot up, or it will operate more slowly than if you used the proper EDO chips.

Tin or Gold

Pins are composed of one or the other of these elements. You'll want to be consistent with the materials in your computer. Mainly, it's the high-end PCs that have modules with pins made of gold. A failure to match metals properly will deteriorate the connections in a computer.

Time to Change

After you've purchased the RAM, it's time to install it. Here are the steps you'll need to follow:

1. Ground yourself again by touching the computer's metal case or power supply box (you bought a grounding strap, didn't you?). Remove the module from its antistatic bag, being careful not to touch any metal parts on the chip. Try to hold the module from the sides.

2. One end of the module has a small notch so you know which way to align it in the socket. The socket has two posts, one on each side. One of these posts has a small plastic tab at its base that will just fit the notch of the module. Depending on the socket type, you'll need to bring the module in either horizontally or at an angle, then lift it to an upright position. On our computer, we pushed the module into the socket at a 45-degree angle, then moved it to a vertical position (see Figure 24.3). You shouldn't have to push very hard to get the module into the socket.

3. When the module is in place, two metal prongs attached to the plastic posts should fit evenly into the slot; one end should not be higher than the other. If everything looks okay, replace whatever components you had to move to install the RAM. You might want to test the machine before replacing the cover.

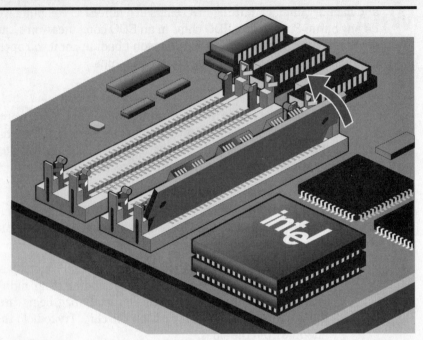

FIGURE 24.3: SIMMs are installed at an angle, then snapped into the metal clip holders.

You'll possibly receive some sort of error message from the BIOS as your computer boots up. All BIOS setup programs are a little different, so you should follow the directions on-screen or in the user's manual. The bottom line is that your computer needs you to update the amount of memory it now has. The setup program might detect the amount of new RAM automatically or you might have to enter the new value yourself.

If you try to boot your PC and nothing happens or your computer recognizes an amount of memory less than you installed, go back over the checklists above to ensure that you are using the right type of memory for your system. If that doesn't shed some light on the problem, try to reseat each of the modules following the steps above.

Once everything is working correctly, you should find that your applications run faster, and your computer generally performs better. And if nothing else, at least you won't have to worry about RAM prices for a while.

WHAT'S NEXT?

In the next chapter, Mark Minasi will talk to you about something important to every computer user: preventive maintenance. Follow his advice now to save yourself headaches in the long run.

Chapter 25

AVOIDING SERVICE:
PREVENTIVE MAINTENANCE

The most effective way to cut down your repair bills is by good preventive maintenance. There are things in the PC environment—some external, some created in ignorance by you through inattention—that can drastically shorten your PC's life. Now, some of these are common-sense things; I don't really imagine that I've got to tell you not to spill soft drinks (or, for that matter, *hard* drinks) into the keyboard. But other PC gremlin sources aren't quite so obvious; so, obvious or not, we'll get to all the environmental hazards in this chapter. A few factors endanger your PC's health:

- ▶ Excessive heat
- ▶ Dust
- ▶ Magnetism
- ▶ Stray electromagnetism
- ▶ Power surges, incorrect line voltage, and power outages
- ▶ Water and corrosive agents

Adapted from *The Complete PC Upgrade & Maintenance Guide*, by Mark Minasi
0-7821-2151-9   1520 pages $59.99

Heat and Thermal Shock

Every electronic device carries within it the seeds of its own destruction. More than half of the power given to chips is wasted as heat—but heat destroys chips. One of an electronic designer's main concerns is to see that a device can dissipate heat as quickly as it can generate it. If not, heat slowly builds up until the device fails. You can help your PC's heat problem in two ways.

▸ You can install an adequate fan in the power supply, or add an auxiliary fan.

▸ Run the PC in a safe temperature range.

Removing Heat with a Fan

Some computers, like most laptops, don't require a fan, as enough heat dissipates from the main circuit board all by itself. But most desktop and tower PCs will surely fail without a fan.

When designing a fan, engineers must trade off noise for cooling power. Years ago, power supplies were quite expensive, running in the $300 range for the cheapest power supply, and great care was exercised in choosing the right fan. Nowadays, power supplies cost under $25, and I doubt that most engineers at PC companies could even tell you what kind of fan is sitting in their machines, any more than they could tell you who makes the case screws. Now, that's a terrible shame, because the $3 fan that's sitting in most PC power supplies is a vital part. If it dies, your PC will cook itself in just a few hours. And they *do* die.

The more stuff that's in your PC, the hotter it runs. The things that make PCs hot inside include:

▸ Chips, memory chips, and CPUs in particular, as they have the most transistors inside them.

▸ Drive motors in hard disks, floppies, and CD-ROMs. Some CD-ROMs run quite warm, like the Plexor 4-Plex models. Large hard disks run *extremely* hot. It seems that the full-height 5.25-inch drives run at a temperature that will almost burn your fingers; I've seen that on old Maxtor 660MB ESDI drives, and more recently on my 1.7GB Fujitsu drive. Newer drives in the 3.5-inch, half-height or third-height format run much cooler.

▶ Some circuit boards can run quite hot, depending on how they're designed (or misdesigned).

In general, heat buildup inside a PC is much less of a problem than it was in the mid-80s.

Good and Bad Box Designs

It's frustrating how totally unaware of heat problems many computer manufacturers are. The first tower computer I purchased was from a company named ACMA, and they put together an impressive machine. There were two fans in the case—a very nice touch—as well as a CPU fan. I've got to say that they spoiled me. A much more recent purchase, from an outfit called Systems Dynamics Group, has been somewhat less enjoyable. The back of the PC chassis has room for two fans, but there's only one fan in the system. There's nothing intrinsically wrong with that, except that the cutout for the second fan—which is right next to the first fan—is left empty. The result is that the fan just sucks in air from the cutout a few inches away from it, and blows it back out.

I noticed this pointless ventilation system pretty quickly, so I took some tape and covered up the extraneous cutout. Within seconds, the air being pumped out the back of the Pentium got 10 degrees warmer. If I'd left the extra cutout uncovered, then the only ventilation that my Pentium system would have gotten was just the simple convection from the heated boards and drives. Even at that, however, the Pentium system—which includes a 1GB drive, 80MB of RAM, a CD-ROM, video capture board, video board, SCSI host adapter, and Ethernet card—only runs 10 degrees hotter inside the box than outside the box.

Things could have been a bit worse if the case was like some I've seen, with the fan *on the bottom of the tower*! This case—it's not too common, fortunately, but it's worth asking so you can avoid it when purchasing a PC—puts the circuit boards on the top of the tower, and the fan on the bottom. I have no idea who designed this case, but it's nice to know that the banjo player kid from *Deliverance* finally has someone to look down upon.

Dead Fans

The point I'm making here is, take a minute and look at the airflow in the box. Of course, even if you have a good box, you can still run into heat problems.

I recently installed Freelance Graphics on my system. Pulling the first floppy out of my A: drive, I noticed that the floppy was warm. My memory flashed back to 1982, when something similar had happened—so I knew what was going on. My system's fan had died. Fortunately, I found the problem early and shut down the computer. I had to travel to Europe for a few weeks to teach classes and consult, but I figured, no problem; I'll just leave the computer off. Unfortunately, while I was gone, one of my employees helpfully started up the computer—reasoning that I always leave my computers on all the time, so what the hey?—and so, despite the "do not turn it on" sign I'd left on it, the computer merrily melted itself down while I lectured in Amsterdam. By the time I returned, the hard disk had self-destructed, as had the Ethernet card in it.

It's actually pretty amazing what *didn't* die in the system. The CPU (a 50 MHz 486DX) still runs to this day, as does the Adaptec 1742 SCSI host adapter. The machine still sees service as a "test" machine, but it stays nice and cool. How? Simple. Other than the memory, CPU, SCSI host adapter, and display board, there's nothing in it. The hard disk and CD-ROM are external devices, with their own fans. It's not a bad idea to do this to help your computer keep its cool.

Heat Sensor Devices

Now, I could have avoided this problem altogether with a 110 Twinalert from a company called PC Power and Cooling Systems. They're a name to know when you're buying power supplies. The 110 Twinalert is a circuit board about the size of a business card that plugs into a floppy power connector. When the PC's internal temperature gets to 110 degrees F, it starts squealing, making an annoying noise. At 118 degrees F, it just shuts the computer down. The device is under $50, and every network server should have one.

While I'm on the subject of PC Power and Cooling, I should mention that the company also makes an interesting variety of power products for the PC, including power supplies with very quiet fans, power supplies with built-in battery backup, and high-quality PC cases. I use their stuff when I want to be 100 percent sure that my PC will be running when I need it.

Safe Temperature Ranges for PCs

Electronic components have a temperature range within which they are built to work. IBM suggests that its PC, for instance, is built to work in the range of 60–85 degrees F. This is because the circuit boards can run as hot as 125 degrees, but a typical machine may, again, be as much as 40 degrees hotter *inside* than outside. And 125 minus 40 yields 85 degrees, the suggested maximum temperature.

Obviously, if you've got a good fan, the acceptable range of room temperatures expands considerably. If you had a really good fan, the inside of the machine would be the same temperature as the outside. You don't want the inside of the PC to get any higher than 110 degrees —hard disks fail at that point, although, again, circuit boards can function in higher temperatures than that (so my old floppy-only laptops could function in the Gobi Desert, although I've had neither the chance nor the inclination to try it yet).

Since the temperature inside the PC is ambient plus some constant, there are two ways to cool the inside of the PC—lower the constant with a good fan, or lower the ambient temperature. Keep the room cooler and the PC will be cooler.

Heat aids the corrosion process. Corrosion is a chemical process, and chemical processes roughly *double* in speed when the temperature of the process is raised by 10 degrees C (about 18 degrees F). Chips slowly deteriorate, the hotter the faster.

How do you measure temperature and temperature changes in your PC? Simple—get a digital temperature probe. (Try Radio Shack or Edmund Scientific Corp.) The easy way to use the probe is to tape it over the exit vents by the fan's power supply. An indoor/outdoor switch lets you quickly view the PC's inside temperature and ambient temperature.

Duty Cycles

We said before that a device should get rid of heat as quickly as it creates it. Not every device is that good, however. Devices are said to have a *duty cycle*. This number—expressed as a percentage—is the proportion of the time that a device can work without burning up. For example, a powerful motor may have a 50 percent duty cycle. This means that it should be active only 50 percent of the time.

Duty cycle is used to describe active versus inactive time for many kinds of devices, although it is (strictly speaking) not correct. Some desktop laser printers, for example, will not run well if required to print continuously.

Thermal Shock

Because a PC is warmer inside than outside, changes in room temperature can become multiplied inside a PC.

This leads to a problem called *thermal shock*. Thermal shock comes from subjecting components to rapid and large changes in temperature. It can disable your computer due to expansion/contraction damage. The most common scenario for thermal shock occurs when the PC is turned on Monday morning after a winter's weekend. Many commercial buildings turn the temperature down to 55 degrees over the weekend: your office may contain some of that residual chill early Monday morning. Inside the PC, though, it may still be 55. Then you turn the machine on. Inside 30 minutes some PCs can warm up to 120 degrees. This rapid, 65-degree rise in temperature over a half hour brings on thermal shock.

This is an argument for leaving the PC on 24 hours/day, seven days/week. (We'll see some more reasons to do this soon.) The temperature inside the PC will be better modulated. By the way, you can't leave portable PCs on all the time, but you should be extra careful with portables to avoid thermal shock. If your laptop has been sitting in the trunk on a cold February day, be sure to give it some time to warm up before trying to use it. And give it some time in a *dry* place, or water vapor will condense on the cold platters of your hard drive. Water on the platters is a surefire way to reduce your drive's life.

Sunbeams

Another heat effect is caused by sunbeams. Direct sunlight isn't a good thing for electronic equipment. A warm sunbeam feels nice for a few minutes, but sit in one for an hour and you'll understand why PCs don't like them. Direct sunlight is also, of course, terrible for floppy disks. Find a shadowy area, or use drapes.

Dealing with Dust

Dust is everywhere. It is responsible for several evils.

First, it sticks to the circuit boards inside your computer. As dust builds up, the entire board can become coated with a fine insulating sheath. That would be fine if the dust were insulating your house, but thermal insulation is definitely a bad thing for computers. You seek, as we have seen, to minimize impediments to thermal radiation from your computer components. To combat this, remove dust from inside the computer and from circuit boards periodically. A good period between cleaning is a year in a house and six months in an office. A simpler approach is to use the "while I'm at it" algorithm—when you need to disassemble the machine for some other reason, clean the insides while you're at it. A tool that can assist you is a can of compressed air. Just as effective for the case and bracket assemblies is a dust-free cloth wetted with a little water and ammonia (just a few drops). Don't use the cloth on circuit boards—get a can of "compressed air" and blow the dust off.

Actually, the "compressed air" isn't compressed air, but some kind of compressed gas. Take a second look when you buy this stuff: a lot of it's freon or some other chlorinated fluorocarbon (CFC), which enlarges the hole in the ozone layer. There are a number of "ozone-friendly" alternatives. One is marketed by Chemtronics.

This should be obvious, but when you blow dust off boards, be aware of where it is going: if you can, have the vacuum cleaner nearby, or take the board to another area, then you'll have better luck. *Please* don't hold the board over the PC's chassis and blow off the dust with compressed air—all it does is move the dust, not *remove* the dust.

The second dust evil is that dust can clog spaces, like the air intake area to your power supply or hard disk or the space between the floppy disk drive head and the disk.

To combat the floppy drive problem, some manufacturers offer a floppy dust cover which you put in place when the machine is off. Unfortunately, you really need the cover when the machine is on. The reason: CRT displays attract dust. Turn your screen on, and all of the dust in the area heads straight for the display. Some of the particles get sidetracked and end up in the floppy drives. Some vendors say that the way to cut down on dust in floppy drives is to close the drive doors. This is wrong because the door *isn't* dust-tight.

A place which creates and collects paper dust is, of course, the printer. Printers should be vacuumed or blown out periodically, *away* from the computer (remember, dust goes somewhere when blown away).

Another fertile source of dust is ash particles. Most of us don't burn things indoors, *unless* we are smokers. If you smoke, fine: just don't do it near the computer. Years ago, I ran across a study by the U.S. Government Occupation Safety and Hazard Administration (OSHA) which estimated that smoke at a computer workstation cuts its life by 40 percent. That's $1200 on a $3000 workstation.

MAGNETISM

Magnets—both the permanent and electromagnetic type—can cause permanent loss of data on hard or floppy disks. The most common magnetism found in the office environment is produced by electric motors and electromagnets. A commonly overlooked electromagnet is the one in older phones that ring or chirp (rather than beep). The clapper is forced against the bell (or buzzer, if the phone has one of those) in the phone by powering an electromagnet. If you absent-mindedly put such a phone on top of a stack of floppy disks, and the phone rings, you will have unrecoverable data errors on at least the top one. Your stereo speakers can do the same thing to floppies.

Don't think you have magnets around? How about:

▶ Magnets to put notes on a file cabinet

▶ A paper clip holder with a magnet

▶ A word processing copy stand with a magnetic clip

Another source of magnetism is, believe it or not, a CRT (video monitor). I have seen disk drives refuse to function because they were situated inches from a CRT. X-ray machines in airports similarly produce some magnetism, although there is some controversy here. Some folks say, "Don't run floppies through the X-ray—walk them through." Others say the X-ray is okay, but the metal detector zaps floppies. Some people claim to have been burned at both. Personally, I walk through an average of three to four metal detectors per week carrying 3.5-inch floppy disks, and have never (knock on wood) had a problem. My laptops have been through X-ray machines everywhere, and I've never lost a byte on the hard disk.

Airport metal detectors should be sufficiently gentle for floppies. Magnetism is measured in a unit called *gauss*—a power of 25 gauss is required to affect a 360K floppy, more for more dense floppies. Metal detectors *in the U.S.* (notice the stress) emit no more than 1 gauss. I'm not sure about Canada and Europe, but I notice that the fillings in my teeth seem to set off the metal detectors in the Ottawa airport.

What about preventive maintenance? For starters, get a beeping phone to minimize the chance of erasing data inadvertently. Another large source of magnetism is the motor in the printer—generally, it is not shielded (the motors on the drives don't produce very much magnetism, in case you're wondering).

Do you (or someone in your office) do a lot of word processing? Many word processors (the people kind, not the machine kind) use a copy stand that consists of a flexible metal arm and a magnet. The magnet holds the copy to be typed on the metal arm.. The problem arises when it's time to change the copy. I watched a word processing operator remove the magnet (so as to change the copy), and slap the magnet on the side of the computer. It really made perfect sense—the case was iron, and held the magnet in a place that was easy to access. The only bad part was that the hard disk on that particular PC chassis was mounted on the extreme right-hand side of the case, right next to the magnet. You can start to see why I hate magnets . . .

Oh, and by the way, *speakers* have magnets in them. Years ago, a friend purchased a "home entertainment system," a VCR, stereo, and some monster speakers. That's when I noticed that he had stacked his videotapes on top of the speakers. I almost didn't have the heart to tell him, but I eventually advised him that his videos were history—and, sad to say, they *were*. Modern multimedia PCs all have speakers that claim to have shielded magnets; but I've got a Sony woofer/satellite speaker system that makes my monitor's image get wobbly when I put the speakers too near the monitor. No matter what the manual says, I think I'll just keep the floppies away from there.

My advice is to go on an anti-magnet crusade. Magnets near magnetic media are disasters waiting to happen.

STRAY ELECTROMAGNETISM

Stray electromagnetism can cause problems for your PC and, in particular, for your network. Here, I'm just referring to any electromagnetism that you don't want. It comes in several varieties.

- ▶ Radiated Electromagnetic Interference (EMI)
- ▶ Power noise and interruptions
- ▶ Electrostatic Discharge (ESD)—static electricity

Electromagnetic Interference

EMI is caused when electromagnetism is radiated or conducted somewhere that we don't want it to be. I discuss two common types—crosstalk and RFI—in the next two sections.

Crosstalk

When two wires are physically close to each other, they can transmit interference between themselves. We're not talking about short circuits here: the insulation can be completely intact. The problem is that the interfering wire contains electronic pulses. Electronic pulses produce magnetic fields as a side effect. The wire being interfered with is touched or crossed by the magnetic fields. Magnetic fields crossing or touching a wire produce electronic pulses as a side effect. (Nature is, unfortunately, amazingly symmetrical at times like this.) The electronic pulses created in the second wire are faint copies of the pulses, i.e. the signal, from the first wire. This interferes with the signal that we're trying to send on the second wire.

Crosstalk can be a problem when bundles of wires are stored in close quarters, and the wires are data cables. There are four solutions to crosstalk:

▶ Move the wires farther apart (not always feasible).

▶ Use twisted-pair (varying the number of twists reduces crosstalk).

▶ Use shielded cable (the shield reduces crosstalk—don't even think of running ribbon cables for distances over six feet).

▶ Use fiber optic cable—it's not electromagnetic, it's photonic (is that a great word, or what?), so there's no crosstalk.

▶ Don't run cables over the fluorescent lights. The lights are noise emitters.

I once helped troubleshoot a network that had been installed in a classroom. The contractor had run the wires through the ceiling, but the network seemed to not work. (Ever notice how often the words "network" and "not work" end up in the same sentence? A Russian friend calls them "nyetworks.") I pushed aside the ceiling tiles and found that the cable installer had saved himself some time and money by forgoing cable trays, instead wrapping the cables around the occasional fluorescent lamp. So, on a hunch, I said to the people that I was working with, "Start the network up again," and I turned off the lights. Sure enough, it worked.

Radio Frequency Interference

Radio Frequency Interference (RFI) is high (10 KHz+) frequency radiation. It's a bad thing. Sources are:

- High-speed digital circuits, like the ones in your computer

- Nearby radio sources

- Cordless telephones, keyboards

- Power-line intercoms

- Motors

Worse yet, your PC can be a *source* of RFI.

RFI is bad because it can interfere with high-speed digital circuits. Your computer is composed of digital circuits. RFI can seem sinister because it seems to come and go mysteriously. Like all noise, it is an unwanted signal. How would we go about receiving a *wanted* RF signal? Simple—construct an antenna. Suppose we want to receive a signal of a given frequency? We design an antenna of a particular length. (Basically, the best length is one quarter of the wavelength.) Now suppose there is some kind of RFI floating around. We're safe as long as we can't receive it. But suppose the computer is connected to the printer with a cable that, through bad luck, happens to be the correct length to receive that RFI? The result: printer gremlins. Fortunately, the answer is simple: shorten the cable.

Electric motors are common RFI-producing culprits. I recently saw a workstation in Washington where the operator had put an electric fan (to cool *herself*, not the workstation) on top of the workstation. When the fan was on, it warped the top of the CRT's image slightly. Electric can openers, hair dryers, electric razors, electric pencil sharpeners, and printers are candidates. Sometimes it's hard to determine whether the device is messing up the PC simply by feeding back noise onto the power line (the answer there is to put the devices on separate power lines), or whether it is troubling the PC with RFI.

Your PC also *emits* RFI which can impair the functioning of other PCs, televisions, and various sensitive pieces of equipment. By law, a desktop computer cannot be sold unless it meets "Class B" specifications. The

Part v

FCC requires that a device 3 meters from the PC must receive no more than the following RFI:

Frequency	Maximum Field Strength (microvolts/meter)
30–88 MHz	100
89–216 MHz	150
217–1000 MHz	200

Protecting your PC from the devices around it and protecting the devices from your PC are done in the same way. If the PC doesn't leak RFI, then it's less likely to pick up any stray RFI in the area. Any holes in the case provide entry/exit points. Use the brackets which come with the machine to plug any unused expansion slots. To prevent unplanned air circulation paths it is also a good idea to plug unused expansion slots. Ensure that the case fits together snugly and correctly. If the case includes cutouts for interface connectors, find plates to cover the cutouts or simply use metal tape.

A simple AM radio can be used to monitor RFI field strength. A portable Walkman-type radio is ideal, as it has light headphones and a small enough enclosure to allow fairly local signal strength monitoring. A cheap model is best—you don't want sophisticated noise filtering. Tune it to an area of the dial as far as possible from a strong station. Lower frequencies seem to work best. You'll hear the various devices produce noises.

The PC sounds different, depending on what it is doing. When I type, I hear a machine gun-like sound. When I ask for a text search, the fairly regular search makes a "dee-dee-dee" sound.

I've also used the radio in a number of other ways. Once, I received a new motherboard, a 486 that I was going to use to upgrade a 286 system. I installed it, and nothing happened. No beeps, no blinking cursor, nothing but the fan. So I removed the motherboard and placed it on a cardboard box (no electrical short fears with a cardboard box). Then I placed a power supply next to it, plugged in the P8/P9 connectors, and powered up. I ran the radio over the motherboard and got no response, just a constant hum. Placing the radio right over the CPU got nothing. I reasoned that what I was hearing was just the clock circuit. I felt even more certain of my guess when I noticed that the CPU had been inserted backwards into its socket. One dead motherboard, back to the manufacturer.

Power Noise

Your wall socket is a source of lots of problems. They basically fall into a few categories:

- ▶ Overvoltage and undervoltage

- ▶ No voltage at all—a power blackout

- ▶ Transients—spikes and surges

We'll look briefly at those issues in a moment. First let's look at the fourth kind of power noise, the one that *you* cause:

- ▶ Power-up power surges

In the process of discussing how to fix this, I'll have to weigh in on The Great PC Power Switch Debate.

Leave Your Machines On 24 Hours/Day

I'd like to discuss one power-related item here: user-induced power surges. What user-induced power surges, you say? Simple: every time you turn on an electrical device you get a power surge through it. Some of the greatest stresses that electrical devices receive is when turned on or turned off. When do light bulbs burn out? Think about it—they generally burn out when you first turn them on or off. One study showed that when a device is first turned on, it draws up to four to six times its normal power for less than a second. For that brief time, your PC may be pulling 600 to 900 watts—not a prescription for long PC life.

The answer? Leave your PCs on 24 hours/day, seven days/week. We've done it at my company for years. Turn the monitor off, or turn the screen intensity down, or use one of those annoying automatic screen blankers so the monitor doesn't get an image burned into it. Turn the printer off, also. Leaving the machines on also modulates temperature.

What? You're still not convinced? I know, it seems nonintuitive—most people react that way. But it really does make sense. First of all, consider the things that you keep on all the time, like:

- ▶ Digital clocks, which obviously run continuously, incorporate some of the same digital technology as microcomputers, and they're pretty reliable.

- ▶ Calculators—I've seen accountants with calculators that are on all the time.

Part v

▶ TVs (part of the TV is powered up all the time so that it can "warm up" instantly, unlike older sets).

▶ Thermostats—the temperature regulating device in your home or business is a circuit that works all the time.

Most of the things that I just named are some of the most reliable, never-think-about-them devices that you work with.

In addition to the things I've already said, consider the hard disk. Disks all incorporate a motor to spin its disks from 3600 to 7200 rpm. You know from real life that it's a lot harder to start something moving than it is to keep it moving. (Ever push a car?) The cost, then, of turning hard disk motors on and off is that sometimes they just won't be able to get started.

Leaving your computer on all the time heads off thermal shock, yet another reason to leave it on. Machines should never be power cycled quickly. I've seen people fry their power supplies by turning their computers on and off several times in a 30-second period "to clear problems" and end up creating bigger problems.

A final word of caution. Leaving the machine on all the time is only a good idea if:

▶ Your machine is cooled adequately. If your machine is 100 degrees inside when the room is 70 degrees, it'll overheat when the room goes to 90 degrees on summer weekends when the building management turns off the cooling in your building. Make sure your machine has a good enough fan to handle higher temperatures.

▶ You have adequate surge protection. Actually, you shouldn't run the machine at all unless you have adequate surge protection.

▶ You have fairly reliable power. If you lose power three times a week, there's no point in leaving the machines on all the time— the power company is turning them off and on for you. Even worse, the power just after a power outage is noise-filled.

Before moving on, let's take a quick peek at the other kinds of power problems.

Transients

A transient is any brief change in power that doesn't repeat itself. It can be an undervoltage or an overvoltage. Sags (momentary undervoltage) and surges (momentary overvoltage) are transients. Being brief, the transient may be of a high enough frequency that it slips right past the protective capacitors and whatever in your power supply and punches holes in your chips. (No, they're not holes you can see, at least not without some very good equipment.) Transients have a cumulative effect—the first 100 may do nothing. Eventually, however, enough chickens come home to roost that your machine decides, one day, to go on vacation. Permanently.

Overvoltage

We say that we have an "overvoltage condition" when we get more than the rated voltage for a period greater than 2.5 seconds. Such a voltage measurement is done as a moving average over several seconds. Chronic overvoltage is just as bad for your system as transient overvoltage: the chips can fail as a result of it.

Undervoltage

Summer in much of the country means air conditioners are running full blast, and the power company is working feverishly to meet the power demands that they bring. Sometimes it can't meet the full needs, however, and so announces a reduction in voltage called a brownout.

Brownouts are bad for large motors, such as you'd find in a compressor for refrigeration. They make your TV screen look shrunken. And they confuse power supplies. A power supply tries to provide continuous power to the PC. Power equals voltage times current. If the voltage drops and you want constant power, what do you do? Simple: draw more current. But drawing more current through a given conductor heats up the conductor. The power supply and the chips get hot, and may overheat.

Surge protectors can't help you here. A power conditioner can—it uses a transformer to compensate for the sagging voltage.

NOTE

In *The Complete PC Upgrade and Maintenance Guide*, Mark Minasi devotes an entire chapter to the topic of power supplies and power protection. There he evaluates the three most common types of protective devices: surge protectors; power conditioners; and backup power supplies, such as Standby Power Supply (SPS) and Universal Power Supply (UPS) devices. For most home and small-office users, a power conditioner may be the best compromise.

Part v

Electrostatic Discharge

Electrostatic discharge—ESD, or, as you probably know it, static electricity—is annoyingly familiar to anyone who has lived through a winter indoors. The air is very dry (winter and forced hot-air ducts bring relative humidity to around 20 percent in my house, for example), and is an excellent insulator. You build up a static charge, and keep it. In the summer, when relative humidity can be close to 100 percent (I live in a suburb of Washington, D.C., a city built over a swamp), you build up static charges also, but they leak away quickly due to the humidity of the air. Skin resistance has a lot to do with dissipating charges, also. The resistance of your skin can be as little as 1,000 ohms when wet and 500,000 ohms when dry.

You know how static electricity is built up. Static can damage chips if it creates a charge of 200 volts or more. If a static discharge is sufficient for the average person to notice it, it is 2000 volts.

Scuffing across a shag rug in February can build up 50,000 volts. This is an electron "debt" which must be paid. The next metal item (metal gives up electrons easily) pays the debt with an electric shock. If it's 50,000 volts, why don't you electrocute when you touch the metal? Simple. Fortunately, the amperage—and the power—is tiny. Different materials generate more or less static. Many people think that certain materials are static-prone, while others are not. As it turns out, materials have a triboelectric value. Two materials rubbed together will generate static in direct proportion to how far apart their triboelectric values are.

Some common materials, in order of their triboelectric values, are:

- ► Air
- ► Human skin
- ► Glass
- ► Human hair
- ► Silk
- ► Paper
- ► Cotton
- ► Hard rubber
- ► Nickel and copper
- ► Polyester

▶ Silicon

▶ Teflon

Once an item is charged, the voltage potential between it and another object is proportional to the distance between it and the other item on the table. For instance, suppose I charge a glass rod with a cotton cloth. The glass will attract things below it on the scale, like paper, but will attract more strongly things below paper.

Why does static damage PC components? The chips which largely comprise circuit boards are devices that can be damaged by high voltage, even if at low current. The two most common families of chips are CMOS (Complementary Metal Oxide Semiconductor) and TTL (Transistor-Transistor Logic). TTLs are an older family. TTLs are faster switching—potentially faster chips (memories, CPUs and such) could be designed with TTL—but TTL has a fatal flaw: it draws a lot of juice. TTL chips need much more electricity than CMOS chips, so they create more heat.

CPUs and memories are all CMOS. This has a lower theoretical maximum speed, but it runs on a lot less power. Sadly, that also means that it is more subject to static electricity problems. TTL chips can withstand considerably more static than CMOS chips. CMOS chips can be destroyed by as little as 250 volts.

Even if static doesn't destroy a chip, it can shorten its life. Static is, then, something to be avoided if possible. Another effect occurs when the static is discharged. When the fat blue spark jumps from your finger to the doorknob, a small ElectroMagnetic Pulse (EMP) is created. This isn't too good for chips, either. (It's the thing you've heard about that could cause a single nuclear explosion to destroy every computer in the country, except a lot smaller.) The easiest way I get rid of my static is to discharge the static buildup on something metal that is not the computer's case. A metal desk or table leg is good, and it's a good idea to leave the power supply plugged in when disassembling a PC; touch the power supply, and you drain off your charges.

For your firm, however, you may want something a trifle more automatic. The options are:

▶ Raise the humidity with a humidifier (evaporative, not ultrasonic—ultrasonic creates dust)

▶ Raise the humidity with plants, or perhaps an aquarium

▶ Install static-free carpet

▸ Put anti-static "touch me" mats under the PCs

▸ Make your own anti-static spray (see below)

From the point of view of comfort, I recommend the first option strongly. Your employees don't feel dried-out, and the static problem disappears. Raise humidity to just 50 percent and the problem will go away.

You can make inexpensive, homemade anti-static spray. Just get a spray pump bottle and put about an inch of fabric softener in it. Fill it the rest of the way with water, shake it up, and you've got a spray for your carpets to reduce static. Just spritz it on the rug, and the rug will smell nice, and everyone will know that you've been busy. (I hear you asking, "How long does it last?" You'll know.)

In a similar vein, a person from a temporary services agency once told me that they tell their word processing operators to put a sheet of Bounce under the keyboard to reduce static.

Technicians who must work with semiconductors all of the time use a ground strap to minimize ESD. The idea with a ground strap is that you never create a spark—and therefore EMP—because you've always got a nice ground connection that's draining off your charges. A good ground strap is an elastic wristband with a metal plate built into it to provide good electrical connection, attached to a wire with an alligator clip. You put the clip on something grounded—the power supply case is the most common place—and put the strap around your wrist. As you're connected to a ground, you continuously drain off your charges.

When you must handle electronic components, take these precautions:

▸ Get an anti-static strap.

▸ If you don't have an anti-static strap, just leave the power supply plugged in and touch the power supply case before touching any component.

▸ Reduce the amount of static that you transfer to a chip with a ground strap, or remember the high-tech equivalent of knocking wood—touch unpainted metal periodically.

▸ Don't handle components in areas having high static potential. For example, avoid carpets unless they are anti-static or low humidity environments. Don't wear an acrylic sweater when changing chips. Get leather-soled shoes. If your work environment allows it, you can really avoid static by removing your shoes and socks.

- ▶ Don't handle chips any more than is necessary. If you don't touch them, you won't hurt them.

- ▶ Use the anti-static protective tubes and bags to transport and store chips.

- ▶ If possible, pick up components by their bodies. Don't touch the pins any more than necessary.

- ▶ Use an anti-static mat.

Use the proper precautions, and your PC won't get a big "charge" out of being touched by you.

AVOIDING WATER AND LIQUIDS

Water is an easier hazard to detect and avoid. You don't need any sophisticated detection devices. Shielding is unnecessary—you just keep the computer away from water. Water and liquids are introduced into a computer system in one of several ways:

- ▶ Operator spills

- ▶ Leaks

- ▶ Flooding

Spills generally threaten the keyboard. One remedy—the one recommended by every article and book I've ever read on maintenance—is to forbid liquids near the computer. For most of us, this is unrealistic. Some people use clear flexible plastic covers on the keyboard, kind of like what Burger King uses on their cash registers. With one of these keyboard "skins," you might say that you can "practice safe typing."

SafeSkin is offered by Merritt Computer Products in Dallas. Their address is in the Vendor's Guide appendix. They offer versions for the various odd keyboards in the PC world.

On the other hand, should someone spill a Coke in a keyboard without one of these covers, all is not lost, so long as you act quickly! Disconnect the keyboard and flush it out at a nearby sink. Let it dry thoroughly and it'll be good as new. The correct way to do this is to use deionized, filtered water. In actuality, the tap water that you find in most parts of North America is clean enough that you'll end up doing more good than harm by simply using the water out of the tap. If, on the other hand, the smell

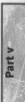

Part V

of rotten eggs lingers in your bathroom after every shower, then I'd think about using some cleaner water for component flushing.

A similar disaster, flooding, sometimes occurs. Don't assume that flooded components are destroyed components. Disassemble the computer and clean the boards by cleaning the contacts and edge connectors: you can buy connector cleaner fluids, or some people use a hard white artist's eraser—do not use pencil erasers! (A Texas Instruments study showed that they contain acids that do more harm than good to connectors.) Blow out crevices with compressed air.

Avoid floods by thinking ahead. Don't store any electrical devices directly on the floor; they'll be damaged when the floor is cleaned. Generally, flooding indoors is under six inches. Be aware of flooding from improper roofing; when installing PCs, don't put one in just under the suspicious stain on the ceiling. ("Oh, that—it was fixed two years ago. No problem now.")

Corrosion

Liquids (and gases) can accelerate corrosion of PCs and PC components. Corrosive agents include:

▶ Salt sweat in skin oils

▶ Water

▶ Airborne sulfuric acid, salt spray, carbonic acid

Your fear here is not that the PC will fall away to rust; the largest problem that corrosion causes is oxidation of circuit contacts. When a device's connector becomes oxidized, it doesn't conduct as well, and so the device does not function, or—worse—malfunctions sporadically. Salt in sweat can do this, so be careful when handling circuit boards; don't touch edge connectors unless you have to. This is why some firms advertise that they use gold edge connectors; gold is resistant to corrosion.

Carbonated liquids include carbonic acid, and coffee and tea contain tannic acids. The sugar in soda is eaten by bacteria who leave behind conductive excrement—like hiring some germs to put new traces on your circuit board. Generally, try to be very careful with drinks around computers.

Don't forget cleaning fluids. Be careful with that window cleaner you're using to keep the display clean. If your PC is on a pedestal on the floor, and the floor is mopped each day, some of the mopping liquid gets into the PC. Cleaning fluids are very corrosive.

You can clean edge connectors with either hard white erasers or connector cleaner products. One of the best-known vendors of these products is Texwipe.

MAKING THE ENVIRONMENT "PC FRIENDLY"

Let's sum up what we've seen in this chapter. Protect your PC by doing the following:

- ▶ Check power considerations:
  - ▶ No heating elements (Mr. Coffee, portable heaters) in the same outlet as a PC
  - ▶ No large electric motors (refrigerators, air conditioners) on the same line as the PC
  - ▶ Some kind of power noise protection
- ▶ Check temperature ranges:
  - ▶ Maximum 110 degrees F (43 degrees C)
  - ▶ Minimum 65 degrees F (18 degrees C)

The minimum temperature can be considerably lower so long as the computer remains *on* all of the time.

- ▶ Heavy dust—you can buy (from PC Power and Cooling) power supplies with a filtered fan that suck air in through the *back* rather than the usual approach of pulling it in through the front.
- ▶ Make sure there isn't a vibration source like an impact printer on the same table as the hard disk.
- ▶ Make sure you're familiar with or (if you're a support person) teach your users about:
  - ▶ Leaving the machines on all the time
  - ▶ Keeping cables screwed in and out of the way
  - ▶ Basic "don't do this" things in DOS, like formatting the hard disk
- ▶ Protect against static electricity.

Part v

WHAT'S NEXT?

Congratulations! This is the last chapter in the book! You can refer to the Appendixes to learn about more about Windows 98, the Internet, and HTML. Or, you can take a break for now and start putting your new Internet skills to use.

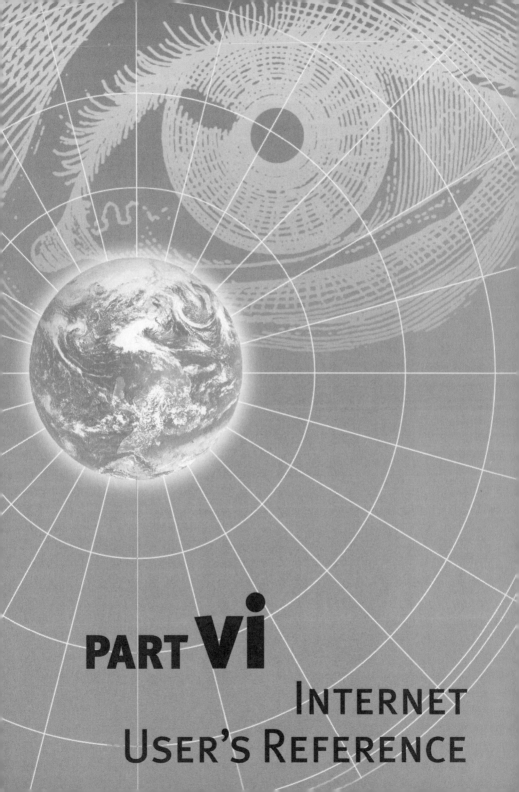

PART VI

INTERNET USER'S REFERENCE

Appendix A

WINDOWS 98 COMMAND AND FEATURE REFERENCE

Adapted from *Windows 98 Instant Reference*, by Peter Dyson
ISBN 0-7821-2191-8   352 pages $14.99

ACTIVE DESKTOP

 In Windows 98, you can use a conventional Windows interface similar to that in earlier versions of Windows, or you can use the Active
Desktop. The Active Desktop brings the world of the Web right to the Windows 98 Desktop, allowing you to replace the static Windows wallpaper
with a fully configurable, full-screen Web page. The Active Desktop can
contain other Web pages, dynamic HTML; even Java components such
as stock tickers and ActiveX controls, and you can add these elements to
the Taskbar or to a folder.

NOTE
You can combine the Active Desktop and Internet Explorer's subscription capabilities to create your own personal push-content client, displaying data on
your Desktop from whatever sources interest you. For example, you can display a continuously updating stock ticker or sports results right on your Desktop; assuming of course that you have continuous Internet access.

To set up your Active Desktop, choose Start ➤ Settings ➤ Active
Desktop, and you will see three options: View As Web Page, Customize
My Desktop, and Update Now. You can also right-click the Desktop and
select Active Desktop from the menu.

View As Web Page

Turns on the Active Desktop interface. Selecting this option a second
time removes the checkmark and turns the Active Desktop off again.

Customize My Desktop

Opens the Display Properties dialog box. You can also right-click the
Desktop and select Properties, or if you prefer, choose Start ➤ Settings ➤
Control Panel and select the Display icon. The Display Properties dialog
box contains six tabs, but we are only concerned with the following two:

Background   Lets you choose an HTML document or a picture
to use as your Desktop background. In the Wallpaper box, select
the background you want to use, or click Pattern to choose or
modify the background pattern. You can also click the Browse
button to locate a file or to go directly to a Web site to find the

HTML document you are interested in using as a background. To cover your entire Desktop with a small wallpaper image, select Tile from the Display box, or choose Center if you prefer to see the image centered. Click the Apply button to see the effect of your changes before you exit the Display Properties dialog box, or click OK to accept the changes and close the dialog box.

TIP
You can also right-click any Web page graphic that takes your fancy and then click Set As Wallpaper.

Web   Lets you select and organize Active Desktop elements. At the top of the tab, you will see a representation of your Desktop, indicating the location of any Active Desktop elements. These same elements are listed in the box below. To add a new element such as a stock ticker or a weather map, click New to open the New Active Desktop Item dialog box. If you want to browse through Microsoft's Active Desktop Gallery on Microsoft's Web site for a component to add, click Yes. To select a different Web site, click No, and then enter the address or URL for the Web site, or click the Browse button to locate it. Be sure that the View my Active Desktop as a Web page box is checked if you want your Desktop to look like a Web page.

NOTE
You can also right-click any link on a Web page, drag it to your Desktop, and then click Create Active Desktop Item Here.

Update Now

Updates the Desktop contents right now to display any changes you have made.

ADD NEW HARDWARE

Guides you through the process of adding new hardware to your system using the New Hardware Wizard. This Wizard automatically makes the appropriate changes to the Registry and to the configuration files so that Windows 98 can recognize and support your new hardware. Be sure you have installed or connected your new hardware before you go any further.

→ *See* Chapter 7 for instructions on installing new hardware with the New Hardware Wizard.

ADD/REMOVE PROGRAMS

Installs or uninstalls individual elements of the Windows 98 operating system itself or certain application programs. Installing or removing application or system software components in this way enables Windows 98 to modify all the appropriate system and configuration files automatically so that the information in them stays current and correct.

To start Add/Remove Programs, choose Start ≻ Settings ≻ Control Panel, and then click the Add/Remove Programs icon to open the Add/Remove Programs Properties dialog box. This dialog box contains four tabs if you are connected to a local area network; otherwise, it contains three tabs.

Install/Uninstall Tab

To install a new program using the Add/Remove Programs applet, follow these steps:

1. Select the Install/Uninstall tab if it isn't already selected, and then click the Install button.

2. Put the application program CD or floppy disk in the appropriate drive, and click the Next button to display a setup or install message, describing the program to be installed.

3. To continue with the installation process, click the Finish button. To make any changes, click Back and repeat the procedure.

To uninstall a program previously installed under Windows 98, you must follow a different process. The programs that have uninstall capability (not all of them do) will be listed in the display box of the Install/Uninstall tab. Click the program you want to uninstall, and then click the Add/Remove button. You may see a warning message about removing the application. You will be to told when the uninstall is finished.

> **NOTE**
>
> Once you remove an application using Add/Remove Programs, you will have to reinstall it from the original program disks or CD if you decide to use it again.

Windows Setup Tab

Some components of the Windows 98 operating system are optional, and you can install or uninstall them as you wish; the Windows Clipboard Viewer is an example. Select the Windows Setup tab to display a list of such components with checkboxes on the left. If the box has a checkmark in it, the component is currently installed. If the checkbox is gray, only some elements of that component are installed; to see what is included in a component, click the Details button. Follow these steps to add a Windows 98 component:

1. Click the appropriate checkbox.

2. If the component consists of several elements, click the Details button to display a list of them, and check the boxes you want to install.

3. Click OK to display the Windows Setup tab.

4. Click the Apply button, and then click OK.

To remove a Windows 98 component from your system, follow these steps:

1. Click the Details button to see a complete list of the individual elements in the component you want to uninstall.

2. Clear the checkmark from the checkboxes of the elements you want to uninstall, and then click OK to open the Windows Setup tab.

3. Click the Apply button, and then click OK.

Startup Disk Tab

A startup disk is a floppy disk with which you can start, or "boot," your computer if something happens to your hard drive. When you originally installed Windows 98, you were asked if you wanted to create a startup disk. If you didn't do it at that time or if the disk you created then is not usable, you can create one now. Simply insert a disk with at least 1.2MB capacity in the appropriate drive, click Create Disk, and follow the instructions on the screen.

Network Install Tab

In some cases, you can also install a program directly from a network using the Network Install tab. If the Network Install tab is not present in the Add/Remove Programs Properties dialog box, this feature may not have been enabled on your computer or on your network; see your system administrator for more details.

If the Install/Uninstall tab is selected, your system is currently connected to the network, and you can click Install followed by Next to find the setup program for your network.

If the Network Install tab is selected, follow the instructions on the screen.

ADDRESS BOOK

Manages your e-mail addresses, as well as your voice, fax, modem, and cellular phone numbers. Once you enter an e-mail address in your Address Book, you can select it from a list rather than type it in every time. To open the Address Book, choose Start ➤ Programs ➤ Internet Explorer ➤ Address Book, or click the Address Book icon on the Outlook Express toolbar.

Importing an Existing Address Book

Address Book can import information from an existing address book in any of the following formats:

- ▶ Windows Address Book
- ▶ Microsoft Exchange Personal Address Book
- ▶ Microsoft Internet Mail for Windows 3.1 Address Book
- ▶ Netscape Address Book
- ▶ Netscape Communicator Address Book
- ▶ Eudora Pro or Lite Address Book

► Lightweight Directory Access Protocol (LDAP)

► Comma-separated text file

To import information from one of these address books, follow these steps:

1. Choose Start ➤ Programs ➤ Internet Explorer ➤ Address Book, or click the Address Book icon on the Outlook Express toolbar.

2. Choose File ➤ Import ➤ Address Book to open the Address Book Import Tool dialog box.

3. Select the file you want to import, and click Import.

Creating a New Address Book Entry

To add a new entry to your Address Book, click the New Contact button on the Address Book toolbar or choose File ➤ New Contact to open the Properties dialog box. This dialog box has six tabs:

Personal   Lets you enter personal information including the person's first, middle, and last names, a nickname, and an e-mail address. If the person has more than one e-mail address, click Add and continue entering addresses.

Home   Allows you to enter additional information about this contact; enter as much or as little information as makes sense here.

Business   Allows you to enter business-related information; again, enter as much or as little information as makes sense.

Other   Offers a chance to store additional information about this contact as a set of text notes.

NetMeeting   Lets you enter NetMeeting information such as a person's conferencing e-mail address and server name. If Net-Meeting is not installed on your system, this tab will be called Conferencing.

Digital IDs   Allows you to specify a digital certificate for use with an e-mail address.

Setting Up a New Group

You can create groups of e-mail addresses to make it easy to send a message to all the members of the group. You can group people any way you like—by job title, musical taste, or sports team allegiance. When you want to send e-mail to everyone in the group, simply use the group name instead of selecting each e-mail address individually. To begin creating a new group, click the New Group icon on the Address Book toolbar or choose File ➤ New Group to open the Group Properties dialog box.

ADDRESS TOOLBAR

| Address 🗁 My Documents ▼ | Shows the location of the page currently displayed in the main window; this may be a

URL on the Internet or an intranet, or it may be a file or folder stored on your hard disk.

To go to another page, click the arrow at the right end of the Address toolbar to select the appropriate entry, or simply type a new location. When you start to type an address that you have previously entered, the Auto-Complete feature recognizes the address and completes the entry for you.

The Address toolbar is available in most Windows 98 applications, including the Explorer, Internet Explorer, My Computer, the Control Panel, and others.

BACKUP

Creates an archive copy of one or more files and folders on your hard disk and then restores them to your hard disk in the event of a disk or controller failure or some other unforeseen event.

BROWSE

| Browse... | The Browse button is available in many common dialog boxes when you have to choose or enter a file name, find a folder, or specify a Web address or URL. Clicking the Browse button or the Find File button opens the Browse dialog box.

You can look through folders on any disk on any shared computer on the network to find the file you want. When you find the file, folder, computer, or Web site, double-click it to open, import, or enter it in a text box.

CD PLAYER

Allows you to play audio compact discs on your CD-ROM drive. Choose Start ➤ Programs ➤ Accessories ➤ Multimedia ➤ CD Player to open the CD Player dialog box.

CHAT

➥ *See* NetMeeting

CLIPBOARD

A temporary storage place for data. You can use the Cut and Copy commands as well as the Windows screen capture commands to place data on the Clipboard. The Paste command then copies the data from the Clipboard to a receiving document, perhaps in another application. You cannot edit the Clipboard contents; however, you can view and save the information stored in the Clipboard by using the Clipboard Viewer, or you can paste the contents of the Clipboard into Notepad.

WARNING

The Clipboard only holds one piece of information at a time, so cutting or copying onto the Clipboard overwrites any existing contents.

CLOSING WINDOWS

Closing an application program window terminates the operations of that program. In Windows 98, you can close windows in a number of ways:

  ▶ Click the Close button in the upper-right corner of the program title bar. ☒

► Choose Control ➤ Close (identified by the icon to the left of the program name in the title bar) or simply double-click the Control Menu icon.

► Choose File ➤ Close or File ➤ Exit within the application.

► If the application is minimized on the Taskbar, right-click the application's icon and choose Close or press Alt+F4.

CONNECTION WIZARD

Walks you through the steps of setting up your Internet connection. All you need is an account with an ISP (Internet Service Provider), and you're all set. You can start the Connection Wizard in several ways:

► Choose Start ➤ Programs ➤ Internet Explorer ➤ Connection Wizard.

► From the Windows 98 Help system, choose the Using the Internet Connection Wizard topic.

► Choose Start ➤ Settings ➤ Control Panel ➤ Internet to open the Internet Properties dialog box, and then select the Connection tab and click the Connect button.

► In Internet Explorer, choose View ➤ Internet Options to open the Internet Options dialog box, and then select the Connection tab and click the Connect button.

No matter which method you use, you first see the Welcome screen; click the Next button to continue. The Setup Options dialog box gives you three choices:

► Open a new account with an ISP. Select the first option if you do not have an account. The Wizard takes you through the steps of finding an ISP and starting an account and sets up the dial-up link for you.

► Establish a connection to an existing Internet account. Select the second option to set up a connection to your existing Internet account or to revise the settings for your current account.

► Make no change to your existing account. If you choose this option and click the Next button, the Wizard closes because there is nothing for it to do.

Creating a New Connection to the Internet

To create a new dial-up connection to the Internet, start the Connection Wizard, click Next at the Welcome screen, and then follow these steps:

1. In the Setup Options dialog box, choose the first option to select an ISP and set up a new Internet account, and then click Next.

2. The Connection Wizard now begins the automatic part of the setup by loading programs from your original Windows 98 CD. You may be asked to restart your computer; the Wizard will resume automatically. Be sure you complete all the steps; otherwise, the Wizard may not be able to set up your connection properly.

3. If you have a modem, the Wizard attempts to locate an ISP in your area and sets up the appropriate Dial-Up Networking software on your system. Follow the prompts on the screen to complete the setup.

Modifying an Existing Connection to the Internet

You can modify your existing Internet account settings at any time. Start the Connection Wizard, click Next at the Welcome screen, and then follow these steps:

1. In the Setup Options dialog box, select the second option to set up a new connection to an existing Internet account.

2. Choose the method you use to connect to the Internet, either by phone line or through your local area network, and click Next.

3. In the Dial-Up Connection dialog box, check the Use an Existing Dial-Up Connection box, select the connection from the list box, and click the Next button.

4. You'll then be asked if you want to modify the settings for this connection. Click Yes, and then click Next to open the Phone Number dialog box where you can enter the phone number to dial to make the connection.

5. In the next dialog box, enter your user name and password information, and click Next.

6. In the Advanced settings dialog box you are asked if you want to change any of the advanced settings for this connection, such as connection type, logon script filename, and IP address. You should only change these settings when your ISP or system administrator tells you to and provides the new information to use. Click Next.

7. You'll then be asked if you want to set up an Internet e-mail account; click Yes and then Next to specify whether you want to use an existing account or create a new one. If you opt to continue using an existing account, you will be asked to confirm your e-mail account settings; if you establish a new account, you will have to enter this information from scratch. Click Next.

8. Next, you'll be asked if you want to set up an Internet news account; follow the instructions on the screen.

9. Finally, click the Finish button to complete the configuration and close the Wizard.

CONTROL PANEL

Provides a way to establish settings and defaults for all sorts of important Windows features. To access the Control Panel, choose Start ≻ Settings ≻ Control Panel.

If you are using the conventional Windows interface, you will see a window that looks like this:

To open an applet, double-click it, or click once on its icon to select it and then choose File ≻ Open.

If you are using the Active Desktop and you have View As Web Page turned on, you will see a much different Control Panel:

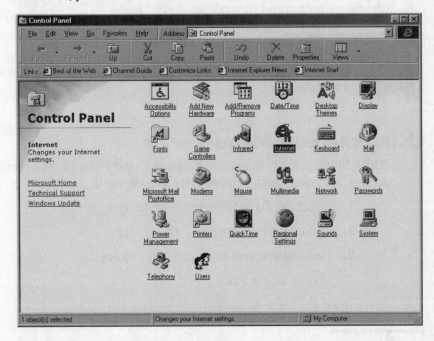

The Control Panel now looks and works like a Web page displayed in a browser. All the names of the applets are underlined, and the mouse pointer turns into a hand when you move the cursor over an icon. You will also see a short description of what each Control Panel applet does on the left side of the window. More important, it now takes only a single mouse-click to open an applet.

COPYING FILES AND FOLDERS

When you copy a file or a folder, you duplicate it in another location and leave the original in place. In Windows, you can copy files and folders in three ways. Let's take a look.

Using Drag-and-Drop

To use the drag-and-drop method, both the source and the destination folders must be open on the Desktop. Press and hold the Ctrl key while holding down the left mouse button, and drag the file or folder from one location to another. When the file or folder is in the correct place, release the mouse button and then release the Ctrl key.

WARNING

Be sure to hold down Ctrl. If you do not, the file or folder will be moved rather than copied.

Using the Edit Menu

The Edit menu in My Computer, Explorer, or any folder window provides a Copy and Paste feature. Follow these steps to use it:

1. Select the file or folder you want to copy.

2. Choose Edit ➤ Copy.

3. Find the destination file or folder and open it.

4. Choose Edit ➤ Paste.

You will see the name of the file in the destination folder.

TIP

You can select multiple files or folders to be copied by holding down Ctrl and clicking them. If the files are contiguous, you can also use Shift to select files.

Using the Right Mouse Button

Right-clicking a file or a folder opens a pop-up menu that you can use to perform a number of functions, including copying. To copy using the right mouse button, follow these steps:

1. Locate the file or folder you want to copy, and right-click to open the pop-up menu. Select Copy.

2. Open the destination folder, click the right mouse button, and select Paste.

You will see the name of the file in the destination folder.

CREATING NEW FOLDERS

Sooner or later you will want to add a new folder to a disk or to another folder, and you can do so in Explorer. Follow these steps:

1. In Explorer, select the disk or folder in which you want to place a new folder.

2. Choose File ➤ New ➤ Folder.

A new folder is added to the disk or the folder you indicated with the name "New Folder" highlighted.

3. Type a new folder name, something that will act as a reminder as to the files it contains, and press Enter.

You can also right-click in the blank part of the Windows Explorer file pane to open a pop-up menu from which you can choose New ➤ Folder.

TIP

If you would rather bypass Explorer altogether, you can create a new folder on the Desktop by clicking My Documents and then choosing File ➤ New ➤ Folder. Give the folder a new name, and then drag it to the Desktop.

DATE/TIME

The clock that appears in the right corner of the Taskbar displays the system clock, which not only tells you the time, but also indicates the time and date associated with any files you create or modify. At any time, you can place the mouse pointer on the time in the Taskbar to display the complete date. To vary the format of the date and time displayed in the Taskbar, select the Regional Settings applet in the Control Panel.

To set the clock, follow these steps:

1. Double-click the time in the Taskbar, or choose Start ➤ Settings ➤ Control Panel ➤Date/Time to open the Date/Time Properties dialog box.

2. Select the Date & Time tab to set the day, month, year, or current time.

3. To change the time, either drag across the numbers you want to change beneath the clock and type the new time, or highlight the numbers and click the up and down arrows to increase or decrease the values.

4. To change the date, click the drop-down arrow to select the month, use the up and down arrows to change the year, and click the appropriate day of the month.

DELETING FILES AND FOLDERS

You can delete a file or a folder in several ways. First, select the file or folder you want in My Computer or Windows Explorer, and then do one of the following:

▶ Choose File ➤ Delete. After you confirm that you want to delete the file or folder, Windows sends it to the Recycle Bin.

▶ Press the Delete key on the keyboard and verify that you want to delete the selected file or folder; Windows then sends it to the Recycle Bin.

▶ Right-click the file or folder to open the pop-up menu. Select Delete and then verify that you want to delete the selected file or folder. Off it goes to the Recycle Bin.

▶ Position the My Computer or Explorer window so that you can also see the Recycle Bin on the Desktop; then simply drag the selected file or folder to the Recycle Bin.

NOTE

If you accidentally delete a file or folder, you can choose Edit ➤ Undo Delete or retrieve the file or folder manually from the Recycle Bin. You cannot retrieve a deleted file or folder if the Recycle Bin has been emptied since your last deletion.

TIP

To delete a file without placing it in the Recycle Bin, select the file and then press Shift+Delete. You cannot recover the file if you do this. You will be asked to confirm the deletion.

DESKTOP

What you see on the screen when you first open Windows. If you are not using any of the Web-like features of the Active Desktop, you see the conventional Windows Desktop. Initially, it contains a set of icons arranged on the left, plus the Taskbar with the Start button across the bottom. As you work with Windows and load application programs, other objects such as dialog boxes and messages boxes are placed on the Desktop.

You can also change the appearance of the Desktop by right-clicking it and selecting Properties. This allows you to change display properties for the Desktop background and screen savers. You can also change the monitor type, as well as font types, sizes, and colors for objects on the screen.

DISK CLEANUP

A quick and convenient way to make more space available on your hard disk. Choose Start ➤ Programs ➤ Accessories ➤ System Tools ➤ Disk Cleanup to open the Disk Cleanup dialog box.

Alternatively, you can open Explorer or My Computer, right-click the disk you want to work with, and then choose Properties from the pop-up menu. On the General tab, click the Disk Cleanup button.

DISK SPACE

To find out how much disk space a file or folder occupies, select it (hold down the Ctrl key to select more than one) in My Computer or Explorer. The window's status bar will display the number of objects selected and the amount of disk space they occupy.

Alternately, you can choose File ➤ Properties or right-click a file or folder and select Properties. The General tab displays the amount of disk space or, in the case of a folder, its size plus the number of files or other folders it contains.

To see how much disk space remains on the entire disk, select the disk name in My Computer or Explorer and then choose File ➤ Properties or right-click and choose Properties. The Properties dialog box displays both the amount of used and the amount of free space. The status bar of My Computer also displays the free space and capacity of a disk drive.

DISPLAY

Controls how the objects on you screen—patterns, colors, fonts, sizes, and other elements—look. Choose Start ➤ Settings ➤ Control Panel ➤ Display (or simply right-click the Desktop and select properties) to open the Display Properties dialog box. It has six tabs: Background, Screen Saver, Appearance, Effects, Web, and Settings.

DOCUMENTS

Choosing Start ➤ Documents displays a list of all the documents you have created or edited recently. If you select a document from the list, Windows opens the document in the appropriate application, making this a quick way to continue working on an interrupted project.

Windows maintains this list of documents and preserves it between Windows sessions even if you shut down and restart your computer. The last 15 documents are preserved in this list, but some of them may look more like applications or folders than documents.

To clear the list of documents and start the list over, choose Start ➤ Settings ➤ Taskbar & Start Menu. Select the Start Menu Programs tab and click the Clear button. Once you do this, only one entry will remain in the list, the shortcut to the My Documents folder.

DRAG-AND-DROP

You can use drag-and-drop to move, copy, activate, or dispose of files and folders on the Desktop and in many accessory and application windows. Place the mouse pointer on a file, press the left button, and drag the file or folder to another disk or folder. Position the pointer over the destination and release the mouse button. The result depends on the file or folder being dragged and the destination:

▶ Dragging a file or folder to another folder on the same disk moves it (hold down the Ctrl key if you want to copy the file or folder).

▶ Dragging a file or folder to another disk copies it.

▶ Dragging a file to a shortcut printer icon on the Desktop prints the document.

▶ Dragging a file or folder to the Recycle Bin disposes of it.

ENTERTAINMENT

Menu used to access the Windows multimedia applications. Choose Start ➤ Programs ➤ Accessories ➤ Entertainment. This menu includes CD Player, Media Player, Sound Recorder, TV Viewer, and others.

EXPLORER

The Windows Explorer (to use its full name) is *the* place to go when working with files and folders in Windows 98. The Explorer lets you look at your disks, folders, and files, in a variety of ways and helps you perform such tasks as copying, moving, renaming, and deleting files and folders, formatting floppy disks, and so on.

Explorer Menus

To access Explorer, choose Start ➤ Programs ➤ Windows Explorer, or right-click the Start button and choose Explore. You may want to create a shortcut for it on the Desktop or in the Start menu itself since it is used so often.

The Explorer menus give you access to all common functions. However, for some menu selections to work, you may first have to select an appropriate object in the main Explorer window, and the type of object you select determines the available options. You may, therefore, not see all these options on any given menu, and you may see some options not listed here. You will also find similar menus in My Computer, the Recycle Bin, and Network Neighborhood.

File Menu

Displays basic file-management options. It allows you to do the following:

▶ Open a folder or file

▶ Explore the contents of a selected computer, disk, or folder

▶ Print a file or get a Quick View of the contents of a file (not shown on the menu unless it is available)

▶ Set parameters for sharing a folder with other users

▶ Send a file to a floppy disk, to an e-mail or fax correspondent (using Windows Messaging), to My Briefcase, or to another destination

- ▶ Create a new folder or a shortcut

- ▶ Make a shortcut to a file or folder

- ▶ Delete or rename a file or folder

- ▶ Display a file's properties

- ▶ Close a file or a folder

If you are working with the Printers folder, you will also see options to Capture Printer Port and to End Capture.

Edit Menu

Allows you to work with the contents of a folder or file. It allows you to do the following:

- ▶ Undo the previous action

- ▶ Cut, copy, and paste folders or files

- ▶ Paste a shortcut within a folder

- ▶ Select all files and folders

- ▶ Select all files except those already selected, which become deselected

View Menu

Allows you to change the window to include or exclude the toolbars, Status bar, and Explorer bar. You can choose how the files and folders are displayed:

- ▶ As a Web page

- ▶ With large icons or small icons

- ▶ In a list

- ▶ With details, describing the size and type of a file and the date modified

You can arrange icons by name, type of file or folder, size, or date created or last modified. You can also arrange icons into columns and rows. Refresh redisplays your screen. Folder Options lets you set defaults for how information is displayed in the main Explorer window, and Customize This Folder lets you change the appearance of the folder.

Go Menu

Lets you go back, forward, or up one level and gives fast access to certain Web sites and other Windows elements such as Mail, News, My Computer, Address Book, and Internet Call.

Favorites Menu

The Favorites menu is divided into two parts. You use the first part to manage your favorite Web sites with Add to Favorites and Organize Favorites, as well as those Web sites to which you subscribe with Manage Subscriptions and Update All Subscriptions. You use the second part for fast access to groups of Web sites with Channels, Links, and Software Updates.

Tools Menu

Gives you quick access to Find so that you can find Files or Folders, Computer, On the Internet, or People. You can also map a networked drive and disconnect a networked drive.

Help Menu

Provides access to the Windows Help system.

TIP

Some functions available from the Explorer menus are also available as buttons on the toolbar.

Explorer Toolbar

The following buttons are available on the standard Explorer toolbar:

Back   Displays the item you last displayed. Click the small down arrow just to the right of this button to see a list of all the items you have displayed in this Explorer session and click an item to go to it directly.

Forward   Displays the item you were viewing before you went back to the current item. Click the small down arrow just to the right of this button to display a list of items. Click an item to go to it directly.

Up   Moves up the directory tree in the left Explorer window, changing the contents displayed in the right window as it goes.

 Cut   Moves the selected items to the Clipboard.

 Copy   Duplicates selected items, placing their content on the Clipboard.

 Paste   Transfers the contents of the Clipboard to a file or folder. A destination folder must already exist and must be selected.

Undo   Cancels the previous action. The label changes depending on what you did last—for example, Undo Delete or Undo Copy.

Delete   Places the selected file or folder in the Recycle Bin.

Properties   Opens the Properties dialog box for the selected disk, file, or folder.

Views   Changes the way information is displayed in the right-hand Explorer window. Click the small down arrow just to the right of this button to display a menu you can use to select the various displays. Alternatively, each time you click the Views button, the display cycles through these four views:

Large Icons   Displays larger-sized icons representing the contents of the selected folder or disk.

Small Icons   Displays smaller-sized icons in a horizontal, columnar list representing the contents of the selected folder or disk.

List   Displays the contents as small icons, except in a vertical rather than horizontal orientation.

Details   Displays the contents in a detailed list with additional information about the file size, file type, and modification date.

The Explorer also contains two other toolbars:

Address   Displays the location of the item currently displayed by the Explorer. The arrow at the right end of the Address toolbar opens a drop-down list of items; select one to open it.

Links   Displays a set of hyperlinks to various parts of Microsoft's Web site; you can also access these links from the Links selection in the Favorites menu.

You will also see a single status line across the bottom of the main Explorer window; it displays messages about your actions and lists information on disk storage space, including the number of items in a folder and the occupied and free disk space.

Explorer Window

When you run the Explorer, all items that make up your computer are listed in the left pane. Some objects have a plus sign (+) next to them, indicating that the object contains other objects that are not currently visible. To display the contents of such an item in the right pane, click the item, not the plus sign.

When you click the plus sign associated with an object, you display all the subelements, usually folders, in the left window, where they become part of the overall tree structure. The plus sign becomes a minus sign (−) if an object's contents are expanded. This tree structure is a graphical representation of how the files and folders on your system are related; the name of each folder appears just after its icon.

Customizing a Folder

Choose View ➤ Customize This Folder to open the Customize This Folder Wizard with these options:

Create or Edit an HTML Document   Lets you create an HTML (Hypertext Markup Language) document in three steps:

1. Open the editor and create the HTML document.

2. Save the document.

3. Close the editor.

Choose a Background Picture   Lets you select a picture that will be displayed as wallpaper when you open this folder.

Remove Customization   Lets you return this folder to its original look and feel.

Selecting a Drive and Choosing a File or a Folder

When you open the Explorer, all the disks and folders available on your computer are displayed in the left pane. The right pane displays the contents of the disk or folder you selected on the left. Follow these steps to find a file or a folder:

1. Scroll up and down using the left scroll bar. On the left, you can see all the disks on your computer, plus those that are shared on your network, and all the folders within each disk. On the right, you will see all the folders and files within the selected disk or folder.

2. If the drive you want is not visible, you may have to expand the My Computer icon by clicking its plus sign. Normally, you will be able to see a floppy disk and at least one hard disk.

3. Click a disk or folder in the left pane to display its contents in the right pane; when a folder is selected, its icon changes from a closed folder to an open one.

4. Once you find the file or folder you want, open it and get to work.

FAVORITES

Contains selections you can use to track your favorite Web sites. You can open your favorite Web sites from many places within Windows 98. You can choose Start ➤ Favorites, or you can use the Favorites menu in Windows Explorer, My Computer, Internet Explorer, Network Neighborhood, and Control Panel; even the Recycle Bin has a Favorites menu.

Add to Favorites

Choose Favorites ➤ Add to Favorites to bookmark a Web site so that you can find it again quickly and easily. Once you place the address, or URL, for the site in this list, you can revisit the site simply by selecting it from the Favorites menu; the result is the same as if you had typed the whole URL into the Address toolbar and pressed Enter. You can also display your Favorites menu from the Explorer Bar; choose View ➤ Explorer Bar ➤ Favorites.

Organize Favorites

Choose Favorites ➤ Organize Favorites to group your Web sites into an arrangement that makes sense to you; a single long list is certainly not the most efficient organization.

Subscribing to a Web Site

In addition to visiting Web sites in the normal way with Internet Explorer, you can also subscribe to a Web site. A subscription is a mechanism that Internet Explorer uses to check for new or updated content on a Web site without your involvement.

FAX

 Sends and receives faxes between computers or fax machines. You can send a fax in several ways:

▸ Drag a text or graphics file to the Microsoft Fax icon in the Printers folder.

▸ Right-click an icon and select the Send to Fax Recipient command.

▸ Select Microsoft Fax as the printer in any application program.

▸ Use Windows Messaging.

▸ Choose Start ➤ Programs ➤ Accessories ➤ Fax ➤ Compose New Fax.

No matter which of these techniques you use, the Compose New Fax Wizard will guide you through creating and sending a fax. Once you have a suitable profile set up under Start ➢ Programs ➢ Windows Messaging, the rest is a breeze.

TIP

To install Fax, you must have Microsoft Exchange, Windows Messaging, or Outlook already installed on your system.

Compose New Fax

Follow these steps to compose a new fax message:

1. Open the Compose New Fax dialog box using one of the techniques discussed earlier.

2. If you are using a laptop (and therefore may not always be calling from the same location), click Dialing Properties and review the methods used to dial an outside line. If you are not using a portable computer, you can click *I'm not using a portable computer, so don't show this to me again.* Click Next.

3. Complete the information on the person to whom you want to send the fax. Type a name, country, fax number, and a recipient list, if applicable.

4. Select whether to send a cover page and its type. Click Options to open the Send Options for This Message dialog box.

5. Specify the following settings for this fax:

   Time to Send   Specifies when the fax will actually be transmitted. Choose from As Soon as Possible, Discount Rates (click Set to specify the times when discount rates take effect), or a Specific Time (which you set using the up and down arrows).

   Message Format   Specifies whether the recipient can edit the fax message. You can send a message that is Editable, if Possible (the fax will be sent in the binary editable format; the recipient must also have Microsoft Fax to be able to edit the fax), Editable Only (Microsoft

Fax will try to send the fax as binary files and will refuse to send the message if the receiving system cannot accept that format), or Not Editable (the fax is sent as a bitmap).

Paper   Establishes the paper specifications, including size, orientation (landscape or portrait), and image quality—choose from Draft (200×100 dpi), Fine (200×200 dpi), 300dpi, or Best Available.

Cover Page   Confirms your choice of cover page.

Dialing   Specifies how fax numbers are dialed, how many times you want to retry a busy or unavailable number, and the waiting period between such retries. Click Dialing Properties to set the default location you normally dial from, the dialing prefix, and credit card information. Click Toll Prefixes to identify phone-number prefixes that are inside your default area code but which require you to use the area code.

Security   Specifies the security method to use with this fax. You can choose from None, Key-Encrypted (which uses a public-key encryption technique), and Password-Protected (the recipient must enter the same password you used when creating the fax to read the message).

6. When you have made your selections, click OK to return to the Compose New Fax dialog box. Click Next.

7. Type the subject of the fax, and in the Note box, type the contents of your fax message. Check the checkbox if you want the Note contents to be part of the cover page. Click Next.

8. If you want to send a file with this fax, click Add File to open the Open a File to Attach dialog box. Locate the file, and then click Open. The name will appear in the Files to Send text box. Click Next.

9. Your fax is now complete, and all you have to do to send it is click the Finish button. You will see two icons in the notification area of the Taskbar for the fax and dialing actions.

Request a Fax

You can also use Fax to call a remote computer, information service, or fax machine to retrieve a specific document; and you can retrieve all the documents available. Once the call is complete, the documents are placed in your Inbox. Follow these steps:

1. Choose Start ➢ Programs ➢ Accessories ➢ Fax ➢ Request a Fax to open the Request a Fax dialog box.

2. To retrieve all faxes stored at the remote site, click Retrieve Whatever Is Available. To retrieve one particular document, click Retrieve a Specific Document, and then type the name of the document and its password (if there is one) in the two boxes in the lower part of the dialog box. Click Next.

3. Type the name of the person to whom the retrieved fax will be routed in the To box. To retrieve a name from the Address Book, click that button, select a name, and then click Add. Verify the country, and type the fax number. Click Next.

4. To specify when you want to call, select from As Soon As Possible, When Phone Rates Are Discounted, or A Specific Time. Click Next.

5. Click Finish to complete the request.

TIP

To review the list of faxes scheduled to be sent, open Inbox and choose Tools ➢ Microsoft Fax Tools ➢ Show Outgoing Faxes to open the Outgoing Faxes dialog box. You'll see the sender, subject, size, recipients, and time to send.

FIND

Windows 98 adds several powerful items to the Find menu, which now includes options for finding files and folders, a computer, information on the Internet, or people. Choose Start ➢ Find and select an option, or choose Tools ➢ Find in Explorer.

Find Files or Folders

To find a file or folder, you can either use My Computer or Explorer to scan the disks yourself, or you can use the Find command to have

Windows 98 conduct the search for you. To use the Find command, choose Start ➤ Find ➤ Files or Folders, or in Explorer, choose Tools ➤ Find ➤ Files or Folders.

In the Find: All Files dialog box, you will see three tabs: Name & Location, Date Modified, and Advanced.

Name & Location Tab
Contains the following options:

Named   Displays the name of the file or folder for which you're searching. Click the down arrow to display a list of your most recent searches.

Containing Text   Lets you specify any text that you want to locate.

Look In   Tells Windows to search a specific path for the file or folder. Click the down arrow to display a list of the disks and folders on your computer.

Browse   Lets you look through the available disks and folders to find the one you want.

Include Subfolders   Searches sublevels of folders as well as the level you specified.

Date Tab
Contains the following options:

All Files   Searches all files in the specified path for the desired file or folder.

Find All Files   Restricts the search to files created, last accessed, or modified between two specified dates, during the previous number of months, or during the previous number of days.

Advanced Tab
Contains the following options:

Of Type   Searches for a specific type of file. Click the down arrow to display a list of registered types.

Size Is   Restricts the search for files to At Least or At Most (selected by the first down arrow) the number of kilobytes specified (typed or entered using the arrow keys).

Enter the Find specifications you want, and then select one of the following buttons:

Find Now   Starts the search.

Stop   Ends the search.

New Search   Allows you to enter new search criteria.

To save a search, including its parameters, choose File ➢ Save Search. To save the results of a search, choose Options ➢ Save Results. To make a search case-sensitive, choose Options ➢ Case Sensitive.

Find a Computer

To locate a computer on your network using the Find command in either the Start menu or Explorer, follow these steps:

1. Chose Start ➢ Find ➢ Computer, or in Explorer, choose Tools ➢ Find ➢ Computer to open the Find Computer dialog box.

2. Enter the computer name or select it from a list of previous searches by clicking the Named down arrow.

3. Click Find Now to activate the search. Stop terminates the search, and New Search allows you to enter the criteria for a new computer search.

Find on the Internet

The Find menu's On the Internet option uses Internet Explorer to connect to the Web site at home.microsoft.com/search/search.asp This site gives you access to some of the most powerful and popular search engines on the Internet, including Infoseek, AOL NetFind, Lycos, Excite, and Yahoo.

You can also use one of the other sites in the categories of General Search, Guides, White Pages, Newsgroups, Chat Guides, Specialty, or International. If you can't find what you are looking for using one of these search engines, what you are looking for doesn't want to be found.

Find People

The Find menu's People option lets you searches public LDAP (Lightweight Directory Access Protocol) directories on the Internet such as Bigfoot (www.bigfoot.com), Four11 (www.four11.com), and WhoWhere? (www.whowhere.com) for particular information. Here are the steps:

1. Choose Start ➤ Find ➤ People, or in Explorer, choose Tools ➤ Find ➤ People to open the Find People dialog box.

2. In the Look In list, select the name of the directory service you want to use

3. Type the information on the person you are looking for, usually just the first name followed by the last name, and then click Find Now.

The results of a search may vary depending on which of the services you use, but you will normally see a long list of names with different e-mail addresses. It is then up to you to decide which of those names is actually the person you want to contact.

FOLDER OPTIONS

In Explorer, choose View ➤ Folder Options (or Start ➤ Settings ➤ Folder Options) to open the Folder Options dialog box, in which you specify how your folders will look and work. The Folder Options dialog box contains three tabs: General, View, and File Types. When you open the Folder Options dialog box in My Computer, Network Neighborhood, and the Recycle Bin, you will see two tabs: General and View.

General Tab

Defines how the following systemwide settings work on your computer:

Web Style   Specifies that your folders work with a single click just like the Web. Icon names will be underlined, and the normal arrow-shaped mouse pointer will turn into a hand as it passes over the icon.

Classic Style   Specifies that your folders behave in the traditional Windows way. Click once to select an item; double-click to open or run an item.

Custom, Based on Settings You Choose   Specifies that you want to choose your own configuration. Click the Settings button to set these preferences.

View Tab

Controls advanced settings for files and folders. The Folder Views box contains two options you can use to make all the folders on your system look and work in the same way:

Like Current Folder   Uses the current settings in effect in the View menu (except for the toolbar settings) on all folders on your computer.

Reset All Folders   Uses the original View menu settings in effect when the program was first installed.

The Advanced Settings box contains a set of checkboxes for certain display options, such as how to treat hidden files, whether file attributes are shown in the Details view, and so on. Click the Restore Defaults button to put everything back into its original state.

File Types Tab

Displays all the file types currently registered with Windows; this is how Windows knows which program to use to open specific data files. When you select a file type in the list, the File Type Details box displays a short summary of which file name extension belongs to that type, its MIME content type, and the name of the program used to open it.

To change or delete one of the existing types, select it in the Registered File Types box, and then choose Edit or Remove. Click the New Type button to register a new file type with Windows. Here are the steps:

1. Click the New Type button to open the Add New File Type dialog box.

2. In the Description of Type field, enter a short text description along the lines of the other entries used, such as Active Streaming File Format.

3. Type the file name extension in the Associated Extension field.

4. Select an existing MIME Content_Type from the drop-down list, or enter a new MIME type.

5. Click the New button, and in the Actions field, enter the oper-
    ation you want to perform; common operations are Open (to
    open the file) and Print. Then, in the Application Used to Per-
    form Action field, enter the full path and file name of the
    application you want to associate with this file type. Click OK
    when you are done.

6. Click OK to return to the File Types tab in the Folder options
    dialog box.

FONTS

The styles of type used when Windows displays or prints text.
Windows maintains a library of fonts that all applications that
run under it use. Choose Start ➤ Settings ➤ Control Panel ➤
Fonts to open the Fonts folder, which displays all the fonts installed on
your computer. Windows applications primarily use two types of fonts:

▶ TrueType fonts (represented by a pair of *T*s in the icon)

▶ Adobe fonts (represented by an *A* in the icon), which are bitmapped
  or vector fonts

The View menu of the Fonts folder offers two unique and quite useful
views for fonts: List Fonts by Similarity, which groups fonts that are reasonably alike; and View ➤ Hide Variations, which hides bold, italics, and
other variant forms of a typeface.

Fonts Used in Windows 98

The defaults for the size and type of fonts used in the Windows 98 windows and dialog boxes are set in the Display Properties dialog box. You
can vary the font and size for text objects and in menus, message boxes,
and title bars.

Right-click the Desktop and choose Properties from the pop-up menu
to open the Display Properties dialog box, or choose Start ➤ Settings ➤
Control Panel ➤ Display. You use the Appearance and Settings tabs to
control the size of fonts on the screen and the size and typeface of fonts
for selected objects on the screen.

Adding a New Font to Your Computer

If you have acquired some new fonts, you can add them to those that come with Windows 98 by following these steps:

1. Choose Start ≻ Settings ≻ Control Panel ≻ Fonts to open the Fonts folder.

2. Choose File ≻ Install New Font to open the Add Fonts dialog box.

3. Select the drive and then select the folder that contains the new font.

4. Click the font you want to add. Hold down the Ctrl key and then click to select more than one font.

Displaying and Printing Font Samples

Once you have collected a large number of fonts, remembering what each one looks like can be difficult. Fortunately, the Windows 98 Font Viewer can help. To use it, follow these steps:

1. Open the Font folder.

2. Select any icon in the folder to open that font in the Font Viewer. Open additional Font Viewer windows if you want to compare two or more fonts.

3. To print an example of the font, click the Print button in the Font Viewer; alternatively, right-click the font in the Font folder and select Print from the pop-up menu.

FORMATTING DISKS

Unless you purchase formatted disks, you must format a floppy disk before you can use it the first time. Formatting a new disk places information on the disk that Windows needs to be able to read and write files and folders to and from the disk. Formatting a used disk erases all the original information it contained and turns it into a blank disk, so be sure that you are formatting the right disk.

FRONTPAGE EXPRESS

A quick-and-easy Web-page editor you can use to create or customize your own Web pages without having to learn the details of Hypertext Markup Language (HTML). You can edit Web-page elements by selecting them in the main FrontPage Express window and then using a toolbar button or menu selection to apply formatting and alignment. →*See* Chapter 20 for instructions on using FrontPage Express.

GAMES

Windows 98 includes four games: FreeCell, Hearts, Minesweeper, and that addictive time-waster, Solitaire. You can play Hearts over the network with other players. To get to the games, choose Start ➤ Programs ➤ Accessories ➤ Games, and then click the game you want to play. If you get stuck, click Help for instructions on how to play.

HELP

Windows 98 contains an extensive help system that provides you with online assistance at almost any time. You can use the main Windows 98 Help System to gain access to a huge amount of information, you can use Windows 98 Troubleshooters to diagnose and isolate a problem relating to specific hardware or software, and you can use Web Help to connect directly to Microsoft's Web site to look for program updates.

Windows Help System

Choose Start ➤ Help to open the main Windows 98 Help System dialog box, which has three tabs:

Contents Lists the main categories in the Help system itself and a general overview of Windows 98.

Index Lists all the subjects in the Help system in one giant alphabetic list. Type the first few letters of the word you're looking for in the text box at the top of this tab, and the list box will automatically scroll to the subject closest in spelling to what you have typed. Or you can scroll to it yourself by using the scroll bars on the right of the display box. When you get to the subject you want, select it and click Display.

Search   Allows you to find specific words or phrases contained within a Help topic. To do this, Windows 98 must create a database containing words used throughout the Help system. When you click the Search tab for the first time, the Search Setup Wizard creates this database. You can then use the Search tab to find the specific word or phrase you want.

When a Windows 98 Help topic is displayed, you may see a link icon. Click it to open the specific application, dialog box, or other element under discussion. When you close the application, you return to the same place in the Help system.

Using the Built-In Troubleshooters

Windows 98 extends the usual concepts of the Help system to include a set of built-in technical support troubleshooters you can use to help diagnose and isolate certain problems. There are two ways to find the right Troubleshooter and start it running on your system:

- ▶ You can choose Start ➢ Help to open the Windows 98 Help System. Select the Contents tab, select the Troubleshooting topic, and then open Windows 98 Troubleshooters. Choose the appropriate Troubleshooter from the list and follow the directions on the screen.

- ▶ Alternatively, you can start a Troubleshooter directly from a page of Help information. As you read through the information the page contains, you will come across a link to a Troubleshooter; click the link to start the Troubleshooter.

Once the Troubleshooter starts, click the Hide button on the Help toolbar to close the left pane. Be sure to follow all the steps the Troubleshooter suggests.

Troubleshooters are available for problems encountered with networking, printing, startup and shutdown, hardware such as modems, and procedures such as dial-up networking and connecting to the Microsoft Network.

Getting Web Help

Click the Web Help button on the Help System toolbar to connect to a Microsoft site to look for updated versions of programs and device drivers. You then select what you want to install; perhaps more important, you can also uninstall a program or a device driver that is causing you problems.

Help in a Dialog Box

Context-sensitive Help is also available in certain dialog boxes and on some property sheets in Windows 98. You may see a Help button on a dialog box; click it to see information specific to that dialog box.

Other dialog boxes and many of the Windows 98 property sheets have a Help button in the upper-right corner (look for the button with a question mark on it) next to the Close button. Click this Help button and the question mark jumps onto the cursor; move the cursor to the entry on the property sheet that you want help with and click again. A small window containing the help text opens; click the mouse to close this window when you are done.

INTERNET

 In Windows 98, you can view or change the configuration options relating to the Internet in two ways:

▶ Via your connection to the Internet

▶ In Internet Explorer

To open the Internet Options dialog box, choose Start ➤ Connections ➤ Control Panel ➤ Internet, or open Internet Explorer and choose View ➤ Internet Options. The Internet Options dialog box has six tabs.

General Tab

The General tab contains these groups of settings:

Home Page   Lets you choose which Web page opens each time you connect to the Internet. The home page is the first Web page you see when you start Internet Explorer.

Temporary Internet Files   Lets you manage those Web pages that are stored on your hard disk for fast offline access.

History   Contains a list of the links you have visited so that you can return to them quickly and easily. You can specify the number of days you want to keep pages in the History folder.

Colors   Lets you choose which colors are used as background, links, and text on those Web pages for which the original author did not specify colors. By default, the Use Windows Colors option is selected.

Fonts   Lets you specify the font style and text size to use on those Web pages for which the original author did not make a specification.

Languages   Lets you choose the character set to use on those Web pages that offer content in more than one language.

Accessibility   Lets you choose how certain information is displayed in Internet Explorer, including font styles, colors, and text size. You can also specify that your own style sheet is used.

Security Tab

Lets you specify the overall security level for each of four zones. Each zone has its own default security restrictions that tell Internet Explorer how to manage dynamic Web-page content such as ActiveX controls and Java applets. The zones are:

Local Intranet   Sites you can access on your corporate intranet; security is set to medium.

Trusted Sites   Web sites you have a high degree of confidence will not send you potentially damaging content; security is set to low.

Internet   Sites you visit that are not in one of the other categories; security is set to medium.

Restricted Sites   Sites that you visit but do not trust; security is set to high.

To change the current security level of a zone, select it from the list box, and then click the new security level you want to use:

High   Excludes any content capable of damaging your system. This is the most secure setting.

Medium Opens a warning dialog box in Internet Explorer before running ActiveX or Java applets on your system. This is a moderately-secure setting that is good for everyday use.

Low Does not issue any warning but runs the ActiveX or Java applet automatically. This is the least secure setting.

Custom Lets you create your own security settings. To look at or change these advanced settings, click the Settings button to open the Security Setting dialog box. You can individually configure how you want to manage certain categories, such as ActiveX controls and plug-ins, Java applets, scripting, file and font downloads, and user authentication.

Content Tab

Contains settings you can use to restrict access to sites and specify how you want to manage digital certificates:

Content Adviser Lets you control access to certain sites on the Internet and is particularly useful if children have access to the computer. Click Settings to establish a password, and then click OK to open the Content Advisor dialog box. Use the tabs in this dialog box to establish the level of content you will allow users to view:

> **Ratings** Lets you use a set of ratings developed by the Recreational Software Advisory Council (RSAC) for language, nudity, sex, and violence. Select one of these categories, and then adjust the slider to specify the level of content you will allow.

> **General** Specifies whether people using this computer can view material that has not been rated; users may see some objectionable material if the Web site has not used the RSAC rating system.

> **Advanced** Lets you look at or modify the list of organizations providing ratings services.

Certificates Lets you manage digital certificates used with certain client authentication servers. Click Personal to view the personal digital certificates installed on this system, click Authorities to list the security certificates installed on your system, or click

Publishers to designate a particular software publisher as a trust-worthy publisher. This means that Windows 98 applications can download, install, and use software from these agencies without asking for your permission first.

Personal Information   Lets you look at or change your own personal profile; this information is sent to any Web sites that request information when you visit their site. Click Edit Profile to review the current information.

Click Reset Sharing to clear the list of sites you previously allowed to access your personal information without asking your permission first. Microsoft Wallet gives you a secure place to store credit card and other information you might need for Internet shopping.

Connection Tab

Allows you to specify how your system connects to the Internet:

Connection   Lets you specify whether your system will connect to the Internet via your corporate network or by modem. Click the Connect button to run the Connection Wizard and set up a connection to an Internet Service Provider (ISP). If you use a modem, click the Settings button to open the Dial-Up Settings dialog box where you can specify all aspects of the phone connection to your ISP.

Proxy Server   Lets you access the Internet via a proxy server system connected to your corporate intranet. A proxy server is a security system designed to monitor and control the flow of information between your intranet and the Internet.

Automatic Configuration   Lets you network system administrator configure your copy of Internet Explorer automatically.

Programs Tab

Lets you set your default program choices for e-mail, newsgroup reader, and so on and specify whether Internet Explorer should check to see if it is configured as the default browser:

Messaging   Lets you choose which application programs are used for mail, news, and Internet calls.

Personal Information   Lets you choose which application programs are used for calendar functions and for your contact list.

Finally, you can specify that Internet Explorer check to see if it is configured as the default browser on your system each time it starts running.

Advanced Tab

Lets you look at or change a number of settings that control much of Internet Explorer's behavior, including accessibility, browsing, multimedia, security, the Java environment, printing and searching, and the Internet Explorer toolbar and how HTTP 1.1 settings are interpreted.

Changes you make here stay in effect until you change them again, until you download an automatic configuration file, or until you click the Restore Defaults button, which returns the settings on the Advanced tab to their original values.

INTERNET EXPLORER

The application that displays Web pages from the Internet or from your corporate intranet. In many ways, Internet Explorer resembles Windows Explorer; it is a *viewer* that presents information in a structured way. Internet Explorer is an easy-to-use program that hides a large part of the complexity of the Internet and Internet operations.

Help Menu

Gives you access to the Internet Explorer Help system through Contents and Index, lets you check for a newer version of Internet Explorer available through Product Updates, guides you through an online tutorial with Web Tutorial, and helps locate information on technical problems with Online Support.

When you choose Help ➤ Microsoft on the Web, the items on the submenu are actually links to different parts of the Microsoft Web site, including:

Free Stuff   Locates Internet Explorer program updates, free stuff, and add-on programs.

Get Faster Internet Access   Displays information about ISDN (Integrated Services Digital Network) service.

Frequently Asked Questions   Answers the most commonly asked questions about Internet Explorer.

Internet Start Page   Opens your home page.

Send Feedback   Lets you send your opinions right to Microsoft.

Best of the Web   Opens Microsoft's Exploring page, which contains a variety of links to useful and interesting sites. This is equivalent to clicking the Best of the Web button on the Internet Explorer Links toolbar.

Search the Web   Opens the same Web site as choosing Go ➤ Search the Web.

Microsoft Home Page   Opens Microsoft's Web site.

Configuring Internet Explorer

To view or set the many configuration options for Internet Explorer, choose View ➤ Internet Options to open the Internet Options dialog box. Or you can choose Start ➤ Connections ➤ Control Panel ➤ Internet. The Internet Options dialog box has six tabs. For a complete discussion of all the settings on these tabs, see the Internet entry earlier in this appendix.

Browsing Offline

You can browse the Web with Internet Explorer without being connected to the Internet. This is because many of the files that you open while browsing the Web are stored in the Temporary Internet Files folder on your hard disk. Choose File ➤ Work Offline, and Internet Explorer will not attempt to connect to the Internet when you select a resource, but will display the copy in the Temporary Internet Files folder instead. To go back to online browsing, choose File ➤ Work Offline a second time.

Speeding Up Internet Explorer

The text component of a Web page downloads quickly, but some of the other common elements, such as graphics, sound files, and animation clips, can take quite a long time to download.

Of course, there is nothing you can do to change the way a Web site is constructed, but you can stop certain types of files from being downloaded to Internet Explorer. You can essentially tell Internet Explorer to ignore all graphics files or all video clips and just collect the text. Here are the steps:

1. In Control Panel, click Internet, or choose View ➤ Internet Options within Internet Explorer to open the Internet Options dialog box.

2. Select the Advanced tab.

3. Scroll down the list box until you see the Multimedia settings, all of which are selected by default.

4. Deselect all the items you want to exclude from the Web pages you download to your system.

5. Click OK to close the Internet Options dialog box.

Remember that these options stay in effect for all subsequent Internet Explorer sessions until you turn them back on.

INSTALLING APPLICATIONS

You can install applications from floppy disks and CD-ROMs using the Add/Remove Programs applet in the Windows 98 Control Panel. You can also choose Start ➤ Run to invoke an individual Install or Setup program.

KEYBOARD

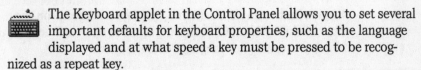 The Keyboard applet in the Control Panel allows you to set several important defaults for keyboard properties, such as the language displayed and at what speed a key must be pressed to be recognized as a repeat key.

To look at or change the keyboard properties, choose Start ➤ Settings ➤ Control Panel ➤ Keyboard to open the Keyboard Properties dialog box. It has two tabs: Speed and Language. The Speed tab contains the following options:

Repeat Delay   Sets the length of time you must hold down a key before the repeat feature kicks in.

Repeat Rate   Sets the speed at which a character is repeated while a key is held down.

Click Here and Hold Down a Key to Test Repeat Rate   Tests the repeat delay and repeat rate speeds that you have chosen.

Cursor Blink Rate   Sets the rate at which the cursor blinks, making the cursor easier to spot in some instances.

The Language tab contains the following options:

Language and Layout   Displays the language and keyboard layout loaded into memory when the computer is first started. Double-click the highlighted language or layout to open the Language Properties dialog box and select another keyboard layout.

Add   Adds a language and keyboard layout to those loaded into memory when the computer is booted.

Properties   Allows you to change the keyboard layout default.

Remove   Deletes the selected language and keyboard layout. It will no longer be loaded into memory when you boot the computer.

Set As Default with More Than One Language Installed
Makes the currently selected language and keyboard layout the default to be used when the computer is started.

Switch Languages   Switches between two or more language and layout settings, as listed above. Click the key combination you want to use to switch the default.

Enable Indicator on Taskbar   Displays a language on the right of the Taskbar. Click this indicator to open a dialog box in which you can switch language defaults quickly.

LOG OFF

Windows 98 maintains a set of user profiles, each containing a different user name, password, Desktop preferences, and accessibility options. When you log on to Windows 98, your profile ensures that your Desktop settings—including elements such as your own desktop icons, background image, and other settings—are automatically available to you.

Windows 98 contains an option you can use to log off and log on again as another user quickly and easily. Click the Start button, and then click

Log Off *username*. In the Log Off Windows dialog box, click Yes. This closes all your programs, disconnects your system from the network, and prepares the system for use by other users.

Log On

When you log on to Windows 98 and are prompted to enter your user name and password, your user profile is loaded to ensure that your Desktop settings—including elements such as your own desktop icons, background image, and other settings—are automatically available to you.

Unfortunately, you can also press the Esc key to bypass this logon screen and completely circumvent all aspects of Windows logon security. This makes Windows 98 a particularly unsecure system.

If you are connected to a local area network and Windows 98 is configured for that network, you will also be prompted to enter your network password.

Maximize/Minimize Buttons

Allows you to change the size of an application window.

The Maximize button is in the upper-right corner of an application window, and when you click it, the window expands to full-screen size. Once the window has expanded, the Maximize button changes to the Restore button, which you can then use to shrink the window back to its original starting size.

You can also place the mouse pointer on the window border, and when the two-headed arrow appears, drag the border in the direction in which you want to change its size.

Use the Minimize button to place an open application on the Taskbar; click the Taskbar icon when you are ready to work with the application again.

Media Player

Allows you to play multimedia files, such as video, animation, and sound clips, depending on the hardware installed on your computer system.

MODEMS

 Allows you to look at or change the settings Windows uses with your modem. Choose Start ➤ Settings ➤ Control Panel ➤ Modems to open the Modem Properties dialog box.

MOUSE

Changes your mouse settings. Choose Start ➤ Settings ➤ Control Panel ➤ Mouse to open the Mouse Properties dialog box, which contains three tabs. If you make changes to the settings in any of these tabs, click the Apply button to make sure your changes are implemented and then click OK.

Buttons Tab

Sets the mouse button configuration and speed with these options:

Button Configuration   Allows you to switch functions from the default right-handed use of the mouse buttons to left-handed.

Double-Click Speed   Allows you to set and then test the speed at which a double-click is recognized.

Pointers Tab

Allows you to change the appearance of the mouse pointer. For example, you can change the pointer used to indicate that Windows is busy from an hour-glass to a symbol or caricature of your choice.

The Scheme box contains the list of pointer schemes available in Windows. By selecting one, you'll see the set of pointers in the scheme displayed in the box below. You can create additional schemes by replacing the individual pointers.

Motion Tab

Controls the pointer speed and the presence of a pointer trail, which makes the mouse pointer much easier to see on LCD screens. If you select a pointer trail, you can also choose whether it is a long or a short trail.

MOVING FILES AND FOLDERS

In Windows, you can move files and folders in three ways:

▶ By dragging-and-dropping

▶ By choosing Edit ➤ Cut and Edit ➤ Paste

▶ By clicking the right mouse button

When you move a file or folder, you move the original to another location—no duplicate is made.

Using Drag-and-Drop

To use drag-and-drop, both the source and the destination folders must be visible, for example, in Explorer or on the Desktop. Hold down the left mouse button and drag the file or folder from one location to the other. When the file or folder reaches the correct destination folder, release the mouse button. The source and destination folders must be on the same drive. If you drag a file or a folder to a different drive, it will be copied rather than moved. If you want to move a file or folder to a different drive, you must drag using the right mouse button.

Using the Edit Menu

The Edit menu in My Computer, Explorer, or any folder window provides a Cut and Paste feature. Here are the steps to follow:

1. Select the file or folder you want to move.

2. Choose Edit ➤ Cut, or click the Cut button on the toolbar.

3. Find the destination file or folder and open it.

4. Choose Edit ➤ Paste, or click the Paste button on the toolbar.

TIP

You can select multiple contiguous files or folders to move by holding down Shift and clicking the first and last file or folder. To select noncontiguous files or folders, hold down Ctrl and click the files or folders you want.

Using the Right Mouse Button

Right-clicking a file or folder opens the pop-up menu, which you can use to perform a variety of functions, including moving. Follow these steps:

1. Right-click the file or folder you want to move and select Cut from the pop-up menu.

2. Open the destination folder, right-click, and then select Paste.

TIP

If you drag a folder or a file with the right mouse button, a pop-up menu opens when you release the button, allowing you to copy the object, move it, or create a shortcut.

MOVING AND ARRANGING ICONS

In Windows, you can arrange icons using any of several methods. In Explorer, Control Panel, and many other windows, you can move or arrange icons using the selections in the View menu:

Large Icons   Displays the files and folders as larger-sized icons.

Small Icons   Displays the files and folders as smaller-sized icons.

List   Displays small icons alongside the names of the files and folders.

Details   Displays files and folders in the List style and adds columns for the size of file, date last modified, and type of file. To sort entries within these columns, simply click the column heading. Click once for an ascending sort (A to Z and 0 to 9); click a second time for a descending sort.

Line Up Icons   Rearranges icons into straight vertical and horizontal lines.

TIP

To rearrange icons on the Desktop, simply drag them to their new location. To tidy up the Desktop quickly, right-click an area of free space, and choose Arrange Icons.

By clicking the Views button on the Explorer toolbar, you can cycle the display through the four presentations of Large Icons, Small Icons, List, and Details; each time you click the button, the display changes to the next format.

MULTIMEDIA

Establishes the default settings for multimedia devices connected to your computer; its contents depend on which multimedia devices you have installed.

Choose Start ➤ Settings ➤ Control Panel ➤ Multimedia to open the Multimedia Properties dialog box, containing tabs appropriate to the hardware installed on your computer. You might see the following tabs:

Audio   Sets playback and recording controls.

Video   Specifies the size of the video playback window.

MIDI   Sets Musical Instruments Digital Interface controls and adds new instruments.

CD Music   Sets the drive letter and head phone volume defaults.

Devices   Lists the multimedia hardware connected to your computer and allows you to set or change properties for any of the hardware listed. Select the hardware component you want to configure, and then click Properties to open the related dialog box.

MY COMPUTER

One of the file-management tools available with Windows. You can use My Computer to locate folders, files, and disks or printers on your computer or on mapped drives on other computers connected to the network.

My Computer Folder

Click the My Computer icon on the Desktop to open the My Computer folder, showing an icon for each drive and drive-level folder on your computer. Click an icon to display the contents of one of these folders or drives in a separate window.

Finding a File or Folder with My Computer

When you open My Computer, the My Computer folder displays all the disks and folders on your computer. Follow these steps to find the file or folder you want:

1. Click the down arrow at the end of the Address toolbar to find the device or folder you want. You will see all the shared disks on your network, important folders such as Control Panel, Printers, and Dial-Up Networking, and other Windows elements, such as Internet Explorer, Network Neighborhood, Recycle Bin, and My Briefcase.

2. Click a disk or a folder to see its contents in the window.

3. Once you find the file or folder (which may be several levels down), click it to open it.

MY DOCUMENTS

A Desktop folder that provides a convenient place to store graphics, documents, or any other files you might want to access quickly. When you save a file in programs such as Paint or WordPad, the file is automatically saved in My Documents unless you specify a different destination folder.

To specify a different destination folder, right-click My Documents and select Properties. Type the name of the new folder in the Target field and click OK. Changing to a different folder does not move existing files stored in My Documents.

NAMING DISKS

You can give a hard or a floppy disk a name that can be a maximum of 11 characters. To name or rename a disk, follow these steps:

1. Open My Computer or Explorer.

2. Right-click the disk you want to name, and select Properties to open the Properties dialog box.

3. Select the General tab, and type the name you want to use for this disk in the Label field. Click OK.

NAMING FILES AND FOLDERS

The first time you save a file using the Save or Save As command, you are asked to provide a name for the file. When you create a new folder, it is always called New Folder until you change the name. Names for files and folders can contain a maximum of 255 characters, including spaces, but cannot contain any of these special characters: / \ ? : * " < > |

You can rename both files and folders in Explorer or My Computer. Follow these steps:

1. Open Explorer or My Computer and find the file or folder you want to rename.

2. Click the name once, pause, and then click it again. A box will enclose the name, and the name will be selected. If you move the mouse inside the box, the pointer will become an I-beam.

3. Type the new name or edit the existing name and press Enter.

NETMEETING

A conferencing application that allows people working in different locations to collaborate simultaneously on the same project, sharing Microsoft applications to edit documents. NetMeeting also supports audio and video conferencing over the Internet (as long as you have the appropriate hardware such as a video camera or microphone attached to your computer system), as well as a file-transfer function.

Choose Start ➤ Programs ➤ Internet Explorer ➤ Microsoft NetMeeting to open NetMeeting.

ONLINE SERVICES

Allows you to access several popular online services such as AOL and the Microsoft Network. Before you can use any of these services, you must first register with it. You can do this using the items in the Online Services menu; each item connects you to a specific service. You can also use the Online Services folder on the Desktop.

Before you start, connect your modem to the phone line, and close any other open applications.

Outlook Express

 Windows application used to send and receive e-mail and read and post messages to Internet news groups. To start Outlook Express, click the Outlook Express Desktop icon, or choose Start ➤ Programs ➤ Internet Explorer ➤ Outlook Express. You can also click the Launch Outlook Express button on the Quick Launch toolbar, or use the Mail menu from within Internet Explorer.

Chapters 4 and 5 show how to use Outlook Express for basic operations such as sending and receiving e-mail, as well as managing address books and mail folders. Following are additional highlights.

Reading the News

Outlook Express is also a newsreader, that you can use to access the thousands of specific-subject newsgroups on the Internet.

WARNING

Anything goes in many of these Internet newsgroups. There is absolutely no censorship, and if you are easily offended (and even if you are not), you might want to stay with the more mainstream Web pages.

In the same way that you set up an e-mail account with an ISP, you must also set up a newsgroup account, complete with password, before you can use Outlook Express as a newsreader.

Configuring Outlook Express

Configuration options for Outlook Express are quite extensive. You can customize the toolbar and add buttons for the tasks you perform most often, and you can define the rules you want Outlook Express to follow when you are creating, sending, and receiving e-mail. Choose Tools ➤ Options to open the Options dialog box. It has the following tabs:

General   Contains general-purpose settings for Outlook Express.

Send   Specifies the format for sending mail and articles to news-groups, as well as several other mail-related options, such as whether to include the text of the original message in any reply.

Read   Specifies options used when displaying articles from newsgroups.

Security   Establishes security zones and specifies how Outlook Express manages digital certificates (also known as digital IDs).

Dial Up   Specifies the options used when connecting to your ISP by dial-up connection.

Advanced   Specifies options only of interest to system administrators.

You can also choose View ➤ Layout to open the Layout Properties dialog box. Click Customize Toolbar to add or remove buttons from the Outlook Express toolbar. To return the toolbar to its original layout, click Customize Toolbar again, and then click Reset followed by Close in the Customize Toolbar dialog box.

PAINT

A program with which you can create lines and shapes, with or without color, and place text within graphics. You can also use it to create backgrounds for the Desktop. Choose Start ➤ Programs ➤ Accessories ➤ Paint to open the main Paint window.

Paint Toolbar

Provides tools for drawing and working with color and text. Below the toolbar is an area containing optional choices depending on the type of tool you chose. For example, if you choose the Brush tool, a selection of brush edges is displayed. If you choose Magnifier, a selection of magnifying strengths is displayed. At the bottom of the main window, the Color Palette displays a series of colored squares.

The toolbox contains the following buttons for drawing lines and shapes and for working with color:

 Free-Form Select   Selects an irregularly shaped area of the image to move, copy, or edit.

Select   Selects a rectangular area of the image to move, copy, or edit.

Eraser/Color Eraser   Erases an area of the image as you move the eraser tool over it.

Fill with Color   Fills an enclosed area with the currently selected color.

Pick Color   Selects the color of any object you click. It is for use with the tool that you chose immediately before you selected Pick Color.

Magnifier   Enlarges the selected area.

Pencil   Draws a free-hand line one pixel wide.

Brush   Draws lines of different shapes and widths.

Airbrush   Draws using an airbrush of the selected size.

Text   Inserts text onto the drawing. Click Text, click the color you want for the text, and then drag a text box to the location where you want to insert the text. In the font window that appears, click the font, size, and style (Bold, Italic, Underline) you want. Click inside the text box, and begin typing your text.

Line   Draws a straight line. After dragging the tool to create a line segment, click once to anchor the line before continuing in a different direction, or click twice to end the line.

Curve   Draws a curved line where one segment ends and another begins. After dragging the tool to create a line segment, click once to anchor the line before continuing. To create a curve, click anywhere on the line and then drag it. Click twice to end the line.

Rectangle   Creates a rectangle. Select the fill style from the toolbar below the main Paint window.

Polygon   Creates a polygon, or figure consisting of straight lines connecting at any angle. After dragging the first line segment, release the mouse, place the pointer where the second line segment is to end, click the mouse button, and repeat until the drawing is complete. Click twice to end the drawing.

Ellipse   Draws an ellipse. Select the fill style from the Color Palette below the main Paint window.

Rounded Rectangle   Creates a rectangle with curved corners. Select the fill style from the Color Palette below the main Paint window.

When you create an image in Paint, first select the tool, then select the tool shape, if applicable, and then click the color you want to use from the Color Palette at the bottom of the Paint window. The currently active color is displayed in the top square on the left of the palette. To change the background color, click Pick Color, and then click the color you want. The next image you create will use the new background color.

Paint Menus

Contain many of the standard Windows options. In addition, you can set a saved paint File to be used as wallpaper, zoom in various ways, flip or rotate an image, invert its colors, define custom colors, and set various image attributes.

PASSWORDS

Allows you to specify a logon password. Windows maintains a set of user profiles, each containing a different user name, password, Desktop preferences, and accessibility options. When you log on to Windows, your profile ensures that your Desktop settings, including elements such as your own Desktop icons, background image, and other settings, are automatically available to you.

Enabling User Profiles

To enable user profiles, follow these steps:

1. Choose Start ➢ Settings ➢ Control Panel ➢ Passwords to open the Passwords Properties dialog box.

2. Select *Users can customize their preferences and Desktop settings.*

3. In the User Profile Settings box; you can select one option or both:

   ▶ Include Desktop icons and Network Neighborhood content in user settings.

   ▶ Include Start menu and Program groups in user settings.

4. You'll have to use Shut Down to restart your computer for these changes to be applied.

Specifying a Password

When you start Windows 98 for the first time, you are prompted to enter a user name and password and then to confirm that password. If you are connected to a network, you may also be asked to enter a network password. On all subsequent startups, this series of dialog boxes will be slightly different. You will only be asked to enter the password; you will not have to confirm it.

Changing a Password

To change a password, follow these steps:

NOTE
You must know the current password in order to change it.

1. Choose Start ➤ Settings ➤ Control Panel ➤ Passwords to open the Passwords Properties dialog box.

2. Select the Change Passwords tab, and then click the Change Windows Password button to open the Change Windows Password dialog box.

3. Type the old password (asterisks will appear as you type), and enter the new password; you will have to retype the new password to confirm it. Click OK to close the Change Windows Password dialog box.

4. Click OK to close the Passwords Properties dialog box and finalize your new password. Next time you log on to Windows, remember to use your new password.

In addition to your logon password, you can establish a password for the following resources:

Dial-Up Connections   To change passwords, click My Computer, click the Dial-Up Networking icon, and select Connections ➤ Dial-Up Server. Click Allow Caller Access to enable the Change Password button.

Disks   To set and change passwords, right-click the disk in the Explorer window and select Sharing from the pop-up menu.

Folders   To change the password or sharing status, open Explorer or My Computer, select the folder, choose File ➤ Properties, and then click the Sharing tab.

Printers   To change the password or sharing status, open the Printers folder from either Explorer, My Computer, or Control Panel. Right-click the printer and select Sharing from the pop-up menu.

Network Administration   Set password access to shared devices from the Access Control tab in the Network applet in the Control Panel.

Screen Savers   You can use a password to prevent others from gaining access to your files when a screen saver is active. To change a password, choose Start ➤ Settings ➤ Control Panel ➤ Display to open the Display Properties dialog box. Select the Screen Saver tab and click Password Protected, and then click the Change button.

Shared Resources   To change the password or sharing status, open Explorer or My Computer, select the resource, choose File ➤ Properties to open the Properties dialog box, and select the Sharing tab. If the resource is shared, you can change the password. You can also change the sharing status from the Access Control tab in the Network applet in the Control Panel.

Click the Change Other Passwords button in the Passwords Properties dialog box to work with these other passwords.

Allowing Remote Administration

You can specify whether a system administrator can create shared folders and shared printers on your computer, and see the user names of anyone who connects to them by using the options on the Remote Administration tab in the Passwords Properties dialog box.

PASTE COMMAND

Copies the contents of the Clipboard into the current document. It is available from the Edit menu and some pop-up menus that are displayed when you right-click a file or a folder.

PLUG AND PLAY

A Windows feature that automatically detects hardware installed in your computer system. Today, most hardware is specifically designed with Plug and Play in mind. You just install the hardware, and Windows takes care of the details, loading the appropriate device drivers and other related software automatically.

Plug and Play adapters contain configuration information stored in permanent memory on the board, including vendor information, serial number, and other configuration data. The Plug and Play hardware allows each adapter to be isolated, one at a time, until Windows identifies all the cards installed in your computer. Once this task is complete, Windows can load and configure the appropriate device drivers. After installing a new Plug and Play adapter in your computer system, Windows will often ask you to restart the system. This is so the new device drivers can be loaded into the correct part of system memory.

PRINTERS

Manages all functions related to printers and printing. From here you can add a new printer, check on a job in the print queue, change the active printer, or modify a printer's properties.

PROGRAMS

Lists the programs available in Windows, either as stand-alone applications or as collections of applications located in submenus or program groups. Any selection that has an arrow pointer to the right of the name is not a single program but a program group. Choosing one of these groups opens another menu listing the items in the group.

Follow these steps to start a program from the Programs menu:

1. Choose Start ➤ Programs to display the current list of program groups.

2. Select a program group to display a list of the programs it contains.

3. Click an application name to start it.

Adding a New Submenu to the Programs Menu

Most Windows programs are added to the Programs menu automatically as they are installed—you are generally asked to verify in which folder or program group any new program should be placed—and the Setup program takes care of the rest. However, you can create a new submenu manually if you wish. Follow these steps:

1. Right-click the Start button and choose Open to open the Start Menu folder.

2. Select the Programs folder, and then choose File ➤ New ➤ Folder. This creates an empty folder in the Program group with the name New Folder.

3. Enter the name you want to use for the submenu as the name of this new folder, press Enter, and then open the folder you just created.

4. Choose File ➤ New ➤ Shortcut to start the Create Shortcut Wizard, which guides you through the process of adding applications to your new folder.

5. Enter the path and file name for the application in the Command Line box, or click the Browse button to locate the file.

6. Type a shortcut name for the program and click Finish.

The next time you open the Programs menu, you will see the entry you just created, and when you select that entry, you will see the list of items that it contains.

PROPERTIES

Characteristics of something in Windows—a computer, a peripheral such as a printer or modem, a file, or a folder—are displayed in the Properties dialog box. The properties for any item depend on what it is. To open any Properties dialog box, follow these steps:

1. Select the item in the Explorer.

2. Choose File ➤ Properties.

You can also open the Properties dialog box by right-clicking an object and then selecting Properties from the pop-up menu.

RECYCLE BIN

 A folder that stores deleted files until they are finally removed from your hard disk. The Recycle Bin is represented on the Desktop by a wastebasket icon. Files are copied to the Recycle Bin both directly and indirectly; you can simply drag a file there, or you can send a file to the Recycle Bin by choosing Delete from a pop-up menu. When you empty the Recycle Bin, the files it contains are permanently removed from your hard disk; once you empty the bin, anything it contained is gone for good.

TIP

If the Recycle Bin contains deleted files, you will see paper protruding from the top of the wastebasket icon.

REGIONAL SETTINGS

Sets the system-wide defaults for country (and therefore language), number, currency, time, and date formatting. If you are using English in the United States, you will probably never need Regional

Settings; if you want to use a different language, this is the place to start. Choose Start ≻ Settings ≻ Control Panel ≻ Regional Settings to open the Regional Settings Properties dialog box.

Regional Tab

On the Regional Settings tab, click the down arrow and select a language and a country.

Number Tab

Sets the defaults for how positive and negative numbers are displayed, the number of decimal places, the separator between groups of numbers, and so on. This tab contains the following options:

Decimal Symbol   Establishes which symbol will be used as a decimal point. The default in the United States is a period.

No. of Digits after Decimal   Specifies how many numbers will be placed to the right of the decimal point. The default is 2.

Digit Grouping Symbol   Determines the symbol that will group digits into a larger number, such as the comma in 999,999. The default is a comma.

No. of Digits in Group   Specifies how many numbers will be grouped together into larger numbers. The default is 3, as in 9,999,999.

Negative Sign Symbol   Establishes which symbol is used to show a negative number. The default is a minus sign.

Negative Number Format   Establishes how a negative number will be displayed. The default is to display the negative sign in front of the number, such as −24.5.

Display Leading Zeroes   Determines whether a zero is shown in front of a decimal number. The default is yes, as in 0.952.

Measurement System   Determines whether the system of measurement will be U.S. or metric. The default is U.S.

List Separator   Specifies which symbol will separate items in a list or series. The default is a comma.

If you make any changes in this tab, click Apply and then OK.

Currency Tab

Determines the format for displaying currency. For example, you might want to vary the number of decimal points or the presentation of negative numbers. This tab contains the following options:

Currency Symbol   Displays the symbol of the currency, such as the dollar sign.

Position of Currency Symbol   Shows where the currency symbol is displayed in the number—usually in front of a number.

Negative Number Format   Specifies how negative numbers are displayed.

Decimal Symbol   Determines which symbol separates the whole from the fractional parts of a number, such as a period or a comma.

No. of Digits after Decimal   Specifies how many digits are shown by default after the decimal—usually two.

Digit Grouping Symbol   Shows which symbol—usually a comma—separates the number groups, such as thousands, millions, and so on.

Number of Digits in Group   Specifies how many digits determine a number group, such as 3 for thousands, millions, and so on.

Click Apply and then OK to put any changes you make into effect.

Time Tab

Establishes the default formatting for the time. The Time tab has the following options:

Time Style   Determines how the time will be formatted.

Time Separator   Determines which symbol separates the hours from the minutes and seconds; the default is a colon.

AM Symbol   Specifies the default for the morning symbol.

PM symbol   Specifies the default for the afternoon symbol.

Click Apply and then OK to activate any changes you make.

Date Tab

Establishes the default formatting for the date. The Date tab has the following options:

Calendar Type   Displays the types of calendars that you can choose from.

Short Date Style   Lists the formats available for displaying the date.

Date Separator   Lists the symbols that can be used to separate the month, day, and year.

Long Date Style   Lists the formats available for displaying a formal date notation.

Click Apply and then OK to activate any changes you make.

RESTORE

Restores an archive copy of one or more files and folders to your hard disk after a disk or controller failure or some other unforeseen event. To start the Windows 98 backup and restore program, choose Start ➣ Programs ➣ Accessories ➣ System Tools ➣ Backup. The first time you start the program, a dialog box welcomes you to Microsoft Backup and leads directly into the Restore Wizard.

Using the Restore Wizard

Using the Restore Wizard is a quick and easy way to learn about restoring backups; it gets you going quickly with a minimum of technical knowledge. Check Restore Backed up Files, and then click OK in this opening dialog box to start the Wizard. If you would rather not use the Wizard, click Close; you can always restart it from the toolbar inside the Backup program if you change your mind.

The Wizard walks you through the following sequence of dialog boxes. Click the Next button when you have made your choice to advance to the next dialog box; click Back to retrace your steps, and click Cancel if you change your mind about using the Wizard.

Restore From   Specify the type and location of the backup you want to restore.

Select Backup Sets   Select a backup set for the restore.

What to Restore   You can restore all files and folders in the backup set, or you can restore selected files and folders.

Where to Restore   Specify the target of the restore; most of the time selecting Original Location to put the file back where it came from makes the most sense.

How to Restore   Specify whether existing files on your hard disk should be overwritten during the restore.

Click the Start button to begin the restore; a small progress indicator tracks the restore as it proceeds.

Using the Restore Tab

Using the Restore tab in the Backup program involves essentially the same tasks that the Restore Wizard does for you—selecting the files, deciding where to put them, and specifying how the restore should actually be made.

NOTE

A check mark in a gray check box means that only some of the files in a folder have been selected. A check mark in a white box means that all files in a folder have been selected.

RUN

Starts a program or opens a folder when you type its path and name. You often use Run with a Setup program or installation programs or to run a program such as Scanreg that does not have a Windows shortcut. Follow these steps:

1. Choose Start ➢ Run to open the Run dialog box.

2. If you have run this program recently, you may find its name already entered in the Open list box. Click the down arrow, select it by name, and then click OK.

3. If you have not run this program recently or if the Open box is blank, type the full path and program name, such as C:*Folder**Program*.

4. If you are not sure of the path or program name, click Browse to find and select the program. Then click OK to load and run the program.

ScanDisk

Checks a disk for certain common errors. Once ScanDisk detects these errors, it can fix them and recover any data in corrupted areas. Windows 98 runs ScanDisk automatically if the operating system is shut down improperly, as might happen during a power outage.

Choose Start ➤ Programs ➤ Accessories ➤ System Tools ➤ ScanDisk to open the ScanDisk dialog box.

Screen Saver

Displays an image on the screen after a fixed period of inactivity. The screen saver hides the normal information displayed by the application you are using and replaces it with another image.

You can change or select a screen saver using the Display applet in the Control Panel. You can set the speed, shape, density, and color of the screen saver, and you can set a password to get back to your work and other settings. You can also use certain active channels as screen savers.

Send To

Send To ▸ Sends items to common destinations, such as floppy disk drives, a fax, an e-mail, or My Briefcase. You can send a file quickly to a destination by following these steps:

1. Right-click the file or folder to open the pop-up menu.

2. Select Send To.

3. Click the appropriate destination.

SETTINGS

 Choose Start ➤ Settings to access all the Windows 98 configuration tools, including the Control Panel, Printers, Taskbar & Start Menu, Folder Options, and the Active Desktop controls.

SHORTCUTS

Quick ways to open an application or access a disk, file, folder, printer, or computer without going to its permanent location using the Windows Explorer. Shortcuts are useful for applications that you use frequently; when you access a shortcut, the file, folder, printer, computer, or program is opened for you. You can create a shortcut using the File menu, pop-up menus, or drag-and-copy.

SHUT DOWN

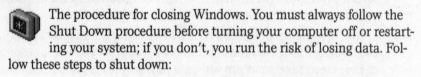 The procedure for closing Windows. You must always follow the Shut Down procedure before turning your computer off or restarting your system; if you don't, you run the risk of losing data. Follow these steps to shut down:

1. When you are ready to turn off your computer, choose Start ➤ Shut Down to open the Shut Down Windows dialog box. It contains the following options:

   Shut Down   Prepares the computer to be turned off.

   Restart   Prepares the computer for shut down and then automatically starts it again.

   Restart in MS-DOS Mode   Closes Windows and restarts the computer in MS-DOS mode.

2. Select the option you want, and then click OK.

3. Respond to any other questions that Windows displays, such as whether it is OK to disconnect network users.

When Windows 98 has finished saving data to your hard disk, it displays a final message telling you that it is now safe to turn off your computer.

SOUNDS

 Assigns sounds to certain system events, such as warning dialog boxes, and to more common events such as opening or closing windows or receiving an e-mail message. Choose Start ➤ Settings ➤ Control Panel ➤ Sounds to open the Sounds Properties dialog box.

START

![Start] The primary way to access files, folders, and programs on your computer. Initially, the Start button is on the bottom left of your screen at the left end of the Taskbar. Click Start to display the Start menu. Some of the options on this menu are standard with Windows 98, but you can add others to give you fast access to your favorite applications.

The Start menu contains the following options:

Shut Down   Prepares the computer to be shut down or restarted.

Log Off   Logs off the system quickly so that you can log back on with a different user profile or so that another user can log on.

Run   Opens the Run dialog box so that you can run a program or open a folder by typing its path and name.

Help   Opens the extensive Windows 98 Help system.

Find   Searches for a file, folder, device, or computer. You can also search the Internet and look for personal contact information.

Settings   Accesses the Control Panel, Printers, Taskbar & Start Menu, Folder Options, and Active Desktop controls so that you can configure the way Windows operates.

Documents   Gives you access to the last 15 documents you opened.

Favorites   Gives you access to Channels, Links, and Software Updates.

Programs   Gives you access to the program groups and files on your computer.

Windows Update   Automatically connects to the Microsoft Web site to check for updates to the Windows 98 operating system.

TIP

To add a program or a shortcut to the Start menu, simply drag its icon to the Start button.

STARTUP

An application that is activated automatically each time you start Windows. If you use certain applications frequently and do not want the bother of starting them manually every time you start Windows, simply put them in your Startup folder. Follow these steps:

1. Choose Start ≻ Settings ≻ Taskbar & Start Menu to open the Taskbar Properties dialog box.

2. Select the Start Menu Programs tab.

3. Click Add, and type the name of the path to the program you want, or click Browse to find it. Click Next.

4. Find the StartUp folder in the list of Start Menu folders, and select it. Click Next.

5. If you don't like the default, type the shortcut name that you want to appear in the StartUp folder, and click Finish.

6. If you are prompted to choose an icon, click one, and then click Finish.

7. To verify that the program you selected is now in the StartUp menu, choose Start ≻ Programs ≻ StartUp.

The next time you start Windows 98, the program you just added to the StartUp folder will be automatically loaded.

TASKBAR

Launches programs and is the primary tool for switching from one application to another. The Taskbar contains several types of icons:

- ▶ The Start button at the left end of the Taskbar is responsible for launching applications, opening documents, and adjusting settings.

- ▶ The Quick Launch toolbar contains buttons you can use to do the following:

  - ▶ Open Internet Explorer

  - ▶ Open Outlook Express

  - ▶ Open TV Viewer

  - ▶ Bring the Desktop to the front

  - ▶ View channels

- ▶ Any shortcut buttons to the right of the Quick Launch toolbar represent the applications currently active in memory or open folders. You can use these icons to switch between the running applications.

- ▶ The system clock at the right end of the Taskbar displays the current time.

The Taskbar may also show other icons from time to time, indicating that an e-mail message is waiting, that you are printing a document, or the battery condition on a laptop computer.

Switching with the Taskbar

When you open a new application, the Taskbar gets another button, and by clicking that button, you can switch to the new application or folder.

Switching with Alt+Tab

You can also use the Alt+Tab key combination to switch between running applications. Press and hold down the Alt key and press the Tab key once to open a dialog box that contains an icon for each application running on your system. Each time you press the Tab key, the outline box moves one icon to the right until it wraps all the way round and reappears on the left side of the box. This outline box indicates the application that will run when you release the Alt key.

TASKBAR & START MENU

 The Taskbar is the main way that you switch from one application to another in Windows 98. The default Taskbar contains two types of buttons: the Start button, and any number of shortcut buttons for the applications currently active in memory.

To change how the Taskbar looks and works, choose Start ➢ Settings ➢ Taskbar & Start Menu to open the Taskbar Properties dialog box. You can also choose a toolbar from a set of default toolbars and add it to your Taskbar; you can even create your own custom toolbar.

> ### TIP
>
> You don't have to leave the Windows Taskbar at the bottom of the screen; you can place it along any of the four edges. To move it, simply drag it to its new location.

Modifying the Taskbar Display

The Taskbar is usually at the bottom of the screen and is always displayed on top of other windows so that you can get to it quickly and easily. To change how the Taskbar is displayed, follow these steps:

1. Choose Start ➢ Settings ➢ Taskbar & Start Menu to open the Taskbar Properties dialog box. You can also simply right-click an empty spot on the Taskbar and select Properties from the pop-up menu.

2. Place a check mark in the box next to the options you want:

   Always on Top   Forces the Taskbar to remain on top of other windows, ensuring that it is always visible to you.

   Auto Hide   Displays the Taskbar as a small thin line on the bottom of the screen. To also display the thin line when a full-screen window is displayed, select both Always on Top and Auto Hide.

   Show Small Icons in Start Menu   Displays a small Start menu with smaller icons.

Show Clock   Displays the time in the left of the Taskbar. By double-clicking the clock, you can reset the time or date.

3. Click Apply to make the changes final, and then click OK.

Adding Toolbars

Windows 98 includes a default set of toolbars that you can add to your Taskbar if you wish:

Address   Allows you to open an Internet address without first opening Internet Explorer.

Links   Contains a set of Internet addresses.

Desktop   Contains all your Desktop icons. Because this toolbar is longer than the screen is wide, you can use the small arrows to see the other icons.

Quick Launch   Contains buttons you can use to do the following:

▸ Open Internet Explorer

▸ Open Outlook Express

▸ Open TV Viewer

▸ Bring the Desktop to the front

▸ View channels

To add one of these toolbars to your Taskbar, right-click an empty spot on the Taskbar, choose Toolbars from the pop-up menu, and then select the toolbar you want to add to your Taskbar.

TIP

You can also add your own shortcut to the Quick Launch toolbar. Open My Computer or Explorer, select the application you want to add, and drag it to the Quick Launch part of the Windows Taskbar. You will see that program's icon appear next to the other icons on the Quick Launch toolbar. To remove an icon from the Quick Launch toolbar, right-click it and choose Delete.

Creating a Custom Toolbar

If the default set of toolbars don't meet your needs, you can always create your own. Follow these steps:

1. Right-click an empty part of the Taskbar to open the pop-up menu.

2. Choose Toolbars ➤ New Toolbar to open the New Toolbar dialog box.

3. Select a folder from the list or type an Internet address that you want to appear as a toolbar.

Another way to build a custom toolbar is to create a new folder, add all your favorite shortcuts to it, and then choose Toolbars ➤ New Toolbar to turn it into a toolbar.

TASK SCHEDULER

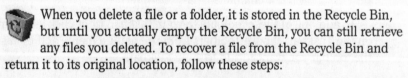 A program you can use to run selected applications at specific times—daily, weekly or even monthly—without any input from you or involvement on your part. The Task Scheduler starts running in the background every time you start Windows 98; it just sits there until it is time to run one of your selected tasks, and then it moves into action.

UNDELETING FILES

When you delete a file or a folder, it is stored in the Recycle Bin, but until you actually empty the Recycle Bin, you can still retrieve any files you deleted. To recover a file from the Recycle Bin and return it to its original location, follow these steps:

1. Click the Recycle Bin on the Desktop.

2. Select the file or files you want to restore.

3. Right-click and choose Restore, or choose File ➤ Restore.

If you have chosen to display the contents of the Recycle Bin as a Web page, you can also click Restore All to return multiple files to their original locations.

TIP

To select multiple files, hold down Ctrl while you click.

UNINSTALLING APPLICATIONS

The Uninstall program removes all traces that an application was ever installed. It removes all references to the program from the Windows directories and subdirectories and from the Windows Registry.

The Uninstall feature is found in the Add/Remove Program Properties dialog box. Follow these steps to uninstall a program:

1. Choose Start ➤ Settings ➤ Control Panel ➤ Add/Remove Programs to open the Add/Remove Programs Properties dialog box.

2. If necessary, select the Install/Uninstall tab.

3. Select the software you want to remove from the list and click Add/Remove.

USERS

Windows 98 maintains a set of user profiles each containing a different user name, password, Desktop preferences, and accessibility options. When you log on to Windows 98, your profile ensures that your Desktop settings—including elements such as your own Desktop icons, background image, and other settings—are automatically available to you.

To set up a new user profile, follow these steps:

1. Choose Start ➤ Settings ➤ Control Panel ➤ Users to open the Enable Multi-User Settings dialog box.

2. Click the Next button.

3. In the Add User dialog box, enter your user name and click Next.

4. In the Enter New Password dialog box, type your password. Type it again in the Confirm Password field and click Next.

5. In the Personalized Items Settings dialog box, select the items from the list that you want to personalize, and then choose whether you want to create copies of these items or create new items in order to save hard-disk space. Click the Next button.

6. Click the Finish button to complete the creation of this new user profile and to close the Wizard.

VOLUME CONTROL

An accessory you can use to control the volume of your sound card and speakers. If you have more than one multimedia capability installed, for example, MIDI or Wave-handling capability, you can control the volume and balance for each device separately. Follow these steps to access the Volume Control:

1. Choose Start ➤ Programs ➤ Accessories ➤ Entertainment ➤ Volume Control to open the Volume Control dialog box. It contains separate features to balance volume for the devices on your computer. Depending on the hardware installed on your computer, the following features may or may not appear:

    Volume Control   Controls volume and balance for sounds coming out of your computer. This is the "master" control.

    Line-In   Controls the volume and balance for an external device that feeds sound into your computer, such as audio tape or an FM tuner.

    Wave Out   Controls the volume and balance for playing .wav files as they come into the computer.

    MIDI   Controls the volume and balance for incoming sounds from MIDI files.

    Audio-CD   Controls the volume and balance for CD-ROM audio files as they come into the computer.

    Microphone   Controls the volume and balance for sound coming in via a microphone.

2. To control the volume of the components, move the vertical slider labeled Volume up or down to increase or decrease volume.

3. To control the balance between two speakers, move the horizontal slider labeled Balance to the left or right to move the emphasis to the left or right speaker.

4. Click Mute All or Mute to silence all components' or one component's contribution to the sound.

Varying the Recording Volume

To vary the volume and balance when you are recording, follow these steps:

1. From the Volume Control dialog box, choose Options ➤ Properties to open the Properties dialog box.

2. Select Recording to display a list of devices that apply to the recording task.

3. If it is not already checked, click the check box to select the device you want.

4. Click OK to open the Recording Control dialog box for the selected device.

5. Move the Balance and Volume sliders to adjust the volume and balance of the sound.

WELCOME TO WINDOWS

Opens an interactive guide to Windows 98. Choose Start ➤ Programs ➤ Accessories ➤ System Tools ➤ Welcome to Windows. The Welcome screen contains the following options:

Register Now   Runs the Windows 98 Registration Wizard so that you can register your copy of Windows 98. In the Welcome screen, click Next to proceed with online registration, or click Register Later if you don't want to register right now.

Discover Windows 98   Starts a three-part Windows 98 tutorial consisting of Computing Essentials, Windows 98 Overview, and What's New.

Tune Up Your Computer   Runs Windows Tune-Up on your
system.

Release Notes   Opens WordPad on the Windows 98 Release
Notes file. You should check the information in this file as it
may contain late-breaking information that didn't make it into
the Windows Help system.

WHAT'S THIS

What's This?   Provides context-sensitive help in some dialog boxes. If
you right-click an item in a dialog box, a small menu
opens containing the single selection What's This. Click What's This to
display help text for that specific item.

Other dialog boxes have a Help button in the upper-right corner (look
for the button with a question mark on it) next to the Close button.
When you click this Help button, the question mark jumps onto the cursor; move the cursor to the entry on the dialog box that you want help
with and click again. A small window containing the help text opens;
click the mouse to close this window when you are done.

WINDOWS TUNE-UP

Optimizes your system for best performance. The Windows Tune-
Up Wizard can help make your programs run faster, free up precious
hard-disk space, and optimize system performance.

The Wizard actually does its work by running three other Windows
system utilities—Disk Defragmenter, ScanDisk, and Disk Cleanup—in
concert with Task Scheduler, which controls when the other utilities run
on your system. To run Windows Tune-Up, follow these steps:

1. Choose Start ➤ Programs ➤ Accessories ➤ System Tools ➤
    Windows Tune-Up to start the Windows Tune-Up Wizard.
    The Wizard welcome screen gives you two choices:

    Express   Uses the most common optimization settings.

    Custom   Allows you to select the tune-up settings.

2. Choose Express and click Next.

The next screen lets you schedule when the Tune-Up Wizard will run on your system. Select a time when your computer will be switched on but you won't be using it, such as in the middle of the night, very early in the morning, or during your lunch break.

3. In the final screen, you will see a list of the optimizations that the Wizard plans to execute on your system. Check the box at the bottom of the screen to run these optimizations when the Wizard closes.

4. Click Finish to close the Wizard.

If you choose Custom in the Wizard welcome screen, you can also specify in more detail how Disk Defragmenter, ScanDisk, and Disk Cleanup will operate on your system.

WINDOWS UPDATE

Connects to the Windows Update Web site and keeps your system up-to-date by automatically downloading new device drivers and Windows system updates as they are needed. Choose Start ➤ Windows Update, or choose Start ➤ Settings ➤ Windows Update. Internet Explorer opens and connects to the Web site. The Wizard scans your system looking for items that could be updated. It makes a list of any new device drivers or system patches that you need and then downloads and installs the files for any items you want to update.

You will also find current information on using Windows 98 on the Windows Update Web site as well as a set of answers to frequently asked questions about Windows. Simply follow the instructions on the screen.

Appendix B

THE INTERNET DICTIONARY

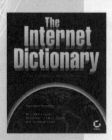

Adapted from *The Internet Dictionary*, by Christian Crumlish
0-7821-1675-2   240 pages $12.99

&   *Ampersand*. In HTML (Web) documents, used with special codes to indicate special characters (the HTML code for an ampersand itself is *&*).

< >   *Angle brackets*, or *brokets*. 1. They surround address return paths in e-mail headers; 2. In IRC, MUDs, and some e-mail and Usenet posts, brackets surround descriptions of actions or expressions, for example, <looking over my left shoulder> or <groan>. Similarly, some use <grin> or <g>.

@   *At*. In Internet e-mail addresses, it separates the username from the domain.

****   *Backslash*, or *backslant*. 1. In DOS paths, it separates directories and subdirectories; 2. In UNIX, it precedes switches (command line arguments).

^   *Caret*, or *hat*. 1. Indicates an exponent (for example, x^2 means x2, that is, x squared); 2. Sometimes used in e-mail and Usenet posts to underscore and emphasize text on the preceding line, as shown below.

```
pc-lover@online.com wrote:
>DOS is a snap once you figure out config.sys.
                 ^^^^^^^^^^
But that's the problem with PC-compatibles in a nutshell!
They make you deal with such awkwardly named setup files.
```

^]   Escape is sometimes represented by this pair of characters. If you're seeing it, some application is misinterpreting something.

:   *Colon*. In URLs, a colon appears after the protocol name. In e-mail and Usenet posts, sometimes indicates included text.

,   *Comma*. In Usenet newsreaders, you can often cross-post your article to several newsgroups by simply listing them one after another, separated by commas. Likewise, in most mail programs, you may list several e-mail recipients the same way, separated by commas.

.   *Dot*. The separator character for domain names, newsgroup names, and other UNIX-oriented files.

..   *Double dot*. In UNIX (as in DOS), the abbreviation for a parent directory.

— *Double hyphen.* Many mail programs and newsreaders automatically include a line containing just two hyphens before appending a signature. Many anonymous remailers strip off any part of a message following such a line to make sure that sig blocks are not included by mistake.

" *Double quotation mark.* They surround URLs in Web HTML documents.

>> *Double right angle brackets.* In UNIX, they append the redirected output of a command to the end of a file.

// *Double slash.* In URLs, the separator between the protocol and the site name. For example, in the URL http://enterzone.berkeley.edu/enterzone .html, *http* is the protocol, *enterzone.berkeley.edu* is the address of the Web server, and *enterzone.html* is the file name of the home page.

! *Exclamation point,* or *bang.* 1. It precedes each site in a UUCP bang path; 2. In some UNIX programs, it enables the user to shell out; 3. Overuse of exclamation marks to punctuate Usenet posts is one of the hallmarks of a newbie or a B1FF.

Number sign, pound sign, hash, or *octo-thorp.* 1. In the UNIX ftp program, if the command hash is given, one hash mark appears on the screen for every kilobyte of data transferred; 2. In Web references, # indicates the start of an anchor within a specified HTML document.

( ) *Parentheses.* They surround users' real names after their e-mail addresses in mail and posts.

% *Percent.* In UNIX, job numbers are preceded by %.

| *Pipe, bar,* or *vertical bar.* 1. In UNIX, used to redirect the output of one program into another. For example, the UNIX command *ls | more* creates a short listing of files in the current directory and displays them one screenful at a time (using the paging program *more*); 2. In e-mail and Usenet posts, sometimes indicates included text.

? *Question mark,* or *query.* A wildcard character in UNIX (and hence in many Internet applications), it stands for any single character.

> *Right angle bracket.* 1. In UNIX, it redirects the output of a command into a file; 2. In e-mail and Usenet posts, this character commonly indicates included (quoted) text.

;   *Semicolon.* In Web documents, special characters are preceded by an ampersand (&) and followed by a semicolon. For example, the less than sign is indicated by *<* (because the plain < indicates the beginning of a tag).

/   *Slash, forward slash, solidus,* or *virgule.* In UNIX (and hence in gopher addresses and URLs), the separator character between directory levels. For example, my home directory where I have my Internet account is /u39/xian.

:-)   The basic *smiley* emoticon (tilt your head to the left and you'll see it). Often used as a disclaimer, as in "just kidding."

*   *Star.* 1. A wildcard character in UNIX (and hence in many Internet applications), it stands for any number of characters; 2. In e-mail, and especially on Usenet, where plain ASCII text is the norm, writers place stars before and after words to emphasize them, like so: "That's what *you* think."

.   *Star-dot-star.* The DOS wildcard for any file name. In UNIX, just * will suffice.

~   A *tilde*, used in the UNIX mail program to issue commands (instead of inserting text).

$0.02   *Two cents.* Appended to a Usenet post, this means "I'm just putting my two cents in."

_   *Underscore,* or *underline.* 1. Used to separate names in some e-mail addresses; 2. Used in place of spaces in the names of files transferred from Macintoshes to other platforms; 3. In e-mail and on Usenet, where plain ASCII text is the norm, writers place underscores before and after titles to suggest underlining or italics, like so: "The origin of fnord is explained in _Illuminati!_"

;-)   *Winkey,* a winking smiley (tilt your head to the left and you'll see it). A more ambiguous sort of disclaimer than

     :-)

a   The command to add a bookmark in the UNIX programs gopher and lynx.

ABE   (rhymes with *babe*) A DOS binary-to-ASCII conversion program for sending files via e-mail.

ABEND   (*ab-end*, n) A computer crash (from "abnormal end" error message).

abstract syntax   A syntax (set of rules for properly formed commands) not limited to a single application or platform.

Abstract Syntax Notation One (ASN.1)   An OSI language used to encode Simple Network Management Protocol packets, part of the infrastructure of the Internet.

acceptable use   Internet service providers require that all their users agree to some guidelines of acceptable use of Internet and Usenet resources. Acceptable use policies vary from provider to provider.

access   (n) 1. A connection to the Internet; 2. A type of Internet connection (network access, dial-up access, etc.); 3. The degree of ability to perform certain activities or read privileged information.

(v) 1. To connect to the Internet; 2. To connect to a site; 3. To open a file.

Access Control List (ACL)   A site's table of services and hosts authorized to use those services.

access privileges   Authorization for a specific level of access.

access provider   An institution providing Internet access, such as a commercial service provider, university, or employer.

account   (n) A form of access to a computer or network for a specific username and password, usually with a home directory, an e-mail inbox, and a set of access privileges.

ACK   (rhymes with *pack*) 1. Acknowledgment from a computer that a packet of data has been received and verified; 2. The mnemonic for ASCII character number 6.

active star   A network design (a way of arranging the devices themselves in a network) in which a central hub retransmits all network traffic.

Addicted to Noise   A music magazine, featuring sound clips, on the Web at http://www.addict.com/ATN/.

Add/Strip   A Macintosh shareware program that inserts or deletes carriage returns (ASCII 13) at the end of each line of a text file, for conversion between Macintosh and UNIX systems.

address   (n) 1. A unique identifier for a computer or site on the Internet—this can be a numerical IP address (logical address) or a textual domain-name address (physical address); 2. A fully specified e-mail address (of the form *username@host.domain*).

address book   In some programs, a list of abbreviations for e-mail addresses.

address command   A UUCP extension that provides additional routing and confirmation options to the basic file-copying transaction that underlies UUCP.

Address Mapping Table (AMT)   A table used to resolve physical addresses into logical addresses.

address mask   The portion of an IP address that identifies the network and subnet.

address resolution   Conversion of a physical address into a logical address.

Address Resolution Protocol (ARP)   A TCP/IP protocol for converting physical addresses to logical addresses.

ADJ   (rhymes with *badge*) [Boolean operator] *Adjacent to*. A text search with ADJ between two words matches only documents in which those words are adjacent.

admin   Administrator, as in *sysadmin*.

Administrative Domain (AD)   The portion of a network overseen by a single administrator.

administrator   1. A system administrator (someone who runs a network); 2. Someone who maintains the addresses and handles the administrative chores for a mailing list or other Internet discussion group.

administrivia   Information regarding the administration of a mailing list or moderated newsgroup, such as the announcement of a new moderator, posted to the list or group.

Asynchronous Digital Subscriber Line (ADSL)   A new technology that utilizes existing copper wire telephone wiring (POTTs) and enables users to connect at anywhere from 640 kbps to 7 Mbps, and possibly faster in the not so distant future. ADSL users do not need to dial in to their Internet service provider, and can use a single line to access the internet, send and receive faxes, and make voice phone calls—all at the same time.

Advanced Interactive Executive (AIX)   IBM's UNIX clone.

Advanced Networks and Services (ANS)   [service provider] maloff@nis.ans.net, (703) 758-7700, (800) 456-8267.

Advanced Program-to-Program Communications (APPC)   An IBM peer-to-peer network protocol.

Advanced Research Projects Agency (ARPA)   A U.S. Department of Defense agency that, along with universities and research facilities, created ARPAnet, the precursor of the Internet.

advTHANKSance   *Thanks in advance.*

agent   1. The process in client/server communication that handles negotiation between the client and the server; 2. A Simple Network Management Protocol program that monitors network traffic; 3. A program that performs some action on the behalf of a user without the direct oversight of the user.

Agent   A newsreader for Windows made by Forté.

Agora   [service provider] info@agora.rain.com, (503) 293-1772.

AIR NFS   A Windows version of NFS (Network File System).

alias   (n) 1. An abbreviation for an e-mail address stored in a mail program, allowing the user to type or select a shorter alias instead of the full address; 2. An alternate name for an Internet address.

ALL-IN-1   A VAX e-mail and conference program.

AltaVista   A search engine developed by Digital Equipment Corporation (at `http://altavista.digital.com`).

alt.   A hierarchy of newsgroups in the Usenet mold but outside of Usenet proper, devoted to "alternative" topics. It is easier to create alt. groups than to create standard Usenet groups, and it's effectively impossible to remove them.

alt.config   A newsgroup for the discussion of new newsgroup formation in the alternative newsgroups hierarchy. Although the alt. hierarchy was created in part to sidestep the consensus rules of Usenet, there are still a range of views about what new alt. newsgroups should be created, how they should be named, and whether or not they will be accepted and propagated by system administrators all over the Net.

alternative newsgroups hierarchy   1. Any hierarchy of newsgroups in the Usenet mold but not strictly speaking part of Usenet; 2. The alt. hierarchy in particular.

alt.fan group   A newsgroup devoted to a real-world or Net celebrity or villain.

alt.plastic.utensil.spork.spork.spork   One of several spork newsgroups (a *spork* is a cross between a spoon and a fork). An example of improper use of a dot instead of a hyphen (plastic.utensil) and of a popular silly group ending.

alt.swedish.chef.bork.bork.bork   The original silly group with a *gag.gag.gag* ending.

American National Standards Institute (ANSI)   U.S. organization that develops and promotes voluntary standards in a wide range of academic and research fields.

Amiga   A line of desktop PCs, famous for their handling of graphics and the evangelical zeal of their users. Many Amiga users include an ASCII graphic double check mark in their sig blocks.

Amoeba   A silly name for Amiga.

ampersand (&) In HTML (Web) documents, used with special codes to indicate special characters (the HTML code for an ampersand itself is *&*).

analog (adj) Representing values as physical states and changes in values as changes in physical states. In a stereo, for example, a CD player converts the digital information encoded on the CD into an analog signal sent to the amplifier.

Anarchie (*anarchy*) A Macintosh program that combines the functions of archie and FTP.

anchor (n) An HTML tag that indicates a hypertext link or the destination of such a link.

AND [Boolean operator] *And*. A text search with AND between two words matches only documents containing both words.

Andrew File System (AFS) A set of network protocols that makes remote files accessible as if they were local (as contrasted with being available via FTP).

angle brackets They surround return addresses in e-mail headers. In IRC channels, MUDs, and some e-mail and Usenet posts, angle brackets surround descriptions of actions or expressions: for example, <looking over my left shoulder> or <groan>. Similarly, some use <grin> or <g>.

In e-mail and Usenet posts, a right angle bracket (>) commonly precedes included (quoted) text.

In UNIX, a right angle bracket redirects the output of a command into a file. A double right angle bracket (>>) appends the redirected output of a command to the end of a file.

annoybot An IRC 'bot that pesters real users.

anonymous FTP The most common use of FTP, the Internet file transfer protocol. FTP sites that allow anonymous FTP don't require a password for access—you only have to log in as *anonymous* and enter your e-mail address as a password (for their records).

anonymous remailer   A service that provides anonymity to users on the Net who wish to send mail and Usenet posts without their actual e-mail address and real name attached. Instead of sending mail or posting articles directly, users send to the anonymous remailer, with special header lines indicating the ultimate destination and the pen name of the user (if any). The remailer strips off any identifying information and sends the message or post on its way.

ANSI   (*antsy*) American National Standards Institute, or various standards promulgated by them.

*.answers   Moderated Usenet newsgroups dedicated to the posting of FAQs (frequently asked questions) and their answers.

any key   Some programs prompt you to continue by telling you to press any key. This means that any key you press will suffice to continue the process. There is no specific "Any" key.

AOL   The standard abbreviation for America Online, from aol.com, the subdomain and domain for that online service.

app   Application, program.

append   To attach a file to the end of another.

Apple   A computer company based in Cupertino, California, that makes the Macintosh computer.

Apple Attachment Unit Interface   Apple's Ethernet interface.

AppleLink   Apple's online service for employees, developers, and industry people, @applelink.apple.com; being phased out in favor of eWorld.

AppleTalk   Apple's built-in LAN software.

application   A computer program that performs a specific function for the user, as contrasted on one hand with a document (which is a file created by an application) and on the other with a shell, environment, or operating system (all of which handle communication between the user and the computer itself).

application layer   The top (seventh) layer of the OSI Model.

Application Programming Interface (API)   Software that controls communication between a program and a computer environment.

April Fool's jokes   Beware strange news or e-mail posted on April 1st.

.arc   A DOS file extension that indicates a compressed archive file.

archie   A client/server application that gives users access to databases (also called *indexes*) that keep track of the contents of anonymous FTP *archives*—hence the name.

archie client   The archie program you run to get information from an archie server.

Archie for the Macintosh   A Macintosh archie client.

Archie for Nextstep   An archie client for the Nextstep operating system.

archie server   The archie program that houses a database listing the contents of anonymous FTP sites, in a searchable form, accessible to archie clients.

archie site   A computer with an archie server running on it.

archive file   A file that has been compressed or that contains a number of related files.

archive site   1. An FTP site, a computer on the Internet that stores files; 2. Any repository of information accessible via the Net.

Are you on the Net?   This question usually means, "Do you have an e-mail address that can be reached from the Internet?"

argument   An additional statement (or subcommand) added to a command to modify how it works or what it works on. For example, to copy a file on most operating systems, you type a copy command, followed by several arguments—the name of the file to be copied and the name of the file to copy it to.

ARMM   Dick Depew's Usenet robot (ARMM stood for *Automated Retro-active Minimal Moderation*) intended to retroactively cancel anonymous posts and post follow-ups. It spun out of control instantly during its first run on March 31, 1993, posting follow-ups to its own follow-ups, spamming several newsgroups, and crashing systems all over the Net. For more on this, see the Net.Legends.FAQ at gopher://dixie.aiss.uiuc.edu:6969/11/urban.legends/Net.Legends.FAQ.

ARPAnet   (*are-pah-net*) The predecessor to the Internet, established in the 1970s by ARPA, which demonstrated the utility of the TCP/IP protocols. It no longer exists, having been superseded by the Internet.

article   A Usenet newsgroup post, that is, a message posted publicly and available for reading by every subscriber to the newsgroup(s) it's been posted to.

Artificial Intelligence (AI)   A field of computer science research aimed at understanding how the human mind thinks and creating intelligent machines that can learn from their experiences.

asbestos   Usenet or e-mail posters expecting flames often speak of donning asbestos overalls or other protective gear.

ASCII   (*askee*) *American standard code for information interchange*. ASCII is a standard character set that's been adopted by most computer systems around the world (usually extended for foreign alphabets and diacriticals).

ASCIIbetical order   A sorting order based on the ASCII character set that corresponds to English alphabetical order but sorts symbols and numbers before letters and uppercase letters before lowercase letters.

ASCII file   A file containing text only. ASCII files are easier and quicker to transfer than binary files.

ASCII file transfer   A method of file transfer by which an ASCII file is sent as a sequence of characters (letters, numbers, and symbols) instead of as a sequence of binary data (1s and 0s). When necessary, newline characters are changed by the file-transfer program.

ASCII font   A "font" created out of plain ASCII characters, usually found in sig blocks, often spelling out the writer's name.

ASCII graphic   A drawing composed of ASCII characters, such as an enormous medieval sword, an attempt to limn Bart Simpson, or a map of Australia.

AskERIC   An educational information service of the Educational Resources Information Center (ERIC), askeric@ricir.syr.edu.

aspect ratio   The proportion of height to width. Most computer displays have a 3 to 4 aspect ratio.

assigned numbers   Standard numbers for ports, sockets, and so on, established by the Internet Assigned Numbers Authority.

Association for Computing Machinery (ACM)   An association of computer researchers and developers that serves as both a source of technical information and an umbrella group for numerous SIGs (Special Interest Groups).

asynchronous   (adj) Not happening at the same time. The word is used both for data transmission and for human communication (e-mail is asynchronous, as opposed to IRC, which is synchronous).

Asynchronous Transfer Mode (ATM)   A standard for handling heavy network traffic at high speeds. Also called fast packet.

asynchronous transmission   A transmission method that uses start bits and stop bits to regulate the flow of data, as opposed to synchronous transmission, which uses a clock signal.

AT commands   (*ay-tee commands*) Hayes-compatible modem commands, most of which begin with *AT* (for "attention"), such as *ATZ*, which resets a modem's factory initialization (the basic settings for the modem when it was created).

aTdHvAaNnKcSe   *Thanks in advance.*

Athene   An online fiction magazine available at ftp://quartz.rutgers.edu/.

atob   (*ay-to-bee*) A UNIX program that converts ASCII files to binary files.

attach   To send a document along with an e-mail message.

attached file   A file sent with an e-mail message.

attachment   A file sent with an e-mail message.

Attachment Unit Interface (AUI)   A universal Ethernet device that connects to a transceiver.

attribute   (n) A setting associated with a file that indicates who can read it, and whether the file is a *system file* (a protected file created by the operating system and not to be tampered with), a *hidden file* (one that won't show up in normal file listings), or an *archive file* (one that has been grouped out of many and/or compressed).

attribution   The portion of a Usenet follow-up post that identifies the author of quoted text (from previous posts). Be very careful to attribute a quotation to the correct author, or face the ire of whomever you are misquoting. (When AOL first made Usenet available to its members, its newsreader software contained a bug that seemed to attribute the text of a follow-up to the author of the preceding post, which annoyed oldbies to no end.)

a2i communications   [service provider] info@rahul.net, (408) 293-8078.

Austin Free-Net   [service provider] jeff_evans@capmac.org, (512) 288-5691.

authentication   Verification of the identity of the sender of a message.

automagically   (adv) Happening automatically and so smoothly that the process appears to be magic.

Autonomous System (AS)   A set of routers overseen by a common administrator, using the same protocol.

autoselect   (v) In Usenet kill files, to select automatically—the opposite of to kill (to mark as already having been read). A kill file comprises instructions to search for certain key words and then either kill or autoselect the articles containing those words.

A/UX   Apple's UNIX clone for the Macintosh.

awk   (rhymes with *gawk*) A UNIX-based programming language for manipulating text.

b   The shortcut for back in many UNIX programs.

back   The command in paging programs, gopher clients, and Web browsers to back up one screenful or return to the previous menu choice or link.

backbone   A large, fast network connecting other networks. The National Science Foundation maintains one of the largest backbones in the United States, NSFnet.

backbone cabal   A now-defunct group of large-site administrators who set in place most of the procedures for Usenet newsgroup creation and orchestrated the Great Renaming of the Usenet hierarchy.

back door   A security loophole that allows a programmer to evade restrictions and enter an otherwise secure system. If a back door remains after the software is released, it becomes a security risk.

background   In a multitasking computer environment, any processes that take place out of sight or with lower priority than the main process are said to take place in the background.

backslash   The \ character, often found above the Enter key on keyboards. In DOS paths, it separates directories and subdirectories; in UNIX, it precedes switches (command-line arguments).

backspace   (v) To use the Backspace key to move a cursor to the left, and, in the process, delete characters on a computer screen.

Backspace key   A key found directly above the Enter key on most computer keyboards, often used to erase characters to the left of the cursor. (On some systems the Delete key plays this role.)

Use of the Backspace key in terminal emulations that don't support it sometimes leaves the original text onscreen, followed by one ^H character for every time Backspace is pressed. This results in the digital equivalent of an unzipped fly.

Bad Thing   Something generally or widely accepted to be bad. Racism is a Bad Thing. So is spamming Usenet.

balanced line   A cable containing electrically equal wires, such as a twisted-pair cable.

balun   (*bal-un*, n) An impedance-matching device that connects a balanced line (containing electrically equal wires), such as a twisted-pair cable, to an unbalanced line (containing electrically unequal wires), such as a coaxial cable.

bandwidth   (n) Literally, the speed at which data can be transmitted across a medium. Also used colloquially throughout the Internet to refer to the speed or capacity of a network connection (which can be described as *low bandwidth* or *high bandwidth*) or network resources in general, something almost everyone at some time or another is accused of wasting.

If you post a uuencoded binary file containing a 9×12 24-bit image to a talk newsgroup, you're definitely wasting bandwidth. But even if you have a sig block of over four lines, if you include too much quoted text in your follow-up post, or if you continue a flame war, you too may be accused of wasting bandwidth.

bandwidth hog   A user or process that consumes more than his, her, or its fair share of bandwidth.

bang   (n) An exclamation point. It precedes each site in a UUCP mail path. In some UNIX programs, it enables the user to shell out.

bang path   A UUCP *mail path* that specifies every site along the way from the sender to the receiver. Although it is rarely necessary any longer to specify the route your mail will take (there are many interchangeable routes on the Internet), mail headers still often include the entire bang path back to the sender.

bar   A popular dummy variable used by programmers in place of specific terms, such as the dummy mail address foo@bar.baz.

barfic   (n) An ugly ASCII graphic. For example:

```
|    .     ,-~'^^`'.     +     .    |
|     ~:.-~.     ",             |
|        :  _  :,  .    *  |
|  :   +  ; (@)   ,.   .      |
|      /          ,:          |
|:  +  <.,;      ,:`          |
|        0  ,/;'  *           |
|         ;  ,;/`             |
|   *  ~,.;;_.;'`             |
```

barney   1. A dummy variable used by programmers in examples in combination with fred (alluding to characters from *The Flintstones* television show); 2. A large, purple, talking dinosaur (star of the children's television show of the same name) who is praised and excoriated in various Usenet newsgroups.

Bart Simpson   A popular subject of ASCII graphics in big, ugly sig blocks. I hope Matt Groening (cartoonist and creator of Bart) doesn't mind, but here's an example:

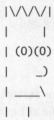

baseband   (adj) Signal transmission that uses the entire bandwidth of the medium, the method used by most LANs.

BASIC   A programming language invented at Dartmouth College in the 1960s as a teaching language. (It stands for *Beginner's All-purpose Symbolic Instruction Code*.) Many feel it teaches bad programming habits.

Basic Encoding Rules (BER)   A technique for encoding data (preparing data for transmission) defined in ASN.1 (Abstract Syntax Notation One).

Basic Rate Interface (BRI)   An ISDN (Integrated Services Digital Network) service that connects LANs (local area networks) via 64 kps data channels.

batch   (adj) 1. Noninteractive, handled without interaction, as in *batch mode*; 2. All at once, or in a bunch, as in *batch printing*.

baud   (*bawd*) Usually confused with bits per second (bps), baud is technically the number of times per second that your modem changes the signal it sends through the phone lines.

baz   A popular dummy variable used by programmers in examples in place of specific terms, such as the dummy mail address foo@bar.baz.

bboard   A BBS. Newbies often refer to Usenet newsgroups as bboards.

BBS   A *bulletin board system*, communications software that runs on a PC and enables users to log in via modem, check messages, communicate in topic groups, engage in real time chats, and (sometimes) access the Internet.

bcc: *Blind carbon copy.* Borrowed from the world of paper memos, the blind carbon copy list is a list of additional recipients of an e-mail message whose names and addresses will not appear in the header. Not all e-mail systems support bcc:, so it is not a perfectly safe way of keeping a recipient's identity secret.

beam   (v) 1. To transfer a file to someone (from *Star Trek* and other science fiction); 2. To wish someone well via e-mail.

(n) An expression of support sent electronically.

Berkeley Internet Name Domain (BIND)   UNIX name server software developed and distributed by the University of California at Berkeley.

Berkeley Software Distribution (BSD)   A version of UNIX developed and distributed by the University of California at Berkeley.

beta   (*bay-ta*) Prerelease software made available to a small group of testers (often called *beta testers*) in the "real world" to put it through its paces and identify any bugs or design flaws that did not show up when it was tested by the developers before being shipped commercially.

Big Blue   Slang term for IBM (from the corporate logo).

B1FF   Also called *BIFF*. A prototypical newbie on Usenet, looking for k00l warez (*k00l* is B1FF-speak for *cool*; *warez*—pronounced *wares*, from *software*—means pirated game software). He posts in all caps, substitutes numbers for letters, uses exclamation marks liberally, and has a huge sig block—all of which are marks of a BBS culture of the 1980s populated mainly by teenage boys.

Big Dummy's Guide to the Internet   The former name of the Electronic Frontier Foundation's excellent free Internet guide, now named *EFF's Guide to the Internet*.

big-endian   (adj) 1. A storage format in which the most significant byte has the lowest address, as opposed to little-endian; 2. The way Internet addresses are written in the United Kingdom, starting with domain, then subdomain, then site (the opposite of the standard order on the rest of the Internet).

big red switch   Sometimes abbreviated *BRS*, the on/off switch on a computer or any crucial toggle switch that, when switched off, will shut down the system.

big seven   The seven top-level Usenet hierarchies (also known as *traditional newsgroup hierarchies*): comp., misc., news., rec., sci., soc., and talk.

binaries newsgroup   A Usenet newsgroup dedicated to the posting of uuencoded binary files, often .gif or .jpg image files. Some sites won't carry binaries newsgroups because their uuencoded binaries consume so much bandwidth (and storage space on the news site computers).

binary   1. Base 2, a numerical system using two digits: *0* and *1* (compare with *decimal*—base 10, a numerical system using 10 digits: *0* through *9*); 2. A binary file.

binary data   Computer information stored in the form of *0*s and *1*s (most program files and image files, as well as some documents, are stored as binary data).

binary file   A file that contains more than simple text, such as an image file, a sound file, or a program file (as opposed to an ASCII file, which contains text only). It must be copied literally, bit for bit, or it will be corrupted. Also called an *image file*.

Binary Synchronous Control (Bisync)   An IBM protocol for controlling communications in synchronous environments.

binary file transfer   A file transfer in which every bit of the file is copied exactly as is (as opposed to a text transfer, in which the text is transferred to whatever format the receiving machine prefers).

BinHex   A Macintosh program that converts binary files to ASCII files so that they may be transmitted via e-mail.

BIOSIS/FS   A database of biological and biomedical research available through the OCLC (Online Computer Learning Center).

Birds of a Feather (BOF)   An ad hoc discussion group on a conference program.

bis   In modem standards, an enhancement to the standard, but not a completely new standard. V.32bis is an improvement on V.32, for example.

bisynchronous   (adj) Communication in which the sending and receiving takes place at the same time.

bit   A binary digit, the smallest unit of computer information, transmitted as a single *on* or *off* pulse symbolized by *1* or *0*.

bit bucket   1. An imaginary place where extra bits land when they "fall off a register"—the computer equivalent of forgetting to "carry the 1" during addition; 2. The computer equivalent of the circular file, or the place where all lost socks and pencils go.

bitnet.   A hierarchy in the Usenet mold populated by newsgroups gated to BITNET listserv mailing lists.

BITNET   *Because It's Time Network*, a huge network distinct from the Internet but fully connected to it, used largely for e-mail and listserv mailing lists.

bits per second (bps)   A measurement of the speed of a medium, meaning the number of bits that can pass through the medium in one second.

bitty box   A derogatory term for a personal computer, from the workstation or mainframe point of view.

BIX   [online service] BYTE Information Exchange, an online service created by *BYTE* magazine. TJL@mhis.bix.com, (800) 695-4775, (617) 354-4137.

biz.   A hierarchy in the Usenet mold dedicated to commercial and business communication. Advertising is explicitly permitted in the biz. hierarchy.

black hole   The place where missing e-mail messages or Usenet posts are said to have disappeared to.

block   (n) A standard unit of data (the size varies from system to system) measured in terms of storage or transmission.

board   (n) 1. A BBS; 2. A computer circuit board.

bogometer   (*boe-gom-i-ter*) A mythical device that measures bogosity or bogon flux.

bogon   (*boe-gon*, n) A mythical basic particle of bogosity.

bogon filter   A mythical device that can limit the flow of bogons.

bogon flux   A mythical measurement of the strength of a field of bogons.

bogosity   (*boe-goss-i-ty*) The extent to which something is bogus.

bogus   (adj) 1. Lame, stupid, false, useless; 2. Fake.

bogus newsgroups   Silly or joke-named Usenet-style newsgroups created by pranksters with the necessary access privileges.

boink   (n) A party at which participants of a Usenet newgroup meet in the flesh.

bomb   (v) To crash, to suffer from an unrecoverable error.

bookmark   In gopher clients and Web browsers, a reference to a menu or page to which you might want to return later. In gopher clients, bookmarks appear together on a gopher menu. In Web browsers, they appear on hotlists.

Insert Bookmark.epsBoolean operator   One of several conjunctions used to limit or specify a search criterion (from George Boole, nineteenth-century English mathematician).

Operator	What it specifies
ADJ	The terms on either side of the operator must appear adjacent to each other in the source text.
AND	The terms on either side of the operator must both appear in the source text.
NAND	The term before the operator must appear in the source text, and the term that appears after the operator must not.

NOT	The term appearing after the operator must not appear in the source text.
OR	One of the terms on either side of the operator must appear in the source text.
XOR	Only one, but not both, of the terms on either side of the operator must appear in the source text.

Boolean operators may be combined with parentheses if necessary to clarify the order of application.

Boolean search   A method of searching a database or text in which Boolean operators are used to limit and specify the search criterion.

boot   (v) To start or restart a computer, or, technically, to load and start the operating system. The term comes from the expression "lifting oneself by one's bootstraps," because the computer kernel must write the remainder of the startup code itself each time the computer is booted.

Bootstrap Protocol (BOOTP)   A protocol for booting diskless nodes on a network.

Border Gateway Protocol (BGP)   An exterior gateway protocol based on the External Gateway Protocol used by NSFnet.

'bot   A robotic entity on the Net that automatically performs some function that people usually do. Many IRC channels are kept open by semipermanent 'bots that stay connected just as real users might. In the past, people have spammed Usenet by employing 'bots to automatically post (robopost) reams of redundant text.

bounce   (v) E-mail that fails to reach its destination and returns to the sender is said to have bounced.

bounce message   A message from a mailer daemon indicating that it cannot find the recipient of an e-mail message and is returning it to the sender.

Bourne shell   A common flavor of UNIX shells.

box   (n) A computer, as in a UNIX box.

bozo   (*boe-zoe*, n) A fool, a kook, a crank, a luser.

bozo filter   A kill file. It allows you to filter out the bozos whose Usenet posts you don't wish to see.

bozotic   (*boe-zot-ic*, adj) Having the qualities of a bozo.

brain dump   (n) An undifferentiated mass of information, often in response to a simple question (by analogy from core dump, screen dump, etc.).

brain-dead   (adj) 1. Completely broken, nonfunctional, usually said of hardware or software; 2. Ridiculously inappropriate, said of an approach to a problem.

branch   (n) 1. An intermediate part of a logical tree, somewhere between the root and a leaf; 2. A participant in a tape tree who receives copies of a tape from her parent and makes copies for her children (who may themselves be branches or leaves).

BRB   (written only) *[I'll] be right back.*

bridge   A device that connects two network components (such as zones) that use the same protocols.

brief   (adj) An operating mode for some systems and applications in which the prompts and reports of activities are abbreviated or skipped altogether.

broadband   (adj) Signal transmission that can carry multiple signals at once, each on separate channels, each taking up a portion of the bandwidth.

broadcast   (n) A transmission sent to all hosts or clients at once, such as "System going down in 10 minutes. Please finish up."

broadcast storm   The confusion and possible network breakdown that occurs when a faulty packet is broadcast, generating multiple incorrect packets in response, ad infinitum.

broket   (*broe-ket*) An angle bracket: < or >.

brouter   (*brow-ter*) A device that combines the functions of a bridge and a router, controlling transmission from one network component to another (as a bridge) and from the network to the Internet (as a router).

browse   To skim an information resource on the Net, such as Usenet, gopherspace, or the Web.

browser   A client program used to read the Web.

btoa   (*bee-to-ay*) A UNIX program that converts binary files to ASCII files.

btw   (written only, also *BTW*) *By the way.*

BUAF   (*bee-you-ay-eff*) Big, ugly ASCII font. Character sets made from ASCII characters, often generated by special programs and often used to spell out names in sig blocks.

Here's a charming example:

```
        iiu.
      x@$$R$$N.
    :$$#`  '$$E @$:        @$~
    W$$`    `$E $$>    :$$"
   4$$      '$E '$$L  :$$~
    ~$&       9$!   R$WW$F
    R$k    . $$    `$$~
    #$$L.u$$$~     9$
     #$$$R~      :$F
               8$>
               #F
```

BUAG   (*bee-you-ay-gee*) Big, ugly ASCII graphic. Large, often crude drawing composed of ASCII characters, such as a map of Australia, a medieval sword, the *U.S.S. Enterprise* (from the TV show Star Trek), etc., often appearing in a sig block.

Below is one of the less elaborate *Enterprise*s:

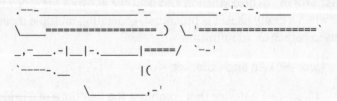

buffer   (n) A memory location that stores a certain amount of data or text until it can be processed or displayed. A screen's *display buffer* is the amount of text you can scroll back to review. If your computer or connection freezes and you type repeatedly until each keypress results in a beep, then you have overflowed your *keyboard buffer*.

bug   (n) A flaw in a program (from the expression "working the bugs out"). Also, jokingly defined as an undocumented feature.

buggy   (adj) Said of software; unstable, unreliable, full of bugs.

bundle   (v) To group packets of data into a single cell for transmission over a cell-switching network.

Bunyip   The company formed by the people who invented archie.

burble   (v) To flame at a very low level of competence or clarity.

bus   (n) An electronic pathway or connector.

bus topology   A network architecture in which all nodes are connected to a single cable.

buzz word   Also *stop word,* a word so common that it is useless to search for it (such as *and*, *address*, *record*, and so on). Most searchable databases have lists of buzz words and filter them out during searches.

by hand   (adv) Executed step-by-step by a human being, instead of automatically by a computer process.

byte   A binary "word" (unit of meaning), usually consisting of eight bits.

bzzzzt, wrong   A rejoinder to an incorrect Usenet post, alluding to radio and TV quiz shows in which a timer buzzes when a contestant answers incorrectly.

c   The catch up command in some UNIX newsreaders.

C   A programming language developed at Bell Labs that has become a standard for scientific and commercial applications. C++ is an object-oriented successor version of C.

cable   A sheathed length of wires used to transmit signals from device to device.

Call for Votes (CFV)   A stage in the Usenet newsgroup creation process, after the Request for Discussion (RFD).

Campus-Wide Information Server (CWIS)   The information system for a college or university, usually including schedules, announcements, job listings, bulletin boards, calendars, and so on.

cancel   On Usenet, to delete an article after you've posted it. It takes a while for the article to vanish everywhere, as the cancel message has to catch up with the propagating article.

canonical   1. Deriving from an official source. In *Star Trek* newsgroups, facts that come from any of the television series or movies is considered canonical; 2. Prototypical, to programmers. For instance,

```
10 GOTO 10
```

and

```
Do x=x+1 until x>x+1
```

are canonical infinite loops.

capture   (v) To save text as it scrolls across the screen. Captured text can be read while offline.

card   A printed circuit board, added to a computer to enable it to control an additional device.

caret   The ^ character. Indicates an exponent (for example, x^2 means x^2, that is, x *squared*).

The caret is also used in e-mail and Usenet posts to underscore and emphasize text on the preceding line, as shown in this example:

```
pc-lover@online.com wrote:
>DOS is a snap once you figure out config.sys.
                  ^^^^^^^^^^
But that's the problem with PC-compatibles in a nutshell!
They make you deal with such awkwardly named setup files.
```

careware   A form of shareware in which the creator of the software requests that payment be made to a charity.

carriage return   A character that moves the cursor back to the beginning of a line (ASCII 13), usually starting a new line in combination with a line feed character.

carrier   A signal constantly transmitted by a modem over a phone line as a reference for the modem on the other end of the line. When a line is disconnected, some modems will report "no carrier."

carrier detect   The notice that a modem has identified the carrier signal from another modem over a phone connection.

Carrier Sense Multiple Access (CSMA)   A protocol that enables multiple devices to transmit on the same channel, by "listening" for the sounds of other devices and only transmitting when the line is clear.

Carrier Sense Multiple Access with Collision Avoidance (CSMA/CA)
A version of CSMA in which devices can detect impending collisions and avoid them.

Carrier Sense Multiple Access with Collision Detection (CSMA/CD)
A version of CSMA in which devices can detect collisions as they occur and resend the corrupted signal.

cascade   A series of one-line follow-up posts, each a play on the previous one. Each post contains all of the previous ones leading up to the latest change, usually in ever-shortening lines, due to the rows of >'s (or sometimes other characters) automatically inserted by newsreader posting commands to indicate an inclusion from a previous post. For example:

```
>>>I'm tired and I'm going to bed.
>>I'm wired and I'm holding my head.
>>I've expired and I'm lacking bread.
>I'm hired! I'm in the red.
>Inspired, I'll quickly wed.
I'm mired in this boring thread.
```

case-insensitive   Not distinguishing between upper- and lowercase characters. In a case-insensitive search, *Internet*, *internet*, and *INTERNET* all match the same key word.

The DOS and Macintosh operating systems are case-insensitive, as are e-mail addresses. UNIX, on the other hand, is case-sensitive.

case-sensitive   Distinguishing between upper- and lowercase characters. To a case-sensitive program, *Peter*, *PETER*, *peter*, and *PeTeR* all mean different things. UNIX is case-sensitive; DOS and Macintoshes are not. E-mail addresses are not case-sensitive.

cat   A UNIX command (short for '*catenate*, from *concatenate*) that can pour the contents of one file into another or dump the contents onto the screen.

catch up   When reading news, to mark all the articles in a newsgroup as read, to clean the slate.

cc: A list of additional recipients for an e-mail message in the header of the message (from *carbon copy*, a carryover from office-memo shorthand). Most e-mail programs enable the sender to add addresses to the cc: list.

CCITT   *Comite Consultatif International de Telegraphique et Telephonique* (International Telegraph and Telephone Consultative Committee), an international standards organization comprising telecommunications companies, part of the United Nations' International Telecommunications Union, creator of the X.25, X.400, and X.500 standards.

cd   A UNIX and DOS command meaning *change directory*.

CD-ROM   *Compact Disc/Read-Only Memory*, a format for storing data on compact discs. Some CD-ROMs contain vast amounts of shareware that can be downloaded for free from the Net.

cell   A packet with a fixed length (in bytes).

cell-switching   A variation on X.25 packet-switching protocol in which data is bundled into equal-sized cells.

Cello   An integrated Web browser and general Internet tool (gopher, WAIS, Usenet, mail) for Windows. Available by anonymous FTP from ftp.law.cornell.edu.

censorship   The public spaces of the Internet (such as Usenet newsgroups, IRC, and so on) are largely free from censorship, and can be noisy and childish at times. Online services, however, take more responsibility for the contents of their networks and may therefore place some restrictions on what can be written in public or even in private.

central processing unit (CPU)   The heart of a computer, the part that does the "thinking."

Cerf, Vinton   Codesigner of the TCP/IP protocols.

CERN European Particle Physics Laboratory   (*surn*) (The acronym CERN comes from an earlier French title of the Lab: *Conseil Européen pour la Recherche Nucleaire*) The creators of the World Wide Web and the first (text-based) Web browser, www. You can reach CERN on the Web at http://www.cern.ch/.

Chameleon NFS   Socket, TCP/IP, and Internet tools software for Windows, made by NetManage. Information is available on the Web at http://www.netmanage.com/.

Chameleon Sampler   A free collection of socket, TCP/IP, and Internet tools available via FTP from ftp.netmanage.com, in the /pub/demos/ sampler directory, in a self-extracting archive file called sampler.exe.

channel   (n) 1. The path along which one device sends a signal to another, meaning a physical cable or wire or an assigned frequency of a physical channel; 2. An IRC topic area; 3. A feature in Microsoft's Internet Explorer browser software, whereby a user can subscribe to special sites.

channel hopping   On IRC, jumping around from channel (definition 2) to channel.

channel op   A privileged user of an IRC channel, able to kick antisocial participants.

character   A letter, number, space, punctuation mark, or symbol—any piece of information that can be stored in one byte.

character-based   (adj) Said of a computer, operating system, environment, or terminal emulation, displaying screens composed entirely of characters (as opposed to graphical images) and accepting input only in the form of characters (as opposed to mouse clicks).

character-based interface   A computer front end which displays only characters on the screen—no graphics, no icons, no mouse pointer, etc. Many dial-up Internet connections are to UNIX boxes with character-based interfaces.

character length   A terminal emulation setting that determines the number of bits in a character (usually seven or eight). ASCII characters require seven bits per byte (one byte per character); binary transfers may require eight bits per character.

character string   A string of characters that must be handled as text, not as numeric data.

charter   The founding document of a Usenet newsgroup, it defines what constitutes on-topic and off-topic discussion, and establishes whether the newsgroup is moderated or not.

chat   (n) 1. Synchronous (happening in real time, like a phone conversation, unlike an e-mail exchange), line-by-line communication with another user over a network; 2. The chat program itself, now largely superseded by the IRC program.
(v) To engage in a chat.

cheapernet   Slang for the "thin" Ethernet specification, generally used in offices.

checksum   An error-checking method in which the sending and receiving modems both sum up the bytes in a data packet and compare the totals.

child directory   A subdirectory.

chmod   (*see-aitch-mode*) The UNIX command for changing the read-write permissions of a file (from *change mode*).

choad   (n) Slang for penis, popularized by the denizens of alt.tasteless.

Church of the SubGenius   A half-serious antireligion founded by the Rev. Ivan Stang and blending the principles of Discordianism with '50s advertising clip art images and mindnumbing homilies. SubGenii can be found in the Usenet newsgroup alt.slack and elsewhere on the Net, often talking about the deity Bob (sometimes BoB).

CIA World Factbook   A source of basic information on every country in the world, reachable by WAIS at world-factbook.src; also, one of the books made available for free by Project Gutenberg.

cipher   (n) A code that involves character-for-character substitution (as contrasted with word-for-word substitution or other schemes), a simple example of which is rot13.

circuit   A channel carrying an electrical current between two devices.

circuit board   A computer card holding printed circuits.

circuit-switched network   A network arrangement in which each node is connected to the next via a dedicated line.

clari.   The Usenet-style newsgroup hierarchy dedicated to ClariNet news items.

ClariNet   An online news service analogous to newspaper wire services. If your service provider gets a ClariNet newsfeed, then the news is part of your overhead cost. Otherwise, you can get ClariNet news by direct subscription. For information, send e-mail to info@clarinet.com.

clear channel   A 64 kps channel with its entire bandwidth available for transmission.

Clearinghouse for Networked Information Discovery and Retrieval (CNIDR)   An organization supporting research and cooperation relating to information resources on the Internet (such as WAIS, gopher, archie, and the Web) and ways to search and retrieve information from them. They distribute free-WAIS, a free version of WAIS. CNIDR can be reached on the Web at http://cnidr.org/welcome.html.

client   An application or computer that communicates with and requests information from a server. In conventional networking, client usually refers to a computer; for Internet client/server applications, client usually refers to a program.

client/server   1. A method of distributing information or files in which a central server application archives (stores) the files and makes them available to requests from client applications; 2. A LAN architecture, in which files and other resources are kept on a central server computer and individuals interact with the network through client computers.

client/server application   A network application that functions with a central server as a repository of information and clients that communicate with the server and request information on behalf of individual users.

clip art   Generic pictures and icons, distributed as image files (or in the days before personal computers, in huge books).

Clipper Chip   A U.S. government-sponsored encryption standard that telecommunications industries will be encouraged to adopt when it becomes final, according to pending proposals. The Clipper Chip includes a back door that would allow government agencies to eavesdrop on communication encrypted with the chip. (The government would need a court order to use the decryption keys, otherwise kept in escrow.)

Opponents of the Clipper Chip are suspicious of the government following its own rules and believe that any individual or company should have access to the best encryption technology available, not just government-approved encryption.

clobber   Kill, delete, erase.

close   (v) To hang up a telnet, FTP, or other remote connection.

clueless newbie   A derogatory term for a beginner who POSTS IN ALL CAPS or betrays some ignorance of the Net. We were all clueless newbies once.

Coalition for Networked Information (CNI)   A coalition of libraries and research organizations dedicated to the sharing of information over computer networks.

coax   (*co-ax*) Slang for coaxial cable.

coaxial cable   (*co-axial*) Cable containing two conductors, one inside the other, used for broadband and baseband networks, as well as for cable TV.

code   (n) Computer program contents.
(v) To write or edit a computer program.

Coffeehousebook.com   A web site at Levity that covers the creative web scene today (http://coffeehousebook.com).

cognitive dissident   The vocation, coined by Electronic Frontier Foundation cofounder John Barlow, for those who challenge the status quo in cyberspace.

Coke machine   At one time or another, there have been many soda machines on the Internet. This usually means that some device monitors the machine, keeping track of how many cans of soda are in each slot and possibly how long they've been there (i.e., how cold they are). This device then updates an information file that can usually be fingered from anywhere on the Internet. To see such a readout for yourself, try fingering drink@drink.csh.rit.edu.

cold boot   (v) To start a computer that's completely off.

collision   What happens when two devices try to use the same channel at the same time.

colon   In URLs, a colon (:) appears after the protocol name. In e-mail and Usenet posts, colons sometimes indicate included text.

Colorado Alliance of Research Libraries (CARL)   An alliance of seven libraries that contribute to a database containing abstracts of thousands of journals. For more information, send e-mail to help@carl.org.

.com   The Internet domain dedicated to commercial entities, generally in the United States.

comm   Communications (sometimes spelled *com*), usually in the context of communications software, a communications port on a computer, and so on.

comma   In Usenet newsreaders, you can often cross-post your article to several newsgroups simply by listing them one after another, separated by commas (,). Likewise, in most mail programs, you may list several e-mail recipients the same way, separated by commas.

command line   A single line of text, with a prompt, often at the bottom of the screen, where the user may enter commands directly. DOS and UNIX are command-line operating systems; Macintosh, Windows, and X Window are graphical environments that do not automatically make a command line available.

command-line interface   A front end that allows or forces the user to memorize and type commands at a prompt, as opposed to one that allows or forces the user to click graphical elements and select commands from pull-down menus.

command mode   A program mode in which you can enter commands. In vi, the UNIX text editor, users start off in command mode and will be frustrated if they try to start typing text. First, they must switch to insert mode.

commercial access provider   A service provider that charges for access to the Internet, as opposed to employers, universities, and free-nets, which provide access for free.

Commercial Internet Exchange (CIE or CIX)   An organization of service providers that represents the interest in making commercial transactions acceptable and secure over the Internet. For more information, send e-mail to info@cix.org.

communications program   A program that operates a modem and provides terminal emulation so that the user can log in to and communicate with a remote computer.

Communications Terminal Protocol (CTERM)   Part of DECnet's virtual terminal service (protocols that allow a user to emulate a different terminal type) specifications.

Communications Toolbox (CTB)   A Macintosh tool that allows a communications program to take advantage of existing communications links.

comp.   A Usenet hierarchy devoted to computers.

Compact Pro   A Macintosh shareware compression program. Files compressed with Compact Pro have a *.cpt* extension.

COM port   The communications port on a computer. On PCs, it's a serial port.

compress   (v) To squish a file in order to save disk storage space.
(n) A UNIX compression program.

compression   A method of squishing a file in order to save disk storage space or the amount of squishing.

Compu\$erve (CI\$)   A mildly derogatory name for CompuServe that refers to its expensive connect time fees.

CompuServe   [online service] Short for *CompuServe Information System* (CIS), an online service with partial Internet access. CompuServe has a long-established presence and provides a large number of services to its nearly two million subscribers. Once only linked via e-mail to the Internet, CompuServe is now in the process of adding new Internet features, most recently Usenet newsgroup access.

For information, contact postmaster@csi.compuserve.com,
(800) 848-8990, (614) 457-0802.

CompuServe Information Manager (CIM)   A program that provides a graphical interface (or front end) for CompuServe, available for both Macintosh and Windows.

Computer Emergency Response Team (CERT)   A network-security task force available round-the-clock to assist Internet users with security problems. For more information, send e-mail to cert@cert.org or call their 24-hour hotline, (412) 268-7090.

computer geek   Someone who enjoys messing around with a computer, not necessarily as a programmer or at the same level of sophistication as a hacker. This is not necessarily a derogatory term. It depends on the context and the company.

computer-mediated communication   Any form of communication aided and abetted by computers, including, but not limited to, e-mail, chat, and conferencing.

Computer Professionals for Social Responsibility (CPSR)   An organization of computer professionals concerned with the impacts computers might have on society. Originally formed to discuss the connections between computer research and the nuclear arms race, it now also addresses such issues as issues as privacy, the role of the computer in the workplace, and research priorities in the coming century.

Computer + Science Network (CSNET)   A computer-science research network that merged with BITNET to create the Corporation for Research and Educational Networking (CREN).

conductor   A particular type of wire, such as copper.

conferencing   (adj) Said of software that enables many users to engage in a more or less public, written conversation, either in real time (as on an IRC channel) or not (as in a Usenet newsgroup).

connection   There are different types, or levels, of connection to the Internet, ranging from a direct network connection, through SLIP or PPP dial-up access, to character-based shell-account dial-up access, and simple e-mail gateways to the Net.

Connection closed by foreign host   A message during a telnet or other remote login session that tells you that the host you've logged in to has closed the connection.

Connection Control Language (CCL)   An AppleTalk scripting language for controlling modem functions.

connectionless communication   A form of communication between applications in which data can be requested and supplied during intermittent connections.

connection-oriented communication   A form of communication between applications in which all data is exchanged during a single connection.

connect time   The amount of time you spend connected to your service provider. Many providers charge a fee based on your connect time. Others are flat-rate providers.

Consortium for School Networking (CoSN)   A nonprofit organization that studies the uses of networking in K–12 schooling. For more information, send e-mail to cosn@bitnic.bitnet.

contention   The situation when two devices both try to use the same channel. Every network must have some protocol in place to deal with issues of contention.

control bus   The channel within a computer along which control signals (signals that control a device or routine) are carried.

control character   A special character, usually nonprinting, that starts or stops a computer function.

Control key   The key marked *Ctrl* on most computer keyboards (the closest Macintosh analogy is the Command key). In combination with other keys, the Control key can send control characters to the computer. It is sometimes symbolized by ^, so Control-C might be written ^C or Ctrl-C.

Conversational Monitor System (CMS)   The command-line interface of IBM's VM operating system.

cookie   1. A file containing identifying information on a user. To accept a cookie, means that you agree to share the information that is on that file with the parties that run the site from which the current request was submitted. 2. A fortune cookie program that spits out a different fortune every time you run it. Some systems run cookie as part of their startup or login procedure.

Cooperative Library Agency for Systems and Services (CLASS)   [service provider] A service provider for member libraries: class@class.org, (800) 488-4559.

Coordinating Committee for Intercontinental Research Networks (CCIRN)   A committee that coordinates research networks in North America and Europe.

copyleft   The General Public License carried by Free Software Foundation software (such as GNU). It grants reuse and reproduction rights to anyone and everyone.

copyright   People debate how standing copyright law applies to articles posted to Usenet or to texts in general made available on the Internet. This is thus far not settled law. Some people attach copyright notices to their Usenet posts.

core   (n) 1. RAM, on UNIX and some IBM machines; 2. The name of a file that appears in your UNIX directory after a core dump. This file contains everything that was in memory at the time of the dump.

core dump   (n) 1. A copy of the contents of memory, dumped into a file when an unrecoverable error occurs; 2. A brain dump.

Corporation for Research and Educational Networking (CREN)   An organization formed by the merger of BITNET and CSNET. CREN can be reached via gopher at info.educom.edu.

corrupted   (adj) Said of a file, block of data, or other communication, damaged in transmission.

cp   The UNIX *copy file* command.

cpio   A UNIX command that makes whole directories into a single file, for easy transportation.

CP/M   A PC operating system that preceded DOS. If someone mentions CP/M, they're bragging about how long they've been working with microcomputers.

.cpt   The extension of a file compressed with Compact Pro, a Macintosh program.

CPU   *Central processing unit*, the heart of a computer, the part that does the "thinking."

cracker   One who breaks into computer systems. What many people in the real world call a hacker.

cracking   The act of breaking into a computer system.

crack root   (v) To break into the root account of a UNIX machine and, most likely, use the root privileges to break into other accounts.

crash (n) An unrecoverable failure of a computer system, requiring rebooting as a minimum response.

(v) To suffer from a crash.

crippleware Shareware that lacks a useful or even crucial functionality, in order to entice you into registering as an owner to obtain the uncrippled version of the program.

crlf A combination of two characters (carriage return and line feed) that on some computer systems constitutes a newline.

crosspost (n) A Usenet article posted simultaneously to more than one newsgroup. Most newsreaders will show you crossposted articles only the first time you encounter them.

cross-post (v) To post a Usenet article to several newsgroups at once. This takes up less disk space than posting it separately and repeatedly.

crosstalk Interference between two wires in a cable.

CrossTalk A communications and terminal emulation program for DOS and Windows.

cryptography The study of codes, ciphers, and other security issues.

C shell A common flavor of UNIX shells.

.cshrc A startup file for the UNIX C shell.

CSLIP *Compressed Serial Line Internet Protocol*, a faster version of SLIP in which Internet address information is compressed.

CSO *Computing Services Office*, a system for searching campus telephone and address listings, reachable by gopher.

CSO name server A searchable white pages listing of real names and associated e-mail addresses, usually reached via gopher.

The Cuckoo's Egg A book by Clifford Stoll describing how he tracked East German crackers breaking into a system at Lawrence Berkeley Labs at the University of California at Berkeley.

CUSeeMe   (*see-you-see-me*) A new Internet protocol for synchronous video and sound communication.

c-ya   (written only) *See you [later]*.

cyber-   A prefix overused to indicate a connection to computers, networks, technology, or futurism.

cybercafé   A coffeehouse that offers Internet access, often via coin-operated or free Internet terminals.

cyberdelics   1. Mind-altering effects brought about by computer technology (as opposed to hallucinogenic drugs); 2. Eye-bending screen savers.

cybernaut   A traveler in cyberspace, someone who uses their Internet connection to explore the furthest realms of cyberspace.

cyberpunk   (n) 1. A largely hype-driven category of popular culture at the crossroads of computer technology, science fiction, and youth culture; 2. A genre of science fiction that appeared in the mid-to-late '80s and combined a bleak, noirish view of the future with a fetishization of technology and human-computer interaction.

cyberspace   A term, coined by author William Gibson, for the shared imaginary reality of computer networks. Some people use cyberspace as a synonym for the Internet. Others hold out for the more complete physical-seeming consensual reality of Gibson's novels.

cycle power   (v) To turn a computer off and then on again.

cyclic redundancy check (CRC)   An error-detection technique used during file transfers and other forms of data transmission. Both the sending and receiving modems perform calculations on the data and then the two results are compared.

cypherpunk   (n) An activist interested in the political potentials of universal Internet access and cheap and foolproof privacy.

daemon (*day-min*) In UNIX and other operating systems, a program that runs all the time, in the background, waiting for things to do (possibly from Maxwell's Demon). When you post an article to a *.test newsgroup, daemons all over the world send you e-mail confirmations when they receive your post.

daisy chain A network architecture, also called bus topology, in which all nodes are connected to a single cable.

dark fiber Unused cable in the fiber-optic network.

DARPA *Defense Advanced Research Projects Agency*, the official name of ARPA during the 1980s and early 1990s.

data Information of any type, usually information stored, transmitted, or processed by computers.

database A repository of information stored on a computer and accessible to searches.

data bits In asynchronous data transmission, the bits between a start bit (and sometimes a parity bit) and a stop bit, the only bits actually carrying data. There are usually seven or eight data bits, depending on the size of a character, or byte.

Data bits is therefore one of the settings you have to specify on your modem to make a connection. Usually 7 or 8, it depends on the modem you're calling.

data block A unit of data sent from one device to another.

data bus The channel within a computer along which communication signals are carried.

data channel Any channel over which data is sent in the form of a signal.

data communications equipment (DCE) Devices such as modems that connect to a serial port and control data communications.

data encryption key (DEK) An element of key encryption that is used to encrypt and decrypt data.

data encryption standard (DES)   A security protocol defined by the U.S. government.

data/fax modem   A modem that can transmit raw data or a fax image.

datagram   The basic unit of data transmission across a network, containing a header and the data itself. The header describes the data, its destination, and its relationship to other datagrams.

Datagram Delivery Protocol (DDP)   An AppleTalk protocol that handles the routing of datagrams over an AppleTalk network.

data link   1. The device that enables data transmission; 2. An active connection for data transmission.

data link layer   The second layer of the OSI Model that deals with transmission of data frames from node to node.

data stream   A series of data blocks sent from one device to another.

data terminal equipment (DTE)   A device at one end or the other of a data transmission. This usually means a PC or terminal.

.dd   The extension of a file compressed with DiskDoubler on the Macintosh.

DEC   (*deck*) *Digital Equipment Corporation*, manufacturer of VAX (and before that PDP-11) boxes and the VMS operating system.

DEChead   (*deck-head*) 1. An employee of Digital Equipment Corporation; 2. A Deadhead (Grateful Dead fan) employee of DEC.

DECnet   (*deck-net*) Network protocols designed for VAX and PDP-11 computers, used by Digital Equipment Corporation operating systems instead of TCP/IP.

DECnet/DNA   DEC's implementation of DNA (Digital Network Architecture).

DECnet tunnel   A protocol for packaging AppleTalk datagrams within DECnet packets.

decrypt   To remove the encryption from a file or e-mail message and make it readable.

decryption key   In key encryption, a key used to decipher an encrypted message and make it readable.

dedicated   (adj) Assigned to a single task or able to perform only a single task.

dedicated line   A separate telephone line dedicated to the tranmission of data.

deep hack   The extreme state of concentration, bordering on a trance, that hackers enter after long hours of hacking.

default   (n) A setting, state, instruction, or selection that a program uses unless you explicitly change it.

default route   An entry in a routing table indicating where to route packets intended for destinations not otherwise listed in the table.

Defense Data Network (DDN)   The network of networks used by the U.S. military, connecting with the Internet in some places and not in others.

Defense Data Network Network Information Center (DDN NIC)
The Network Information Center for the DDN, a source of information as well as an administrative authority over the DDN.

Defense Information Systems Agency (DISA)   The U.S. government agency that oversees the Defense Data Network.

DejaNews   A search engine for searching Usenet newsgroups (at http://www.dejanews.com).

delete   (v) To erase a character, file, or directory.

Delete key   A key used in most environments to erase the character that the cursor or insertion point is on or just before. On some systems, Delete erases the character just typed or to the left of the cursor.

delimiter   A character or symbol that indicates a break between two pieces of information, items in a table, or fields in a database.

delurk   (*dee-lurk*, v) To post to a list or newsgroup for the first time.
    (n) A first post to a newsgroup or list after the writer has lurked for a while.

demon   A routine in a program that waits until it is needed (possibly from Maxwell's Demon).

Depew, Dick   The inventor of ARMM, a roboposting utility designed to retroactively cancel off-topic Usenet posts. Depew's 'bot had a serious flaw and followed up its own posts, eventually bringing down part of the Internet in sorcerer's apprentice mode.

deprecated   (adj) Being phased out in favor of a new standard.

despew   (v) From [Dick] Depew, to robotically post reams of junk to the Net.

developer   A software publisher.

device   Any piece of computer equipment, though the term is often used to specify peripheral devices.

/dev/null   On UNIX boxes, the null device. Data piped to /dev/null disappears. People posting controversial articles to Usenet sometimes add the notice "flames to /dev/null."

dial up   (v) To use a modem to call up another computer or network and log in to it.

dial-up   (adj) Said of an Internet access that requires the user to connect via a modem.

dial-up account   An Internet account on a host machine that you must dial up with your modem to use.

DIALOG Information Retrieval Database   A commercial online database service with hundreds of databases and millions of records. To connect to DIALOG, telnet to dialog.com.

dictionary flame   A flame that focuses on someone's use of a particular word or their vocabulary, a weak sort of flame that indicates that the flamer has nothing substantial to say against the flamee.

digest   (n) A collection of mailing list posts, sent out as one message.

digestified   (adj) Turned into a digest. Not all mailing lists are available in a digestified form.

digital   (adj) Representing values as discrete bits. CD is a digital medium because the sound or other information is *digitized* (converted into bits) and then stored. A CD player converts the digital information encoded on the CD into an analog signal sent to the amplifier.

Digital Data Communications Message Protocol (DDCMP)   A DECnet data link protocol that can handle both synchronous and asynchronous links.

Digital Equipment Corporation (DEC)   Manufacturer of VAX (and before that PDP-11) boxes and the VMS operating system.

Digital Network Architecture (DNA)   A set of protocols for network architecture.

DIP   *Dual in-line package*, the housing for an integrated circuit.

DIP switch   A switch used to select the operating mode of a device.

directed information   Information intended for a particular recipient, such as private e-mail.

directory   An organizing structure for files. In most operating systems, directories can themselves be organized hierarchically into a "tree" of parent and children directories.

Directory Access Protocol (DAP)   An X.500 protocol governing communication between a Directory User Agent and a Directory System Agent.

directory listing   A summary list of available files, possibly including file sizes, attributes, date and time of creation or last changes, and the owner, where appropriate.

directory service   A database of sites and usernames that enables users to locate other users, hosts, and services.

Directory System Agent (DSA)   X.500 software that serves directory information to Directory User Agents.

Directory User Agent (DUA)   X.500 software that queries a Directory System Agent for directory information.

disable   (v) To temporarily disconnect or make nonfunctional (without necessarily shutting off).

disclaimer   The line in some sig blocks asserting that the opinions of the writer are not necessarily those of the organization providing her Internet access.

Discordianism   The principles of the Discordian Society, as set down in the *Principia Discordia* and other sacred (or profane) texts.

Discordian Society   Followers of the goddess Eris (or Discordia), a mostly farcical organization spawned from Robert Anton Wilson's *Illuminati!* trilogy.

discussion group   Any online group of likeminded people who may communicate via a mailing list, in a newsgroup, on an IRC channel, etc.

disk   A medium for storing computer data, either built into the computer (a hard disk) or removable (a floppy disk).

disk drive   The mechanism that spins, reads from, and writes to the disk itself.

diskette   A $5\frac{1}{4}$" or $3\frac{1}{2}$" removable floppy disk used for storing data.

disk server   A network program that enables a computer to use a disk drive on another computer (or a partition of such a disk drive) as if it were a local disk drive.

Distinct TCP/IP Tools   A set of Internet tools for Windows sold by Distinct Corporation.

distributed computing   An approach to computing that allows applications to run the same way across different types of networks.

Distributed Computing Environment (DCE)   A set of standards for servers, interfaces, and protocols promoted by the Open Software Foundation to enable distributed computing.

distributed database   A repository of information stored on various hosts and accessible to searches as if stored in a single location.

distributed server   Peer-to-peer network architecture, in which server functions are shared among the peer computers in the network, and disk drives, printers, and other devices are available to all.

distribution   The geographic range that a Usenet post is distributed to. By default, most newsreaders will give posts *World* distribution.

distribution list   A simple form of mailing list in which an alias is assigned to a list of e-mail addresses. Mail directed to the alias is sent to every address on the list.

disusered   (adj) Denied access to the Net, having an account canceled.

DIX   Digital, Intel, and Xerox, together the developers of the Ethernet protocol.

doc   Slang for a document.

documentation   Paper or online manuals that describe the functions of a computer system, often in incomprehensible terms.

dogpile   (v) To quickly follow up a Usenet post with a large volume of critical replies.

domain   The main subdivision of Internet addresses, the last part of an Internet address after the final dot. In the United States, the standard domains are as follows:

DOMAIN	Meaning
.com	Commercial
.edu	Educational
.gov	Government
.mil	Military
.org	Non-profit organization
.net	Network

Outside the United States, the top-level domain is usually the country domain, such as *.ca* for Canada, *.de* for Germany (Deutschland), *.uk* for the United Kingdom, and so on.

domain name   A complete description of an Internet site including a host name, subdomain, and domain, all separated by dots.

domain name address   An Internet address expressed in terms of host, subdomain, and domain, as opposed to the numerical IP address. Also called a *fully qualified domain name*.

domain name resolution   The process of converting domain names to numerical IP addresses, by consulting domain name servers.

domain name server   An application that maintains a table of domain names and corresponding IP addresses in order to resolve the domain names of messages.

Domain Name System (DNS)   A collection of distributed databases (domain name servers) that maintain the correlations between domain name addresses and numerical IP addresses, for example, the domain name address ruby.ora.com gets resolved into the numeric Internet address 134.65.87.3, and vice versa. DNS allows human beings to use the Internet without remembering long lists of numbers.

d00dz   B1FFspeak for *dudes*, a term of address.

DOS   *Disk Operating System*, the operating system developed for IBM PCs.

dos2unix   A UNIX program that converts DOS text files to UNIX format (by stripping of the carriage return character from the end of each line).

dot   The separator character for domain names, newsgroup names, and other UNIX-oriented files. Dots should only be used to separate hierarchical levels in newsgroup names, not to split compound names. So, for example, alt.fan.dave.barry would be improper, but alt.fan.dave-barry is fine.

dot address   A 32-bit numerical IP address of the form *number-dot-number-dot-number-dot-number* (such as 192.100.81.101).
Each of the four numbers can range from 0 to 255.

dot file   A UNIX file whose name begins with a dot, such as .profile, .netrc, .cshrc, and so on. Dot files will not show up in a normal directory listing.

doubled sig   A sig block that appears twice at the end the of an e-mail message or Usenet post, a sign that the writer is a newbie or that the software is hiccupping.

down   (adj) Said of a network or device that is not functioning.

download   (v) To transfer a file over a modem from a remote computer to your desktop computer. (Technically, to transfer a file from a larger computer to a smaller computer.)

downstream   Where your newsfeed goes after it has reached your host and your host has sent it along to other sites.

DRECnet   A derogatory name for DECnet.

driver   Software that controls peripheral devices, such as monitors, printers, or keyboards.

drop-ins   Random characters that appear on the screen due to a faulty connection and/or line noise.

drop-outs   Characters that are missing from the screen or not passed on by the keyboard.

DS4   *Digital Signal Level 4* is 274.176 Mbps, a standard level of digital transmission service (also called T4).

DS1   *Digital Signal Level 1* is 1.544 Mbps, a standard level of digital transmission service (also called T1).

DS3   *Digital Signal Level 3* is 44.736 Mbps, a standard level of digital transmission service (also called T3).

DS2   *Digital Signal Level 2* is 6.312 Mbps, a standard level of digital transmission service (also called T2).

DS0   *Digital Signal Level 0* is 64 Kbps, a standard level of digital transmission service (also called *fractional* T1).

dual in-line package   The housing for an integrated circuit.

dumb terminal   A keyboard-and-monitor device that sends keystrokes to a computer and displays output on the screen. If you dial up to a UNIX shell, then your PC is being used as a dumb terminal.

dummy variable   A meaningless variable used in an example to demonstrate correct syntax, such as foo, bar, or baz.

dump   (v) To send the contents of a file (or other data) to a device or another file, in order to print, display, or store the data.

dup killer   (*doop killer*) FidoNet software that tries to detect and eliminate duplicate copies of the same message that may have arrived via different routes.

duplex   Transmission of signals in two directions at once.

dup loop   (*doop loop*) A series of nearly identical messages that have eluded the dup killer.

dynamic adaptive routing   A method of directing network traffic based on the current state of the network.

dynamic node addressing   A method of addressing used on AppleTalk networks in which nodes are assigned network addresses as needed, but do not have stable consistent network addresses, as in an IP network.

dynamic SLIP   A type of SLIP access to the Internet, in which the user is supplied with a new IP address, drawn from a pool of possibilities, every time she connects. This enables the service provider to assign fewer IP addresses to its SLIP customers, with the trade-off being that the users cannot function as a host without a consistent address.

EBCDIC   (*eb-sa-dic* or *eb-see-dic*) *Extended Binary Coded Decimal Interchange Code*, a proprietary IBM character set that is not entirely compatible with ASCII.

echo   (n) 1. A discussion group on FidoNet; 2. The method by which the characters you type are displayed on your screen, also known as *local echo*; 3. The method by which characters sent from a remote system are displayed on your screen, also known as *remote echo*.

EcoNet   (*ee-coe-net*) A BBS dedicated to environmental issues. Its Internet domain name is igc.org.

ed   (rhymes with *bed*) A UNIX, line-at-a-time text editor.

EDGAR   *Electronic Data Gathering Archiving and Retrieval*, a database of corporate disclosure, transaction, and financial status data maintained by the United States Security Exchange Commission. For more information, see the Web page at http://town.hall.org/edgar/edgar.html.

editor   1. A text editor, a program used to edit simple text files; 2. Any program used to edit any type of file, such as a .WAV (Windows sound file) editor.

EDLIS   *Exchange of Dylan Lyrics—Internet Service,* an underground organization whose agents respond to requests posted in rec.music.dylan and elsewhere on the Net.

EDT   A text editor available on VMS machines and at Delphi Information Service.

.edu   The Internet domain dedicated to educational institutions, generally in the United States.

Educational Resources Information Center (ERIC)   A service for schools providing online bibliography and journal abstracts, via gopher at ericir.syr.edu and via e-mail at askeric@ricir.syr.edu.

EDUCOM   (*ed-you-com*) An organization dedicated to facilitating the use of computers in educational institutions. It is a supporter of the National Research and Education Network (NREN). Gopher: educom.com, e-mail: inquiry@bitnic.educom.com.

ee   (*ee-ee*) A UNIX text editor.

EFF's Guide to the Internet   Formerly *Big Dummy's Guide to the Internet*, the Electronic Frontier Foundation's excellent free Internet guide, available via FTP, gopher, and the Web.

ego search   To use Internet search engines to look for mentions of one's own name.

ego surfing   Searching for one's own name on the Internet.

EIA/TIA-568   A document coauthored by the American National Standards Institute, the Electronics Industry Association, and the Telecommunications Industry Association that specifies a wiring standard for buildings suitable for both LANs and telecommunications systems.

8-bit clean   (adj) Said of a modem connection with 8 data bits and no corruption of the signal from line noise.

802.x   A set of communications standards (802.1 through 802.5) for physical and electrical connections in LANs, defined by the Institute of Electrical and Electronic Engineers.

80-character line length   The standard line length for an IBM or UNIX terminal, a recommended maximum line length for e-mail and Usenet posts (some prefer 75 characters to allow for quotation, since most e-mail and newsreader programs quote text by preceding it with a > or other character).

e-journal   An *electronic journal*, an academic journal that circulates via an e-mail mailing list. One advantage e-journals have over print journals is that they are searchable.

Electronic Frontier Foundation (EFF)   A lobbying and advocacy organization, founded by Mitch Kapor and John Barlow, working for the preservation of freedom on the cyberspace frontier.

electronic journal   Also called an *e-journal*, an academic journal that circulates via an e-mail mailing list. One advantage e-journals have over print journals is that they are searchable.

electronic mail   Usually called e-mail, messages carried electronically from computer to computer.

Electronics Industries Association (EIA)   A standards organization for the electronics industry, the coauthor of EIA/TIA-568.

elm   (rhymes with *helm*) A full-screen UNIX e-mail program, easier to use than the basic, line-at-a-time mail but still more difficult than pine, which is much closer to modern word processors.

.elmrc   A setup file for elm.

emacs   (*ee-macs*) Also written *EMACS*, a UNIX text editor that doubles as an operating environment, mail program, and newsreader.

e-mail   (n) Also *email*, short for *electronic mail*, one of the most popular features of networks, online services, and the Internet in general, but you already knew that, didn't you? The term *e-mail* is used both for the overall process and for the messages carried electronically from computer to computer.

(v) To send e-mail.

e-mail address   1. An Internet mail address of the form *username@host .domain*; 2. The username portion of a mail account on a network.

e me   Send me e-mail, please reply by e-mail.

emoticon   A smiley or other sideways punctuation face such as these:

:-)   :-(:-P   %^)   ;-)   B-)   :D

Emoticons can convey some insight into the writer's emotional state.

emulation   For a computer, operating system, or application, the process of imitating the functions of another environment.

encapsulate   To embed a higher-level protocol within a lower-level protocol to create a single frame for transportation over a network.

Encapsulated PostScript (EPS)   A device-independent file format for PostScript files. EPS files are portable and can be printed with any PostScript printer.

encoding   The process of converting data to a coded format, generally to make it more easily transportable.

encrypt   To scramble the contents of a file or e-mail message so that only those with the key can unscramble and read them.

encryption   A process of rendering a file or e-mail message unreadable to anyone lacking the encryption key.

encryption key   A unique, secret data block used to encrypt e-mail.

end-to-end   (adj) Direct, said of a connection between two computers.

end-user   (n) From a programmer's perspective, the ultimate customer, the regular person using the program, operating system, or computer.

Enter key   A large key on the right side of most keyboards (sometimes called the *Return key*) used to submit commands or insert hard returns (newlines) into text.

enterprise computing   Corporate network computing, bridging a variety of platforms, operating systems, and networking protocols.

Enterzone   A hyperzine on the World Wide Web (at http://ezone.org/ez).

environment   Also called *operating environment,* a front end for an operating system, a set of tools and a consistent look and feel that allow the user to interact with the computer. Windows is an environment that runs on top of the MS-DOS operating system.

EOF   (*ee-oh-eff*) An *end-of-file* marker.

.eps   The file extension for an Encapsulated PostScript file.

Eris   The Goddess of Discord (from Greek mythology), worshipped by members of the Discordian Society.

error   An unexpected action or result, or incorrectly transmitted data. Any process that causes results which a computer cannot properly interpret.

error control   Any method for verifying the correctness of transmitted data.

error message   A message from the operating system, alerting a user that something has gone wrong. Error messages can be as cryptic as a random number or as informative as a complete explanation of the problem.

escape character   1. ASCII 26; 2. Any character which, when preceded by an escape (usually ASCII 26, the character that is transmitted when the Escape key is pressed), sends a command to a device, such as a terminal or printer. They are often represented on the screen as capital letters preceded by carets, such as ^E, ^X, etc.

escape out   (v) 1. To substitute a special symbol for a character that would otherwise be misinterpreted (e.g., to escape out slash characters so they don't get interpreted as directory separators); 2. To run a temporary shell from within an application in order to send commands to the operating system (e.g., to escape out to UNIX to check your mail without exiting the newsreader).

escape sequence   A sequence of characters reserved for a special meaning by a computer's operating system; may be used to send commands (for example, to a printer).

e-text   Written works made available electronically.

Ethernet   A LAN network protocol and set of cabling specifications, originally developed by Digital, Intel, and Xerox, employing a bus topology and providing a transfer rate of up to 10 Mbps. Ethernet nodes may be connected with unshielded twisted-pair wiring or thick or thin coaxial cable. Ethernet uses CSMA/CD to prevent collisions, as opposed to token rings, which use token passing.

EtherTalk   AppleTalk protocols for Ethernet LANs, encapsulating DDP datagrams into Ethernet frames.

EtherTalk Link Access Protocol (ELAP)   AppleTalk's Ethernet data-link protocol.

ETLA   (*ee-tee-ell-ay*) *Extended three-letter acronym* (i.e., a four-letter acronym). The acronym is a facetious comment on the proliferation of bewildering TLAs in the technical world. Too many TLAs and ETLAs thrown around make MEGO (my eyes glaze over).

.etx   File extension for a setext file.

Eudora   An e-mail program for Windows or the Macintosh that can use the Post Office Protocol and function as an offline mail reader. Available via anonymous FTP from ftp.qualcomm.com.

European Academic and Research Network (EARN)   A network of universities and research facilities in Europe that has e-mail and file-transfer connections to BITNET.

even parity   A method of verifying the correctness of transmitted data by summing each byte, adding a parity bit of 1 if necessary to make the sum even before sending the data, and then repeating the summation on the receiving end.

exclamation mark (!)   1. A bang—it precedes each site in a bang path; 2. In some UNIX programs, an exclamation mark enables the user to shell out; 3. Overuse of exclamation marks to punctuate Usenet posts is one of the hallmarks of a newbie or a B1FF.

.exe   A DOS file extension used to indicate an executable file (such as a program or self-extracting archive file).

execute   To perform a command or run a program, something operating systems do.

exit   (v) To quit a program or leave a shell.

expansion slot   Inside a PC, a connector that gives an adapter access to the system bus, allowing the installation of additional peripheral devices.

expire   Applied to Usenet articles, to be removed after an expiration date to keep the newsfeed from growing too large.

export   (v) 1. To save a file in a different format (that of another program); 2. To send a product to a foreign country (whether physically or over the Internet).

Extended Binary Coded Decimal Interchange Code (EBCDIC)   A proprietary IBM character set that is not entirely compatible with ASCII.

extension   The portion of a file name after the last dot, often used to indicate the type of file. DOS extensions have a three-character maximum length.

External Gateway Protocol (EGP)   A routing protocol by which connected networks signal their availability to each other.

extranet   An enterprise's private intranet that relies on secure use of the public Internet to connect disparate locations.

e-zine   Also *ezine*, an electronically distributed fanzine or magazine. Many are sent as e-mail. Others are made available via gopher or the Web.

f   1. The forward command in many UNIX mail programs; 2. The follow up command in some UNIX newsreaders.

face time   (n) Time spent meeting with a person, as contrasted with time spent communicating via e-mail, voice mail, etc.

fair use   The legal doctrine that allows limited quotation of other people's work if the use of their work does not undercut its market value.

fall off   (v) Said of a portion of data that exceeds the size of a memory register and is lost.

fanzine   An underground, do-it-yourself magazine, often dedicated to a band, celebrity, or cult figure.

FAQ   (*fack*, n) 1. A *frequently asked question*; 2. A file containing frequently asked questions and their answers, sometimes called a FAQL (*frequently asked question list*). To find FAQs, look in the *.answers newsgroups or the FTP archive at rtfm.mit.edu. Many mailing lists and Usenet newsgroups maintain FAQs so that participants won't have to spend lots of time answering the same set of questions.

FAQL   (*fackle*, n) *Frequently-asked-question list*, a file containing frequently asked questions and their answers, usually compiled and maintained by a newsgroup, mailing list, or Internet site.

FARNET (Federation of American Research Networks)   A nonprofit organization that works to promote the use of computer networks for research and education.

fast packet   A standard for high-speed, high-traffic, cell-switching networks. Also called *Asynchronous Transfer Mode (ATM)*.

fax   (n) 1. A *facsimile* of a document, digitized and transmitted over phone lines. While faxes are usually sent and received with a stand-alone fax machine, faxes may also be sent to and from computers using fax software and a fax modem; 2. A machine that can send and receive faxes.
(v) To send a fax.

fax modem   A modem that can fulfill some of the functions of a fax machine.

Federal Information Exchange (FIX)   A gateway linking U.S. government networks with the Internet.

Federal Information Processing Standards (FIPS)   A United States Department of Defense document specifying U.S. government networking plans.

Federal Networking Council (FNC)   An organization that coordinates the networking standards of U.S. government agencies.

FEDIX   An online information service linking educational institutions and the U.S. government. It offers the Minority On-Line Information Service (MOLIS).

fetch   (v) To transfer a file from a remote site on the Internet to your host computer.

(n) A Macintosh FTP program.

Fiber Distributed Data Interface (FDDI)   A backbone system for large networks, employing two rings of fiber-optic cabling, with a signaling rate of 80 Mbps.

fiber-optic cable   Glass cabling designed to carry light pulses, often used for backbones; more dependable, lighter, and smaller than copper cable carrying electronic signals, but much more expensive and more difficult to repair.

FidoNet   A network of BBSs with Internet e-mail access.

Fiction Rag & Gossip   A web site about writers maintained by the novelist Martha Conway (at http://www.syx.com/pilgrim/rag.html).

field   (n) A defined area containing a fixed number of characters, found in online forms and some databases.

56K   (adj) Said of a telephone circuit with a 64-Kbps bandwidth that uses 8K for signaling and the remaining 56K for traffic.

File Attach   A FidoNet procedure for attaching a file to an e-mail message to send it to another BBS.

file locking   Preventing all but the first user from making changes to a file that is opened by more than one user on a network.

File Request   A FidoNet procedure for transferring a file from one BBS to another.

file server   A computer that makes files available to other users on a network.

file transfer   The copying of a file over a network connection from a remote site to the local host.

film at 11   A common tag line in Usenet follow-up posts mocking the timeliness (or lack thereof) of the original article. (This is an allusion to a once-popular evening news teaser.) Often follows "Imminent death of the Net predicted!"

filter   (n) 1. A program that converts one file format into another; 2. In e-mail, a program that allows certain messages to reach the user while eliminating other messages. On UNIX machines, it is easy to set up an e-mail filter to prevent unwanted mail from making it to your inbox.

(v) To ignore unwanted information by using a filter (definition 2).

finger   (v) To seek the identity of a user or the status of a network.

(n) The UNIX command that performs the finger function.

finn   (v) To pull rank on someone else in IRC by showing that you've been around a lot longer than the other person—a relative newbie compared to you. (The IRC protocol was first used on servers in Finland, hence the term *finn*.)

firewall   (n) A security measure on the Internet, protecting information, preventing access, or ensuring that users cannot do any harm to underlying systems. Some networks are connected to the Internet via a firewall machine.

FirstSearch Catalog   A catalog maintained by the Online Computer Library Center that gives member libraries access to many databases of books and magazines in print.

flame   (n) An insulting e-mail or Usenet post. Flames are often ill-considered knee-jerk expressions of anger, but they can also be cruelly detailed and intended for the amusement of the general audience at the expense of the flamee.

(v) To post a flame.

flamebait   (n) A post to a mailing list or newsgroup designed to elicit flames. Flamebait can be recognized by the fact that it goes beyond the premises of the list or newsgroup. Nobody objects to provocative or even argumentative posts, but posts to the alt.fan.frank-zappa newsgroup saying "Zappa was a no-talent potty-mouthed dweeb" betray a lack of legitimate interest in the subject at hand.

flamefest   A flame war, particularly one involving many participants.

flame on   A comment in a post meaning either "Here is where I start flaming" or "I'm prepared to be flamed for the following comment."

flamer   1. One who flames; 2. One who flames habitually or incessantly.

flames to /dev/null   A tag line in posts to mailing lists and newsgroups meaning "I'll ignore (or delete) any flames," from the UNIX name for the null device, a sort of trash can.

flame war   Often written *flamewar*, a prolonged series of flames and counterflames, drowning out the on-topic posts in a newsgroup or mailing list. Traditionally, flame wars end when Nazis are mentioned.

flavor   (n) A variety, as in "BSD is a flavor of UNIX."

flood   (v) To spam an IRC channel, that is, to type or paste in huge amounts of text, effectively drowning out the conversation.

floppy disk   A removable storage medium.

flow control   The method by which two devices, generally modems, signal to each other when to start and stop sending data.

fnord   (n) A nonsense word embedded in posts or sig blocks, alluding to Robert Anton Wilson's *Illuminati!* trilogy (in which children are taught not to see the fnords as part of their fnord conditioning by fnord the state fnord).

FOAF   (written only, n) A *friend of a friend*, the most common source or attribution for urban legends, implying that the teller doesn't personally know the participants, but knows someone who does.

folder   1. A directory, especially on a Macintosh; 2. An e-mail file containing related messages.

follow up   (v) To respond to a post with a replying post.

follow-up   (n) A post that replies to and possibly quotes an earlier post.

follow-up line   A line in the header of some Usenet posts directing follow-ups to a particular newsgroup or newsgroups. Newbies who fail to heed the follow-up line can be tricked into posting replies to inappropriate newsgroups (or worse, to *.test groups, resulting in thousands of automated replies stuffing their inbox).

foo   A dummy variable used by programmers as a stand-in for a real variable, often paired with bar.

foobar   A dummy variable used by programmers as a stand-in for a real variable.

footprint   The portion of a surface that a computer or other device occupies.

foreground   In a multitasking computer environment, a process that takes place in full view or with higher priority than other running processes is said to take place in the foreground.

FORTRAN   An early computer programming language (the name comes from *FORmula TRANslator*).

fortune cookie   A program that spits out a different fortune every time you run it. Some systems run cookie as part of their startup or login procedure.

forum   A discussion group on CompuServe and other online services and BBSs where users with similar interests may find valuable information, exchange ideas, and share files.

forward   (v) To send received e-mail along to another address, either manually or automatically.

forward slash   /, used to divide directories in a path in UNIX and, hence, in many Internet applications).

FQA   Frequently questioned acronym.

frame   1. An area of the screen of some graphical web browsers (such as Netscape and Microsoft Internet Explorer), which can be updated independently and may also scroll separately.
2. (n) A block of data encapsulated with a header and trailer for transmission over a network.

frame relay   A standard for transmission of frames over a packet-switching network, a variant of the X.25 standard.

fred   1. An easy-to-use X.500 interface; 2. A dummy variable used by programmers to stand for a real variable.

FrEdMail   (*fred-mail*) A network of BBSs for students and teachers.

free-net   A free public network providing Internet access to members of a community.

Free Software Foundation (FSF)   An organization dedicated to the production and distribution of free software, the creators of GNU, reachable via FTP at prep.ai.mit.edu.

free-WAIS   A free version of a WAIS server produced and distributed by CNIDR (Clearinghouse for Networked Information Discovery and Retrieval).

freeware   Software distributed for free (or for bragging rights) via the Net. The culture of the Internet encourages freeware.

frequency   A measurement of the number of cycles per second of an electronic signal, roughly a measurement of the speed of a process or device.

fringeware   Software of dubious stability, commercial value, or appeal, made available as freeware.

front end   The part of a computer process that the end-user interacts with. In client/server applications, the client acts as a front end for the server.

FSLIST   The *Forgotten Site List*. A list of Internet service providers available via anonymous FTP from freedom.nmsu.edu in the /pub/docs/fslist/ directory.

ftp   The UNIX FTP program.

FTP   Internet *file transfer protocol*, the standard TCP/IP protocol for transferring files over the Internet, across any platforms.

FTPmail   A way to use FTP by e-mail if you don't have an FTP application. One address for an FTPmail server is ftpmail@pa.dec.com.

FTP server   An FTP file server, a computer serving files from an FTP archive.

FTP site   A host on the Internet containing archives and set up for FTP.

f2f   (written only, adv or adj) Face-to-face, meeting in person.

full duplex   Two-way communication in which the computers at either end of the transmission both send and receive at the same time.

full name   The real name associated with an e-mail address; can be an alias.

full-screen editor   A text editor that allows the user to move around the screen, editing the entire file.

fully qualified domain name (FQDN)   The complete domain name that identifies a specific computer (or host network, at the very least) on the Internet, including a host name, a subdomain name, and a domain name. Also called *domain name address*.

furrfu   (*fur-foo*) ROT-13 for *sheesh!*

fwiw   (written only) *For what it's worth*.

fyi   (*eff-why-eye*) *For your information*.

FYI   (n) An Internet document that provides information about the Internet itself, but which does not define standards. Available via anonymous FTP from rtfm.mit.edu.

g   The *go* command in the UNIX programs gopher and lynx, used to go to a specific address.

G   Abbreviation for gigabyte (roughly one billion bytes).

<g>   Also *<grin>*, indicates that the author is grinning, similar to
   :-)

gate   (n) Also called a *gateway*, a computer providing a connection between two networks, two e-mail handling systems, or a Usenet newsgroup and a mailing list. A gate reformats the data so that it will be acceptable to the system it is passing into.
(v) To establish a gate.

gated   (adj) Connected to another network or discussion group via a gateway.

gated newsgroup   A newsgroup whose posts are sent to a mailing list and which receives (or includes) posts from the mailing list.

gateway   Also called a *gate*, a computer providing a connection between two networks, two e-mail handling systems, or a Usenet newsgroup and a mailing list. A gateway reformats the data so that it will be acceptable to the system it is passing into.

<gd&r>   *Grinning, ducking, and running* (what you post after you've tweaked someone). Also *<gr&d>*.

geek   Someone who knows a lot about computers, networks, or the Internet and thinks they're interesting (not necessarily an insult).

geek code   A set of coded ratings in a sig block, describing the poster in humorous, geeky terms. For example, if I put the following geek code in my signature:

```
GLP d- H s-:+ g? p0 au- a w v+++ C++ US N++ K+++ W+ M+ !V
-po+ Y+ t+ j+ R- tv+ b++ !D B- e++ u** h- f+ r++ !n y?
```

I'd be saying "I'm a geek of literature and philosophy, I dress casually (jeans at work), have normal hair, am shorter and rounder than average, can't find my glasses, generally have no pens in my pockets, drive an old car, am between 30 and 39, am slightly weird, talk a mile a minute, use computers a lot, work in the Sun OS/Solaris version of UNIX, keep up with a number of newsgroups, have gotten mail from Kibo, am overly committed to Microsoft Windows, like Macintoshes, have never used VMS, hate both sides of the conventional political debate, am concerned about privacy and security in cyberspace, watch *Star Trek*, enjoy *Jeopardy*, am down on role-playing games, watch some TV just about every day, read a lot, have never played Doom, find Barney slightly annoying, have a bachelor's degree, listen to lots of strange music, live in a fairly nongeeky home, have a lot of geeky friends, have dated my current SO for a long time, will eat anything, and I'm male.

The code is maintained by Robert A. Hayden. For a complete key to all of the categories, finger hayden@vax1.mankato.msus.edu.

geek out   (v) 1. To get lost in the minutiae of a computer process; 2. To talk computers or networking in a social setting.

General Public License (GPL)   Also called *copyleft*, the license carried by Free Software Foundation software (such as GNU), granting reuse and reproduction rights to anyone and everyone.

get   (v) To copy a file from a remote source to your host computer, particularly via FTP.

(n) The FTP command to get a file.

Get a life!   A common flame, suggesting that the flamee is too involved in the Internet or her/his computer.

Get a real...!   A common geeky type of flame (such as "Get a real computer," "Get a real operating system," "Get a real service provider," and so on) directed at someone's inferior hardware, software, or network connection.

Ghod   An alternative spelling for God preferred by some hackers and other netizens (also spelled *ghod*).

Ghu   A deity some hackers and other netizens offer their praises and curses to, as in "Great Ghu! Where'd you get an idea like that?"

.gif   The file extension for GIFs.

GIF (Graphics Interchange Format)   1. An extremely popular compressed graphics (image) file format originated by CompuServe but readable in most platforms; 2. A file in the GIF format.

GIF! GIF! GIF!   A ritual follow-up to a post mentioning an image (such as a photograph), requesting that someone scan the image, save it a as a GIF, uuencode it, and post it to the newsgroup.

giga-   Prefix meaning one billion.

gigabyte   Roughly one billion bytes (actually 1,073,741,824 bytes), a large amount of storage.

GIGO   (written only) *Garbage in, garbage out*, a longstanding computer truism meaning that the computer won't produce meaningful results if you feed it useless data.

gilley   (n) A unit of bogosity, specifically applied to bogus analogies.

glitch   An unexplainable small computer lapse, causing a faulty result.

global   (adj) Affecting an entire document or system (for example, a global search and replace is a search and replace operation performed on an entire document, rather than a small selection or a single item).

gnu.   A hierarchy in the Usenet mold devoted to the Free Software Foundation and to its free products, such as GNU and emacs.

GNU   (*noo*) A freely distributed set of applications and utilities intended as a replacement for UNIX. GNU is distributed by the Free Software Foundation. (Its name is a recursive acronym that stands for *GNU's not UNIX*.)

GNUMACS   A contracted form of GNU emacs.

Godwin's Rule   Usenet Rule #4, which states that a thread in which Nazis or Hitler have been invoked has reached irrelevancy and will end soon. For some (but not all) of the other Rules see the net.legends FAQ at gopher:// dixie.aiss.uiuc.edu:6969/00/urban.legends/net.legends/Net.Legends.FAQ.

Good Times virus hoax   An oft-circulated false warning about an imaginary virus called Good Times that is said to come in the guise of an e-mail message and wreak havoc on your poor computer. There is no Good Times virus, but the hoax itself is a virulent type of meme.

gopher A client/server application that allows you to browse huge amounts of information by performing FTP transfers, remote logins, archie searches, and so on, presenting everything to the end-user in the form of menus. This saves the user from having to know (or type in) the addresses of the Internet resources being tapped.

Gopher Book for Windows A gopher client for Windows, available via anonymous FTP from sunsite.unc.edu.

gopher client The gopher program that an end-user runs to get information from a gopher server. The gopher client retrieves the menus and documents and displays them for the user.

gopher.micro.umn.edu The site of the University of Minnesota Gopher, the original gopher server.

Gopher for Nextstep A gopher client for the Nextstep operating system, available via anonymous FTP from sonata.cc.purdue.edu.

gopher server An application that provides documents and menus to gopher clients, a starting point for a gopher search.

gopher site A computer with a gopher server running on it.

gopherspace A conceptual space encompassing all of the menus and documents that can be reached via the interconnected system of gopher servers on the Internet.

gorets (n) A generic noun that can have any meaning, especially as elaborated in the alt.gorets newsgroup.

go root (v) To log in as root, a UNIX superuser or system administrator account, in order to exercise the extended privileges of that account.

.gov An Internet domain corresponding to U.S. government, including federal, state, and local governments.

Government OSI Profile (GOSIP) A set of OSI standards that the U.S. government follows in the procurement of computers in order to preserve compatibility among various government computer networks.

graphical user interface (GUI)   A full-screen graphical interface (meaning not limited to just letters and numbers) that allows users to run programs, execute commands, and generally interact with the computer by using a pointing device such as a mouse to manipulate graphical screen elements, as opposed to typing commands at a prompt.

Dial-up Internet users generally need SLIP or PPP access to be able to interact directly with Internet facilities within their GUI.

<gr&d>   (written only) *Grinning, running, and ducking* (what you post after you've tweaked someone). Also *<gd&r>*.

Great Renaming   A day in 1985 on which nonlocal Usenet newsgroup names were changed from the form *net.** to the hierarchy still in use today.

Great Worm   The 1988 worm that got out of control and crashed systems all over the Internet, throwing a scare into many.

grep   (rhymes with *prep*, v) To globally search a document, set of files, or newsfeed for a particular word or expression, from the UNIX grep command.

<grin>   Also *<g>*, just kidding, similar to

    :-)

grok   (v) To understand deeply or intimately, from Robert A. Heinlein's *Stranger in a Strange Land.*

group   (n) Generally, a newsgroup, a Usenet or similar-style discussion group.

groupware   Software that gives multiple users access to the same information over a network, allowing collaboration on documents, scheduling of meetings, tracking of mission-critical projects, and so on.

grovel   1. To beg for something in a Usenet newsgroup; 2. For a programmer, to hunt through code looking for a problem.

guest   A special login account reserved for visitors checking out a BBS, online service, or service provider.

GUI   (*gooey*) A full-screen *graphical user interface* (meaning not limited to just letters and numbers) that allows users to run programs, execute commands, and generally interact with the computer by using a pointing device such as a mouse to manipulate graphical screen elements, as opposed to typing commands at a prompt.

Dial-up Internet users generally need SLIP or PPP access to be able to interact directly with Internet facilities within their GUI.

guiltware   Shareware that reminds you to register (and pay for) the product.

gunzip   (n) The UNIX uncompression program for gzipped files.

guru   A helpful expert, someone to whom regular users turn to solve problems with their computer or network.

.gz   A file extension for files that have been compressed with gzip.

gzip   (n) A UNIX file compression program.

h   The help command in some UNIX applications. Also try *?* (question mark).

-h-   The letter *h* is often stuck inside other words to make them appear odd, as in Ghod.

^H   The backspace character. Use of the Backspace key in terminal emulations that don't support it sometimes leaves the original text on-screen, followed by one ^H character for every time Backspace is pressed, as in "Let me be the first to call you a fool^H^H^H^Hfriend."

hack   (v) To write code, to work on a computer, to cleverly diagnose and fix a problem, to dig beneath the surface of a computer process, reinventing things when necessary. (Outside of the Internet, the word *hack* suggests the action of breaking into computer networks. On the Internet, the word crack is used for that meaning.)

hack around   To figure a software program out for yourself, by trial and error, rather than by reading the manual.

hacker   A computer adept, someone who enjoys working with computers and testing the limits of systems, an enthusiastic or fast (or both) programmer. (Outside of the Internet, the word *hacker* has unsavory connotations, suggesting someone who breaks into computer networks and steals or vandalizes information. On the Internet, such malevolent hackers are called crackers.)

hacker ethic   The philosophy, common among hackers, that information, technology, and clever tricks should be shared and disseminated rather than hoarded.

Hacker's Dictionary   *The New Hacker's Dictionary, Second Edition*, compiled by Eric S. Raymond and published by MIT Press: the paper book equivalent of the jargon file, an invaluable resource of hacker slang (much of which overlaps Internet slang and jargon).

half bridge   A device that connects a network to a communications link via a modem without passing routing information, which must be supplied by the network software.

half duplex   Two-way communication in which the computers at each end of the transmission take turns sending.

half router   A device that connects a network to a communications link via a modem, passing routing information along with data.

HAND   (written only) *Have a nice day* (usually sarcastic).

handle   A nickname or one-word name, such as a nick on IRC or a username. Network connections provided by employers often assign a strung-together version of a person's full name (using hyphens, underlines, dots, or capitalization to separate first and last name and sometimes even middle initials) as their username, instead of a handle.

handshaking   For two connected devices, the sending of signals to alert each other when ready to receive data.

hang   (v) Said of a computer, to stop working, to freeze, to become unresponsive, to wait for something that will never happen.

HappyNet   Kibo's proposed reorganization of Usenet into three major hierarchies—*nonbozo.*, *bozo.*, and *megabozo.* The entire text of the original HappyNet proclamation and manifesto can be found on the Web at ftp://ftp.std.com/pub/alt.religion.kibology/happynet/HappyNet.1994.

hard disk   A fixed computer storage medium.

hardware   Computer equipment—the actual pieces of metal and plastic, as opposed to the programs that run on computers (software).

hardware address   A specific physical address (as contrasted with a variable logical address) assigned to a device.

hardware flow control   A form of flow control that is governed by devices themselves, instead of by communications software.

Harris' Lament   "All the good ones are taken!" (that is, all the good domain names).

hash   1. A symbol (usually #) echoed at regular intervals to show that a process is still underway; 2. The ftp command that causes the hash symbols to be displayed.

hat   A common name for the caret character, ^ (ASCII 94), used to indicate exponents and to underscore text on the previous line in e-mail and Usenet posts.

Hayes-compatible   Said of a modem that understands the Hayes AT instruction set. (Hayes is a name-brand modem maker.) Most modems today are Hayes-compatible.

header   1. The rows of information at the top of an e-mail message that include who the message is from, who it's to, when it was sent, and what it's about; 2. Information preceding the data in a packet, specifying the addresses of the source and the destination as well as error-checking information.

Hello world.   The output of most C programmers' first program, from Kernighan & Ritchie's canonical C text, *The C Programming Language*.

help   A command that will bring up help information in some programs and in some operating systems. When you are stuck, it never hurts to type *help*, or *h*, or *?*, and press Enter to see what happens.

HEPnet   A network for physicists, not part of the Internet, but accessible via the Web at http://info.cern.ch/hypertext/DataSources/bySubject/Physics/HEP.html.

heterogeneous network   A network that includes various types of computers, operating systems, network cards, and so on, which therefore must be capable of different network protocols.

hexadecimal   (adj) Pertaining to a numerical system using base 16 (as opposed to our more common decimal system, which uses base 10, or the binary system, which uses base 2). Hexadecimal digits are represented by the numerals 0 through 9 and the letters A through F. Because 16 is a multiple of 2, it is easy to convert binary numbers into hexadecimal numbers, and some programs display data in hexadecimal form.

HGopher   A gopher client for Windows, available via anonymous FTP from lister.cc.ic.ac.uk.

hiccup   (v) Said of a network or application, to mistakenly skip some data or send it more than once.

hierarchical file system   A system of arranging files in directories and subdirectories in order to maintain hierarchical relationships between the files and make them easier to find and retrieve.

hierarchical routing   A system of routing in which different parts of a large network are arranged in a hierarchical tree and each level takes care of routing information to subordinate levels.

The Internet maintains three different routing levels: backbone networks, mid-level networks, and stub networks.

hierarchy   1. In file storage, the arrangement of directories into a tree of parents and children; 2. In networks, the arrangement of levels for routing purposes; 3. In Usenet, the organization of newsgroups into general areas, topics, and subtopics, or the major groupings themselves.

High-Level Data Link Control (HDLC)   An ISO protocol for the data link layer of X.25 and OSI networks. It specifies that data is sent in frames that may vary in length.

High Performance Parallel Interface (HPPI)   An ANSI standard for connecting supercomputers to other devices, such as routers and other computers.

hing   (n) A hint (originally from a typo) on IRC, used in initgame.

history   1. A list of a user's recent actions or commands; 2. A list of the gopher menus a user has passed through; 3. A list of the hypertext links a Web browser has followed.

hit   1. A connection made to a Web server; 2. A successful match in a database search (in some searches, you can specify a maximum number of hits).

hog   (v) To reserve an undue amount of some resource for yourself, as in "hogging bandwidth."
(n) One who hogs some resource.

holy war   An neverending argument between intractable sides, such as over gun control, abortion, or IBM vs. Mac. There are usually special talk. newsgroups set up for the people who can't resist arguing with their opposites, and it's considered bad form to bring up a holy war topic in an inappropriate forum. (Newsgroups and mailing lists often have their own local holy wars.)

$HOME   In UNIX, a variable that serves as an abbreviation for the path of your home directory.

home directory   The directory allotted to your specific account, where you start off when you log into your UNIX account, and where you store your files.

home page   On the Web, a starting page with links to other related pages. Many people have personal home pages with biographical information and a hotlist of favorite Web destinations.

homogeneous network   A network that includes only one type of computer, operating system, network card, and so on, and therefore a single network protocol.

hop   (n) Each short individual trip that packets (or e-mail messages) make many times over, from router to router, on their way to their destinations.

hop count   The number of hops it will take for a packet to make it from a source to a destination.

host   (n) A computer on a network that allows many users access at once. If you connect to the Internet by dialing up a provider via a modem, then the computer you log into is your local host. If you connect via FTP to an archive site, then the computer you're getting the files from is a remote host.

host address   A numerical IP address of the form *number-dot-number-dot-number-dot-number* (such as 192.100.81.101).

host name   Also *hostname*, the leftmost portion of a fully qualified domain name, uniquely identifying a specific computer (host) on a network in a subdomain in a domain.

hotlist   A list of frequent destinations, or sites, arranged on a menu, such as a list of Web pages.

HotBot   A search engine powered by Inktomi and sponsored by HotWired (at http://www.hotbot.com).

HotJava   A web browser made by Sun Microsystems to demonstrate the use of Java.

HotWired   The online sibling of *Wired* magazine, a Web site, a publication, and an online service, at http://www.hotwired.com./

HP-UX   Hewlett-Packard's version of UNIX.

.hqx   A file extension that indicates the file has been compressed with the Macintosh BinHex compression.

HTML   *Hypertext markup language*, the hypertext language used in Web pages. It consists of regular text and tags that tell the browser what to do when a link is activated. It is a subset of SGML, a preexisting markup language.

HTTP   *Hypertext transport protocol*, the Internet protocol that defines how a Web server responds to requests for files, made via anchors and URLs.

hub In networks arranged with star topology, the central connecting device, a device that allows a network to add workstations by extending the transmission signal.

humma A nonsense word used to fill dead air on IRC.

hung (adj) Said of a computer, unresponsive, frozen, and possibly stuck in an infinite loop.

HyperCard The Macintosh hypermedia program that features cards that may contain text, pictures, sounds, movies, and so on, with clickable links to other cards.

hyperlink A hypertext link or a hypermedia link.

hypermedia An extension of the concept of hypertext to include pictures, sounds, movies, and so on, along with text and links to other documents.

hypermedia link A link from one document to another, from an anchor to a named location, or from an anchor to another form of media entirely, such as a picture, sound, or movie.

Hypernews An experimental Web news format, in some ways analogous to Usenet, found at http://ginko.cecer.army.mil:8000/hypernews/ hypernews.html.

hypertext Text that contains links to other text documents, allowing the reader to skip around and read the documents in various order.

hypertext link A link from one text document to another or from a text anchor to a named location.

HyperWais A WAIS client for HyperCard (for the Macintosh), available via anonymous FTP from sunsite.oit.unc.edu.

hyperzine An electronic hypermedia magazine or 'zine.

hyphen On computer keyboards, the - character, used also to indicate a dash. Compound portions of newsgroup names are hyphenated, as in alt.fan.dave-barry (alt.fan.dave.barry would be incorrect), as are some usernames.

Hytelnet   A telnet shell that runs in UNIX; it helps you find the telnet site you want and then runs the telnet session for you. It contains a huge list of university and public library catalogs, as well as gopher servers, WAIS servers, BBSs, and so on.

Hytelnet for DOS   A version of Hytelnet that runs in MS-DOS on a PC, available via anonymous FTP from access.usask.ca.

IANAL   (written only) *I am not a lawyer* (used as a disclaimer before offering quasi-legal advice on the Net).

IBM   *International Business Machines*, at one time the world's dominant computer company, maker of mainframes and PCs.

ice   Slang for security software, popularized in William Gibson's *Neuromancer* trilogy.

ignore   On IRC or in any other type of chat, to screen out the contributions of a participant who is annoying you.

image file   Another name for a binary file.

IMAP   *Internet Message Access Protocol*, a protocol for the storage and retrieval of e-mail, not yet a widespread standard.

imho   (written only, also *IMHO*) *In my humble opinion.*

imnsho   (written only, also *IMNSHO*) *In my not so humble opinion.*

imo   (written only, also *IMO*) *In my opinion.*

impression   (n) A web server's record of a browser's visit to a single page of a web site. (The word is used to distinguish from a hit, in that a single impression may register as several hits—one on the HTML document, one for each graphic on the page, and so on.)

In Some Unrelated Land   A novel by Martha Conway published as shareware on the Web (at http://syx.com/pilgrim/land.html) by Pilgrim Press.

inbox   Also *in box*, *in-box*, a file in which a mail program stores incoming e-mail messages.

include   To copy some or all of the message to which you are responding. Most e-mail programs and newsreaders will add a character such as > before each line of included text.

#include <disclaimer.h>   A C joke that appears in sig blocks, meaning that a standard disclaimer should be understood to have been included there.

include war   (n)   A flame war in which so many previous posts have been included that it's impossible to follow the argument amidst all the >s.

index   (n) 1. A file in a directory at a site that describes the contents of the directory; 2. An archie database; 3. A default Web page that a Web server provides when no file is specified.

INET   An annual conference put on by the Internet Society; 2. An abbreviation for Internet.

infinite loop   A computer process that repeats forever due to a programming error, causing the computer to hang. The instructions on the back of many a shampoo bottle—lather, rinse, repeat—would cause an infinite loop in a computer.

info   A common username for a mailbot (info@*host.subdomain.domain*) providing information about a network, service provider, or information service.

Infobahn   A euphemism for Internet that conjures up images of elevated freeways through a Bauhaus cyberscape.

info-deli   Peter Kaminski's information server (e-mail info-deli@netcom.com).

Info-Mac archives   A huge collection of Macintosh software at the sumex-aim.stanford.edu FTP site, in the /info-mac directory. It's also mirrored at wuarchive.wustl.edu in the /mirrors/info-mac directory.

information agent   A program that searches databases for information without requiring that the user know where the information is stored.

info-server   An e-mail address that triggers a mail server, responding to messages that contain key words by sending stored information.

initgame   An IRC variation on the guessing game called Botticelli, in which one participant changes their nick to the initials of a famous or fictional person and the other participants ask yes-or-no questions trying to guess the secret identity. Winner gets to start the next game.

initialization string   A string of seemingly nonsense characters (really AT commands) sent to a modem to get it ready to make a connection.

Inktomi   A search engine developed at the University of California at Berkeley and now found at http://www.inktomi.com. Inktomi now powers the HotBot search site.

inline graphic   An illustration on a Web page (as opposed to a linked graphic).

insert mode   In text editors such as vi, a special mode the user has to switch into (from command mode) to insert text.

Institute of Electrical and Electronic Engineering (IEEE)   A professional organization that, among other things, has defined a number of networking standards, such as the 802.x protocols.

integrated circuit   A computer chip—a tiny circuit housing many electronic components.

intelligent agent   A (mostly theoretical so far) type of computer program that can handle a user's mail, database searches, file transfers, and so on over the Internet without the user having to oversee the process directly or even remain connected to the Net.

interactive   (adj) Said of programs or environments, able to respond and give feedback to a user and to take instruction from user commands.

Interagency Interim National Research and Education Network (IINREN)   A set of network and operating system protocols under development for the National Research and Education Network.

INTERCAL   A mock programming language designed to be written only (INTERCAL is said to stand for *Compiler Language with No Pronounceable Acronym*) that is the subject of the alt.lang.intercal newsgroup.

interface   The "face" presented to a user by a computer operating system or application, and the set of rules governing how information is displayed and how users may enter commands.

Interior Gateway Protocol (IGP)   A protocol that defines how routing information is distributed among routers in a network.

Intermediate System (IS)   An OSI system that moves packets across a network.

Intermediate System to Intermediate System Protocol (IS-IS)   An OSI Interior Gateway Protocol that can route both OSI and IP packets.

intermittent   (adj) Said of a connection, not constant, occurring irregularly.

internal modem   A modem chip mounted on a board installed inside a computer.

International Organization for Standardization (ISO)   An international standards organization attempting to foster international cooperation in science, engineering, and technology. Creator of the OSI Model.

International Telegraph and Telephone Consultative Committee (Comité Consultatif International de Telegraphique et Telephonique—CCITT)   An international standards organization comprising telecommunications companies, part of the United Nations' International Telecommunications Union, creator of the X.25, X.400, and X.500 standards.

internet   Any network that uses the TCP/IP protocol suite. (Now most often referred to as an intranet).

Internet   An international network of well over ten thousand networks linked using the TCP/IP protocols. Also used more loosely to mean either the worldwide information net or the conglomeration of all computers and networks that can be reached via an Internet e-mail address.

Internet Adapter, The (TIA)   A UNIX program that enables a dial-up shell account to emulate a SLIP connection, allowing the user to run Internet software native to his or her desktop environment without the full costs (or full functionality, either) of real SLIP. TIA is available from Cyberspace Development at http://marketplace.com/.

Internet Architecture Board (IAB)   A group that oversees the maintenance of TCP/IP protocols and promulgates other Internet standards.

Internet Assigned Numbers Authority (IANA)   A group that assigns the standard numbers used for ports, sockets, and so on. Assigned numbers can be found in the Internet document called STD2 (one of the RFCs).

Internet Control Message Protocol (ICMP)   An Internet protocol that defines error messages and governs how test packets and the ping command function.

Internet-Draft (I-D)   Draft documents written by the Internet Engineering Task Force dealing with potential problems and networking developments. They are archived at the rtfm.mit.edu anonymous FTP site.

Internet Engineering Steering Group (IESG)   A group that manages the Internet Engineering Task Force and reviews Internet standards.

Internet Engineering Task Force (IETF)   A voluntary group made up of researchers that studies technical problems and proposes solutions to the Internet Architecture Board.

Internet Experiment Note (IEN)   A now-obsolete series of reports on the development of the Internet, parallel to the RFCs.

Internet Explorer   Microsoft's web browser, which is rapidly morphing, version to version, into the basic Windows desktop interface. (Download it from http://www.microsoft.com/ie/.)

Internet Hunt   A monthly contest consisting of ten questions whose answers must be dug up on the Internet. The contest is reachable by gopher via gopher.cic.net in the hunt directory. Here's a sample question from the October, 1994 hunt (question designed by Dan Marmion):

    "Surrey With the Fringe on Top." How many stars did Down Beat
    magazine give that album?

Internet Monthly Report (IMR)   A monthly publication about the Internet, produced for the Internet Research Task Force.

Internet Protocol (IP)   The protocol that handles routing of datagrams from one Internet host to another. It works along with the Transmission Control Protocol (TCP) to ensure that data is trasmitted accurately across the Internet.

Internet Research Steering Group (IRSG)   A group that manages the Internet Research Task Force.

Internet Research Task Force (IRTF)   A voluntary group that projects long-term issues and problems for the Internet and proposes solutions and new directions, reporting to the Internet Architecture Board.

Internet service provider (ISP)   A company or enterprise that provides Internet access.

Internet Services List   An exhaustive list of Internet services, maintained by Scott Yanoff and available via anonymous FTP from csd4.csd.uwm.edu, in the /pub directory, with the file name inet.services.txt.

Internet Society (ISOC)   A nonprofit organization that promotes the use of the Internet in academic and research communities and supports networking research, publishing the *Internet Society News* and putting on the INET conference every year.

Internet Talk Radio (ITR)   A set of audio programs, similar to radio broadcasts, distributed over the Internet via the MBONE. For more information, send e-mail to info@radio.com.

Internet tools   A set of utility programs that can use various Internet facilities and that have interoperability.

Internet Underground Music Archive (IUMA)   A database of (mostly unsigned) bands, including sound clips, video clips, information, and many other music-related links, available via the Web at http://www.iuma.com.

Internetwork Packet Exchange (IPX)   Novell's NetWare network-layer protocol that specifies addressing, routing, and switching packets between a server and workstations and across interconnected LANs. Encapsulated IPX packets can be carried by Ethernet packets and token ring frames.

InterNIC Short for the Internet Network Information Center, a service of the National Science Foundation. It provides information about the Internet and registers domain names, available via e-mail at info@internic.net or on the Web at http://www.internic.net/.

interoperability The ability of devices made by different manufacturers or as part of different computer systems to communicate and share information over a network.

InterSLIP Macintosh SLIP software, developed by InterCon Systems Corporation and available as freeware via anonymous FTP from ftp.intercon.com.

InterText An online fiction magazine distributed via the Web from http://www.etext.org/Zines/InterText/.

intranet A private network that uses the standard Internet protocols.

IP *Internet Protocol*, the protocol that handles routing of datagrams from one Internet host to another. It works along with the Transmission Control Protocol (TCP) to ensure that data is transmitted accurately across the Internet.

IP address Also called a *dotted quad*, the numerical Internet Protocol address that uniquely identifies each computer on the Internet, made up of four numbers separated by three dots.

irc UNIX client software for IRC.

IRC *Internet Relay Chat*, a protocol for client/server programs that allows you to chat with people in real time (synchronously) all over the Internet in channels devoted to different topics.

Ircle Macintosh client software for Internet Relay Chat, available via anonymous FTP from mac.archive.umich.edu.

ISDN *Integrated Services Digital Network*, a digital circuit-switched network that can carry both voice and data communication over a single cable. ISDN standards have been specified by the CCITT. (Some people joke that ISDN stands for *It Still Does Nothing*.)

ISO   The *International Organization for Standardization*, which attempts to foster international cooperation in science, engineering, and technology. Creator of the OSI Model.

ISO Development Environment (ISODE)   Software that enables networks using OSI standards to communicate with TCP/IP networks.

IWBNI   (written only, also *iwbni*) *It would be nice if.*

IYFEG   (written only) *Insert your favorite ethnic group.*

jack in   To log onto the Internet (from a cyberpunk term popularized by William Gibson).

Janet   The major United Kingdom backbone network.

jargon file   A list of hacker jargon and slang—compiled and maintained collectively since the 1960s—with excellent definitions, great humor, and lots of interesting anecdotes, available via the Web at http://www.ccil.org/jargon/jargon.html and as a paper book from MIT Press under the name *The New Hacker's Dictionary, Second Edition* (buy the book!).

Java   A programming language for making software that can be run on any type of computer over an Internet connection.

JavaScript   A scripting language developed by Netscape to add dynamic (interactive) capabilities to web pages.

joe   A UNIX text editor.

Joint Photographics Experts Group   An ISO committee that proposed the JPEG image compression standard.

JPEG   A compressed file format for images that is more efficient than GIF (but newer and therefore not so widespread).

.jpg   A file extension that indicates JPEG compression.

Jughead   An index of high-level gopher menus. (After the creation of archie, other Internet tool developers have not been able to resist naming their applications after other Archie Comics characters. Besides Jughead, there is also Veronica. What's next, Big Moose?)

jupiter   (v) To kill an IRC 'bot or kick a user and then keep the 'bot or user from reconnecting by adopting its nick. (Jupiter is the handle of the first user to use this tactic.)

k   1. An abbreviation for kilobit; 2. The kill command in many UNIX newsreaders.

K   An abbreviation for kilobyte.

KA9Q   An adaptation of TCP/IP protocols for radio systems.

Kb   An abbreviation for kilobit.

KB   An abbreviation for kilobyte.

Kbps   An abbreviation for kilobits per second, a measurement of transmission speed (such as modem speed or network speed).

Kbyte   An abbreviation for kilobyte.

ken   Ken Thompson, the primary inventor of UNIX, a net.god (to some) who appears in the jargon file.

Kermit   A very common, but now relatively slow, protocol for downloading and uploading via a modem.

kevork   (v) To abort a process or reboot a computer (from Dr. Jack Kevorkian, a.k.a. Dr. Death, a Michigan physician who routinely assists terminally ill patients in committing suicide).

key   1. In encryption, a phrase or string that allows you to decrypt encrypted text. In public-key encryption, there are two kinds of keys, public keys and private keys; 2. A key word.

key encryption   A form of encryption that relies upon keys for the encrypting and decrypting of messages or files.

key word   (Also *keyword*.) 1. In a database search, a word to search for in target documents—hits (successful matches) must include the key word; 2. In online services, a word used to jump directly to a topic area.

kgbvax   One of the machines on the bang path of the famous April Fool's kremvax post.

Kibo   The username of James F. Parry, acclaimed by some as the first deity of the Internet. Also known as "he who greps," Kibo reportedly notes every mention of his name on Usenet and follows up worthy posts. He is also the founder of HappyNet. Students of kibology can read more on the subject in the alt.religion.kibology newsgroup.

kibology   The religion (or is it a science?) of Kibo. Its main doctrine is You're Allowed. Only Spot, Kibo's dog, is Not Allowed. For more adept instruction in the ways of kibology, try to follow the alt.religion.kibology newsgroup or wait for the kibologists to start cross-posting their meta-posts into your favorite newsgroup. Beware of trolls.

Kibo number   Also *Kibo #*, a number that represents how close you are to Kibo in terms of e-mail. Kibo's Kibo number is 0. Anyone who has gotten mail from Kibo has the Kibo number 1. Mail from someone with a lower Kibo number than yours lowers your Kibo number to that person's Kibo number plus 1.

kiboze   (v) To grep the newsfeed to find every single post that mentions the key word you're grepping for.

kick   (v) To eject a participant from an IRC conversation and prevent the user from rejoining (done by the channel op).

kill   (v) 1. To delete a post (mark it as having been read); 2. To delete posts automatically, using a kill file; 3. To stop a process; 4. To erase a file.

kill file   Also a *killfile*, a file containing search instructions for automatically killing or autoselecting Usenet posts. Sometimes called a bozo filter, a kill file can be used to screen out annoying posters and avoid uninteresting threads.

kilobit   (Abbreviated *k* or *Kb*.) Roughly one thousand (actually 1,024) bits. Kilobits per second (kps or Kbps) is a common measurement of transmission speed (such as modem speed or network speed).

kilobits per second   (Abbreviated *kps* or *Kbps*.) A measurement of the speed of a medium, meaning the number of kilobits that can pass through the medium in one second.

kilobyte   (Abbreviated *K*, *KB*, or *Kbyte*.) Roughly one thousand (actually 1,024) bytes, usually a measurement of memory or storage capacity.

kludge   (*klooj*, n) The more common spelling of *kluge*, a clumsily assembled program or feature of a program that functions well enough but is not elegant, similar to the noncomputer expression *jury-rigged*.

kluge   (*klooj*, n) The original and more phonetically correct spelling of *kludge*, a clumsily assembled program or feature of a program that functions well enough but is not elegant, similar to the noncomputer expression *jury-rigged*.

Knowbot Information Services (KIS)   An experimental information service on the Net, intended to function as a robotic librarian that can search databases and, among other things, help find e-mail addresses. To access the Knowbot, telnet to nri.reston.va.us. For more information, send e-mail to kis@nri.reston.va.us.

Korn shell   A common flavor of UNIX shells.

kps   An abbreviation for kilobits per second, a measurement of transmission speed (such as modem speed or network speed).

kremvax   An imaginary Usenet site, the source of a famous April Fool's hoax posting in 1984, supposedly the first Soviet communication over the Internet, a direct message from Premier Konstantin Chernenko (actually written by Piet Beertema). The post was met with both welcoming and scornful responses.

k12.   An alternative newsgroup hierarchy in the Usenet mold, dedicated to elementary and secondary school (kindergarten through 12th grade) education.

l   The UNIX *directory list* command, producing full information about the files (except dot files) in the working directory.

LAN   (n) *Local area network*, a computer network, usually confined to a single office or building, that allows for the sharing of files and other resources (such as printers) among several users and makes interoperability among various systems possible.

LAN adapter   Also called a *network interface card* or *network interface controller*, a card installed into a PC to attach it to a LAN.

LAN Workplace   Novell's TCP/IP client software for Macintosh and DOS computers.

lcd   The UNIX ftp command to change the local directory (as opposed to the working directory at the ftp host site).

leaf   1. In network architecture, a computer that receives a signal from a more central computer but does not pass a signal along to a more remote computer; 2. In (audio cassette) tape trees, a participant who receives a copy of the tape being distributed but does not make copies of the tape for anyone else.

leaf site   A Usenet computer that receives a newsfeed from another site but does not distribute news to any other computers.

League for Programming Freedom   A group that opposes software patents and copyrights; information available via anonymous FTP at prep.ai.mit.edu in the pub/lpf directory or by e-mail at league@prep.ai.mit .edu.

leased line   A telephone line leased from the telephone company to provide a permanent connection from a LAN to an Internet service provider or to a WAN.

letterbomb   An e-mail message containing either escape characters that can lock up certain types of terminals, or harmful commands to be interpreted by the user's shell.

Levity   A writers' web site run by Dan Levy (at http://www.levity.com).

Lexis/Nexis   A proprietary system of searchable databases of legal briefs (Lexis) and newspaper and magazine articles (Nexis).

lharc   A file compression program for DOS.

.lhz   A file extension that indicates lharc compression.

library catalogs   Most university and public library catalogs are available via telnet (and some via gopher). Hytelnet has an excellent index of library catalogs.

Library of Congress   The main repository of information of the U.S. government, available by telnet at locis.loc.gov or on the Web at http://www.loc.gov/.

line eater   A bug in older versions of Usenet newsreader software for UNIX that caused certain lines at the beginning of posts to vanish. To appease the line eater, posters would include lines of spurious text to be sacrificed instead of the actual contents of the message.

line feed   Also *linefeed*, a character that moves the cursor down one line (ASCII 10), usually starting a new line in combination with a carriage return character.

line length   The number of characters that fit on a line—fixed on some systems, settable on others. The standard line length on the Internet is 80 characters; e-mail or Usenet posts produced with software using longer line lengths will wrap irregularly and appear awkward to users with 80-character lines.

line noise   Static or interference on a wire that corrupts the signal. On a character-based modem connection, for example, line noise might result in random gibberish and escape characters interpolated with the intended text.

line-oriented   (adj) Said of applications and interfaces that display text one line at a time, rather than making an entire screenful of text available at once.

link   (n) 1. In UNIX, a reference to a directory or file contained elsewhere that appears in directory listings just as if the remote directory or file were in the current directory (also called a *symbolic link*); 2. On Web pages, a hypertext connection, a button or highlighted bit of text that, when selected, jumps the reader to another page.

Link Access Protocol (LAP)   A data link layer protocol for AppleTalk that specifies the interface to network hardware.

Linux   (*line-ux*) An implementation of UNIX for IBM PC-compatibles. It has been developed as a collaborative effort by widespread Internet users and is distributed for free.

LISP   The acronym for *List Processor*, a popular Artificial Intelligence programming language.

list   (v) 1. To view the names of files in a directory; 2. To display the contents of a file.

(n) An Internet or BITNET mailing list.

listserv   A type of automated mailing list software that runs on IBM mainframes and originated on the BITNET network.

little-endian   (adj) A storage format in which the most significant byte has the highest address, as opposed to big-endian.

liveware   People (as opposed to hardware or software), also known as *wetware*.

local   (adj) Said of a computer to which a user is connected directly or of a device (such as a printer) or process under the user's direct control, as contrasted with remote hosts, devices, and processes.

Local Area Transport (LAT)   Digital (DEC) architecture for connecting terminal servers on Ethernet networks to host computers.

local echo   1. A copy of the data being sent (usually typed) over a communications device (such as a modem) displayed in a terminal window so that the sender can monitor the process; 2. A terminal mode in some communications programs, specifying half duplex transmission, in which the communications program displays the user's input on the screen, instead of relaying an echo from the host.

localhost   (n) Also *local host*, the host computer a user is currently logged in to. The *loopback address* of any user's current localhost is always 127.0.0.1.

local node   The computer on a network to which a user is connected directly.

LocalTalk   Shielded, twisted-pair wiring and connectors for using the Macintosh's built-in AppleTalk network hardware.

locative domain name   A two-letter geographical domain name, such as *.us* for the United States, *.uk* for the United Kingdom, *.de* for Germany (Deutschland), and so on.

LOCIS   The *Library of Congress Information Service*, available by telnet at locis.loc.gov or on the Web at http://www.loc.gov/.

lock up   (v) To freeze, as when certain sequences of characters freeze a keyboard, preventing the user from typing.

logical   (adj) Said of a computer address or device, identified by a numerical reference, which may or may not correspond to a physical address or device.

logical conjunction   A word that joins two or more key words by specifying a logical relationship between them.

Logical Link Control (LLC)   1. The Institute of Electrical and Electronic Engineering 802 standard that specifies a uniform user interface; 2. A data link layer defined in IEEE 802.2.

logical tree   Any logical arrangement of devices, files, data, and so on in which all relationships stem from a root; child branches are subordinate to parent branches, and an element without any children is called a leaf.

Logical Unit   Software that communicates with an IBM SNA network.

log in   (v) To connect to a network or computer, identify oneself as a user, supply a password, and start a session.

login   (n) 1. A username, the *handle* a user logs in with, corresponding to an account; 2. An instance of logging in.

login script   A prerecorded sequence of login (definition 2) steps that can play back automatically to connect a user to a computer or network. Login scripts can breach security if they automate the process of supplying a password, thereby allowing anyone who runs the script to log in.

log out   (v) To end a session and disconnect from a computer or network.

LOL   (written only, also *lol*) *Laughing out loud.*

loopback   (n) A test in which a signal is sent from a source to an intermediate point and then back to the original source to evaluate the accuracy of the transmission.

loopback address   The Internet address (127.0.0.1) that always points back to the localhost.

low-bandwidth   (adj) 1. Said of a connection that can only manage a slow connect speed or of a resource on the Internet that a user with a slow connection will still find useful; 2. Colloquially, containing little useful information.

ls   The UNIX *short directory list* command.

lurk   To read a mailing list or newsgroup without posting to it. Every new user should lurk for a while before posting to get a feel for what the group is all about and how others in the group behave.

lurker   One who lurks. On any mailing list or in any newsgroup, there are usually many times more lurkers than regular contributors.

luser   (*loser*) A hacker's term for a clueless newbie.

Lycos   A search engine (at http://www.lycos.com).

lynx   An excellent, text-based, UNIX browser for the Web that was created at the University of Kansas. To try out lynx (if it's not installed on your system), telnet to ukanaix.cc.ukans.edu and log in as *www*.

m   The mark as unread command in some UNIX newsreaders.

M   Abbreviation for megabyte.

^M   One way that the carriage return character (ASCII 13) can appear. Some computers use a carriage return to indicate a newline, some use a linefeed, and some use both. If an ASCII file is transferred from a computer that uses carriage returns to one that doesn't, and a binary file transfer rather than an ASCII file transfer is used, ^M may appear at the end of each line.

MaasInfo Package   A set of documents written by Robert E. Maas explaining how to use various Internet resources, available via anonymous FTP from aarnet.edu.au in the pub/doc subdirectory.

MAC address   The address that identifies a particular piece of hardware out of several connected to shared media.

MacBinary   A Macintosh file transfer protocol that specifies how files should be transmitted over modems.

Macintosh   A line of personal computers made by Apple..

Macintosh archive   The largest source of Macintosh shareware and files is the Macintosh archive at Stanford University. Connect via anonymous FTP to sumex-aim.stanford.edu and look in the info-mac directory. This site is also mirrored at the wuarchive.wustl.edu FTP site in the /mirrors/infomac directory.

MacPPP   PPP (Point-to-Point Protocol) software for the Macintosh, developed by Merit Computer Network and available as freeware via anonymous FTP from ftp.merit.edu in the internet.tools/ppp/mac directory.

macro   A shortcut consisting of a sequence of memorized keystrokes or a more elaborate set of scripting commands used to automate repetitive tasks, similar to a rudimentary program.

MacSLIP   SLIP (Serial Line Internet Protocol) software for the Macintosh, developed by Hyde Park Software.

MacTCP   TCP/IP protocol software for the Macintosh, built into versions 7.5 through 7.5.2 of the Macintosh operating system. For more information, send e-mail to apda@applelink.apple.com.

MacWeb   A Web browser for the Macintosh, created by EINET and available via anonymous FTP from ftp.einet.net in the /einet/mac/macweb directory.

Magellan   A search engine maintained by McKinley corporation (at http://www.magellan.com).

magick   Magic in the sense of the occult, natural or supernatural mysteries, study of the kaballah, and so on, spelled with a *k* to distinguish from stage magic. For more information, See newsgroups such as alt.magick, alt .magick.ethics, etc.

mail (n) 1. On the Internet, synonymous with e-mail, that is, *electronic mail*, messages carried electronically from computer to computer; 2. The name of a simple UNIX mail program.

(v) To send an e-mail message.

mail address 1. An Internet e-mail address of the form *username@host .domain*; 2. The *username* portion of a mail account on a network.

mailbomb (n) A huge number of messages or an enormous chunk of data, such as a core dump, sent to an e-mail address as a prank or attack on the recipient, in hopes that the bomb will overload or even crash the user's mailer program.

(v) To send or encourage others to send a huge number of messages or an enormous chunk of data.

mailbot A *mail server*, a program that automatically responds to mail by sending information or performing functions specified in the incoming mail.

mailbox A file, directory, or area of hard disk space used to store e-mail messages.

mail bridge A device that connects networks and filters mail between them, passing only messages that meet certain criteria.

mail-enabled application A program that, in addition to its normal capabilities, can also handle the sending and receiving of mail.

Mail Exchange Record A record type in the Domain Name System that identifies the mail-serving host for a given domain.

mail exploder A program that forwards an e-mail message to all the addresses on a mailing list.

mail gateway A computer that passes e-mail from one network to another, from a network to the Internet, or vice versa, reformatting the headers as necessary.

mailing list A discussion group, commonly referred to on the Internet simply as a *list*, consisting of people with a common interest, all of whom receive all the mail sent, or posted, to the list. Mailing lists are often more specialized than Usenet newsgroups. Lists can be moderated or unmoderated.

mail-news gateway   A computer that collects posts from a mailing list and forwards them to a corresponding newsgroup, and vice versa.

mail path   Also bang path, a list of sites an e-mail message must pass through on the way from the sender to the receiver. Although it is rarely necessary any longer to specify the route your mail will take, mail headers still often include the entire mail path back to the sender.

mail program   Also *mail reader*, the program a user reads, replies to, forwards, and saves mail with. Common UNIX mail programs include mail, elm, and pine. Eudora is a popular mail program for PCs and Macs.

.mailrc   A setup file for UNIX mail programs (other than elm).

mail reflector   A mail address that automatically forwards any mail it receives to a list of other addresses.

mail server   A *mailbot*, a program that automatically distributes files or information in response to e-mail requests.

mainframe   (n) A large, fast, multiuser computer (larger than a minicomputer or microcomputer), capable of handling large quantities of data and complicated tasks, generally designed for batch (as opposed to interactive) use, and most often used by large corporations, universities, and military organizations.

majordomo   A type of automated mailing list management software, similar to listserv.

MAKE.MONEY.FAST   A chain letter still making its rounds on the Net after many years. A classic Ponzi/pyramid scheme.

As someone replied last time I saw this garbage reposted, "Don't make your first Federal crime one that includes your name and address at the top!"

man   The UNIX command that displays the man pages, online documentation for UNIX programs and commands.

MAN   A Metropolitan Area Network, a high-speed (100 Mbps) public network, capable of voice and data transmission over long distances (but smaller than a WAN), connecting LANs across a city or campus.

Management Information Base (MIB)   A database on a host, router, or bridge that stores information about a network's configuration and performance.

Management Information System (MIS)   A computer-organized system of synthesizing information from various departments in a corporation in order to provide information, assessments, and recommendations to management; a corporate computer center.

Manchester encoding   A method of data-transmission that enables network interface cards to transmit digital signals using direct current, encoding data, and timing signals in the same data stream, as opposed to non-return to zero (NRZ) encoding, which employs two voltage levels—negative and positive—to represent 0 and 1.

mang   1. An undefined expletive, uttered or written in response to statements or actions so outrageous or bewildering as to overload a civilized person's ability to respond; 2. The sound the boo tree makes, straining to express the ineffable.

man pages   The *manual pages*—online documentation for UNIX commands and programs.

Marble Teleconnect   SLIP (Serial Line Internet Protocol) software for the Nextstep operating system, developed by Marble Associates.

mark as unread   To save a newsgroup article as if it were still unread.

Martian   (adj) Said of a packet that arrives with an incorrect or impossible source address.

Mass ACK   A message sent to a mailing list requesting a response, in order to test the currency of the addresses on the list.

massage   (v) To edit, extract information from, or format a file, as in "I'll have to massage this data some to figure out what it means."

match   (n) In a search, a record or document that meets the specified criteria, also called a hit.

Matrix News   A newsletter of the Matrix Information and Directory Services, on the subject of networks, available via WAIS at matrix_news.src.

Maximum Transmission Unit (MTU)   The greatest datagram length allowed on a particular network.

Maxwell's Demon   Nineteenth-century Scottish philosopher James Clerk Maxwell postulated that temperature could be regulated in a room by posting a demon at the entrance who would only allow air molecules moving at a certain speed or higher to enter. This theory is the probable source for the computer terms daemon and demon.

Mb   Abbreviation for megabit.

MB   Abbreviation for megabyte.

MBONE   The *multicast backbone*, an experimental, high-speed virtual network that can send packets simultaneously to a large number of Internet sites, suitable for audio and visual transmission. In 1994, a Rolling Stones concert was multicast to workstations around the world via the MBONE.

Mbps   Abbreviation for megabits per second.

Media Access Control (MAC)   The lower component of the data link layer, which defines how computers on a LAN share access to a transmission medium, used in CSMA/CD (Carrier Sense Multiple Access with Collision Detection) and token ring LANs.

media filter   A device that converts the signal from a token ring adapter board for a particular type of wiring.

medium   Any substance that conveys a signal from a sender to a receiver, such as copper or other wire, coaxial cable, optical fiber, and so on.

megabit   Roughly one million (actually 1,048,576) bits.

megabits per second   A measurement of transmission speed (such as modem speed or network speed).

megabyte   Roughly one million (actually 1,048,576) bytes, usually a measurement of memory (RAM) or storage (HD).

MEGO   (written only) *My eyes glaze over.*

meltdown   What happens when a network is so overloaded that it crashes.

meme (rhymes with *seem*, n) A self-replicating and self-perpetuating idea, concept, saying, pun, or way of thinking. For example, how many times have you heard "The Eskimo language has a thousand words for *snow*" or words to that effect? It doesn't matter that it's not actually true; it is such an infectious or useful metaphor that it sticks in the mind and circulates from person to person perpetually.

The word *meme* was coined as an analogy to *gene* (in the sense of the "selfish" gene that propagates itself, using people as a medium) as well as *phoneme* and *morpheme* (in the sense of a "unit" of thought). The study of memes is called *memetics*. When a powerful set of memes is unleashed on the Internet (such as a religious philosophy), it is called a *meme plague*.

MemeWatch A web site (at http://syx.com/MemeWatch/) that tracks prevalent memes on the Net and off.

memory Generally synonymous with RAM (random access memory), a location where files and processes a computer is currently working on are stored. The operating system reads applications and documents into memory and also writes (saves) the results back to the disk (or other storage medium).

menu A list of options available to a user. Options can usually be selected with a mouse or other pointing device, or by typing the number of the desired menu item and pressing Enter.

menu-driven program A program whose commands are accessible via menus, relieving the user of the need to memorize commands.

message 1. An e-mail letter; 2. A comment sent to a specific person on IRC and not to the entire channel; 3. A packet.

message cancel A feature of some mail programs that allows the user to catch a message and "unsend" it (for only a short while after sending).

message of the day A message from a network's system administrator that is displayed whenever a user logs in.

message handling service (MHS) A popular e-mail protocol for storage, management, and exchange, especially in corporate offices, licensed by Novell.

message handling system   The CCITT X.400 protocol for store-and-forward messaging.

message switching   Also called packet switching, a store-and-forward method for routing messages in which each message is passed from a source through intermediate nodes to a destination address.

metanetwork   A network made up of other networks. The Internet is one.

metapost   A Usenet post, such as troll, whose actual purpose is different from its literal content.

metasyntactic variable   A dummy variable, a stand-in variable used in an example to clarify a point of syntax.

mget   The command in the UNIX ftp program for *multiple get*, to get a number of files at once.

Microcom Networking Protocol (MNP)   An error-checking feature built into many modems. MNP organizes data into frames, then transmits the frames, sometimes compressing the data as well.

microcomputer   A small computer with a single-chip processor, smaller than a minicomputer or a mainframe, though currently as powerful as either of these earlier computer types once were. Scorned at first by the mainframe establishment, PCs (personal computers) ushered in the microcomputer revolution, bringing computing power into the hands of laypeople for the first time.

Microcomputers can range in size from desktops to portables to laptops to notebooks.

MicroDroid   An employee of Microsoft, especially one who defends the company in Usenet newsgroups.

Microphone   A communications program for the Macintosh.

microprocessor   A CPU (central processing unit) housed on a single integrated circuit, as in a microcomputer. The processor is the part of the computer that communicates with RAM, the storage medium (hard disk), the keyboard, the printer, and any other devices; performs arithmetic and logical comparisons; and controls the operations of the computer.

The Pentium, PowerPC, 680x0 series, 80x86 series, and 80x8 series are all microprocessors.

MicroSerf   An employee of Microsoft.

Microsloth Windows   A derogatory term for Microsoft Windows.

Microsoft   A computer company founded in 1975 that sells MS-DOS (the operating system for IBM PCs and compatibles), the Microsoft Windows operating environment, and a host of applications for PCs and Macintoshes. Some believe it to exert hegemony over the PC market.

Microsoft Network   An online service from Microsoft, access to which comes built-in with Windows 95.

Microsoft Windows   A multitasking operating environment that runs on top of MS-DOS and provides IBM PCs and compatibles with a GUI (graphical user interface) not unlike that of the Macintosh, including icons, dialog boxes, menus, and a mouse pointer.

mid-level network   A regional network, a vague Internet level category between backbone and rib levels.

.mil   An Internet domain corresponding to U.S. military organizations.

Military Network (MILNET)   A network of U.S. military sites (it was part of the original ARPAnet) that carries nonclassified military communication.

MIME   *Multipurpose Internet Mail Extensions*, a protocol that allows e-mail to contain simple text plus color pictures, video, sound, and binary data. Both the sender and the receiver need MIME-aware mail programs to use it.

minicomputer   A medium-sized computer (larger than a microcomputer but smaller than a mainframe), such as DEC's VAX, which can handle multitasking and over one hundred users (compared with over one thousand for mainframes).

Minority On-Line Information Service (MOLIS)   A service maintained by the U.S. government offering educational and other information, as part of Fedix, available via telnet at fedix.fie.com (log in as *fedix*).

MIPS   *Millions of instructions per second*, a measurement of chip (CPU) processing speed. Also, humorously, *meaningless indication of processor speed*.

mIRC   A windows IRC program.

mirror   (v) To store an exact copy of files at another archive site (in order to minimize the load at the original site or provide an archive site geographically closer to some users).

mirror site   An archive site (generally FTP) containing an exact copy of the files at another site.

misc.   A Usenet hierarchy devoted to whatever doesn't fit in the other hierarchies.

mkdir   The UNIX command to make a directory.

mnemonic   (*ne-mon-ic*, n) A word that helps one remember a command or shortcut. For example, in WordStar (an archaic word processing language), the *cut text* command is Ctrl+Y; the mnemonic to help remember this is *yank* (because you're yanking the text out of the document).

By association, the term has also taken on the meaning of the shortcut or command itself; thus, in the WordStar example, *Ctrl+Y* can also be called the mnemonic for *cut*.

mode   One of several possible states a program can be in. The most common example of this is the requirement some older text editors such as vi have that the user must first enter insert mode before typing anything.

modeless editor   A text editor that does not require the user to execute a special command to enter insert mode in order to begin typing. Most new text editors are modeless. On UNIX systems, pico is a modeless editor and vi is not.

modem   (n) Short for *modulator/demodulator*, a device that connects your computer to a phone jack and, through the phone lines, to another modem and computer, transmitting data by converting the computer's digital signal into the telephone's analog carrier signal, and vice versa.

The standard 14400 bps modem is 46 times faster than the 300 bps modems of 15 years ago.

modem bank A set of shelved modems connected to a host or BBS to allow many callers to log in.

moderate (v) To review articles submitted to a list or newsgroup and post only those which meet certain criteria (minimally, they must be on topic).

moderated (adj) Said of lists and newsgroups whose posts must pass muster with a moderator before appearing.

moderator The volunteer who decides which submissions to a moderated list or newsgroup will be posted.

monospace font A font in which all the characters are the same width (as opposed to a proportional-width font, in which the letters *w* and *i*, for instance, vary greatly in width).

```
This text is written in a monospace font.
```

For e-mail and newsgroup posts, the 80-character line length standard presupposes a monospace font (as do ASCII graphics and many people's sig blocks).

more A common UNIX paging program. Type

```
more filename
```

to see *filename* displayed one screenful at a time.

MorF (written only) Short for *Male or Female*, asking another user's sex.

Morning Star PPP PPP (Point-to-Point Protocol) software for Nextstep, developed by Morning Star Technologies.

Mosaic The first graphical Web browser, developed by National Center for Supercomputing Applications, which greatly popularized the Web in its first few years, and by extension the Internet, as it made the multimedia capabilities of the Net accessible via mouse clicks.

Mosaic exists in freeware and shareware versions for the Macintosh, Windows, and X Window systems and is available via anonymous FTP at ftp.ncsa.uiuc.edu.

moskvax One of the sites in the path of the famous April Fool's kremvax post in 1984.

MOTAS   (written only) *Member of the appropriate sex.* A way of referring to a potential partner without specifying that person's sex.

motd   (written only) *Message of the day.*

Motion Picture Experts Group   An ISO committee that proposed the JPEG audiovideo compression standard.

MOTOS   (written only) *Member of the opposite sex.*

MOTSS   (written only) *Member of the same sex.*

motto!   A follow-up post on a newsgroup, proposing the previous post as a motto for the group or for Usenet as a whole, perhaps facetiously.

mouse potato   A human being who spends inordinate chunks of his or her waking life glued to a computer screen, mouse in hand.

Mozilla   A slang name for the Netscape Web browser.

MPEG   A compressed file format for movies (audiovideo files).

.mpg   A file extension that indicates MPEG compression.

mput   The command in the UNIX ftp program for *multiple put*, to send a number of files at once.

MS-DOS   An operating system for IBM PCs and compatibles, made by Microsoft.

MU*   An abbreviation for any one of a series of acronyms for *multi*user role-playing game environments.

mud   (v) To explore a MUD.

MUD   A *multiuser domain/dimension/dungeon.* A role-playing game environment that allows people all over the Net to play together in something like interactive text adventures. Other names for MUDs include *MOO, MUSE, Muck, Mush, Fugue, TinyFugue,* and *TinyMUD.*

MUDs are said to be highly addictive and it sometimes seems that only college students have enough time to explore them thoroughly.

They are also now used as conference spaces and educational aids.

For more information, see the newsgroups rec.games.mud.announce and alt.mud or the FTP site actlab.rtf.utexas.edu.

multicast   (v) To send a packet simultaneously to multiple sites.

(adj) Said of a packet intended to be received by a number of hosts.

Multics   A late '60s predecessor to UNIX.

multimedia   A form of communication combining text with graphics, page layout, motion pictures, animation, sounds, and so on.

Multiple Virtual Storage (MVS)   IBM's standard mainframe operating system, similar to VM (Virtual Machine).

multiplex   (adj) Using a single transmission medium to transmit over multiple logical channels at once, such as when an Internet site maintains HTTP, FTP, SMTP, telnet, and other channels.

multitasking   (n) The simultaneous execution of two or more programs by a single computer.

MUSE   A *multiuser simulation environment* (for role-playing games).

MYOB   (written only) *Mind your own business.*

my two cents   A tag appended to Usenet or list posts, indicating "this is just my opinion," or "I just wanted to get my two cents in."

n   The next article command in many UNIX newsreaders.

nagware   Shareware that reminds the user, automatically and frequently, to register the software and pay for it.

NAK   (rhymes with *pack*) A *negative acknowledgment* from a computer that a packet of data has not been received successfully, i.e., the checksum figure does not match that of the sent packet (ASCII 21).

Name Binding Protocol (NBP)   AppleTalk's transport layer protocol. It resolves numeric AppleTalk addresses into names and vice versa.

name server   1. Also *domain name server*, an application that maintains a table of domain names and corresponding IP addresses in order to resolve the domain names of messages; 2. Also *CSO name server*, a searchable white pages listing of real names and associated e-mail addresses, usually reached via gopher.

NAND   (rhymes with *hand*) [Boolean operator] *Not and*. A text search with NAND between two words will match any documents that fail to contain both words.

nastygram   1. An e-mail chastisement from a net.god for violating neti-quette; 2. A particularly vicious flame; 3. A letterbomb.

National Center for Supercomputing Applications (NCSA)   Part of the National Science Foundation and the creator of NCSA telnet and Mosaic.

National Information Infrastructure (NII)   The U.S. government's name for the Internet and other public networks. More information about the government's plans for the NII is available via anonymous FTP from ftp.ntia.doc.gov in the /pub directory in a file called NIIAGENDA.ASC.

National Information Standards Organization (NISO)   A U.S. organization for standards in information, technology, and computing, most specifically as related to the Internet and WAIS, author of the revised WAIS standard.

National Institute for Standards and Technology (NIST)   A U.S. government organization that promotes national standards of measurement, technology, computing, and networking (formerly the National Bureau of Standards).

National Public Telecommunications Network (NPTN)   A nonprofit network that promotes free-nets and public networking in general.

National Research and Education Network (NREN)   The network established by the High-Performance Computing Act of 1991, intended to link government agencies, research organizations, and schools.

National Science Foundation (NSF)   The U.S. government agency that funds and runs NSFnet, and consequently many university links to the Internet. Besides its involvement with the Net, NSF promotes science and research.

natural language   The way real human beings communicate, as contrasted with computer languages, which are generally much more logical, literal, and inflexible.

natural language query   A query written in natural language (for example, plain English) seeking information from a database.

navigate   A computer jargon term meaning to get around a program, find commands, move through a document, or hunt around the Internet.

Navigator   CompuServe's graphical software for browsing its online service.

ncftp   A sophisticated UNIX FTP program (a cut above ftp) that helps to automate and streamline FTP operations.

NCSA telnet   A free telnet client for Macintosh or Windows, available via anonymous FTP from ftp.ncsa.uiuc.edu.

net.   1. The original Usenet hierarchical distinction, superseded by the big seven hierarchies (comp., news., misc., rec., sci., soc., and talk.) in the Great Renaming; 2. A prefix added to a lot of common words to suggest their counterparts on the Internet (such as net.cop, net.god, and so on).

.net   An Internet domain, corresponding to constituent networks.

Net   Also *net* and *'net*, often used as an abbreviation for the Internet or for Usenet, really a more general term for the lump sum of interconnected computers on the planet.

net address   An Internet address.

netcasting   A method for distributing information over the Web (also called push or webcasting), wherein, after initial setup or subscription by the user, web sites are automatically checked for updates and displayed in a window or on the desktop, automatically.

net.celebrity   Someone famous on the Net (usually meaning on Usenet).

net.citizen   A responsible member of an online community.

Netcom   [Service Provider] A large ISP (info@netcom.com).

NetComplete   An all-in-one software tool for connecting to Netcom.

net.cop   A derogatory term for someone who tries to censor or control the posts of others on Usenet.

NetCruiser   Netcom's old connection software, now superseded by NetComplete.

netdead   (adj) Said of someone who has signed off IRC and can no longer be reached.

Netfind   An Internet resource for finding e-mail addresses, reachable by telnet (the exact address depends on where you are).

net.god   An apparently powerful being on the Net.

nethack   A popular text-adventure dungeon game, similar to *Rogue*.

nethead   1. A Deadhead (fan of the Grateful Dead) who participates in the rec.music.gdead newsgroup (which is gated to the dead-flames mailing list) or any of the many Dead discussion groups on online services; 2. Any obsessed Internet user (a more recent definition of the term).

net.heavies   People who know a lot about how the Internet and Usenet work and whose opinions carry a lot of weight.

netiquette   Accepted proper behavior on the Net, especially in regard to e-mail and Usenet. Violate netiquette at your peril. Although the Internet and Usenet are effectively anarchies, they still have strong social cultures, and most of the rules and regulations of the Net are enforced by peer pressure.

netizen   A net.citizen.

net.kook   Any frequent Usenet poster whose posts reveal a strange and possibly obsessive personality. For more information, see the newsgroup alt.usenet.kooks.

netlag   An excessive delay on IRC that causes messages to bunch up.

net.legend   A net.celebrity, net.kook, or other famous Internet/Usenet figure, many of whom are discussed in the Net.Legends FAQ.

Net.Legends FAQ   A FAQ document that praises and excoriates various net.legends, available via gopher from dixie.aiss.uiuc.edu port 6969 (choose urban.legends, then Net.Legends FAQ and other assorted FAQs, then Net.Legends.FAQ or any of the other related FAQs).

NetManage Chameleon   TCP/IP software for Windows and DOS.

netnews   Also *net news*, another name for Usenet.

net.personality   A somewhat well-known person on the Net.

.netrc   A setup file for the UNIX ftp and ncftp programs.

Netscape   1. A popular web browser. The current version is a suite of programs called Netscape Communicator. The web-browser portion of the suite is called Netscape Navigator, but most people refer to the program generically as Netscape; 2. The company that makes Netscape Communicator and other software for the Internet.

netter   Someone who explores the Net.

network   A group of computers or other devices connected by a communications channel, to enable the sharing of files and resources among users. Networks typically provide for the sharing of printers and distribution of e-mail.

network address   1. The unique name of a node on a network; 2. An e-mail address.

Network File System (NFS)   Not to be confused with *NSF* (the National Science Foundation), a UNIX presentation layer protocol developed by Sun Microsystems that makes it possible for a user to access files elsewhere on the network just as if they were on the user's own computer.

Network Information Center (NIC)   An organization that provides information and help to users of a network, as the InterNIC does for the Internet.

network interface card   Also called a *LAN adapter*, a card installed into a PC to attach it to a LAN.

network layer   The third layer of the OSI Model. (IP governs the network layer in the TCP/IP protocol suite.)

network news   A synonym for Usenet.

Network News Transfer Protocol (NNTP)   The protocol used to distribute Usenet newsgroups.

network operating system (NOS)   A set of programs that enables networked computers to share files and devices.

Network Operations Center (NOC)   An organization that oversees a network, monitoring its traffic and solving problems.

network peripheral   A device, such as a printer, that is directly connected to a network and not to one of the computers or workstations.

Network Time Protocol (NTP)   A protocol that synchronizes time information on the Internet.

newbie   (n) A beginner on the Internet or especially Usenet (not as derogatory as clueless newbie).

newgroup   A special kind of control message that creates a new newsgroup.

newgroup wars   Competing newgroup and rmgroup messages repeatedly posted by people who alternately want and don't want a new newsgroup to be propagated.

The New Hacker's Dictionary   The printed-book version of the jargon file, published by MIT Press and well worth owning in book form.

The contents of the jargon file are also available via the Web at http://www.ccil.org/jargon/jargon.html.

newline   Any character or group of characters used to indicate the start of a new line in an ASCII text file. The newline characters vary from system to system. An ASCII file that is mistakenly transmitted as a binary file to an incompatible system can end with garbage characters such as ^M at the end of each line.

news   Usenet articles, posted to newsgroups.

news.   A Usenet hierarchy devoted to Usenet policy, guidelines, and administrative issues.

newsfeed   The packet of news articles passed along from one computer to the next on Usenet.

newsfroup   A common typo for newsgroup, now accepted (facetiously) as an alternative spelling.

newsgroup   A Usenet discussion group.

newsgroup creation   In the big seven Usenet newsgroup hierarchies, new newsgroups can be created only after a formal RFD (Request for Discussion) and a subsequent CFV (Call for Votes).

In the alternative newsgroup hierarchies, it is much easier to create a new newsgroup, which accounts for the proliferation of abandoned silly groups.

newsgroup name   The hierarchical name of a Usenet newsgroup, starting with the first-level hierarchical distinction, followed by a dot, then one or more further qualifying names, none of which may be longer than 15 characters, each of which is separated by a dot.

In proper newsgroup naming, hyphens or underscores rather than dots should be used to break up compound words. For example, alt.fan.jimi.hendrix is incorrect (and implies other jimis besides hendrix with their own fans), but alt.fan.jimi-hendrix is correct.

newshroup   A common typo for newsgroup which, unlike newsfroup, has *not* been accepted as a humorous alternative spelling.

.newsrc   A setup file for newsreaders on UNIX systems that keeps track of which Usenet newsgroups the user is subscribed to and which articles have been read.

newsreader   A program used to read Usenet articles, and usually also to save, respond to, and post follow-ups to articles, as well as to post new articles.

news server   A program or computer that supplies a newsfeed.

NewsWatcher   A newsreader for the Macintosh, available via anonymous FTP from sumex-aim.stanford.edu.

newsweeding   A pun on *newsreading*, meaning the process of killing or ignoring uninteresting threads and zeroing in on the worthwhile content of a high-volume newsgroup.

News Xpress   A newsreader for Windows.

Nexis   An information service of Mead Data giving access to a searchable database of news and magazine articles and abstracts.

Nextstep   An operating environment for UNIX that offers a graphical user interface.

NeXT-WAIStation   Nextstep software that functions as both a WAIS server and as a client.

nibble   Half a byte (generally four bits).

nick   A nickname used on IRC, not necessarily the same as your username.

nickname   An alias or address book entry in some e-mail programs (such as Eudora).

nixpub   A list of Internet service providers, posted regularly to comp.bbs.misc and alt.bbs, also available via anonymous FTP from vfl.paramax.com in the /pub/pubnetc directory.

nn   A UNIX newsreader (it stands for *no news*, as it tries to hide everything you don't want to see).

nntpd   A UNIX news server program.

NO CARRIER   The message a modem displays when it detects no carrier signal from the phone line.

Nodal Switching System (NSS)   The routing method of the NSFnet backbone.

node   1. In a network, any computer or other device (such as a printer); 2. Any computer on the Internet, a host.

nodename   The unique name of a device attached to a network.

noninteractive   Automated, taking place all at once, without input from a user.

non-return to zero (NRZ) encoding   A data-transmission method that employs two voltage levels—negative and positive—to represent 0 and 1, as opposed to Manchester encoding, which enables network interface cards to transmit digital signals using direct current, encoding data, and timing signals in the same data stream.

NOT   [Boolean operator] *Not.* Used to reverse the logical relationship to one of the search elements. A text search for *x* AND NOT *y* will match only documents that contain *x* and do not contain *y*.

notwork   A network that isn't working.

NRIE   *(written only)* No reply is expected (appended to e-mail messages that do not require a courtesy reply).

NSA line eater   A (probably) mythical National Security Agency program that would sift through the entire Usenet newsfeed (and perhaps all e-mail traffic as well) looking for telltale words (such as *glock*, *Uzi*, *TNT*, and so on) that would incriminate terrorists and anarchists. Some people deliberately put such words in their sig blocks to confuse the NSA line eater.

NSFnet   A major Internet backbone, operated by the National Science Foundation.

nuke   To kill a file or a process.

null device   A logical device that corresponds to no actual physical device, functioning as a sort of wastebasket.

numeric string   Any sequence of numbers taken as text rather than as a numeral.

Nuntius   A newsreader for the Macintosh, available via anonymous FTP from sumex-aim.stanford.edu.

NUPop   A newsreader for Windows, available via anonymous FTP from ftp.acns.nwu.edu.

nyetwork   A network that isn't working.

o   The *options* command (for setting user preferences) in many UNIX programs.

oak.oakland.edu   A huge FTP archive at Oakland University.

Ob-   A prefix for an obligatory addendum to an off-topic Usenet or list post. Say you get into a political debate in the rec.music.dylan newsgroup. To keep your post technically relevant to the group, you might add:

> ObDylan: Ah, but I was so much older then/I'm younger than that now.

object-oriented   Said of an operating system, programming language, or application that makes use of self-contained *objects* that can contain both programming code and data, and which function as modular program pieces.

obligatory * content   Something added to a mailing list or Usenet post to make it relevant to the charter of the list or newsgroup (replacing the * with the subject of the group, as in *obligatory Amiga content* or *obligatory cat content*, and so on).

octet   Eight bits, especially on a system in which eight bits do not equal a byte.

octothorpe   A number sign (#).

odd parity   A method of verifying the correctness of transmitted data by summing each byte, adding a parity bit of 1 if necessary to make the sum odd, before sending the data, and then repeating the summation on the receiving end.

offline   (adj) 1. Not currently connected to the Net; 2. Not responding to network requests; 3. Said of a person no longer involved in a chat.

offline mail reader   A program that connects to the Net, downloads your e-mail, and then disconnects, allowing you to read, reply to, and send mail without being charged for connect time.

offline newsreader   A newsreader that connects to the Net, downloads all unread articles in all subscribed newsgroups, and then disconnects, allowing you to read, reply to, and post articles without being charged for connect time.

oic   *Oh, I see.*

oldbie   A longtime user of the Net, coined by analogy to newbie.

Oldie   A text editor available in the Delphi Information Service.

127.0.0.1   The Internet *loopback address*, it is always the address of your localhost, the computer you are currently logged in to.

online   (adj) 1. Currently connected to the Net; 2. Available for network requests; 3. Said of a person, participating in a chat.

Online Book Initiative (OBI)   An organization that publishes uncopyrighted (or no longer copyrighted) books via the Internet, reachable via anonymous FTP at world.std.com.

Online Career Center   A nonprofit organization that maintains a searchable database of employment information. It offers free access to job listings and résumés to both employers and job-seekers. For more information, gopher to gopher.msen.com or send e-mail to occ@msen.com.

online community   Also *virtual community*, a group of people with shared interests who meet, communicate, and interact via a network, BBS, Internet discussion group, or any other form of electronic common space. Online communities have many of the properties of real-world communities.

Online Computer Library Center (OCLC)   A nonprofit organization providing computer services (such as cataloging and interlibrary loans) for over ten thousand libraries and educational institutions. OCLC maintains the FirstSearch Catalog. For more information, send mail to listserv@oclc.org

online service   A company that maintains a proprietary network and provides e-mail, forums, chats, games, databases of information, downloadable files, and information services (stocks, airlines, and so on), such as America Online, CompuServe, Delphi, eWorld, GEnie, Prodigy, Microsoft Network, and so on.

Most online services have e-mail connections to the Internet (though some charge extra for that e-mail). More and more are adding other Internet facilities, such as FTP, gopher, and the Web, blurring the distinction further between online services and Internet service providers.

open   (adj) Said of a protocol, using algorithms and technologies available to anyone (as contrasted with proprietary).

(v) To make a connection to a remote host.

open protocol   A protocol that may be utilized by a variety of developers, not just the organization that formulated the protocol.

Open Software Foundation (OSF)   An alliance of DEC, IBM, and Hewlett-Packard.

Open Systems Interconnection (OSI)   An international organization sponsored by the ISO with a mission to create international computer communications standards, such as the OSI Model, specifically to facilitate internetworking among incompatible systems.

operating environment   A front end for an operating system, a set of tools and a consistent look and feel that allow the user to interact with the computer. For instance, Microsoft Windows is an operating environment that runs on top of the MS-DOS operating system.

operating system   The software that governs all communication with and use of a computer's system resources, such as memory, disk space, the attention of the processor, and peripheral devices (monitor, keyboard, mouse, printer, modem, and so on). It also mediates between applications and system resources. The operating system starts running before any other software and stays in memory the whole time a computer is on.

Popular operating systems include DOS, Macintosh, OS/2, UNIX, and VMS.

option   A command or selection available on a menu or list.

OR   [Boolean operator] *Or*. A text search with OR between two words matches any documents containing either word.

.org   An Internet domain corresponding to (nonprofit) organizations.

OS/2   An IBM operating system for PCs and compatibles.

OSF/1   A port of UNIX that runs on VAXen.

OSI   *Open Systems Interconnection*, an international organization sponsored by the ISO with a mission to create international computer communications standards, such as the OSI Model, specifically to facilitate internetworking among incompatible systems.

OSI Model   The seven-layer networking reference model (sometimes called the *seven-layer cake*) defined by the ISO's OSI to facilitate the internetworking of incompatible computers and networks.

The organization of the seven layers, together known as a protocol stack, represents the dependence of each layer on the next lower layer in the stack.

From lowest to highest:

Layer number	Layer Name	Defines Protocols For
1	Physical layer	Interface hardware, cabling, communications medium
2	Data link layer	Transmission of data frames from node to node
3	Network layer	Data routing, addressing, and verification
4	Transport layer	Structure of messages, delivery, some error checking
5	Session layer	Connecting, maintaining communications, security, logging, tracking
6	Presentation layer	Encoding, conversion, file format, data presentation
7	Application layer	Interaction between the network and applications

otoh   (written only) *On the other hand.*

Open Transport (OT)   Apple's Open Transport technology is a comprehensive collection of Networking and Internet connectivity protocols, which was introduced with System 7.5.3, and is included with each subsequent Operating System upgrade.

otth   (written only) *On the third hand.*

Outernet   A collective name for all the networks, BBSs, and online services that have e-mail gateways with the Internet but no full connection.

overhead   (n) The accumulation of protocol information wrapped around data transmitted over networks.

packet   Any unit of data (the size varies) sent across a network. Besides the data, a packet also includes the addresses of the sender and the recipient, as well as error-control information. On the Internet, a packet is the same thing as a datagram. A large piece of data will be split into several packets, each of which may take an independent route to the destination, where they will be reassembled.

Packetized Ensemble Protocol (PEP)   A proprietary feature of Telebit brand modems that allows two modems to be connected directly.

packet sniffer   1. A person who tries to "listen in" on Internet traffic in search of information to steal; 2. The program that such a person employs to "sniff out" interesting packets.

packet-switched network   A network made up of interconnected circuits that route packets over a variety of alternative paths, as opposed to a circuit-switched network, in which packets are routed over dedicated lines.

packet switching   A method of transmitting data in which packets for many unconnected operations are routed simultaneously over a communications channel (often a telephone line) to make best use of the line. Related packets are reassembled at the destination.

packet switch node (PSN)   The computer that handles the routing of packets in a packet-switched network.

page   (v) To display a document one screenful at a time in a character-based interface.

(n) A document published on the Web.

paging program   A program (sometimes called a *pager*) that displays documents one screenful at a time, such as the UNIX utility more.

paper-net   The U.S. Postal Service.

parallel   (adj) Said of a connection in which bits are transmitted simultaneously.

parallel port   A port in the back of a PC that can connect via a cable to a parallel device.

paren   (n) A parenthesis.

parent directory   1. In a hierarchical file system, the directory for which the current directory is a subdirectory, symbolized in UNIX, DOS, and OS/2 by a two dots (..); 2. Any directory which contains other directories.

parity   An error-checking method in data transmission in which an extra bit is added to each byte (between the data bit and the stop bit) to round off bit-total values to even or odd numbers. The parity bit must match at both ends of the transmission.

Parity is therefore one of the settings you have to specify on your modem to make a connection. It's usually set to None or Even, but it depends on the modem you're calling.

parity bit   A redundant bit added to a byte in data transmission as part of an error-checking technique.

parity error   An error caused by mismatched parity bits in a byte of transmitted data.

parse   (v) To interpret an instruction by breaking it down and analyzing its parts.

Pascal   A beginner's programming language, often used as a stepping stone to C.

passive star   A network design with a central hub that connects all the branches but does not retransmit signals that pass through it.

password   A secret code used to restrict access to an account, channel, file, and so on, only to authorized users who know the password.

A bad password is one that is a real word or is otherwise easily guessable (a birth date, a pet's name, and so on). A good password contains upper- and lowercase letters and numerals, and the longer it is, the better.

passwd   The UNIX command to change an account's password.

patch   (n) A quick-and-dirty correction that fixes a bug, or at least works around it.

(v) To fix a problem with a temporary work-around or kluge.

path   1. A bang path, the route an e-mail message takes between its sender and receiver; 2. The channel through which a signal passes; 3. A completely specified location of a directory or file, starting from the root directory.

PC   A *personal computer*, generally a microcomputer, usually either an IBM PC or compatible, a Macintosh, or perhaps an Amiga.

PC-compatible   Said of a computer that emulates the functionality of an IBM PC.

PC Eudora   A Windows mail program (a port of Eudora for the Macintosh) that uses Post Office Protocol (POP) and can function as an offline mail reader. It is available via anonymous FTP from ftp.qualcomm.com.

PC Gopher for DOS   A gopher client for the IBM PC or compatible running any flavor of DOS, available via anonymous FTP from sunsite.unc.edu.

PC Pursuit   A SprintNet service that allows users to connect directly to another computer (as opposed to an online service).

PC/TCP Plus for DOS   DOS software that enables an IBM PC or compatible to connect via modem to a computer connected to the Internet for FTP and telnet.

PC-Xware   Windows software that includes TCP/IP, NFS, FTP, and server access for X Window applications, developed by Network Computing Devices, Inc.

PDIAL   *Public Dial-Up Internet Access List*, Peter Kaminski's excellent list of Internet service providers, complete with cost information, posted regularly to alt.internet.access.wanted and alt.bbs.lists, and available via anonymous FTP from rtfm.mit.edu in the /pub/usenet/news.answers directory, with the file name pdial.

PDP-11   A series of DEC computers now largely superseded by VAXen. PDP stands for *programmed data processor*. The PDP-11 series was preceded by PDP-10, according to hacker lore the first real timesharing machine.

PeaceNet   A BBS for nonprofits, religious organizations, and people concerned with peace and justice. For more information, anonymous FTP to igc.org in the /pub directory.

peer   A network device that communicates directly with other devices on the network.

peer-to-peer   (adj) A network architecture in which each computer on the network can communicate directly with other nodes and function as both a client and a server.

Pegasus Mail   Also known as *p-mail*, a freeware e-mail program for IBM PCs and compatibles and Macintoshes, available via FTP from risc.ua.edu.

PENpages   A database and information service covering every imaginable aspect of rural life in general and agriculture in particular, administrated by Pennsylvania State University. It is updated daily and the latest additions are always available on the main menu.

To connect, telnet to psupen.psu.edu and log in as your two-letter state abbreviation (no password).

Pentium   A 64-bit microprocessor, Intel's successor to the 80486 chip (named Pentium after the courts decided that Intel could not defend as a trademark the number 586 or 80586).

The discovery of an error in the much-vaunted chip has spun off a long series of jokes about rounding errors (for example, "Q: How many Pentiums does it take to screw in a lightbulb? A: 1.9999998657586.").

peon   An ordinary user with no special privileges.

peripheral   (adj) Said of a device that is not essential to the computer or physically a part of it (as opposed to the processor or hard-disk drive), such as a printer or modem.

(n) A peripheral device.

Perl   A programming language (it stands for *practical extraction and report language*) distributed over Usenet, favored by UNIX system administrators.

permissions   Settings associated with an account on a network or multi-user system that define a level of access (to certain system resources) permitted to the user of the account.

PGP   A shareware public-key encryption program (it stands for *pretty good privacy*), developed by Phillip Zimmerman. For more information see the Web page at http://www.mantis.co.uk/pgp/pgp.html.

phage   (n) A program that modifies other programs or databases in unauthorized ways.

phreak   (v) To crack (break into) a network or phone system.

(n) One who enjoys cracking secure networks or phone systems.

physical   (adj) Said of hardware and mechanical connections, as opposed to logical.

physical layer   Layer 1 (the bottom layer) of the OSI Model; it defines protocols for connecting cables and other hardware.

pico   A full-screen, modeless text editor for UNIX machines based on the built-in editor in the pine e-mail program.

pile-on   (n) A flame war in which many participants take turns attacking a single victim, creating long posts of polymorphous abuse.

Pilgrim Press   A collective online publishing venue on the Web (at http://syx.com/pilgrim).

pine   A UNIX e-mail program whose name is a recursive acronym (pine stands for *pine is not elm*). Pine has a built-in full-screen modeless editor, MIME support, and the ability to attach files.

ping   (v) 1. To check the presence of a host with PING; 2. To send e-mail to an entire mailing list, requesting a response, in order to check which addresses are still valid.

(n) The UNIX command that uses the PING protocol.

PING   Said to stand for *Packet Internet Groper*, a protocol for sending a signal to see whether another network host or other device is online and responding. (It's probably actually named for the sound made by submarine sonar/depth equipment.)

pipe   (v) To send the output of a process or dump the contents of a file to a device (such as a printer), program (such as one that will process the data), or another file.

(n) The | character (also called a *vertical bar*), used in the piping process.

.pit   The file extension for Macintosh PackIt files. (PackIt has largely been superseded as a Macintosh compression standard by StuffIt.)

pita   (written only) *Pain in the arse.*

pixel   A single dot on a monitor or in a bit-mapped image (from *picture element*).

.pkg   The file extension for an AppleLink Package file.

pkunzip   The uncompression program for pkzipped files.

pkzip   A DOS file compression program.

plain ASCII   (adj) Said of an ASCII text file (a document with no word-processor formatting).

.plan   (*dot plan*) A text file that is displayed when your username is fingered. Originally intended to alert people to your whereabouts or immediate plans, .plan files have evolved into personalized files sometimes filled with information or absurdities. Here's my old .plan:

```
Released December 1:
Enterzone, a quarterly hyperzine on the World Wide Web
<http://enterzone.berkeley.edu/enterzone.html>
Current Project:
Internet Dictionary (Sybex)
Available Now:
A Guided Tour of the Internet (Sybex)
WordPerfect 6 Roadmap (Sybex)
Word for Windows Quick & Easy (Sybex)
Last Story:
No Bird but An Invisible Thing (hypertext version)
<http://enterzone.berkeley.edu/homies/nobird/nobird.html>
```

platform   A computer or operating system type.

plokta   (written only, v) *Press lots of keys to abort.* Many newbie posts end
with a series of attempts to quit while still in insert mode, like so:

```
This is my first post so please don't flame me.
-b1ff
~BL
:wq
~BL
~BL
ZZ
~BL
quit
:wq
~BL
help
?
~BL
bye
```

plonk   A follow-up post that means "I just put you in my kill file." (It's
supposed to be the sound of the bozo falling into the kill file.)

p-mail   1. Pegasus Mail; 2. Physical mail, as opposed to e-mail.

point at   To start a client program, such as a Web browser, by supplying it
with an address, as in "Point your Web browser at http://ezone.org/ez to
see the latest episode of Enterzone."

PointCast   A program for receiving pushed netcasts, most popularly used as
a screen saver. You can download it for free from http://www.pointcast.com.

point of presence (POP)   A local phone number connected to a modem
connected to the network of a service provider, to enable users to log in to
the network without paying long distance charges.

Point-to-Point Protocol (PPP)   A TCP/IP protocol, similar to SLIP, for
transmitting IP datagrams over serial lines such as phone lines. With
PPP, PC users can connect to the Internet and still function in their
native environment (instead of having to deal with a character-based
UNIX environment).

poll   (v) 1. To check a port to see whether a device is connected and available for network or communications activity; 2. To connect to another system to check for new mail or news.

port   (n) 1. A socket on the back of a computer for connecting cables and hence modems, printers, etc.; 2. On Internet hosts, a channel dedicated to a specific program, so that a multiplexing host can run telnet sessions on one port, FTP connections on another, logins on another, etc.; 3. The interface between a router and a network; 4. A version of a program that was originally designed for a different platform.

(v) To translate software designed for one platform so that it will run on another.

post   (v) 1. To send a message to a mailing list or an article to a newsgroup; 2. To publish information in any medium on the Internet. (The word *post* comes from the bulletin-board metaphor, in which scraps of paper are posted to the board to be read by anyone who comes by, as opposed to the British usage, which means to send mail.)

(n) A message sent to a mailing list or newsgroup.

postcardware   Shareware that's almost free, except the programmer requests that satisfied users send a postcard (so she can see how far the software has spread).

poster   One who posts.

postmaster   A person who oversees a network's e-mail connection to the Internet. Questions about users at a host or problems with e-mail to or from that host can often be addressed to postmaster@*hostname.domain*.

Post Office Protocol (POP)   A protocol that specifies how a personal computer can connect to a mail server on the Internet and download e-mail.

PostScript   A proprietary "page-description" computer language developed by Adobe Systems. It describes pages (text, graphics, layout) in mathematical terms. PostScript files generally have a .ps or .eps extension.

Pot. Kettle. Black.   A shorthand newsgroup or mailing list follow-up, criticizing the previous poster for exhibiting the same foibles she was faulting another for. (It's short for the aphorism "that's like the pot calling the kettle black.")

pour   (v) To pipe the output from a process or file to a device or other file.

power cycling   Turning the hardware off, waiting, and then turning it on again.

PPP   *Point-to-Point Protocol*, a TCP/IP protocol similar to SLIP for transmitting IP datagrams over serial lines such as phone lines. With PPP, users connect to the Internet and still function in their native environment (instead of having to deal with a character-based UNIX environment).

presentation layer   Layer 6 of the OSI Model, it defines how data is formatted, encoded, converted, and presented.

prime time   The period of heaviest usage of a network, usually 9–to–5 during the work week.

Principia Discordia   An underground tract that elucidates the worship of Eris, ancient goddess of discord.

printed circuit   A computer chip with microcircuits literally printed (via a photographic process) onto it.

Printer Access Protocol (PAP)   The AppleTalk protocol that defines how a workstation and a printer communicate.

privacy   Because the Internet is not inherently secure, users are cautioned to e-mail and post only information that they don't mind being public, or take steps to increase the privacy of their communication, either via encryption, anonymity, or by using other communications channels entirely.

privacy-enhanced mail (PEM)   E-mail—handling systems that incorporate encryption techniques to secure privacy and verification of message integrity.

private key   In public-key encryption, the secret key the user reveals to no one and uses to sign outgoing messages and to decrypt incoming messages that were encrypted with the public key.

private virtual circuit (PVC)   Software circuits that maintain a private line between hosts.

privatization   On the Internet, generally refers to the U.S. government's process of placing maintenance of backbone networks in the hands of private organizations. So far this has not significantly changed the pricing structure for individual users.

privileges   Also called *access privileges*, a set of system resource and directory actions that a user is permitted to perform.

process   A program or part of a program being executed in a multitasking operating system. More generally, one task of many that a computer is doing.

ProComm Plus   A popular communications package for IBM PCs and compatibles, sold by Datastorm Technologies, Inc.

Prodigy Information Service   [Online service]; (800) PRODIGY [776-3449]

.profile   A startup file in some flavors of UNIX.

programmer   A person who writes computer programs.

programming   The process of writing programs.

.project   (*dot project*) On some systems, a file similar to a .plan that is displayed when a user is fingered, intended to discuss the project the user is currently working on.

Project Gutenberg   An organization that publishes uncopyrighted books on the Internet, reachable via anonymous FTP at mrcnext.cso.uiuc.edu.

prompt   (n) Also *command-line prompt*, a string of text that a character-based operating system displays on the screen to tell a user that it is ready to accept input (such as a command or the name of a program to run).

propagation   The process of dissemination for packets in general, and Usenet newsfeeds in particular, as they are passed from computer to computer. Propagation delays are responsible for the confusing situation that sometimes occurs when you read a follow-up to a post that hasn't yet appeared at your site.

proprietary   (adj) Said of a technology, architecture, or set of protocols whose design is the property of the company that developed it.

Prospero   A distributed directory system, file system, and index service (and the protocol that underlies it) that allows users to access both local and remote directories in the same way. For more information, connect via anonymous FTP to prospero.isi.edu and go to the /pub/prospero directory.

protocol   An agreed-upon set of rules that allows otherwise incompatible machines or software to communicate. Protocols can govern a wide range of the aspects of communications, from the order in which bits are transmitted to the rules for opening and maintaining a connection to the format of an electronic mail message.

protocol layer   One portion of a set of protocols that handles one aspect of the transmission of data.

protocol stack   A set of protocol layers that work together to provide reliable communication between a computer and a network or another computer, also called a *protocol family* or *protocol suite*. The TCP/IP protocol stack includes such protocols as TCP, IP, FTP, SMTP, telnet, and so on.

proxy server   A security measure that enables users behind a firewall to browse the Web (visited resources are actually downloaded by the intervening proxy server and then viewed internally from there) without exposing the contents of the intranet to public scrutiny. A proxy server may render some web services inaccessible to the user.

.ps   The file extension for PostScript files.

pseudo   (n) A new identity assumed on Usenet in order that the user might act (provocatively or otherwise) without those actions being associated with the user's real (or better-known) name.

/pub   A UNIX directory often found on FTP hosts, where public information is stored and made available.

pubic directory   Slang for an FTP public directory.

public data network (PDN)   A type of commercial packet-switched network offering wide-area services to customers, with sophisticated error-checking, buffering, and handling of protocols. Tymnet, SprintNet, and the CompuServe Packet Network are all PDNs.

Public Dial-Up Internet Access List (PDIAL)   Peter Kaminski's excellent list of Internet service providers, complete with cost information, posted regularly to alt.internet.access.wanted and alt.bbs.lists, and available via anonymous FTP from rtfm.mit.edu in the /pub/usenet/news.answers directory, with the file name pdial.

public domain   (adj) Available for free to the public, uncopyrighted, as are much of the information, system software, and applications available on the Internet.

public key   In public-key encryption, the key a user distributes freely and which correspondents use to encrypt messages to the user and decrypt the user's signature (encrypted with the user's private key) on messages from the user.

public-key encryption   A form of key encryption which uses two keys, a public key (for encrypting messages) and a private key (for decrypting messages) to enable users to verify each other's messages without having to securely exchange secret keys.

public libraries   Many public libraries have made their card catalogs available and searchable via the Internet, often from telnet addresses. The easiest way to search many libraries is with Hytelnet.

publishing   Posting on the Net (to newsgroups, the Web, gopher, etc.) is considered equivalent to publishing, though the paradigm is different—the reader comes to you and you do not distribute the information.

push   (n) A method of distributing information over the Web, by which updates are (scheduled and then) automatically sent to the user's screen or window, as if the content were being "broadcast" to a receiver (hence the synonymous terms netcast and webcast).
(v) To distribute content over the Web via netcasting.

put   (v) To copy a file from your host computer to a remote site, particularly via FTP.
(n) The FTP command to put a file.

'puter   (*pewter* or *pooter*) A computer, usually a personal computer.

pwd   The UNIX command (short for *print working directory*) that displays the current working directory (the directory the user is "in").

q   The quit command in many UNIX programs. (Often a capital *Q* will mean *quick quit* and will allow you to quit without any questions.)

qotd   (written only) *Quotation of the day.* Some systems display a quotation when you log in. Some Usenet posters change the quotations in their sig block daily (or more often).

query   (n) 1. A search request submitted to a database to find a particular record (piece of information) or all records that meet certain criteria, such as an archie query; 2. A question mark.

question mark   ? 1. a wildcard character in UNIX (and hence in many Internet applications), it stands for any single character; 2. A help command in some character-based applications.

questionnaires   Usenet newsgroups are often bombarded by purveyors of questionnaires, hoping to exploit a ready-made audience. That the responders are self-selecting doesn't seem to bother the questioneers, but to regular readers of the newsgroups, these posts and the ubiquitous surveys get tiresome awfully fast.

queue   (*cue*, n) A list of items (such as print jobs or messages) waiting to be sent from one device to another.

QuickTime   An Apple technology that compresses, stores, translates, and plays back files combining text, sound, animation, and video, on both the Windows and Macintosh platforms. QuickTime clips are distributed via the Internet and the Web.

quit   To stop running an application and (usually) return to the operating system.

quoting   Including a relevant portion of a preceding article when posting a follow-up. Most newsreaders precede quoted text with a symbol, such as >, and try to indicate who said what, though multiple embedded quotations often require that the latest author untangle the attributions.

It is bad netiquette to quote no text (unless the follow-up makes it absolutely clear what it is responding to), and it's both bad netiquette and an unmistakable marker of a clueless newbie to quote an entire article merely to add "I agree" or "Right on, d00d!!" at the end.

QWERTY   (n) The standard typewriter and computer-keyboard layout, so named for the first six characters of the first alphabetical row.

r   The reply command in many UNIX mail programs; 2. The *reply by e-mail* command in many UNIX newsreaders.

RAM   (*ram*) *Random access memory*, memory that any application or process can read or write to. It's frequently confused with storage, because both resources are often measured in megabytes.

ranking   The order in which a WAIS program displays the results of a database search—from most likely to least likely.

rb   The Ymodem command for receiving (uploading) a file.

rc file   A UNIX text file with a file name of the form . *rc*, containing command line instructions or other startup information for an application or for the operating system itself. Examples include .newsrc, .pinerc, and so on.

rcp   The UNIX *remote copy* command.

read   To copy data from a disk into memory.

README file   An information file describing the contents of an FTP directory or the files associated with an application.

readme.txt   Typical name for a README file.

read notification   A feature of some e-mail programs that lets you know when the recipient of your e-mail has received and opened the message.

read-only   (adj) Said of a file that can be read but not altered.

read-write   (adj) Said of a file that can be both read and written to (altered).

RealAudio   Progressive Networks' original streaming audio format. The latest version is called RealPlayer.

RealPlayer   Progressive Networks' format for streaming audio and movies.

real life   The offline world, as in the question "What do you do in real life?"

real name   Also called a *full name*, a user's full name as it appears on e-mail messages and Usenet posts, as opposed to their username (the real name can also be a pseudonym). On UNIX systems, the user's real name is a variable that can be set with the chfn command. Many Windows and Macintosh Internet applications allow the user to enter or change a real name on the fly.

Real Soon Now   Also *RSN*, similar to *as soon as possible* but with a subtext that it ain't really gonna happen any time soon.

real time   Also *realtime*, the time used for synchronous communication, in which both participants must be available (as in a telephone conversation). Also, taking place at the present time, live, not delayed or recorded.

reboot   To restart a crashed operating system, either through a designated key combination (a warm boot), or by turning it off and on again (power cycling).

rec.   A Usenet hierarchy devoted to recreation.

receipt notification   A proof-of-delivery feature provided by some e-mail programs (similar to the idea of registered mail in the real world).

record   (n) A set of related data from a database.

recursive acronym   An acronym that contains the acronym itself in its spelled out form, such as GNU, which stands for *GNU's not UNIX*, and pine, which stands for *pine is not elm*.

redirection   Sending output from one device or file to another device or file.

redundant path   A secondary path that a router can assign to a packet when the normal route is not available.

refresh   To redraw the screen, usually either to reflect changes to the data or to restore the screen when something has marred its intended appearance.

register   (v) To sign up and pay for shareware.
(n) A designated area of memory.

registered jack (RJ)   Any of a series of specialized jacks used for connecting wires, such as RJ-11 and RJ-45.

rehi   (*ree-high*) *Hi again*, typed on IRC when you rejoin a channel.

relevance feedback   A system used by WAIS applications to rank documents retrieved in a search in order of relevance to the search criteria. Documents are ranked based on the number of times that key words from the query appear in them.

reliable   Said of networks with dedicated connections.

remailer   A program that receives e-mail and then resends it, with different information attached.

remote   Said of a host or other network resource that is located on a computer or network elsewhere, as opposed to a local host or resource.

remote access   The process of accessing another computer's resources, such as files or printers. Dial-up accounts and telnet are both forms of remote access.

remote login   To connect to a remote computer over a network, usually done on the Internet with telnet or rlogin.

remove   To kill or erase a file or directory.

rename   To change the name (or path) of a file or directory.

repeater   A device that connects two stretches of cable and boosts the power of the signal it passes, to reduce line noise and the risk of errors.

reply   (v) To respond to an e-mail message or Usenet post.
(n) 1. A message sent in response to a previous message or post; 2. An e-mail command that takes the return path from the current message and makes that address the recipient of a new message, possibly quoting the previous message as well.

repost   (n) An article posted again in full. (Many newsgroups expect that reposts be labeled as such in their subject lines.)
(v) To post the same information again.

Request for Discussion (RFD)   The first stage in the formal process of Usenet newsgroup creation.

-request   A suffix appended to the username of a human-administered mailing list to form the username of the administrative address for the list. (So a human-administered mailing list called atoz@netcom.com would have an administrative address called atoz-request@netcom.com associated with it.) It is a Bad Thing to post administrative requests (generally to subscribe or unsubscribe) to the actual mailing list rather than to the -request address.

Research Libraries Information Network (RLIN)   An online catalog of catalogs with information from most major research libraries in the United States, reachable by telnet at rlg.stanford.edu (it's not free). For information, send e-mail to bl.ric@rlg.standord.edu or call (800) 537-RLIN.

Reseaux Associés pour la Recherche Europèenne (RARE)   A European group of research networks. For more information, connect via anonymous FTP to ftp.rare.nl.

Reseaux IP Europèenne (RIPE)   A group of European TCP/IP networks.

resolution   1. Conversion of a physical address into a logical address (*address resolution*); 2. The degree of detail, sharpness, or fineness of an image.

resolve   (v) To convert a physical address to a logical address or vice versa.

return from the dead   (v) To be reconnected to the Internet after a hiatus.

return path   An address in the header of an e-mail program that tells the recipient's mail program where to send a reply message.

Reverse Address Resolution Protocol (RARP)   A TCP/IP protocol for converting logical addresses to physical addresses.

RFC   *Request for Comments*, one of a set of documents that contain Internet protocols, standards, and information, and together more or less define the Internet, in an open way. The standards contained in them are followed carefully by software developers (both commercial and freeware). The name Request for Comments can be confusing, since the contents are settled, but they arrived from free and open discussion on the Net.

RFCs can be found via anonymous FTP at the ftp.internic.net site, among others.

rib site   A computer with a high-speed link to a backbone site that distributes traffic to smaller networks.

rights   Another name for privileges.

ring topology   A network architecture in which the nodes are arranged in a circle.

RINGO   An experimental service at MIT that that allows you to rate a list of musicians and bands and receive back some suggestions about other music you might like. To participate, send e-mail to ringo@media.mit.edu.

RJ   A registered jack.

RJ-11   A typical phone jack.

RJ-45   A modular jack that can hold up to four pairs of wires, used most often to connect unshielded twisted-pair wiring in LANs. An RJ-45 looks like a phone jack (RJ-11) except bigger.

RL   (written only) Real life.

rlogin   A protocol (and program) for remote login from one UNIX machine to another. It automatically supplies the username and password given when the user first logged in.

rm   The UNIX *remove* command, for deleting a file. (Be very careful not to type *rm* * and press Enter by mistake—there's no "undelete" in UNIX!)

rmdir   The UNIX *remove directory* command, for deleting a directory.

rmgroup   A special kind of control message that removes a newsgroup.

rn   The most common UNIX newsreader. It's not a threaded newsreader.

robocancel   (v) To automatically cancel articles. A controversial (because it's a form of censorship) method for dealing with spammers and roboposters.

robopost   (v) To post automatically, usually done by a 'bot that is programmed to post reams of articles and responses to Usenet.

roboposter   1. A 'bot that automatically posts and reposts huge numbers of articles to Usenet; 2. The programmer behind the roboposting 'bot.

A reputed roboposter using the name of Serdar Argic singlehandedly rendered soc.history (and a number of other newsgroups) unreadable without a kill file to screen him out. His howling through the wires (ranting holocaust revisionism about the Turks and the "x-Soviet" Armenians) came to an unexpected but welcome halt in the spring of 1994.

robot   A user on IRC or in a MUD (or, less commonly, on Usenet) that is actually a program. Some perform useful functions while others are merely annoying.

robust   (adj) Said of software that doesn't crash often and recovers well when it does.

rofl   (written only, also *ROFL*) *Rolling on the floor laughing*.

Rogue   A widely circulated text-adventure role-playing game, with a dungeon/swords-and-sorcery motif.

role-playing game   A game or activity, such as a MUD, in which participants take on fictional identities and strive to remain in character.

ROM   (rhymes with *prom*) *Read-only memory*. Fixed memory that can't be altered.

root   1. In a hierchical file system, the first directory, to which all other directories are subdirectories; 2. On UNIX machines, a superuser account with unlimited permissions.

rot13   (*rot-thirteen*) A simple cipher in which each letter is replaced with the one 13 letters away from it in the alphabet, traditionally used to hide spoilers and off-color jokes from sensitive eyes. (Because the alphabet has 26 letters, the same rotation will both encode and decode.)

rotfl   (written only) *Rolling on the floor laughing*.

route   (n) The path a packet takes from sender to destination.
(v) To send a packet along a path.

router   A device that physically connects two networks or a network to the Internet, converting addresses and sending on only the messages that need to pass to the other network.

routing information protocol (RIP)   A TCP/IP protocol that specifies how routers exchange information.

routing table   A list used by a router to determine the best route for a packet.

RS-232C   A 25-pin connector, such as the one used to connect a computer to an external modem.

rtfm.mit.edu   A huge FTP archive, with FAQs from many Usenet newsgroups, RFCs, FYIs, and more.

RTM   (written only, also *rtm*) *Read the manual!*

rx   The Xmodem command for receiving (uploading) a file.

rz   The Zmodem command for receiving (uploading) a file.

s   The save command in many UNIX applications.

samizdat   (*sam-is-dot*) Also *samizdata*, from the Russian word for self-published underground pamphlets, a word used to describe the flow of unofficial information on the Internet, particularly e-zines.

sat   (*written only*, abbrev.) Sorry about that.

save   Literally, to copy a file or some data from memory (RAM) to a disk (or other storage medium). More loosely, to preserve the work you're doing by storing it on a disk.

Savvy   [service provider] info@savvy.com, (800) 275-7455.

sb   The Ymodem command for sending (downloading) a file.

sci.   A Usenet hierarchy devoted to science.

screen dump   A copy of the contents of a screen, saved to a file or sent to a printer.

screen name   An America Online term for a user's real name or one of several allowable pseudonyms.

screen-oriented   (adj) Said of applications that permit the user to move the cursor around the screen.

script   A sequence of commands to be executed by an application or operating system, often saved as a text file.

scroll   (v) To browse through a document, moving the text up the screen as if on a continuous parchment. Usually suggests being able to move as little as a line at a time, as opposed to the display of a paging program, which always moves through a document one screenful at a time.

scroll-back   The ability to scroll to an earlier part of a document, which in a terminal-emulation program requires that it be saved in a buffer.

SCSI   (*scuzzy*) Stands for *Small Computer Systems Interface*, a standard for connecting personal computers to certain peripheral devices, including CD-ROM drives and external hard drives.

.sea   A file extension that indicates a Macintosh self-extracting archive.

search   (v) To seek information from a database, document, or other source, usually by specifying key words to match.

(n) The process of seeking specific information from a source.

(adj) Said of programs, interfaces, or tools that facilitate the process of seeking specific information.

searchable   (adj) Said of indexes, databases, and documents that are formatted to facilitate searches by standard Internet search tools, such as WAIS, gopher, and Web clients.

search criterion   A set of keywords separated by Boolean operators (such as AND, OR, and NOT) specified in a query in order to find matching documents or entries in a database, such as an archie or WAIS server.

search engine   Database software, usually fronted by a web site for searching the Internet, the Web, or some other computer domain, such as AltaVista (at http://altavista.digital.com). Most search engines feature, at minimum, a text box for typing key words and a Search (or Go or Do it Now! or whatever) button.

secondary service provider   An organization that provides a direct Internet connection to a regional set of networks.

security   The Internet is not inherently secure. For example, e-mail messages are in some ways more like postcards than like letters sealed in envelopes. Your mail generally passes through many sites on the way to its destination, and postmasters and other superusers can read your mail if they want, although it would be unethical for them to do so.

If you are interested in making your e-mail more private or secure, look into encryption software, such as PGP. New Web products are exploring methods of making private transactions over the Internet as well.

seed   In a tape tree, the original master tape from which the first set of copies is made.

segment   (n) 1. A length of cable in a network; 2. A unit of data packaged by TCP for IP.

select articles   (v) In a newsreader, to choose which articles to read (by their titles or authors).

self-extracting archive   An executable file, containing one or more compressed files, that will extract the files it contains when run.

sequenced packet exchange (SPX)   A Novell NetWare transport layer protocol that coordinates messages between workstations.

serial   Said of a connection, such as a phone line, in which bits are transmitted one at a time.

Serial Line Internet Protocol (SLIP)   A TCP/IP protocol for transmitting IP datagrams over serial lines, such as phone lines. With SLIP, personal computer users can connect to the Internet and still function in their ·native environment (instead of having to deal with a character-based UNIX environment).

serial port   A port in the back of a PC that can connect via a cable to a serial device, such as a modem or printer.

server   A network application or computer that supplies information or other resources to client applications that connect to it. In conventional networking, server usually refers to a computer; for Internet client/server applications, server usually refers to a program.

Many Internet features are provided by servers: file servers, mail servers, WAIS servers, Web servers, FTP servers, archie servers, name servers, finger servers, and so on.

service provider   A company that provides direct access to the Internet.

session   A period of connection and exchange of communications between hosts.

session layer   Layer 5 of the OSI Model, it specifies how computers make and maintain connections.

setext   A sophisticated text-formatting program for UNIX.

shareware   Software available for a free trial that must be registered and paid for if you decide to use it. Payment may also buy you manuals, support, and updates. Much shareware is distributed via the Internet. A large FTP archive for Macintosh software can be found at sumex.aim .stanford.edu; another large FTP site for IBM PC and compatible software can be found at wuarchive.wustl.edu in the /systems/ibmpc directory.

shar file   Also called a *sharchive*, a UNIX archive file that contains one or more compressed files. It can be uncompressed in a UNIX shell without any special software.

shell   1. An operating environment, that is, a program through which a user communicates with the operating system. There are many flavors of UNIX shell, such as Bourne, Korn, Bourne again (bash), C shell, and so on; 2. A command in many applications that allows you to enter shell commands without quitting the program.

shell account   An Internet account that provides access to a UNIX shell, usually via a modem and a terminal-emulation program.

shell command   An operating-system command entered at a command-line prompt or from within an application.

shell out   (v) To temporarily escape an application and get access to a shell without quitting the program.

Shergold, Craig   If you get the chain mail telling you to send this poor kid a get well card, don't! He is the famous "dying boy" (no longer dying and no longer a little boy) who, according to a perennially circulating meme, is hoping to become the *Guinness Book of World Records* champion for post-cards received. Due to the persistence of this story (it was true once, over 10 years ago), the hospital he stayed in still gets postcards.

shielded cable   A cable protected from electromagnetic interference by wire mesh and plastic, such as a coaxial cable. Shielded cable will not interfere with other electronic devices and is secure from wire tapping.

shielded twisted-pair (STP)   A cable shielded with foil and a copper braid surrounding the wire in twisted pairs, suitable for high-speed trans-mission over long distances, often used in token ring networks.

shouting   On the Internet, TYPING IN ALL CAPS is frequently interpreted as shouting.

Shub-Internet   A mythical god or demon thought to be responsible for all slowdowns on the Net. It lives under the Pentagon and is worshipped by some MUD people. Its name is spoken aloud at great peril.

sig block   Also *sig, .sig, signature,.signature*, or *signature block, or signature file*, a text file containing a user's name and, optionally, e-mail address, other identifying information, aphorisms, ASCII graphics, etc., automati-cally attached to the ends of e-mail messages and Usenet posts. A UNIX sig block is a file called .signature in the user's home directory.

It is generally considered a breach of netiquette to have a sig block over four lines long. Sig blocks are the bumper stickers of the information highway.

signal   (n) An electronic impulse passing over a medium such as a wire, carry-ing data from one device to another; 2. More loosely, any useful information.

signal-to-noise ratio   1. Literally, an electrical engineering measurement of the quality of a communication medium; 2. On the Internet, colloquially used as a metaphor for the proportion of useful information to junk on a list or in a newsgroup.

sig quote   A quotation contained in a sig block, not unlike yearbook quota-tions and frequently about as interesting.

sig virus   A meme in sig blocks that became very popular around late 1991 to early 1992, usually some variation on "Hi! I'm a sig virus. Copy me into your signature file and join the fun."

silicon   The mineral that computer chips (and sand) are made from.

silly group   A newsgroup created simply for the sake of amusement, either because the name itself is silly or because the topic to be discussed in it is silly, many of which can be found in the alt.silly-group.* hierarchy. Some silly groups have a *gag.gag.gag* ending, for instance, alt.tv.dinosaurs.barney .die.die.die.

Simple Mail Transfer Protocol (SMTP)   The TCP/IP protocol that specifies how computers exchange electronic mail. It works with Post Office Protocol, and is one of the reasons that Internet e-mail functions so well.

Simple Network Management Protocol (SNMP)   A TCP/IP protocol that specifies how nodes are managed on a network, using agents to monitor network traffic and maintain a management information base.

Simple Wide Area Information Server (SWAIS)   A WAIS interface for VT100 terminals that shows sources in numbered lists.

simplex   Transmission of a signal in one direction at a time.

.sit   The file extension of a Macintosh StuffIt file.

site   An Internet host that allows some kind of remote access, such as FTP, telnet, gopher, and so on.

site name   Also *sitename*, the portion of an Internet address that precedes the (subdomain, if any, and the) domain. In the address mang@garnet .blob.com, *garnet* is the site name.

64K line   A 64 kps telephone circuit, also called a DS0 line. A 64K line is called a clear channel when its entire 64 kps bandwidth is available for transmission.

slack   (n) 1. Unused storage space on a disk; 2. According to the teachings of the Church of the SubGenius, the prerequisite of all human happiness. For more information, see the newsgroup alt.slack.

slash   /, in UNIX (and hence in gopher addresses and URLs), the separator character between directory levels.

SLIP   *Serial Line Internet Protocol*, a TCP/IP protocol for transmitting IP datagrams over serial lines, such as phone lines. With SLIP, personal computer users can connect to the Internet and still function in their native environment (instead of having to deal with a character-based UNIX environment).

SLIP emulator   A UNIX program, such as TIA, that runs in a shell account and mimics the behavior of a SLIP connection, enabling a shell user to run Internet applications on a personal computer.

SlipKnot   A program made by MicroMind that provides graphical access to the Web for people with character-based Unix accounts.

slot   A rack inside a computer where an expansion card can be put.

Small Computer Systems Interface

smart terminal   A terminal that can handle some of the display processing, taking some of the load off the computer it's connected to (an obsolete term in the PC world).

smiley   A sideways smiley face, also called an emoticon, used to indicate an emotion. Here some examples of smileys:

    :-)
    ;)
    %^$

smurf   (n) A sickly-sweet newsgroup participant (from the icky-cute little blue elf characters from Saturday morning television rot).

snail   (n) A snail mail address, especially labeled as such in a sig block.
    (v) To send snail mail.

snail mail   Internet slang for U.S. Postal Service mail, so called for its relative slowness, compared to electronic mail.

snarf   (v) To fetch a set of files across a network, as with FTP.

sneakernet   The kind of network in which you copy the file to a diskette, walk the diskette over to another computer (that's the sneaker part), and then copy the file onto the new computer. The lowest-tech LAN.

'Snooze   A derogatory term for Usenet News, commenting on the low signal-to-noise ratio.

SO   (*ess-oh*) *Significant other*, a genderless term for partner, spouse, lover, etc., common on Usenet.

soc.   The Usenet hierarchy devoted to society (and usually sectarian groups in it).

socket   A subdivision of a network node reserved for a single application or process.

socket client   An application or process that reserves a socket for a specific purpose.

socket number   A unique number assigned to a socket by a network.

soda remailer   An anonymous remailer. For information, send mail to remailer@soda.csua.berkeley.edu with remailer-info as your subject.

soft boot   (v) To reboot only part of a system without restarting the whole thing.

software   1. A program—either an application or operating system—that a computer can execute, as opposed to hardware (the computer itself); 2. A suite of related programs.

software description database (SDD)   A list of file names and directories accessible via archie.

solidus   A slash (/).

sorcerer's apprentice mode   What happens when a program or process spins out of control, spawning more and more processes from itself until it eventually crashes its system, or worse, slows down or crashes parts of the Internet.

source   A remote database storing files available to WAIS searches.

source code   The original, uncompiled program instructions that make up a piece of software.

SPACEWAR   The original spaceship combat game, first created on DEC PDP machines, then ported to UNIX, and eventually inspiring one of the first video games.

spam   (v) To post (or robopost) huge amounts of material to Usenet, or to post one article to huge numbers of inappropriate groups. (The term comes from the commercial meat product Spam and the Monty Python routine in which rowdy Vikings in a diner chant "Spam, Spam, Spam, Spam Spam, Spam, Spam, Spam, wonderful Spam, marvelous Spam," and so on, *ad nauseam*.)

Crossposting, even to an inappropriately large number of groups, is not the same thing as spamming, because any decent newsreader will ignore the same crossposted article after it has displayed it once, no matter in what newsgroup it appears.

Special Interest Group (SIG)   1. An e-mail discussion group; 2. One of several technical discussion groups sponsored by ACM (the Assocation for Computing Machinery).

spelling flame   The lowest type of flame, a criticism of the spelling of your opponent, a cheap shot given the crude editors available to many users, and evidence that you have nothing of substance to add to the argument.

spew   To post excessively.

splat   (n) An asterisk (*).

spoiler   A post that reveals a plot twist or the solution to a puzzle or riddle. It is good netiquette to label such a post with the word *spoiler* in the subject line and/or to encode the post with rot13.

SprintNet   A global public data network providing local dial-up access from six hundred locations. SprintNet is a packet-switched network using X.25 protocols. It used to be called *Telenet* (not to be confused with telnet).

squick   (v) To exceed someone's threshold for violent or tasteless imagery.

standard   (n) A description of the expected performance of a device or system.

standard disclaimer   A disclaimer attached to the end of a Usenet or mailing list post, usually to the effect that the user is not speaking in an official capacity for the user's employer or access provider.

standard generalized markup language (SGML)   A set of formatting tags designed to show the logical relationships between text elements. The language of Web documents, HTML (hypertext markup language), is a subset of SGML.

star   * 1. A wildcard character in UNIX (and hence in many Internet applications), it stands for any number of characters; 2. In e-mail and especially on Usenet, where plain ASCII text is the norm, writers place a * before and after words to emphasize them: "I'm *really* sorry about posting your phone number."

star-dot-star   *.*, the DOS wildcard for any file name. (In UNIX, just * will suffice.)

start bit   A bit, set to 0, preceding the transmission of a byte, to tell the receiving computer that the following bits are a character.

star topology   A network architecture in which all the nodes are connected to a central hub computer and not to each other.

startup   (adj) Said of a process or set of instructions that take place when a system or application is started up, usually in order to set user preferences.

STD   An RFC that has been adopted as an Internet standard. (*STD* stands for *standard*.) STDs are numbered consecutively.

stop bit   A bit, set to 1, following the transmission of a byte, to tell the receiving computer that the character is complete. Also, the number of stop bits is one of the things you have to set to use your modem (usally 1 or 2; it depends on the modem you're calling).

stop word   A word so common that it is useless to search for (such as *and*, *address*, *record*, and so on). Most searchable databases have lists of stop words and filter them out during searches. (Also called *buzz words*.)

store-and-forward   (n) 1. A method of transmitting messages in which they reside at intermediate nodes before being sent to their eventual destination in order to wait for a more cost-effective transmission time or to wait until the receiving network is available; 2. The usual method of e-mail distribution, in which e-mail is stored on a server until the user connects to check her mail, at which point it is forwarded to the user.

streaming   (adj) Said of a media format that enables a player program to begin playing back or displaying the media content quite soon after the data starts flowing (in a *stream*) from the server (as opposed to formats that require that the browser download an entire, possibly huge, file before playing anything).

string   A sequence of characters (letters, numbers, or symbols) to be input or output as data.

stroke   A slash (/).

Structured Query Language (SQL)   An ANSI and ISO standard language used to search relational databases.

stub network   A network that transmits data only among localhosts.

StuffIt   An extremely popular Macintosh compression program that was originally distributed as shareware. It is now a commercial product, but StuffIt Expander, which can uncompress StuffIt and other compressed files, is freeware, available from the sumex-aim.stanford.edu FTP site.

subdirectory   In a hierarchical file system, a directory that is the child of another directory.

subdomain   A named portion of an Internet domain, usually a network, university, or company. In editor@enterzone.berkeley.edu, berkeley is the subdomain.

Subject says it all.   What some people write as the contents of a post or e-mail message for which the entire question or comment is contained in the Subject line.

subnet   A subdivision of a network.

subnet address   The portion of an IP address that identifies a subnet.

subscribe   To join a mailing list or start reading a newsgroup.

substring search   An archie option that specifies that the text to be searched for may be contained within a longer file name and need not match the file name exactly.

suite   1. A group of related protocols; 2. A group of related programs that make up a software package.

summarize   To collect the results of a survey or voting process via e-mail and then post the results to a newsgroup to prevent all the votes or opinions from being posted individually to the Net.

Sun Microsystems   A computer company that makes workstations.

SunOS   (*sun-oss* or *sun-oh-ess*) A flavor of UNIX for Sun Microsystems workstations.

supercomputer   The most powerful type of computer. Supercomputers cost tens of millions of dollars and are used for very complex calculations and modeling.

SuperTCP/NFS for Windows   Windows TCP/IP software, developed by Frontier Technologies Corp.

superuser   A special user account with unlimited permissions.

surf   (v) To browse, following tangents (trendy slang). You can surf Usenet or gopherspace, but the Web is best suited for surfing, since hypertext links allow you to follow digressions more or less infinitely.

switch   (n) A command-line instruction that modifies a command, often preceded by a slash in UNIX and DOS.

(v) To send packets along whatever route is best without attempting to send related packets via the same routes.

switched access   A network connection that disappears when not needed, such as the type used for SLIP or PPP connections.

Switched Multimegabit Data Service (SMDS)   A new high-speed technology for data networks, developed by Bell Labs.

sx   The Xmodem command for sending (downloading) a file.

synchronous   (adj) Said of communication that happens for both participants at the same time. IRC is a synchronous form of communication, while e-mail is asynchronous.

Synchronous Data Link Control (SDLC)   A data link layer protocol used on IBM SNA networks.

synchronous transmission   A transmission method that uses a clock signal to synchronize the sending and receiving computers in order to regulate the data flow, instead of using start bits and stop bits, as in asynchronous transmission. Data is then sent at a fixed rate.

syntax   Rules for properly formed commands.

system   1. A program that supervises a computer and coordinates all its functions, also called an operating system; 2. An entire computer taken together with all its devices; 3. A large program.

system administrator   Someone who runs or maintains a network.

system file   A file reserved for use by the system and not ordinarily killable by a user (at least not without a warning).

system operator   Someone who runs or maintains a BBS.

Systems Application Architecture (SAA)   A set of standards that specify interfaces (user interface, programming interface, and communications) for IBM software.

Systems Network Architecture (SNA)   A set of communications protocols for networks running on IBM mainframe computers, incompatible with the OSI Model.

sz   The Ymodem command for sending (downloading) a file.

table of services   A service provider's internal list of Internet services (such as FTP, finger, IRC, and so on) offered to users.

talk   (n) 1. One-to-one synchronous chatting over the Net; 2. The UNIX command for initiating or accepting a talk request (the form of the command is talk *username@address*).

talk.   A Usenet hierarchy devoted to discussion, argument, and debate.

talk mode   A UNIX feature in which two or more users can participate in an online conversation.

TANSTAAFL   (written only, also *tanstaafl*) *There ain't no such thing as a free lunch*, often pointed to as a general principal of the universe, probably taken from economist Milton Friedman's book *There's No Such Thing as Free Lunch*.

tape tree   A distributing mechanism for audio cassette tapes employed in some of the music-related newsgroups and mailing lists (see the rec.music.* Usenet hierarchy), in which a seed tape is copied by a root participant for a number of branches, each of which, in turn, dub copies for their children on the tree, until copies of the tapes reach leaf participants, who have parents but no children in the tree structure.

tar   (n) A UNIX program (*tape ar*chiver) that concatenates a number of files into a single file (without compressing them).
(v) To create an archive file with the tar program.

.tar   A file extension indicating that the file is a tarred file, an *archive* consisting of several concatenated files.

tar file   A file containing several files, concatenated with the UNIX tar program.

.tar.Z   A file extension indicating that the file is tarred *and* compressed with the UNIX compress program.

T-carrier   A series of long-distance, digital, point-to-point communications circuits numbered T1, T2, T3, T4.

TCP   *Transmission Control Protocol*, part of the TCP/IP stack. It functions on the transport layer (layer 4) of the OSI Model, establishing and verifying the data connection.

TCP Connect/II   A suite of Macintosh software comprising Internet tools such as e-mail, a Usenet newsreader, FTP, and telnet, developed by InterCon Systems Incorporated.

TCP/IP   A protocol stack, designed to connect different networks, on which the Internet is based. The suite includes protocols for remote login (telnet), file transfer (FTP), e-mail (SMTP), and so on. TCP/IP can work with any hardware or operating system.

TCP/IP was developed by DARPA in the late 1970s as a set of robust internetworking protocols that could survive the partial destruction of constituent networks (as might occur in a nuclear war).

TECO   A once popular text editor with a powerful built-in programming language, now largely supplanted by emacs.

Telenet   The original name of SprintNet (often confused with telnet).

telex   An international communications system made up of linked terminals that can send and receive data. Some online services offer telex access.

telnet   (n) 1. A terminal-emulation protocol (defined in RFC 854) for remote login over the Internet, part of the TCP/IP suite; 2. The UNIX program that uses that protocol.

(v) To log in to a remote computer via the telnet protocol.

10BaseF   The Ethernet specification (802.3 standard) for fiber-optic cable (*10* for the 10 Mbps bandwidth, *base* for baseband, and *F* for fiber-optic).

10Base5   The Ethernet specification (802.3 standard) using "thick" coaxial cable, also known as *thicknet*. (*10* for 10 Mbps bandwidth, *base* for baseband, and *5* for 500-meter-long cable segments.)

10BaseT   The Ethernet specification (802.3 standard) using two pairs of unshielded twisted-pair (UTP) wire. (*10* for 10 Mbps bandwidth, *base* for baseband, and *T* for twisted-pair cable.)

10Base2   The Ethernet specification (802.3 standard) using "thin" coaxial cable (~FB3/8~FE~"), also known as *thinnet*, or *cheapernet*. (*10* for 10 Mbps bandwidth, *base* for baseband, and *2* for 200-meter long cable segments.)

term   A DOS program that enables a personal computer to function as a UNIX terminal-emulation program over a dial-up connection.

terminal   A keyboard-and-monitor combination, one of many, connected to a computer. The terminal passes the user input from the keyboard to the computer and displays the computer's output on the monitor (screen). Large, multiuser computers such as mainframes have traditionally been accessed via terminals, as have UNIX machines.

Terminal Access Controller (TAC)   A device that provides and maintains a dial-up terminal connection to the Internet.

terminal emulation   Behaving like a specific type of terminal (such as a DEC VT100 or VT52 or an IBM 3270), passing keyboard input to a computer and displaying computer output on the screen (possibly in a window).

terminal-emulation program   Software a personal computer uses to imitate a specific type of terminal (such as a VT100, ANSI, or TTY terminal) and connect to a host.

terminal/host computing   The model of computing used by dumb terminals and host computers, in which the terminal is only a messenger and the host does all of the processing.

terminal server   A device that enables several modems (usually assembled on a modem bank) or terminals to connect to a host on one channel by sending a combined signal.

terminal window   A window in a graphical user interface in which a terminal-emulation program displays an emulated terminal screen connected by network to a remote computer.

terminator   A device connected to the end of a LAN cable to prevent signals from being transmitted.

*.test   Any of the newsgroups with names such as misc.test, alt.test, rec.test, and so on, designated for test posts. If you post to a *.test newsgroup, daemons all over the Internet send you e-mail acknowledgments when your post reaches their site. It is a breach of netiquette to post test messages to any newsgroup other than *.test newsgroups.

One trap often set for newbies is a post with its follow-up line set to a *.test newsgroup. Anyone who responds to the post without noticing and removing the *.test group will suffer a mailbox flooded by well-meaning daemons.

test post   A post with no meaningful content, posted to a newsgroup (preferably a *.test newsgroup) so that the user can determine if her newsreader software and Internet connection are working properly.

T^EX   (*tekh*) Also written *TeX*, a free, very powerful, macro-based typesetting/text-formatting system for UNIX.

text editor   An application for editing text files, usually less fully featured than a word processor. The Notepad accessory in Windows is a text editor, as are the UNIX programs vi, pico, emacs, ee, and joe, among others.

text file   Also *ASCII file* or *ASCII text file*, a file containing only ASCII characters. This means no formatting—no bold or italics, no headers, footers, margin adjustments, nonbreaking hyphens, and so on.

text file transfer   A form of file transfer, both with FTP and with uploading/downloading programs (kermit, zmodem, etc.) used to transfer files containing only ASCII characters. (Newline characters are automatically converted for the operating system being transferred to.)

text transfer   1. A text file transfer; 2. A transfer of text directly from a local file to a remote computer, as if typed directly from the keyboard, or from the output of a remote program running on a remote host computer to the terminal window and/or to a text file on the local computer.

T4   A long-distance, digital, point-to-point communications circuit developed by AT&T that transmits a signal at 274.176 Mbps, with up to 168 T1 channels (4,032 channels of 64 Kbps), handling both voice and data.

TFTP   *Trivial File Transfer Protocol*, a simplified version of FTP that does not include password protection.

thanks in advance   Often abbreviated *TIA* or more whimsically as aTdHvAaNnKcSe, a common sign-off for requests made in Usenet or elsewhere on the Internet.

The Internet Adapter (TIA)   A UNIX program that enables a dial-up shell account to emulate a SLIP connection, allowing the user to run Internet software native to his desktop environment without the full costs (or full functionality, either) of real SLIP. TIA is available from Cyberspace Development at http://marketplace.com/.

Thomas   U.S. Congressional archives on the Web, administered by the Library of Congress, named for Thomas Jefferson, at http://thomas.loc.gov/.

thread   (n) 1. A series of messages related to the same topic in a discussion group, such as an original post and related follow-ups. It is appropriate to read an entire thread before contributing to it to avoid repeating something that may already have been contributed one or more times; 2. A process that is part of a larger process or program.

threaded newsreader   A newsreader that organizes posts according to thread and allows you to read your way up or down a thread, such as trn, tin, and Newswatcher.

3270   An IBM terminal type.

throughput   A measure of the rate of data transmitted, expressed as bits per second.

thwap   A virtual slap, as on IRC, indicating that you've just smacked the recipient for writing something stupid or inappropriate.

TIA   1. An abbreviation for thanks in advance; 2. The Internet Adapter, a SLIP-emulation program for UNIX.

TidBITS   A weekly newsletter about the Internet and Macintosh computers, distributed via e-mail by Adam Engst. For more information, contact info@tidbits.com.

tidy   Cool, stylish, and confident, from the idea of well-structured, well-organized, and easy-to-read programming code.

tilde   The ˜ character, used to issue commands in the UNIX mail program.

tilde escape   A command in the UNIX mail program that starts with a tilde character (˜) and performs a function, rather than inserting text into the mail.

Time to Live (TTL)   An IP packet header field that tells how long the packet should be held before it's purged.

time out   (v) To fail, as a network process, because the remote server or computer has not responded in time, to close a connection after waiting too long for acknowledgment.

timeout   (n) The occasion when a remote computer times out.

tin   A threaded newsreader for UNIX.

TLA   (written only) *Three-letter acronym*, many of which persist throughout the Internet.

tn3270   A program similar to telnet that emulates a 3270 terminal connected to an IBM mainframe.

toggle   (n) A logical or physical switch (or even a single bit) that can be set to two positions, usually on and off. A light switch is a toggle.

(v) To change a switch or bit from one state to the other (from 0 to 1 or back again).

token ring   A (typically IBM) type of network architecture in which nodes are connected in a closed circle. The nodes continually pass a token (a special message) around the circle. To transmit data, a node has to wait until it's "it." Then the data rides along with the token and gets off at the right stop.

TokenTalk   An Apple product that enables AppleTalk protocols to work on a token ring network.

T1   A long-distance, digital, point-to-point communications circuit, developed by AT&T, that transmits a DS1 signal at 1.544 Mbps, with 24 (voice) channels of 64 Kbps. If the circuit uses fewer than 24 channels, it's called *FT1* or *fractional T1*. T1 is also called *High-Cap*, *T-span*, and *T-carrier*.

tool   A utility program, a useful program that performs a set function.

topic drift   As threads wear on in discussion groups, they frequently stray from the original topic, as listed in the Subject header. Some posters take the initiative of changing the Subject line to spawn new threads.

This same phenomenon is noticed in e-mail conversations, in which the original header, perhaps preceded by *Re: Re: Re:* outlasts its relevance.

topic group   Any electronic common space for people who share an interest.

topology   Any type of physical network layout, organizing the devices and the cables connecting them. Most LANs have bus topology, star topology, or ring topology.

toy   A computer or system less powerful than the one used by the speaker, not necessarily derogatory. (Toys can be fun.)

traditional newsgroup hierarchy   The seven newsgroup hierarchies in Usenet news proper: comp., misc., news., rec., sci., soc., and talk. New newsgroups in any of the traditional hierarchies can only be created after a formal process, including a request for discussion and a call for votes.

traffic   1. Mailing list or newsgroup posts, taken as a whole; 2. Network activity, measured in bits per second, kilobits per second, or megabits per second.

trailer   Information following the data in a packet, signifying the end of the data and possibly including error-checking information.

transceiver   A device that both transmits and receives signals, exchanging frames between a node and a network.

Transmission Control Protocol (TCP)   Part of the TCP/IP stack. It functions on the transport layer (layer 4) of the OSI Model, establishing and verifying the data connection.

transmit network   A network that communicates with at least two other networks and transmits data among networks as well as among local nodes.

transport layer   Layer 4 of the OSI Model, controlling delivery and verification of messages.

tree administrator   In a tape tree, the person who designs the tree and administers the process, not necessarily the person who provides the seed (usually not, in fact).

tree-killer   A printer.

trn   A threaded newsreader for UNIX, based on rn.

troff   A UNIX text processor that can produce output for typesetting equipment, superseded largely by T^EX.

Trojan horse   An attack program, hidden inside a seemingly benign program, that enables the program's creator to gain access to the user's system.

troll   (v) 1. To deliberately post egregiously false information to a newsgroup in hopes of tricking dense know-it-alls into correcting you; 2. From the fishing term, to explore information sources or communication methods on the Net, looking for something specific, as in the *New Yorker* cartoon in which a boss tells his employee: "I hear you've been trolling for babes on the Internet."

(n) A deliberately false post.

TrueSound   Microsoft's own streaming sound format.

Trumpet newsreader   Windows newsreader software that works with NNTP, available by anonymous FTP from biochemistry.cwru.edu.

Trumpet for Windows   Windows Internet software featuring a newsreader and a mail program, available by anonymous FTP from biochemistry .cwru.edu.

T3   A long-distance, digital, point-to-point communications circuit, developed by AT&T, that transmits a signal at 44.746 Mbps, with up to 28 T1 channels (762 voice channels of 64 Kbps), running over a leased line, usually fiber-optic cable.

T2   A long-distance, digital, point-to-point communications circuit, developed by AT&T, that transmits a signal at 6.3 Mbps, with up to four T1 channels (92 channels of 64 Kbps). T2 is used within telephone company networks, not commercially.

tunafish test   A series of posts in 1994 to a *.test newsgroup via the anon.penet.fi anonymous remailer service that may have compromised the identities of some of the remailer's users.

tunneling   Encapsulating a datagram of one protocol within that of a different protocol to transport the enclosed data across an intervening backbone that does not support the former protocol.

tuple   (*toople*) A pair of related values in a routing table (the network number and the number of hops to that network).

TurboGopher   1. A gopher client for the Macintosh, available via anonymous FTP from sumex-aim.stanford.edu; 2. An improved version of the original gopher software developed at the University of Minnesota.

Tweak   1. To make small changes in order to get something just exactly perfect; 2. To tease someone in a minor way.

twiddle   A tilde (~).

twilight zone   An imaginary place where only IRC channel ops may go.

twisted-pair cable   Cable comprising four or more copper wires, twisted in pairs (one grounded, one carrying a signal) to reduce interference, usually one pair for sending, one for receiving. There are two types of twisted-pair cable: shielded twisted-pair (STP) and unshielded twisted-pair (UTP).

.txt   A file extension indicating a text file.

Tymnet   A global public data network, offering local dial-up access in one hundred countries, including access to some online services and Internet service providers.

Ultrix   A port of UNIX that runs on VAXen.

UN*X   A generic term for the various flavors and ports of UNIX, used also to refer to UNIX without including the ~TM notice erroneously thought to be required by AT&T.

unbalanced line   A cable containing electrically unequal wires, such as a coaxial cable.

uncompress   (v) To unsquish a compressed file.
(n) A UNIX uncompression program.

uncompression   A method of unsquishing a compressed file.

UnCover   A search service provided by CARL with access to over ten thousand journals.

undelete   To restore a deleted file. This is not possible on UNIX systems.

undernet   A network of IRC servers formed as an alternative to EFnet, the "mainstream" IRC net. Undernet IRC servers always have domain names of the form *city.state*.undernet.org or *city.country*.undernet.org.

underscore   In e-mail and Usenet posts, only plain text may appear, so to suggest underlining and italics, users often precede and follow text with the underscore character (_), like so: "The origin of fnord is explained in _Illuminati!_"

undirected information   Information intended for the public at at large, such as Usenet or mailing list posts.

Unicode   A standard 16-bit character code (as compared with ASCII, which is a 7-bit character code) with 65,536 possible characters, as well as the ability to encode color and graphics. A possible eventual successor to ASCII.

uniform resource locator (URL)   (also universal resource locator) A web address. It consists of a protocol, a host name, a port (optional), a directory (optional), and a file name (optional). In the URL http://ezone.org/ez, the protocol is HTTP, the host name is ezone.org, and the file name is ez. URLs can be used to address other Internet resources besides web pages, such as FTP sites, gopher servers, telnet addresses, and so on.

Universal Asynchronous Receiver/Transmitter (UART)   A device that combines the transmitting and receiving functions of asynchronous communications over a serial line.

Universal Time Coordinate (UTC)   Greenwich mean time, used to synchronize computers on the Internet.

University of Maryland Info Database   A huge information resource intended to demonstrate the breadth of potential information on the Net. Telnet to info.umd.edu and log in as *info*.

UNIX   (*you-nix*) An 32-bit, multiuser, multitasking operating system common to workstations and dominant (but getting gradually less so) on the Internet. It was originally developed at Bell Labs in 1969 by Ken Thompson, and is now owned by Novell, although it has spawned many ports and clones.

Dealing with UNIX is a frustrating barrier to most Internet newbies, what with its arbitrary command abbreviations, rigorous syntax, case-sensitivity, lack of an undelete feature, and so on. Fortunately, alternative routes to the Internet that require no knowledge of UNIX (or very little) are sprouting up every day.

UNIX box   A computer running the UNIX operating system.

unix2dos   A program that converts UNIX text files to DOS format, by changing the line breaks.

UNIX wizard   A helpful UNIX expert, such as those who answer questions in the comp.unix.wizards newsgroup.

unmoderated   (adj) Said of lists and newsgroups whose posts are not vetted by a moderator.

unread   (adj) Said of newsgroup articles that the user has not yet read or has marked as such. Unread articles will show up again the next time the user returns to the newsgroup.

unselect articles   (v) To remove the selection tag from Usenet articles selected for reading.

unshielded cable   Cable that's not protected from electromagnetic or radio-frequency interference by a foil shield.

unshielded twisted-pair (UTP)   A cable containing unshielded wire in twisted pairs.

unsubscribe   1. To remove one's name from a mailing list. 2. To remove the name of a newsgroup from the list of subscribed groups.

untar   (v) To separate a tarred file into its component parts.

up   (adj) Working, functioning just fine, turned on.

upload   To transfer a file over a modem from a desktop computer to a remote computer.

upstream   (adv) Where your newsfeed comes from.

URL   (*you-are-ell*) *Uniform resource locator*, a Web address. It consists of a protocol, a host name, a port (optional), a directory (optional), and a file name (optional). In the URL http://enterzone.berkeley.edu/enterzone.html, the protocol is HTTP, the host name is enterzone.berkeley.edu, and the file name is enterzone.html. URLs can be used to address other Internet resources besides Web pages, such as FTP sites, gopher servers, telnet addresses, and so on.

U.S. Department of Defense (DoD)   The original funder of ARPA and hence ARPAnet, the predecessor to the Internet.

Usenet   1. From *User's Network* and often written *USENET*, the collection of computers and networks that share news articles. Usenet is *not* the Internet (though it overlaps pretty well). It's sometimes called the world's largest electronic bulletin board. 2. The newsgroups in the traditional newsgroup hierarchies.

Usenet cabal   A imaginary set of net.gods who establish the policy for Usenet.

Usenet News   The traffic of posted articles in the Usenet newsgroups.

Usenet newsgroup   A newsgroup in one of the seven traditional newsgroup hierarchies. Newsgroup names go from the general to the specific: rec.music.makers.bass (pronounced *rec-dot-music-dot-makers-dot-base*) is the newsgroup for musicians who play the bass.

Usenet Oracle   A cooperative project of mostly humorous questions and oracular responses. Anyone can submit questions or answers. To find out more about the Oracle, send mail to oracle@cs.indiana.edu with the word *help* in the Subject line, or read the rec.humor.oracle newsgroup.

user   Anyone logged on to a computer system or network.

user agent   One way to refer to a mail program.

User Datagram Protocol (UDP)   A connectionless transport protocol in the TCP/IP suite. UDP is used for Simple Network Management Protocol, database lookups, and other functions instead of TCP, because it does not add overhead to the transmission.

user-friendly   (adj) Said of computers, systems, and applications that are easy to understand and learn and that function as expected once some basic principles are understood.

username   A login, the name a user logs in with. Also, the first part of an Internet e-mail address (up to the @).

Choose your username well. In many ways it is more important (on the Net) than your real name. It's the name people see most often.

/usr   A directory on many UNIX machines containing users' home directories.

utility   A program that performs some useful function, often something that helps monitor or tweak an operating system.

.uu   A file extension that indicates a uuencoded file.

UUCP   From *Unix to Unix Copy Program*, a protocol and a program for copying files, news, and mail from one UNIX box to another during intermittent dial-up connections.

UUCPNET   An international store-and-forward network of UNIX machines (and others) that use the UUCP protocol to exchange mail and news, which is where Usenet originated.

.uud   A file extension that indicates a uuencoded file.

uudecode   (*you-you-decode*, n) A UNIX program that converts uuencoded files back into their binary form.

(v) To turn a uuencoded file back into its normal form.

.uue   A file extension that indicates a uuencoded file.

uuencode   (*you-you-encode*, n) A UNIX program that converts binary files into an ASCII format suitable for inclusion in an e-mail message (and one-third again as long as the original).

(v) To convert a binary file into a text form that can be sent as part of an e-mail message.

uupc   A Macintosh program that can transfer files using the UUCP protocol.

vacation   A UNIX program that sets up a return message to be sent to anyone who sends you e-mail, telling them that you're on vacation.

vanilla   (adj) Plain, unmodified, fresh out of the box, said of applications, systems, and hardware.

vaporware   Software that a developer has been promising for a long time (possibly as a marketing strategy), but which is nowhere in sight.

VAX   A DEC minicomputer (the name comes from *Virtual Address Extension*) with 32-bit architecture, a successor to the PDP-11 series, favored by hackers.

VAXen   A whimsical plural of VAX.

verbose   (adj) A mode of certain programs, such as ftp, in which they return as much information as possible and narrate their processes for the user's benefit.

Veronica   An searchable index of gopher menus (it supposedly stands for *Very Easy Rodent-Oriented Netwide Index to Computerized Archives*, but more likely is named after the Archie Comics character Veronica (note the other applications archie and Jughead). The results are themselves presented to you as a gopher menu.

v.42   A modem standard defined by CCITT, describing error control.

v.42bis   A modem standard defined by CCITT, describing data compression.

vi   A common but difficult to learn UNIX text editor with two modes, edit and insert. (To start inserting text, press *i*; to stop inserting, quit, and save, press Escape, then *ZZ*.)

viewer   1. An application used to view image files, such as GIFs and JPEGs; 2. By extension, any auxiliary application that enables the user to open, see, or play a file in a special format.

vine   A variation on the tape tree concept used for digital tapes (for which there is no generational loss of quality from one copy to the next), in which the source tape is passed along to each participant in the vine, copied, and then passed again.

Viola   Also called *ViolaWWW*, a Web browser for the X Window operating environment.

virtual   (adj) Said of something that exists only in software, not physically.

virtual circuit   A technology used in packet-switched networks, in which users share communication paths that appear to each as a dedicated end-to-end connection.

virtual community   Also *online community*, an electronic community of people who share some discussion groups or chat rooms and behave socially much like people in a small village who know all their neighbors. The Well is often cited as a virtual community.

virtual reality   An overused term for computer-simulated three-dimensional environments with which the user can interact, often by wearing equipment such as gloves and goggles. By analogy, role-playing environments such as MUDs are sometimes considered examples of virtual reality.

virus   A program that deliberately does damage to the computer it's on, often hidden inside an apparently benign program.

VM   An IBM mainframe operating system (it stands for *Virtual Machine*), similar to MVS.

VMS   A operating system used on VAXen (it stands for *Virtual Memory System*).

vmsnet.   An alternative hierarchy in the Usenet mold dedicated to discussion of the VMS operating system.

vn   A now rare UNIX newsreader (it stands for *visual newsreader*), on which the Windows newsreader WinVN is loosely based.

.voc   The audio format for the SoundBlaster sound card.

voice   (v) To call someone on the telephone.

voice-net   A facetious name for the telephone system, as often cited with phone numbers in sig blocks.

volume   A generic name for a storage medium or portion thereof, such as a disk, diskette, or network file server.

Vote ACK   Also called a *Mass ACK*, a Usenet post listing the e-mail address of each person who votes for and against a proposed newsgroup.

VRML   Virtual Reality Modeling Language; VRML files usually have a .wrl extension.

VT52   A DEC terminal type, less commonly emulated than the VT100.

v.32   A modem standard defined by CCITT, describing 9600-bps modems.

v.32bis   A modem standard defined by CCITT, describing 14400-bps modems.

VT100   A terminal type, originally designed by DEC for VAXen, that has become the standard terminal. If you dial up a UNIX shell, then your communications program probably emulates a VT100.

WAIS   (*ways*) *Wide Area Information Server*, a client/server database-search system with access to over four hundred sources. WAIS uses the Z39.50 standard for data searches. A WAIS search is made with a natural language query, and successful matches are ranked according to relevance feedback. WAIS searches ignore buzz words (also called *stop words*), extremely common words that might be found in any database or document. There are many different client programs for WAIS, with many different appearances. WAIS was developed by Thinking Machines Corp., Apple Computer, and Dow Jones.

WAIS-for-Mac   Macintosh WAIS client software made by WAIS Incorporated, available via anonymous FTP from ftp.wais.com.

WAIS Manager for Windows   Windows WAIS client software available via anonymous FTP from sunsite.unc.edu.

WAN   *Wide area network*, a long-distance computer network using dedicated phone lines and/or satellites to interconnect LANs across large geographical distances up to thousands of miles apart.

warez   (*wares*) An old BBS term for pirated game software, still heard mostly in B1FFspeak.

warlord   (v) To post someone else's large, ugly, or stupid sig block to the alt.fan.warlord newsgroup and then cut it down to size (from the username of a newbie with a BUAG medieval sword in his sig).

warm boot   (v) To reboot a computer without turning it off.

Washington University Services   A gateway to many Internet services, libraries, and other information resources. To use it, telnet to wugate.wustl.edu and log in as services.

waste bandwidth   (v) To misuse system resources (even having too long a sig block is sometimes enough to bring out accusations of wasting bandwidth).

.WAV   Wave format, from Microsoft; perhaps the most widespread sound format on the Internet.

weather   There are many weather information servers on the Internet. For weather information, telnet to madlab.sprl.umich.edu, port 3000; or wind.atmos.uah.edu, port 3000.

Web   (proper noun) The most commonly used name for the *World Wide Web*, an interlinked collected of hypertext documents (Web pages) residing on Web servers and other documents, menus, and databases, available via URLs (uniform resource locators). Web documents are marked for formatting and linking with HTML (hypertext markup language), and Web servers use HTTP (hypertext transport protocol) to deliver Web pages.

The Web was invented as an online documentation resource by physicists at the CERN European Particle Physics Laboratory in Switzerland.

web   (adj) Pertaining to the World Wide Web or to HTML or HTTP.

web address   A URL, consisting of a protocol, a host name, a path, and a file name. In the address of my home page, http://ezone.org:1080/homies/xian.html, the protocol is HTTP, the host name is ezone.org, the port number is 1080, the path is /homies/ and the file name is xian.html.

web browser   Client software for the World Wide Web, such as Lynx, Netscape, or Internet Explorer. A web browser displays HTML and other documents, and allows the user to follow hypertext links.

webcasting   Also called netcasting or push, a method of distributing information on the Web by pre-arranged downloading and scheduled updates. It gives the impression of information being broadcast from a web server to your desktop.

web page   An HTML document on the World Wide Web, usually containing hypertext links to other documents on the Web, often on other web servers entirely. Surfing the Web consists of following links from page to page.

web server   An application that stores web pages and associated files, databases, and scripts, and serves up the pages to web browsers, using HTTP.

web site   A site on the Internet that hosts a web server.

The WELL (Whole Earth 'Lectronic Link)   Famous service provider and on-line community (info@well.sf.ca.us).

well-connected   (adj) Said of a network with dependable e-mail links and a relatively full newsfeed.

wetware   Also *liveware*, slang for human beings, seen as part of a greater computer system including software and hardware.

whatis   An archie command that looks for key words in a software-description database containing file names and associated descriptions, used to find key words to search for.

wheel   (n) A privileged user, someone with unrestricted access to some particular system resource.

whitehouse.gov   The domain of the executive branch of the U.S. government. The White House Web server is at http://www.whitehouse.gov/. Send e-mail to the president at president@whitehouse.gov or the vice president at vice.president@whitehouse.gov.

white pages   Informal name for databases of Internet e-mail addresses or other information. For example, telnet to wp.psi.net and log in as *fred*.

whois   1. One of many online databases of Internet e-mail addresses and other identifying information about users, admins, domains, and so on; 2. The UNIX command that draws on the whois resource.

who owns the Internet?   A perpetual question on the Net. The answer is no one in particular. All the hardware that composes the Net is owned by various people; the Internet itself, taken as an electronic space, belongs to its users.

WhoWhere?   A search engine on the Web used to look for people (at http://www.whowhere.com).

WIBNI   (written only) *Wouldn't it be nice if* (also *wibni*).

wildcard   A special character used to represent either any single character or any number of characters. Usual wildcard characters are ? (for single characters) and * (for any number of characters).

WIMP   (adj) From *Window, Icon, Menu, Pointing device*, said of a graphical user interface such as Macintosh, Windows, or X Window).

WinCIM   *CompuServe Information Manager for Windows.*

Windows   Short for *Microsoft Windows*, a multitasking operating environment that runs on top of MS-DOS and provides IBM PCs and compatibles with a GUI (graphical user interface) not unlike that of the Macintosh, including icons, dialog boxes, menus, and a mouse pointer.

Windows 95   The current version of Windows.

Windows NT   A 32-bit operating system based on the Windows operating environment with built-in networking capabilities and no remaining traces of DOS.

Windows socket   The conventional method of configuring the Windows operating environment for TCP/IP networking.

Windows for Workgroups   A version of Windows with built-in peer-to-peer networking capabilities.

WinGopher   A gopher client for Windows.

winkey   A winking smiley:

  ;-)

Winqvt/Net   Combined mail, news, telnet, and FTP software for Windows. Available via anonymous FTP from wuarchive.wustl.edu.

Winsock   A type of Windows application that sets up a socket and works with TCP/IP protocols to establish an Internet connection.

WinVN   A newsreader for Windows based on the UNIX vn newsreader that communicates with Network News Transfer Protocol-based news servers, available via anonymous FTP from titan.ksc.nasa.gov.

WinWAIS   A Windows WAIS client program, available via anonymous FTP from ridgisd.er.usgs.gov.

WinWeb   A Web browser for Windows, created by EINET, and available via anonymous FTP from ftp.einet.net in the /einet/pc/winweb directory.

WinZip   A Windows compression file that can handle pkzip and other compression formats.

wizard   Someone who really understands how a piece of hardware or software works and is willing to help newbies

word wrap   The property most word processors but not all text editors have of automatically starting new lines to fit into a window or onto a page.

workaround   A temporary patch for a bug that avoids but does not fix the underlying problem.

workgroup   A group of users, often on a LAN, working on the same project.

working directory   The current directory, the directory you're "in" right now.

workstation   A computer on a network, usually of a type somewhere in the range between microcomputers and minicomputers.

world   The default distribution choice for newsgroup posts. Post distribution can also be limited to geographical areas (by their two-letter abbreviations) or to *local*.

World Wide Web   Also called the *Web*, *WWW*, *W3*, and *w³*, an interlinked collected of hypertext documents (Web pages) residing on Web servers and other documents, menus, and databases, available via URLs (uniform resource locators). Web documents are marked for formatting and linking with HTML (hypertext markup language), and Web servers use HTTP (hypertext transport protocol) to deliver Web pages.

The Web was invented as an online documentation resource by physicists at the CERN European Particle Physics Laboratory in Switzerland.

worm   A program that duplicates itself repeatedly, potentially worming its way through an entire network.

:wq   The *save and quit* command in vi, often seen at the end of newbies' posts when they fail to switch back from insert mode to edit mode before typing the command.

write   To save, to copy the contents of memory onto a storage medium such as a disk.

wrt   (written only) *With respect to.*

WS_FTP   A Windows FTP client program made by John A. Junod, available via anoymous FTP from 129.29.64.246 in the /pub/msdos directory.

WSArchie   A Windows archie client.

WSGopher   A Windows gopher client.

WSIRC   A Windows IRC client.

w³   (Also *W3.*)

wumpus   A game, originally written in BASIC, in which the user hunts a monster called the Wumpus, in a sort of maze of rooms containing various hazards. Depending on how near the Wumpus is, the user can hear, smell, or see it, and the user has "crooked" arrows with which to shoot through up to three connected rooms.

wustl archives   A huge FTP archive at wuarchive.wustl.edu.

www   The original text-based UNIX Web browser, developed at CERN European Particle Physics Laboratory. To try out www (if it's not installed on your system), telnet to info.cern.ch.

WWW   Abbreviation for World Wide Web.

WWW Browser for the Macintosh   A Macintosh Web browser available via anonymous FTP from info.cern.ch.

www.whitehouse.gov   The White House Web server.

WYSIWYG   (*whizzy-wig*) *What you see is what you get*, a description of display technology (as in GUIs) that closely matches printed output on the screen, or claims to.

x   The exit command in many UNIX programs.

.x   The extension for SuperDisk self-extracting archive files and More Disk-Space compressed files.

X Consortium A group of hardware developers that oversees the X Window standard.

Xerox Network System (XNS) A suite of communications protocols, similar to TCP/IP, developed by Xerox Corporation and later used by Novell and other network developers.

Xerox PARC Xerox's legendary Palo Alto Research Center, where the modern GUI (which combines the use of a mouse, windows, and icons) was invented, not to mention laser printers and LANs.

X.500 A CCITT- and ISO-recommended standard for electronic directory services, using a distributed database of X.400 information, including usernames, postal addresses, telephone numbers, fax numbers, and so on.

X.400 A CCITT and ISO standard for international e-mail handling. X.400 is different from Internet e-mail standards, but mail can be transferred from one system to the other via gateways.

XGopher X Window gopher client software, available via anonymous FTP from boombox.micro.umn.edu.

Xibo The evil anti-Kibo. This unfortunate devil has many fewer adherents than his nemesis.

XLibrary for the Macintosh Macintosh software for designing SLIP front ends to network services, available via anonymous FTP from sumexaim .stanford.edu.

Xmodem A file-transfer protocol supported by just about every communications program. Xmodem sends 128-byte blocks and is used for uploading and downloading to and from dial-up Internet accounts and BBSs.

Xmodem-CRC An extension of Xmodem using more stringent error-checking (called a *cyclical redundancy check*).

XOFF Ctrl+S (ASCII 19), a character that pauses data transmission.

XON Ctrl+Q (ASCII 17), a character that resumes data transmission.

XON/XOFF A form of flow control, using ASCII characters 17 and 19 to control the flow of data over an asynchronous connection, usually one of the choices for configuring a modem to connect to a dial-up service.

XOR   [Boolean operator] *Exclusive or*. A text search with XOR between two words matches any documents containing one word or the other, but not both.

XRemote   X Window software for connecting to a network over phone lines.

X.25   A CCITT-recommended standard for connecting computers to public packet-switched networks that specifies transmission and error-correction protocols, now largely superseded by frame relay.

XWAIS   X Window WAIS client software available via anonymous FTP from sunsite.unc.edu.

X Window   Also called *X*, an open, nonproprietary graphical user interface often used with UNIX. It was developed at MIT and is independent of the hardware or operating system it runs on. It's easy to find Internet client software for X Window. There are implementations of X called Motif and OpenLook.

YA-   (written only, also *ya-*) *Yet another . . . .*

YAA   (written only, also *yaa*) *Yet another acronym*.

YABA   (written only, also *yaba*) *Yet another bloody acronym*.

YAFIYGI   (*yaffy-yiggy*, also written *yafiygi*) *You asked for it, you got it*, applied to certain forms of word-processing and desktop publishing applications in which the user gets no preview of the eventual appearance of the document (the opposite of WYSIWYG).

Yahoo   A popular Internet directory (at http://www.yahoo.com).

Yanoff's Internet Services List   A thorough and frequently updated list of Internet services, maintained by Scott Yanoff of the University of Wisconsin. It's available via anonymous FTP from csd4.csd.uwm.edu in the /pub directory, with the file name inet.services.txt. It's also posted regularly to alt.bbs.internet.

yellow pages   1. An informal name for the database of machine names and addresses of the InterNIC Registration Service; 2. An informal name for the security and file-access database of a UNIX system.

YHBT   (written only) *You have been trolled.*

YHBT. YHL. HAND.   (written only) *You have been trolled. You have lost. Have a nice day.*

YHL   (written only) *You have lost.*

YMMV   (written only) *Your mileage may vary (used metaphorically).*

Ymodem   Also called *Xmodem 1K*, a file-transfer protocol supported by many communications programs. Ymodem sends 1024-byte blocks, is faster than Xmodem, and can send multiple files.

You misspelled...   A form of silly follow-up post favored by kibologists (followers of kibology), in which the original poster is accused of spelling some entirely different word from the one obviously intended, but perhaps what the poster meant or should have meant.

YR   (written only, also *yr*) *Yeah, right.*

.z   A file extension indicating a file that has been compressed with GNU Zip.

.Z   A file extension indicating a file that has been compressed with the UNIX compress program.

'zine   Also *zine*, a fanzine or other underground publication, possibly produced on company time or using office equipment. Most 'zines are still produced on paper and mailed to subscribers, but many are archived on the Internet, and there are also some e-zines, electronic 'zines distributed by e-mail, by gopher, or on the Web.

zip   (v) To compress a file with pkzip or another program.
   (n) A compression program.

.zip   A file extension indicating the file has been compressed with the programs pkzip, zip, or WinZip.

zip codes   U.S. postal zip codes as of 1991 can be found via anonymous FTP from oes.orst.edu in the /pub/almanac/misc with the file name zicode.txt.Z.

zip file   A compressed file.

zip up   (v) To compress a file with pkzip or with another program.

Zmodem   A batch file-transfer protocol supported by some communications programs. Zmodem is faster than Ymodem and Xmodem and recovers from disconnections more gracefully.

zone   (n) A logical (as opposed to physical) group of users on a LAN, such as an AppleTalk network, within a larger group of interconnected networks.

Zone Information Protocol (ZIP)   The protocol AppleTalk routers use to exchange zone names and network numbers.

Zone Information Table (ZIT)   A list of zone names and corresponding network numbers used by AppleTalk routers.

zone list   A list of AppleTalk zones in the Chooser.

zone name   1. The text name of a zone, corresponding to a network number; 2. The name of an AppleTalk network zone.

.zoo   A file extension indicating a file compressed with the zoo210 program.

zoo210   A UNIX file compression program.

Zork   A text adventure first written in the late '70s and distributed with BSD UNIX, also ported as *Dungeon*. Now sold in a commercial form as the *Zork Trilogy*.

zorkmid   A unit of currency used in many computer games, originally from Zork.

Zterm   A Macintosh communications and terminal emulation application.

Z39.50   The ANSI information-retrieval service definition and protocol specification for library applications, a format by which all Internet database information could potentially be made available.

ZZ   A *quit and save* command in vi.

Appendix C

A COMPREHENSIVE HTML QUICK REFERENCE

Adapted from *HTML 4.0: No experience required.*, by
E. Stephen Mack and Janan Platt-Saylor
0-7821-2143-8   704 pages $29.99

If you start to get into Web design seriously, you'll need a good HTML reference; this one is as compact and convenient as possible. Here you'll find a list of the RGB color codes you can use, several lists of the special HTML characters you can include in your HTML documents (either by the entity's name or number), and an alphabetical list of HTML elements, including the start and end tags, attributes, description, and any warnings.

SPECIFYING COLOR NAMES AND RGB VALUES

You can use colors by name (<FONT COLOR="RED">) or by RGB code (<BODY TEXT="#FF0000">). Several HTML elements use colors: the <FONT> tag and <BASEFONT> tag can include a COLOR attribute to set the font color, and the <BODY> tag can specify background color, text color, and three types of link colors. Tables also specify background.

In addition, some style sheet properties such as COLOR and BACKGROUND can use color names or RGB codes for a value. HTML 4.0 recommends you use a style sheet to set colors instead of HTML attributes.

NOTE

Some HTML tools and older browsers have difficulty with color names, so it's safest to always use the RGB code. The RGB code is a hexadecimal number preceded by a number sign (surrounded by quotes).

Table C.1 shows the 16 colors named in HTML 3.2 and HTML 4.0. These 16 colors come from the names and colors used on the IBM PC.

TABLE C.1:   The 16 Named Colors of HTML 3.2 and HTML 4.0

COLOR NAME	RGB CODE	COLOR NAME	RGB CODE
black	"#000000"	green	"#008000"
maroon	"#800000"	navy	"#000080"
silver	"#C0C0C0"	lime	"#00FF00"
red	"#FF0000"	blue	"#0000FF"
gray	"#808080"	olive	"#808000"

COLOR NAME	RGB CODE	COLOR NAME	RGB CODE
purple	"#800080"	teal	"#008080"
white	"#FFFFFF"	yellow	"#FFFF00"
fuchsia	"#FF00FF"	aqua	"#00FFFF"

WARNING

All colors vary by computer system. The shade of red you see on your screen can be different from what your audience will see. Also, many systems are black and white (including most printers).

Table C.2 is a longer list of color names. These color names, which are always without spaces, are recognized by Netscape Navigator 3 and Microsoft Internet Explorer 3 (and later versions) but not by any other browsers. They are not official HTML color names, so you should *always* use the RGB code instead of the color name shown in Table C.2. However, it's helpful to be able to look up a color by name, even if some of these names are a little strange ("blanchedalmond"?).

TABLE C.2: The 125 Named Colors Supported by Navigator and IE, with Their Equivalent RGB Codes

COLOR NAME	RGB CODE	COLOR NAME	RGB CODE
aliceblue	"#F0F8FF"	gainsboro	"#DCDCDC"
mintcream	"#F5FFFA"	antiquewhite	"#FAEBD7"
ghostwhite	"#F8F8FF"	mistyrose	"#FFE4E1"
aquamarine	"#7FFFD4"	gold	"#FFD700"
moccasin	"#FFE4B5"	azure	"#F0FFFF"
goldenrod	"#DAA520"	navajowhite	"#FFDEAD"
beige	"#F5F5DC"	greenyellow	"#ADFF2F"
oldlace	"#FDF5E6"	bisque	"#FFE4C4"
honeydew	"#F0FFF0"	olivedrab	"#6B8E23"
blanchedalmond	"#FFEBCD"	hotpink	"#FF69B4"
orange	"#FFA500"	blueviolet	"#8A2BE2"
indianred	"#CD5C5C"	orangered	"#FF4500"

COLOR NAME	RGB CODE	COLOR NAME	RGB CODE
brown	"#A52A2A"	indigo	"#4B0082"
orchid	"#DA70D6"	burlywood	"#DEB887"
ivory	"#FFFFF0"	palegoldenrod	"#EEE8AA"
cadetblue	"#5F9EA0"	khaki	"#F0E68C"
palegreen	"#98FB98"	chartreuse	"#7FFF00"
lavender	"#E6E6FA"	paleturquoise	"#AFEEEE"
chocolate	"#D2691E"	lavenderblush	"#FFF0F5"
palevioletred	"#DB7093"	coral	"#FF7F50"
lawngreen	"#7CFC00"	papayawhip	"#FFEFD5"
cornflowerblue	"#6495ED"	lemonchiffon	"#FFFACD"
peachpuff	"#FFDAB9"	cornsilk	"#FFF8DC"
lightblue	"#ADD8E6"	peru	"#CD853F"
crimson	"#DC143C"	lightcoral	"#F08080"
pink	"#FFC0CB"	cyan	"#00FFFF"
lightcyan	"#E0FFFF"	plum	"#DDA0DD"
darkblue	"#00008B"	lightgoldenrodyellow	"#FAFAD2"
powderblue	"#B0E0E6"	darkcyan	"#008B8B"
lightgreen	"#90EE90"	rosybrown	"#BC8F8F"
darkgoldenrod	"#B8860B"	lightgrey	"#D3D3D3"
royalblue	"#4169E1"	darkgray	"#A9A9A9"
lightpink	"#FFB6C1"	saddlebrown	"#8B4513"
darkgreen	"#006400"	lightsalmon	"#FFA07A"
salmon	"#FA8072"	darkkhaki	"#BDB76B"
lightseagreen	"#20B2AA"	sandybrown	"#F4A460"
darkmagenta	"#8B008B"	lightskyblue	"#87CEFA"
seagreen	"#2E8B57"	darkolivegreen	"#556B2F"
lightslategray	"#778899"	seashell	"#FFF5EE"
darkorange	"#FF8C00"	lightsteelblue	"#B0C4DE"
sienna	"#A0522D"	darkorchid	"#9932CC"
lightyellow	"#FFFFE0"	skyblue	"#87CEEB"
darkred	"#8B0000"	limegreen	"#32CD32"

COLOR NAME	RGB CODE	COLOR NAME	RGB CODE
slateblue	"#6A5ACD"	darksalmon	"#E9967A"
linen	"#FAF0E6"	slategray	"#708090"
darkseagreen	"#8FBC8F"	magenta	"#FF00FF"
snow	"#FFFAFA"	darkslateblue	"#483D8B"
maroon	"#800000"	springgreen	"#00FF7F"
darkslategray	"#2F4F4F"	mediumaquamarine	"#66CDAA"
steelblue	"#4682B4"	darkturquoise	"#00CED1"
mediumblue	"#0000CD"	tan	"#D2B48C"
darkviolet	"#9400D3"	mediumorchid	"#BA55D3"
thistle	"#D8BFD8"	deeppink	"#FF1493"
mediumpurple	"#9370DB"	tomato	"#FF6347"
deepskyblue	"#00BFFF"	mediumseagreen	"#3CB371"
turquoise	"#40E0D0"	dimgray	"#696969"
mediumslateblue	"#7B68EE"	violet	"#EE82EE"
dodgerblue	"#1E90FF"	mediumspringgreen	"#00FA9A"
wheat	"#F5DEB3"	firebrick	"#B22222"
mediumturquoise	"#48D1CC"	whitesmoke	"#F5F5F5"
floralwhite	"#FFFAF0"	mediumvioletred	"#C71585"
yellowgreen	"#9ACD32"	forestgreen	"#228B22"
midnightblue	"#191970"		

If you're designing a GIF image with regions of solid color, you shouldn't use any of the RGB color values in Table C.1 or C.2 since they might dither on a system that only displays 256 colors. Instead, you'll want to use a special 216-color palette that consists of RGB codes that only include 00, 33, 66, 99, CC, or FF. See Lynda Weinman's Browser Safe Color Palette page (http://www.lynda.com/hex.html).

REFERENCING AN ENTITY LIST

You can use either the numerical entity code or the named entity code. For example, either ë or ë would display an e with an umlaut (ë), a character used in words like Zoë or Noël.

ASCII Table in Entity Format

ASCII is the American Standard Code for Information Interchange, consisting of 128 codes used by most computers, as formalized by the American National Standards Institute (ANSI) in 1968. The first 32 codes (numbered from #0 to #31) as well as the 128th code (#127) are not used in HTML since they are control characters with no specified visual appearance. The rest of the codes, from 32 to 126, correspond to commonly used keyboard characters (see Table C.3). These characters are universally supported.

NOTE

Only the ASCII characters with a special meaning in HTML (&, <, >, and ") have an entity name. You should use either the numeric or name entity code instead of the &, >, and < characters in your documents.

TABLE C.3:   ASCII Character Chart in HTML Entity Format

ASCII CHARACTER NUMBER	APPEARANCE	NUMERICAL ENTITY CODE	NAME (COMMENTS) AND NAMED ENTITY CODE, IF ANY
32	N/A	&#32;	space
33	!	&#33;	exclamation mark
34	"	&#34;	quotation mark (double quote) **Named Entity Code**: "
35	#	&#35;	number sign (hash, pound sign)
36	$	&#36;	dollar sign
37	%	&#37;	percent sign
38	&	&#38;	ampersand **Named Entity Code**: &
39	'	&#39;	apostrophe (single quote)

ASCII CHARACTER NUMBER	APPEARANCE	NUMERICAL ENTITY CODE	NAME (COMMENTS) AND NAMED ENTITY CODE, IF ANY
40	(	&#40;	left parenthesis (open parenthesis)
41	)	&#41;	right parenthesis (close parenthesis)
42	*	&#42;	asterisk
43	+	&#43;	plus sign
44	,	&#44;	comma
45	-	&#45;	hyphen-minus (dash)
46	.	&#46;	full stop (period)
47	/	&#47;	solidus (forward slash)
48	0	&#48;	digit zero
49	1	&#49;	digit one
50	2	&#50;	digit two
51	3	&#51;	digit three
52	4	&#52;	digit four
53	5	&#53;	digit five
54	6	&#54;	digit six
55	7	&#55;	digit seven
56	8	&#56;	digit eight
57	9	&#57;	digit nine
58	:	&#58;	colon
59	;	&#59;	semicolon
60	<	&#60;	less-than sign **Named Entity Code**: <
61	=	&#61;	equals sign
62	>	&#62;	greater-than sign **Named Entity Code**: >
63	?	&#63;	question mark
64	@	&#64;	commercial at (at sign)
65	A	&#65;	Latin capital letter A
66	B	&#66;	Latin capital letter B
67	C	&#67;	Latin capital letter C

ASCII Character Number	Appearance	Numerical Entity Code	Name (Comments) and Named Entity Code, If Any
68	D	&#68;	Latin capital letter D
69	E	&#69;	Latin capital letter E
70	F	&#70;	Latin capital letter F
71	G	&#71;	Latin capital letter G
72	H	&#72;	Latin capital letter H
73	I	&#73;	Latin capital letter I
74	J	&#74;	Latin capital letter J
75	K	&#75;	Latin capital letter K
76	L	&#76;	Latin capital letter L
77	M	&#77;	Latin capital letter M
78	N	&#78;	Latin capital letter N
79	O	&#79;	Latin capital letter O
80	P	&#80;	Latin capital letter P
81	Q	&#81;	Latin capital letter Q
82	R	&#82;	Latin capital letter R
83	S	&#83;	Latin capital letter S
84	T	&#84;	Latin capital letter T
85	U	&#85;	Latin capital letter U
86	V	&#86;	Latin capital letter V
87	W	&#87;	Latin capital letter W
88	X	&#88;	Latin capital letter X
89	Y	&#89;	Latin capital letter Y
90	Z	&#90;	Latin capital letter Z
91	[	&#91;	left square bracket (open bracket)
92	\	&#92;	reverse solidus (backslash)
93	]	&#93;	right square bracket (close bracket)
94	^	&#94;	circumflex accent (caret, exponent)
95	_	&#95;	low line (underscore, underline)
96	`	&#96;	grave accent

ASCII Character Number	Appearance	Numerical Entity Code	Name (Comments) and Named Entity Code, If Any
97	a	&#97;	Latin small letter a
98	b	&#98;	Latin small letter b
99	c	&#99;	Latin small letter c
100	d	&#100;	Latin small letter d
101	e	&#101;	Latin small letter e
102	f	&#102;	Latin small letter f
103	g	&#103;	Latin small letter g
104	h	&#104;	Latin small letter h
105	i	&#105;	Latin small letter i
106	j	&#106;	Latin small letter j
107	k	&#107;	Latin small letter k
108	l	&#108;	Latin small letter l
109	m	&#109;	Latin small letter m
110	n	&#110;	Latin small letter n
111	o	&#111;	Latin small letter o
112	p	&#112;	Latin small letter p
113	q	&#113;	Latin small letter q
114	r	&#114;	Latin small letter r
115	s	&#115;	Latin small letter s
116	t	&#116;	Latin small letter t
117	u	&#117;	Latin small letter u
118	v	&#118;	Latin small letter v
119	w	&#119;	Latin small letter w
120	x	&#120;	Latin small letter x
121	y	&#121;	Latin small letter y
122	z	&#122;	Latin small letter z
123	{	&#123;	left curly bracket (left French brace)
124			|	vertical line (vertical bar)

ASCII CHARACTER NUMBER	APPEARANCE	NUMERICAL ENTITY CODE	NAME (COMMENTS) AND NAMED ENTITY CODE, IF ANY
125	}	&#125;	right curly bracket (right French brace)
126	~	&#126;	tilde

Latin-1 Entities

The Latin-1 characters are available as character number 160 up to character number 255 (see Table C.4). Many foreign languages require the characters in Latin-1; many of the special symbols will be useful for your documents.

WARNING

Don't use the characters numbered from 127 to 159. Although a particular character may appear on your system, it will not be the same on other systems. In particular, Macintosh and PC systems have different characters in this range.

TABLE C.4:   Latin-1 Character Chart with Name and Numerical Entity Codes

LATIN-1 CHARACTER NUMBER	APPEARANCE	NUMERICAL ENTITY CODE	NAMED ENTITY CODE	NAME (COMMENTS)
160	N/A			non-breaking space
161	¡	&#161;	&iexcl;	inverted exclamation mark
162	¢	&#162;	&cent;	cent sign
163	£	&#163;	&pound;	pound sterling sign
164	¤	&#164;	&curren;	general currency sign
165	¥	&#165;	&yen;	yen sign
166	¦	&#166;	&brvbar;	broken (vertical) bar
167	§	&#167;	&sect;	section sign
168	¨	&#168;	&uml;	umlaut (dieresis)

LATIN-1 CHARACTER NUMBER	APPEARANCE	NUMERICAL ENTITY CODE	NAMED ENTITY CODE	NAME (COMMENTS)
169	©	&#169;	&copy;	copyright sign
170	ª	&#170;	&ordf;	ordinal indicator, feminine
171	«	&#171;	&laquo;	angle quotation mark, left
172	¬	&#172;	&not;	not sign (logical not sign)
173	-	&#173;	&shy;	soft hyphen
174	®	&#174;	&reg;	registered sign (registered trademark)
175	¯	&#175;	&macr;	macron
176	°	&#176;	&deg;	degree sign
177	±	&#177;	&plusmn;	plus-or-minus sign
178	^{2}	&#178;	&sup2;	superscript two
179	^{3}	&#179;	&sup3;	superscript three
180	´	&#180;	&acute;	acute accent
181	µ	&#181;	&micro;	micro sign
182	¶	&#182;	&para;	pilcrow (paragraph sign)
183	·	&#183;	&middot;	middle dot
184	¸	&#184;	&cedil;	cedilla
185	^{1}	&#185;	&sup1;	superscript one
186	º	&#186;	&ordm;	ordinal indicator, masculine
187	»	&#187;	&raquo;	angle quotation mark, right
188	¼	&#188;	&frac14;	fraction one-quarter
189	½	&#189;	&frac12;	fraction one-half
190	¾	&#190;	&frac34;	fraction three-quarters
191	¿	&#191;	&iquest;	inverted question mark

LATIN-1 CHARACTER NUMBER	APPEARANCE	NUMERICAL ENTITY CODE	NAMED ENTITY CODE	NAME (COMMENTS)
192	À	&#192;	&Agrave;	capital A, grave accent
193	Á	&#193;	&Aacute;	capital A, acute accent
194	Â	&#194;	&Acirc;	capital A, circumflex accent
195	Ã	&#195;	&Atilde;	capital A, tilde
196	Ä	&#196;	&Auml;	capital A, dieresis or umlaut mark
197	Å	&#197;	&Aring;	capital A, ring
198	Æ	&#198;	&AElig;	capital AE diphthong (ligature)
199	Ç	&#199;	&Ccedil;	capital C, cedilla
200	È	&#200;	&Egrave;	capital E, grave accent
201	É	&#201;	&Eacute;	capital E, acute accent
202	Ê	&#202;	&Ecirc;	capital E, circumflex accent
203	Ë	&#203;	&Euml;	capital E, dieresis or umlaut mark
204	Ì	&#204;	&Igrave;	capital I, grave accent
205	Í	&#205;	&Iacute;	capital I, acute accent
206	Î	&#206;	&Icirc;	capital I,circumflex accent
207	Ï	&#207;	&Iuml;	capital I, dieresis or umlaut mark
208	Ð	&#208;	&ETH;	capital Eth, Icelandic
209	Ñ	&#209;	&Ntilde;	capital N, tilde
210	Ò	&#210;	&Ograve;	capital O, grave accent
211	Ó	&#211;	&Oacute;	capital O, acute accent
212	Ô	&#212;	&Ocirc;	capital O, circumflex accent
213	Õ	&#213;	&Otilde;	capital O, tilde

LATIN-1 CHARACTER NUMBER	APPEARANCE	NUMERICAL ENTITY CODE	NAMED ENTITY CODE	NAME (COMMENTS)
214	Ö	&#214;	&Ouml;	capital O, dieresis or umlaut mark
215	×	&#215;	&times;	multiply sign
216	Ø	&#216;	&Oslash;	capital O, slash
217	Ù	&#217;	&Ugrave;	capital U, graveaccent
218	Ú	&#218;	&Uacute;	capital U, acute accent
219	Û	&#219;	&Ucirc;	capital U, circumflex accent
220	Ü	&#220;	&Uuml;	capital U, dieresis or umlaut mark
221	Ý	&#221;	&Yacute;	capital Y, acute accent
222	Þ	&#222;	&THORN;	capital THORN, Icelandic
223	ß	&#223;	&szlig;	small sharp s, German (sz ligature)
224	à	&#224;	&agrave;	small a, grave accent
225	á	&#225;	&aacute;	small a, acute accent
226	â	&#226;	&acirc;	small a, circumflex accent
227	ã	&#227;	&atilde;	small a, tilde
228	ä	&#228;	&auml;	small a, dieresis or umlaut mark
229	å	&#229;	&aring;	small a, ring
230	æ	&#230;	&aelig;	small ae diphthong (ligature)
231	ç	&#231;	&ccedil;	small c, cedilla
232	è	&#232;	&egrave;	small e, grave accent
233	é	&#233;	&eacute;	small e, acute accent
234	ê	&#234;	&ecirc;	small e, circumflex accent
235	ë	&#235;	&euml;	small e, dieresis or umlaut mark

LATIN-1 CHARACTER NUMBER	APPEARANCE	NUMERICAL ENTITY CODE	NAMED ENTITY CODE	NAME (COMMENTS)
236	ì	&#236;	&igrave;	small i, grave accent
237	í	&#237;	&iacute;	small i, acute accent
238	î	&#238;	&icirc;	small i, circumflex accent
239	ï	&#239;	&iuml;	small i, dieresis or umlaut mark
240	ð	&#240;	&eth;	small eth, Icelandic
241	ñ	&#241;	&ntilde;	small n, tilde
242	ò	&#242;	&ograve;	small o, grave accent
243	ó	&#243;	&oacute;	small o, acute accent
244	ô	&#244;	&ocirc;	small o, circumflex accent
245	õ	&#245;	&otilde;	small o, tilde
246	ö	&#246;	&ouml;	small o, dieresis or umlaut mark
247	÷	&#247;	&divide;	divide sign
248	ø	&#248;	&oslash;	small o, slash
249	ù	&#249;	&ugrave;	small u, grave accent
250	ú	&#250;	&uacute;	small u, acute accent
251	û	&#251;	&ucirc;	small u, circumflex accent
252	ü	&#252;	&uuml;	small u, dieresis or umlaut mark
253	ý	&#253;	&yacute;	small y, acute accent
254	þ	&#254;	&thorn;	small thorn, Icelandic
255	ÿ	&#255;	&yuml;	small y, dieresis or umlaut mark

WARNING
All named entity codes are case-sensitive.

NOTE

Portions of Tables C.4 and C.5 are Copyright © International Organization for Standardization 1986: Permission to copy in any form is granted for use with conforming SGML systems and applications as defined in ISO 8879, provided this notice is included in all copies.

New HTML 4.0 Language, Symbol, and Math Entities

HTML 4.0 adds several new named entity codes that are available from the Unicode character set. Many of these entity names are for symbols (available through a Symbol font or a Unicode font); some are for mathematical symbols or foreign languages. (Note that the named Greek entities here are for math, not the Greek language.)

In Table C.5, we list the Unicode number in hexadecimal so that you may check its appearance at the Unicode home page (`http://www.unicode.org/`). While future browsers will allow you to use the hexadecimal number, for now all of the browsers require the (decimal) numerical entity code.

WARNING

Because these entity names are new, support is currently mixed. Older browsers can't display these entity names properly at all.

If you use any of the named entities from Table C.5, Navigator 4 and earlier and IE 3 and earlier won't display them. Instead, your named entity itself will be displayed literally (that is, you'll see the letters "√" instead of the square root/radical symbol).

If you use the numerical entities, IE 3 displays the wrong character. Navigator 3 and earlier display only a question mark for any of the characters in Table C.5. (Navigator 4 can display some of them.)

IE 4 displays both the numerical and named entity codes perfectly (with the two exceptions noted)—as long as the Universal Alphabet Font (UTF-8) font is selected from the View ➤ Fonts command. If the default Western font is used, then only some of these symbols are displayed correctly.

TABLE C.5: New HTML 4.0 Named Entities from the Unicode Character Set

UNICODE HEXADECIMAL NUMBER	APPEARANCE	NUMERICAL ENTITY CODE	NAMED ENTITY CODE	NAME (COMMENTS)
&#x0152;	Œ	&#338;	&OElig;	Latin capital ligature OE
&#x0153;	œ	&#339;	&oelig;	Latin small ligature oe
&#x0160;	Š	&#352;	&Scaron;	Latin capital letter S with caron
&#x0161;	š	&#353;	&scaron;	Latin small letter s with caron
&#x0178;	Ÿ	&#376;	&Yuml;	Latin capital letter Y with dieresis
&#x0192;	ƒ	&#402;	&fnof;	Latin small f with hook (function, florin)
&#x02C6;	ˆ	&#710;	&circ;	modifier letter circumflex accent
&#x02DC;	˜	&#732;	&tilde;	small tilde
&#x0391;	A	&#913;	&Alpha;	Greek capital letter Alpha
&#x0392;	B	&#914;	&Beta;	Greek capital letter Beta
&#x0393;	Γ	&#915;	&Gamma;	Greek capital letter Gamma
&#x0394;	Δ	&#916;	&Delta;	Greek capital letter Delta
&#x0395;	E	&#917;	&Epsilon;	Greek capital letter Epsilon
&#x0396;	Z	&#918;	&Zeta;	Greek capital letter Zeta
&#x0397;	H	&#919;	&Eta;	Greek capital letter Eta
&#x0398;	Θ	&#920;	&Theta;	Greek capital letter Theta
&#x0399;	I	&#921;	&Iota;	Greek capital letter Iota
&#x039A;	K	&#922;	&Kappa;	Greek capital letter Kappa
&#x039B;	Λ	&#923;	&Lambda;	Greek capital letter Lambda
&#x039C;	M	&#924;	&Mu;	Greek capital letter Mu
&#x039D;	N	&#925;	&Nu;	Greek capital letter Nu
&#x039E;	Ξ	&#926;	&Xi;	Greek capital letter Xi
&#x039F;	O	&#927;	&Omicron;	Greek capital letter Omicron
&#x03A0;	Π	&#928;	&Pi;	Greek capital letter Pi

Unicode Hexadecimal Number	Appearance	Numerical Entity Code	Named Entity Code	Name (Comments)
&#x03A1;	Ρ	&#929;	&Rho;	Greek capital letter Rho
&#x03A3;	Σ	&#931;	&Sigma;	Greek capital letter Sigma
&#x03A4;	Τ	&#932;	&Tau;	Greek capital letter Tau
&#x03A5;	Υ	&#933;	&Upsilon;	Greek capital letter Upsilon
&#x03A6;	Φ	&#934;	&Phi;	Greek capital letter Phi
&#x03A7;	Χ	&#935;	&Chi;	Greek capital letter Chi
&#x03A8;	Ψ	&#936;	&Psi;	Greek capital letter Psi
&#x03A9;	Ω	&#937;	&Omega;	Greek capital letter Omega
&#x03B1;	α	&#945;	&alpha;	Greek small letter alpha
&#x03B2;	β	&#946;	&beta;	Greek small letter beta
&#x03B3;	γ	&#947;	&gamma;	Greek small letter gamma
&#x03B4;	δ	&#948;	&delta;	Greek small letter delta
&#x03B5;	ε	&#949;	&epsilon;	Greek small letter epsilon
&#x03B6;	ζ	&#950;	&zeta;	Greek small letter zeta
&#x03B7;	η	&#951;	&eta;	Greek small letter eta
&#x03B8;	θ	&#952;	&theta;	Greek small letter theta
&#x03B9;	ι	&#953;	&iota;	Greek small letter iota
&#x03BA;	κ	&#954;	&kappa;	Greek small letter kappa
&#x03BB;	λ	&#955;	&lambda;	Greek small letter lambda
&#x03BC;	μ	&#956;	&mu;	Greek small letter mu
&#x03BD;	ν	&#957;	&nu;	Greek small letter nu
&#x03BE;	ξ	&#958;	&xi;	Greek small letter xi
&#x03BF;	ο	&#959;	&omicron;	Greek small letter omicron
&#x03C0;	π	&#960;	&pi;	Greek small letter pi
&#x03C1;	ρ	&#961;	&rho;	Greek small letter rho
&#x03C2;	ς	&#962;	&sigmaf;	Greek small letter final sigma
&#x03C3;	σ	&#963;	&sigma;	Greek small letter sigma
&#x03C4;	τ	&#964;	&tau;	Greek small letter tau
&#x03C5;	υ	&#965;	&upsilon;	Greek small letter upsilon

Unicode Hexadecimal Number	Appearance	Numerical Entity Code	Named Entity Code	Name (Comments)
&#x03C6;	φ	&#966;	&phi;	Greek small letter phi
&#x03C7;	χ	&#967;	&chi;	Greek small letter chi
&#x03C8;	ψ	&#968;	&psi;	Greek small letter psi
&#x03C9;	ω	&#969;	&omega;	Greek small letter omega
&#x03D1;	ϑ	&#977;	&thetasym;	Greek small letter theta symbol
&#x03D2;	ϒ	&#978;	&upsih;	Greek upsilon with hook symbol
&#x03D6;	ϖ	&#982;	&piv;	Greek pi symbol
	N/A			en space (a space as wide as the letter N)
	N/A			em space (a space as wide as the letter M)
	N/A			thin space
&#x200C;	N/A	&#8204;	&zwnj;	zero width non-joiner (used in foreign languages such as Arabic and Persian to prevent characters from joining each other)
&#x200D;	N/A	&#8205;	&zwj;	zero width joiner (used in foreign languages such as Arabic and Persian when a character must join with another, but no character is available due to context)
&#x200E;	N/A	&#8206;	&lrm;	left-to-right mark (see also the DIR attribute)
&#x200F;	N/A	&#8207;	&rlm;	right-to-left mark (see also the DIR attribute)
&#x2013;	–	&#8211;	&ndash;	en dash (dash as wide as the letter N)
&#x2014;	—	&#8212;	&mdash;	em dash (dash as wide as the letter M)
&#x2018;	'	&#8216;	&lsquo;	left single quotation mark
&#x2019;	'	&#8217;	&rsquo;	right single quotation mark

Unicode Hexadecimal Number	Appearance	Numerical Entity Code	Named Entity Code	Name (Comments)
&#x201A;	‚	&#8218;	&sbquo;	single low-9 quotation mark
&#x201C;	"	&#8220;	&ldquo;	left double quotation mark
&#x201D;	"	&#8221;	&rdquo;	right double quotation mark
&#x201E;	„	&#8222;	&bdquo;	double low-9 quotation mark
&#x2020;	†	&#8224;	&dagger;	dagger
&#x2021;	‡	&#8225;	&Dagger;	double dagger
&#x2022;	•	&#8226;	&bull;	bullet (black small circle)
&#x2026;	...	&#8230;	&hellip;	horizontal ellipsis (three dot leader)
&#x2030;	‰	&#8240;	&permil;	per mille sign
&#x2032;	¢	&#8242;	&prime;	prime (minutes, feet)
&#x2033;	"	&#8243;	&Prime;	double prime (seconds, inches)
&#x2039;	‹	&#8249;	&lsaquo;	single left-pointing angle quotation mark
&#x203A;	›	&#8250;	&rsaquo;	single right-pointing angle quotation mark
&#x203E;	–	&#8254;	&oline;	overline (spacing overscore)
&#x2044;	/	&#8260;	&frasl;	fraction slash
&#x2118;	℘	&#8472;	&weierp;	script capital P (power set, Weierstrass p)
&#x2111;	ℑ	&#8465;	&image;	black letter capital I (imaginary part)
&#x211C;	ℜ	&#8476;	&real;	black letter capital R (real part symbol)
&#x2122;	™	&#8482;	&trade;	trademark sign (**NOTE:** IE 3 understands this entity name)
&#x2135;	ℵ	&#8501;	&alefsym;	alef symbol (first transfinite cardinal)
&#x2190;	←	&#8592;	&larr;	leftwards arrow
&#x2191;	↑	&#8593;	&uarr;	upwards arrow
&#x2192;	→	&#8594;	&rarr;	rightwards arrow

Unicode Hexadecimal Number	Appearance	Numerical Entity Code	Named Entity Code	Name (Comments)
&#x2193;	↓	&#8595;	&darr;	downwards arrow
&#x2194;	↔	&#8596;	&harr;	left right arrow
&#x21B5;	↵	&#8629;	&crarr;	downwards arrow with corner leftwards (used to symbolize the carriage return)
&#x21D0;	⇐	&#8656;	&lArr;	leftwards double arrow
&#x21D1;	⇑	&#8657;	&uArr;	upwards double arrow
&#x21D2;	⇒	&#8658;	&rArr;	rightwards double arrow
&#x21D3;	⇓	&#8659;	&dArr;	downwards double arrow
&#x21D4;	⇔	&#8660;	&hArr;	left right double arrow
&#x2200;	∀	&#8704;	&forall;	for all
&#x2202;	∂	&#8706;	&part;	partial differential
&#x2203;	∃	&#8707;	&exist;	there exists
&#x2205;	∅	&#8709;	&empty;	empty set (null set, diameter)
&#x2207;	∇	&#8711;	&nabla;	nabla (backward difference)
&#x2208;	∈	&#8712;	&isin;	element of
&#x2209;	∉	&#8713;	&notin;	not an element of
&#x220B;	∋	&#8715;	&ni;	contains as member
&#x220F;	∏	&#8719;	&prod;	n-ary product (product sign)
&#x2211;	∑	&#8721;	&sum;	n-ary summation
&#x2212;	−	&#8722;	&minus;	minus sign
&#x2217;	∗	&#8727;	&lowast;	asterisk operator
&#x221A;	√	&#8730;	&radic;	square root (radical sign)
&#x221D;	∝	&#8733;	&prop;	proportional to
&#x221E;	∞	&#8734;	&infin;	infinity
&#x2220;	∠	&#8736;	&ang;	angle
&#x2227;	∧	&#8743;	&and;	logical and (wedge)
&#x2228;	∨	&#8744;	&or;	logical or (vee)
&#x2229;	∩	&#8745;	&cap;	intersection (cap)
&#x222A;	∪	&#8746;	&cup;	union (cup)

Unicode Hexadecimal Number	Appearance	Numerical Entity Code	Named Entity Code	Name (Comments)
&#x222B;	∫	&#8747;	&int;	integral
&#x2234;	∴	&#8756;	&there4;	therefore
&#x223C;	~	&#8764;	&sim;	tilde operator (varies with, similar to)
&#x2245;	≅	&#8773;	&cong;	approximately equal to
&#x2248;	≈	&#8776;	&asymp;	almost equal to (asymptotic to)
&#x2260;	≠	&#8800;	&ne;	not equal to
&#x2261;	≡	&#8801;	&equiv;	identical to
&#x2264;	≤	&#8804;	&le;	less-than or equal to
&#x2265;	≥	&#8805;	&ge;	greater-than or equal to
&#x2282;	⊂	&#8834;	&sub;	subset of
&#x2283;	⊃	&#8835;	&sup;	superset of
&#x2284;	⊄	&#8836;	&nsub;	not a subset of
&#x2286;	⊆	&#8838;	&sube;	subset of or equal to
&#x2287;	⊇	&#8839;	&supe;	superset of or equal to
&#x2295;	⊕	&#8853;	&oplus;	circled plus (direct sum)
&#x2297;	⊗	&#8855;	&otimes;	circled times (vector product)
&#x22A5;	⊥	&#8869;	&perp;	up tack (orthogonal to, perpendicular)
&#x22C5;	·	&#8901;	&sdot;	dot operator
&#x2308;	⌈	&#8968;	&lceil;	left ceiling (apl upstile)
&#x2309;	⌉	&#8969;	&rceil;	right ceiling
&#x230A;	⌊	&#8970;	&lfloor;	left floor (apl downstile)
&#x230B;	⌋	&#8971;	&rfloor;	right floor
&#x2329;	⟨	&#9001;	&lang;	left-pointing angle bracket ("bra") **WARNING:** IE 4 does not display this symbol
&#x232A;	⟩	&#9002;	&rang;	right-pointing angle bracket ("ket") **WARNING:** IE 4 does not display this symbol

Unicode Hexadecimal Number	Appearance	Numerical Entity Code	Named Entity Code	Name (Comments)
&#x25CA;	◊	&#9674;	&loz;	lozenge
&#x2660;	♠	&#9824;	&spades;	black spade suit
&#x2663;	♣	&#9827;	&clubs;	black club suit (shamrock)
&#x2665;	♥	&#9829;	&hearts;	black heart suit (valentine)
&#x2666;	♦	&#9830;	&diams;	black diamond suit

ALPHABETICAL SUMMARY OF HTML 4.0 ELEMENTS, TAGS, AND ATTRIBUTES

In this section, we'll list the 91 valid HTML 4.0 elements with their tags and attributes. We won't list any extensions to HTML. Any elements that are new to HTML 4.0 will be marked as so. Everything else is valid in HTML 3.2 as well as HTML 4.0.

NOTE

Elements only introduced in HTML 3.0 are not listed here since HTML 3.0 was never approved. Other versions of HTML before 4.0 included only three elements that are not listed here: the listing, plaintext, and xmp elements (all three of which behaved similarly to the pre-formatted text element). HTML 4.0 has made these elements obsolete; use <PRE> and </PRE> instead.

Table C.6 is alphabetical by start tag. Included for each of the 91 elements are several items:

▶ The element's description (sometimes including an example or a warning)

▶ The element's start tag, and whether it's optional or required

▶ For elements with end tags, the tag is listed and we indicate whether the end tag is optional or required. For elements without end tags (such as <IMG>), we'll list "forbidden (empty element)."

▶ The element's attributes, if any. All attributes are optional unless marked as required.

▶ What type of content is allowed within the element, if anything (the special term *DATA* refers to ordinary characters and entities, called "CDATA" by the HTML 4.0 specification)

▶ The element's category

There are several possible categories for an element. Elements are either part of HTML's basic structure, the head section, or the body section's block-level and text-level elements, or a special category. In addition, some elements only occur inside another element. Here's how the elements break down (listed by start tag):

▶ Basic structure elements: <BODY>, <HEAD>, <HTML>, and <TITLE>

▶ Head section elements: <BASE>, <ISINDEX>, <LINK>, <META>, <SCRIPT>, and <STYLE>

▶ Block-level elements: <ADDRESS>, <BLOCKQUOTE>, <CENTER>, <DIV>, <FIELDSET>, <FORM>, <H1>, <H2>, <H3>, <H4>, <H5>, <H6>, <HR>, <ISINDEX>, <NOFRAMES>, <NOSCRIPT>, <P>, <PRE>, and <TABLE>

▶ Block-level list elements: <DL>, <DIR>, <MENU>, <OL>, and <UL>

▶ Text-level special elements: <A>, <APPLET>, <BASEFONT>, <BDO>, <BR>, <FONT>, <IFRAME>, <IMG>, <MAP>, <OBJECT>, <Q>, <SCRIPT>, <SPAN>, <SUB>, and <SUP>

▶ Text-level phrase elements: <ACRONYM>, <CITE>, <CODE>, <DFN>, <EM>, <KBD>, <SAMP>, <STRONG>, and <VAR>

▶ Text-level font elements: <B>, <BIG>, <I>, <S>, <SMALL>, <STRIKE>, <TT>, and <U>

▶ Text-level form controls: <BUTTON>, <INPUT>, <LABEL>, <SELECT>, <TEXTAREA>.

▶ Special hybrid elements: <DEL> and <INS>

▶ Special SGML constructs: <!DOCTYPE> and <!-

▶ Special frame structure: <FRAMESET>

▶ Table model elements: <CAPTION>, <COL>, <COLGROUP>, <TBODY>, <TD>, <TFOOT>, <TH>, <THEAD>, and <TR>

▶ Child elements: The definition list element contains <DD> and <DT>. Other types of list elements contain <LI>. The select element contains <OPTION>. The map element contains <AREA>. The frameset element contains <FRAME>. The fieldset element contains <LEGEND>. Finally, the applet and object elements contain <PARAM>.

NOTE

The script element is both a head section element and a text-level element. The isindex element is both a head section element and block-level element.

You'll notice that many elements can use the "generic 4.0 attributes." These are the language attributes (LANG and DIR), the advisory TITLE attribute, the style and identification attributes (CLASS, ID, and STYLE), and the event attributes.

SUMMARY OF CASE-SENSITIVITY

To end this appendix, we'll summarize case-sensitivity in HTML.

▶ Tags are *not* case-sensitive (<B> and <b> are the same).

▶ The attribute names are *not* case-sensitive (HREF and href are the same).

▶ The values for attributes are generally *not* case-sensitive (COLOR="RED" is the same as COLOR="red"), but there are a few exceptions. For example, ordered list types *are* case-sensitive (TYPE="a" is different from TYPE="A"), as are URLs, general text (for example, alternate content with the ALT attribute or the meta element's CONTENT attribute), and embedded active scripts used with the event attributes.

▶ Some browsers treat anchor and target names as case-sensitive (<A NAME="ROXANNE"> is different from <A NAME="Roxanne"> in some browsers, despite HTML's declaration that they should not be different).

• Names of entities are *always* case-sensitive (© won't display a copyright symbol, only © will).

▶ The four special target names are case-sensitive.

- Some parts of URLs are *not* case-sensitive: the protocol is not case-sensitive (HTTP: and http: are the same), and the domain name is *not* case-sensitive (WWW.IBM.COM and www.ibm.com are the same), but everything else in a URL *is* usually case-sensitive (depending on the Web server's operating system).

- The components of a <!DOCTYPE> declaration *are* case-sensitive (for example, dtd html 4.0 and DTD HTML 4.0 are not the same).

- Cascading Style Sheet rules are *not* case-sensitive except for URLs and some font family names. To be safe, you should treat CLASS and ID attribute names as if they were case-sensitive since some browsers treat them that way (incorrectly).

- Most active script statements *are* case-sensitive (exactly how much so depends on the programming language; for example, JavaScript is case-sensitive).

TABLE C.6:   Alphabetical List of HTML 4.0 Elements

Element	Description
<!DOCTYPE> **document type declaration**	Declares the precise version of HTML you are using. or example: <!DOCTYPE HTML PUBLIC "-//W3C//DTD HTML 4.0//EN">
Category:	special SGML construct; can only occur in the very beginning of an HTML document, before any tags
Starting Tag:	<!DOCTYPE>, required
Ending Tag:	forbidden (empty element)
Attributes:	special
Content:	none (empty element)
<!– **comment**	Inserts comments into an HTML document that won't be displayed by a browser (unless the surfer views source) Also used to hide style sheets and active scripts from older browsers
Category:	special SGML construct
Starting Tag:	<!–, required
Ending Tag:	–>, required
Attributes:	none
Content:	Any DATA except for two dashes (—). Also, greater-than signs (>) can cause problems and are not recommended inside a comment

ELEMENT	DESCRIPTION
<A> **anchor element**	Inserts hyperlink anchors and can name a section of a document
Category:	text-level element (special)
Starting Tag:	<A>, required
Ending Tag:	</A>, required
Attributes:	HREF to create a link, NAME to create a named section (either an HREF or NAME attribute, or both, is required), CHARSET to indicate the character encoding used at the other end of the link, TARGET to indicate where the link should be displayed, REL and REV to indicate relationships (not commonly used in anchors) ACCESSKEY and TABINDEX to define a keyboard shortcut and tab order for the, SHAPE and COORDS to define an image map (see the Web site), plus generic 4.0 attributes (including ONFOCUS and ONBLUR)
Content:	DATA and/or text-level elements (excluding other anchor elements)
<ACRONYM> **acronym/abbreviation element**	Indicates that the enclosed text is an acronym or abbreviation
Category:	text-level element (phrase)
Starting Tag:	<ACRONYM>, required
Ending Tag:	</ACRONYM>, required
Attributes:	none except generic 4.0 attributes
Content:	DATA and/or text-level elements
<ADDRESS> **address element**	Indicates the author's address
Category:	block-level element
Starting Tag:	<ADDRESS>, required
Ending Tag:	</ADDRESS>, required
Attributes:	none except generic 4.0 attributes
Content:	DATA, paragraph elements, and/or text-level elements
<APPLET> **applet element**	Inserts a Java applet **NOTE:** This element is not recommended by HTML 4.0 in favor of the object element, but for now you should continue to use the applet element since it is currently compatible with more browsers
Category:	text-level element (special)
Starting Tag:	<APPLET>, required

ELEMENT	DESCRIPTION
Ending Tag:	</APPLET>, required
Attributes:	CODE, to indicate the `.class` filename of the applet (this attribute should be used in most cases), ARCHIVE to indicate the location of a `.jar` format Java Archive, OBJECT to indicate a special serialized-format applet (at least one of CODE, OBJECT, or ARCHIVE is required), CODEBASE to indicate the directory URL where the applet is located, WIDTH and HEIGHT to size the applet (both of these attributes are required), ALIGN to place the applet in relation to the rest of the line (either "BOTTOM", "MIDDLE", "TOP", "LEFT", or "RIGHT"), HSPACE and VSPACE to determine the amount of pixels of space around the applet's region, ALT to provide a text description of the applet for browsers that are not Java-enabled, and NAME to give the applet a name (useful if two applets on a page need to communicate with each other), plus the ID, CLASS, STYLE, and TITLE generic attributes
Content:	One or more param elements (to control the applet's behavior), followed by DATA and/or text-level elements (used as alternate content for browsers that can't display the applet)

<AREA> **area element**	Defines a clickable hot spot in an image map
Category:	child element: can only be used in a map element
Starting Tag:	<AREA>, required
Ending Tag:	forbidden (empty element)
Attributes:	SHAPE (to set the shape of the hot spot; either "RECT", "POLYGON" or "CIRCLE"), COORDS (the x and y coordinates of the hot spot; see Web site for format and example), HREF (the URL for the hot spot's link), TARGET (where the link should be targeted), NOHREF (to declare a hot spot region with no link), ALT (required, to describe the resource being linked to), and TABINDEX (to control the hotspot's position in the tab key navigation order), ACCESSKEY (for a keyboard shortcut), plus generic 4.0 attributes
Content:	none

<B> **bold element**	Makes enclosed text bold **WARNING:** <STRONG> is preferred over <B>
Category:	text-level element (physical font)
Starting Tag:	<B>, required
Ending Tag:	</B>, required
Attributes:	none except generic 4.0 attributes
Content:	DATA, and text-level elements

ELEMENT	DESCRIPTION
<BASE> **base element**	Indicates the location of a document and can set a default link target
Category:	head section element
Starting Tag:	<BASE>, required
Ending Tag:	forbidden (empty element)
Attributes:	HREF (required, to indicate the full URL of the current document) TARGET (to indicate the default targeted location of all links in the current document)
Content:	none (empty element)
<BASEFONT> **basefont element**	Indicates the default font settings for the rest of the document **WARNING:** This element is not recommended by HTML 4.0; use a style sheet instead
Category:	text-level element (special)
Starting Tag:	<BASEFONT>, required
Ending Tag:	forbidden (empty element)
Attributes:	SIZE (required, to set the font size—must be a number from "1" to "7"), COLOR (to set the font color), and FACE (to specify the desired font face; use a comma-delimited list, for example FACE="Verdana, Helvetica, Arial"), plus the generic ID attributes
Content:	none (empty element)
<BDO> **bdo element (bi-directional text override element)** ported	Overrides the current direction of text (either right-to-left or left-to-right),only useful when working with documents written in a language that reads from right-to-left such as Hebrew **WARNING:** This element is not yet widely sup-
Category:	text-level element (special)
Starting Tag:	<BDO>, required
Ending Tag:	</BDO>, required
Attributes:	DIR (required, to indicate the direction of text; must be either DIR="RTL" for right-to-left text or DIR="LTR" for left-to right text), and LANG (to indicate the language used for the bdo element's content), plus the ID, Class, STYLE, and TITLE generic attributes
Content:	DATA and/or text-level elements
<BIG> **big element**	Makes enclosed text one size larger

Category:	text-level element (physical font)

ELEMENT	DESCRIPTION
Starting Tag:	<BIG>, required
Ending Tag:	</BIG>, required
Attributes:	none except generic 4.0 attributes
Content:	DATA and/or text-level elements
<BLOCKQUOTE> **blockquote element**	Indicates a quotation from another source; often the quote is indented but not every browser does this
Category:	block-level element
Starting Tag:	<BLOCKQUOTE>, required
Ending Tag:	</BLOCKQUOTE>, required
Attributes: 4.0 attributes	CITE (to indicate the URL of the quote's source) plus generic
Content:	DATA, block-level elements, and/or text-level elements
<BODY> **body element**	Contains the body section of an HTML document
Category:	basic structure element
Starting Tag:	<BODY>, optional
Ending Tag:	</BODY>, optional
Attributes:	BACKGROUND (to set a background image), BGCOLOR (to set a background color), TEXT (to set the text color), LINK (to set the link color), ALINK (to set the active link color), and VLINK (to set the visited link color). HTML 4.0 recommends the use of a style sheet instead. In addition the <BODY> tag can use the ONLOAD and ONUNLOAD event attributes, plus generic 4.0 attributes
Content:	DATA, block-level elements, text-level elements, plus ins and del elements
** ** **line-break element**	Creates a line-break
Category:	text-level element (special)
Starting Tag:	 , required
Ending Tag:	forbidden (empty element)
Attributes:	CLEAR (either "LEFT", "RIGHT", "ALL", or "NONE") to determine how far down the line-break should move, plus the ID, CLASS, STYLE, and TITLE generic 4.0 attributes (not the language or event generic attributes)

Content:	none (empty element)

ELEMENT	DESCRIPTION
<BUTTON> **button element**	Creates a button form control **WARNING:** The button element is not yet widely supported
Category:	form control element
Starting Tag:	<BUTTON>, required
Ending Tag:	</BUTTON>, required
Attributes:	VALUE (to give the button a value that's passed to the form processor when the form is submitted), NAME (to give the button a name for use with a script), TYPE (either "SUBMIT" or "RESET" to make this button submit or reset the form), DISABLED (to make this button "grayed out" and unavailable by default), TABINDEX (to control this button's position in the tab key navigation order), ACCESSKEY (for a keyboard short-cut), plus generic 4.0 attributes, including the special ONFO-CUS and ONBLUR event attributes
Content:	DATA, text-level elements, and/or block-level elements (except for anchor elements, form elements, fieldset elements, and form control elements)
<CAPTION> **caption element**	Creates a caption for a table
Category:	table model element
Starting Tag:	<CAPTION>, required
Ending Tag:	</CAPTION>, required
Attributes:	ALIGN (to indicate where the caption should go; either "TOP", "BOTTOM", "LEFT", or "RIGHT" although most browsers only support top and bottom), plus generic 4.0 attributes
Content:	DATA, and/or text-level elements
<CENTER> **center element**	Horizontally centers its content; identical to <DIV ALIGN="CENTER"> **WARNING:** This element is not recommended in HTML 4.0. Use a style sheet instead
Category:	block-level element
Starting Tag:	<CENTER>, required
Ending Tag:	</CENTER>, required
Attributes:	none except generic 4.0 attributes
Content:	DATA, block-level elements, and/or text-level elements

ELEMENT	DESCRIPTION
\<CITE\> **cite element**	Indicates a source that is being used as a citation
Category:	text-level element (phrase)
Starting Tag:	\<CITE\>, required
Ending Tag:	\</CITE\>, required
Attributes:	none except generic 4.0 attributes
Content:	DATA and/or text-level elements
\<CODE\> **code element**	Indicates that the contents is computer code—browsers will often render a code element in a fixed-width font
Category:	text-level element (phrase)
Starting Tag:	\<CODE\>, required
Ending Tag:	\</CODE\>, required
Attributes:	none except generic 4.0 attributes
Content:	DATA and/or text-level elements
\<COL\> **column element**	Creates a column or range of columns in a table
Category:	table model element
Starting Tag:	\<COL\>, required
Ending Tag:	forbidden (empty element)
Attributes:	SPAN (to indicate the number of columns to create), WIDTH (to specify the width of the columns in pixels, a percentage of the table width, or the special asterisk notation), horizontal cell alignment attributes: ALIGN (to set the default alignment of the cell data, either "LEFT", "CENTER", "RIGHT", "JUSTIFY", or on a particular character with "CHAR"), CHAR (to specify which alignment character to use if ALIGN="CHAR"), CHAROFF (to specify a length in pixels or percentage of the column's width to use as an offset for determining the character alignment), and vertical cell alignment: VALIGN (to specify the vertical position of cell data: "TOP", "MIDDLE", "BOTTOM", or "BASELINE"), plus generic 4.0 attributes **WARNING:** Character alignment is not yet supported in the popular browsers
Content:	none (empty element)
\<COLGROUP\> **column group element**	Creates groups of columns in a table, allowing many columns to be formatted together with one set of attributes
Category:	table model element

ELEMENT	DESCRIPTION
Starting Tag:	<COLGROUP>, required
Ending Tag:	</COLGROUP>, optional
Attributes:	Same as for the column element (see <COL>)
Content:	One or more column elements (see <COL>)
<DD> **definition element**	Creates a definition in a definition list
Category:	child element: can only be used in a definition list
Starting Tag:	<DD>, required
Ending Tag:	</DD>, optional
Attributes:	none except generic 4.0 attributes
Content:	DATA, text-level elements, and/or block-level elements
<DEL> **del element**	Indicates elements and text that are considered removed from a document **WARNING:** Not yet widely supported
Category:	special hybrid element (used in the body section, similar to a block-level element except doesn't cause a paragraph break)
Starting Tag:	<DEL>, required
Ending Tag:	</DEL>, required
Attributes:	CITE (with a URL explaining why the contents were removed), DATETIME, us generic 4.0 attributes
Content:	DATA, text-level elements, and/or block-level elements
<DFN> **definition element**	Indicates that the contents is a definition
Category:	text-level element (phrase)
Starting Tag:	<DFN>, required
Ending Tag:	</DFN>, required
Attributes:	none except generic 4.0 attributes
Content:	DATA and/or text-level elements
<DIR> element **directory list element**	Creates a list in the "directory" style **WARNING:** This element is not recommended; use an ordered list or unordered list instead
Category:	block-level element (list)
Starting Tag:	<DIR>, required
Ending Tag:	</DIR>, required

ELEMENT	DESCRIPTION
Attributes:	COMPACT (to indicate that the list should be reduced in size; ignored by most browsers and not recommended) plus generic 4.0 attributes
Content:	One or more list item elements (see <LI>)
<DIV> **division element**	Divides a document into logical sections; useful when used with style sheets
Category:	block-level element
Starting Tag:	<DIV>, required
Ending Tag:	</DIV>, required
Attributes:	ALIGN (for horizontal alignment; possible values are "LEFT", "RIGHT", "CENTER", or "JUSTIFY", but this attribute is not recommended; use style sheets instead) plus generic 4.0 attributes
Content:	DATA, text-level elements, and/or block-level elements
<DL> **definition list element**	Creates a definition list
Category:	block-level element (list)
Starting Tag:	<DL>, required
Ending Tag:	</DL>, required
Attributes:	COMPACT (to indicate that the list should be reduced in size; ignored by most browsers and not recommended), plus generic 4.0 attributes
Content:	One or more definition terms (see <DT>) and/or one or more definitions (see <DD>); however it is recommended that each term be followed by a definition
<DT> **definition term element**	Creates a term that can be defined in a definition list
Category:	child element: can only be used in a definition list element
Starting Tag:	<DT>, required
Ending Tag:	</DT>, optional
Attributes:	none except generic 4.0 attributes
Content:	DATA and/or text-level elements
<EM> **emphasis element**	Indicates that the contents should be emphasized, often displayed using italics
Category:	text-level element (phrase)
Starting Tag:	<EM>, required

ELEMENT	DESCRIPTION
Ending Tag:	</EM>, required
Attributes:	none except generic 4.0 attributes
Content:	DATA and/or text-level elements
<FIELDSET> **fieldset element**	Groups one or more form controls; you should usually use a fieldset element only within a form element
Category:	block-level element
Starting Tag:	<FIELDSET>, required
Ending Tag:	</FIELDSET>, required
Attributes:	none except generic 4.0 attributes
Content:	a legend element, followed by form controls (including DATA, block-level elements, and/or text-level elements)
<FONT> **font element**	Sets the font size, font color, and/or font face **WARNING:** This element is not recommended by HTML 4.0; use a style sheet instead.
Category:	text-level element (special)
Starting Tag:	<FONT>, required
Ending Tag:	</FONT>, required
Attributes:	SIZE (to set the font size—must be a number from "1" to "7"), COLOR (to set the font color), and FACE (to specify the desired font face; use a comma-delimited list, for example FACE="Verdana, Helvetica, Arial"), plus the ID, class, style, and title generic attributes
Content:	DATA and/or text-level elements
<FORM> **form element**	Marks an area containing an interactive form (consisting of one or more form controls); attributes indicate how the form is to be processed using CGI, e-mail, or an active script
Category:	block-level element
Starting Tag:	<FORM>, required
Ending Tag:	</FORM>, required
Attributes:	ACTION (required, to indicate the URL of the form handler that will process the form when it's submitted), METHOD (either "GET" or "POST"), ENCTYPE (to indicate what MIME type should be used to send the data), TARGET (to indicate where the results of the form should appear), ACCEPT-CHARSET (to indicate what character encodings the form processor can understand), plus generic 4.0 attributes—as well the special ONSUBMIT and ONRESET event attributes

ELEMENT	DESCRIPTION
Content:	DATA, block-level elements, and/or text-level elements (except for other form elements: a form cannot be nested inside another form) **NOTE:** Form elements should contain one or more fieldset elements and one or more form controls (button elements, input elements, label elements, select elements, and/or textarea elements)
<FRAME> **frame element**	In a frameset document, indicates the file the URL used as the contents of a frame
Category:	child element: can only be used in a frameset element
Starting Tag:	<FRAME>, required
Ending Tag:	forbidden (empty element)
Attributes:	SRC (a URL for the frame's content), NAME (the name of the frame for targeting purposes), MARGINWIDTH and MARGIN-HEIGHT (the distance in pixels between the frame's border and the content), FRAMEBORDER ("0" for no border, "1" for a border), NORESIZE (to indicate whether the frame can be resized by the surfer), and SCROLLING ("YES", "NO", or "AUTO" to determine whether or not a scroll bar is present), plus the generic ID attributes
Content:	none (empty element)
<FRAMESET> **frameset element**	Creates a frameset that defines how multiple documents can appear in different frames of a browser's window
Category:	special frame structure element; replaces the body element in the basic structure
Starting Tag:	<FRAMESET>, required
Ending Tag:	</FRAMESET>, required
Attributes:	Either ROWS or COLUMNS is a required attribute to define the number of frames, or use both to create a grid; in addition, you can use the ONLOAD or ONUNLOAD events
Content:	Any number of frame elements and any number of frameset elements. Also you should use a noframe element (not required but highly recommended)
<H1> **heading level-one element**	Creates a first-level heading
Category:	block-level element
Starting Tag:	<H1>, required
Ending Tag:	</H1>, required

ELEMENT	DESCRIPTION
Attributes:	ALIGN (for horizontal alignment; either "LEFT", "RIGHT", "CENTER", or "JUSTIFY", although this attribute is not recommended in favor of style sheets), plus generic 4.0 attributes
Content:	DATA and/or text-level elements
\<H2\> **heading level-two element**	Creates a second-level heading
Category:	block-level element
Starting Tag:	\<H2\>, required
Ending Tag:	\</H2\>, required
Attributes:	ALIGN (for horizontal alignment; either "LEFT", "RIGHT", "CENTER", or "JUSTIFY", although this attribute is not recommended in favor of style sheets), plus generic 4.0 attributes
Content:	DATA and/or text-level elements
\<H3\> **heading level-three element**	Creates a third-level heading
Category:	block-level element
Starting Tag:	\<H3\>, required
Ending Tag:	\</H3\>, required
Attributes:	ALIGN (for horizontal alignment; either "LEFT", "RIGHT", "CENTER", or "JUSTIFY", although this attribute is not recommended in favor of style sheets), plus generic 4.0 attributes
Content:	DATA and/or text-level elements
\<H4\> **heading level-four element**	Creates a fourth-level heading
Category:	block-level element
Starting Tag:	\<H4\>, required
Ending Tag:	\</H4\>, required
Attributes:	ALIGN (for horizontal alignment; either "LEFT", "RIGHT", "CENTER", or "JUSTIFY", although this attribute is not recommended in favor of style sheets), plus generic 4.0 attributes
Content:	DATA and/or text-level elements
\<H5\> **heading level-five element**	Creates a fifth-level heading
Category:	block-level element
Starting Tag:	\<H5\>, required
Ending Tag:	\</H5\>, required

Attributes:	ALIGN (for horizontal alignment; either "LEFT", "RIGHT", "CENTER", or "JUSTIFY", although this attribute is not recommended in favor of style sheets), plus generic 4.0 attributes
Content:	DATA and/or text-level elements

<H6>
heading level-six element

Creates a sixth-level heading

Category:	block-level element
Starting Tag:	<H6>, required
Ending Tag:	</H6>, required
Attributes:	ALIGN (for horizontal alignment; either "LEFT", "RIGHT", "CENTER", or "JUSTIFY", although this attribute is not recommended in favor of style sheets), plus generic 4.0 attributes
Content:	DATA and/or text-level elements

<HEAD>
head element

Contains the head section of a document

Category:	basic structure element
Starting Tag:	<HEAD>, optional
Ending Tag:	</HEAD>, optional
Attributes:	The generic 4.0 attributes for language (LANG and DIR) and the PROFILE attribute
Content:	Must contain exactly one title element. In addition, can contain one isindex element and/or one base element. Can also contain multiple script elements, style elements, meta elements, and link elements

<HR>
horizontal rule element

Inserts a horizontal line to divide two different sections

Category:	block-level element
Starting Tag:	<HR>, required
Ending Tag:	forbidden (empty element)
Attributes:	ALIGN (to determine the horizontal alignment of the rule; either "LEFT", "CENTER", or "RIGHT"), SIZE (to specify the height of the rule in pixels), WIDTH (to specify the width of the rule in pixels or as a percentage of the window's size), NOSHADE (to indicate that the rule should be solid, and not given the default shading and three-dimensional appearance), plus the generic 4.0 attributes (except for the two language attributes, LANG and DIR). HTML 4.0 recommends using style sheets instead of the ALIGN, SIZE, or WIDTH attributes.
Content:	none (empty element)

ELEMENT	DESCRIPTION
<HTML> **html element**	Contains the head element and body element of a document; if frames are used, then a frameset element can be substituted for the body element
Category:	basic structure element
Starting Tag:	<HTML>, optional
Ending Tag:	</HTML>, optional
Attributes:	generic 4.0 attributes for language (LANG and DIR), plus a VERSION attribute (to indicate the version of HTML you're using; not recommended—use a DOCTYPE declaration instead, see <!DOCTYPE>)
Content:	One head element, and either a body element or a frameset element
<I> **italics element**	Makes the enclosed text italic **WARNING:** <EM> is preferred over <I>
Category:	text-level element (physical font)
Starting Tag:	<I>, required
Ending Tag:	</I>, required
Attributes:	none except generic 4.0 attributes
Content:	DATA and/or text-level elements
<IFRAME> **iframe element**	Creates an inline frame—that is, a region containing a different HTML document **WARNING:** Not supported by Navigator 4 or earlier
Category:	text-level element (special)
Starting Tag:	<IFRAME>, required
Ending Tag:	</IFRAME>, required
Attributes:	SRC (a URL for the frame's content), NAME (the name of the frame for targeting purposes), HEIGHT and WIDTH (to set the frame's size in pixels or a percentage), ALIGN to place the frame in relation to the rest of the line (either "BOTTOM", "MIDDLE", "TOP", "LEFT", or "RIGHT"), MARGINWIDTH and MARGINHEIGHT (the distance in pixels between the frame's border and the content), FRAMEBORDER ("0" for no border, "1" for a border), and SCROLLING ("YES", "NO", or "AUTO" to determine whether or not a scroll bar is present)
Content:	DATA, text-level elements, and/or block-level elements (used as alternate content for browsers that cannot display inline frames)

ELEMENT	DESCRIPTION
<IMG> **image element**	Inserts an inline image
Category:	text-level element (special)
Starting Tag:	<IMG>, required
Ending Tag:	forbidden (empty element)
Attributes:	SRC (required, with the URL of the image), ALT (required for the alternate text of the image, displayed by browsers that don't display images), LONGDESC (for a URL to a longer description of the image), ALIGN to place the image in relation to the rest of the line (either "BOTTOM", "MIDDLE", "TOP", "LEFT", or "RIGHT"), HEIGHT and WIDTH (to determine the dimensions of the image, in pixels), BORDER (to determine the image's border width, in pixels), HSPACE and VSPACE (to determine the space between the image and the text around it, in pixels), and USEMAP and ISMAP (for use with image maps, see the Web site), plus generic 4.0 attributes
Content:	none (empty element)
<INPUT> **input element**	Creates one of several types of form controls, including text boxes, radio buttons, and submit buttons
Category:	form control element
Starting Tag:	<INPUT>, required
Ending Tag:	forbidden (empty element)
Attributes:	YPE (to indicate what type of form control to create; either "TEXT", "PASSWORD", "CHECKBOX", "RADIO", "SUBMIT", "RESET", "FILE", "HIDDEN", "IMAGE", or "BUTTON"), VALUE (determines the value of a radio button, the text label used in a button, or the default text in a textbox; required for the "RADIO" and "CHECKBOX" types), NAME (required for most input types, to give the form control a value that's passed to the form processor when the form is submitted and to give the form control a name for use with a script), SIZE (to determine how large a text box is or indicate the size of a button in pixels), CHECKED (for radio buttons and check boxes to indicate the control's initial state), MAXLENGTH (to limit the text box entries to a particular number of characters), ACCEPT (a list of MIME types that the file input type can accept, indicating what types of files your CGI can process), DISABLED (to make this button "grayed out" and unavailable by default), READONLY (to prevent changes from being made to the text in a text box), TABINDEX (to control this button's position in the tab key navigation order), ACCESSKEY (for a keyboard shortcut), ALIGN (to determine where the control is placed relative to its surroundings; either "TOP", "MIDDLE", "BOTTOM",

ELEMENT	DESCRIPTION
	"LEFT", or "RIGHT"), a number of attributes to control buttons that are images (SRC, ALT, and USEMAP), plus generic 4.0 attributes, including the special ONFOCUS, ONSELECT, ONCHANGE, and ONBLUR event attributes
Content:	none (empty element)
\<INS\> **ins element**	Indicates elements and text that are considered inserted into a document **WARNING:** Not yet widely supported
Category:	special hybrid element (used in the body section, similar to a block-level element except doesn't cause a paragraph break)
Starting Tag:	\<INS\>, required
Ending Tag:	\</INS\>, required
Attributes:	CITE (with a URL explaining why the contents were inserted), DATETIME, plus generic 4.0 attributes
Content:	DATA, text-level elements, and/or block-level elements
\<ISINDEX\> **isindex element**	Indicates that the document is a searchable index; requires that you set up CGI to handle the search **WARNING:** No longer recommended; use forms instead
Category:	head section element (HTML 4.0 now allows it to be block-level element as well)
Starting Tag:	\<ISINDEX\>, required
Ending Tag:	forbidden (empty element)
Attributes:	PROMPT attribute for a search prompt, plus generic 4.0 attributes (but not the event attributes)
Content:	none (empty element)
\<KBD\> **keyboard element**	Indicates that the contents is a keyboard command, often displayed using bold text
Category:	text-level element (phrase)
Starting Tag:	\<KBD\>, required
Ending Tag:	\</KBD\>, required
Attributes:	none except generic 4.0 attributes
Content:	DATA and/or text-level elements

ELEMENT	DESCRIPTION
<LABEL> **label element**	Associates a text label with a form control; for example: <LABEL>Name:<INPUT TYPE="TEXT" NAME="your name"></LABEL> **WARNING:** This element is not widely supported
Category:	form control element
Starting Tag:	<LABEL>, required
Ending Tag:	</LABEL>, required
Attributes:	ACCESSKEY (to create a keyboard shortcut for the control), DISABLED (to make the label and its contents disabled or "grayed-out" initially), FOR (to associate this label with a form control elsewhere in the document that has a matching ID name), plus generic 4.0 attributes, including the special ONFOCUS and ONBLUR events
Content:	ATA and/or text-level elements (excluding another label); mostly will be used to contain a single form control
<LEGEND> **legend element**	Adds a legend (caption) to a fieldset
Category:	child element: can only be used in a fieldset element
Starting Tag:	<LEGEND>, required
Ending Tag:	</LEGEND>, required
Attributes:	ALIGN (to specify where in the fieldset the legend should appear: use "TOP", "BOTTOM", "LEFT", or "RIGHT"), ACCESSKEY (to set a shortcut key), plus generic 4.0 attributes
Content:	DATA and/or text-level elements
<LI> **list item element**	Creates a list item in an ordered list, unordered list, menu list, or dir list
Category:	child element: can only be used in a ul element, ol element, menu element, or dir element
Starting Tag:	<LI>, required
Ending Tag:	</LI>, optional
Attributes:	TYPE (to indicate the list item style; for list items in unordered lists, can be one of the bullet types, and for list items in ordered lists, can be one of the numbering styles; see the unordered list element and ordered list element), VALUE (for list items in ordered list, used to set a specific number) plus generic 4.0 attributes
Content:	DATA, text-level elements, and/or block-level elements (except dir and menu lists cannot contain list items that contain block-level elements)

ELEMENT	DESCRIPTION
\<LINK\> **link element**	Creates link relationships to other documents and resources such as the author's e-mail address, and links to external style sheets. For example: \<LINK REL="next" HREF="chapter2.html"\> or \<LINK REV="made" HREF="mailto:estephen@emf.net"\> or \<LINK REL="stylesheet" HREF= "mystyle.css" TYPE="text/css" MEDIA="screen" TITLE="My Style Sheet"\> **WARNING:** The relationships other than style sheets are not well supported
Category:	head section element
Starting Tag:	\<LINK\>, required
Ending Tag:	forbidden (empty element)
Attributes:	REL or REV (one of these are required) with a relationship name, HREF (the URL of the linked resource), TARGET (where the linked resource should be displayed), TYPE (for the style sheet language), MEDIA (defining when to use the style sheet), CHARSET (to indicate a character encoding for foreign languages), plus generic 4.0 attributes (including the TITLE attribute for the style sheet's title)
Content:	none (empty element)
\<MAP\> **map element**	Creates a collection of hotspots for use with a client-side image map
Category:	text-level element (special)
Starting Tag:	\<MAP\>, required
Ending Tag:	\</MAP\>, required
Attributes:	NAME (to name the map, for reference via an image's USEMAP attribute) plus generic 4.0 attributes
Content:	One or more area elements
\<MENU\> **menu list element**	Create a list in the "menu" style **WARNING:** This element is not recommended; use an ordered list or unordered list instead.
Category:	block-level element (list)
Starting Tag:	\<MENU\>, required
Ending Tag:	\</MENU\>, required
Attributes:	COMPACT (to indicate that the list should be reduced in size; ignored by most browsers and not recommended) plus generic 4.0 attributes
Content:	One or more list item elements (see \<LI\>)

ELEMENT	DESCRIPTION
<META> **meta element**	Defines information about the document; can be used to help index-ing robots, to define the document's default style sheet language, scripting language, or for meta refresh. For example:`<META NAME="Description" CONTENT= "Meredith's page about The Simpsons">`
Category:	head section element
Starting Tag:	<META>, required
Ending Tag:	forbidden (empty element)
Attributes:	NAME or HTTP-EQUIV (to define the type of meta information you're specifying) along with a CONTENT attribute (required, with the actual information), SCHEME, plus the generic 4.0 language attributes (LANG and DIR)
Content:	none (empty element)
<NOFRAMES> **noframes element**	Marks content that should only be displayed when the browser is not frames-enabled **NOTE:** This element has two uses. The first use is inside the frameset element of a frame set document, where the noframes element should contain a body element. The second use is in any document, when you want to display any section (such as a navigation bar) only in the event that the document is not being displayed in a frame. The second use is not widely supported yet, but the first use is very important.
Category:	block-level element
Starting Tag:	<NOFRAMES>, required
Ending Tag:	</NOFRAMES>, required
Attributes:	none except generic 4.0 attributes
Content:	First use: body element (which may in turn contain DATA, block-level elements, and/or text-level elements) Second use: DATA, block-level elements, and/or text-level elements
<NOSCRIPT> **noscript element**	Marks content that should only be displayed if the browser is not active script-enabled
Category:	block-level element
Starting Tag:	<NOSCRIPT>, required
Ending Tag:	</NOSCRIPT>, required
Attributes:	none except generic 4.0 attributes
Content:	DATA, block-level elements, and/or text-level elements

ELEMENT	DESCRIPTION
\<OBJECT\> **object element**	Inserts an object of some kind, such as a sound, image, applet, movie object, text file, or another HTML document
Category:	text-level element (special)
Starting Tag:	\<OBJECT\>, required
Ending Tag:	\</OBJECT\>, required
Attributes:	DATA (the object's URL), HEIGHT and WIDTH (to define the object's size, in pixels or a percentage), TYPE (the MIME type of the object), ALIGN to place the object in relation to the rest of the line (either "TOP", "MIDDLE", "BOTTOM", "LEFT", or "RIGHT"), HSPACE and VSPACE (space in pixels between the object and the surrounding text), BORDER (size in pixels of the object's surrounding border), NAME (to give the object or applet a name), TABINDEX (where the object fits in the tab key navigation order), CLASSID (to identify the URL and CLSID implementation of ActiveX controls), CODEBASE (the URL of the applet's source code), CODETYPE (the MIME type of the applet's source code), STANDBY (a message to show while the object is loading), DECLARE (to indicate that an applet should be loaded but not beginning running immediately), ARchIVE (to indicate the location of an applet file), plus generic 4.0 attributes
Content:	One or more param elements (to control an applet object's behavior), followed by DATA, text-level elements, and/or block-level elements (used as alternate content for browsers that can't display the object); notably you can nest several objects within each other to allow the browser to negotiate for an object it is able to display
\<OL\> **ordered list element**	Creates an ordered list, with numbers preceding each list item
Category:	block-level element (list)
Starting Tag:	\<OL\>, required
Ending Tag:	\</OL\>, required
Attributes:	COMPACT (to indicate that the list should be reduced in size; ignored by most browsers and not recommended), TYPE (to indicate the numbering style: "1" for numbers: 1 2 3..., "A" for capital letters: A B C..., "a" for small letters: a b c..., "I" for large Roman numerals: I II III..., and "i" for small Roman numerals: i ii iii...), START (to indicate what number to start at, for example \<OL TYPE="A" START="9"\> would create a list where the numbering will start with "I" then "J" and so on), plus generic 4.0 attributes
Content:	One or more list item elements (see \<LI\>)

ELEMENT	DESCRIPTION
<OPTION> **option element**	Creates menu items for a select element form control
Category:	child element: can only be used in a select element
Starting Tag:	<OPTION>, required
Ending Tag:	</OPTION>, optional
Attributes:	VALUE (to indicate the default value for this menu item when it is selected and submitted to the form processor; by default, it's equal to the contents), SELECTED (to indicate that this menu item is initially selected as the default value), DISABLED (to make this menu item "grayed out" and unavailable by default), plus generic 4.0 attributes
Content:	DATA
<P> **paragraph element**	Creates a paragraph
Category:	block-level element
Starting Tag:	<P>, required
Ending Tag:	</P>, optional
Attributes:	ALIGN (for horizontal alignment; either "LEFT", "RIGHT", "CENTER", or "JUSTIFY", although this attribute is not recommended in favor of style sheets), plus generic 4.0 attributes
Content:	DATA and/or text-level elements
<PARAM> **param element**	Passes a parameter to an applet element or object element; this parameter controls the applet's behavior
Category:	child element: can only be used in an applet element or object element
Starting Tag:	<PARAM>, required
Ending Tag:	forbidden (empty element)
Attributes:	NAME (required, the name of the parameter as dictated by the applet; varies from applet to applet), VALUE (the data content for the parameter; usually data of some kind such as a name or number), VALUETYPE (not used often, but indicates whether the VALUE attribute contains data, with VALUETYPE="DATA", as is the default; or a URL, with VALUETYPE="REF"; or the specific ID name of another applet or HTML element, with VALUETYPE="OBJECT"), and TYPE (to indicate the MIME type of the file given in the VALUE URL if VALUETYPE is "REF"), plus the generic ID attributes
Content:	none (empty element)

ELEMENT	DESCRIPTION
<PRE> **pre-formatted text element**	Creates a block of preformatted text (in which the normal rules of collapsing white space do not apply) so that you can arrange lines in a particular way and create text art **NOTE:** Most browsers will display the pre element using a mono spaced font, such as Courier
Category:	block-level element
Starting Tag:	<PRE>, required
Ending Tag:	</PRE>, required
Attributes:	WIDTH to indicate the number of characters the widest line of the preformatted text has (but this attribute is not widely supported) plus generic 4.0 attributes
Content:	DATA and/or text-level elements (except for the img, big, small, sub, sup, basefont, font, applet, and object elements)
<Q> **quote element**	Creates inline quotes **NOTE:** This element is not widely supported yet; it's similar to the blockquote element, but the quote element is a text-level element while blockquote is a block-level element
Category:	text-level element (special)
Starting Tag:	<Q>, required
Ending Tag:	</Q>, required
Attributes:	CITE (to indicate the URL of the quote's source) plus generic 4.0 attributes
Content:	DATA and/or text-level elements
<S> **strike element**	Makes the enclosed text appear with a strike-out through the middle; see also <STRIKE> (which is more widely supported than <S>) **WARNING:** HTML 4.0 does not recommend the use of this element; use the del element or a style sheet instead
Category:	text-level element (physical font)
Starting Tag:	<S>, required
Ending Tag:	</S>, required
Attributes:	none except generic 4.0 attributes
Content:	DATA and/or text-level elements
<SAMP> **sample element**	Indicates that the contents is a sample output from a computer program, often displayed using a fixed-width font
Category:	text-level element (phrase)
Starting Tag:	<SAMP>, required

ELEMENT	DESCRIPTION
Ending Tag:	</SAMP>, required
Attributes:	none except generic 4.0 attributes
Content:	DATA and/or text-level elements
<SCRIPT> **script element**	Contains an active script
Category:	head section element; also text-level element (special)
Starting Tag:	<SCRIPT>, required
Ending Tag:	</SCRIPT>, required
Attributes:	TYPE and LANGUAGE, to specify the scripting language (HTML 4.0 recommends using the TYPE attribute, but current browsers expect the LANGUAGE attribute, so both methods are currently necessary), plus SRC to specify an external active script file
Content:	DATA that's an active script written in a scripting language (such as JavaScript or VBScript); be sure to surround the script with an HTML comment so older browsers don't display it inadvertently
<SELECT> **select element**	Creates a selection menu form control, either as a drop-down menu or list box
Category:	form control element
Starting Tag:	<SELECT>, required
Ending Tag:	</SELECT>, required
Attributes:	NAME (required, to give the form control a value that's passed to the form processor when the form is submitted, and to give the form control a name for use with a script), SIZE (to determine how many items are displayed at once; if this attribute is omitted, most browsers will display a drop-down menu, but if it's included, you'll get a list box instead), MULTIPLE (if you want to allow the surfer to select more than one item from a list box), DISABLED (to make this form control "grayed out" and unavailable by default), TABINDEX (to control this form control's position in the tab key navigation order), plus generic 4.0 attributes, including the special ONFOCUS, ONCHANGE, and ONBLUR event attributes
Content:	One or more option elements
<SMALL> **small element**	Makes the enclosed text one size smaller
Category:	text-level element (physical font)

ELEMENT	DESCRIPTION
Starting Tag:	<SMALL>, required
Ending Tag:	</SMALL>, required
Attributes:	none except generic 4.0 attributes
Content:	DATA and/or text-level elements
<SPAN> **the span element**	A generic text-level element, useful for indicating where style sheets should be applied, to give a name to section using the generic CLASS or ID attributes, or to assign a language to a section; for example: <SPAN LANG="FR" CLASS="foreign">Bonjour!</SPAN>
Category:	text-level element (special)
Starting Tag:	<SPAN>, required
Ending Tag:	</SPAN>, required
Attributes:	none except generic 4.0 attributes
Content:	DATA and/or text-level elements
<STRIKE> **strike element**	Makes the enclosed text appear with a strike-out through the middle; see also <S>, but <STRIKE> is more widely supported than <S> **WARNING:** HTML 4.0 does not recommend the use of this element; use the del element or a style sheet instead
Category:	text-level element (physical font)
Starting Tag:	<STRIKE>, required
Ending Tag:	</STRIKE>, required
Attributes:	none except generic 4.0 attributes
Content:	DATA and/or text-level elements
<STRONG> **strong emphasis element**	Indicates that the contents should be given a strong emphasis, usually displayed with bold
Category:	text-level element (phrase)
Starting Tag:	<STRONG>, required
Ending Tag:	</STRONG>, required
Attributes:	none except generic 4.0 attributes
Content:	DATA and/or text-level elements

ELEMENT	DESCRIPTION
\<STYLE\> **style element**	Creates an embedded style sheet
Category:	head section element
Starting Tag:	\<STYLE\>, required
Ending Tag:	\</STYLE\>, required
Attributes:	TYPE (required, to specify the style sheet language's MIME type such as TYPE="text/css" for Cascading Style Sheets), MEDIA (to specify what display the style sheet should be used with), and TITLE (to name the style sheet); you may also use the generic HTML 4.0 language attributes (LANG and DIR) to specify the language used in the TITLE attribute
Content:	DATA that's a style sheet written in a style sheet language (such as Cascading Style Sheets); be sure to surround the style sheet with an HTML comment so older browsers don't display it inadvertently
\<SUB\> **subscript element**	Used to indicate a subscripted section; for example: H\<SUB\>2\</SUB\>0
Category:	text-level element (special)
Starting Tag:	\<SUB\>, required
Ending Tag:	\</SUB\>, required
Attributes:	none except generic 4.0 attributes
Content:	DATA and/or text-level elements
\<SUP\> **superscript element**	Used to indicate a superscripted section; for example: E=MC\<SUP\>2\</SUP\>
Category:	text-level element (special)
Starting Tag:	\<SUP\>, required
Ending Tag:	\</SUP\>, required
Attributes:	none except generic 4.0 attributes
Content:	DATA and/or text-level elements
\<TABLE\> **table element**	Creates a table of data
Category:	block-level element
Starting Tag:	\<TABLE\>, required
Ending Tag:	\</TABLE\>, required

ELEMENT	DESCRIPTION
Attributes:	ALIGN (for the table position, "LEFT", "RIGHT", or "CENTER"), BGCOLOR (for the table's background color), WIDTH (in pixels or percentage, for the table's width), COLS (the number of columns in the table), BORDER (to create a visible border; use BORDER="SIZE" to determine how big the border is in pixels), FRAME (which sides of the table will have a border, either "VOID", "ABOVE", "BELOW", "HSIDES", "LHS", "RHS", "VSIDES", "BOX", or "BORDER"), RULES (to determine which sides of the whole table will have a border, either "NONE", "GROUPS", "ROWS", "COLS", or "ALL"), CELLSPACING (how much space between cells, in pixels), CELLPADDING (how much space between the edge of the cell and the cell's contents, in pixels) plus generic 4.0 attributes
Content:	An optional caption element, followed by any number of optional colgroup and/or col elements, followed by an optional thead element, followed by an optional tfoot element, followed by one or more tbody elements (the <TBODY> and </TBODY> tags are optional if there's no thead element, no tfoot element, and only one tbody element). One tbody element is required. The tbody element contains one or more table row elements (see the <TR> tag), and each row contains one or more cells of data
<TBODY> **table body row group** **element (tbody element)**	Creates a group of rows in a table, used as the body of the table; convenient for setting the attributes of many rows of data at once
Category:	table model element
Starting Tag:	<TBODY>, optional (required if a thead or tfoot element is present in the table)
Ending Tag:	</TBODY>, optional
Attributes:	horizontal cell alignment attributes: ALIGN (to set the default alignment of the cell data, either "LEFT", "CENTER", "RIGHT", "JUSTIFY", or on a particular character with "CHAR"), CHAR (to specify which alignment character to use if ALIGN="CHAR"), CHAROFF (to specify a length in pixels or percentage of the column's width to use as an offset for determining the character alignment), and vertical cell alignment: VALIGN (to specify the vertical position of cell data: "TOP", "MIDDLE", "BOTTOM", or "BASELINE"), plus generic 4.0 attributes **WARNING:** Character alignment is not yet supported in the popular browsers
Content:	one or more table rows (see <TR>)

ELEMENT	DESCRIPTION
\<TD\> **table data element**	Creates a cell of data in a table
Category:	table model element
Starting Tag:	\<TD\>, required
Ending Tag:	\</TD\>, optional
Attributes:	BGCOLOR (background color for the cell), ROWSPAN and COLSPAN (number of rows or columns spanned by the data), NOWRAP (to indicate that the cell's data shouldn't be word wrapped), AXIS and AXES (to set up the cell's name and coordinates), horizontal cell alignment attributes: ALIGN (to set the default alignment of the cell data, either "LEFT", "CENTER", "RIGHT", "JUSTIFY", or on a particular character with "CHAR"), CHAR (to specify which alignment character to use if ALIGN="CHAR"), CHAROFF (to specify a length in pixels or percentage of the column's width to use as an offset for determining the character alignment), and vertical cell alignment: VALIGN (to specify the vertical position of cell data: "TOP", "MIDDLE", "BOTTOM", or "BASELINE"), Width and height (in pixels, to specify a cell's minimum dimensions), plus generic 4.0 attributes **WARNING:** Character alignment is not yet supported in the popular browsers
Content:	DATA, text-level elements, and/or block-level elements
\<TEXTAREA\> **textarea element**	Creates a textarea form control, displayed as a box where the surfer can type information
Category:	form control element
Starting Tag:	\<TEXTAREA\>, required
Ending Tag:	\</TEXTAREA\>, required
Attributes:	NAME (required, to give the textarea form control a value that's passed to the form processor when the form is submitted, and to give the textarea form control a name for use with a script), ROWS and COLS (both required, to set the size of the textarea box), DISABLED (to make this form control "grayed out" and unavailable by default), READONLY (to make the contents of the textarea form control unchangeable by default), TABINDEX (to control this form control's position in the tab key navigation order), plus generic 4.0 attributes, including the special ONFOCUS, ONSELECT, ONCHANGE, and ONBLUR event attributes
Content:	DATA (the default information in the textarea control)

ELEMENT	DESCRIPTION
<TFOOT> **table foot row group element (tfoot element)**	Creates a row group in a table that's used as the table's footer, repeated on the bottom of each page of a printout
Category:	table model element
Starting Tag:	<TFOOT>, required
Ending Tag:	</TFOOT>, optional
Attributes:	Same as for the tbody element (see <TBODY>)
Content:	one or more table rows (see <TR>)
<TH> **table heading element**	Creates a cell with table heading data, usually centered and in bold
Category:	table model element
Starting Tag:	<TH>, required
Ending Tag:	</TH>, optional
Attributes:	Same as for the table data element (see <TD>)
Content:	DATA, text-level elements, and/or block-level elements
<THEAD> **table head row group element (thead element)**	Creates a row group in a table that's used as the header for the table, repeating on each page of a printout **WARNING:** This element is not yet widely supported
Category:	table model element
Starting Tag:	<THEAD>, required
Ending Tag:	</THEAD>, optional
Attributes:	Same as for the tbody element (see <TBODY>)
Content:	one or more table rows (see <TR>)
<TITLE> **title element**	Creates the document's title. Every HTML document requires a title
Category:	head section element that's part of the basic structure
Starting Tag:	<TITLE>, required
Ending Tag:	</TITLE>, required
Attributes:	none except the generic HTML 4.0 language attributes (LANG and DIR)
Content:	DATA

ELEMENT	DESCRIPTION
<TR> **table row element**	Creates a row of cells in a table
Category:	table model element
Starting Tag:	<TR>, required
Ending Tag:	</TR>, optional
Attributes:	Same as for table body row groups (see <TBODY>), plus BGCOLOR can be used to set the row's background color
Content:	One or more cells; cells can be table data elements (see <TD>) or table heading elements (see <TH>) or a mixture of both
<TT> **teletype element**	Makes enclosed text appear in a fixed-width, typewriter-style font, such as Courier
Category:	text-level element (physical font)
Starting Tag:	<TT>, required
Ending Tag:	</TT>, required
Attributes:	none except generic 4.0 attributes
Content:	DATA and/or text-level elements
<U> **underline element**	Makes enclosed text appear with an underline **WARNING:** HTML 4.0 does not recommend the use of this element at all; underlined text is easily confused with a link
Category:	text-level element (physical font)
Starting Tag:	<U>, required
Ending Tag:	</U>, required
Attributes:	none except generic 4.0 attributes
Content:	DATA and/or text-level elements
<UL> **unordered list element**	Creates an unordered list, with bullets preceding each list item
Category:	block-level element (list)
Starting Tag:	<UL>, required
Ending Tag:	</UL>, required
Attributes:	COMPACT (to indicate that the list should be reduced in size; ignored by most browsers and not recommended), TYPE (to indicate the bullet style, either "DISC" for a normal solid bullet, "SQUARE" for a solid square, or "CIRCLE" for a hollow bullet), plus generic 4.0 attributes
Content:	One or more list item elements (see <LI>)

ELEMENT	DESCRIPTION
<VAR> **variable element**	Indicates that the contents is a computer program variable or user-specified piece of information
Category:	text-level element (phrase)
Starting Tag:	<VAR>, required
Ending Tag:	</VAR>, required
Attributes:	none except generic 4.0 attributes
Content:	DATA and/or text-level elements

INDEX

Note to the Reader: Throughout this index first level entries are in **boldface**. **Boldface** page numbers indicate the principal discussion of a topic. *Italic* page numbers indicate illustrations.

D

E

F

N

Y

Z

ABOUT THE CONTRIBUTORS

Some of the best—and best-selling—Sybex authors have contributed chapters from their current books to *Internet Complete*.

Laura Arendal   contributed chapters from *America Online Amazing Secrets*.

Ms. Arendal has long labored behind the scenes at Sybex—editing, re-writing, even ghostwriting—to produce books of the highest possible quality. *America Online Amazing Secrets* is the first book to bear her name—and the latest of many that have benefited from her knowledge and abilities.

Pat Coleman   contributed chapters from *Mastering Internet Explorer 4* (coauthored with Gene Weisskopf).

Ms. Coleman is the co-author of *Mastering Intranets, Windows 95/NT Edition*, as well as many other Sybex books.

Gini Courter and Annette Marquis   contributed material from *The Learning Guide to Computers*.

Ms. Courter and Ms. Marquis are co-owners of TRIAD Consulting, a computer consulting firm specializing in training and database design for schools, health care systems, and companies. Ms. Courter has extensive experience teaching computer applications in college and high school settings and designing and implementing school staff training. Ms. Marquis' background is in health care administration, where she implemented technological solutions to improve patient care and information management. Ms. Courter and Ms. Marquis are the authors of numerous books, including *The Learning Guide to Windows 95*, *The Learning Guide to Access for Windows 95*, and *The Learning Guide to Microsoft Office Professional for Windows 95*, all from Sybex.

Christian Crumlish   contributed material from *The Internet: No experience required.* and *The Internet Dictionary*.

Mr. Crumlish is co-owner of an Internet and network consulting firm. He has written several books on the Internet, including *A Guided Tour of the Internet* and *The ABCs of the Internet*, all from Sybex. Crumlish is known for his easy, witty writing style and ability to simplify difficult topics.

Peter Dyson   contributed material from *Windows 98 Instant Reference*.

Mr. Dyson is a writer and consultant software engineer with more than twenty years of experience in engineering, software development, and technical support. His computer-related publications include numerous technical research papers and over two dozen books. Among his recent Sybex titles are *ABCs of Intranets* and *Mastering Microsoft Internet Information Server*.

E. Stephen Mack   contributed material from *HTML 4.0: No experience required.* (coauthored with Janan Platt-Saylor).

Mr. Mack is a Web designer, software trainer, and computer consultant. He has worked with several major companies over the last 10 years, written computer articles, and co-created two best-selling computer books.

Michael Meadhra   contributed chapters from *The ABCs of Netscape Composer.*

Mr. Meadhra is the author of *The ABCs of Online Banking with Quicken* and has served as a contributor to several Sybex books, including *Mastering CorelDRAW 7.*

Mark Minasi   contributed chapters from *The Complete PC Upgrade and Maintenance Guide.*

Mr. Minasi is a noted lecturer and writer in the fields of PC computing, data communications, and operating systems. His best-selling books include *Expert Guide to Windows 98*, *Mastering Windows NT Server 4*, *Mastering Windows NT 4 Workstation*, *Mastering TCP/IP for NT*, *The Hard Disk Survival Guide*, and *Troubleshooting Windows*, all from Sybex.

Janan Platt-Saylor   contributed material from *HTML 4.0: No experience required.* (coauthored with E. Stephen Mack).

Ms. Platt-Saylor has 13 years experience as a controller and consultant teaching people to use computers. She publishes multimedia poetry, often from her online poetry workshop, Alien Flower.

John Ross   contributed chapters from *ABCs of Internet Explorer 4.*

Mr. Ross has been writing about computers and telecommunications for more than fifteen years. He has written award-winning user's manuals and articles for AT&T, Motorola, and many other communication equipment manufacturers. His other books include *Connecting with Windows 95* and *All About WinFax PRO 7 for Windows 95*, both from Sybex.

Daniel A. Tauber and Brenda Kienan   contributed material from *Mastering Netscape Communicator 4.*

Mr. Tauber has led technical development of Web sites for Fortune 500 companies and holds a degree in Computer Science. Ms. Kienan produces Web content for the publishing and search engine industries. Their other books include *Mosaic Access to the Internet*, *The Complete Linux Kit*, and the best-selling *SimCity 2000 Strategies and Secrets*, all from Sybex.

Gene Weisskopf   contributed chapters from *Mastering Internet Explorer 4* (coauthored with Pat Coleman).

Mr. Weisskopf has been involved in the PC revolution since the early 1980s. He has developed software applications for business and science and has taught a variety of classes and training sessions. His articles have appeared in a number of computer magazines, and he has written several books for Sybex, including *The ABCs of Excel 97*, *Mastering Quattro Pro 6*, and *Murphy's Laws of PCs*.